The Essential Client/Server Survival Guide

Second Edition

Robert Orfali • **Dan Harkey** • **Jeri Edwards**

WILEY COMPUTER PUBLISHING

JOHN WILEY & SONS, INC.

New York   Chichester   Brisbane   Toronto   Singapore

Publisher: Katherine Schowalter
Editor: Theresa Hudson
Managing Editor: Frank Grazioli
Text Design & Composition: Robert Orfali, Dan Harkey, and Jeri Edwards
Graphic Art: David Pacheco

Designations used by companies to distinguish their products are often claimed as trademarks. In all instances where John Wiley & Sons, Inc. is aware of a claim, the product names appear in initial capital or all capital letters. Readers, however, should contact the appropriate companies for more complete information regarding trademarks and registration.

This text is printed on acid-free paper.

This publication is designed to provide accurate and authoritative information in regard to the subject matter covered. It is sold with the understanding that the publisher is not engaged in rendering legal, accounting, or other professional service. If legal advice or other expert assistance is required, the services of a competent professional person should be sought.

The authors and publisher of this book have used their best efforts in preparing this book. The authors and publisher make no warranty of any kind, expressed or implied, with regard to the documentation contained in this book. The authors and publisher shall not be liable in any event for incidental or consequential damages in connection with, or arising out of the use of, the information in this book.

The product descriptions are based on the best information available at the time of publication. Product prices are subject to change without notice.

Some illustrations incorporate clip art from Corel Systems Corporation's Corel Draw 5.0 clip art library.

All the views expressed in this book are solely the authors' and should not be attributed to IBM or MATISSE, Inc., or any other IBM or MATISSE, Inc. employee. The three authors contributed equally to the production of this book.

Library of Congress Cataloging-in-Publication Data:

ISBN 0-471-15325-7

Printed in the United States of America
10 9 8 7 6 5

Foreword

by Zog the Martian

Captain Zog

Greetings, Earthlings! I'm Zog, the captain of the Martian team. My team and I first visited earth over two years ago to understand what client/server was all about. During that visit, we discovered **The Essential Client/Server Survival Guide** and found it to be absolutely vital in our mission to explore this new technology. So we were very excited to hear about this second edition. We returned to Earth to pick up a copy of this new book. It was just what we were looking for. It gives us an update on all the new technologies we've been hearing about—including distributed objects, the Web, data warehousing, TP Monitors, DBMSs and groupware.

It's hard to believe the pace at which you Earthlings keep coming up with new technologies. You seem to be reinventing client/server every year. We thought the Java Web was the hottest thing in the universe. Now we hear that even Java is not enough; you also need an Object Web. Or, as the authors put it, you need "to morph distributed objects with the Web." Yes, things keep changing so fast that this second edition reads like a new book. Over half the material is completely new, and the rest was completely updated. Not a single page was left untouched since our last visit. Does it ever stop? Don't get me wrong: I know it's not the authors' fault that things keep changing so fast. They're just trying to help us understand these constant upheavals, which is why we keep buying their books.

So what did I like about this book? It felt like it was talking directly to me and to my crew in a friendly voice. That's very important when you're from a foreign planet. We like books that are painless, fun to read, and contain good Martian humor. We were apprehensive at first about client/server technology. The first edition helped us overcome this barrier. Then here comes this new edition with a ton of new technologies. As it turns out, the timing is perfect. We now believe that objects are the only way to build an intergalactic client/server Web. Yes, we will be connected to the Internet. Hopefully, our Java objects will be connected to yours.

In summary, this new Survival Guide helped us understand the "latest and greatest" client/server technology and how to use it in practical Martian situations. The personal touch was great; it felt like we had our own private tour guides. The artwork and cartoons were wonderful. I love to see pictures of myself in books (and especially on the cover). The Soapboxes really helped us understand the issues and what the latest Earthling debates are all about. We like to hear strong opinions instead of just sterilized information. I cannot recommend this book enough to my fellow Martians. Through this foreword, I highly recommend this book to you Earthlings. If I can understand this intergalactic client/server technology, so can you.

Zog

Preface

Client/Server: The Perpetual Revolution

Client/server computing has created a deep paradigmatic shift in our industry. It's replacing monolithic mainframe applications with applications split across client and server lines. The client—typically a PC—provides the graphical interface, while the server provides access to shared resources—typically a database. Distributed objects and the Internet are a paradigm shift within a paradigm shift—they're a new client/server revolution within the client/server revolution. Objects break-up the client and server sides of an application into smart components that can play together and roam across networks. The Java Web is the killer application that is bringing objects to the masses. The combination of distributed objects and the Web (or the *Object Web*) is reinventing client/server computing.

Why Another Revolution?

So why is there another client/server revolution when the first one is still in full swing? The answer—as usual—is newer and better hardware and the demand for applications that match the new hardware. The first client/server revolution was driven by new hardware—PCs and Ethernet LANs forever changed the way we interact with our applications. Gone are the green-screen uglies associated with terminal-attached mainframes. Instead, we have GUIs. There's no way to turn back the clock.

The second client/server revolution is also being fueled by advances in hardware. This time, Wide Area Networks (WANs) are breaking the proximity barriers associated with Ethernet LANs. Millions of us are getting a firsthand taste—thanks to the Internet—of the joys of intergalactic networking. We will soon want a lot more. We won't be satisfied with just navigating through information and chatting; we will want to conduct our business on these networks. Money will start changing hands. People will either transact directly or through their electronic agents. In the age of intergalactic transactions, there's no going back to single-server, departmental client/server LANs. The Java Web has changed that forever.

So, the second era of client/server is being driven by very high-speed, low-cost, wide-area bandwidth. The telephone companies and WAN providers are getting ready to unleash almost unlimited bandwidth—they're wiring the entire planet for fiber-optic speeds. In addition, network-ready PCs running commodity multi-threaded operating systems—such as NT Workstation and OS/2 Warp Connect—are now capable of running as both clients and servers.

The Object Web

We may soon have millions of servers interconnected across the planet at ten times LAN speeds. This is the good news. The bad news is that our existing client/server infrastructure is geared for single-server departmental LANs; it cannot cope with the new intergalactic demands—millions of servers and applications that can spawn trillions of distributed transactions. 3-tier client/server solutions using distributed objects and the Web—or the *Object Web*—are our only hope for dealing with the new infrastructure requirements. Distributed Web objects—such as Java applets, ActiveXs, and OpenDoc parts—are changing the way we architect, develop, package, distribute, license, and maintain our client/server software. Object request brokers built on top of the Internet promise to provide the ultimate middleware.

We Live in Uncertain Times

A paradigm shift is akin to a revolution: Dominant structures crumble, vacuums are created, and the world is in turmoil. The transition period is marked by confusion, deep uncertainty, and exhilaration. Confusion is the result of seeing familiar bedrock structures disappear. Uncertainty comes from not knowing what the next day will bring. And the exhilaration comes from realizing the new possibilities that are being created by the new paradigm. **The Essential Client/Server Survival Guide** is our attempt to understand this revolution. The new client/server paradigm is fielding a lineup of competing technologies, each vying to become the new emperor. We hope the new emperor will have clothes.

And We Can't Turn Back the Clock

Before we tell you all about this book, let's answer some questions that we've been wrestling with: Is client/server just a passing fad? Can things go back to the way they were? We're the first to admit that client/server has become the industry's most overhyped and overloaded term; but it's not a passing fad. This is because the world is populated with more than 120 million PCs that need to be served in the style they expect. The client is the heart of the application; servers extend the client's universe. And in the age of the Internet, this service must be provided on an intergalactic scale. Servers are expected to do a lot more work for their clients. Client/server computing is unabashedly network-centric, and there's no turning back the clock. Yes, the revolutionary chaos of the client/server world may make some of us yearn for the good old days, but the time machine only marches forward.

What This Survival Guide Covers

This Survival Guide explores client/server computing from the ground up. It consists of ten parts; each one can almost be read independently. (One of our reviewers even read the book backwards and found that it made sense.) We'll give you a short description of what the parts cover. If you find the terminology too foreign, then by all means read the book to find out what it all means.

- **Part 1** starts with an overview of what client/server is and what the fuss is all about. We develop a client/server model that will serve as a map for the rest of the book. We go over the state of the client/server infrastructure to get a feel for how much of it is already here, and what remains to be built. We take a close look at how much bandwidth we can expect, and when.

- **Part 2** examines the client/server capabilities of our current crop of operating systems—including Windows 95, OS/2 Warp, Windows NT, Unix, and NetWare. We feel like war correspondents covering the battlefield of the operating system wars. We also look at how Internet PCs, shippable places, and compound documents are changing the client landscape.

- **Part 3** explores the NOS and transport middleware substrate. We take a look at communication stacks, RPCs, MOMs, global directories, network security, and the products that provide these functions.

- **Part 4** explores the very popular database server model of client/server. We cover SQL-92, SQL3, ODBC, DRDA, stored procedures, and triggers. We spend a lot of time looking at new database technologies such as data warehouses, OLAP, data mining, and data replication. We also cover products in all these areas.

- **Part 5** explores the TP Monitor model of client/server. We cover the different transaction types—including flat transactions, sagas, nested transactions, chained transactions, and long-lived transactions. We bring you up-to-date on what's happening with TP Monitors. Then we dive into the great debate that's pitting the TP Lite model offered by the database servers against the TP Heavy model offered by TP Monitors. We explain why TP Monitors are needed in a world dominated by database servers.

- **Part 6** explores the groupware model of client/server. We look at the world of Lotus Notes, Exchange, Collabra Share, workflow, and interpersonal applications. Groupware shows us what client/server can really do—its paradigm goes much further than just recreating mainframe-like applications on PCs.

- **Part 7** explores the distributed object model of client/server. We look at CORBA ORBs, OpenDoc, OLE, and DCOM. We explore how objects and components can be used to create a new generation of client/server information systems.

- **Part 8** explores the Internet from a client/server perspective. We start with the Web as we know it today. Then we look at Java objects. Finally, we look at how distributed objects, components, and the Web are morphing into a new Object Web. This is real revolutionary technology that's going to completely overhaul the way we build client/server systems.

- **Part 9** is about how to manage client/server applications. The biggest obstacle to the deployment of client/sever technology is the lack of integrated system management platforms. Fortunately, the situation is changing. We will look at some exciting technologies that will semi-automate the management of client/server systems. We also cover system management standards—including SNMPv2, RMON2, CMIP, DMI, CORBA, X/Open, and CORBA.

- **Part 10** is about how to design, build, and deploy 3-tier client/server applications. We look at what tools can and cannot do for you. This part ends the survival journey and ties all the pieces together.

What's New in This Edition?

We thank the 80,000+ readers of our first edition for making it a bestseller. As a result, our publisher asked us to do a "minor" update to bring the book up-to-date. Much to our chagrin, we soon discovered that there's no such thing as a minor update in the client/server field. Time is measured in dog years. Almost everything in the book had changed. So what started as a minor upgrade became an eight-month effort. The result is this new book. Over half of it is entirely new material—including the parts on data warehousing, the Web, and distributed objects. We introduced "meet the players" chapters in every part. Finally, almost every page in the old book was updated. It was an amazing amount of work. We pity the practitioners of client/server because the field is a moving target; it takes a certain amount of stability to develop applications. We also pity the readers of our first edition because you must now read an entire new book. There are no shortcuts. Of course, we kept some of the old cartoons. The Martians appear to be timeless.

How To Read This Book

As we recommend in all our books, the best way to approach this Survival Guide is to ask your boss for a one-week, paid sabbatical to go sit on a beach and read it. Tell him or her that it's the cheapest way to revitalize yourself technically and find out all there is to know about client/server technology, which now covers almost the entire computer science discipline. Once you sink into that comfortable chair overlooking the ocean, we think you'll find the book a lot of fun—maybe even downright relaxing. You won't get bored; but if you do, simply jump to the next part until you find something you like. You can jump to any part of the book and start reading it. We recommend, however, that you carefully go over the cartoons so that you have something to tell the boss back at the office.

What Are the Boxes For?

We use shaded boxes as a way to introduce concurrent threads in the presentation material. It's the book version of multitasking. The Soapboxes introduce strong opinions or biases on some of the more controversial topics of client/server computing. Because the discipline is so new and fuzzy, there's lots of room for interpretation and debate—so you'll get lots of Soapboxes that are just another opinion (ours). The Briefing boxes give you background or tutorial type information. You can safely skip over them if you're already familiar with a topic. The Detail boxes cover some esoteric area of technology that may not be of interest to the general readership. Typically, the same readers that skip over the briefings will find the details interesting (so you'll still get your money's worth). Lastly, we use Warning boxes to let you know where danger lies—this is, after all, a Survival Guide.

Who Is This Book For?

This book is for anybody who's associated with the computer industry and needs to understand where it's heading. We are all involved with client/server technology in some form or another—as users, IS managers, students, integrators, system developers, and component developers. All new software is being built using some form of client/server technology.

How Does It Compare With Our Distributed Objects Survival Guide?

Our other book, **The Essential Distributed Objects Survival Guide** (Wiley, 1996) provides an overview of distributed objects. It covers CORBA, OLE, COM, OpenDoc, and OpenStep. It explains how you can use distributed components in intergalactic client/server computing situations. If you read our Distributed Objects Survival Guide, you'll notice that we borrowed about 70 pages from it to make this one stand on its own. Which of our Survival Guides should you read first? If you have not read any of our books, then start with this one. The Distributed Objects Survival Guide starts out where this one leaves off.

We hope you enjoy the reading, the cartoons, and the Soapboxes. Drop us a line if you have something you want to "flame" about. We'll take compliments too. We're relying on word-of-mouth to let people know about the book, so if you enjoy it, please spread the word. Finally, we want to thank you, as well as our Martian friends, for trusting us to be your guides.

Contents at a Glance

Contents

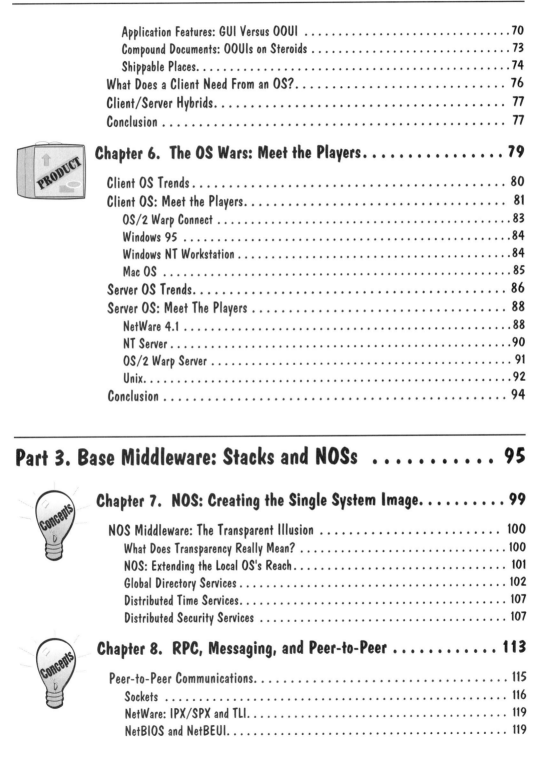

Part 7. Client/Server With Distributed Objects 375

Chapter 25. The OpenDoc Component Model 437

Chapter 26. OLE/DCOM: The Other Component Bus 449

Part 1
The Big Picture

An Introduction to Part 1

Welcome to our client/server planet. We hope you will like it here, because there's no turning back now! You've long passed the point of no return. Don't panic: You're in good hands. We'll somehow find our way through the swamps, deserts, and roaring waters. We will show you how to avoid the dangerous paths infested with rattlesnakes and scorpions. Our adventure will be challenging—and exciting. In the course of the journey, we may even help you find the fabled land of client/server "milk and honey."

Part 1 of any good Survival Guide always starts with mapping the treacherous terrain. This is where you get the bird's-eye view of things—continents, oceans, forests, and Manhattan traffic jams. We create such a map for the world of client/server.

We start with an overview of what client/server is and what the fuss is all about. We explain what client/server computing can do, as well as what makes a product client/server. Then we develop a game using client/server building blocks that will help you navigate through the treacherous terrain. Finally, we go over the state of the client/server infrastructure—the equivalent of roads, bridges, and airports for client/server.

Chapter 1

Your Guide to the New World

Don't stand in the doorway
Don't block the hall
For he that gets hurt
Will be he who has stalled...
  For the times they are
  a-changin

— *Bob Dylan, 1963*

THE GOOD OLD DAYS

Back in the days when mainframes roamed the Earth, life was simple. The big choice of the day was how to pick the "right" computer vendor. And there were only a few you could choose. Once that choice was behind you, everything else fell into place. A staff of superbly trained analysts supervised the powering up of a great big box with a matching operating system. Data communications specialists could fine-tune, in a matter of hours, the octopus-like front-end network that brought hundreds of remote terminals into the fold. They were followed by storage specialists who would hookup "farms" of disk and tape drives. Maintenance and system management were built into every component. If anything went wrong, you knew exactly who to call—your on-site systems engineer.

If you had to write applications, your vendor would provide the "right" set of top-down methodologies, case tools, and run-time subsystems. There were, of course, five-year plans and grand architectures to help you design your future growth and budget for it. Most importantly, there was job security, a career path, and a bright future for everybody in the computer industry. And revenues were good for mainstream computer vendors and for the niche players that marketed within their orbits. These were the good old days before the client/server and "open" systems revolution.

LIFE AFTER THE REVOLUTION

Life is not as simple in the new world of client/server and open systems. Client/server computing is the ultimate "open platform." Client/server gives you the freedom to mix-and-match components at almost any level. You can put together an incredible variety of networked client and server combinations. Everything in the client/server world is sold *a la carte*.

At every turn, you will be presented with a Chinese restaurant menu of choices: Which server platform? Which client platform? Which network protocols? Which distributed computing infrastructure? Which database server? Which set of middleware? Which system management base? If you get past the first set of choices, you will face even tougher new choices in the area of client/server application development and tools. There are at least five major technologies that can be used to create client/server applications: database servers, TP Monitors, groupware, distributed objects, and Intranets. Which one is best?

You're the one who makes the tough decisions in this new world order. To succeed, you'll need to pick the right client/server platform, tools, vendors, and architecture base. You must identify and ride the *right* client/server technology wave. If the winning wave is distributed objects, it doesn't make sense to invest time and energy in database servers. But if you pick the object wave too soon, it may shipwreck your business. So it's important that you know exactly what the technology can do for you at a given point in time. To figure this out, you must be able to sort your way through the marketing slogans and architectural promises. Most importantly, you need to know exactly what existing products can do for you *today*.

The good news in all of this is that client/server technology is liberating, flexible, and allows you to do the great things we will describe later in this book. The bad news is that you're on your own. The vendors will sell you their products at near-commodity prices, but you'll have to figure out how to make the pieces work together. If they don't work, it's your problem. No promises were made when the

goods were sold. Yes, system integrators can help, but they don't come cheap. So what happened to the good old days? They're gone. Vendors now sell piecemeal components. Everything is unbundled. Even service is priced separately. In this new *a la carte* world, you are the system integrator.

THE SURVIVAL PLAN

We, the authors, have been roaming in the wilderness for quite some time, and the result is this Client/Server Survival Guide. It will help you survive, but it won't be easy. Nobody, unfortunately, has that magic map with all the correct paths. We will share with you our insights which, when combined with yours, may help you take the least treacherous path. A Survival Guide is more than just a map. It contains instructions for how to find food, build shelter, navigate in strange terrain, and protect yourself from snakes and scorpions. We'll provide all of this.

We will first go over the client and server sides of the equation. We will then work on the slash (/) in client/server—that's the glue that ties the client with the server. We will go over the five leading technologies for developing client/server applications: database servers, TP Monitors, groupware, distributed objects, and the Internet. We will conclude by covering system management platforms and tools.

Chapter 2

Welcome to Client/Server Computing

In no way does Internet computing replace client/server computing. That's because it already is client/server computing.

— Herb Edelstein, Principal
Euclid Associates
(April, 1996)

At times, it seems as if everyone associated with computing has something to say about the client/server relationship. In this chapter, you get one more "definitive" viewpoint of what this all means. We will first look at the market forces that are driving the client/server industry today. After coming this far, we feel we can handle even more danger in our lives, so we tackle the big issue of trying to answer the question: *Just what is client/server anyway*? We then get into a diatribe on fat clients versus fat servers. Finally, we peek through our crystal ball to give you a little glimpse of where things are going with the client/server industry. And we introduce the forthcoming *intergalactic* client/server era.

THE CLIENT/SERVER COMPUTING ERA

Client/server computing is an irresistible movement that is reshaping the way computers are being used. Although this computing movement is relatively young, it is already in full force and is not leaving any facet of the computer industry untouched. In addition, the Internet is like a tsunami; it is introducing a new form of client/server computing—*intergalactic* client/server. It's a revolution within the revolution.

What will the brave new world of client/server computing look like? What effect will it have on IS shops? What does it mean to compete in an open client/server computing market? What new opportunities does it create for software developers? Let's try to answer these questions now.

What's the Real Client/Server Vision?

Client/server computing has the unique distinction of having strong champions across the entire spectrum of the computer industry. For the "PC can do it all" crowd, client/server computing means scrapping every mainframe that can't fit on the desktop and the demise of host-centric computing. For mainframe diehards, client/server computing means unleashing a new breed of "born-again" networked mainframes that will bring every PC in the enterprise back to the fold. For the middle of the roaders, client/server is "computer glasnost," which really means a new era of co-existence and openness in which all can play.

There is some truth in all these visions. Client/server computing provides an open and flexible environment where mix-and-match is the rule. The client applications will run predominantly on PCs and other desktop machines that are at home on LANs. The successful servers will also feel at home on LANs and know exactly how to communicate with their PC clients. Beefy PCs make natural superservers. For mainframes to succeed as servers, however, they will have to learn how to meet PCs as equals on the LAN. In this world of equals, mainframe servers cannot treat PCs as dumb terminals. They need to support peer-to-peer protocols, interpret PC messages, service their PC clients' files in their native formats, and provide data and services to PCs in the most direct manner. Ultimately, the server platform with the best cost/performance and the most services wins.

Client/Server and the "New IS"

Client/server application development requires hybrid skills that include transaction processing, database design, communications experience, and graphical user interface savvy. The more advanced applications require a knowledge of distributed objects and the Internet. Mastering these skills will require renaissance programmers who can combine the best of "big-iron," reliability-driven thinking with the PC LAN traditions. Where will these renaissance programmers come from? Will IS shops be able to provide solutions and services in this new computing environment? Or will that service be provided by consultants and system integrators who have taken the time to learn these new skills?

Most client/server solutions today are PC LAN implementations that are personalized for the group that uses them. Everything from LAN directories to security requirements must be properly configured, often by the users themselves. IS departments have the skills to not only manage and deploy large networks but also to provide interoperability standards. They also know how to fine-tune applications, distribute fixes, and ensure data integrity. IS traditionally caters to the large data centers—not to the line departments that own the PCs and LANs. The key is for them to do what they do well in a distributed client/server environment where they share the power, responsibility, computing know-how, and financial budgets with the line business managers (the end-users). Consequently, distributing the IS function is essential.

Client/server computing may be best served by two-tiered IS organizations: a line IS for managing and deploying departmental systems, and an enterprise IS for managing the global network and setting interoperability standards. This type of aligned federation will not only preserve departmental autonomy but will also allow the local LANs to be part of the multiserver, multivendor global network.

Competition in the Client/Server Market

Client/server, the *great equalizer* of the computer business, encourages openness and provides a level playing field on which a wide variety of client and server platforms can participate. The open client/server environment serves as the catalyst for "commoditizing" hardware and system software. The PC is a good example of a computer commodity; it can be obtained from multiple suppliers and is sold in very price-competitive market situations. LAN adapters, LAN protocol stacks, network routers, and bridges are also becoming commodities. On the software side, PC operating systems, SQL Database Management Systems (DBMSs), and Web servers and browsers are approaching commodity status. CORBA, Network OLE, and the Distributed Computing Environment (DCE) will make instant commodities out of distributed objects, network directory software, security services, and system management. These trends are good news for computer users.

But where are the *great differentiators* that will set vendors apart in this highly competitive commodity environment? What will happen to the computer vendors when commodity-priced client/server computing power satisfies the needs for computerization as we know it today?

Computer vendors will in the short run differentiate themselves by the power of the superservers they provide. This will last until commodity operating systems start to routinely support multiprocessor hardware platforms. We anticipate that the most sustained differentiation will be in the area of new client/server software and not hardware platforms. PCs and client/server solutions will unleash a massive new wave of computerization. For example, image and multimedia enhanced client/server solutions have ravenous appetites for storage, network bandwidth, and processing power. These solutions will easily consume the new supply of low-cost client/server systems, as long as software providers can create enough applications.

We foresee a brave new era of ubiquitous client/server computing. Clients will be everywhere. They will come in all shapes and forms—including desktops, palmtops, pen tablets, intelligent appliances, mobile personal communicators, electronic clipboards, TV sets, intelligent books, robots, automobile dashboards, Internet PCs, and myriads of yet-to-be-invented, information-hungry devices. These clients, wherever they are, will be able to obtain the services of millions of other servers. In this brave new world, every client can also be a server. This bullish view of the industry puts us in the camp of those who believe that *the supply of low-cost MIPs creates its own demand.*

The Internet and Intranets

The World Wide Web is redefining client/server computing. In many cases, it is causing departmental LANs and corporate WANs to morph into the Internet— technically, they're *Intranets* because they hide behind firewalls. But these Intranets are breaking down the traditional barriers between departmental and enterprise client/server computing. Instead, we have webs of servers that are interconnected at an intergalactic level. The corporate LANs and WANs become part of the Internet, and vice versa.

WHAT IS CLIENT/SERVER?

Even though client/server is the leading industry buzzword, there is no consensus on what that term actually means. So, we have a fine opportunity to create our own definition. As the name implies, clients and servers are separate logical entities that work together over a network to accomplish a task. So what makes client/server different from other forms of distributed software? We propose that all client/server systems have the following distinguishing characteristics:

- **Service:** Client/server is primarily a relationship between processes running on separate machines. The server process is a provider of services. The client is a consumer of services. In essence, client/server provides a clean separation of function based on the idea of service.

- **Shared resources:** A server can service many clients at the same time and regulate their access to shared resources.

- **Asymmetrical protocols:** There is a many-to-one relationship between clients and server. Clients always *initiate* the dialog by requesting a service. Servers are passively awaiting requests from the clients.

- **Transparency of location:** The server is a process that can reside on the same machine as the client or on a different machine across a network. Client/server software usually masks the location of the server from the clients by redirecting the service calls when needed. A program can be a client, a server, or both.

- **Mix-and-match:** The ideal client/server software is independent of hardware or operating system software platforms. You should be able to mix-and-match client and server platforms.

- **Message-based exchanges:** Clients and servers are loosely coupled systems that interact through a message-passing mechanism. The message is the delivery mechanism for the service requests and replies.

- **Encapsulation of services:** The server is a "specialist." A message tells a server what service is requested; it is then up to the server to determine how to get the job done. Servers can be upgraded without affecting the clients as long as the published message interface is not changed.

- **Scalability:** Client/server systems can be scaled horizontally or vertically. Horizontal scaling means adding or removing client workstations with only a slight performance impact. Vertical scaling means migrating to a larger and faster server machine or multiservers.

- **Integrity:** The server code and server data is centrally maintained, which results in cheaper maintenance and the guarding of shared data integrity. At the same time, the clients remain personal and independent.

The client/server characteristics described here allow intelligence to be easily distributed across a network. These features also provide a framework for the design of loosely coupled, network-based applications.

WILL THE REAL CLIENT/SERVER PLEASE STAND UP?

Many systems with very different architectures have been called "client/server." System vendors often use client/server as if the term can only be applied to their specific packages. For example, file server vendors swear they first invented the term, and database server vendors are known in some circles solely as *the* client/server vendors. To add to the confusion, this book adds distributed objects, TP Monitors, groupware, and the Internet to the list of client/server technologies. So who is right? Which of these technologies is the real client/server? The answer to both of these questions is all of the above.

The idea of splitting an application along client/server lines has been used over the last ten years to create various forms of Local Area Network (LAN) software solutions. Typically, these solutions sell as shrink-wrapped software packages, and many are sold by more than one vendor. Each of these solutions, however, is distinguished by the nature of the service it provides to its clients, as shown in the following sections.

File Servers

With a file server, the client (typically a PC) passes requests for file records over a network to the file server (Figure 2-1). This is a very primitive form of data service that necessitates many message exchanges over the network to find the requested data. File servers are useful for sharing files across a network. They are indispensable for creating shared repositories of documents, images, engineering drawings, and other large data objects.

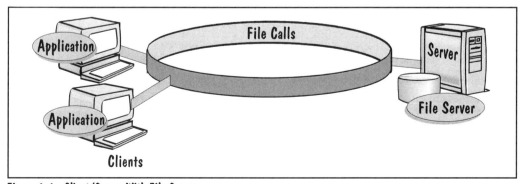

Figure 2-1. Client/Server With File Servers.

Database Servers

With a database server, the client passes SQL requests as messages to the database server (Figure 2-2). The results of each SQL command are returned over the network. The code that processes the SQL request and the data reside on the same machine. The server uses its own processing power to find the requested data instead of passing all the records back to a client and then letting it find its own data, as was the case for the file server. The result is a much more efficient use of distributed processing power. With this approach, the server code is shrink-wrapped by the vendor. But you often need to write code for the client application (or you can buy shrink-wrapped clients like Quest or Paradox). Database servers provide the foundation for decision-support systems that require ad hoc queries and flexible reports.

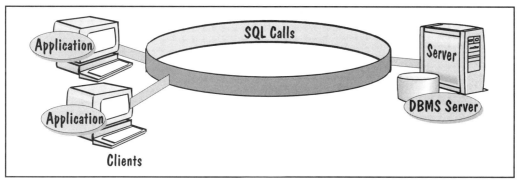

Figure 2-2. Client/Server With Database Servers.

Transaction Servers

With a transaction server, the client invokes *remote procedures* that reside on the server with an SQL database engine (Figure 2-3). These remote procedures on the server execute a group of SQL statements. The network exchange consists of a single request/reply message (as opposed to the database server's approach of one request/reply message for each SQL statement in a transaction). The SQL statements either all succeed or fail as a unit. These grouped SQL statements are called *transactions*.

With a transaction server, you create the client/server application by writing the code for both the client and server components. The client component usually includes a Graphical User Interface (GUI). The server component usually consists of SQL transactions against a database. These applications are called *Online Transaction Processing, or OLTP.* They tend to be mission-critical applications that require a 1-3 second response time 100% of the time. OLTP applications also

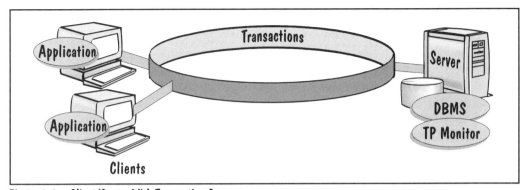

Figure 2-3.   Client/Server With Transaction Servers.

require tight controls over the security and integrity of the database. Two forms of OLTP will be discussed in this book: *TP Lite*, based on the stored procedures provided by database vendors; and *TP Heavy*, based on the TP Monitors provided by OLTP vendors.

Groupware Servers

Groupware addresses the management of semi-structured information such as text, image, mail, bulletin boards, and the flow of work. These client/server systems place people in direct contact with other people. Lotus Notes is the leading example of such a system, although a number of other applications—including document management, imaging, multiparty applications, and workflow—are addressing some of the same needs. Specialized groupware software can be built on top of a vendor's canned set of client/server APIs. In most cases, applications are created using a scripting language and form-based interfaces provided by the vendor. The communication middleware between the client and the server is vendor-specific (Figure 2-4). Eventually, the Internet will become the middleware of choice for groupware.

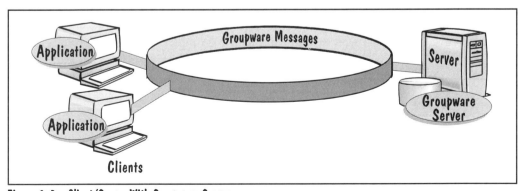

Figure 2-4.   Client/Server With Groupware Servers.

Object Servers

With an object server, the client/server application is written as a set of communi-cating objects (Figure 2-5). Client objects communicate with server objects using an *Object Request Broker (ORB)*. The client invokes a method on a remote object. The ORB locates an instance of that object server class, invokes the requested method, and returns the results to the client object. Server objects must provide support for concurrency and sharing. The ORB brings it all together. After years of incubation, some "real life" commercial ORBs are now in production. Examples of commercial ORBs that comply with the Object Management Group's CORBA standard include Digital's *ObjectBroker*, IBM's *SOM 3.0*, Sun's *NEO*, HP's *ORB Plus*, Expersoft's *PowerBroker*, Iona's *Orbix*, and PostModern's *BlackWidow*. However, CORBA is not the only game in town. As we go to press, Microsoft is getting ready to ship its own ORB, which it calls *Distributed COM (DCOM)* or *Network OLE*.

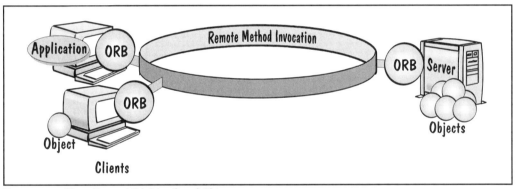

Figure 2-5. Client/Server With Distributed Objects.

Web Servers

The World Wide Web is the first truly intergalactic client/server application. This new model of client/server consists of thin, portable, "universal" clients that talk to superfat servers. In its simplest incarnation, a Web server returns documents when clients ask for them by name (see Figure 2-6). The clients and servers communicate using an RPC-like protocol called HTTP. This protocol defines a simple set of commands; parameters are passed as strings, with no provision for typed data. The Web is being extended to provide more interactive forms of client/server computing. In addition, the Web and distributed objects are starting to come together. Java is the first manifestation of this new Object Web.

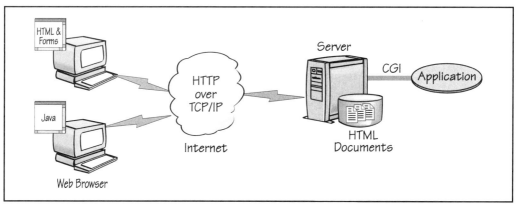

Figure 2-6.   Client/Server With Web Servers.

So What Is "Middleware"?

Briefing

Mid.dle.ware: 1) a hodgepodge of software technologies; 2) a buzzword; 3) a key to developing client/server applications.

— *Information Week*

Middleware is a vague term that covers all the distributed software needed to support interactions between clients and servers. Think of it as the software that's in the middle of the client/server system. In this Survival Guide we refer to middleware as the slash (/) component of client/server. It's the glue that lets a client obtain a service from a server. Where does the middleware start and where does it end? It starts with the API set on the client side that is used to invoke a service, and it covers the transmission of the request over the network and the resulting response. Middleware does not include the software that provides the actual service—that's in the server's domain. It also does not include the user interface or the application's logic—that's in the client's domain.

We divide middleware into two broad classes:

■ *General middleware* is the substrate for most client/server interactions. It includes the communication stacks, distributed directories, authentication services, network time, remote procedure calls, and queuing services. This category also includes the network operating system extensions such as distributed file and print services. Products that fall into the general middleware category include DCE, ONC+, NetWare, Named Pipes, LAN Server, LAN Manager, Vines, TCP/IP, APPC, and NetBIOS. We also include the Message-

Oriented Middleware (also known as MOM) products from Peerlogic, Covia, Message Express, System Strategies, and IBM.

■ *Service-specific middleware* is needed to accomplish a particular client/server type of service. This includes:

◆ Database-specific middleware such as ODBC, DRDA, EDA/SQL, SAG/CLI, and Oracle Glue.

◆ OLTP-specific middleware such as Tuxedo's ATMI and /WS, Encina's Transactional RPC, and X/Open's TxRPC and XATMI.

◆ Groupware-specific middleware such as MAPI, VIM, VIC, SMTP, and Lotus Notes calls.

◆ Object-specific middleware such as OMG's CORBA and Microsoft's Network OLE (or DCOM).

◆ Internet-specific middleware such as HTTP, S-HTTP, and SSL.

◆ System management-specific middleware such as SNMP, CMIP, and ORBs.

You can probably tell by now that middleware was created by people who love acronyms. To the best of our knowledge, few technologies have as many buzzwords and acronyms as client/server middleware. We will cover, in gruesome detail, the middleware standards that apply to the different client/server application types. By the time you finish reading this Survival Guide, you'll know exactly what all these middleware acronyms mean. In the meantime, please bear with us as we gradually pull together the pieces of this story. ❑

FAT SERVERS OR FAT CLIENTS?

So far, we've shown you that client/server models can be distinguished by the service they provide. Client/server applications can also be differentiated by how the distributed application is split between the client and the server (see Figure 2-7). The *fat server model* places more function on the server. The *fat client model* does the reverse. Groupware, transaction, and Web servers are examples of fat servers; database and file servers are examples of fat clients. Distributed objects can be either.

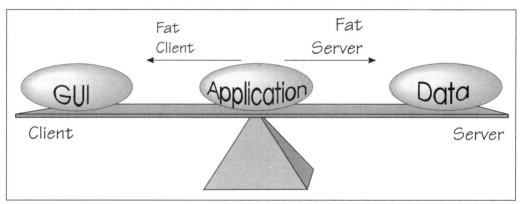

Figure 2-7.   Fat Clients or Fat Servers?

Fat clients are the more traditional form of client/server. The bulk of the application runs on the client side of the equation. In both the file server and database server models, the clients know how the data is organized and stored on the server side. Fat clients are used for decision support and personal software. They provide flexibility and opportunities for creating front-end tools that let end-users create their own applications.

Fat server applications are easier to manage and deploy on the network because most of the code runs on the servers. Fat servers try to minimize network interchanges by creating more abstract levels of service. Transaction and object servers, for example, encapsulate the database. Instead of exporting raw data, they export the procedures (or methods in object-oriented terminology) that operate on that data. The client in the fat server model provides the GUI and interacts with the server through remote procedure calls (or method invocations).

Each client/server model has its uses. In many cases, the models complement each other, and it is not unusual to have them coexist in one application. For example, a groupware imaging application could require an "all-in-one" server that combines file, database, transaction, and object services. Fat servers, used for mission-critical applications, represent the new growth area for PC-based client/server computing.

2-TIER VERSUS 3-TIER

High-brow client/server pundits prefer to use terms like 2-tier and 3-tier client/server architectures instead of fat clients and fat servers. But it's the same basic idea. It's all about how you split the client/server application into functional units that you can then assign to either the client or to one or more servers. The most typical functional units are the user interface, the business logic, and the shared data. There many possible variations of multi-tier architectures depending on how you split the application and the middleware you use to communicate between the tiers.

In 2-tier client/server systems, the application logic is either buried inside the user interface on the client or within the database on the server (or both). In 3-tier client/server systems, the application logic (or process) lives in the middle-tier; it is separated from the from the data and user interface (see the next Warning). Processes become first-class citizens; they can be managed and deployed separately from the GUI and the database. In theory, 3-tier client/server systems are more scalable, robust, and flexible. In addition, they can integrate data from multiple sources. Examples of 3-tier client/server systems are TP Monitors, distributed objects, and the Web. Examples of 2-tier client/server systems are file servers and database servers with stored procedures. According to Gartner Group, 3-tier will grow from 5% of all client/server applications in 1995 to 33% in 1998.

3-Tier Is an Overloaded Word

Warning

3-tier is an overloaded word in the client/server literature. It was first used to describe the physical partitioning of an application across PCs (tier 1), departmental servers (tier 2), and enterprise servers (tier 3). Later it was used to describe a partitioning across client (tier 1), local database (tier 2), and enterprise database (tier 3). Now, the in vogue definition is client (tier 1), application server (tier 2), and database server (tier 3). ❏

INTERGALACTIC CLIENT/SERVER

If you're like most of us—just starting to feel comfortable with your Ethernet departmental LAN and local database server—you may not want to hear this: Our industry is poised for a second client/server revolution. Fasten your seat belts because this second revolution promises to be just as traumatic as the one we just went through when client/server applied a giant chainsaw to mainframe-based monolithic applications and broke them apart into client and server components.

Client/server applications stand at a new threshold brought on by: 1) the exponential increase of low-cost bandwidth on Wide Area Networks—for example, the Internet and CompuServe; and 2) a new generation of network-enabled, multi-threaded desktop operating systems—for example, OS/2 Warp Connect and Windows 95. This new threshold marks the beginning of a transition from *Ethernet* client/server to *intergalactic* client/server that will result in the irrelevance of proximity. The center of gravity is shifting from single-server, 2-tier, LAN-based departmental client/server to a post-scarcity form of client/server where every machine on the global "information highway" can be both a client and a server. Table 2-1 contrasts these two eras of client/server computing.

Table 2-1. Web Client/Server Versus Traditional Client/Server.

Application Characteristic	Intergalactic Era Client/Server	Ethernet Era Client/Server
Number of clients per application	Millions	Less than 100
Number of servers per application	100,000+	1 or 2
Geography	Global	Campus-based
Server-to-server interactions	Yes	No
Middleware	ORBs on top of Internet	SQL and stored procedures
Client/server architecture	3-tier (or n-tier)	2-tier
Transactional updates	Pervasive	Very infrequent
Multimedia content	High	Low
Mobile agents	Yes	No
Client front-ends	OOUIs, compound documents, and shippable places	GUI
Time-frame	1997-2000	1985 till present

The Intergalactic Vision

The big insight for the next ten years is this: What if digital communications were free? The answer is that the way we learn, buy, socialize, do business, and entertain ourselves will be very different.

> — Bill Gates, Chairman
> Microsoft
> (January, 1995)

When it comes to intergalactic client/server applications, the imagination is at the controls. The promise of high bandwidth at very low cost has conjured visions of an information highway that turns into the world's largest shopping mall. The predominant vision is that of an electronic bazaar of planetary proportions—replete with boutiques, department stores, bookstores, brokerage services, banks, and travel agencies. Like a Club Med, the mall will issue its own electronic currency to facilitate round-the-clock shopping and business-to-business transactions. Electronic agents of all kinds will be roaming around the network looking for bargains and conducting negotiations with other agents. Billions of electronic business transactions will be generated on a daily basis. Massive amounts of multimedia data will also be generated, moved, and stored on the network.

Obviously, what we're describing is not the Internet as we know it today—there is a lot more to this vision than just surfing through hypertext webs of HTML-tagged information. We're talking about transaction rates that are thousands of times larger than anything we have today. In addition, these transactions are going to be more long-lived and complex. The data these transactions operate on will also be more complex and rich in multimedia content. So we're talking about the next generation of Internet technology, which we call in this book the *Object Web* (see Part 8). This technology will also be used on small "i" Internets—or Intranets—including LANs, interbusiness networks, and private wide-area networks.

What Do We Need?

Some key technologies are needed at the client/server application level to make all this happen, including:

■ ***Rich transaction processing***. In addition to supporting the venerable flat transaction, the new environment requires nested transactions that can span across multiple servers, long-lived transactions that execute over long periods of time as they travel from server to server, and queued transactions that can be used in secure business-to-business dealings. Most nodes on the network should be able to participate in a secured transaction; superserver nodes will handle the massive transaction loads.

■ *Roaming agents*. The new environment will be populated with electronic agents of all types. Consumers will have personal agents that look after their interests; businesses will deploy agents to sell their wares on the network; and sniffer agents will be sitting on the network, at all times, collecting information to do system management or simply looking for trends. Agent technology includes cross-platform scripting engines, workflow, and Java-like mobile code environments that allow agents to live on any machine on the network.

■ *Rich data management*. This includes active multimedia compound documents that you can move, store, view, and edit in-place anywhere on the network. Again, most nodes on the network should provide compound document technology—for example, OLE or OpenDoc—for doing mobile document management. Of course, this environment must also be able to support existing record-based structured data including SQL databases.

■ *Intelligent self-managing entities*. With the introduction of new multi-threaded, high-volume, network-ready desktop operating systems, we anticipate a world where millions of machines can be both clients and servers. However, we can't afford to ship a system administrator with every $99 operating system. To avoid doing this, we need distributed software that knows how to manage and configure itself and protect itself against threats.

■ *Intelligent middleware*. The distributed environment must provide the semblance of a single system-image across potentially millions of hybrid client/server machines. The middleware must create this Houdini-sized illusion by making all servers on the global network appear to behave like a single computer system. Users and programs should be able to dynamically join and leave the network, and then discover each other. You should be able to use the same naming conventions to locate any resource on the network.

This is a tall order of requirements. Can our client/server infrastructure—conceived to meet the needs of the single-server Ethernet era—meet the new challenges? Is our client/server infrastructure ready for intergalactic prime time? Can our existing middleware deal with millions of machines that can be both clients and servers? We answer these questions in the rest of this book.

Chapter 3

Client/Server Building Blocks

What are you able to build with your blocks? Castles and palaces, temples and docks.

— **Robert Louis Stevenson**
A Child's Garden of Verses

We are all familiar with the concept of *architecture* as applied in the construction of buildings. Architectures help us identify structural elements that may be used as building blocks in the construction of ever more complex systems. Just like we buy homes, instead of plans, users in the computer industry buy solutions to business problems, instead of grand client/server architectures. But architecture determines the structure of the houses, high rises, office buildings, and cities where we live and work. In the computer analogy, architecture helps us determine the structure and shape of the client/server systems we can build to meet various needs.

The "million dollar" architectural questions we will cover here are: How is the application split between the client and the server? What function goes in the client and what function goes in the server? Can the client/server model accommodate businesses of all sizes? How are the new tribes of nomadic laptop users brought into the client/server fold? Can client/server play in the home? Where do peer networks fit in this picture? Will client/server disappear in a post-scarcity computing world?

CLIENT/SERVER: A ONE SIZE FITS ALL MODEL

Can a single client/server model accommodate all these types of users? We think we have such a model. It is deceptively simple, and it works well with today's technologies. It is ideally suited for dealing with the needs of a *post-scarcity computing* world, where client/server becomes the ultimate medium for sharing and collaborating.

The model we present in this section is really a game of putting together things with building blocks. We will show you how we can meet a wide spectrum of client/server needs—from the tiny to the intergalactic—with just three basic building blocks: a client, a server, and the slash (/) that ties the client to the server (see Figure 3-1). Kids of all ages will love this game. It should help you identify some durable structures in the design of client/server systems.

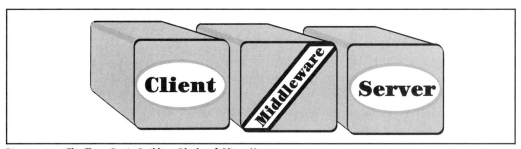

Figure 3-1. The Three Basic Building Blocks of Client/Server.

In the next few sections, we explain (and illustrate) how the building-block arrangements are used in four situations:

- *Client/server for tiny shops and nomadic tribes* is a building-block implementation that runs the client, the middleware software, and most of the business services on the same machine. It is the suggested implementation for the one-person shops, home offices, and mobile users with well-endowed laptops. This is a new opportunity area for client/server technology.

- *Client/server for small shops and departments* is the classic Ethernet client/single-server building-block implementation. It is used in small shops, departments, and branch offices. This is the predominant form of client/server today.

- *Client/server for intergalactic enterprises* is the multiserver building-block implementation of client/server. The servers present a single system image to the client. They can be spread out throughout the enterprise, but they can be made to look like they're part of the local desktop. This implementation meets the initial needs of intergalactic client/server computing.

■ *Client/server for a post-scarcity world* transforms every machine in the world into both a client and a server. Personal agents on every machine will handle all the negotiations with their peer agents anywhere in the universe. This dream is almost within reach.

You will discover many similarities in the four arrangements. This is because they all use the same type of software, middleware, and communications infrastructure.

Client/Server for Tiny Shops and Nomadic Tribes

The nice thing about client/server is that it's infinitely malleable. It is easy to run the client and server portion of an application on the same machine. Vendors can easily package single-user versions of a client/server application (see Figure 3-2). For example, a client/server application for a dentist's office can be sold in a single-user package for offices consisting of a single dentist and in a multiuser package for offices with many dentists. The same client/server application covers both cases. The only caveat is that you need to use an operating system that is robust enough to run both the client and server sides of the application.

The example of the tiny dentist's office also works for the tiny in-home business office and the mobile user on the road. In all cases, the business-critical client/server

Figure 3-2.   Client/Server for Tiny Shops and Nomadic Users.

application runs on one machine and does some occasional communications with outside servers to exchange data, refresh a database, and send or receive mail and faxes. For example, the one-person dentist's office may need to communicate with outside servers such as insurance company billing computers. And, of course, everyone needs to be on the Internet, even dentists.

Client/Server for Small Shops and Departments

The client/server architecture is particularly well-suited for the LAN-based single server establishments. So, it's no wonder that they account for around 80% of today's client/server installations. This is the "archetypical" Ethernet model of client/server. It consists of multiple clients talking to a local server (see Figure 3-3). This is the model used in small businesses—for example, a multiuser dentist office—and by the departments of large corporations—for example, the branch offices of a bank.

The single-server nature of the model tends to keep the middleware simple. The client only needs to look into a configuration file to find its server's name. Security is implemented at the machine level and kept quite simple. The network is usually relatively easy to administer; it's a part-time job for a member of the group. There are no complex interactions between servers, so it is easy to identify failures— they're either on the client or on the local server.

Braver souls may be using their server to interact in a very loosely-coupled way with some enterprise server. For example, data (such as a price list) may be downloaded once a day to refresh the local server. Or inventory data may be uploaded to an

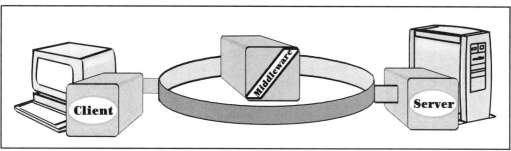

Figure 3-3. Client/Server for Small Shops and Departments.

enterprise server. Fax and mail can be sent or received any time through the mail server gateway. Typically, the software that interacts with remote servers will reside on the departmental server.

Departmental servers will continue to be popular, even in large enterprises, because they provide a tremendous amount of user autonomy and controls. Users feel that it is *their* server, and they can do anything they please with it. A departmental server's applications typically address the specific needs of the local clients first, which make users very happy. With fiber optics and high-speed ATM connections, it will be hard to detect a performance difference between a local departmental server and an enterprise server a continent away. However, the psychology (and politics) of ownership will always provide a powerful motivator for holding on to that local server.

In summary, this implementation of client/server uses our three building blocks to create the classical single-server model of client/server that is so predominant in the Ethernet era. This model works very well in small businesses and departments that depend on single servers or on very loosely-coupled multiserver arrangements.

Client/Server for Intergalactic Enterprises

The client/server enterprise model addresses the needs of establishments with a mix of heterogeneous servers. This is an area that's getting a lot of industry attention as solutions move from a few large computers to multiple servers that live on the Internet, Intranets, and corporate backbone networks (see Figure 3-4). One of the great things about the client/server model is that it is upwardly scalable. When more processing power is needed for various intergalactic functions, more servers can be added (thus creating a pool of servers), or the existing server machine can be traded up for the latest generation of superserver machine.

We can partition servers based on the function they provide, the resource they control, or the database they own. In addition, we may choose to replicate servers for fault tolerance or to boost an application's performance. There can be as many

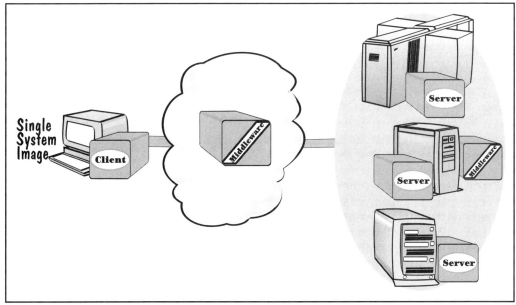

Figure 3-4. Client/Server for Intergalactic Enterprises.

server combinations as your budget will tolerate. Multiserver capability, when properly used, can provide an awesome amount of compute power and flexibility, in many cases rivaling that of mainframes.

To exploit the full power of multiservers, we need low-cost, high-speed bandwidth and an awesome amount of middleware features—including network directory services, network security, remote procedure calls, and network time services. Middleware creates a common view of all the services on the network called a "single system image."

Good software architecture for intergalactic enterprise client/server implementations is all about creating system "ensembles" out of modular building blocks. With some practice, you may develop creative skills akin to those of a symphony composer in the articulation of software components that run on multiple servers. You will need to find creative ways to partition work among the servers. For example, you may partition the work using distributed objects. You will also need to design your servers so that they can delegate work to their fellow servers. A complex request may involve a task force of servers working together on the request. Preferably, the client should not be made aware of this behind-the-scenes collaboration. The server that the client first contacts should be in charge of orchestrating the task force and returning its findings to the client.

Intergalactic client/server is the driving force behind middleware standards such as distributed objects and the Internet. We're all looking for that magic bullet that will make the distributed multivendor world as integrated as single-vendor mainframes. Tools for creating, deploying, and managing scalable client/server applications are getting a lot of attention. There are fortunes to be made in intergalactic client/server because nobody has yet put all of the pieces back together.

Client/Server for a Post-Scarcity World

In this section, we up the ante. We will investigate what new systems can be created on a client/server platform when memory and hardware become *incredibly afford-able*. Every machine is both a client and a full-function server (see Figure 3-5). We call this plentiful environment *the post-scarcity world*. We imagine the typical post-scarcity machine as a $2000 cellular notebook powered by a 200 MHz Pentium and loaded with 100 MBytes of RAM and 100 GBytes or more of disk space. And, of course, this machine runs all the middleware that vendors will be able to dream of over the next few years.

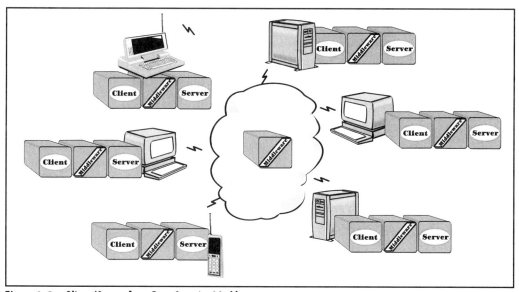

Figure 3-5.   Client/Server for a Post-Scarcity World.

What do we do with all this power other than run middleware? What happens when every machine in the world becomes a universal server and client? Because every machine is a full-function server, we should assume it will run, at a minimum, a file server, database server, workflow agent, TP Monitor, and Web server—all connected via an ORB. This is in addition to all the client software and middleware.

What we're saying is that in the next few years, a hundred million machines or more may be running *almost all* the forms of client/server software described in this book. This should be good news to TP Monitor, ORB, groupware, Internet, and database vendors—it's a huge opportunity. Are they thinking about it? Do they have the proper packaging and marketing channels to go after it? After you read this book, you'll have a better appreciation for how complex, powerful, and essential this software is. So who will manage and run all that software on behalf of the user? *Personal agents*, of course (see next cartoon).

INSIDE THE BUILDING BLOCKS

In the last sections we introduced the three *building blocks* of client/server: the client, the server, and the middleware slash (/) that ties them together. Figure 3-6 peels the next layer off the onion and provides more detail about what goes into each of the building blocks. What you see in this figure is, in a nutshell, the entire client/server software infrastructure. Let's go over the pieces:

■ **The client building block** runs the client side of the application. It runs on an Operating System (OS) that provides a Graphical User Interface (GUI) or an Object Oriented User Interface (OOUI) and that can access distributed services, wherever they may be. The operating system most often passes the buck to the middleware building block and lets it handle the non-local services. The client also runs a component of the *Distributed System Management (DSM)* element. This could be anything from a simple agent on a managed PC to the entire front-end of the DSM application on a managing station.

■ *The server building block* runs the server side of the application. The server application typically runs on top of some shrink-wrapped server software package. The five contending server platforms for creating the next generation of client/server applications are SQL database servers, TP Monitors, groupware servers, object servers, and the Web. The server side depends on the operating system to interface with the middleware building block that brings in the requests for service. The server also runs a DSM component. This could be anything from a simple agent on a managed PC to the entire back-end of the DSM application (for example, it could provide a shared object database for storing system management information).

■ *The middleware building block* runs on both the client and server sides of an application. We broke this building block into three categories: transport stacks, network operating systems (NOSs), and service-specific middleware. Middleware is the nervous system of the client/server infrastructure. Like the other two building blocks, the middleware also has a DSM software component.

The Distributed System Management application runs on every node in a client/server network. A *managing* workstation collects information from all its *agents* on the network and displays it graphically. The managing workstation can also instruct its agents to perform actions on its behalf. Think of management as running an autonomous "network within a network." It is the "Big Brother" of the client/server world, but life is impossible without it.

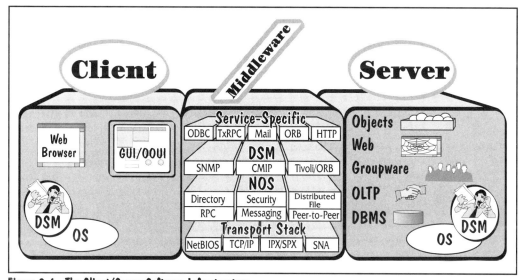

Figure 3-6. The Client/Server Software Infrastructure.

Server-to-Server Middleware

Middleware does not include the software that provides the actual service. It *does*, however, include the software that is used to coordinate inter-server interactions (see Figure 3-7). Server-to-server interactions are usually client/server in nature— servers are clients to other servers. However, some server-to-server interactions require specialized server middleware. For example, a two-phase commit protocol may be used to coordinate a transaction that executes on multiple servers. Servers on a mail backbone will use special server-to-server middleware for doing store-and-forward type messaging. But most modern software (even on operating system kernels) follows the client/server paradigm.

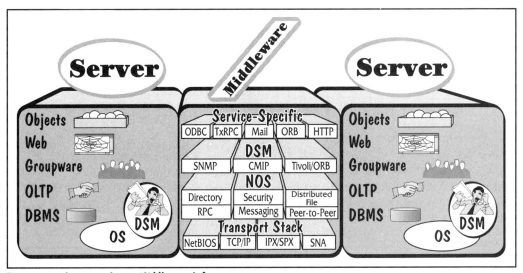

Figure 3-7. Server-to-Server Middleware Infrastructure.

The Client/Server Roadmap

The building blocks we just described will serve as our roadmap throughout this Survival Guide. It will keep you from getting lost in the client/server maze. In the next chapter, we look at the state of the networking infrastructure: When can we expect bandwidth heaven? *Part 2* covers what clients and servers need from an OS. *Part 3* is about the intergalactic NOS. We then start our ascent into the application space by covering the five competing technologies for intergalactic client/server: *Part 4* covers SQL databases and data warehousing; *Part 5* covers TP Monitors; *Part 6* covers groupware; *Part 7* covers distributed objects, components, and compound documents; and *Part 8* covers the Internet and the Web. We're almost there. *Part 9* is about how to manage these systems; it deals with the issues of distributed systems management. Finally, *Part 10* introduces a model for looking at client/server application tools and speculates on where all this is going.

Chapter 4

The Road
To Bandwidth
Heaven

If something inert is set in motion, it will gradually come to life.

— *Lao Tzu*

We hope to have convinced you that our planet will soon be covered with ubiquitous client/server webs. Using these webs, we will be able to communicate more effectively with other humans—customers, suppliers, the boss, coworkers, family, and friends. We will also be able to communicate with the everyday machines that serve us—cars, gas pumps, TV sets, and even intelligent homes.

This chapter provides an overview of the extensive networking infrastructure that supports these client/server webs. Even though this book is really about client/server software, we need to take a short detour to look at the physical networking infrastructure on which the software builds. Today, it is a very extensive infrastructure that can interconnect every network on the planet. But for intergalactic client/server to really take off, these webs must become even more ubiquitous. They must extend deep into our homes. Just as importantly, they must provide low-cost, abundant bandwidth. So what is the state of this infrastructure? When can we expect this bandwidth heaven? What obstacles remain? These are the questions we need to answer in this chapter.

SO WHAT DOES A MODERN NETWORK LOOK LIKE?

A physical network is a collection of communication links, cables, routers, switching equipment, and the transport stacks that glue it all together. Networks can be divided into two broad categories: *Local Area Networks (LANs)* that cover short distances—typically a building or campus; and *Wide Area Networks (WANs)* that cover extended geographical areas. A WAN may use physical links from multiple carriers. This section explains how LANs and WANs are interconnected into global backbones. And we briefly explain where transport stacks fit in this equation.

Bridges, Routers, and Gateways

Transport stacks—for example, TCP/IP, NetBIOS, IPX/SPX, DECnet, AppleTalk, and SNA/APPN—provide reliable end-to-end communications across WANs and LANs. So how do these protocols provide end-to-end networking on a global scale? They use the magic of LAN/WAN/LAN interconnect technology—such as routers, bridges, and gateways—to transport multiprotocol traffic across a campus or wide area network in an integrated fashion. Groups can decide for themselves what protocols to run on their local networks. And they can leave it up to the backbone providers to collect these protocols and route them across networks.

Figure 4-1 shows how bridges, routers, and gateways are used in a modern backbone network. As you can see, today's enterprise networks consists of a combination of LANs, including Token Rings and Ethernets; WANs, including public and private packet switched networks that run X.25, Frame Relay, and ATM; and the bridges, routers, and gateways that provide the internetworking, multiprotocol "glue" that ties the LANs and WANs together.

Bridges are computers or devices that interconnect LANs using link layer routing information and physical addresses; protocols that do not support internetworking, like NetBIOS, are bridged. *Routers* interconnect LANs using protocol-dependent routing information. Routers create and maintain dynamic routing tables of the destinations they know. They are typically used with protocols that support a network layer—such as TCP/IP, IPX/SPX, APPN, XNS, AppleTalk, and OSI. *Multiprotocol Routers* support different combinations of network layer protocols. *Bridge/Routers* are single devices that combine the functions of bridges and routers; they are quite popular today. *Gateways* are devices that perform brute force translations between protocols. They are used in situations where the backbone can only support one protocol, and all other protocols get translated to it.

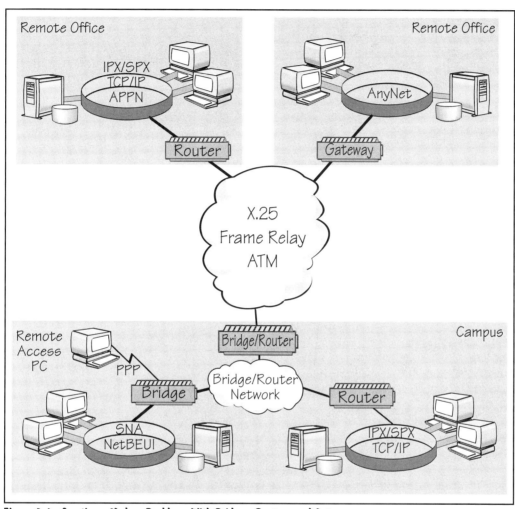

Figure 4-1. Creating a Modern Backbone With Bridges, Routers, and Gateways.

Bridge/Routers started as a bottom-up phenomenon—they solved practical problems and were not part of a grand architecture. The router products from Cisco, Bay Networks, 3Com, Digital, HP, and IBM can now encapsulate NetBIOS, Apple-Talk, SNA, and IPX/SPX to allow only a single protocol to run on the backbone (usually IPX/SPX, APPN, or TCP/IP). The industry is still learning how to make these products work in environments that require the load balancing of traffic between links and the handling of high-priority traffic. Bridges use fixed path, one-route only schemes; only a few know how to re-route traffic to alternate paths when a link fails. While they can handle any LAN-based protocols, they do not perform very well when large amounts of broadcast packets are propagated throughout the network. But the Bridge/Router industry is extremely competitive, and it will undoubtedly solve these problems. This fast-growing industry—$3 billion in 1995—is continuously introducing newer features and more robust models. For example, the newest routers use specialized protocols to determine the best paths for network traffic and can even perform load balancing across multiple parallel paths.

Despite their popularity, bridges and routers are no panacea. Segmenting LANs with bridge and routers is a band-aid, not a long-term cure. When the widespread use of multimedia starts to dramatically increase our traffic loads, routers will become *incredibly expensive* band-aids. Routers will become much harder to manage and will introduce delays that are unacceptable for real-time data flows, like motion pictures. We anticipate that routers will eventually be replaced by ATM-based backbones, which we discuss later in this chapter. Of course, if you're in the router business, you may call these high-speed ATM switches the new routers of the late-1990s.

The Transport Stacks Middleware

The Bridge/Router phenomenon is not the only area that experienced great progress. Modern operating systems—like Windows 95, OS/2 Warp Connect, NetWare, Windows NT, and Unix SVR4—are becoming much more network friendly. They've introduced features that allow multivendor communication stacks and network adapters to easily plug into them. And they also make life easier for programmers by providing APIs that are stack independent.

Here's a summary of some of the new operating system features that make that possible:

■ **The stack sandwich** provides the hooks for snapping multivendor protocol stacks into an operating system. To accommodate multivendor networks, modern operating systems must support multiple protocols, redirectors, and APIs. To do that effectively, the operating system must provide well-defined interfaces between components. A modern operating system usually "sandwiches" the transport stacks between a transport-independent interface at the top of the stacks and a logical interface to the network device drivers at the bottom of the stacks (see Figure 4-2).

■ **The logical network driver** provides a single interface to all the network adapters. This interface between the network adapter and the transport stacks is particularly important. The last thing vendors who provide transport stacks want is to write a driver for every possible network adapter. And, of course, network adapter vendors want to avoid having to interface to every possible stack. Microsoft/3Com's NDIS and Novell's ODI are the two most widely supported de facto standards for interfacing protocol stacks to network adapter

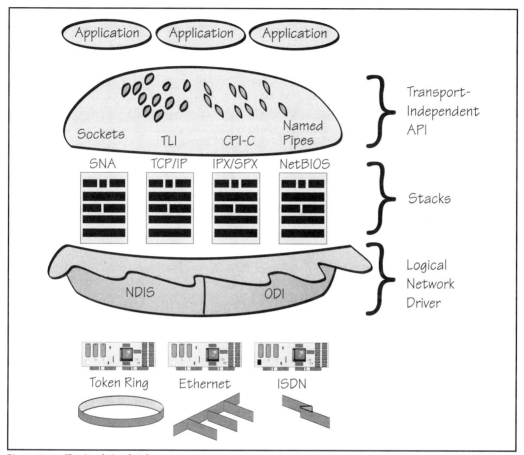

Figure 4-2. The Stack Sandwich.

device drivers. They do so by providing a logical network board that makes it easy to interface different network adapters with multiple protocol stacks (see Figure 4-2). Transport stack providers can use NDIS or ODI as the common interface to all network adapters. And network adapter vendors can use NDIS or ODI as the top layer for their network drivers. NDIS and ODI take care of sending and receiving data and managing the adapter card.

■ *The transport-independent APIs* sit on top of the transport stacks and allow developers to plug their programs into a single interface that supports multiple protocols. The *Sockets* interface is becoming the premier choice on most operating system platforms for interfacing to multivendor multiprotocol stacks. Other choices include the *Transport Layer Interface (TLI)* used in NetWare and many Unix implementations; *CPI-C*, the modern SNA peer-to-peer API that can now run over both SNA and TCP/IP stacks; and *Named Pipes* that runs on top of NetBIOS, IPX/SPX, and TCP/IP stacks.

■ *The protocol matchmakers* allow applications written for a specific transport, such as SNA, to run across other networks, such as TCP/IP or IPX/SPX (see Figure 4-3). This strategy eliminates the need for gateways and works well with existing applications. For example, a Lotus Notes application written for NetBIOS could be made to run over SNA networks without changing a line of code. IBM's *AnyNet* product line is an example of a protocol matchmaker.

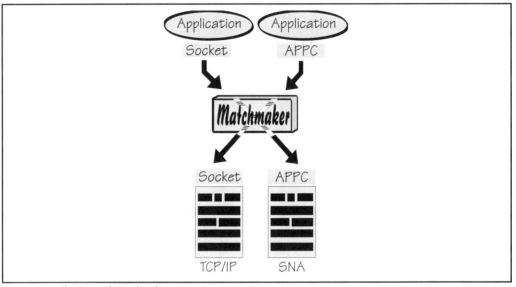

Figure 4-3. The Protocol Matchmaker.

In summary, today's network environment is a truly heterogeneous hodgepodge of protocols and media options. Network routers, gateways, and bridges insulate the application developer from having to worry about cabling, network adapters, or protocol transport choices. Multiprotocol API sets make it easier for service providers to develop client/server applications that run over multiple protocol stacks. And we're getting closer to the day when client/server programs can be plugged into any protocol stack (on any machine) almost as easily as appliances plug into electrical outlets.

IS BANDWIDTH HEAVEN AROUND THE CORNER?

Is bandwidth heaven around the corner? To answer this question, we must first take a stab at defining bandwidth heaven, and then we can determine if the networking infrastructure can meet our expectations. As you will discover, some of us are already in bandwidth heaven. For the rest of us, a few more roadblocks need to be overcome before we get there.

Boundless Bandwidth: How Much Is Enough?

So how much bandwidth do you need? It really depends on your tastes (see Table 4-1). If you have expensive tastes, then you will need at least 9 Mbit/s to get high-quality video, audio, and data on your network connections. Many of us will be in heaven with just under 1 Mbit/s—at least until we compare ourselves with the Jones. According to Morgan Stanley's U.S. Investment Research Group, the typical user's demand for bandwidth has grown between 16 and 55 times over the past three years. So it's all very subjective. In this book, we define heaven as 2 Mbit/s or more of dedicated, isochronous bandwidth.

Table 4-1. How Much Bandwidth Do You Need?

Content	Bandwidth Requirements	Remarks
Audio		
■ CD quality	706 Kbit/s	44,100 samples/sec, 16-bit per sample
■ Digital phone quality	64 Kbit/s	8,000 samples/sec, 8-bit samples
Minimum-quality, full-motion video	566 Kbit/s	1024 X 768 pixels, 30 frames/sec 3 colors; 8 bits each
TV-quality, full-motion video		
■ Uncompressed	96 Mbit/s	
■ MPEG-2 compression	6 Mbit/s	
Data requirements	2 Mbit/s	For LAN-speed responsiveness

Must It Be Isochronous?

First, what is an *isochronous* network? It's a network that provides very low and predictable node-to-node delays (or latencies). Isochronous networks are capable of dealing with the steady, immediate delivery, and high-bandwidth requirements of multimedia technology. For example, networks that support desktop training videos or videoconferencing need to supply, on demand, 1.5 Mbit/s (or more) to each PC. We can accommodate some of that demand by exploiting the prioritized traffic services of existing Token Ring and Ethernet networks. Higher-priority frames are assigned to the delay-sensitive traffic. But what we really need are high-speed networks with separate voice/video and data traffic channels (also called virtual circuits) that can guarantee a fixed delivery time for multimedia traffic (see the next Briefing box). At another level, the Internet community is working on a *Real-Time Protocol (RTP)* for delivering multimedia data over the Net.

FYI

What's a Virtual Circuit?

Briefing

Virtual circuits are like the phone system. They get established when two nodes need to communicate, and then get relinquished after they're not needed. Because video and voice are carried over the network in streams within virtual circuits, delays are low and constant. For example, the WAN-based Frame Relay packet switching technology uses virtual circuits to allocate bandwidth on demand and optimize the use of the existing bandwidth.

In contrast, today's LAN technology allocates bandwidth by *contention*. Everybody is bidding with everybody else to obtain the use of the broadcast medium. To get on the LAN, you must either wait for a token (Token Ring) or start broadcasting; you must be prepared to back off if you detect a collision (Ethernet). Contention methods cannot guarantee deterministic response times (or delays). It's a matter of luck, and things get worse around rush hour. The situation can be improved by assigning priorities, but there's still contention within the same priority levels.

Some of the new isochronous LAN technologies propose a *hybrid* environment that allocates a certain amount of bandwidth to contention traffic and gives the rest to virtual circuits. For example, isochronous FDDI allocates a certain percentage of the network bandwidth to multiple 64 Kbit/s virtual circuits and gives the remainder to normal contention-based data.

Another approach is to use LAN switches to eliminate contention. For example, *Switched Ethernet* provides a dedicated 10 Mbit/s pipe to each station by giving it its own LAN segment; each cable segment is directly wired to a centralized Ethernet switch, which acts as a hub. The hub provides a high-speed internal bus to switch packets between multiple cable segments and still offers 10 Mbit/s to each station. Many LAN switches are designed to be interconnected via high-speed uplinks such as FDDI (100 Mbit/s), Fast Ethernet (100 Mbit/s), and, in limited situations, ATM (up to 2.4 Gbit/s). LAN switching is now a big business; IDC estimates it will generate revenues in excess of $2 billion in 1996.

Asynchronous Transfer Mode (ATM) is the ultimate isochronous technology. It allocates LAN/WAN bandwidth on demand via virtual circuits. ATM uses high-speed, hardware-based, circuit-switching technology that is potentially capable of unleashing an awesome amount of isochronous bandwidth at very low cost (every node is given its own dedicated LAN segment into the switch). ❑

How Much Bandwidth Can We Really Expect?

You're only as fast as your weakest link.

> — *Gopi Bala, Senior Analyst*
> *Yankee Group*
> *(May, 1996)*

The amount of bandwidth you get generally depends on which side of the firewall you're on. Many corporate users are already in bandwidth heaven, at least on their LANs. However, if you're outside the corporate firewall, you're probably in "bandwidth hell"—this includes home users, mobile users, and corporate users when they're outside their inner sanctum. In addition, even traffic on corporate LANs must occasionally traverse a slow WAN—the big cloud in the sky—to connect with other LANs in far away places (see Figure 4-4).

Assuming no contention, the bandwidth you get at work is primarily a function of the capacity of your LANs, WANs, and the links that connect them. The bandwidth you get at home is primarily determined by the link that connects you to an access

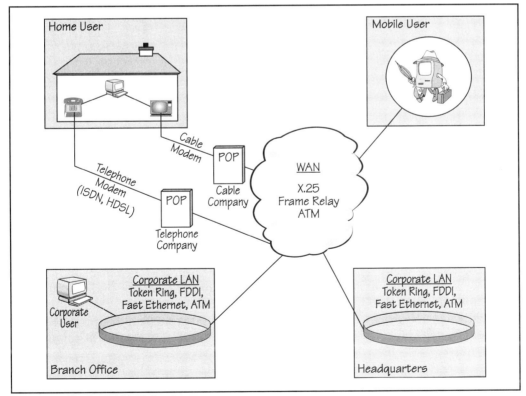

Figure 4-4. The Bandwidth Chokepoints.

point—or *Point of Presence (POP)*—on the WAN; it is also a function of the capacity of the WAN. Finally, if you're a mobile user, the bandwidth you get will be determined by your wireless link to the WAN or LAN. So to understand bandwidth, we need to look at the performance of the five potential chokepoints: LANs, WANs, LAN-to-WAN, home-to-WAN, and wireless-to-WAN. The next five sections give you a quick update of the state of these five networking technologies and their infrastructures.

The State of the LAN

We're at an intersection between the old LAN technology and ATM—a moment in history in which the most blood will be lost.

> — *Jamie Lewis, President*
> *Burton Group*
> *(September, 1995)*

Table 4-2. LAN Transmission Technologies.[1]

LAN Type	Speed	Market Share	Adapter Cost	Deployment
Ethernet	10 Mbit/s	75%	Under $100	Widespread (Over 40 million nodes)
Token Ring	4/16 Mbit/s	16%	Under $250	Growing
Fast Ethernet	100 Mbit/s	1%	Under $150	Growing very rapidly.
FDDI	100 Mbit/s	<1%	Under $1,000	Growing
ATM	25 Mbit/s-2.4 Gbit/s	<1%	$500 and up	Nascent, but accelerating

1. Table source: Wessels, Arnold, and Henderson, **Industry Report** (April 22, 1996). Note that we updated some of the numbers to reflect the latest product prices.

As you can see from Table 4-2, LANs are not the bottleneck in our quest for bandwidth heaven. However, except for ATM and switched Ethernet, all these LAN technologies use some form of contention to access the broadcast medium. This means that the various stations on a LAN must contend for the same bandwidth, especially under heavy loads. But, as we explained in the previous briefing, switched Ethernet gives each user a dedicated 10 Mbit/s of bandwidth.[1] If this is not enough, you can move to Fast Ethernet using existing wiring. You should also

---

[1] Token Ring switching hubs are also becoming available. Token Ring is inherently more scalable than Ethernet, and it can provide switching at the backbone level. Consequently, the demand for Token Ring switching at the departmental level is not as strong.

note that workstation ATM now sells for around $500, which means that it is affordable. Consequently, you can now use ATM switching technology on both LANs and WANs.

The State of the WAN

*P*utting large file-oriented applications over WANs is like herding hippos through a garden hose.

> — *David Willis, Network Computing*
> *(April, 1996)*

WAN performance is primarily determined by two factors: 1) the switches that route data across networks, and 2) the type (and quality) of the wide-area cabling infrastructure. For example, the faster switches require a fiber-optic cabling infrastructure to achieve their maximum speeds. Yes, the physical world still matters when it comes to networks.

Table 4-3 shows the progression of physical links that are used in WAN backbones. Until recently, the Internet backbone was a collection of T1 lines. Today, it runs at T3 speeds. And, of course, we all know the Internet is already on its knees, just carrying text and occasional pictures. So T3 is not enough. As a result, Internet backbone providers are now stepping up to ANSI's *Synchronous Optical Network*

Table 4-3. WAN Backbone: Physical Interconnect Technology.

Line Type	Speed	Comments
T1 (or DS1)	1.54 Mbit/s	North American standard
E1	2.04 Mbit/s	European CCITT standard
E2	8.44 Mbit/s	European CCITT standard
E3	34.36 Mbit/s	European CCITT standard
T3 (or DS3)	44.73 Mbit/s	North American standard
OC1	51.84 Mbit/s	Sonet fiber standard
OC2	103.68 Mbit/s	Sonet fiber standard
OC3	155.52 Mbit/s	Sonet fiber standard
OC12	622.08 Mbit/s	Sonet fiber standard
OC24	1.244 Gbit/s	Sonet fiber standard
OC48	2.488 Gbit/s	Sonet fiber standard

(Sonet) transmission standards for high-speed fiber-optic links. The Sonet standard is specified in multiples of 51.84 Mbit/s. The top-of-the-line is OC48, which specifies a line speed of 2.4 Gbit/s; ANSI is now working on 10 Gbit/s Sonet. Sonet also specifies a ring-like wiring topology for instantly rerouting traffic around outages.

The good news is that all the major carriers worldwide are deploying Sonet on their backbones. And many are starting to offer Sonet services to corporate users and Internet service providers but it's not cheap. By the year 2000, most public WANs will be close to 100% Sonet. In the U.S., most long distance carriers have installed Sonet fiber coast-to-coast, and many local carriers are installing Sonet fiber rings within major cities. Sprint is the furthest along, with 32 interconnected Sonet rings nationwide. Over 50% of Sprint's network is Sonet today; it will reach 100% by 1998. Sprint is now carving out Sonet OC12 trunks into lower-capacity T1 and T3 circuits and selling them to individual users; the idea is to provide a low-cost fiber service at the low-end. Now that Sonet is being deployed around the world, the question is: What will run on top of it? Of course, the answer must be ATM; it alone can support switching speeds of up to 2.488 Gbit/s.

Modern WANs make use of packet switching technology to provide the link layer on top of T1, T3, or Sonet physical backbones. Packet switches break data streams into packets that they then launch into the network. The address headers are used to direct each packet to its destination. You should note that protocols like TCP/IP or IPX/SPX run on top of these packet-switched networks.

Table 4-4 compares the three leading packet switching technologies—*Frame Relay, Switched Multimegabit Data Services (SMDS)*, and *Asynchronous Transfer Mode (ATM)*. Clearly, ATM gives us the best bandwidth. However, Frame Relay is a seasoned technology that works on the existing T1 WAN infrastructure. SMDS is mostly used in Europe as a precursor to ATM. Both Frame Relay and SMDS can run on top of ATM packet switches (see the next Briefing box).

Table 4-4. WAN Backbone: The Packet-Switching Alternatives.

WAN Technology	Maximum Speed	Applications	Packet Size	Deployment
Frame Relay	1-2 Mbit/s (T1/E1)	Data	Variable length 4,096 bytes max	Wide
SMDS	45 Mbit/s (T3)	Data	Variable length 9,188 bytes max (can be broken into 53-byte cells)	Limited
ATM	2.4 Gbit/s	Data, voice, and video	53-byte cells	Limited but growing

B-ISDN: Frame Relay, SMDS, and ATM

Briefing

The public network, which is essentially 20 years old, has been overwhelmed by the sudden and dramatic increase in traffic. And conditions are getting worse.

> — Joe McGarvey
> Inter@ctive Week
> (April, 1996)

Fiber optics is taking us from a modest to an almost infinite bandwidth, with nothing in between.

> — Nicholas Negroponte, Author
> Being Digital
> (Knopf, 1995)

What Is Frame Relay?

Frame Relay is currently the most popular packet-switching technology for WANs; it is supported by over 90 U.S. carriers. The technology first appeared in 1992 as a streamlined implementation of the older X.25 packet switching technology. Frame Relay can route variable-length packets at T1 (or E1) speeds over existing routers, switches, and other HDLC-based equipment; it only requires a software upgrade. In contrast, X.25 can only deliver a maximum of 64 Kbit/s over the same physical infrastructure. Frame Relay achieves its magic by bypassing error checks at each network segment (the midpoints). Instead, it relies on the endpoints to provide end-to-end error checking. The demand for Frame Relay is very strong. According to Vertical Systems Group, the Frame Relay market is expected to grow from $1.6 billion in 1995 to $5.4 billion in 1998. Note that Frame Relay is being continuously improved; T3-speed implementations are in the works.

What Is SMDS?

SMDS was originally designed to fill the gap for high-speed WAN services until ATM became widely available. It supports variable-length packets that can be broken into ATM-size fixed cells to facilitate the migration. SMDS today can run at T3 speeds (45 Mbit/s); it obtains its high throughput by not providing support for virtual circuits—each packet is on its own. In contrast, both ATM and Frame Relay support virtual circuits. SMDS is not a runaway market success. According to Vertical Systems Group, the market for SMDS was less than $45 million in 1995. In the U.S., only MCI offers SMDS services. The other major carriers seem to have passed over SMDS in favor of Frame Relay and ATM.

What Is ATM?

ATM is the current darling of the network industry—and its greatest hope for the future. It is a packet-switching protocol that achieves very high speeds by using fixed-length data cells—or packets on top of *virtual circuits*. *Permanent Virtual Circuits (PVCs)* are statically assigned; *Switched Virtual Circuits (SVCs)* are dynamic. In either case, a virtual circuit can guarantee quality of service—including bandwidth and priority.

ATM was designed from the start to mix different types of traffic—including data, voice, and video. ATM's system of transmitting small 53-byte cells of information—or packets—is flexible enough to work at capacities ranging from megabits to gigabits (see Figure 4-5). The small, fixed size cell makes it possible to implement very high-speed switches in hardware. ATM's bandwidth is demand-based and scalable, meaning that each node can access the network at the speeds required by an application. ATM promises to provide seamless networking and remove the current distinctions between LANs and WANs. However, at this stage, LAN and WAN implementations of ATM continue to be separate markets.

The *ATM Forum* is a multivendor body with over 800 members whose purpose is to accelerate the introduction of ATM standards. In May 1995, the Forum passed two critical standards: *LAN Emulation (LANE 1.0)* and an *Interim Interswitch Protocol (IISP)*. In November 1995, the Forum approved the 25 Mbit/s ATM interface for desktops. In February 1996, it approved further bandwidth specifications—up to 622 Mbit/s. The *Available Bit Rate (ABR)* specification is complete and waiting for approval; it specifies automatic traffic congestion control and bandwidth allocation. Also waiting for approval is the ATM *Private Network-to-Network Interface (PNNI)*; it defines how to route a connection through a series of ATM switches. The Forum is expected to complete some key ATM specifications in 1996—including multiprotocol over ATM, T1/E1 support, ATM interworking with Frame Relay, and ATM systems management.

More than 35 vendors make ATM products for LANs and WANs—including Fore Systems, 3Com, Bay Networks, IBM, Cisco, and Digital. What's surprising is that some of this equipment even interoperates. In addition, all the major local and long-distance telephone carriers in the U.S. and Canada now offer ATM. Nearly every carrier says its ATM network will handle all types of traffic—including Frame Relay and SMDS. And most carriers plan to offer Frame Relay to ATM conversions in 1996. So what's holding ATM back? Sky-high prices. But the good news is that the price of an ATM connection is declining by about 40% each

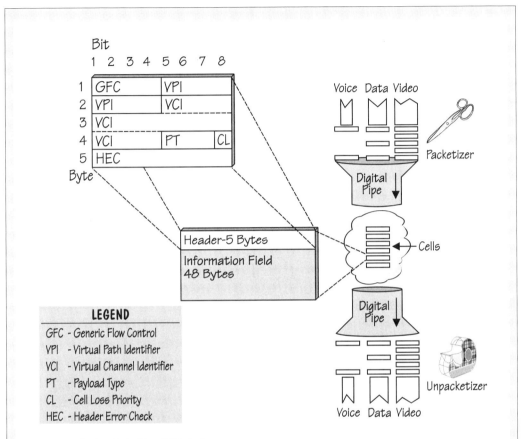

Figure 4-5. Packet-Switching, ATM-Style.

year. Consequently, the ATM market is on the verge of explosive growth. According to the Vertical Systems Group, ATM LAN equipment revenues will grow from $159 million in 1995 to $947 million in 1998. ATM WAN sales will grow from $305 million in 1995 to $1.9 billion in 1998. This means that ATM may become a $3 billion industry by 1998.

What Is B-ISDN?

So what is the *Broadband-Integrated Services Digital Network (B-ISDN)*. The CCITT defines B-ISDN as a cell-switched WAN that supports speeds of over 1.54 Mbit/s. B-ISDN is really ATM over Sonet. The B-ISDN standard defines an *ATM adaptation layer (AAL)* that is responsible for mapping data, voice, and video information to and from ATM-defined cell formats. So B-ISDN is really the Information Highway built on fiber links and ATM switches. SMDS and Frame Relay are the precursors to this technology. ❏

The State of the LAN-to-WAN Interconnect

Today's LANs connect to WANs via routers. The router connects to either a private or public WAN via dedicated leased lines (usually T1 or T3). The switching technology is typically Frame Relay, X.25, or just point-to-point (PPP). Some of the larger corporations are now using ATM over Sonet for their LAN-to-WAN connections. Others are looking at Intranet service providers as a way to replace private networks with public WANs.

In contrast to individuals, corporations can require a guaranteed "fat pipe" from their WAN providers via bandwidth reservation schemes (or *quality of service*).[2] And corporations can afford to maintain sophisticated high-speed routers on their premises. This means that the LAN becomes just another segment on the WAN. Consequently, the technology that we described in the previous section applies to the LAN-to-WAN connection. So today's LAN-to-WAN connection is Frame Relay; tomorrow's connection will be ATM. And if ATM runs on the LAN, separate routers won't even be required. The LAN simply morphs into the WAN. There is no longer an impedance mismatch.

The State of the Home-to-WAN Connection

So how do we bring the digital highway into the home? As most Internet Web users are painfully aware, the home is on the wrong side of the bandwidth track. To extend the WAN into the home requires a solution to the impedance mismatch (or bottleneck) created by the "last mile" of telephone cable that connects homes and offices to the long-distance service providers. In the U.S. alone, telephone companies still own more than 100 million pairs of copper wire local loops. But, over the past decade, the long-distance carriers replaced their copper wire backbones with a network of superfast, high-bandwidth, low-tariff, and fiber-optic cables (i.e., Sonet). However, bringing these advantages into the home requires the upgrading of that last mile of local cable to fiber—a mind-boggling expense.

Today's 28.8 Kbit/s modems are pushing the analog telephone system to the limit. These "blazingly fast" modems won't deliver their advertised throughput, except under prime conditions. But there's good news on the horizon in the form of two competing technologies from the local telephone companies that promise to speed up the local loops without replacing the existing wiring: *Integrated Services*

---

[2] *Internet Service Providers (ISPs)* are also getting into the guaranteed bandwidth business. For example, starting in 1997, BBN Planet plans to offer "quality of service" Internet access to corporate customers. It will use a new Internet protocol called the *Resource Reservation Protocol (RSVP)*. In May 1996, Cisco announced it would incorporate RSVP in its routers.

Digital Network (ISDN) and the *High-Bit-Rate Digital Subscriber Line (HDSL)*. And if these don't work out, there's always the *cable modem* alternative from the cable TV companies (see next Briefing box).

Eventually, fiber-optic cable will be strung into homes. Fiber is several hundred times faster than even coaxial cable, and more versatile. U.S. local phone companies are already expanding fiber beyond their switching offices to the curbs of their residential customers. They will eventually extend it all the way into the home. Pacific Bell—which covers all of California—is leading the pack. In addition, some cable operators (such as Time Warner) are installing fiber as a replacement for coax. Table 4-5 compares these various alternatives (also see the next Briefing box).

Table 4-5. The Home-to-WAN Connection: Comparing the Alternatives.

Connection Technology	Speed	When Available	Comments
V.32bis	14.4 Kbit/s	Now	■ Dial-up analog modem ■ Modem under $100
V.34	28.8 Kbit/s	Now	■ Dial-up analog modem ■ Modem under $250
ISDN BRI	128 Kbit/s	Now	■ Dial-up digital modem ■ $300 - $1000 for ISDN card ■ $100 install ■ $25 per month + usage
ISDN PRI	1.544 Mbit/s	Now	■ Requires T1 ■ $500 - $750 per month
T1	1.544 Mbit/s	Now	■ Leased line ■ More than $700 per month
HDSL	1.5 Mbit/s	Late 1996	■ Uses existing telephone wire ■ 2 twisted pairs ■ Modem under $300 (estimate)
ADSL 3	6 Mbit/s 640 Kbit/s (return)	1997	■ Asymmetrical bandwidth ■ Single twisted pair ■ Modem under $300 (estimate) ■ $35 - $100 per month
Cable modem	10 Mbit/s (one-way)	1997	■ Modem under $400 ■ Separate telephone return ■ Cable fee ■ Cable company support
B-ISDN (ATM/Sonet)	100 Mbit/s (and up)	1999	■ Bandwidth nirvana ■ Voice, multimedia, and data ■ Requires fiber to the curb

FYI

Briefing

Medium Bandwidth:
ISDN, HDSL, and Cable Modems

What Is ISDN?

ISDN—not to be confused with B-ISDN—is a digital telephony technology that supports the high-speed transfer of voice and data over telephone lines. The most prevalent ISDN service is the *Basic Rate Interface (BRI)*, also known as *2B + D*. This service works over regular telephone lines by creating two independent 64 Kbit/s "B channels" for information (data or voice), and one 16 Kbit/s "D channel" for signaling and placing calls. The Basic Rate telephone line is clocked at 192 Kbit/s and uses time division multiplexing to allocate the two B and D channels; the extra 48 Kbit/s is reserved. Basic Rate uses the standard 4-wire telephone jack that is used in homes and offices. A higher-capacity version of ISDN is also available; it is called the *Primary Rate Interface (PRI)*, or *23B + D*. PRI can deliver 1.544 Mbit/s, but it is rarely used.

ISDN BRI is the digitization of the telephone line. It is five times faster than anything you can do with a modem today. In addition, ISDN provides a lower-cost form of communication because it charges by connect time (like normal voice calls) rather than by the packet (like some packet-switched WANs). Its higher speeds can reduce the connect time and save you some money. Today, more than 70% of U.S. homes can access ISDN. In contrast, more than 90% of European phones are ISDN-friendly. However, the number of ISDN users in the U.S. is less than 500,000; Europe has slightly less than a million ISDN users, but it's growing at 40% per year.

Why isn't everyone using ISDN? The problem with ISDN is that obtaining the service can be a nightmare. There are at least 50 options that you can specify. Some U.S. telephone companies, such as Bell Atlantic and Pacific Bell, are very ISDN-friendly. Others, such as Nynex, are not—for example, you may have to wait four months to get ISDN service in Manhattan. Local ISDN surcharges can also vary wildly. However, proponents of ISDN claim that it still provides the ideal end-user entry point to the "data highway" because the telephone is ubiquitous. Detractors argue that 128 Kbit/s does not provide enough band-width for multimedia; it's not worth the pain to upgrade.

What Is HDSL/ADSL?

The *High-Bit-Rate Digital Subscriber Line (HDSL)* was developed at Bellcore Labs as a way to use existing telephone copper twisted-pair to deliver low-cost video on demand in competition with cable modems. HDSL delivers 1.5 Mbit/s of bandwidth over the two telephone twisted pairs that are found in most U.S. homes. The beauty of HDSL is that it offers repeaterless spans of 12,000 feet over existing copper loops. In contrast, a T1 circuit requires the carrier to install repeaters every 6,000 feet, and the last one can't be more than 3,000 feet from your home. A variation of HDSL called the *Asymmetric Digital Subscriber Line (ADSL)* offers up to 6 Mbit/s incoming and 640 Kbit/s outgoing. Asymmetrical, in this case, means that the line has more bandwidth going into the home than out. ADSL runs on a single telephone twisted-pair; its repeaters can span 18,000 feet.

HDSL and ADSL are both screamingly fast when compared with ISDN. AT&T Paradyne's division developed a 2-chip set—called *GlobeSpan*—that supports both protocols. Local telephone companies plan to introduce HDSL service in late 1996 and ADSL in 1997. The word on the street is that they will charge flat rates of less than $50 per month for these types of connections. For example, U.S. West plans to charge a flat $35 per month for its ADSL service by 1998. We expect the modem to sell for less than $300. Welcome to the age of medium-high bandwidth!

What Are Cable Modems?

Of course, the telephone companies are not the only ones trying to solve the last mile problem. They face stiff competition from the cable TV companies. Cable wires snake past 97% of all U.S. households. Cable has over 60 million subscribers in the U.S. The secret weapon of the cable companies is to introduce a cheap cable modem that can provide more than 10 Mbit/s of bidirectional bandwidth by emulating Ethernet over a cable. You will even be able to connect your computer to the cable modem via a standard Ethernet adapter. Such modems are now available from Digital, LANcity, Intel, Motorola, and Zenith.

Even though the modems are bidirectional, most home cable systems are unidirectional—the bandwidth only comes into the home. So generally you will be using the cable modem to download information from the WAN at Ethernet speeds and a plain old telephone modem to upload (or return) information. A number of cable companies—including TCI—have launched ventures to provide bidirectional data. By the end of 1996, 16% of the U.S. will have two-way cable (up from 8% in 1995). You will be able to get 10 Mbit/s of bandwidth—incoming and outgoing—using two separate cable channels. On the average, a cable modem sells for around $400, but you must also pay a cable fee to the service provider. A new start-up called @Home is partnering with the major cable companies to provide a high-speed Internet *Point of Presence (POP)* at the cable head-end. The competition for local service allowed by the *Telecommunications Act of 1996* is just starting to heat up. We are sure to have cable modem versus HDSL/ADSL price wars. So who are you betting on: cable or telephone? ❏

The State of the Wireless-to-WAN Connection

Be-all end-all wireless-communications technology always seems a couple of years away.

— Angela Hickman, PC Magazine
(May, 1996)

Wireless networks promise to provide the ultimate connection to the digital highway by letting you communicate "anywhere, anytime." With the mobile workforce growing at nearly 15% per year, wireless is becoming a necessity. But while cellular phones are everywhere (over 58 million in use), ubiquitous wireless data connections are still off into the future. Table 4-6 compares the leading wireless data technologies. Not one is ideal for high-volume traffic. So you may have to live with your wired connections for another year, until the new *Personal Communication Services (PCSs)* give us all the bandwidth we need in the friendly skies.

Table 4-6. The Wireless Alternatives.

Wireless Service	Bandwidth	Call Setup Time	Pricing
Cellular-Switched	14.4 Kbit/s (or less)	30 secs	By-the-minute (35 cents per minute)
Cellular-Packet (CDPD)	19.2 Kbit/s	5 secs	By-the-packet (15 cents per KByte)
Private Packet Radio	19.2 Kbit/s	5 secs (or more)	By-the-packet (15 cents per KByte)

But first, what is the state of today's wireless WAN connection? Here's a quick update on what's available:

■ *Circuit-switched cellular* simply provides a modem that lets you connect your laptop with a cellular phone. You can then connect to any phone (with a modem) on the nationwide cellular network. And you can still use your cellular phone for voice. So all you need to go wireless is a cellular phone and a cellular modem (about $400 for both). Of course, you must still pay cellular rates by the minute (35 cents or more), which is where the fun stops.

■ *Cellular Digital Packet Data (CDPD)* lets you transmit data packets over unused portions of the existing cellular network. CDPD can dynamically pick the open voice channels and use them for data traffic. You will need a $400 CDPD modem to get on the network, and you then pay by-the-packet—*Cellular One* charges about 15 cents per KByte. CDPD modems do not require an existing cellular phone—they include their own radio transceivers.

■ ***Private packet radio providers*** offer a nationwide wireless alternative to the cellular network. The two leading private packet radio providers in the U.S. are *RAM Mobile Data* and *Ardis*. RAM claims that it can provide two-way wireless services to over 94% of the U.S. urban population (it covers 260 metropolitan areas). Ardis—the IBM/Motorola digital wireless network—is available in over 400 U.S. cities. In addition, AT&T spent $12.6 billion to acquire McCaw Cellular Communications to round-out its end-to-end wireless suite of offerings. AT&T/McCaw plan to provide a single wireless network based on PCS that covers 80% of the U.S.

In addition to these nationwide services, you should shop around for local wireless alternatives. For example, in the San Francisco Bay Area, Ricochet (http://www.ricochet.net) offers unlimited wireless Internet access for a flat fee of $29.95 per month. And it will rent you a 28.8 Kbit/s wireless modem for another $10 per month. Ricochet built its own private packet radio network by mounting digital repeaters on city street lights (on the average, one repeater each 1/2 mile).

Wireless Standards: IEEE 802.11 and NDIS

Briefing

The ideal wireless panacea would be to tell people they can take their laptop computer on the road and have it work as if it were wired into their company's LAN.

> — *Dan Croft, Senior VP*
> *Ardis*
> *(March, 1996)*

But who will maintain order in the friendly skies? Currently, each wireless network provider is building its own "skyway." To bring order out of that chaos, the IEEE 802.11 committee was given the thankless task of creating standards for wireless networks. The standards are intended to cover the following areas: wireless modems, APIs, PCMCIA devices, data security in the sky, bridges from wired-to-wireless LANs, guidelines to prevent broadcast interference, and a media-access protocol for radio and infrared transmissions. The good news is that after three long years in gestation, the IEEE 802.11 standard is expected to be approved by the time you read this. In addition to the IEEE standard, a new NDIS standard for wireless was completed in early 1996. This means that existing communication stacks will be able to transparently access any wireless modem—including cellular, Ardis, CDPD, RAM, and future PCS networks. These standards will make wireless more affordable and easier to deploy. ❑

The up-and-coming attraction in the wireless world is PCS—the all-digital alternative to today's cellular network. *Narrowband PCS (N-PCS)* will be used for data only; *Broadband PCS (B-PCS)* will carry data and voice. So where did the additional PCS bandwidth come from? It came from the U.S. federal regulators— the FCC. The FCC allocated 140 MHz of government-held radio frequency to be auctioned to private developers. This is four times the spectrum originally allocated to the cellular phone industry. The allocated frequencies—between 1.85 GHz and 1.99 GHz—can be supported by low-cost, low-power, small-cell, one-chip transceivers. The first auction was held in March 1995; the government sold an 80 MHz chunk of the PCS spectrum for $7.7 billion. This is one way to get rid of the U.S. federal deficit.

We anticipate that the PCS wireless network will open up entire new industries based on low-cost and ubiquitous wireless technology for data transmissions. It could conceivably lead to a day when wired phones are seldom used and are replaced by small mobile phones carried by nearly everyone at all times. Phone numbers will be assigned to individuals, not locations. In Europe, the PCS counterpart is called the *Personal Communications Network (PCN)*. PCN operates in the 1.8 GHz frequency range; it uses a proven technology called the *Global System for Mobile Communications (GSM)*.

CONCLUSION

Bandwidth is intrinsically abundant.

> — *George Gilder*
> *(November, 1995)*

In conclusion, the global networking infrastructure is coming together at a fast pace. Everything can physically exchange bits with everything else via the magic of WANs and routers. The next step is to do something meaningful with these bits, which is what client/server computing is all about. Of course, without low-cost and abundant bandwidth, client/server will remain a departmental technology. We hope to have made the case that abundant bandwidth is already here for most corporate users. For the home user, it appears to be just around the corner.

Will the cost of bandwidth come down? Yes, especially in the U.S. The *Telecommunications Act of 1996* will unleash intensive competition between long-distance carriers, local carriers, and cable companies. They can now all play in each other's turf. It's goodbye to the age of the telephone monopoly. As George Gilder points out, bandwidth is intrinsically plentiful. It's also intrinsically cheap. For example, one Mbit/s of ATM bandwidth is an order of magnitude cheaper than its Ethernet equivalent. Of course, supply also creates its own demand.

Part 2
Clients, Servers, and Operating Systems

An Introduction to Part 2

Now that you've got the "bird's-eye" view, are you ready for some action? We've got a dangerous journey ahead. Did you bring your bullet-proof vests? We're only going to cross an active war zone. No, it's not Star Wars. It's the client/server operating system wars, and they're just as dangerous. You'll feel the bullets coming right out of the book. But don't worry. You're in good hands.

Part 2 is an overview of what clients and servers do in life and what they require from their operating systems. We'll briefly look at various OSs and see what they have to offer on both the client and server sides. There's no right or wrong when it comes to OSs—it's one big balancing act with hundreds of shades of gray. Everything is fuzzy and constantly in flux. If you make the wrong decision or ride the wrong client/server wave, you simply go broke (or take the next spaceship back to Mars). Some of the big players in client/server can afford to take a more secular view of OSs by simply porting to all the platforms. If you can afford to be secular, do it. Otherwise, you'll have to pick your OSs very carefully.

Chapter 5

Clients, Servers, and Operating Systems

Look at every path closely and deliberately. Try it as many times as you think necessary. Then ask yourself, and yourself alone, one question...Does this path have a heart? If it does, the path is good; if it doesn't, it is of no use.

— Carlos Castaneda,
The Teachings of Don Juan

This chapter starts with a brief description of what typical clients and servers do in life. We then examine what each side of the client/server equation needs from an operating system. By the time you reach the end of this chapter, you should be better prepared to know what to look for in a client/server platform.

THE ANATOMY OF A SERVER PROGRAM

The role of a server program is to *serve* multiple clients who have an interest in a shared resource owned by the server. This section describes a day in the life of a typical server. Here's what a typical server program does:

■ ***Waits for client-initiated requests***. The server program spends most of its time passively waiting on client requests, in the form of messages, to arrive over a communication session. Some servers assign a dedicated session to every client. Others create a dynamic pool of reusable sessions. Some provide a mix of the two environments. Of course, to be successful, the server must always be responsive to its clients and be prepared for *rush hour traffic* when many clients will request services at the same time.

■ ***Executes many requests at the same time***. The server program must do the work requested by the client promptly. Clearly a client should not have to depend on a single-threaded server process. A server program that does not provide multitasking will run the risk of having a client hog all the system's resources and starve out its fellow clients. The server must be able to concurrently service multiple clients while protecting the integrity of shared resources.

■ ***Takes care of VIP clients first***. The server program must be able to provide different levels of service priority to its clients. For example, a server can service a request for a report or batch job in low priority while maintaining OLTP-type responsiveness for high-priority clients.

■ ***Initiates and runs background task activity***. The server program must be able to run background tasks triggered to perform chores unrelated to the main program's thrust. For example, it can trigger a task to download records from a host database during non-peak hours.

■ ***Keeps running***. The server program is typically a mission-critical application. If the server goes down, it impacts all the clients that depend on its services. The server program and the environment on which it runs must be very robust.

■ ***Grows bigger and fatter***. Server programs seem to have an insatiable appetite for memory and processing power. The server environment must be upwardly scalable and modular.

WHAT DOES A SERVER NEED FROM AN OS?

In distributed computing environments, operating system functions are either *base* or *extended* services. The base services are part of the standard operating system, while the extended services are add-on modular software components that are layered on top of the base services. Functionally equivalent extended services are usually provided by more than one vendor. There is no hard rule that determines what gets bundled in the base operating system and what goes into the extensions. Today's extensions are usually good candidates for tomorrow's base system services.

Base Services

It should be apparent from the previous description that server programs exhibit a high level of concurrency. Ideally, a separate task will be assigned to each of the clients the server is designed to concurrently support. Task management is best done by a multitasking operating system. Multitasking is the natural way to simplify the coding of complex applications that can be divided into a collection of discrete and logically distinct, concurrent tasks. It improves the performance, throughput, modularity, and responsiveness of server programs. Multitasking also implies the existence of mechanisms for intertask coordination and information exchanges.

Servers also require a high level of concurrency within a single program. Server code will run more efficiently if tasks are allocated to parts of the same program rather than to separate programs (these tasks are called *coroutines* or *threads*). Tasks within the same program are faster to create, faster to context switch, and have easier access to shared information. Figure 5-1 shows the type of support that servers require from their operating system. Let's go over the server operating system requirements.

■ *Task Preemption*. An operating system with preemptive multitasking must allot fixed time slots of execution to each task. Without preemptive multitasking, a task must voluntarily agree to give up the processor before another task can run. It is much safer and easier to write multitasking server programs in environments where the operating system automatically handles all the task switching.

■ *Task Priority*. An operating system must dispatch tasks based on their priority. This feature allows servers to differentiate the level of service based on their clients' priority.

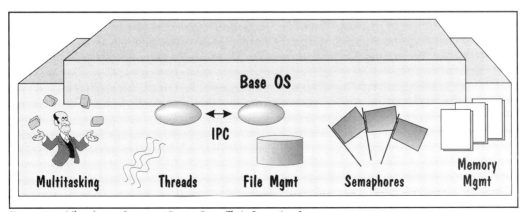

Figure 5-1. What Server Programs Expect From Their Operating System.

■ **Semaphores**. An operating system must provide simple synchronization mechanisms for keeping concurrent tasks from bumping into one another when accessing shared resources. These mechanisms, known as *semaphores*, are used to synchronize the actions of independent server tasks and alert them when some significant event occurs.

■ **Interprocess Communications (IPC)**. An operating system must provide the mechanisms that allow independent processes to exchange and share data.

■ **Local/Remote Interprocess Communications**. An operating system must allow the transparent redirection of interprocess calls to a remote process over a network without the application being aware of it. The extension of the interprocess communications across machine boundaries is key to the development of applications where resources and processes can be easily moved across machines (i.e., they allow servers to grow bigger and fatter).

■ **Threads**. These are units of concurrency provided within the program itself. Threads are used to create very concurrent, event-driven server programs. Each waiting event can be assigned to a thread that blocks until the event occurs. In the meantime, other threads can use the CPU's cycles productively to perform useful work.

■ **Intertask Protection**. The operating system must protect tasks from interfering with each other's resources. A single task must not be able to bring down the entire system. Protection also extends to the file system and calls to the operating system.

■ **Multiuser High-Performance File System**. The file system must support multiple tasks and provide the locks that protect the integrity of the data. Server programs typically work on many files at the same time. The file system must support large number of open files without too much deterioration in performance.

■ **Efficient Memory Management**. The memory system must efficiently support very large programs and very large data objects. These programs and data objects must be easily swapped to and from disk, preferably in small granular blocks.

■ **Dynamically Linked Run-Time Extensions**. The operating system services should be extendable. A mechanism must be provided to allow services to grow at run time without recompiling the operating system.

Extended Services

Extended services provide the advanced system software that exploits the distributed potential of networks, provide flexible access to shared information, and make the system easier to manage and maintain. They also make it easier for independent software vendors (ISVs) and system integrators to create new server applications. Figure 5-2 shows some of the extended services server programs can expect from their operating system. We will go over these expectations, starting from the bottom layer and working our way up. Some of these expectations read more like wish lists. They will eventually find their way into most operating systems.

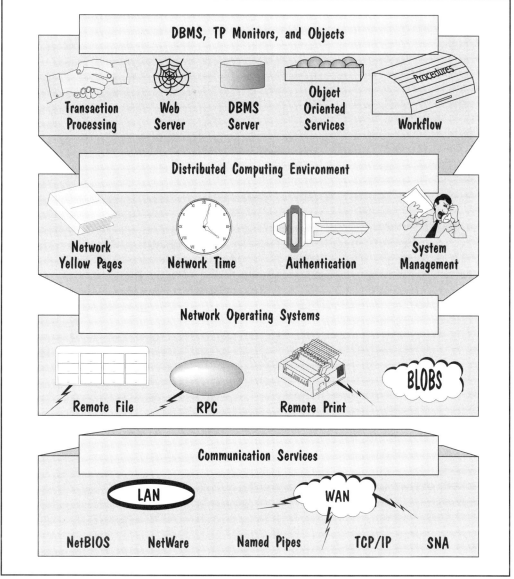

Figure 5-2. What Server Programs Hope To Get From Their Extended Operating Systems.

■ ***Ubiquitous Communications***. The operating system extensions must provide a rich set of communications protocol stacks that allow the server to communicate with the greatest number of client platforms. In addition, the server should be able to communicate with other server platforms in case it needs assistance in providing services.

■ ***Network Operating System Extensions***. The operating system extensions must provide facilities for extending the file and print services over the network. Ideally, the applications should be able to transparently access any remote device (such as printers and files) as if they were local.

■ ***Binary Large Objects (BLOBs)***. Images, video, graphics, intelligent documents, and database snapshots are about to test the capabilities of our operating systems, databases, and networks. These large objects (affectionately called BLOBs) require operating system extensions such as intelligent message streams and object representation formats. Networks must be prepared to move and transport these large BLOBs at astronomic speeds. Databases and file systems must be prepared to store those BLOBs and provide access to them. Protocols are needed for the exchange of BLOBs across systems and for associating BLOBs with programs that know what to do when they see one.

■ ***Global Directories and Network Yellow Pages***. The operating system extensions must provide a way for clients to locate servers and their services on the network using a global directory service. Network resources must be found by name. Servers must be able to dynamically register their services with the directory provider.

■ ***Authentication and Authorization Services***. The operating system extensions must provide a way for clients to prove to the server that they are who they claim to be. The authorization system determines if the authenticated client has the permission to obtain a remote service.

■ ***System Management***. The operating system extensions must provide an integrated network and system management platform. The system should be managed as a single server or as multiple servers assigned to domains. An enterprise view that covers multiple domains must be provided for servers that play in the big leagues. System management includes services for configuring a system and facilities for monitoring the performance of all elements, generating alerts when things break, distributing and managing software packages on client workstations, checking for viruses and intruders, and metering capabilities for pay-as-you-use server resources.

■ ***Network Time***. The operating system extensions must provide a mechanism for clients and servers to synchronize their clocks. This time should be coordinated with some universal time authority.

■ *Database and Transaction Services*. The operating system extensions must provide a robust multiuser Database Management System (DBMS). This DBMS should ideally support SQL for decision support and server-stored procedures for transaction services. The server-stored procedures are created outside the operating system by programmers. More advanced functions include a *Transaction Processing Monitor (TP Monitor)* for managing stored procedures (or transactions) as atomic units of work that execute on one or more servers.

■ *Internet Services*. The Internet is a huge growth opportunity for servers. We expect that over time the more common Internet services will become standard server features—including HTTP daemons, Secure Sockets Layer (SSL), firewalls, Domain Name Service, HTML-based file systems, and electronic commerce frameworks.

■ *Object-Oriented Services*. This is an area where extended services will flourish for a long time to come. Services are becoming more object-oriented. The operating system will provide object broker services that allow any object to interact with any other object across the network. The operating system must also provide object interchange services and object repositories. Client/server applications of the future will be between communicating objects (in addition to communicating processes).

As you can see, extended does mean "extended." It covers the universe of current and future services needed to create distributed client/server environments. No current operating system bundles *all* the extended functions, but they're moving in that direction. You can purchase most functions *a la carte* from more than one vendor.

SERVER SCALABILITY

What are the upper limits of servers? The limits really depend on the type of service required by their clients. One safe rule is that clients will always want more services, so scalable servers are frequently an issue. Figure 5-3 shows the different levels of escalation in server power. It starts with a single PC server that reaches its limits with the top-of-the-line processor and I/O power. The next level of server power is provided by superservers populated with multiprocessors. If that is not enough power, the client/server model allows you to divide the work among different servers. These multiservers know no upper limits to power. But they must know how to work together.

Multiservers (or *clusters*) are used in environments that require more processing power than that provided by a single server system—either SMP or uniprocessor (see the next Briefing box). The client/server model is upwardly scalable. When you need more processing power, you can add more servers (thus creating a pool of servers). Or, the existing server machine can be traded up to the latest generation of PC superserver machine. Multiservers remove any upward limits to the growth of server power. Ordinary servers can provide this power by working in all kinds of ensembles. As we explain in Part 3, network operating system extensions like the *Distributed Computing Environment (DCE)*, and TP Monitors like CICS, Encina, and Tuxedo provide the plumbing needed to create cooperating server ensembles. Eventually, ORBs will also play in this arena.

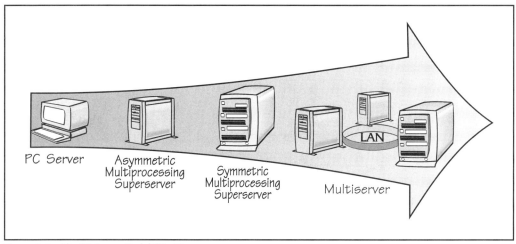

Figure 5-3. The PC Server Scalability Story.

MULTIPROCESSING SUPERSERVERS

Briefing

If you need more server power, you'll be looking at a new generation of *superservers*. These are fully-loaded machines; they include multiprocessors, high-speed disk arrays for intensive I/O, and fault-tolerant features. Operating systems can enhance the server hardware by providing direct support for multiprocessors. With the proper division of labor, multiprocessors should improve job throughput and server application speeds. A multiprocessor server is upwardly scalable. Users can get more performance out of their servers by simply adding more processors instead of additional servers. Multiprocessing comes in two flavors: asymmetric and fully symmetric (see Figure 5-4).

Asymmetric multiprocessing imposes hierarchy and a division of labor among processors. Only one designated processor, the master, can run the operating system at any one time. The master controls (in a tightly-coupled arrangement)

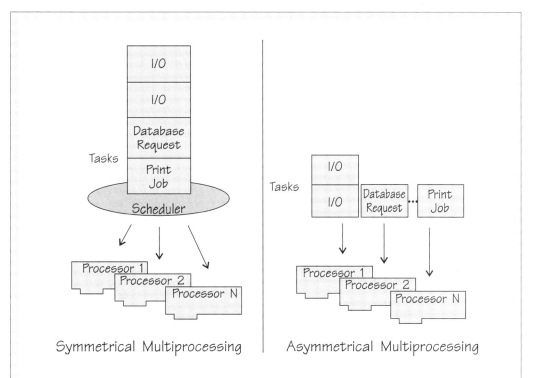

Figure 5-4. Symmetric and Asymmetric Multiprocessing.

slave processors dedicated to specific functions such as disk I/O or network I/O. A coprocessor is an extreme form of codependency; one processor completely controls a slave processor through interlocked special-purpose instructions. The coprocessor has unique special-purpose hardware that is not identical to the main processor. An example is a graphic coprocessor.

Symmetric Multiprocessing (SMP) treats all processors as equals. Any processor can do the work of any other processor. Applications are divided into threads that can run concurrently on any available processor. Any processor in the pool can run the operating system kernel and execute user-written threads. Symmetric multiprocessing improves the performance of the application itself, as well as the total throughput of the server system. Ideally, the operating system should support symmetric multiprocessing by supplying three basic functions: a reentrant OS kernel, a global scheduler that assigns threads to available processors, and shared I/O structures. Symmetric multiprocessing requires multiprocessor hardware with some form of shared memory and local instruction caches. Most importantly, symmetric multiprocessing requires new applications that can exploit multithreaded parallelism. The few applications on the market that exploit SMP are SQL database managers such as Oracle7 and Sybase.

The major 32-bit operating systems—including Unix, NetWare, OS/2, and NT—all support SMP. These operating systems will run on commodity superserver platforms; the hardware vendors have been gearing up for these OSs for quite some time. Commodity Intel-based servers supplemented with SMP are powerful enough to handle more than 90% of client/server application needs. These servers can run ordinary PC software and have a strong affinity with clients. The current breed of 32-bit OSs are finally taking advantage of the Intel hardware. It's not clear that there's a pressing need to move to RISC. The next step in servers and OSs will be support for megaclusters (i.e., clusters of SMP machines). Servers can also take advantage of loosely-coupled multiservers using TP Monitors and ORBs.

Beyond SMP, we see loosely-coupled, parallel computers like Tandem's NonStop systems, IBM's SP2, AT&T's GIS, and Oracle's NCube. Their "shared nothing" architectures eliminate the bottlenecks found in SMP architectures, allowing them to scale to hundreds or even thousands of processors, all working together. ❑

CLIENT ANATOMY 101

Client/server applications are *client-centric*. The client side provides the "look and feel" for the services a system provides. All client applications have this in common: they request the services of a server. What makes client applications different is what triggers the requests and what GUI, if any, is needed. Based on these differences, we can classify clients into three categories: *Non-GUI Clients*, *GUI Clients*, and *OOUI Clients* (see Figure 5-5).

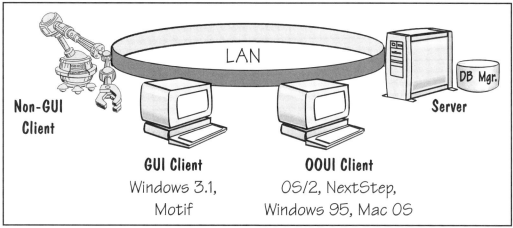

Figure 5-5. Three Client Types: Non-GUI, GUI, and OOUI.

Non-GUI Clients

Non-GUI client applications generate server requests with a minimal amount of human interaction (see Figure 5-6). Non-GUI clients fall into two sub-categories:

■ ***Non-GUI clients that do not need multitasking.*** Examples include automatic teller machines (ATMs), barcode readers, cellular phones, fax machines, smart gas pumps, and intelligent clipboards (coming soon). These clients may provide a simple human interface in the request generation loop.

■ ***Non-GUI clients that need multitasking.*** Examples include robots, testers, and daemon programs. These clients often require very granular, real-time, event-driven multitasking services.

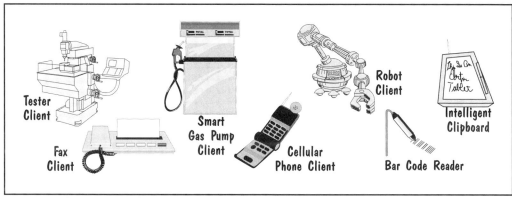

Figure 5-6. The Many Faces of Non-GUI Clients.

GUI Clients

Simple GUI Clients are applications where occasional requests to the server result from a human interacting with a GUI. The simple GUI interface is a good fit for mainstream, OLTP-type business applications with repetitive tasks and high-volumes. They also make good front-end clients to database servers. Simple GUI client applications are graphical renditions of the dialogs that previously ran on dumb terminals. GUIs replace the "green-screen uglies" with graphic dialogs, color, menu bars, scroll boxes, and pull-down and pop-up windows (see Figure 5-7). Simple GUI dialogs use the object/action model where users can select objects and then select the actions to be performed on the chosen objects. Most dialogs are serial in nature. This model of user interaction is predominantly used in Windows 3.X and OSF Motif applications. It is also known as the CUA 89 graphical model.

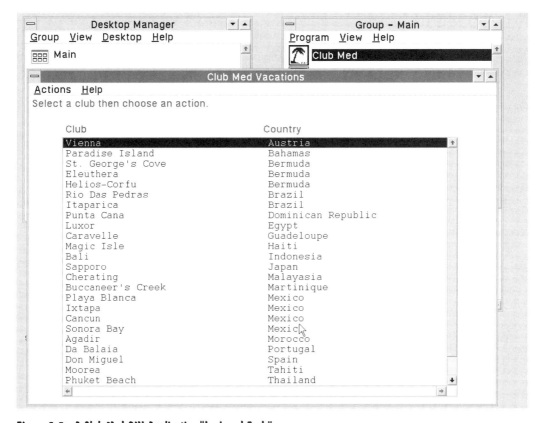

Figure 5-7. A Club Med GUI Application "Look and Feel."

Object-Oriented User Interface (OOUI) Clients

The *Object-Oriented User Interface (OOUI)* metaphor is used to provide what Microsoft Chairman Bill Gates calls *information at your fingertips*. This is a highly-iconic, object-oriented user interface that provides seamless access to information in very visual formats. OOUIs are used by information workers doing multiple, variable tasks whose sequence cannot be predicted. Examples include executive and decision-support applications, multimedia-based training systems, system management consoles, and stockbroker workstations. OOUIs have an insatiable appetite for communications. OOUI desktop objects need to communicate among themselves and with external servers. The communications are, by necessity, real time, interactive, and highly concurrent.

Examples of OOUIs are the OS/2 Workplace Shell, NextStep, Mac OS, and, to some extent, Windows 95. Current OOUIs provide a visual desktop metaphor (think of it as an arcade game) where you can bring together related objects and programs to perform a task. The desktop can contain multiple workplaces running concurrently

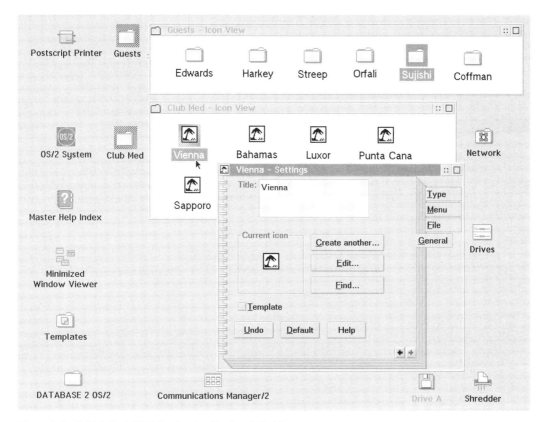

Figure 5-8. A Club Med OOUI Application "Look and Feel."

(see Figure 5-8). Each workplace may be running parallel dialogs, also called *modeless dialogs*, over parallel sessions with the server. With advanced multimedia-type applications, you can use these parallel dialogs to display images, video, multiobject folders, and voice-annotated mail. Information is displayed to the user in the foreground windows, while background tasks are constantly moving information to and from servers. For example, the first page from a multimedia document is displayed in a window while a background task is busy prefetching the rest of the document from the server.

OOUIs focus on the objects required to accomplish a task. They provide folders, workareas, shadows, and associations that allow users to personalize their desktops and manage their objects. OOUIs provide a common metaphor for creating, copying, moving, connecting, and deleting any object on the desktop. One of the major features of OOUIs is the concept of multiple views of objects.

In an OOUI, the application is transparent to the user. The desktop is a collection of objects (icons) and windows associated with those objects, as opposed to GUIs, where the desktop is a collection of windows or icons representing windows associated with applications. In OOUI environments, the user interacts with objects rather than with the operating system or with separate programs. The interaction has the same look and feel across all tasks. The OOUI is a simulation of how users interact with objects in real life. It is a computer visual of the real-life situation.

Application Features: GUI Versus OOUI

The best way to compare GUIs and OOUIs is to put the two side-by-side and contrast some of their features. Let's go back to Figures 5-7 and 5-8, the GUI and OOUI vintages of our Club Med application.[1] By just looking at these two pictures, can you tell what the OOUI fuss is all about?

- The OOUI Club Med is an extension of the operating system's user interface. You can't tell where the application starts and the OS desktop ends. They appear to be seamlessly integrated.

- The OOUI Club Med invites the user to manipulate the visual Club Med objects through drag-and-drop. For example, a transaction may be triggered by dragging a guest object to the shredder to delete it. Or, if we want to be kind, we'll drop it on the Fax machine icon to send a confirmation of the reservation.

---

[1] The GUI Club Med was developed in the first edition of our book, **Client/Server Programming with OS/2** (VNR, 1991). The OOUI Club Med was developed for the second and third editions of the same book. It's a true Workplace Shell application.

■ The OOUI Club Med icon can be opened at any time to reveal a notebook view of the information inside it. The notebook control makes it possible to visually staple together many dialog windows and let the user find the information needed. This is a giant step forward for OLTP-type of applications.

■ The OOUI Club Med setup will reappear the way the user left it when the machine is turned on again. The desktop configuration is persistent.

■ The OOUI Club Med is very familiar, especially to kids. It feels like a video game. Kids feel quite at home with drag-and-drop, icons, and direct manipulation. The OOUI is a simulation of reality that they can easily recognize. Can we say the same about adults?

■ The OOUI Club Med can be extended to seamlessly work with any other OOUI object (with very little new code). We could easily think of mail-enabling it or allowing scanned pages to be dragged into the notebook view. The OLTP transaction is starting to look more like its real-world counterpart.

■ The GUI Club Med, on the other hand, is your typical Windows interface. The icon is just there to represent the application to the desktop. You're not invited to play with it. You start the application by clicking on the icon. From then on, you're in menu land. The user is quite aware that there is a running Club Med application.

Table 5-1 provides a detailed summary of the features that distinguish OOUIs from GUIs.

Table 5-1. GUI Versus OOUI.

Feature	Graphical User Interface (GUI)	Object-Oriented User Interface (OOUI)
Application Structure	A graphic application consists of an icon, a primary window with a menu bar, and one or more secondary windows. The focus is on the main task. Ancillary tasks are supported by secondary windows and pop-ups. Users must follow the rigid task structure (and may get trapped in a task). An application represents a task.	A graphic application consists of a collection of cooperating user objects. Everything that you see is an object. Each object is represented by an icon and has at least one view. Objects can be reused in many tasks. The application's boundaries are fuzzy. The user defines what's an application by assembling a collection of objects. These objects may come from one or more programs and are integrated with the desktop objects the system provides (like printers and shredders). The users can innovate and create their own "Lego-like" object collections.
Icons	Icons represent a running application.	Icons represent objects that may be directly manipulated.
Starting an Application	Users start applications before selecting an object to work with.	Users open the object on the desktop, which causes a window view of the object to be displayed.
Windows	Users open a primary window and then specify the objects they want to interact with. The same window can be used to display other objects.	A window is a view of what's inside an object. There is a one-to-one relationship between a window and an object.
Menus	Menus provide the primary method for navigating within an application.	Each object has a context menu. You navigate within an application or across applications by directly manipulating objects. The desktop functions as one big menu; icons represent the objects that you can manipulate.
Active Application Visual	Icons represent minimized windows of active applications.	Icons are augmented with the *in-use* emphasis to represent an active object.
Direct Manipulation	An application may provide direct manipulation on an ad hoc basis.	Objects are created, communicated with, moved, and manipulated through drag-and-drop manipulation.
Creating New Objects	Objects are created in an application-specific manner, usually through some form of copy mechanism or using the menu choices: new or open.	A templates folder contains a template for every object type. To create a new instance of an object, drag its template to where you want the new object to reside.

Table 5-1. GUI Versus OOUI. (Continued)

Feature	Graphical User Interface (GUI)	Object-Oriented User Interface (OOUI)
Actions	Choose object; then choose action from menu bar.	In addition to choosing actions from menus, a user can drag objects to icons to perform operations; for example, dragging a file to a printer icon.
Containers	Text-based list boxes provide the primary form of containment.	In addition to list boxes, OOUIs provide container objects, including folders and notebooks. These in turn can contain other objects. Actions performed on container objects affect all the objects inside them.
Focus	Focus is on the main task.	Focus is on active objects and tasks.
Who Is in Control?	Control alternates between the user and the application.	All the applications behave the same and the user acts as the conductor. Think of the user as the visual programmer of the desktop.
Product Examples	Windows 3.X, NT 3.5, and Motif.	OS/2 Workplace Shell, NextStep, Mac OS, Windows 95, and NT 4.0.

Compound Documents: OOUIs on Steroids

Compound documents frameworks—like OLE and *OpenDoc*—are the latest and greatest OOUI technology (see Figure 5-9). You can think of compound documents as OOUIs on steroids. Every visual object on the screen is a live component. Some components are also containers, which means that they can embed other components. You can edit the contents of any component "in-place," regardless of how deeply embedded it is within other components. A component is an independent piece of software that you can separately purchase on the market. Components can play together in visual suites that mimic applications.

In today's OOUIs, visual objects are typically rectangular icons with underlying views. With compound documents, components can take any shape, and you can move them around and embed them at will. You can resize components, zoom in on their contents, and visually rearrange them within a visual container in any way you want. The components automatically share the document's menu, clipboard, and palette. Everything looks very seamless—it's like a visual tapestry. So compound documents are a better simulation of reality than CUA-91 vintage OOUIs. 3-D compound documents will provide even more realistic simulations. The document becomes a virtual world populated with components.

OLE and OpenDoc are available today in the form of free toolkits. OLE is also part of Windows 95; it provides the component foundation for Microsoft's desktop,

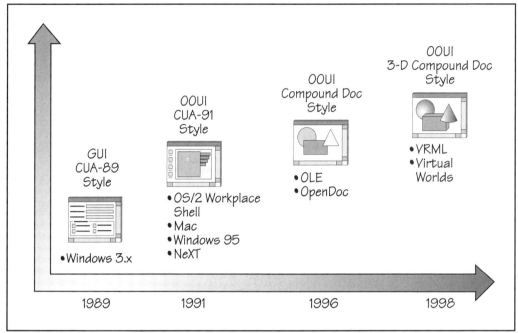

Figure 5-9. The GUI/OOUI Evolution.

enterprise, and Internet/Intranet products. OpenDoc is shipping on the Mac and OS/2; it will be available on Windows 95 and AIX in late 1996. In 1997, the Mac and OS/2 desktops will become fully-enabled OpenDoc containers, and Windows 97 will become a fully-enabled OLE container. So welcome to the age of compound documents. We cover compound documents in more detail in Parts 7 and 8.

Shippable Places

Imagine a world in which we assume that everyone is always a member of a network—not necessarily attached, but always belonging.

— *Amy Wohl*
(October, 1995)

A *place* is a visual ensemble of related components. A *shippable place* is a mobile container of components; it's a place that can be shipped over the Net. Today's user interfaces are centered around a primitive place that represents a desktop. In contrast, shippable places let you interact with multiple places that represent collaborative environments based on real-world models; it's like having multiple desktops.

So a place is a mini *virtual world* that servers can ship to their clients; it's a shippable front-end for all kinds of specialized Internet services and server objects. Places allow servers to automatically update their client's desktop. It also gives them a visual place on the client in which to display information in real time. So a place can be a dynamic assembly of ever-changing data, video feeds, and other live content.

Figure 5-10 shows the evolution of shippable client front-ends. Web technology made it possible for servers to ship HTML pages to clients where they are displayed in GUI format. The Web then evolved to support HTML-based forms that let clients send data to their servers. With Java, servers can now embed code—in the form of applets—within HTML pages; Java makes the Web page active and smart. Finally, we have shippable places. These are shippable compound documents—in the OLE and OpenDoc sense. Like a page, a place can contain Java components. But unlike a page, a place does not go away after you switch pages; it can live on your desktop for as long as you need it. A place also has its own storage, so it can remember your preferences and maintain active links to the outside world. Again, we will have a lot more to say about the objects, places, and the Web in Parts 7 and 8.

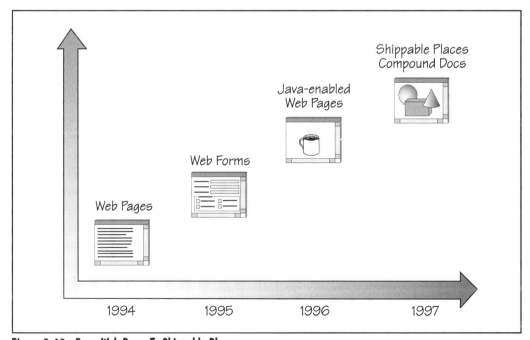

Figure 5-10. From Web Pages To Shippable Places.

WHAT DOES A CLIENT NEED FROM AN OS?

Each of the three types of clients described here place a different set of requirements on the operating system. These requirements are listed in Table 5-2. As you
can see, all client applications need some mechanism to communicate service
requests and files to a server. All three client categories will function best in a
robust, multitasking environment. It is particularly important for the client environment to be robust because it is impossible for system providers to test the client
software on all possible hardware/software combinations (you can't dictate what
people run on their PCs). It is important to use an operating system that can protect
programs from clashing and crashing. No client program should cause the system
to hang (requiring a reboot).

GUI and OOUI clients work best with a thread-like mechanism for handling the
background requests. By using separate threads for the user interface and background processing, the program can respond to user input while a separate thread
handles the interaction with the server. This is how GUIs avoid the notorious
"hourglass" icon, a sure sign that the computing environment is not keeping up with

Table 5-2. What Does a Client Need From an OS?

Requirements From an OS	Non-GUI Client		Simple GUI Client	OOUI Client
	Without Multitasking	With Multitasking		
Request/reply mechanism (prefera-bly with local/remote transparency)	Yes	Yes	Yes	Yes
File transfer mechanism to move pictures, text, and database snapshots	Yes	Yes	Yes	Yes
Preemptive multitasking	No	Yes	Desirable	Yes
Task priorities	No	Yes	Desirable	Yes
Interprocess communications	No	Yes	Desirable	Yes
Threads for background communi-cations with server and receiving callbacks from servers	No	Yes	Yes (un-less you like the hourglass icon)	Yes
OS robustness, including intertask protection and reentrant OS calls	No	Yes	Desirable	Yes
Window 3.X GUI (CUA-89 vintage)	No	No	Yes	Yes
OOUI and compound documents	No	No	No	Yes

the human users. Threads also help clients respond to asynchronous calls from a server (i.e., they implement *callbacks*). Priority-based preemptive multitasking is also required to respond to multimedia devices and to create client applications where multiple dialogs are displayed in parallel.

CLIENT/SERVER HYBRIDS

Another point to consider is that the industry is moving beyond the pure client/server model. This is because more intelligence (and data) is moving onto the client. Database clients keep snapshots of tables locally. TP Monitor clients coordinate multiserver transactions. Groupware clients maintain queues. Multimedia clients check-in and check-out folders. And distributed object clients accept requests from objects anywhere. These "New Age" clients must provide a *server lite* function— an interim step toward fulfilling the post-scarcity vision of a full client and server function on every machine. Note that even the simplest Internet PCs should be able to download shippable places, run Java applets, and receive calls from a server. For example, someday the dashboard on your car may receive a call from a server to display your location on a map.

A server lite provides a thread, queue, or background process on the client machine that can accept *unsolicited* network requests—usually from a server. For example, a server may call its clients to synchronize locks on a long duration transaction, refresh a database snapshot, or recall a checked-out multimedia document. A server lite implementation (as opposed to a full-blown server) does not need to support concurrent access to shared resources, load balancing, or multithreaded communications. We call clients that provide a server lite function *hybrids* (as opposed to pure).

CONCLUSION

Going through the motions of picking a client/server platform is a good mental exercise. It helps sharpen our understanding of the issues and platform trade-offs. In the real world, things are not black and white. There are no hermetically sealed computer worlds at the intergalactic client/server level. And very few machines started life as green-field client/server systems—most of the world's computers, even the PCs, are "legacy systems." You'll typically be dealing with heavy doses of platform mixing. Luckily, client/server middleware is starting to become the *cross-platform unifier*. So, once you're fully proficient with one platform, you'll be able to work with the next one without too much sweat. In the meantime, diversity is what makes client/server so much fun.

Chapter 6

The OS Wars:
Meet the Players

Picking a client/server platform is not an easy task. New operating systems for the desktop seem to be sprouting like weeds, while older operating systems are fragmenting into mutant "sibling" variants. This is not necessarily bad news for the client/server architecture model, which thrives on diversity. However, it can be bad news if you're trying to develop a software product and you end up picking the wrong client/server platform.

The popular press has declared the OS wars to be over: Windows 95 won the desktop, and Windows NT is winning the server. So what is there left to write about? As it turns out, quite a bit. Microsoft may have won the standalone desktop, but it certainly does not control either the client or the server. The client environment is just too diversified for one winner to take it all—especially in the age of Java, the Internet, and smart appliances. And the battle for the server—at both the departmental and intergalactic levels—is just starting. NT happens to have finally joined the fray—it is just now considered to be a mainstream OS contender. This chapter starts by looking at some of the key client and server OS trends; yes, we enjoy danger. Then we introduce you to the key players.

CLIENT OS TRENDS

Very few computers will be on the desktop in 10 years. Today's workstation capacity will be in wristwatches, on the wall, off the wall, and so on.

— *Ted Nelson, Guru*
(November, 1995)

In the last chapter, we covered what clients require from their OSs. Here are some of the trends we see developing in the client industry:

■ ***The desktop is becoming more fragmented***. The move to 32-bit OSs is fragmenting the desktop. Unlike its predecessors—DOS and Windows 3.X— Windows 95 does not own the client (see Figure 6-1). In fact, the Microsoft world has four competing client OSs to choose from: Windows 3.X, Windows for Workgroups, Windows 95, and NT Workstation—not to mention MS-DOS. In addition to Windows, OS/2 Warp is well-entrenched on corporate desktops, and Mac OS has its dedicated following among the Internet crowd. So diversity is in. The old homogeneous DOS-Windows fabric is starting to split at the seams.

■ ***The Web will generate a huge demand for Java PCs***. These are PCs that natively run a Java OS. Sun calls its forthcoming Java OS *Kona*. We anticipate a huge demand for $500 "Network PCs" that run Kona and download applets to perform a task. As we explained in Part 1, there's currently enough bandwidth

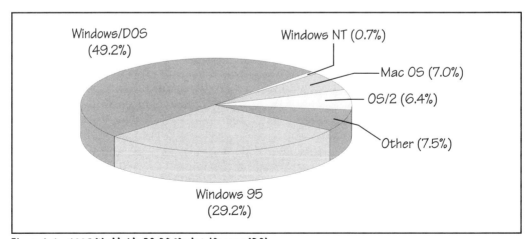

Figure 6-1. 1995 Worldwide PC OS Market (Source: IDC).

behind corporate firewalls to effectively download applets on demand. So Kona may be all the OS you need. The idea here is that Java PCs may be easier to use, maintain, and upgrade than current PCs. They will be bring to the Web millions of users who can't afford, comprehend, or deal with the cost of ownership of a full-blown OS. Web clients (or Java machines) may become as ubiquitous as the telephone. Of course, someone must first write these applets.

■ ***There will be a huge demand for fat PCs***. These are ordinary PCs that act as both clients and servers. These servers must be shrink-wrapped; you can't afford a system administrator with every server.

■ ***Shippable places will become the new desktops***. Today, you mostly live within the Windows desktop. Soon, you will be living in your favorite shippable places. These are the virtual worlds that connect you with the network at large. For example, there will be places for lawyers, dentists, and 12-year olds. So you will spend your time in the virtual worlds that make you feel the most at home. The desktop is no longer a single monolithic place. Instead, you now have multiple places to choose from.

■ ***Embedded clients will be everywhere***. This is the Novell vision of "the billion-node network by the year 2000." To get to this number, millions of little network nodes will be installed in fuel injectors, copy machines, crockpots, refrigerators, cash registers, telephony devices, automated teller machines, and pick-up trucks. Sun estimates that by 1999, the typical home will contain 100 microcontrollers. These nodes require an OS with a small footprint that can also run some form of client/server middleware. Again, a Java OS—augmented with a CORBA ORBlet—may be all we need in this embedded environment. Novell is also working on an OS called *Nested NetWare*.

In summary, the client is transforming itself. The desktop OS will not be the absolute center of the client universe. Servers—via Web browsers and shippable places—will have more say over what gets displayed inside the client's visual space. New clients—such as Internet PCs and intelligent appliances—will require network-savvy OSs with very small footprints; Kona seems to be a good fit. At the high-end, the client must also be a full-function personal server. So can one client OS do it all? We wouldn't bet on it.

CLIENT OS: MEET THE PLAYERS

As you can see in Figure 6-2, most of today's client platforms belong to Microsoft. The only other competition on the desktop comes from *OS/2 Warp Connect* and *Mac OS*. *Java OS* may eventually become a formidable competitor—especially in the area of Internet PCs and embedded clients. Though ubiquitous, *DOS* and *Windows 3.x* do not make very good client platforms. Their poor little computer brains are too weak to give us what it takes to build universal clients and fulfill the vision of post-scarcity client/server computing, where each machine is both a client and a server. For client/server computing to unleash its potential, we must move to 32-bit client platforms with full multithreaded support, robust memory management, and preemptive multitasking.

What about desktop Unix? So far, the desktop has been almost a Unix-free zone. In an industry that numbers desktop systems in tens of millions, desktop Unix sales are in the noise level. You still can't call an 800 number or walk into your local Egghead store and buy standard Unix. Installing Unix is a chore; Unix SVR4.2

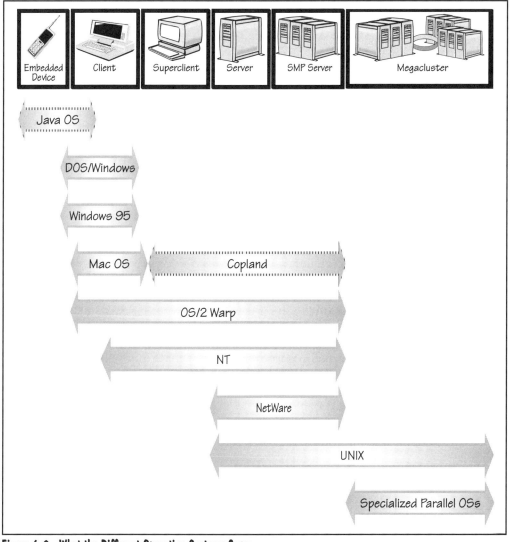

Figure 6-2. What the Different Operating Systems Cover.

requires 93 diskettes (versus 18 for OS/2, which is still a lot). Unix is also tough to administer and can easily intimidate your average desktop user. And finally, Unix's limited market means that common desktop software, when available, is 2-3 times more expensive than standard PC software.

This leaves us with four client contenders: *OS/2 Warp Connect*, *Windows 95*, *Windows NT Workstation*, and *Mac OS*. Here's a brief update on their status as client platforms.

OS/2 Warp Connect

OS/2 Warp Connect is a robust and proven 32-bit client OS. Its advanced OOUI, preemptive multitasking and page-based virtual memory are ideal for multimedia-intensive client applications. Warp Connect is network-ready; it includes a complete TCP/IP stack, NetBEUI, IPX/SPX, PPP, SLIP, and an IP router. Warp Connect is also very laptop-friendly—it supports PCMCIA plug-and-play and provides advanced power management. OS/2 runs DOS and Windows 3.X applications seamlessly in a protected-mode environment. By the time you read this, a new version of Warp Connect—code-named *Merlin*—will be shipping. Merlin will provide an enhanced user interface, extended plug-and-play, OpenDoc support, a Java runtime, built-in security, integrated systems management, advanced voice recognition, and improved installation.[1]

So what are the cons? First, OS/2 still suffers from a poor market image—much of it self-inflicted by IBM. The company as a whole cannot seem to align itself behind OS/2 and do whatever it takes to win. In contrast, Microsoft is 100% behind Windows. So the market is confused by the conflicting messages it receives from the different IBM divisions (and executives). This confusion creates unnecessary Fear, Uncertainty, and Doubt (FUD) around OS/2.

Despite all this, OS/2 has a very loyal customer base—especially within corporations and in Europe. These customers seem to keep OS/2 alive regardless of what IBM does.[2] Finally, OS/2 does not have as many native 32-bit applications as Windows, and it does not currently support 32-bit Windows 95 applications. To make up for this shortcoming, IBM—with help from Lotus—must develop a strong core of OpenDoc-based client/server components and applets. If this happens, it could put OS/2 in the *avant garde* of component software (along with Mac OS).

---

[1] Merlin will provide continuous speech recognition for a built-in vocabulary of 10,000 words; it doesn't require training the software. You will be able to automatically start dictating to it in a window.

[2] With over 13.7 million copies shipped, OS/2 has the second largest 32-bit operating system installed base; Windows 95 has the largest. However, second place does not seem to be good enough for IBM.

Windows 95

You can think of Windows 95 as Windows 3.X on steroids. It's an entry-level desktop OS that provides an OOUI-like user interface, plug-and-play, and convenient hardware autodiscovery features. It also provides many useful networking features such as a network neighborhood, the remote registry editor, and a built-in SNMP agent. Windows 95 is also network-ready. It comes with a minimal TCP/IP stack, NetBEUI, IPX/SPX, and PPP.

So what are the cons? First, the Windows 95 OOUI is inconsistent. It mixes the OOUI and GUI paradigms, which can be quite confusing. Second, Windows 95 is still built on DOS; it is DOS with a pretty face. This means that 16-bit applications have no crash protection, and only have limited multitasking (it is not preemptive). Third, Windows 95 does not appear to be robust enough for the corporate client market. Only 10% of corporations are migrating to it, versus 30% of consumers. Corporations seem to be either upgrading to OS/2 or NT Workstation; many are waiting for NT 4.0 with its new Windows 95 user interface shell.

Windows NT Workstation

Windows NT Workstation is a robust 32-bit client OS. It supports preemptive multitasking, multithreading, memory protection, and a transactional file system. Windows NT is network-ready; it supports TCP/IP, NetBEUI, IPX/SPX, PPP, and AppleTalk. NT has very few system upper limits. It also provides C2-level security. NT 4.0—now in beta—will support the new Windows 95 OOUI instead of the Windows GUI. It will also become the first Microsoft platform to support Network OLE (or DCOM).

So what are the cons? First, NT is a resource hog. It requires a minimum of 16 MBytes of RAM and 512 MBytes of disk. Second, compared to Windows 95 and OS/2 Warp, NT's support for laptops is very poor; it has limited PCMCIA support and power management. Third, NT provides poor emulation of DOS and 16-bit Windows applications; it does not support virtual device drivers (VxDs). In addition, NT does not support plug-and-play, which makes it harder to configure. Compared to Windows—and even OS/2—NT has limited device driver support. Finally, NT Workstation is an expensive client platform. It sells for $250 versus $100 (or less) for Windows 95. Because of all these limitations, NT Workstation does not get the same level of ISV support as the rest of the Windows platforms. Consequently, fewer applications run on it. NT Workstation only sold 480,000 copies in 1995, which is a small number by client standards. Of course, this may all change after NT 4.0 ships.

Mac OS

With 10-15 million users, the Mac is a key player on the desktop. Mac users also have a disproportionate presence on the Web. They may account for almost 20% of the Web client population. Apple views the Web as a key software and hardware initiative. The idea is to extend the Mac's friendliness to the Web. Mac can then become the client platform of choice for the Internet and Intranets. As a hardware vendor, Apple is well-positioned to enter the Internet PC sweepstakes with *Pippin*—a low-cost Web PC based on the Power Mac.

Apple's secret weapon to win the client is called Cyberdog, which is an OpenDoc component suite for the Internet. Web access will be totally integrated with the rest of the OS. Apple is counting on OpenDoc's seamless visual experience to provide a killer user interface; the Mac will feel like a video arcade game. People will buy Macs just to get the best Internet multimedia experience. As we go to press, over 500 ISVs are developing OpenDoc parts for the Mac. So OpenDoc may lead to a renaissance of visual programming on the Mac. It may help the Mac regain its position as the number one visual platform in the industry.

So what are the cons? First, Mac OS is not a very good server platform; it's not even a good advanced client platform. It does not scale well and has limited multithreading. But all this will change next year when Apple ships its new microkernel-based Mac OS—code-named *Copland*.

SERVER OS TRENDS

There will be a clear winner in the server space, but it's far too early to say who.

> — *Paul Cubbage, Dataquest*
> *(November, 1995)*

According to IDC, server OS sales are going through the roof and will continue to do so over the next few years (see Figure 6-3). The fastest growing category is what IDC calls *application servers*. These are your Web, DBMS, TP Monitor, object, and groupware servers.

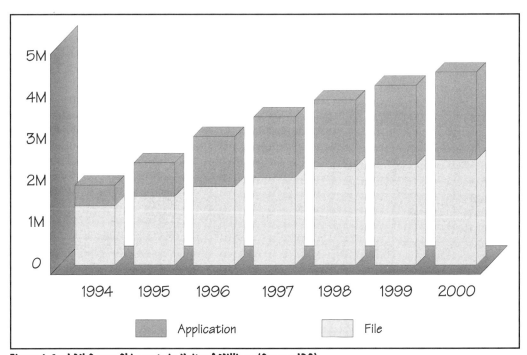

Figure 6-3. LAN Server Shipments in Units of Millions (Source: IDC).

Figure 6-4, from Summit Strategies, shows where application servers fit in the scheme of things. They started out from the department and are now spreading in two directions: 1) downward into the space held by traditional NetWare LAN servers; and 2) upward into the space held by Unix servers running downsized

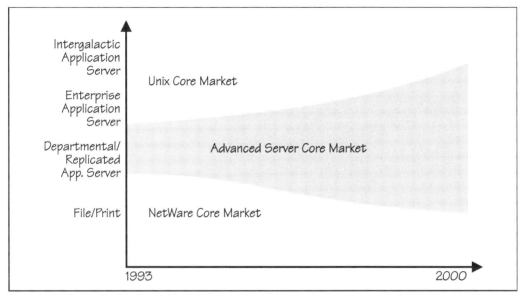

Figure 6-4. The Application Server Market (Source: Summit Strategies).

mainframe applications. Of course, all server OSs—including NetWare, OS/2, NT, and all the Unixes—are going after this high-growth market.

Figure 6-5, also from IDC, shows the breakdown of worldwide OS server shipments in 1995.[3] Novell had record sales in 1995. It sold 923,000 NetWare licenses; 25% were for NetWare 4.1. The Unixes combined sold 514,000 server licenses, and 900,000 desktop licenses. Microsoft sold 393,000 copies of NT Server, and 565,000 copies of NT Workstation. Finally, IBM sold 299,000 copies of OS/2 Warp for servers, and 4.25 million copies for clients.[4]

These numbers tell us that the server market is fragmented. And, we didn't even mention the significant players that fall into the "other" category—including Tandem's NonStop Kernel, Digital's VMS, and IBM's MVS and OS/400. So how do you navigate through this crowded field? First, stay with whatever server platform you currently own—it should only get better with time (unless your OS vendor is going out of business).

Second, if you're starting from ground zero, look for an application server OS that can also be a client. Make sure it can scale to handle your future needs. Also look for things that make your life easier—OOUI-based installation and configuration, plug-and-play, available device drivers, built-in system management, server applica-

---

[3] These are IDC's best numbers as of May, 1996.
[4] Sales of OS/2 servers picked up in April 1996 after the new *OS/2 Warp Server* product shipped; over 50,000 copies were sold in the first month.

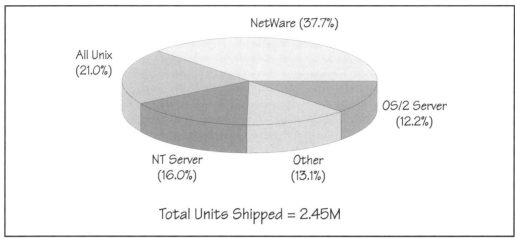

NetWare (37.7%)

All Unix (21.0%)

OS/2 Server (12.2%)

NT Server (16.0%)

Other (13.1%)

Total Units Shipped = 2.45M

Figure 6-5. Worldwide Server OS Shipments in 1995 (Source: IDC).

tion suites, and so on. The days are gone when only the "high priests" of computer-dom were allowed to play with servers. You should expect a modern server OS to have the same friendly look-and-feel as your ordinary desktop.

SERVER OS: MEET THE PLAYERS

Well, it may be the devil, or it may be the Lord, but you're gonna have to serve somebody.

— Bob Dylan

As you can tell from the last section, the competition in the server market is intense. Again, Figure 6-2 shows how the different server platforms are dividing the turf. The players in the low-to-medium end of the server market include NetWare 4.1, OS/2 Warp Server, NT Server 4.0, and Unixes on Intel such as SCO and Solaris. The high-end belongs to Unix clusters and to any mainframe or supermini that can act as a server to PCs. The most formidable competitors at the very high-end are the RISC mainframe vendors that can provide massively parallel computing, scalability, and/or fault tolerance (for example, Tandem, Pyramid, Stratus, IBM, and Sequent). The parallel, MVS-based IBM mainframes—with their transaction engines, enter-prise-based system management, and large databases—are also key players.

NetWare 4.1

By a big margin, the largest server installed base belongs to Novell's NetWare. NetWare is a very fast, effective, well-supported file server that seamlessly supports OS/2, Mac, and Windows clients. The product also includes an X.500-like global

directory service and the tools that make it usable. NetWare is a well-managed server platform; the global directory provides a single point of network administration. *NetWare 4.1 SMP* is similar to NetWare 4.1, except for a second kernel that handles and executes threads across processors.

Today over 4,000 applications run on NetWare—including the major DBMSs. NetWare has a very large support and sales infrastructure—including 200,000 *Certified NetWare Engineers (CNEs)*, and 20,000 reseller partners across the world. Future releases of NetWare will provide C2-level security. They will also provide built-in support for the Internet—including a server-side Java environment.

So what are the cons? The biggest problem is that NetWare makes a poor application server. To become a general-purpose application server vendor, Novell needs to find a way to open its server platform. To try to address this problem, Novell introduced *NetWare Loadable Modules (NLMs)* in NetWare 3.1, which are special namespaces set aside on the server that allow programmers to provide new system services (or write new applications). The NLM server modules you create get loaded by NetWare to manage these namespaces. Your NLMs, in effect, become part of the NetWare operating system kernel. Novell provides tools and a programming environment for the development of NLMs.

But while they open NetWare up to application development, NLMs have become the Achilles' heel of NetWare. They have been slow to catch on with third-party developers who are used to writing applications for conventional server operating systems such as Unix, NT, and OS/2. There are many problems with NLMs that make it very difficult (if not impossible) to use NetWare as a general-purpose application server platform. The three worst culprits are: 1) limited memory protection; 2) lack of memory management—NetWare does not provide virtual memory; and 3) no support for preemptive multitasking. According to Richard Finkelstein, NetWare's non-preemptive status puts too much of the burden on the application developer because it requires applications to be bug free, "a virtual impossibility with the complexity of software we are talking about."

To ease some of the NLM problems and help prevent conflicts between software, Novell established an NLM certification program. In general, it's not a good idea to run application NLMs on the same machine that provides the file or database servers. Some people even recommend that you only run one NLM on each server, but that's untenable.

NT Server

NT Server provides the following additional features over *NT Workstation*: file/print server support, built-in Internet server, disk mirroring and striping, and SMP. NT Server code can be compiled to run on different microprocessor platforms—including Intel, Alpha, PowerPC, and MIPS. The turning point for NT Server came in September 1994, with the release of *NT 3.5* and the *BackOffice 1.0* server application suite. The new release enhanced the TCP/IP stack, provided better support for NetWare, and improved the performance. NT 4.0—expected in late 1996—will add Network OLE support, enhanced security, multiprotocol routing, and ISDN communications.

NT is a good application, database, and file/print server platform. Its tight coupling with Windows, BackOffice, and Network OLE makes it a natural server in Microsoft environments. NT comes from the PC LAN tradition, which means that it is easy to install, manage, and configure. Finally, the NT programming environment and tools are familiar to programmers versed in Microsoft tools.

So what are the cons? First, NT does not scale well. Its SMP engine seems to hit a brick wall with four processors, even when running Microsoft's own SQL Server. Adding a fifth processor only slows it down. In contrast, Unix platforms—for example, Solaris—have demonstrated linear scalability of up to 64 processors using clusters. Second, NT does not provide an enterprise directory server; its directory does not even integrate with other BackOffice applications. Third, only NT Workstations have passed the C2 security certification; NT servers still have security holes. Fourth, NT's backup facilities are not as good as its competitors.

NT also trails its competitors in the area of enterprise services and support channels. For example, there are fewer than 4,000 certified Microsoft Professional Engineers. This is obviously not enough. An enterprise server platform requires a long sales cycle and a lot of customer hand-holding. NT must learn how to coexist with every form of legacy system if it is to play a role in the enterprise. In contrast, NetWare is supported by Novell's vast army of certified resellers who are very experienced at installing and supporting networks. OS/2 is supported by thousands of IBM system engineers who have some of the industry's best system integration skills. And, Unix can count on enormous pools of client/server specialists. Microsoft's forte is still shrink-wrapped products.

OS/2 Warp Server

Like NT, OS/2 is also an excellent application server for departments. It's a seasoned, 32-bit operating system that has incubated some leading-edge server software—including Lotus Notes and CORBA services. OS/2's database, middle-ware, system management, and communications offerings are—in many cases—as rich as their Unix counterparts, but they are almost always easier to install, use, and manage.

In February 1996, IBM introduced *OS/2 Warp Server*, which combines OS/2 Warp's application server environment with LAN Server—a very fast file and print server.[5] Warp Server provides an OOUI user interface for easy installation, configuration, and system management. You do everything via point-and-click. The installation also autodetects hardware, which makes it easier to find and configure all these strange network adapters. Warp Server also provides disk mirroring, remote administration, remote software distribution, a backup server, and software metering.

---

[5] According to benchmarks conducted by PC Week Labs, OS/2 Warp Server elbowed out NetWare 4.1 SMP and NT Server to become the fastest file server on the market. (Source: **PC Week**, "State of the Server," April 1, 1996).

Finally, IBM is introducing—throughout 1996—a family of integrated, turn-key, server offerings code-named *Eagle*. There are Eagle servers for database, Lotus Notes, Internet commerce, TP Monitor, CORBA object services, and DCE security and directory. IBM's idea is to make client/server solutions more accessible by providing shrink-wrapped server packages that have common installation, maintenance, and support features. All Eagle servers will run on OS/2 and take advantage of its user-friendly environment. They will also run on AIX and NT.

So what are the cons? First, OS/2 is an Intel-only server platform; OS/2 for the Power PC appears to be dead on arrival. Note that Intel-only may also be a benefit in this case. It means that OS/2 does not incur the extra burden of a portability layer. It can take full advantage of Intel hardware and SMP buses and become the fastest OS for the ubiquitous Intel servers, which account for over 80% of all servers. Except for the very high-end of the server market, it doesn't hurt to be Intel-only.

OS/2's second shortcoming is its system limits. For example, the largest file size OS/2 supports is 2 GBytes. Disk partitions are limited to 512 GBytes. These may appear like reasonable limits now, but they will hit us as we move into multimedia. Finally, many of OS/2's high-end server functions are still "futures." This includes C2 security, Unicode support (for internationalization), support for megaclusters, transactional file systems, and memory-mapped files. Many of these features will find their way in the forthcoming *OS/2 Merlin Server*.

Unix

Unix provides a seasoned, function-rich operating system that is scalable from the desktop to the supercomputer. Unix is the melting pot of the computer industry. Its close connection with universities makes it a great incubator of new ideas. Most of these ideas first appear on the commercial market as Unix extensions and variants. The Unix mainstream, on the other hand, moves a lot more cautiously. Unix can claim an army of trained programmers, integrators, and technicians.

The Unix server industry grew out of the downsizing of mainframe applications. In the last 15 years Unix was able to successfully surround the mainframe. It then provided "a poor man's mainframe" alternative. However, in the PC LAN environment Unix, is viewed as a "rich man's server." Unix is now surrounded by low-cost PC alternatives such as NT, OS/2, and NetWare. However, Unix continues to thrive. It is a $30 billion market with 25% annual growth rates. The latest high-growth area for Unix servers is the Internet. Unix standards have become Internet standards—including mail, FTP, TCP/IP, and the domain name service. In a sense, the Internet is a showcase of distributed Unix technology.

Unix vendors have always been at the forefront of client/server middleware. Now they are introducing Java and CORBA objects to the world, again by incorporating

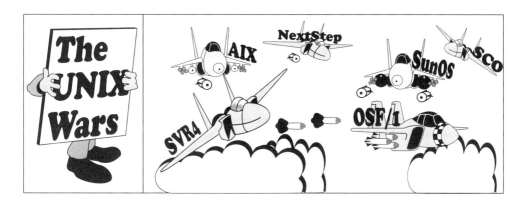

them into the Internet infrastructure. Unix is also a well-regarded choice for database servers, especially ones that scale. Finally, the Unix world is now working on a 64-bit standard, which should help Unix leapfrog its competitors—including NT, OS/2, and NetWare.

So what are the cons? The main problem with Unix has always been: Which Unix do you choose? At last count, there were over 45 variants of Unix on the market. Because Unix is a hardware-independent operating system, an application should be able to run on any machine that supports Unix, from a PC to a Cray supercomputer. This server scalability story is very attractive, but it is not realistic. In the real world, what keeps this from happening are two factors:

- ■ *Lack of binary compatibility.* The Unix world is different from the PC world where software comes in low-cost, shrink-wrapped floppy packages that can run on any PC clone that runs MS-DOS, NT, Windows 95, or OS/2. Unlike these operating systems that are developed by one company and marketed on many types of hardware platforms, Unixes vary widely. There is still no broadly supported binary standard. Unix applications, at a minimum, must be recompiled to be ported from platform to platform. This is a major headache and expense for software providers.

- ■ *Functional differences among the Unixes*. There will always be differences among the Unixes: Vendors like to sell products, and functional differences are required to avoid relentless, no-win price wars. Even though X/Open's *Spec 1170*—which supports over 1,170 kernel APIs selected from the top 50 Unix applications—will be used to "brand" Unixes as such, it will only define the least common denominator functions. To get what you paid for out of a platform, you will likely need to use its extensions and lose portability.

The NT threat is pushing Unix vendors toward some kind of unification. SCO has become the new guardian of the Unix standard, but Sun is still the "odd man out." It seems that for Unix to effectively compete, it must change its model. Instead of each vendor reinventing the wheel with their Unix extensions, they must learn to cross-license each other's technology.

CONCLUSION

If you can run the same OS on both clients and servers—do it!

— John Dvorak

Yes, it is true that client/server allows us to "mix-and-match," but it's simpler to avoid this. Running the same OS on both clients and servers makes LANs simpler to administer, and you can easily move programs (and functions) between clients and servers. In addition, the installation procedures, the file systems, and the interfaces to the operating system are the same on both the client and the server. This familiar setting makes it easy for departments and small organizations to introduce client/server solutions. Unfortunately, for most of us, there is no one-size-fits-all operating system. So we must learn to live with client/server diversity, and then grow to love it.

Part 3
Base Middleware:
Stacks and NOSs

An Introduction to Part 3

Multivendor systems have serious barriers to cooperation. An articulated aim of the industry is to increase the capacity of systems to cooperate.

— **Hal Lorin, Author**
Doing IT Right
(Prentice-Hall, 1996)

Congratulations, you're still alive after going through the OS wars. Wasn't that exciting? Yes, Earthlings are always fighting over one thing or another. That seems to be in their nature. But we're going to change the pace now and take you through some more secular terrain. Instead of fighting each other, the client/server vendors will now try to hide their differences behind a facade called the "single-system image."

Now don't get us wrong. The folks you met in Part 2 are far from burying the hatchet. Instead, they're all trying to make everybody else's system look like their own. If they can't get rid of the other systems, the next best thing is to make them disappear (the politically correct term is to "make them transparent"). So how do they do that disappearing trick? By throwing layer upon layer of middleware until everything becomes one. Now that's magic!

Part 3 is about the base middleware that is used to create the "single-system illusion." We will start with a brief tutorial on *Network Operating System (NOS)* middleware. You'll discover the "bag of tricks" NOSs use to create illusions that would put to shame the great Houdini himself—that's one of our better magicians who lived on Earth not too long ago. There were no NOSs in Houdini's time.

After exploring the NOSs, we go into the *stacks* middleware, which introduce their own repertoire of tricks. Eventually, nothing is what it appears to be. Everything gets deconstructed, reconstructed, and then repackaged so that it "appears to work" with everything else. But you'll know better, of course.

You'll soon discover that each vendor will be glad to sell you a different set of middleware products. Unfortunately, middleware does not extend its disappearing act to make the products themselves transparent. This is because middleware is a lucrative business in its own right. Yes, when there's money to be made, nothing disappears. And we pay for the pleasure of seeing the heterogeneous world look like it's one happily integrated system. Yes, we pay for illusions on Earth. Look at our movie industry.

Finally, we will introduce you to some of the products you'll need to create the type of illusions that meet your fancy (or real needs). You can create almost any type of facade as long as you have the money to pay for it. Another important reason to look at products is to get a reality check of what's really there. The middleware vendors are practitioners of magic who, like all magicians, sometimes forget what's

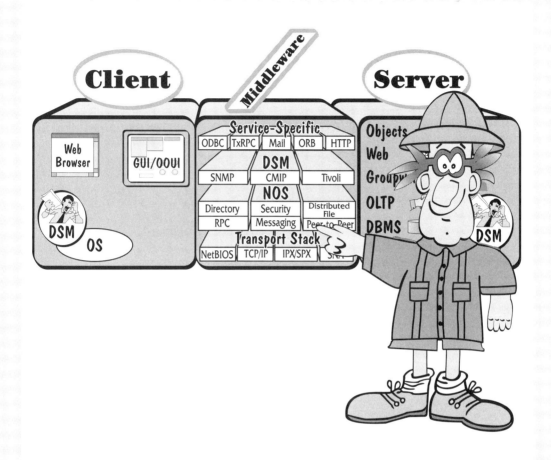

real. So it's essential to go behind the stage and see what's really there, at least in terms of product. We hope you'll enjoy the show.

Chapter 7

NOS: Creating the Single System Image

---

*S*ingle system image creates an illusion in the minds of users that all the servers on the network are part of the same system or behave like a single computer.

— Andrew Tanenbaum, Author
Modern Operating Systems
(Prentice-Hall, 1992)

This chapter goes over the functions that the Network Operating System (NOS) middleware must provide to create a "single-system image" of all the services on the network. As we explained earlier, this is really a Houdini-sized illusion that makes all servers of the world—we're talking about a multiserver, multiservice, multivendor, and multinetwork world—appear to the client as one big happy family. In a sense, the NOS middleware provides the glue that recreates the single system out of the disparate elements. It's a thankless job, but without it there can be no client/server computing. By the end of this chapter, you'll get a better appreciation of the "bag of tricks" that are used by clients and servers to create the *grand illusion*.

NOS MIDDLEWARE: THE TRANSPARENT ILLUSION

NOSs are evolving from being a collection of independent workstations, able to communicate via a shared file system, to becoming real distributed computing environments that make the network *transparent* to users.

What Does Transparency Really Mean?

Transparency means fooling everyone into thinking the client/server system is totally seamless. It really means hiding the network and its servers from the users and even the application programmers. Here are some of the types of transparencies the NOS middleware is expected to provide as part of its "network disappearing act":

■ *Location transparency*—You should not have to be aware of the location of a resource. Users should not have to include the location information in the resource's name. For example, *Machine**directory**file* surfaces the name of the server machine. This is a transparency violation.

■ *Namespace transparency*—You should be able to use the same naming conventions (and namespace) to locate any resource on the network. The whole universe is one big tree (see Figure 7-1). This includes every type of resource on any vendor's product.

■ *Logon transparency*—You should be able to provide a single password (or authentication) that works on all servers and for all services on the network.

■ *Replication transparency*—You should not be able to tell how many copies of a resource exist. For example, if a naming directory is shadowed on many

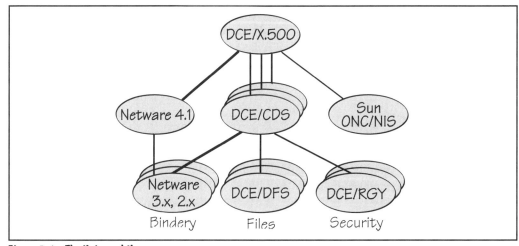

Figure 7-1. The Universal Namespace.

machines, it is up to the NOS to synchronize updates and take care of any locking issues.

■ *Local/remote access transparency*—You should be able to work with any resource on the network as if it were on the local machine. The NOS must handle access controls and provide directory services.

■ *Distributed time transparency*—You should not see any time differences across servers. The NOS must synchronize the clocks on all servers.

■ *Failure transparency*—You must be shielded from network failures. The NOS must handle retries and session reconnects. It must also provide some levels of service redundancy for fault-tolerance.

■ *Administration transparency*—You should only have to deal with a single-system management interface. The NOS must be integrated with the local management services.

The challenge for the NOS middleware is how to provide this high level of transparency *without sacrificing the autonomy of the local OS.*

NOS: Extending the Local OS's Reach

One of the functions of a NOS is to make the physical location of resources (over a network) transparent to an application. The early NOSs were in the business of virtualizing the file and printer resources and redirecting them to LAN-based file and print servers. These NOSs provided agents on the local machines—the *requesters*—that intercepted calls for devices and *redirected* them to servers on the LAN. The only way an application (or user) could tell the difference between a local or remote resource was from a pathname, which included its machine name. But aliases could be used to even hide the pathnames from the users. The NOS thus extends the local OS's device support transparently across the network. Practically anything that can be done on a local OS can be done remotely and transparently. The NOS allows applications written for the local OS to become networked without changing a line of code. Most NOSs allow clients that run on different OSs (such as DOS, Mac, and Unix) to share files and other devices. For example, a Mac client sees DOS files in the Mac format.

A new generation of network file servers promises to introduce even more transparency into the file systems. For example, the DCE *Distributed File Service (DFS)* provides a single-image file system that can be distributed across a group of file servers (see Figure 7-2). The DFS file naming scheme is location-independent. Each file has a unique identifier that is consistent across the network. Files use the DCE global namespace just like the rest of the network resources. And the file system is integrated with the DCE security mechanisms.

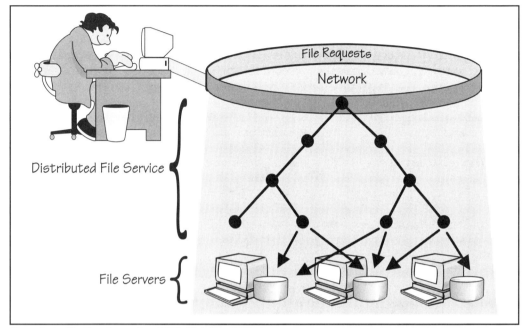

Figure 7-2. The New Generation: DCE's Distributed File Server.

DFS provides a *Local File System (LFS)* with many advanced features, including replication facilities that make the file system highly available. Fast response is achieved with a distributed cache. A snapshot of the file system can reside on the client, which can operate on files even if the server is down. Backups and file relocations can take place without making LFS unavailable. LFS also provides transactional log support. In case of a system crash, file records can be replayed to bring the system to a consistent state. LFS still has a few problems that need to be ironed out; but when it is ready, it will raise the bar for distributed file systems. DFS can work with other local file systems, such as NFS, or the Unix file system.

Global Directory Services

The state of a client/server system is always in flux. Users join and leave the network. Services can be added and moved around at will. Data is always being created and moved around. So who keeps track of all this activity? How do clients find their servers in a constantly changing universe? Where is the single-system image kept? It's kept in the NOS directory service, of course (see Figure 7-3). This essential component tracks all the NOS's resources and knows where everything is. Without it, we would be lost. Ideally, a distributed directory should provide a single image that can be used by all network applications—including e-mail, system management, network inventory, file services, RPCs, distributed objects, databases, authentication, and security.

What's in a Name?

Briefing

In client/server systems, names must be unique within the context in which they are resolved (and used). You can think of a context as an autonomous naming authority. It's like the area code in the telephone system. A federated naming scheme (or *namespace*) is a conglomeration of independent naming authorities. In a federated namespace, each name must include its naming authority. For example, if you're within the US telephone naming authority, you can only call somebody in Switzerland by including the country code for Switzerland along with the person's telephone number. It's a tree-like (or hierarchical) naming scheme. If you create enough layers of hierarchy, you'll end up with a namespace that includes every communicating entity in the universe. In summary, a local directory allows us to locate entities within our own network neighborhood; a federated—or global—directory allows us to find things outside the local neighborhood. ❏

Directories and name servers solve the same problem: How to resolve human understandable names into machine addresses? In a modern NOS, the directory service is implemented as a distributed, replicated, object database. It is *distributed* to allow different administration domains to control their environment. It is *replicated* to provide high availability and performance where needed. Remember, if the directory is down, all the network activity comes to a grinding halt. Nothing can be found. It's an *object database* in the sense that everything that is tracked is an instance of an object class. You can use inheritance to derive new object types.

A typical directory is implemented as a set of named entries and their associated attributes. For example, "MyServer" may be an instance of an application server type (or class). Its attributes can be: room number = 54, status = up, and CPU utilization = 54 percent. MyServer may also contain a list of the functions it exports and their interface definitions.

Modern NOS directories have APIs and user interfaces that allow programs (or humans) to locate entities on the network by querying on the name or attributes. For example, a program can issue a query to locate all the 1200-dpi printers that are not busy. If you know the name of an entity, you can always obtain its attributes. The directory service itself is a well-known address known to all the trusted users on the network (and sometimes even intruders).

How do directories maintain their autonomy in a global network environment? How do they let us create unique names on the network without bumping into each other? How do we accommodate legacy naming services? This is usually accomplished by

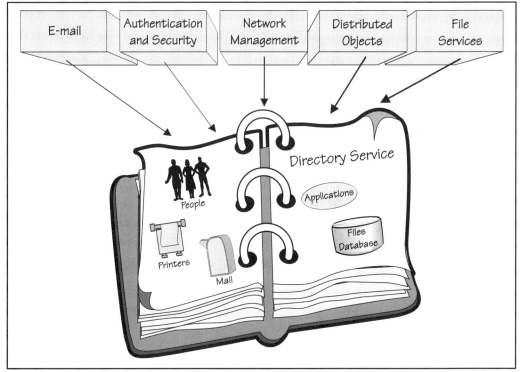

Figure 7-3. Global Directories: Keeping Track of NOS Resources.

introducing hierarchical namespaces like in a file system (see Figure 7-4). In each name, there is a *global component* and a *local component*. The global component is the name by which the local directory is known at the intergalactic level. The global component manages a federation of loosely-coupled local directories. You can name the local component according to local conventions. In addition, a gateway agent can reside on each local directory and can forward queries for non-local names to a global directory (or naming service).

How are directories replicated? Typically, a directory maintains a master copy and read-only shadow replicas. Two types of synchronization schemes are used to refresh the replicas:

- ■ ***Immediate replication*** causes any update to the master to be immediately shadowed on all replicas.

- ■ ***Skulking*** causes a periodic propagation (for example, once a day) to all the replicas of all changes made on the master.

In summary, the new generation of NOS directory services uses some of the most advanced distributed database and object technology to keep track of distributed system resources. The technology is flexible enough to manage and track today's coarser network entities—such as printers, users, programs, and servers—and the more fine-grained entities that are beginning to appear—such as distributed objects.

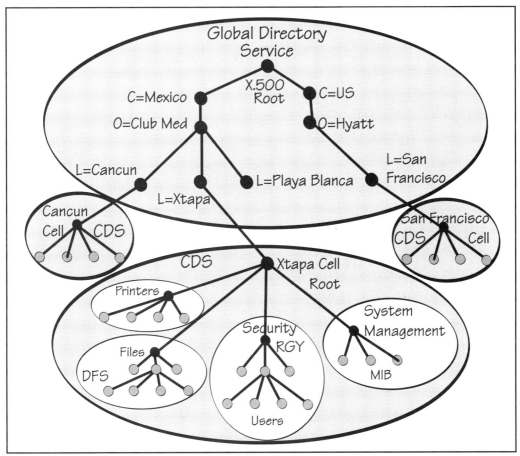

Figure 7-4. Federated Directories—Creating a Unified Namespace.

FYI

The X.500 Global Directory Standard

Briefing

X.500 is the only standard out there that's the Esperanto of the directory world.

— Tim Sloane, Aberdeen Group

Warning: This box is filled with TLAs (Three-Letter Acronyms).

The industry standard for global directories, X.500, is based on a replicated distributed database (see Figure 7-5). Programs can access the directory services using the X/Open Directory Service (XDS) APIs. The XDS APIs allow programs to read, compare, update, add, and remove directory entries; list directories; and search for entries based on attributes. You use the X/Open Management (XOM) API for defining and navigating through the information objects that are in the directory. Think of XOM as an object metalanguage. Each object in an X.500 directory belongs to a class. A class can be derived from other classes. XOM provides an API for defining object classes and their attributes. XOM APIs also define basic data types such as string.

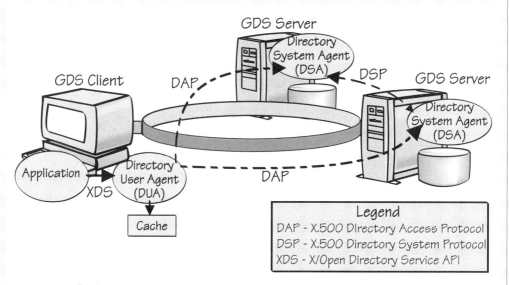

Figure 7-5. The X.500 Directory Components.

The X.500 client component—the Directory User Agent (DUA)—and server component—the Directory System Agent (DSA)—communicate using the Directory Access Protocol (DAP). Servers talk to each other using the Directory System Protocol (DSP). The DAP and DSP formats and protocols are defined in the X.500 standard and provide worldwide interoperability among directory services.

The X.500 standard was written to run on top of the OSI communication protocol. OSI is not very popular, so most implementations of X.500 cheat and use alternatives like TCP/IP or IPX/SPX. X.500 is being implemented—fully or partially—in a number of products—including *DCE, Microsoft Exchange, Lotus Notes, NetWare Directory Service,* and *NT Cairo.* X.500 is a standards success story. It is our best hope for finding things on intergalactic networks. Sorry for all the acronyms! ❑

Distributed Time Services

Maintaining a single notion of time is important for ordering events that occur on distributed clients and servers. So how does a client/server system keep the clocks on different machines synchronized? How does it compensate for the unequal drift rates between synchronizations? How does it create a single system illusion that makes all the different machine clocks tick to the same time? With the NOS's distributed time services, of course.

Typically, the NOS addresses the problem of distributed time using two complementary techniques:

- *It periodically synchronizes the clocks on every machine in the network.* The NOS typically has an agent on each machine—DCE calls it a *Time Clerk*—that asks *Time Servers* for the correct time and adjusts the local time accordingly. The agents may consult more than one Time Server, and then calculate the probable correct time and its inaccuracy based on the responses it receives. The agent can upgrade the local time either gradually or abruptly.

- *It introduces an inaccuracy component to compensate for unequal clock drifts that occur between synchronizations.* The local time agents are configured to know the limits of their local hardware clock. They maintain a count of the inaccuracy factor and return it to an API call that asks for the time. The time agent requests a synchronization after the local clock drifts past an inaccuracy threshold.

As you can see, today's NOSs may have even surpassed the Swiss in their attention to intricate timing details.

Distributed Security Services

The client/server environment introduces new security threats beyond those found in traditional time-shared systems. In a client/server system, you can't trust any of the operating systems on the network to protect the server's resources from unauthorized access. And even if the client machines were totally secure, the network itself is highly accessible. Sniffer devices can easily record traffic between machines and introduce forgeries and Trojan horses into the system. This means the servers must find new ways to protect themselves without creating a fortress mentality that upsets users.

To maintain the single-system illusion, every trusted user must be given transparent access to all resources. How is that done when every PC poses a potential threat to network security? Will system administrators be condemned to spend their working lives granting access level rights to users, one at a time, for each individual application on each server across the enterprise? Let's find out what the NOSs have to offer.

Can We Obtain C2-Level Security on the LAN?

C2 is a U.S. government security standard for operating systems; it requires that users and applications be authenticated before gaining access to any operating system resource. To obtain C2 certification on a network, all clients must provide an authenticated user ID, all resources must be protected by access control lists, audit trails must be provided, and access rights must not be passed to other users that reuse the same items. Let's go over the security mechanisms a modern NOS can provide to meet (and even beat) C2 level security on the network.

■ *Authentication: Are you who you claim to be?* In time-shared systems, the authentication is done by the OS using passwords. NOSs must do better than that. Any hacker with a PC and network sniffer knows how to capture a password and reuse it. OK, so let's encrypt the password. Oh boy! Who is going to manage the secret keys and all that good stuff? Luckily, NOSs have an answer: *Kerberos*. Kerberos is the trusted third party that allows two processes to prove to each other that they are who they claim to be. It's a bit like two spies meeting on a street corner and whispering the magical code words that establish the "trust" relationship. Both parties obtain the magic words separately from Kerberos (see the next Briefing box).

Kerberos: "You Can't Trust Anyone"

Briefing

MIT's project Athena adopted the position that it is next to *impossible* to make sure each workstation on the network is secure. Instead, the MIT folks took it as a given that some "impersonation" would take place on the LAN and decided to protect themselves against it. The result was a software fortress called *Kerberos* that delivers a higher level of security than traditional passwords and access control lists. Kerberos automatically authenticates every user for every application. The Kerberos protocol, especially with the add-ons introduced by the OSF DCE, fulfills the authentication requirement of C2. It allows servers to trust their clients (mostly PCs), and vice versa. You must remember that we could always put a Trojan horse on the server side, so the servers also need to prove their identity. ❑

■ **Authorization: Are you allowed to use this resource?** Once clients are authenticated, the server applications are responsible for verifying which operations the clients are permitted to perform on the information they try to access (for example, a payroll server may control access to salary data on a per-individual basis). Servers use *Access Control Lists (ACLs)* to control user access. ACLs can be associated with any computer resource. They contain the list of names (and group names) and the type of operations they are permitted to perform on each resource. NetWare's administration services, for example, make it easy for network managers to add new users to groups without having to specify access rights from scratch. NOSs can easily meet C2's ACL requirements.

■ **Audit Trails: Where have you been?** Audit services allow network managers to monitor user activities, including attempted logons and which servers or files are used. Audit services are a piece of the arsenal needed by network managers to detect intruders in their own organizations. For example, they can monitor all the network activity associated with a suspect client workstation (or user). Knowing an audit trail exists usually discourages insiders from tampering with servers using their own logon, but they can do it under somebody else's logon. Most NOSs support audit trails, and that should make the C2 accreditation people happy.

In summary, it looks like C2 security on a LAN is within the reach of a modern NOS.

Can We Do Better Than C2 on the LAN?

But we need to have security better than C2 when traffic moves over unsecured wide area networks. How can we guarantee that vital messages are not tampered with? You don't want the data in an electronic fund transfer to be intercepted and rerouted from your account to somebody else's. In addition, electronic commerce on the Internet is introducing the need for a new security feature called *non-repudiation*. This is the electronic equivalent of a notarized signature that can hold in court. Modern NOSs, like the OSF DCE, provide at least two mechanisms for dealing with these type of situations:

- *Encryption* allows two principals to hold a secure communication. Each principal must obtain a copy of a *session key* from a trusted third party (for example, a Kerberos server). This session key can then be used for encoding and decoding messages. Another approach is to use a public/private key encryption technique. The advantage of the public/private key scheme is that it can also be used for electronic signatures and non-repudiation (see the next Briefing box).

- *Cryptographic checksums*, a less extreme solution, ensure that data is not modified as it passes through the network. The sender calculates a checksum on the data, using a session key to encrypt it, and appends the result to the message. The receiver recalculates the checksum, decrypts the one received in the message using the session key, and then compares the two. If they don't match, the message is suspect. Without the session key, intruders will not be able to alter the data and update the checksum.

Encryption may be an overkill in some situations because it introduces performance overheads and may be subject to governmental restrictions.

Single Logon Makes it Easier for the User

Users are already complaining about having to do multiple logons to different servers and resource managers. Modern NOSs provide the technology that allows a user to access any server resource from anywhere—including hotel rooms, offices, homes, and cellular phones—using a single signon. How's that done? With Kerberos-like security, of course. You simply log on once (see Figure 7-6), get authenticated, and then obtain a set of security tickets (also called tokens) for each server with which you want to communicate. All this activity is conducted under-the-cover by the NOSs security agents. No password is stored in the login script on the client, and no telephone callbacks are required. It doesn't get any easier, as long as you can remember your password.

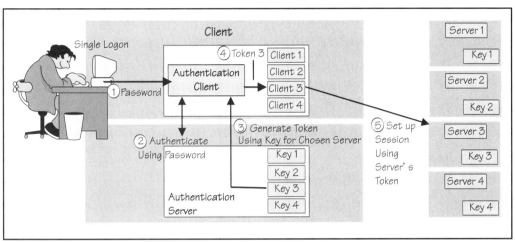

Figure 7-6. Logon Once and Get To Everything You Need.

 FYI

The Battle Between Public and Private Keys

Briefing

Encryption has been used to protect information for at least 4000 years. Today, the two predominant approaches to electronic encryption are based on shared cypher keys and public cypher keys:

■ *The shared private key approach* uses a single key to encrypt or decrypt information. Each pair of users who need to exchange messages must agree on a private key and use it as a cypher to encode and decode their messages. This method works well, as long as both sides maintain the secrecy of the private key. It's their shared "little secret."

The *Data Encryption Standard (DES)* is based on this public key approach and has been the official U.S. national cryptographic standard since 1977. DES was originally proposed by IBM as a 128-bit cypher, but the NSA (the U.S. spy agency) insisted that it be trimmed to 56 bits before accepting it as the basis for the national cryptographic standard—the NSA didn't want an algorithm that they could never break. DES has been the encryption algorithm of choice for interbank electronic fund transfers. In all its years of service, there has not been a reported case of DES cracking. A machine performing one DES decryption per microsecond would take 2000 years to crack a given key. The DES algorithm enables 72 quadrillion possible keys.

Kerberos uses an encryption cypher based on DES. As far as keys go, Kerberos uses a shared, session-specific, private key approach.

■ ***The public key approach*** uses two keys: a *public* key and a *private* key. The public key may be listed in directories and is available for all to see. You encrypt your message with your private key, and the recipient uses your public key to decode it. In addition, anybody can send you an encrypted message by using your public key as a cypher (you decode it with your private key). This way, you don't even have to know who the sender is. Again, all this works well, as long as you keep your private key secret (see Figure 7-7).

RSA is a public key algorithm invented at MIT. RSA stands for the initials of its three inventors. It is considered the public key algorithm of choice and is used mostly for authentication. RSA can also be used for encrypting very short messages. The problem is that RSA is too slow for encrypting longer messages and requires DES to do that. If the encryption is done in software, DES is about 100 times faster than RSA. In hardware, DES is between 1000 and 10,000 times as fast, depending on the implementation (Source: Stang and Moore, **Network Security Secrets**, IDC Books, 1993).

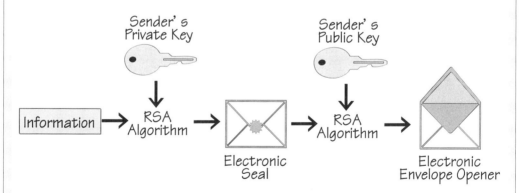

Figure 7-7. Public Keys: The Sealed Digital Envelope.

So why would anybody want RSA? Because it lets you encrypt messages without the prior exchange of secrets (or tokens), and it provides an unforgeable electronic signature. Only you can know your private key—there is no "trusted third party" like Kerberos. An RSA signature can be binding in legal courts because there can be no fingerpointing. And if you loose control of your private key, you're the only one to blame. One of the problems with RSA is that the private key part must be delivered to each node on the network without breaching security. They need something like Kerberos to do that. An alternative is to use a *Certificate Authority (CA)* that authenticates the public key. The CA digitally signs the public key (more on this in Part 8). ❏

Chapter 8

RPC, Messaging, and Peer-to-Peer

Therefore, ye soft pipes, play on.

— *Keats*

Client/server applications are split across address spaces, physical machines, networks, and operating systems. How do clients and servers talk to each other? How are the requests and responses synchronized? How are the dissimilar data representations on different computers handled? What happens if one of the parties is unavailable? You guessed it: The modern NOS is taking on a lot of these responsibilities. It comes with the territory. The purpose of the NOS is to make distributed computing transparent. This means it must create an environment that hides the nastiness of dealing with communication protocols, networks, and stacks.

All NOSs offer *peer-to-peer* interfaces that let applications communicate using close to the wire send/receive semantics. Most NOSs provide some form of *Remote Procedure Call (RPC)* middleware that hides "the wire" and makes any server on the network appear to be one function call away. An alternative type of model—message queuing, or simply *Message-Oriented Middleware (MOM)*—is gaining new converts. It turns out that messaging is incredibly helpful in situations where you do not want the clients and servers to be tightly synchronized. The current NOSs don't include MOM in their offerings. However, some very powerful product offerings are available from companies that specialize in this field. Let's take a closer look at what each type of interface has to offer (also see the next Briefing box).

What's a Stack Anyway?

Briefing

Like everything else on the network, RPCs, MOM, and peer-to-peer APIs sit on top communications stacks (see Figure 8-1). So what exactly is a stack? Communications software vendors have tackled the problem of network complexity by breaking down complex protocols into layers. Each layer builds on top of the services provided by the layers below it. Eventually, you get a *stack* of layers that looks like a birthday cake. Vendors sell their communication products as stack offerings that are architected to work together. In theory, each stack layer has a well-defined set of APIs and protocols so that it should be possible to mix-and-match different vendor offerings within the same stack. In practice, this is not the case. You buy an entire stack from a single vendor and pray that it works with the hardware.

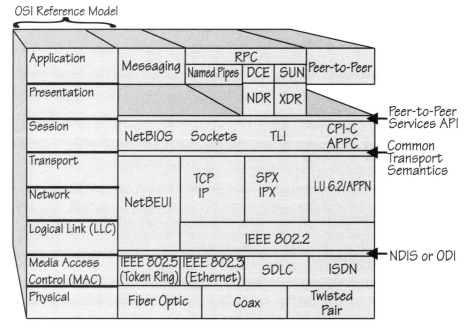

Figure 8-1. Where the Most Popular Stacks Fit in the OSI Reference Model.

The lowest layer of communication software belongs to the device drivers that provide an interface to several types of communication hardware adapters. The bottom of the stacks sits on top of the device drivers. The top of the stacks sits right below the NOS. The stacks and NOS are simply divisions that help us create a survival map. The *OSI Reference Model* defines seven layers of functions that a complete stack should ideally provide. To help you navigate through this chapter, we couldn't resist coming up with our own interpretation of where the most popular commercial stacks fit in the OSI reference model (see Figure 8-1). Remember, it's just a reference model. So take it in with a grain of salt. *Real* products don't have any notion of architectural boundaries or reference models—they just get a job done.

So what do stacks provide? At the lower layers, they interface to the hardware using the physical *Media Access Control (MAC)* protocols defined by the IEEE. The *Logical Link Control (LLC)* provides a common interface to the MACs and a reliable link service for transmitting communication packets between two nodes. The OSI *link* layer combines the LLC and MAC functions. On top of this layer is the *network* layer that allows packets to be routed across multiple networks. The *transport* layer sits on top of the network layer and provides some form of reliable end-to-end delivery service. The *session* layer deals with network etiquette—who goes first, who reconnects in case of failure, and synchronization points. On top of the session layer is a *presentation* layer that deals with data representation. Finally, the *application layer* provides network services and interfaces to an application.

The boundary between the stacks and NOS gets fuzzy at the upper layers. For example, is the peer-to-peer interface an application, presentation, or session layer service? Does it belong to the NOS or to the stacks? But, then, everything in client/server is a bit fuzzy. ❏

PEER-TO-PEER COMMUNICATIONS

Most early client/server applications were implemented using low-level, conversational, peer-to-peer protocols—such as sockets, TLI, CPIC/APPC, NetBIOS, and Named Pipes. There were very few alternatives then. These low-level protocols are hard to code and maintain, so they are loosing their popularity. Instead, programmers are now using RPCs, MOMs, and ORBs, which provide higher levels of abstraction. So the conversational protocols should only be used by very demanding user applications or system-level software.

The term "peer-to-peer" indicates that the two sides of a communication link use the same protocol interface to conduct a networked conversation. Any computer can initiate a conversation with any other computer. The protocol is symmetrical, and it is sometimes called "program-to-program." The peer-to-peer interface tends to

be "close to the wire" in the sense that it does not fully mask the underlying network from the programmer. For example, the interface will surface transmission time-outs, race conditions, and network errors, and then leave it to the programmer to handle. The peer-to-peer protocols started as stack-specific APIs. But as we explained in Part 1, most of these APIs now support multiple stacks. So their association with a particular stack is only of historical interest. Here's a brief description of the major peer-to-peer protocols and their associated stacks.

Sockets

Sockets were introduced in 1981 as the Unix BSD 4.2 generic interface that would provide Unix-to-Unix communications over networks. In 1985, SunOS introduced NFS and RPC over sockets. In 1986, AT&T introduced the *Transport Layer Interface (TLI)* that provides functionality similar to sockets but in a more net-work-independent fashion. Unix SVR4 incorporates both sockets and TLI. As it stands, sockets are far more prevalent than TLI. Sockets and TLI are very similar from a programmer's perspective. TLI is just a cleaner version of sockets. An application written to TLI is, in theory, stack independent. It should run on IPX/SPX or TCP/IP with very few modifications. The TLI API consists of about 25 API calls.

Sockets are supported on virtually every operating system. The Windows socket API, known colloquially as *WinSock*, is a multivendor specification that standard-izes the use of TCP/IP under Windows. The WinSock API is based on the Berkeley sockets interface. In the BSD Unix system, sockets are part of the kernel and provide both a standalone and networked IPC service. Non-BSD Unix systems, MS-DOS, Windows, Mac OS, and OS/2 provide sockets in the form of libraries. So it is safe to say that sockets provide the current *de facto* portable standard for network application providers on TCP/IP networks.

The three most popular socket types are *stream*, *datagram*, and *raw*. Stream and datagram sockets interface to the TCP and UDP protocols, and raw sockets interface to the IP protocol. The type of socket is specified at creation time. In theory, the socket interface can be extended, and you can define new socket types to provide additional services. A socket address on the TCP/IP internet consists of two parts: an internet address (IP_address) and a port number (see Figure 8-2). So what's an internet address? And what's a port number?

Figure 8-2. Socket = Internet Address (IP) + Port Address.

An *internet address* is a 32-bit number, usually represented by four decimal numbers separated by dots, that must be unique for each TCP/IP network interface card within an administered AF_INET domain. A TCP/IP *host* (i.e., networked machine) may have as many internet addresses as it has network interfaces.

A *port* is an entry point to an application that resides on a host. It is represented by a 16-bit integer. Ports are commonly used to define the entry points for services provided by server applications. Important commercial server programs—such as Oracle and Sybase DBMSs—have their own *well-known* ports.

 FYI

Datagrams Versus Sessions

Briefing

Connection-oriented protocols—also known as *session-based protocols*, *virtual circuits*, or *sequenced packet exchanges*—provide a reliable two-way connection service over a session. Each packet of information that gets exchanged over a session is given a unique sequence number through which it gets tracked and individually acknowledged. Duplicate packets are detected and discarded by the session services.

The price you pay for this reliable class of service is the overhead associated with creating and managing the session. If a session is lost, one of the parties must reestablish it. This can be a problem for fault-tolerant servers that require automatic switchovers to a backup server if the primary server fails. The backup server needs to reestablish all the outstanding sessions with clients. In addition, sessions are inherently a two-party affair and don't lend themselves well to broadcasting (one-to-many exchanges).

Datagrams—also known as *connectionless* protocols or *transmit and pray* protocols—provide a simple but unreliable form of exchange. The more powerful datagram protocols such as NetBIOS provide broadcast capabilities. NetBIOS allows you to send datagrams to a named entity, to a select group of entities (multicast), or to all entities on a network (broadcast). Datagrams are unreliable in the sense that they are not acknowledged or tracked through a sequence number. You "send and pray" that your datagram gets received. The recipient may not be there or may not be expecting a datagram (you will never know). Novell literature estimates that about 5% of datagrams don't make it. You may, of course, design your own acknowledgement schemes on top of the datagram service. Some stacks (for example, LAN Server's Mailslots) provide an acknowledged datagram service.

Datagrams are very useful to have in "discovery" types of situations. These are situations where you discover things about your network environment by broadcasting queries and learning who is out there from the responses. Broadcast can be used to obtain bids for services or to advertise the availability of new services. Broadcast datagrams provide the capability of creating electronic "bazaars." They support the creation of very dynamic types of environments where things can happen spontaneously. In situations where the name of the recipient is not known, broadcast datagrams are the only way to get the message out. The cost of broadcast datagrams is that, in some cases, recipients may get overloaded with "junk mail." The multicast facility helps alleviate this problem because broadcast mail can then be sent only to "special interest" groups. The alternative to broadcast is to use a network directory service.

Datagrams are also very useful in situations where there is a need to send a quick message without the world coming to an end if the message is not received. The typical situation is sending control-like information, such as telling a network manager "I'm alive." It doesn't make sense to go through all the overhead of creating a session with the network manager just to say "I'm alive," and what if there are 500 nodes on the network? The manager will need 500 permanent sessions, an exorbitant cost in resources. This is where the datagram alternative comes in. With datagrams you can send your "I'm alive" message. And if the manager misses your message once, it will get another one when you send your next heartbeat (provided you're still alive). ❏

NetWare: IPX/SPX and TLI

Because Novell owns—depending on whose numbers you quote—between 50% and 60% of the network market, it follows that IPX/SPX, NetWare's native stack, must be the most widespread stack in the industry. IPX/SPX is also popular with network managers in large enterprises who are delighted with its internetworking capabilities. This means that IPX/SPX covers the entire spectrum, from PC LANs to enterprise LANs. IPX/SPX is an implementation of the *Xerox Network Services (XNS)* transport and network protocol. Banyan Vines is also an adaptation of XNS, but it uses a TCP/IP-like addressing scheme. XNS, developed by the Xerox PARC research institute, is a much cleaner architecture than the older TCP/IP protocol. It's ironic that XNS (in the form of IPX/SPX) is the world's most predominant stack. This is another example of a PARC technology that Xerox was not able to exploit.

The IPX/SPX network layer is provided by the *Internet Packet Exchange (IPX)* protocol. This is a "send and pray" datagram type of protocol with no guarantees. It is used as a foundation protocol by sophisticated network applications for sending and receiving low-overhead datagram packets. Novell's SPX builds a reliable protocol service on top of IPX. NetWare provides 12 API calls that you can use to obtain datagram services using IPX. The transport layer of IPX/SPX is provided by the *Sequenced Packet Exchange (SPX)* protocol—a reliable connection-oriented service over IPX. The service consists of 16 API calls. NetWare provides four peer-to-peer protocols on top of the IPX/SPX stack: NetBIOS, Named Pipes, TLI, and the IPX/SPX APIs. These protocols are supported in the DOS, Windows, NT, Windows 95, OS/2, Unixware, and NLM environments.

NetBIOS and NetBEUI

NetBIOS is the premier protocol for LAN-based, program-to-program communications. Introduced by IBM and Sytek in 1984 for the IBM PC Network, NetBIOS now runs with almost no changes on every LAN. NetBIOS is used as an interface to a variety of stacks—including IBM/Microsoft LANs (NetBEUI), TCP/IP, XNS, Vines, OSI, and IPX/SPX. Support for a NetBIOS platform exists on a multiplicity of operating system environments, including MS-DOS, Windows, Windows 95, OS/2, Windows NT, Unix, and some mainframe environments. One of the many reasons for NetBIOS's success is its intuitive simplicity.

NetBEUI is the protocol stack that comes with IBM and Microsoft LAN products—including Windows for Workgroups, NT, LAN Manager, Windows 95, OS/2 Warp Connect, and OS/2 Warp Server. It came to life as the original transport for NetBIOS commands. The literature often uses the term NetBIOS to refer to the combination of the NetBIOS interface and the NetBEUI stack. This can be misleading. NetWare, for example, has nothing to do with NetBEUI, yet it uses NetBIOS as an interface to both IPX/SPX and TCP/IP.[1] IBM and Microsoft use NetBIOS as an interface to both TCP/IP and NetBEUI. So be careful, especially when you read our books; we've been known to use NetBIOS and NetBEUI interchangeably.

NetBEUI offers powerful datagram and connection-oriented services. It also offers a dynamic naming service based on discovery protocols. NetBEUI's main weakness is the lack of a network layer. Its other weakness is the lack of security. The broadcast mechanism, used to dynamically "discover" names, can be a liability on an unsecured network where it's not a good idea to expose names. Broadcasting names also causes unwanted traffic on the network. Luckily, most bridges and routers have ways to filter the discovery packets and block them from propagating to other networks.

The NetBIOS services are provided through a set of commands, specified in a structure called the *Network Control Block (NCB)*. The structure also contains the parameters associated with the command and the fields in which NetBIOS will return information to the program. A command can be issued in either wait or no-wait mode. In the *wait* mode, the requesting thread is blocked until the command completes. In the *no-wait* mode, control is returned to the calling thread at the earliest time possible, usually before the command completes. When the command completes, the NetBIOS DLL places a return code in the NCB.

Named Pipes

Named Pipes provide highly reliable, two-way communications between clients and a server. They provide a file-like programming API that abstracts a session-based two-way exchange of data. Using Named Pipes, processes can exchange data as if they were writing to, or reading from, a sequential file. Named Pipes are especially suitable for implementing server programs that require many-to-one pipelines. A server application can set up a pipeline where the receiving end of the pipe can exchange data with several client processes. Then it lets Named Pipes handle all the scheduling and synchronization issues.

A very important benefit of Named Pipes, at least for Windows, OS/2, and NT client/server programmers, is that they're part of the base interprocess communications service. The Named Pipes interface is identical, whether the processes are running on an individual machine or distributed across the network. Named Pipes run on NetBIOS, IPX/SPX, and TCP/IP stacks. Named Pipes are built-in networking features in Windows NT, Windows for Workgroups, Windows 95, and Warp Server. Unix support for Named Pipes is provided by LAN Manager/X.

---

[1] The confusion may have started with Microsoft's naming of NetBEUI. It stands for *NetBIOS Extended User Interface* (NetBEUI).

The New SNA: APPC, APPN, and CPI-C

IBM is evolving SNA into a true distributed operating system that supports cross-network directory services, transparent network access to resources (such as servers, applications, displays, printers, and data), common data streams, and integrated network management. *Advanced Peer-to-Peer Network (APPN)* is the network infrastructure responsible for this "true distribution." APPN creates an SNA network without the mainframe-centric hierarchy of traditional SNA configurations. The mainframe is just another node on the network. APPN allows LU 6.2 SNA applications, using APPC or CPI-C APIs, to take full advantage of peer networks. It also greatly simplifies SNA configuration, provides better availability through dynamic routing, makes it easier to maintain SNA networks, and meets the flexibility requirements of modern networks.

Common Programming Interface for Communications (CPI-C) builds on top of APPC and masks its complexities and irregularities (see Figure 8-3). Every product that supports APPC has a slightly different API. CPI-C fixes that problem. Writing to the CPI-C API allows you to port your programs to all SNA platforms. The CPI-C API consists of about 40 calls; APPC consists of over 60 calls. Most of these calls deal with configuration and services.

The X/Open consortium has licensed the CPI-C interface from IBM; so have several other companies (including Novell and Apple). In addition to *all* the IBM platforms, CPI-C APIs are provided by Insession (for Tandem Computers), Systems Strategies (for Unix), Rabbit Software (for DOS), and DCA (for DOS and OS/2).

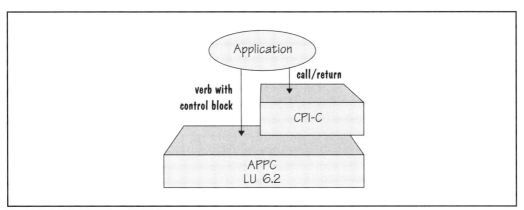

Figure 8-3. CPI-C on Top of APPC.

REMOTE PROCEDURE CALL (RPC)

An essential problem is that RPCs are not procedure calls at all, they are truly process invocations. The invoked program runs across the wire in a different resource domain.

> — *Hal Lorin, Author*
> *Doing IT Right*
> *(Prentice-Hall, 1996)*

RPCs hide the intricacies of the network by using the ordinary procedure call mechanism familiar to every programmer. A client process calls a function on a remote server and suspends itself until it gets back the results. Parameters are passed like in any ordinary procedure. The RPC, like an ordinary procedure, is synchronous. The process (or thread) that issues the call waits until it gets the results. Under the covers, the RPC run-time software collects values for the parameters, forms a message, and sends it to the remote server. The server receives the request, unpacks the parameters, calls the procedure, and sends the reply back to the client.

While RPCs make life easier for the programmer, they pose a challenge for the NOS designers who supply the development tools and run-time environments. Here's some of the issues they face:

■ *How are the server functions located and started?* At a minimum, somebody's got to provide a run-time environment that starts a server process when a remote invocation is received, passes it the parameters, and returns the response. But what happens when multiple clients go after the same function? Is each function packaged as a process? Pretty soon you discover that an entire environment is needed to start and stop servers, prioritize requests, perform security checks, and provide some form of load-balancing. It also becomes quickly obvious that threads are much better at handling these incoming requests than full-blown processes. And it is better to create a server loop that manages a pool of threads waiting for work rather than create a thread for each incoming request. What is really needed on the server side is a full-blown *TP Monitor.* This is, of course, a lot more function than what the current NOSs provide.

■ *How are parameters defined and passed between the client and the server?* This is something NOSs do quite well. The better NOSs provide an *Interface Definition Language (IDL)* for describing the functions and parameters that a server exports to its clients. An *IDL compiler* takes these descriptions and produces source code stubs (and header files) for both the client and server (Figure 8-4). These stubs can then be linked with the client and server code. The client stub packages the parameters in an RPC packet, converts the

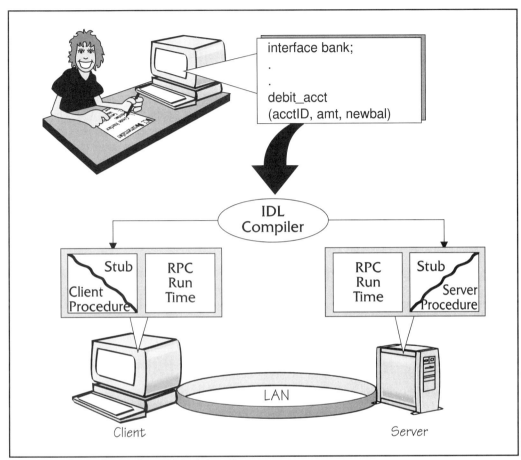

interface bank;

.
.

debit_acct
(acctID, amt, newbal)

IDL
Compiler

Stub
Client
Procedure

RPC
Run
Time

RPC
Run
Time

Stub
Server
Procedure

LAN

Client

Server

Figure 8-4. The Mechanics of an RPC Stub Compiler.

data, calls the *RPC run-time library,* and waits for the server's reply. On the server side, the server stub unpacks the parameters, calls the remote procedure, packages the results, and sends the reply to the client.

■ *How are failures handled?* Because both sides of the RPC can fail separately, it is important for the software to be able to handle all the possible failure combinations. If the server does not respond, the client side will normally block, time out, and retry the call. The server side must guarantee *only once semantics* to make sure that a duplicate request is not re-executed. If the client unexpectedly dies after issuing a request, the server must be able to undo the effects of that transaction. Most NOSs provide connection-oriented and connectionless versions of their RPCs. If you need a more robust environment, use the connection-oriented RPC.

■ ***How is security handled by the RPC?*** Modern NOSs—like DCE—make it easy to automatically incorporate their security features into the RPC. All you need to specify is the level of security required (authentication, encryption, and so on); then the RPC and security feature will cooperate to make it happen.

■ ***How does the client find its server?*** The association of a client with a server is called *binding*. The binding information may be hardcoded in the client (for example, some services are performed by servers with *well-known* addresses). Or a client can find its server by consulting a configuration file or an environment parameter. A client can also find its server at run time through the network directory services. The servers must, of course, advertise their services in the directory. The process of using the directory to find a server at run time is called *dynamic binding*. The easiest way to find a server is let the RPC do it for you. This is called *automatic binding*, meaning that the RPC client stub will locate a server from a list of servers that support the interface.

■ ***How is data representation across systems handled?*** The problem here is that different CPUs represent data structures differently (for example, *big-endian* versus *little-endian*). So how is data transparency achieved at the RPC level? To maintain machine independence, the RPC must provide some level of data format translation across systems. For example, the Sun RPC requires that clients convert their data to a neutral canonical format using the *External Data Representation (XDR)* APIs.

In contrast, DCE's *Network Data Representation (NDR)* service is multicanonical, meaning that it supports multiple data format representations. The client chooses one of these formats (in most cases, its own native data representation), tags the data with the chosen format, and then leaves it up to the server to transform the data into a format it understands. In other words, the *server makes it right*. DCE assumes that in most cases, the client and server will be using the same data representation, so why go through the translation overhead? Sun assumes that client MIPs are cheap, so it lets the client do the translation, which makes life easy for the server. With Sun, all clients look the same to the server: *The client makes it right*.

Figure 8-5 shows how the RPC mechanism all comes together. The scenario shows a simple seat reservation application. The seating server first starts up, advertises its location and service in the network directory, and begins its continuous cycle of receiving and servicing requests. A ticketing client keeps in its cache the location of the server. When a customer is ready to buy a ticket for a Madonna concert, an RPC is issued to reserve a seat. Notice how the client and server stubs cooperate to make that happen. It takes a lot of work to make that reservation for the Madonna concert. RPCs take away some of that drudgery.

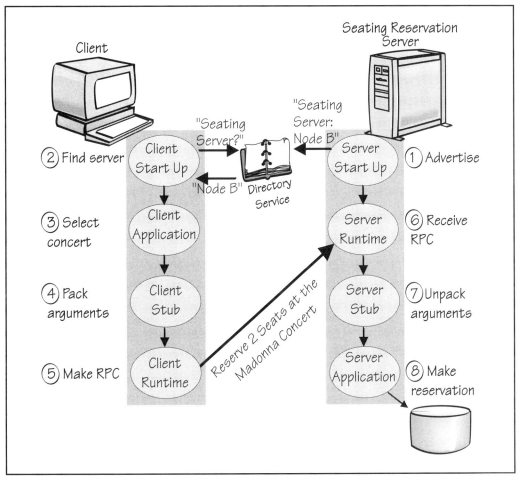

Figure 8-5. Getting a Seat for a Madonna Concert Using RPCs.

MESSAGING AND QUEUING: THE MOM MIDDLEWARE

Every DAD needs a MOM.

> — *The Message-Oriented Middleware*
> *(MOM) Consortium*

"Every DAD needs a MOM" is the unofficial motto of the MOM Consortium. In this context, DAD stands for *Distributed Application Development* and MOM stands for *Message-Oriented Middleware*. We agree with the motto. MOM is a key piece of middleware that is absolutely essential for a class of client/server products. If your application can tolerate a certain level of time-independent responses, MOM provides the easiest path for creating enterprise and inter-enterprise client/server systems. MOM also helps create nomadic client/server systems that can accumulate outgoing transactions in queues and do a bulk upload when a connection can be established with an office server.

MOM allows general-purpose messages to be exchanged in a client/server system using message queues. Applications communicate over networks by simply putting messages in queues and getting messages from queues. MOM hides all the nasty communications from applications and typically provides a very simple high-level API to its services. A MOM Consortium was formed in mid-1993 with the goal of creating standards for messaging middleware. Members are product providers, including IBM (*MQSeries*), Covia (*Communications Integrator*), Peerlogic (*PIPES*), Horizon Strategies (*Message Express*), and System Strategies (*ezBridge*). So what can you do with MOM?

MOM's messaging and queuing allow clients and servers to communicate across a network without being linked by a private, dedicated, logical connection. The clients and servers can run at different times. Everybody communicates by putting messages on queues and by taking messages from queues (see Figure 8-6). Notice that the server sends back the reply via a message queue. Messaging does not impose any constraints on an application's structure: If no response is required, none is sent.

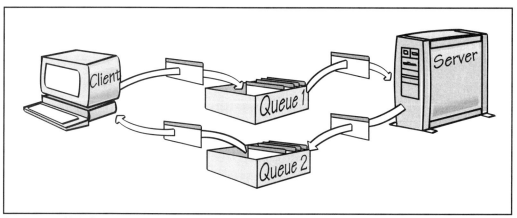

Figure 8-6. MOM: Two-way Message Queuing.

MOM products provide their own NOS services—including hierarchical naming, security, and a layer that isolates applications from the network. They use virtual memory on the local OS to create their queues. Most messaging products allow the sender to specify the name of the reply queue. The products also include some type of *format field* that tells the recipient how to interpret the message data.

MOM-enabled programs do not talk to each other directly, so either program can be busy, unavailable, or simply not running at the same time. A program can decide when it wants to retrieve a message off its queue—there are no time constraints. The target program can even be started several hours later. Or, if you're using a laptop on the road, you can collect outgoing requests in a queue and submit them to the server when you get to a phone or to an office LAN. Messaging allows either the client or the server to be unavailable (see Figure 8-7).

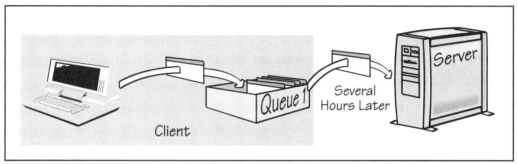

Figure 8-7. MOM: Save Your Messages Until You Get To a Server.

Messaging queues are very versatile. You can use them to create one-to-many or many-to-one relationships (see Figure 8-8). In the figure, many clients are sending requests to one server queue. The messages are picked off the queue by multiple instances of the server program that are concurrently servicing the clients. The server instances can take messages off the queue either on a first-in/first-out basis or according to some priority or load-balancing scheme. In all cases, a message queue can be concurrently accessed. The servers can also use messaging filters to throw away the messages they don't want to process, or they can pass them on to other servers.

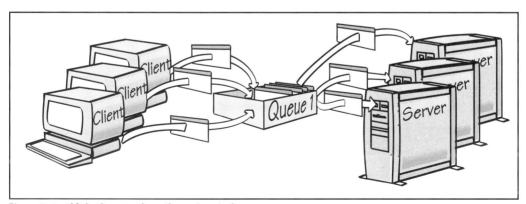

Figure 8-8. MOM: Many-to-Many Messaging via Queues.

Most MOM messaging products make available a simple API set that runs on multiple operating system platforms. Most also provide *persistent* (logged on disk) and *non-persistent* (in memory) message queues. Persistent messages are slower, but they can be recovered in case of power failures after a system restart. In both cases, messages can be either copied or removed from a queue. A message queue can be *local* to the machine or *remote*. System administrators can usually specify the number of messages a queue can hold and the maximum message size.

Most messaging products provide a minimum level of fault-tolerance in the form of persistent queues. Some of the products provide some form of *transactional protection*, allowing the queue to participate in a two-phase commit synchronization protocol. And some may even reroute messages to alternate queues in case of a network failure.

MOM VERSUS RPC

Comparing the RPC and messaging paradigms is like doing business via a telephone call versus exchanging letters or faxes (see Figure 8-9). An interaction using a telephone call is immediate—both parties talk to each other directly to conduct their business. At the end of the phone conversation, a unit of work is concluded. In contrast, conducting business via mail allows you to stage work, prioritize it, and do it when you're ready for it. You're in control of the workflow, not that ringing phone. On the other hand, it may be frustrating on the client side not to receive immediate feedback.

Table 8-1 compares the messaging and RPC architectures. Messaging is, of course, more flexible, loosely-coupled, and time-tolerant than RPC. However, messaging only skews things in time and may create its own level of complications. In the telephone analogy (RPC), you complete the work as it arrives; you don't have to manage stacks of incoming letters (or faxes). Your clients are happy to get immediate service. When you close shop at the end of the day, you're all done with your work. In the mail analogy, letters may start to pile up, and clients may be polling their incoming mailboxes continuously, waiting for a response. We may have made life easier for the server at the expense of the client. On the other hand, messaging does free clients from being synchronized to their servers; this can be very liberating for mobile and home users.

Messaging encourages an event-driven model of communications. You can send off multiple requests to multiple servers and then accept the responses as they come back. Your application doesn't block waiting for the responses. Instead, responses are treated like events. They just happen. Of course, you must be prepared to deal with them when they happen. RPCs can mimic this type of asynchronous, loosely-coupled, event-driven behavior using threads.

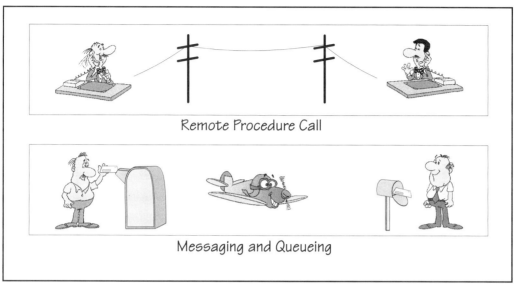

Remote Procedure Call

Messaging and Queueing

Figure 8-9. MOM Versus RPC: Do You Like the Post Office or Telephones?

Table 8-1. Comparing MOM and RPC.

Feature	MOM: Messaging and Queuing	Remote Procedure Call (RPC)
Metaphor	Post office-like.	Telephone-like.
Client/Server time relationship	Asynchronous. Clients and servers may operate at different times and speeds.	Synchronous. Clients and servers must run concurrently. Servers must keep up with clients.
Client/Server sequencing	No fixed sequence.	Servers must first come up before clients can talk to them.
Style	Queued.	Call-Return.
Partner needs to be available	No.	Yes.
Load-balancing	Single queue can be used to implement FIFO or priority-based policy.	Requires a separate TP Monitor.
Transactional support	Yes (some products). Message queue can participate in the commit synchronization.	No. Requires a transactional RPC.
Message filtering	Yes.	No.

Table 8-1. Comparing MOM and RPC. (Continued)

Feature	MOM: Messaging and Queuing	Remote Procedure Call (RPC)
Performance	Slow. An intermediate hop is required.	Fast.
Asynchronous processing	Yes. Queues and triggers are required.	Limited. Requires threads and tricky code for managing threads.

In summary, there's plenty of room for MOMs, RPCs, and peer-to-peer styles of communication on the modern NOS. Each distinctive style presents its own paradigm for conducting business. You'll end up choosing the style that provides the best fit for your particular needs.

FYI

3-Tier Client/Server, MOM-Style

Briefing

If you really like the loosely-coupled, event-driven programming style, then MOM is made for you. But can you really build robust 3-tier client/server applications using just MOMs? It may come as a surprise, but the answer is yes. And, boy, do we have a deal for you. It's called *MQSeries Three Tier (MQ3T)*—a stealth product from IBM's Hursley Lab. MQ3T lets you build 3-tier client/server applications using MOM and nothing but MOM—in this case, *MQSeries*.

The first tier of MQ3T consists of *presentation objects* that hook into the client's window event queue. You define the messages a client emits or receives, and then leave the rest to MOM. In the middle tier are *business objects* that sit between the clients and the *data logic* objects that form the third tier. Objects in all three tiers communicate using MOM. MQ3T will deliver the message to the right object instance—and it may even start the object for you.

MQ3T essentially routes MOM messages between object instances. It also lets you visually define the logic and the rules for processing these messages on all tiers (see Figure 8-10). You define rules to route, broadcast, and filter messages. You can send messages to object replicas for increased fault-tolerance. And you can define rules for how to handle multiple replies, timeouts, late-arriving messages, and a variety of messaging errors. MQ3T supports multiple client and server platforms—including Windows, NT, OS/2, AIX, and mainframes. So, yes, MOM can do 3-tier client/server. ❑

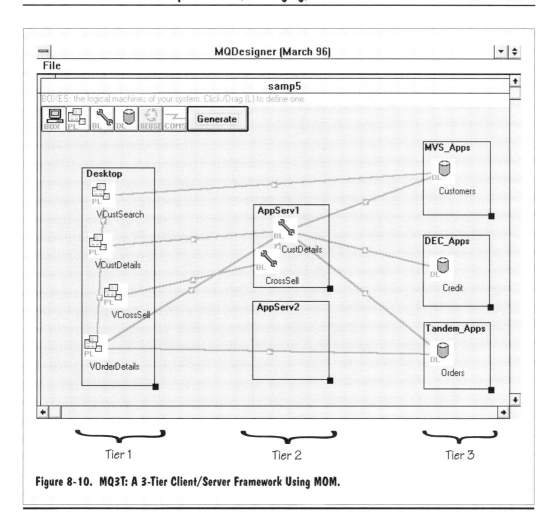

Figure 8-10. MQ3T: A 3-Tier Client/Server Framework Using MOM.

CONCLUSION

As you may have surmised from this long chapter, the NOS middleware pieces are of interest to all client/server apps. If you don't acquire the pieces "off-the-shelf," you'll have to recreate them in some shape or form. After all, a network is almost unusable without security, directory, and naming services. And everybody needs MOM, RPC, or peer-to-peer communications. The NOS creates a "gentle and civilized environment" on raw networks that hides the underlying nastiness and lets you focus on your client/server business.

Chapter 9

NOS: Meet the Players

---

*C*hoosing a NOS can seem like part blind luck, part mysticism—just like the feeling when you step into a casino. The NOS newcomer must learn the rules of each network offering and discover which vendor requires the steep ante, which game is most likely to pay off at high odds, and which best suits the situation.

— *PC Magazine*

This may come as a surprise, but you've already met most of the NOS players in Part 2. This is because the server operating systems have by now subsumed most of the functions independent NOSs used to provide. The server OSs have morphed into NOSs. The key NOSs are Novell's *NetWare 4.1*, Microsoft's *NT Server 4.0*, and IBM's *OS/2 Warp Server*. In addition, the Unix world has two NOSs to choose from: Sun's *ONC+* and OSF's *DCE*. Interestingly, none of these NOSs provide MOM functions. So you still have to buy these *a la carte* from the MOM vendors.

In this chapter, we first look at NOS technology and market trends. Then we briefly introduce you to the key players. Finally, we go over the OSF's *Distributed Computing Environment (DCE)* in some detail. DCE is important because it provides the most comprehensive NOS solution on the market for integrating multivendor servers in a heterogeneous client/server environment. Although there are some partial NOS solutions for the heterogeneous server environment, no existing product matches DCE's integration technology. This is because DCE was built on top of the industry's best-of-breed commercial NOS technology. DCE is the archetypical example of an intergalactic postmodern NOS. It is intended to become the "mother of all NOSs." But we're getting ahead of our story.

NOS TRENDS

According to IDC, NOSs are growing at a rate of 13% yearly. Figure 9-1 shows how the different players size up.[1] IDC is betting on Windows NT, which it thinks will overcome NetWare by 1999. Keep in mind that industry analysts and journalists made similar predictions when Microsoft introduced NT in 1992. However, NT's adoption rates fell well short of these expectations. Of course, NT is currently winning both mindshare and marketshare. But it still faces a formidable set of competitors.

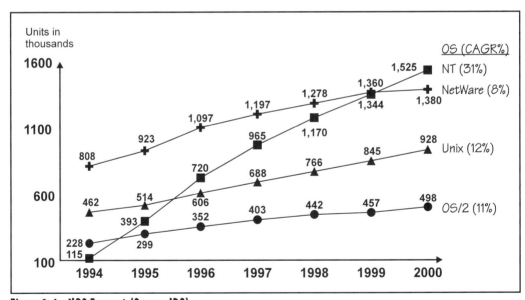

Figure 9-1. NOS Forecast (Source: IDC).

We already discussed server OS trends in Part 2. Here's our take on where NOSs are heading:

- ■ **_NOS functions are being subsumed by server OSs._** The early NOSs, like _NetWare 3.X_ and _LAN Manager_, were mainly in the business of providing

---

[1] Source: IDC, **NOS Forecast** (May, 1996).

shared file and printer access to DOS client machines. However, the newer server OSs—such as *Windows NT Server*, *OS/2 Warp Server*, and various *Unixes*—are now bundling the NOS functions in the OS. As far as these vendors are concerned, the NOS is dead. Of course, Novell's fortunes depend on providing specialized NOS servers. Novell believes there is a market for OS-independent NOS services—including global directory, network security, and distributed files. NetWare is the epitome of a pure NOS product.

- *NOSs are becoming intergalactic.* NOSs are transcending their LAN origins and are now moving into the enterprise. *DCE* and the *NetWare Directory Services (NDS)* are examples of the new intergalactic services NOSs now provide. In addition, many of the popular Internet services are built on top of NOS technology, much of it contributed by Sun—for example, NFS and Sun RPC.

- *Global directories are becoming strategic.* In the age of intergalactic networking, companies without a global directory will be at a disadvantage. We learned from the Internet just how painful life can be without one. The competing global directories include Novell's *NDS*, Banyan's *Universal Street-Talk*, and DCE. The next big challenge is to get these directories to interoperate, which is where X.500 will play a big role. It will help customers create federations of loosely-coupled directories.

- *ORBs will subsume the NOS and expand their scope.* In a sense, ORBs are the new NOSs. It's not surprising that both CORBA and OLE are creating competing object interfaces on top of traditional NOS services—including directories, events, RPCs, and system management. Of course, ORBs extend the reach of the NOS deep into the application space, so they're much more than just NOSs (we cover ORBs in Part 7).

- *NOSs are becoming turn-key commodities.* NOSs are being delivered as "shrink-wrap" software in the form of commodity server OSs—for example, *NT Server*, *NetWare*, and *OS/2 Warp Server*. They are becoming increasingly easier to install, use, and maintain.

- *NOSs are becoming Internet-savvy.* NOSs are starting to include the more common Internet services. Next they will integrate these services with their global directories to obtain a competitive advantage, especially in the lucrative Intranet market. Most NOS vendors have announced support for the Internet's *Lightweight Directory Access Protocol (LDAP)* specification. So the NOS is also becoming a vehicle for packaging turn-key Internet servers and related middleware.

In summary, the NOS—which has been with us since the earliest days of client/server computing—is reinventing itself in two ways. First, it is becoming intergalactic in function. Second, it is being repackaged as a turn-key server OS. The NOS is the closest thing to a shrink-wrapped client/server solution. Consequently, there is a lot we can learn from it.

DCE: THE POSTMODERN NOS

DCE is a big system, designed for solving big problems.

— *Sandy Rockowitz, Minaret Software*
(April, 1996)

The *Distributed Computing Environment (DCE)* from the Open Software Foundation (OSF)—and now X/Open—creates an open NOS environment that spans multiple architectures, protocols, and operating systems. The X/Open standards consortium is including the DCE specifications in Version 4 of its *X/Open Portability Guide (XPG)*. The importance of DCE is that *almost* all software vendors are planning to support it in one way or another. DCE provides key distributed technologies, including a remote procedure call, a distributed naming service, a time synchronization service, a distributed file system, a network security service, and a threads package (see Figure 9-2). These six key technologies will be incorporated into virtually every operating system. The sections that follow contain a brief summary of the main DCE components, including their origins.

DCE allows a client to interoperate with one or more server processes on other computing platforms, even when they are from different vendors with different operating systems. In addition, DCE provides an integrated approach to security, naming, and interprocess communications. All these pieces are used to create a coherent heterogeneous client/server environment. DCE is the best architectural example of an intergalactic *postmodern NOS*. It is intended to become the "mother of all NOSs."

DCE RPC

The DCE RPC initially came from HP—it is an adaptation of the Apollo RPC. DCE provides an *Interface Definition Language (IDL)* and compiler that facilitate the creation of RPCs. The IDL compiler creates portable C code stubs for both the client and server sides of an application. The stubs are compiled and linked to the RPC run-time library, which is responsible for finding servers in a distributed system, performing the message exchanges, packing and unpacking message parameters, and processing any errors that occur.

The most powerful feature of the DCE RPC is that it can be integratcd with the DCE security and naming services. This integration makes it possible to authenticate

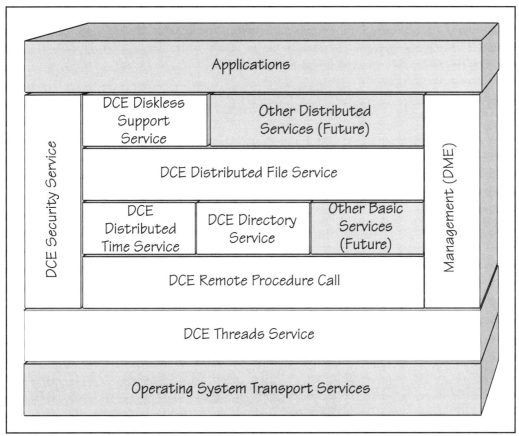

Figure 9-2. The DCE Components.

each procedure call and to dynamically locate servers at run time. Servers can concurrently service RPCs using threads. The RPC mechanism provides protocol and network independence.

DCE: Distributed Naming Services

OSF adopted the DCE distributed naming services from Digital's *DECdns* product and Siemens' *DIR-X X.500* services. The DCE naming services allow resources such as programs, servers, files, disks, or print queues to be identified by user-oriented names in a special-purpose distributed database that describes the objects of interest. Object names are independent of their location on the network.

DCE divides the distributed environment into administrative units (or domains) called *cells*. A DCE cell is a combination of client and server workstations. The cell's domain is defined by the customer. A cell usually consists of the set of machines used by one or more groups working on related tasks. The cell size is dictated only by how easy it is to administer. At a minimum, a DCE cell must have one cell directory server and one security server.

As shown in Figure 9-3, the DCE directory service consists of two elements: *Cell Directory Service (CDS)* and *Global Directory Service (GDS)*. This two-tier hierarchy provides local naming autonomy (at the cell level) and global interoperability (at the intercell level). Global access is provided using X.500's intergalactic naming system or with TCP/IP's Internet *Domain Name System (DNS)*. All the names in the DCE system taken together make up the DCE *namespace*, which looks like a hierarchical file system. The DCE namespace is used by the different DCE services. For example, the security service uses a part of the namespace to maintain its information on user accounts and principals. The DFS file system uses another part of the namespace for the file system.

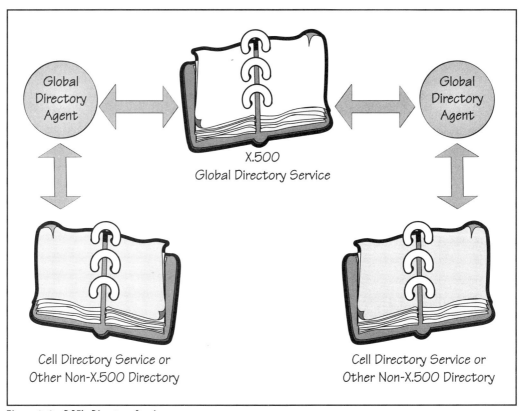

Figure 9-3. DCE's Directory Services.

DCE: Distributed Time Service

OSF adopted the Distributed Time Service from Digital. This technology provides a mechanism for synchronizing each computer in the network to a recognized time standard. The DCE Time Service provides APIs for manipulating timestamps and for obtaining universal time from public sources such as the Traconex/PSTI radio clock. DCE requires at least three *Time Servers*; one (or more) must be connected to an *External Time Provider* (see Figure 9-4). The Time Servers periodically query one another to adjust their clocks. The External Time Provider may be a hardware device that receives time from a radio or a telephone source. DCE uses the UTC standard, which keeps track of time elapsed since the beginning of the Gregorian calendar—October 15, 1582.

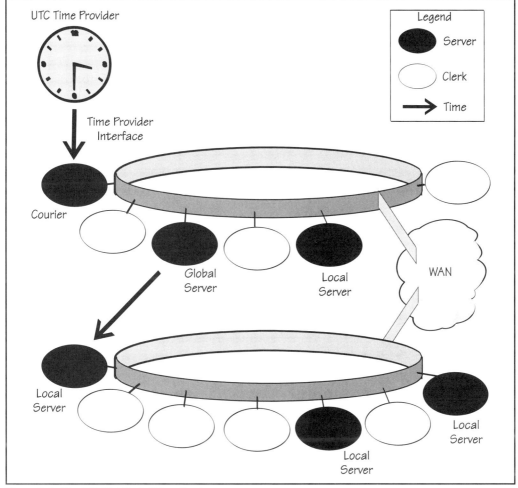

Figure 9-4. The DCE Distributed Time Service.

DCE: Distributed Security Services

Kerberos—A three-headed dog that guarded the gates of Hades.

— *Greek Mythology*

OSF adopted MIT's Kerberos authentication system and enhanced it with some HP security features. Kerberos, a protocol that Machiavelli would have loved, is based on total mutual distrust. The MIT folks who built it named it after a three-headed mythological monster that guarded the gates of Hades (yes, Hell). Why would anyone want to crash the gates of Hell? We'll let security administrators answer that one. The Kerberos monster consists of three "heads," all residing on the same secured server: the *Authentication Server*, *Security Database*, and *Privilege Server*. The MIT three-headed monster gives network administrators the heavy-duty security they need to keep "intruding hackers" from crashing into their network's gates.

DCE's network security services provide authentication, authorization, and user account management. *Authentication* validates that a client, typically a user or program, is who or what it claims to be. This validation is accomplished through the secure communications capability provided by the RPC and the Kerberos ticketing mechanism. Each DCE machine must run a security agent.

The DCE *security server* is a physically secured server that stores security-related information such as names and associated passwords. Each DCE cell must have a security server; it is usually a dedicated machine. A cell may have replicated security servers for backup. The DCE *login facility* enables users (DCE calls them

principals or *units of trust*) to establish their identity by authenticating themselves using a password. The DCE security system never sends a password in "clear text" across the network.

The security agent works with the authenticated RPC to provide secure access to all the DCE services—not just authentication. The RPC mechanism hides all the complexity of the security system from the user. It obtains the tickets, provides encryption when needed, and performs authenticated checksums if the policy requires it. Under-the-covers, both the RPC client and server must mutually authenticate one another by exchanging tickets (little secrets) with a trusted third party (the Kerberos server). Each party trusts the Kerberos server to identify the other party on the network. This is called *trusted third-party, secret-key encryption*. In addition, information is timestamped so that the usefulness of a ticket expires within a relatively short period of time, measured in hours.

Authorization comes after authentication; it determines whether the authenticated client has permission to access a resource. DCE supports authorization through *Access Control Lists (ACLs)*. Each DCE implementation that uses ACLs must implement an ACL manager that controls access to services and resources managed by it (DCE provides sample code that shows how to create an ACL manager). *Data integrity* is provided by DCE using cryptographic data checksums to determine whether a message was corrupted or tampered with while passing through the network. In addition, *data privacy* can be ensured by encrypting data that is transferred across a network.

DCE and Access Control Lists

Briefing

Modern NOSs, like the OSF DCE, provide a set of APIs that allow servers to create and manage their ACLs. The DCE NOS also provides hooks that help the clients present their authorization credentials to the server applications. DCE calls it the *Privilege Attribute Certificate (PAC)*—a security-server issued ticket the client must present to the server. PACs contain authorization information specific to the client, such as its designated group. DCE provides a set of server APIs that can read the information contained in the PACs and match them with the information in the ACLs. ❏

In summary, DCE solves the problems associated with user authentication in distributed networks. Passwords are never sent in the "clear text." The security database (DCE calls it the *registry*) can be propagated across trusted servers.

DCE's Kerberos, in addition to solving the authentication problem, helps with the authorization issue. And better yet, the whole scheme can work on heterogeneous systems. No other NOS can match DCE when it comes to security.

Distributed File System (DFS)

For its distributed file server, OSF chose the *Andrew File System (AFS)* from Transarc (and Carnegie Mellon University) and the diskless client from HP (also based on AFS protocols). The DCE *Distributed File System (DFS)* provides a uniform namespace, file location transparency, and high availability. DFS is log-based and thus offers the advantage of a fast restart and recovery after a server crash. Files and directories can be replicated (invisibly) on multiple servers for high availability. A cache-consistency protocol allows a file to be changed in a cache. The changes are automatically propagated to all other caches where the file is used, as well as on the disk that owns the file. The DFS file system APIs are based on the POSIX 1003.1a (portable OS interface). DFS is interoperable with Sun's NFS, giving NFS sites an easy migration path to the more function-rich DFS file server.

DFS provides a single-image file system that can be distributed across a group of file servers. The DFS file naming scheme is location independent. Each file has a unique identifier that is consistent across the network. Files use the DCE global namespace just like the rest of the network resources. And the file system is integrated with the DCE security and RPC mechanisms. Because DFS fully exploits the DCE services, you can administer it from any DCE node, which helps keep costs down in a widely distributed system. Note that you do not need DFS to use the rest of the DCE services.

Threads

For its thread package, OSF chose the *Concert Multithread Architecture (CMA)* from Digital. This portable thread package runs in the user space and includes small wrapper routines to translate calls to a native kernel-based thread package (like OS/2, NT, or Mach threads). Threads are an essential component of client/server applications and are used by the other DCE components. The DCE thread package provides granular levels of multitasking on operating systems that do not provide kernel-supported threads. The DCE thread APIs are based on the POSIX 1003.4a (Pthreads standard). The DCE threads also support multiprocessor environments using shared memory. DCE provides a semaphore service that helps threads synchronize their access to shared memory.

Coming Attractions: DCE 1.2

DCE has been out in some form or another since 1992. The current version—*DCE 1.1*—was released by OSF in November 1994; it is now available in many commercial products. You should note that it takes commercial products at least a year to incorporate OSF code releases. The next major OSF release—*DCE 1.2*—is expected in late 1996. Digital, HP, IBM, and Hitachi are developing this new release under the sponsorship of OSF.

So what's new in DCE 1.2? The primary objective of this new release is to facilitate the enterprise-wide deployment of DCE by making it more scalable, more interoperable, and easier to manage. DCE 1.2 provides several new features that will help you integrate DCE with Novell's *NetWare* and Sun's *ONC+*. DCE 1.2 will also guarantee wire protocol compatibility with *Kerberos Version 5* as defined by the Internet Engineering Task Force (IETF) in *RFC 1510*. The current version of DCE only supports the Kerberos private key authentication. In contrast, DCE 1.2 will also provide support for public key encryption mechanisms such as RSA. A new IETF standard API called *Generic Security Services API (GSSAPI)*—defined in *RFC 1508*—should make it easier for non-DCE middleware to use DCE security services. Finally, DCE 1.2 will support C++ in addition to C. The DCE IDL will be extended to support C++ inheritance using HP's *OO-DCE* object mappings.

So Who Is Implementing DCE?

DCE began as a Unix facility, but it now exists on systems ranging in scale from PCs running Windows to mainframes running MVS. DCE implementations are available on all the Unixes. Even Sun now provides DCE support on Solaris in addition to ONC+. NetWare may be the last bastion of resistance to DCE. But OSF is building DCE bridges into NetWare and IBM is working on a DCE for NetWare.

So where do you buy DCE? Typically, you won't go out and purchase a shrink-wrapped version of DCE. Instead, you will be using products that incorporate DCE under the hood. For example, DCE provides the foundation for Transarc's *Encina* TP Monitor, HP's new CORBA-based *ORB Plus*, and Microsoft's forthcoming *Network OLE* (or DCOM).[2] Portions of DCE are also being incorporated into the middleware products of Sybase and Oracle. Finally, DCE is the basis for IBM's *Directory and Security* servers. They are part of IBM's "Eagle" server suites, which offer turn-key client/server solutions on AIX, OS/2 Warp Server, and NT.

---

[2] Microsoft has reversed engineered the DCE RPC so as not to pay OSF licensing fees. As far as we know, it has still not implemented the rest of DCE.

CONCLUSION

Intergalactic NOSs are creating brave new possibilities for client/server application developers. There are no limits to the possible system ensembles that can be built on top of these distributed NOS substrates. And the best is yet to come. Distributed objects are the ultimate NOS. They extend the distributed NOS all the way into the application space, and then meld it with the Internet (more on this in Parts 7 and 8). The winners in the software development game will be those who learn how to harness the extensive NOS power and use it to create exciting new software packages.

Part 4
SQL Database
Servers

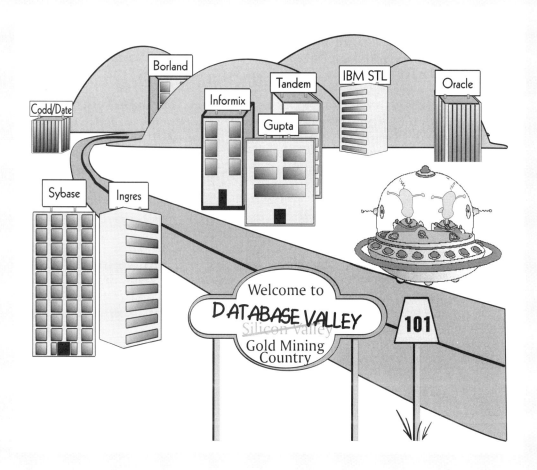

An Introduction to Part 4

The relational model is over 25 years old, predicate logic and set theory are each over 100 years old, and propositional logic dates back to the ancient Greeks (4th century BC).

— *Chris Date*
(October, 1995)

Ah! You're still with us, so you must have enjoyed the "single system illusion" in the last part. NOSs and stacks are great—there can be no client/server computing without them. But the real hot area in client/server today is in SQL databases. Have you Martians heard about Database Valley? That's a strip of highway south of San Francisco where database companies are creating a new California gold rush. But in the new gold rush, they mine SQL instead of gold.

So pack your luggage: We're heading west. What? You Martians don't have cowboy boots? No problem. They wear sneakers in Database Valley. You won't need mining gear, either. All the modern mining is done on computer screens by looking at SQL tables and relational calculus. The guy who discovered the gold, a guru named Codd, is a mathematician. Yes, an abstract mathematician created a new gold rush with tables. No, the tables are not made of gold. They're computer creations that point to other tables and store and organize information. In this part, we're going to visit the gold country and understand how putting SQL databases on client/server networks could have created such a commotion.

Even though all these new database barons live within a few miles from each other, they all speak different SQL dialects. They can't understand each other. And the biggest barons are always charging ahead with new features that bring in more gold. So how do they ever work together? By throwing tons of middleware onto networks. These folks have agreed to create loosely coupled database federations fueled by middleware. The more ambitious are now proposing to pull all the world's data into warehouses that transform it into information. The warehouses could turn into perpetual gold-generating machines.

The plan for Part 4 is to first look at what this SQL stuff is all about: What standards are being created? What awesome new extensions are the barons concocting? We then look at the middleware needed to create the database federations. With all this preparation behind us, we can look at these fabulous warehouses—the new gold-mining machines. We close with an overview of some representative products that give us some form of reality check. When you deal with gold rushes and California dreams, you really need reality checks.

Chapter 10

SQL
Database
Servers

At present the majority of existing client/server-based software is to be found in the area of databases, and it is here that the greatest challenge to any corporation currently lies.

— *Richard Finkelstein, President*
Performance Computing

This chapter covers SQL databases from a client/server perspective. SQL servers are the dominant model for creating client/server applications. SQL server vendors—including Oracle, Sybase, Informix, Ingres, and Gupta—have almost become household names. Why is SQL so popular from a client/server connectivity perspective? Can relational databases hold the fort against newer models of client/server computing—including object databases, object request brokers, the Web, and groupware? Are TP Monitors needed, or can we do just fine with the stored procedures provided by the database vendors? In this chapter, we give you a snapshot of where things are in database-centric client/server computing. This sets the stage for answering these questions later in the book.

Our plan for this chapter is to first look at the magic of SQL and the relational model from a client/server perspective. We go over the standards—including SQL-89,

SQL-92, and SQL3. We conclude with the important SQL "extensions" that add active intelligence to tables—including stored procedures, rules, and triggers.[1]

THE FUNDAMENTALS OF SQL AND RELATIONAL DATABASES

Perhaps the most important trend among database servers of any size is the emergence of SQL as the *lingua franca* for the manipulation, definition, and control of data. SQL, now an ISO standard, is a powerful set-oriented language consisting of a few commands; it was created as a language for databases that adhere to the *relational model*.

SQL's Relational Origins

The relational model of database management was developed at IBM's San Jose Research Lab in the early 1970s by E.F. Codd. SQL—pronounced "sequel"— originally stood for Structured Query Language; now the acronym is the name. It was also developed by IBM Research in the mid-1970s to serve as an "English-like" front-end query language to the System R relational database prototype. Even though the SQL language is English-like, it is firmly rooted in the solid mathematical foundation of set theory and predicate calculus. What this really means is that SQL consists of a short list of powerful, yet highly flexible, *commands* that can be used to manipulate information collected in tables. Through SQL, you manipulate and control *sets* of records at a time. You tell the SQL database server what data you need; then it figures out how to get to the data.

The relational model calls for a clear separation of the physical aspects of data from their logical representation. Data is made to appear as simple tables that mask the complexity of the storage access mechanisms. The model frees you from having to concern yourself with the details of how the data is stored and makes the access to data purely logical. Using SQL statements, you only need to specify the tables, columns, and row qualifiers to get to any data item.

Oracle Corporation was the first company to offer a commercial version of SQL with its Oracle database in 1979. In the early 1980s, IBM came out with its own SQL products: SQL/DS and DB2. Today, over 200 vendors offer SQL products on PCs, superminis, and mainframes. Most of these products incorporate the SQL-89

---

[1] In spite of its length, this chapter is not a general introduction to programming with SQL. Here's a shameless advertisement: You'll find a lengthy introduction to SQL and 400 pages of detailed SQL programming examples in our book, **Client/Server Programming with OS/2** (Wiley, 1993).

standard features, some include SQL-92 features, and a few have even implemented their proprietary versions of SQL3 functions.

SQL has become the predominant database language of mainframes, minicomputers, and LAN servers; it provides the focus for a market-share battleground. The emergence of SQL client tools that can work across servers is heating up the competition even more, making SQL a horizontal industry where you can "mix-and-match" front-end tools with back-end servers.

What Does SQL Do?

The SQL language is used to perform complex data operations with a few simple commands in situations that would have required hundreds of lines of conventional code. Physicists might call SQL "the grand unified theory of database" because of the multifaceted roles it plays. Here is a partial list of roles:

■ *SQL is an interactive query language for ad hoc database queries.* SQL was originally designed as an end-user query language. However, modern graphical front-ends to SQL databases are much more intuitive to use. And they do a good job hiding the underlying SQL semantics from end-users.

■ *SQL is a database programming language.* It can be embedded in languages such as C, C++, and COBOL to access data or it can be called using the X/Open callable interface API set. Vendors, like Sybase and Oracle, even offer SQL-specific programming languages. SQL provides a consistent language for programming with data. This raises programmer productivity and helps produce a more maintainable and flexible system.

■ *SQL is a data definition and data administration language.* The data definition language is used to define simple tables, complex objects, indexes, views, referential integrity constraints, and security and access control. All the SQL-defined objects are automatically tracked (and maintained) in an active data dictionary (that is, system catalogs). The structure and organization of an SQL database is stored in the database itself.

■ *SQL is the language of networked database servers.* It is being used as a universal language to access and manipulate all types of data. For example, the IBM data warehouse uses SQL as the network access standard for both relational and non-relational data (like IMS and Indexed files). Even the object database vendors have adopted a derivative of SQL as a query language for objects.

■ *SQL helps protect the data in a multiuser networked environment.* It does that by providing good reliability features such as data validation, referential integrity, rollback (undo transaction), automatic locking, and deadlock detection and resolution in a multiuser LAN environment. SQL also enforces security and access control to database objects.

SQL provides a number of advantages to system builders because the same language that is used to define the database is also used to manipulate it. The SQL language makes it easy to specify product requirements in an unambiguous manner. This helps communications between customers, developers, and Database Administrators (DBAs).

The ISO Standards: SQL-89, SQL-92, and SQL3

Although many commercial implementations of SQL have existed since 1979, there was no official standard until 1986, when one was published jointly by the American National Standard Institute (ANSI) and the International Standards Organization (ISO). The 1986 standard was revised in 1989 to introduce referential (and check constraints) integrity; it is now known as *SQL-89* or ANSI SQL. In late 1989, a separate ANSI addendum for Embedded SQL was added to SQL-89.

SQL-89

The SQL-89 standard was an "intersection" of the SQL implementations of that time, which made it easy for existing products to conform to it. SQL-89 was a "watered-down" SQL that made the term "SQL compliant" almost meaningless. Vendors (like Gupta, Oracle, and XDB) would usually add DB2 compliance to their checklist of compliances. And even that didn't mean too much, at least in terms of creating a unified SQL.

SQL-92

The ISO *SQL-92* (also called SQL2), ratified in late 1992, is over five times the length of the original SQL-89 standard. SQL-92 standardizes many of the features previously left to the implementor's discretion (i.e., the loopholes) and is essentially a superset of SQL-89. C.J. Date estimates that it's going to take a big implementation effort to bring the current relational databases to SQL-92 standards. To get around that problem, ISO suggests a staged approach with three levels of compliance: entry, intermediate, and full. To help you understand where you're at, the SQL-92 standard introduces the concept of a *flagger*—a program that examines the source code and "flags" all SQL statements that do not conform to SQL-92.

What's New in SQL-92?

Details

Incidentally, the word "relation" does not appear anywhere in the standard. And the word "database" is used only informally (it is formally replaced by "SQL data"). This is a relational database standard?

— C.J. Date
(May, 1993)

This section provides a quick summary of what's new in SQL-92 for readers who are already familiar with SQL and the previous SQL-89 standard. If you're not familiar with SQL, first read this chapter and then come back to this box.

The previous SQL-89 standard supports the SQL Data Definition Language (DDL) for creating tables, indexes, views, and referential integrity constraints. The standard also supports GRANT/REVOKE security privileges. The SQL-89 Data Manipulation Language (DML) consists of the SELECT, INSERT, UPDATE, and DELETE commands. COMMIT and ROLLBACK are used for transaction management. A cursor mechanism provides row-at-a-time navigation. The SQL-89 Embedded SQL addendum defines the mechanism for embedding SQL statements in FORTRAN, COBOL, PL/I, and Pascal.

The "new" SQL-92 standard supports all the SQL-89 features and adds the following features:

- *SQL agents*—these are defined as programs or interactive users that produce SQL statements. In the previous standard, SQL statements were associated with Authorization IDs (an ambiguous concept).

- *SQL client/server connections*—before performing any database operations, an SQL agent must ask the SQL client code to CONNECT to some SQL server. A connection establishes an SQL session. SQL-92 supports concurrent connections (or sessions) but only one can be active at a given time. Agents can explicitly switch between connections using the SET CONNECTION command.

- *More granular transaction controls*—using the SET TRANSACTION command, we can specify a transaction as read-only or read/write. A read-only transaction cannot change the state of the database. In addition, we can set the *isolation level* (i.e., the level of automatic lock protection) for a given transaction to *read-uncommitted, read-committed, read-repeatable,* or *serializable.*

■ ***Standardized catalogs for describing the structure of a database—*** a catalog, in the new standard, is a collection of *SQL-schemas* describing "one database." The schemas are SQL tables that describe the structure of base tables, views, privileges, constraints, and so on. Each SQL-session has one *cluster* of catalogs describing all the data available to that session.

■ ***Embedded SQL support for new languages—*** including C, Ada, and MUMPS.

■ ***Support for dynamic SQL—*** including dynamic cursors and the typical commands (with minor surprises) that have been used by most database vendors to generate SQL code at run time.

■ ***Support for new data types—*** including BLOBs, VARCHAR, DATE, TIME, and TIMESTAMP.

■ ***Support for temporary tables—*** including local and global tables. Temporary tables are used as working storage and are automatically dropped at the end of a session. Think of them as memory variables created using the SQL DDL statement with the TEMPORARY attribute.

■ ***Support for join operators—*** including outer join, union join (no matching), cross join (all combinations), and inner join. All of these joins are supported with special operators in the FROM clauses of queries. SQL-89 did not specify mechanisms for creating the different types of joins.

■ ***Standardized error codes and diagnostics—*** the use of SQLCODE is not recommended any more; the preferred approach is to use SQLSTATE, which contains a five-character text string with standard values for the different error conditions. A GET DIAGNOSTICS statement was introduced to return more error information.

■ ***Domain checks and constraints—*** including domain constraints (acceptable values), assertions, and base table constraints. *Constraints* are rules that a user defines to restrict the values of what goes into the table columns. Any constraint can be defined to be immediate or deferred.

■ ***Miscellaneous improvements—*** including new string functions, support for backward and forward scrollable cursors, commands for altering and dropping objects, refinements to the referential integrity model, support for data type conversions, improvements in revoking privileges, and a CASE statement.

Some of the "new" SQL-92 features are already implemented in existing database products. However, be prepared for a few surprises in almost every area, regardless of how familiar they may seem. ❏

SQL3

*T*he changes in SQL3 are substantial enough that they'll change the way your organization designs and builds systems.

> — David Menninger, Director
> Oracle
> (November, 1995)

Even though it may take vendors a few more years to become fully SQL-92 compliant, a new 1000-page SQL3 draft is already in circulation. It's a multipart standard with each part progressing independently through the standards process. The following should give you an idea of what's coming down the pipeline:

■ Part 1, **SQL/Framework**, provides basic definitions and explains the structure of the SQL3 specification.

■ Part 2, **SQL/Foundation**, includes the bulk of the SQL3 effort. It covers triggers, roles, recursive queries, collections, and object SQL—including user-defined *Abstract Data Types (ADTs)*. An ADT is like a C++ class—it consists of a set of properties and methods. The SQL3 ADTs can be public, private, or protected. ADTs can also be inherited using the keyword *UNDER*; for example, *CREATE TYPE Dog UNDER Animal*. Your ADTs can appear in columns like any other built-in SQL data type.

Recursive queries solve the SQL parts explosion problem. For example, you'll be able to discover all the descendants of a parent by issuing one SQL statement (instead of successively searching for the children of each intermediary parent in the family tree). *Roles* are permissions (and privileges) that you assign to groups, not to individuals; users are assigned to roles so that they inherit the permissions and privileges that come with a role. We cover triggers later in this chapter.

■ Part 3, **SQL/CLI**, defines the *Callable Level Interface (CLI)*. It's an extension of the X/Open SQL Access Group (SAG) CLI that was started over seven years ago. The interest in the SQL CLI was so high that it was put on the fast track; it became ISO standard 9075-3 in early 1996. Note that Microsoft has stated publicly that "a future version" of ODBC will conform to the ISO CLI standard. We cover the SQL CLI, SAG, and ODBC in the next chapter.

■ Part 4, **SQL/PSM**, defines the SQL *Persistent Storage Modules (PSMs)*. This is a fancy name for stored procedures and procedural language extensions for SQL. The standard also specifies specialized exception handlers for doing *undo*, *redo*, and *commit*. The PSM specification is also being "fast-tracked." So expect it to become an ISO standard by late 1996. We cover stored procedures later in this chapter.

- Part 5, *SQL/Bindings*, defines the mechanics of intermingling SQL with other languages via precompilers and embedded SQL. We cover these topics in the next chapter.

- Part 6, *SQL/Transactions*, defines how SQL databases participate in global transactions. The SQL3 committee is "fast-tracking" SQL/Transactions by conforming to ISO X/Open's XA standard with very minor modifications. We cover XA in Part 5.

- Part 7, *SQL/Temporal*, defines how SQL databases handle time-series data. The idea is for SQL databases to model time so that you are able to submit queries with time as a variable. An example of a query is, "What were Q4 sales in 1990?" The SQL3 committee was about to standardize on work done by Richard Snodgrass—a temporal database researcher from the University of Arizona. Unfortunately, the U.K. participants were not in agreement. So don't hold your breath waiting for a standard.

The SQL3 draft also contains suggested SQL improvements—including persistent (or "held") cursors that remain open after a commit, new join types, temporary views, column specific privileges, and a better definition of how to update views. It also deals with esoteric topics—including syncpoints over sessions, subtables and supertables, and asynchronous SQL statement execution.

SQL3 may also include specifications for multimedia SQL, called *SQL/MM*. The ISO group commissioned to look at the implications of "full text" data for SQL expanded its charter to include the more general issue of multimedia data—including full text, digitized audio, video clips, spatial and seismic data, and other forms of real-life data structures. SQL/MM will use abstract data types to define the operations supported on each multimedia object type. Unlike today's BLOBs, abstract data types provide methods to manipulate each of the multimedia data types. Providing the storage is the easy part; the harder part is providing the methods and multimedia-specific data fields that allow us to do something meaningful with these BLOBs (like rotating or playing them). As Jim Melton, one of the key SQL3 strategists, puts it, "BLOBs and objects are two very different animals."

SQL3 adds many new features to an already bloated SQL-92 standard. ISO estimates that SQL3, in its entirety, will be ratified in July 1998 (they think they may have a draft standard in February 1997). Just to calibrate you, it took three years before the early SQL-92 draft, which appeared sometime in 1989, became a standard. However, it's important to get a cursory understanding of what's being proposed in the SQL3 standard to get an idea of where SQL is heading (see Figure 10-1).

Figure 10-1. The Evolution of the SQL Specification.

WHAT DOES A DATABASE SERVER DO?

DBMS product differentiation has resulted in no single DBMS being best in all function categories.

— *Meta Group*
(November, 1995)

In a database-centric client/server architecture, a client application usually requests data and data-related services (such as sorting and filtering) from a database server. The database server, also known as the SQL engine, responds to the client's requests and provides secured access to shared data. A client application can, with a single SQL statement, retrieve and modify a set of server database records. The SQL database engine can filter the query result sets, resulting in considerable data communication savings.

An SQL server manages the control and execution of SQL commands. It provides the logical and physical views of the data and generates optimized access plans for executing the SQL commands. In addition, most database servers provide server administration features and utilities that help manage the data. A database server also maintains dynamic catalog tables that contain information about the SQL objects housed within it.

Because an SQL server allows multiple applications to access the same database at the same time, it must provide an environment that protects the database against a variety of possible internal and external threats. The server manages the recovery, concurrency, security, and consistency aspects of a database. This includes controlling the execution of a transaction and undoing its effects if it fails. This also includes obtaining and releasing locks during the course of executing a transaction and protecting database objects from unauthorized access.

Most SQL servers provide, at a minimum, SQL-89 level functionality. Most servers also include some SQL-92 features. Quite a few servers offer proprietary versions of SQL3 stored procedures, triggers, and rules. Some server engines (for example, Illustra and DB2 V2) have implemented some form of SQL extensions for objects.

So what is an SQL server? It's a strange mix of standard SQL and vendor-specific extensions. The leading database-only vendors—including Sybase, Oracle, Informix, and Ingres—have a vested interest in extending their database engines to perform server functions that go far beyond the relational data model. The more diversified system software vendors—including IBM, Digital, Tandem, and Microsoft—are inclined to stick with SQL standards and offload the non-standard procedural extensions to NOSs (like DCE), TP Monitors, Object Databases, and Object Request Brokers. Finally, some of the smaller database vendors—including Gupta, XDB, and Watcom—are making their mark by creating "best-of-breed," standard-compliant implementations of SQL.

In this section, we briefly go over the architecture of database servers. We then review some of the major features they provide—including shared data access, transactional protection, referential and domain integrity, and database catalogs.

SQL Database Server Architectures

Figures 10-2, 10-3, and 10-4 show three server architectures that databases use to handle remote database clients: process-per-client, multithreaded, and hybrid. Here are the trade-offs of the three approaches:

■ **Process-per-client architectures** provide maximum bullet-proofing by giving each database client its own process address space. The database runs in one or more separate background processes. The advantages of this architecture are that it protects the users from each other, and it protects the database manager from the users. In addition, the processes can easily be assigned to different processors on a multiprocessor SMP machine. Because the architecture relies on the local OS for its multitasking services, an OS that supports SMP can transparently assign server processes to a pool of available processors. The disadvantage of process-per-client is that it consumes more memory and CPU resources than the alternative schemes. It can be slower because of process context switches and interprocess communications overhead. However, these problems can easily be overcome with the use of a TP Monitor that manages a pool of reusable processes. Examples of database servers that implement this architecture include DB2/2 V1, Informix, and Oracle6.

■ **Multithreaded architectures** provide the best performance by running all the user connections, applications, and the database in the same address space.

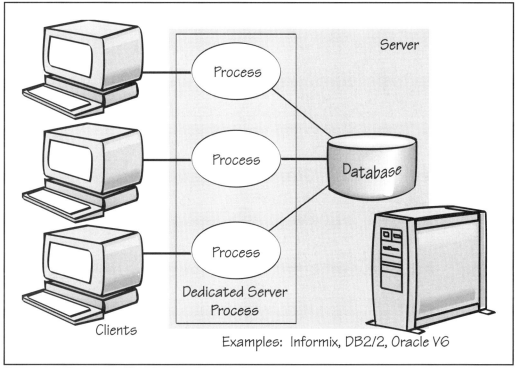

Figure 10-2. Process-per-Client Database Server Architecture.

This architecture provides its own internal scheduler and does not rely on the local OS's tasking and address protection schemes. The advantage is that it conserves memory and CPU cycles by not requiring frequent context switches. In addition, the server implementations tend to be more portable across platforms because they don't require as many local OS services. The disadvantage is that a misbehaved user application can bring down the entire database server and all its tasks. In addition, user programs that consist of long-duration tasks (for example, long queries) can hog all the server resources. Finally, the preemptive scheduling provided by the server tends to be inferior to the native OS's scheduler. Examples of database servers that implement this architecture include Sybase and SQL Server (SQL Server uses Windows NT's SMP scheduler).

■ *Hybrid architectures* consist of three components: 1) multithreaded network listeners that participate in the initial connection task by assigning the client to a dispatcher; 2) dispatcher tasks that place messages on an internal message queue, and then dequeue the response and send it back to the client; and 3) reusable shared server worker processes that pick the work off the queue, execute it, and place the response on an out queue. The advantage of this architecture is that it provides a protected environment for running the user

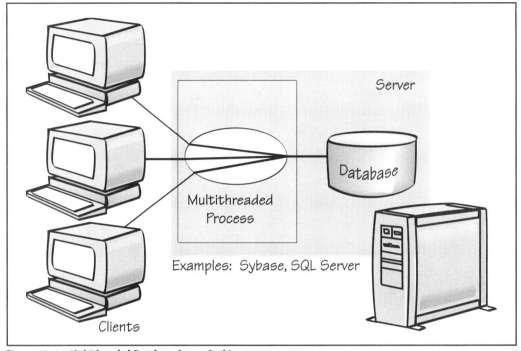

Figure 10-3. Multithreaded Database Server Architecture.

tasks without assigning a permanent process to each user. The disadvantages are queue latencies. While this architecture appears on the surface to be good, its load balancing is not as good as that provided by a TP Monitor. In fact, the queues may get in the way of the TP Monitor's own scheduling algorithms. The first database server to implement this architecture is Oracle7. According to Rich Finkelstein, you can expect anywhere from 20% improvements to 20% degradation of performance between Oracle V6 and Oracle7.

So which architecture is best for client/server? It's a tough choice. The process-per-client architectures perform poorly when a large number of users connect to a database, but they provide the best protection. The multithreaded architectures can support large number of users running short transactions, but they do not perform well when large queries are involved. They also do not provide bullet-proof protection. Hybrid architectures are, in theory, very promising. But are they better than using a TP Monitor with a process-per-client database server? As a rule of thumb, these architectures don't matter much if you're just doing simple LAN-based decision support. However, they do matter if you're planning to create a bullet-proof OLTP system. If you're planning the latter, we suggest that you check references carefully and go for the maximum amount of bullet-proofing.

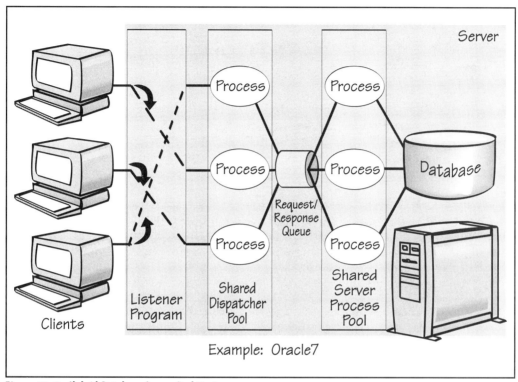

Figure 10-4. Hybrid Database Server Architecture.

STORED PROCEDURES, TRIGGERS, AND RULES

Relational databases now have built-in procedural extensions—including stored procedures, triggers, and rules. These extensions are very useful but extremely non-standard. So why are database servers moving into the procedural turf? What are these extensions and what new services do they provide? We answer the first question with an opinionated Soapbox. The contents of this section attempt to answer the second question.

What Is a Stored Procedure?

Many database vendors are now offering an RPC-like mechanism for database. This mechanism is sometimes referred to as "TP lite" or "stored procedures." A stored procedure is a named collection of SQL statements and procedural logic that is compiled, verified, and stored in the server database. A stored procedure is

Look Who's Cheating

Soapbox

Relational database vendors are cheating big time. They're adding all sorts of procedural extensions to SQL that deviate from the original vision of a "pure declarative language for relational data." Database purists used to scoff at procedural languages for being "relationally incomplete and insecure."

So what are today's newest and hottest SQL extensions? They are procedural constructs of all types—including stored procedures, triggers, rules, and proprietary scripting languages. So instead of keeping the data separate from the code, the relational vendors have simply brought the code to the database. Not only do databases store procedures, but they have also given them the keys to the data kingdom. Procedural constructs, as you will find out in this section, are simply taking over the database.

So the current message we're getting from the relational vendors is: "Procedures are OK as long as they're *ours* and we get to store them on *our* databases." But we believe database vendors are stepping out of their territory. They should stick to managing the data and leave the procedural extensions to the NOS RPCs, MOMs, TP Monitors, Object Databases, and Object Request Brokers (ORBs). Of course, what will happen instead is that everybody will step into everybody else's turf; most client/server systems will become hybrids of some sort. ❏

typically treated like any other database object and registered in the SQL catalog. Access to the stored procedure is controlled through the server's security mechanisms.

Stored procedures accept input parameters so that a single procedure can be used over the network by multiple clients using different input data. The client invokes a remote procedure and passes it the parameters required to do a job. A single remote message triggers the execution of a collection of stored SQL statements. The result is a reduction of network traffic (compared to remote SQL) and better performance. Table 10-1 shows the results of a TPC-like benchmark we ran on a DB2/2 database to compare the performance of dynamic SQL, static SQL, and two flavors of stored procedures. The results explain why stored procedures are so attractive—they're much faster in client/server situations than the other SQL alternatives.

Table 10-1. Server Network Performance.[1]

LAN Database Servers		LAN Stored Procedures	
Dynamic SQL (RDS/NETBIOS)	**Static SQL (RDS/NETBIOS)**	**Application Remote Interface (RDS/NETBIOS)**	**Roll-Your-Own Named Pipes (NetBIOS)**
2.2 TP1s/sec	3.9 TP1s/sec	10.9 TP1s/sec	11.6 TP1s/sec

[1] The benchmarks are from our book: **Client/Server Programming with OS/2, Third Edition** (Wiley, 1993). The book contains about 100 pages of code for running these benchmarks. The benchmarks were run on a slow 486-class machine; they do not represent best-case performance.

The concept of stored procedures was pioneered by Sybase in 1986 to improve the performance of SQL on networks. Stored procedures are used to enforce business rules and data integrity; to perform system maintenance and administration functions; and to extend the database server's functions. However, the primary use of stored procedures (in all of its variations) is to create the server side of an application's logic. The encapsulation features of stored procedures are well suited for creating performance-critical applications known as Online Transaction Processing, or *OLTP*. These applications typically: 1) receive a fixed set of inputs from remote clients; 2) perform multiple precompiled SQL commands against a *local* database; 3) commit the work; and 4) return a fixed set of results (see Figure 10-5).

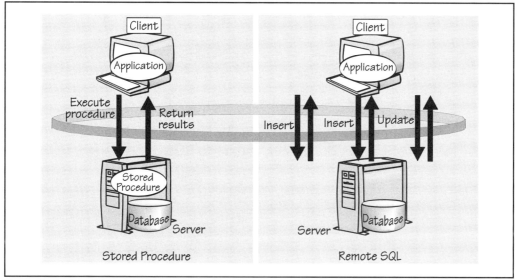

Figure 10-5. Stored Procedures Versus Networked SQL.

In other words, a stored procedure is a database-centric, RPC-like SQL entity that is persistent, shared, and has a name. It reduces network traffic, improves response times, and provides an object-oriented flavor of database service that is well suited for OLTP applications. Stored procedures also provide better *site autonomy* because the remote modification of tables can only occur through locally executing programs. If the tables change, you don't need to recompile all your remote applications. In general, stored procedures provide better distribution of intelligence than static or dynamic remote SQL.

Static and Dynamic SQL

Briefing

Static SQL statements are defined in your code and converted into an access plan at program preparation time. The SQL statement is known before your program is run. The database objects need to exist when precompiling static SQL statements. You can think of static SQL as being a compiled form of the SQL language. Static SQL is a performance enhancement feature.

Dynamic SQL statements are created and issued at run time. They offer maximum flexibility at the expense of execution speed. You can think of dynamic SQL as an interpretive form of the SQL language. The database objects need not exist when precompiling dynamic SQL statements. The compilation of dynamic SQL statements is done at run time and must be repeated every time the same statement gets executed again.

Static SQL is used for writing highly optimized transaction programs. Dynamic SQL is used for writing general database programming utilities and by GUI front-end tools that need to create ad hoc queries. ❑

Stored Procedures Versus Static and Dynamic SQL

Table 10-2 compares the client/server functional characteristics of stored procedures with other forms of SQL programming. You can see that stored procedures offer many advantages.

Table 10-2. Stored Procedures Versus Static and Dynamic SQL.

Feature	Stored Procedure	Remote SQL	
		Embedded Static	Dynamic
Named function	Yes	No	No
Shared function	Yes	No	No
Persistently stored on server	Yes	Yes	No
Input/output parameters	Yes	No	No
Tracked in catalog	Yes	Yes	No
Procedural logic	Within object	External	External
Flexibility	Low	Low	High
Abstraction level	High	Low	Low
Standard	No	Yes	Yes
Performance	Fast	Medium	Slow
Tool-friendly	No	No	Yes
Client/Server shrink-wrap friendly	Yes (call procedure)	No (messy)	Yes (CLI calls)
Network messages	One request/reply for many SQL commands	One request/reply per SQL command	One request/reply per SQL command

So, What's Wrong With Stored Procedures?

One drawback of stored procedures is that they provide less ad hoc flexibility than remote dynamic SQL. In addition, stored procedures may perform very poorly if their plans are not refreshed (rebound) to take advantage of the optimizer statistics—dynamic SQL creates a fresh plan with every execution. Another drawback is that there is no transactional synchronization—that is, two-phase commit—between stored procedures; each stored procedure is a separate transaction.

However, the main drawback of stored procedures is that they're totally non-standard. This results in a number of problems. No two vendor implementations are alike. The language for describing the stored procedures and their functionality varies from server to server; stored procedures are not portable across vendor platforms. There is no standard way to pass or describe the parameters. It is difficult for database tools to create and manage stored procedures. Dealing with the parameters is very messy (there is no standard interface definition language or stub compiler tool).

Alternatives to Stored Procedures

Soapbox

OK, we'll admit it. Stored procedures are better than the embedded SQL alternative. But now that you've seen what these stored procedures are all about, you may agree with us that they're not a panacea, and they're certainly not the only game in town. Stored procedures (or "TP lite") will face some stiff competition from other types of RPC-like extensions that offer more sophisticated functions and are further along in their standardized implementations. For example, NOSs and Transaction Monitors have their own architectures for implementing function that is equivalent to the database stored procedures. You've already encountered the NOS's DCE RPC and the MOM implementations in Part 3. In Part 5, we'll go over the "TP Heavy" implementation of stored procedures. You'll discover that Transaction Monitors provide an OS-like environment for scheduling and managing transactions. Transaction Monitors execute stored procedures "in style" by providing message queuing, load balancing, routing, nesting, and two-phase commit synchronization. In addition, object request brokers are defining their own versions of stored procedures (that is, method invocations) through the CORBA and Network OLE standards. ❑

Which Stored Procedure?

The following examples illustrate some of the differences in vendor implementations of stored procedures:

- ■ *Sybase and SQL Server* stored procedures can return multiple rows, but they do not support cursors. They require the use of *Transact-SQL*, a proprietary procedural language, to create the stored procedures that are compiled and stored in the catalog. The procedures are invoked using the SQL EXECUTE command and passing it the name of the stored procedure and server on which it resides.

- ■ *Oracle7* stored procedures only return a single row, but they support cursors. They require the use of *PL/SQL*—a proprietary procedural language. The procedures are invoked by following the procedure or function name with a database link that points to the remote server.

- ■ *IBM's DB2 v2.1* family implements stored procedures as ordinary DLL functions written in standard programming languages. The stored procedures reside on the same server as the database, but they are not stored within the database.

Client applications calling DB2 stored procedures don't need to know what language was used to code the procedure. IBM intends to release—in late 1996—a visual tool for building stored procedures, triggers, and userdefined data types. The tool will let you create the procedural logic using a 4GL-like language that is very similar to Microsoft's Visual Basic. Note that, in addition to stored procedures, DB2 V2.1 supports SQL3-like, user-defined data types. You can use these abstract data types to extend your database with new functions and data types. IBM currently offers *extenders* for text, image, audio, video, and fingerprints. DBAs and third parties can add their own extenders.

■ **Gupta's SQLBase** allows a set of SQL commands (known as a *command chain*) to be stored on the server and later executed. SQLBase does not support procedural extensions within the command chain. Three SQL-extended commands—STORE, EXECUTE, and ERASE—are used to manage the command chains. In 1995, SQLBase 6.0 introduced stored procedures that return multiple-row result sets. You can now define these stored procedures using Gupta's *SQLWindows Application Language (SAL)*. Gupta also provides an SQLWindows-like tool to help you create these stored procedures.[2]

■ **Informix** provides a proprietary language called *Stored Procedure Language*. It won't let you share stored procedures between transactions.

The list of vendor differences goes on. The bad news is that SQL-92 does not address stored procedures; SQL3 does, but we won't see it soon enough in products.

Triggers and Rules

Triggers are special user-defined actions—usually in the form of stored procedures—that are automatically invoked by the server based on data-related events. Triggers can perform complex actions and can use the full power of a procedural language. A *rule* is a special type of trigger that is used to perform simple checks on data. Both triggers and rules are attached to specific operations on specific tables. In other words, an event tells you something happened to the database; a trigger or rule is an event handler you write to take the proper action in response to that event (see Figure 10-6).

Triggers and rules are typically used to perform tasks related to changes in tables, such as auditing, looking for value thresholds, or setting column defaults. Enabled triggers or rules are executed whenever a table is updated by an SQL DELETE, INSERT, or UPDATE command. A separate trigger or rule can be defined for each of these commands, or a single trigger may be defined for any updates to a table.

---

[2] Note that in January 1996, Gupta was renamed *Centura Software Corporation*; Centura is also the new name for their product line and tools.

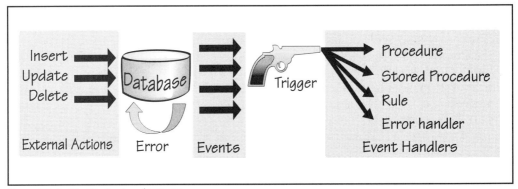

Figure 10-6. The Mechanics of SQL Triggers.

In general, triggers can call other triggers or stored procedures. So what makes a trigger different from a stored procedure? Triggers are called implicitly by database generated events, while stored procedures are called explicitly by client applications. Server implementations of triggers are extremely non-standard and vendor-specific. Here are some examples of vendor implementation differences:

- **Sybase and SQL Server** support only one trigger per INSERT/UPDATE/DELETE operation.

- **Ingres** supports multiple triggers, but the execution of the triggers is non-deterministic.

- **Oracle7** supports up to 12 triggers per table. It does this by allowing you to specify for each INSERT/UPDATE/DELETE the following: a *before trigger* that fires before the SQL statement executes, and an *after trigger* that fires after the SQL statement executes. In addition, Oracle lets you specify the number of times a trigger fires. *Row-level triggers* fire once for each updated row; *statement-level triggers* fire once for the entire SQL statement, even if no rows are inserted, updated, or deleted. Both can be defined to be active simultaneously. Oracle7's implementation of triggers is close to the SQL3 draft standard (but it's not fully compliant).

- **Informix** supports before and after triggers and more than one trigger per operation; it uses the column numbers to determine the sequence of trigger firings.

- **DB2 V2.1**—introduced in June 1995—now supports triggers on the OS/2, AIX, and NT versions. You can define multiple triggers to be executed for each INSERT/UPDATE/DELETE to a table. DB2 executes the triggers in the order that you create them. A DB2 trigger consists of one or more SQL INSERT, UPDATE, or DELETE functions. In addition, DB2 V2 introduced a special type of trigger called an *alert*; it has the ability to inform an external application of a database state change.

- **SQLBase 6.0** now supports before and after triggers. You can execute a trigger on a per-row or per-command basis. In addition, SQLBase 6.0 introduced a special type of trigger called an *event*; it executes a procedure at a specified time or at periodic time intervals.

Triggers are written in proprietary SQL procedural extensions. Different implementations limit what triggers can do. For example, Oracle7 will not let you issue commits or rollbacks from within a trigger; DB2 does not let you write procedural code within a trigger or call a stored procedure. Triggers and rules are also used, in a very *non-standard* manner, by Sybase (prior to System 10) and by SQL Server to enforce referential integrity. For example, a trigger associated with a particular table is invoked when data in the table is modified or updated. However, trigger-enforced referential integrity has many drawbacks, and very few database servers use it (see the following Warning box). Instead, most servers implement the SQL-89 defined *declarative referential integrity* standard. In summary, triggers are extremely non-standard, and the situation will not improve until SQL3 becomes a standard.

The Pitfalls of Referential Integrity

Warning

Trigger-enforced referential integrity is non-standard, error-prone, and difficult to implement and maintain. Triggers require programming efforts to implement referential integrity; declarative integrity doesn't. Because a server has no way of knowing that a trigger is being used for referential integrity, it cannot do anything to help optimize it. For example, a transaction that adds 100 new parts to a trigger-enforced relationship between a supplier and parts table will cause the trigger to be executed 100 times. It will check the same key value each time; the execution of triggers is not deferrable. In contrast, a server-enforced referential implementation would check the value only once for the entire transaction.

In addition, referential triggers are hard to document (and query) because they consist of procedural code. In contrast, declarative integrity provides better documentation and clarity by using catalog-based standard DDL SQL statements. Finally, some trigger implementations only support three triggers (or fewer) per table, which may not be enough to exhaustively cover all the referential constraints and rules that need to be enforced. ❑

Chapter 11

SQL Middleware and Federated Databases

The issue of deciding how to handle an organization's real systems is like trying to remodel the bathroom without rebuilding the whole house. Perfect synchronization is only possible if the world stands still...Only stagnant companies are able to unify their environments.

— **Don Haderle, Director of Database**
IBM
(October, 1995)

How does an SQL database client access data that's on multivendor database servers? With database-specific middleware, of course. Why not use straight SQL? Because it's not that simple. A heavy dose of *middleware* is needed to smooth over the different SQL dialects and extensions, network messaging protocols, and vendor-specific "native" APIs. It's sad to report that after ten years of intense standardization efforts, multivendor SQL clients cannot talk to SQL servers without layer upon layer of middleware. Fierce competition is driving vendors to build database engines and APIs that increasingly diverge from each other. Despite vendor efforts to conform to SQL-92, the complete set of SQL APIs from each vendor are further apart today than they were when we wrote the first edition of this book. The best we can do today is to allow a "federation" of loosely-coupled, autonomously-owned, multivendor database servers to communicate using a "least common denominator" approach. The industry calls this compromise *federated database systems*.

This chapter looks at the middleware that's needed to make SQL clients and servers work across multivendor, heterogeneous, database networks—or more simply put, federated databases. How well does this middleware provide a "single database illusion" in a federated world?

To create the "single database illusion," the middleware must make two sets of customers happy: 1) the developers of applications and front-end tools who need a single OS-independent SQL API to get to any database server; and 2) the MIS connectivity people who must make the disparate desktop clients talk to the "federated" database servers on their enterprise networks. The middleware must address difficult issues such as: How does a client program issue multivendor SQL calls? How do federated database desktops interoperate with federated database servers? Can all this be done transparently?

The good news is that there is middleware that you can use to glue together disparate systems. The bad news is that you cannot use this middleware to create production-strength, federated databases. It does, however, provide an adequate foundation for decision-support systems and data warehousing.

SQL MIDDLEWARE: THE OPTIONS

True database independence will not be possible without 3-tiered architectures.

— *Meta Group*
(November, 1995)

Based on our previous definition, middleware starts with the API on the client side that is used to invoke a service, and it covers the transmission of the request over the network and the resulting response. Middleware does not include the software that provides the actual service. So the questions we need to answer are: What APIs do SQL database servers provide to clients? And how is the request/reply exchanged with the server? As you will discover, there are too many answers to both of these questions.

Before going into detailed answers, let's first create a common mindset that will help us understand the solutions. We'll start with SQL "Nirvana"—these are the integrated single-vendor offerings. We then look at the problems created in a multivendor, federated SQL environment. Next we give you a quick overview of the two leading architectures for smoothing over the federated database discrepancies. Finally, we give you our two cents worth on what *federated* SQL Nirvana should include.

SQL Nirvana: The Single Vendor Option

If a single vendor SQL solution can fulfill all your shared data needs, consider yourself *very* lucky. All you need to do is read this section and then move on to the next chapter. Figure 11-1 shows what a typical single-vendor middleware solution currently provides:

- *A vendor-proprietary SQL API that works on a multiplicity of client platforms.* Most vendors support DOS, Windows, and OS/2 clients; quite a few also support Macintosh and some Unix variants. Most vendor APIs support SQL-89 with proprietary extensions. Some of the vendor APIs use *Embedded SQL (ESQL)*, and others support a call-level interface (CLI). More on that later in this chapter.

- *A vendor-proprietary SQL driver.* This is a thin client run-time element that accepts the API calls, formats an SQL message, and handles the exchanges with the server. The format of the SQL message and the handshake are known affectionately as the FAP, which stands for *Format and Protocols*. The SQL FAPs are typically vendor-defined.

- *FAP support for multiple protocol stacks.* As a result of user pressures, most vendors now support multiple protocol stacks. Some vendors bundle the stacks with their drivers; others support a common transport interface (like Sockets or Named Pipes) and require that you provide your own stacks. At the server side, the vendor typically provides "listeners" for the different stacks. However, some vendors provide their own internal protocol gateways—for example, Oracle7 on Unix translates IPX/SPX packets to TCP/IP on the server side.

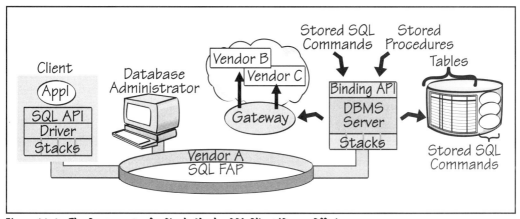

Figure 11-1. The Components of a Single-Vendor SQL Client/Server Offering.

- *Gateways to other vendor databases.* Some vendors provide gateways that make other vendors' databases look like their own. For example, Oracle, Sybase, Informix, Gupta, and XDB all provide gateways to DB2. Most vendor-supplied database gateways only provide an intersection of the features supported by the two databases—the least common denominator. This means that most vendor-supplied database gateways only support dynamic SQL. They are only good for simple data extracts and queries—not for transaction processing (also see the following Soapbox). Most vendor-supplied gateways require two database engines: the vendor's own database, which acts as a middle tier on the gateway server; and the "foreign" database. The middle-tier database server provides a directory of connected databases, catalog services, and handles the shipping and routing of "foreign" requests.

- *Client/Server database administration tools.* Most vendors will let you manage and administer the database from a remote workstation using a graphical user interface. You have a single point of management for the middleware, the clients, and the servers, as long as they're from the *same* vendor.

- *Front-end graphical application development and query tools.* These help you create visual interfaces to the database server. Of course, each vendor supplies GUI tools for its own database servers. Most third-party tools do a good job for a particular database (see the following Warning box).

Tools: Not All Databases Are Equal

Warning

The SQL database server peculiarities and extensions create major headaches for the vendors of multiplatform client/server database tools. As a result, the support of server extensions tends to be highly uneven. Most tool vendors usually do an excellent job supporting their "preferred" server platform, they do a mediocre job on the second platform, and they do an atrocious job for the rest of the platforms (they provide almost no support for server-specific extensions). Let's face it: Front-end tool vendors have their plate full just trying to keep up with the graphical engines on which they run—Windows 3.x, Windows 95, Motif, Macintosh, and the OS/2 Workplace Shell—and they can only deal with so many server idiosyncracies. You'll find that each database server has its GUI tool specialists. With over 200 GUI tool vendors out there, many are trying to stay alive by becoming best-of-breed—or specialists—for a particular database server. ❑

Vendor Gateways: Are They Just a Band-Aid?

Soapbox

A vendor gateway solution is not really open. It ties you into the vendor's database offering, and you get whatever gateway connectivity the vendor chooses to implement. Typically, the vendor will not support the smaller platforms (and if they do, support is very spotty). The vendor also has no incentive to create a level playing field for their competitor's databases. Everybody supports data extracts from DB2 and Digital's Rdb; but what incentive does Oracle have to provide gateways to Sybase and Informix (or vice versa)?

In all fairness, Sybase, Oracle, and Informix are trying to make their gateways more "open" by exposing some of the internal programming interfaces. For example, the Sybase *Open Data Server (ODS)* and the corresponding Microsoft *Open Data Services (ODS)* are general-purpose, event-driven server APIs that third parties can use to create gateways. The MDI *Database Gateway for DB2* was developed jointly by Micro Decisionware and Microsoft using ODS as their gateway base. The MDI gateway translates Sybase (DB-Library) or ODBC client API calls to DB2 calls. The clients run on DOS, Windows, or OS/2, and use Named Pipes to communicate to the MDI gateway server, which in turn uses an APPC stack to talk to the mainframe (see Figure 11-2). MDI supports, in addition to DB2, Teradata and SQL/DS. Note that MDI was acquired by Sybase in 1994; its product was recently renamed *Sybase Enterprise Connect*.

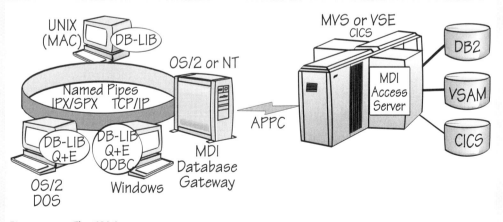

Figure 11-2. The MDI Gateway.

Some gateways go out of their way to "compensate" for missing functions on the "foreign" database engines. For example, the Sybase/MDI gateway provides a mainframe component called the *DB2 CICS Access Server.* It uses the CICS TP Monitor to simulate Sybase stored procedures on DB2 (but it doesn't come cheap). Oracle7 and Ingres gateways support some level of two-phase commit for updating foreign data, but it's still a least common denominator approach.

In our opinion (this is a Soapbox), if you're already locked into a single vendor database solution, then you might as well enjoy the convenience provided by the vendor's gateway. It's good for occasional decision-support access to foreign databases. And it's highly convenient because you use the same APIs and middleware to get to that foreign data almost transparently. However, you're at the total mercy of your vendor, and it locks you in deeper. But given the chaotic state of "open database middleware," locking yourself into a single vendor solution may not be such a bad idea (you'll understand why after you finish reading this chapter). For most large enterprises, a single vendor database solution is not in the cards. They have too many diverse database management requirements that go all the way from PC-based decision support systems to high-volume OLTP production data. ❏

SQL Nightmare: The Multivendor Option

Interoperability between N vendor databases ends up being an N^2 problem.

> — *Mohsen Al-Ghosein, TP Architect*
> *Microsoft*
> *(September, 1995)*

Figure 11-3 shows what happens when you move into a multivendor database world. Here's the short list of obvious inconsistencies that you will immediately face:

- **Different SQL APIs** make it a nightmare to write a common set of applications. Even if common API semantics were magically to show up later in this chapter, we still need a way to deal with all the proprietary SQL extensions.

- **Multiple database drivers** eat up precious memory space on the client machines (especially for DOS). Can these drivers use the same protocol stacks or do we need duplicate stacks? If multiple stacks are needed, how will they share the LAN adapter? Who do we call when a problem occurs?

■ *Multiple FAPs and no interoperability* means that the database protocols from the different vendors are simply sharing the LAN; they cannot talk to one another.

■ *Multiple administration tools* means that database administrators must familiarize themselves with a set of managing workstations, each of which have their own semantics and user interfaces.

We have not even addressed some of the thornier issues, such as federated database joins, federated commits, or concurrent access to federated data.

The federated middleware solutions concentrate on simple SQL access to a federated database—one connection at a time. More ambitious schemes, such as RDA and DRDA, aim at creating a federated environment that matches the power of a single-vendor distributed database approach. But they're far from accomplishing that goal. The best we can do today is focus on the issues of submitting simple SQL statements against one federated database at a time.

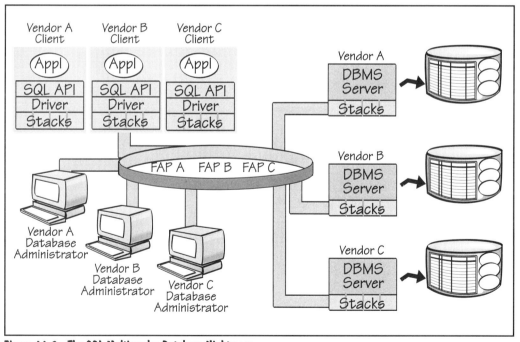

Figure 11-3. The SQL Multivendor Database Nightmare.

Middleware Solution #1: The Common SQL Interface

The first step towards regaining some level of sanity in a federated database environment is to *standardize on a common SQL Interface* (see Figure 11-4). The idea is to create a common SQL API that is used by all the applications, and then let the server differences be handled by the different database drivers. This is, of course, easier said than done. Here are the problems:

■ *Which SQL API to standardize on?* You'll soon discover that there are many SQL "standard APIs" on the table. How are stored objects on the server defined and invoked (remember the stored procedures and static SQL)? Should we use a call-level API or the ISO-defined embedded SQL? How do we deal with the non-standard SQL extensions? Will the common interface be slower than the native vendor implementation?

■ *Multiple drivers are still required.* Should the drivers reside on the client or on the server side? Who provides the drivers to the "common APIs"? What's the incentive for the vendors to support a "common" driver over their own "native" driver? Can the drivers coexist on the same stacks or on the same LAN adapters?

■ *Multiple managing stations and multiple FAPs are still required.* We haven't solved those problems; we just made them invisible to the developer. So the system administration people are still not happy.

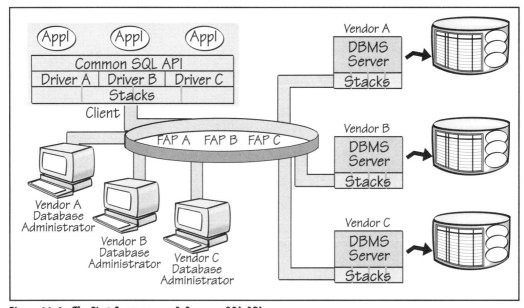

Figure 11-4. The First Convergence: A Common SQL API.

Later in this chapter, we will go over the contending schemes for creating a common SQL interface—including Embedded SQL, the X/Open SAG CLI, ODBC, and the EDA/SQL API.

Middleware Solution #2: The Open SQL Gateway

Let's assume that we have all magically agreed on a common SQL interface. What is the next middleware improvement that can be *realistically* accomplished to better articulate the federated database environment? Figure 11-5 shows a middleware solution that's currently in vogue: *the open gateway.* The idea is to standardize on one (or most likely two) open industry FAPs, supply a common client driver for the FAP, and develop a gateway catcher for each server. The gateway catcher will "catch" the incoming FAP messages and translate them to the local server's native SQL interface. The good news is that the industry has at least three "common" FAPs to choose from: the ISO/SAG RDA, IBM's DRDA, and the EDA/SQL FAP. Later in this chapter we will spend some time looking at the three approaches.

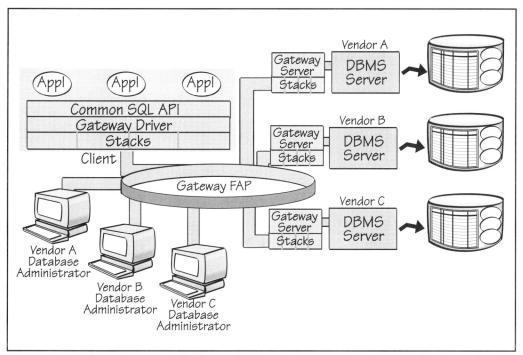

Figure 11-5. The Second Convergence: A Common FAP Using Gateways.

Middleware Solution #3: Federated Nirvana

Let's assume that we have both the common FAP and the common API. What else is needed to create a federated SQL environment that provides the same level of completeness as the single vendor implementation? Figure 11-6 shows what this "ideal" would look like. Notice that we've removed the gateway catchers, which improves server performance, reduces cost, and simplifies maintenance. And, we've created a single database administration interface.

To eliminate the gateway catchers, the common FAP must either support a superset of all the SQL dialects or it must tolerate native SQL dialects (meaning that it must allow pass-throughs). The SQL vendors must also agree to replace their own private FAPs with the common FAP.

The database administration facility will be the last proprietary stronghold to fall. There is just too much variety in the database server implementations to create a common interface. Even if we solved the technological issues, there are still some thorny political issues to be resolved. For example, is there a single point of administration control in a federated database environment? IBM's *DataHub*, an OS/2-based tool, is an example of a federated (but single-vendor) database administration tool. Third-party database management products—like Compuware's *EcoTools*, BMC's *Patrol*, and Platinum's *DBVision*—are also beginning to address these issues. The good news is that database vendors now have a DBMS MIB

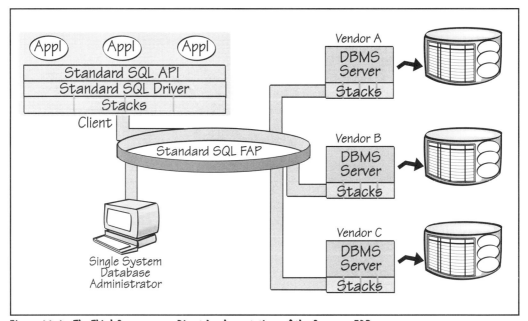

Figure 11-6. The Third Convergence: Direct Implementations of the Common FAP.

standard that defines database configuration and control parameters to SNMP
management stations.

WILL THE REAL SQL API PLEASE STAND UP?

How do you access SQL data? Can an application transparently access a system of
federated databases? Can an application built for one SQL database be deployed
on another? What's the state of the SQL data access standards? The answers, as
you will discover in this long section, are a fuzzy yes, no, and maybe.

The early SQL architects felt it was very important to keep SQL language-neutral.
In fact, SQL was created as a higher-level declarative language that was to isolate
us from low-level procedural constructs. Remember, it was designed as an end-user
query language. But to create applications that use SQL, it became obvious that
SQL constructs needed to be integrated within existing programming languages.
Incidentally, "SQL first" people view this process as extending SQL with procedural
capabilities, while programmers think of it as providing an interface to SQL
services. Two competing approaches are currently in vogue for supporting SQL
from within programming languages: *embedded SQL*, and the SQL *Call-Level
Interface (CLI)*. Figure 11-7 shows the two approaches.

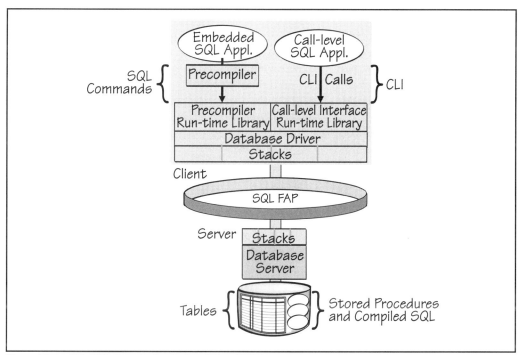

Figure 11-7. SQL APIs Come in Two Styles: CLI and ESQL.

This section looks at the SQL interface from the point of view of how it helps create a federated middleware solution. We will first look at embedded SQL because it is an ISO standard. We then look at the CLI alternatives, including the SAG CLI and some of its more famous mutants: ODBC and the X/Open SQL CLI. We will defer the discussion of the EDA/SQL CLI to the gateway section.

The SQL-92 Embedded SQL (ESQL)

Embedded SQL (ESQL) is an ISO SQL-92 defined standard for embedding SQL statements "as is" within ordinary programming languages. The SQL-92 standard specifies the syntax for embedding SQL within C, COBOL, FORTRAN, PL/I, Pascal, MUMPS, and ADA. Each SQL statement is flagged with language-specific identifiers that mark the beginning and end of the SQL statement. This approach requires running the SQL source through a *precompiler* to generate a source code file that the language compiler understands. As an example, for C, an embedded SQL statement must start with the **EXEC SQL** keyword pair and end with a semicolon (**;**). These bracketed statements will be processed by the precompiler and anything else in your source code will be passed through unchanged.

From a client/server packaging perspective, the biggest hurdle with ESQL is that the target database must be known (and available) when the program is being developed. This makes it hard to target a client program to a database at run time. In addition, the installation process involves binding applications to each server database they connect to—a process that may be too complicated for the "shrink-wrapped" client/server software market. Finally, precompilers have traditionally been tied to a particular database product; you must recompile your embedded SQL code for each vendor's database server. The same features that make precompilers so popular with IS shops and corporate developers have turned into liabilities for the providers of shrink-wrapped client/server software.

The SQL Call Level Interfaces (CLIs)

The alternative to Embedded SQL is to use a callable SQL API for database access. An API does not require a precompiler to convert SQL statements into code, which is then compiled and bound to a database. Instead, an API allows you to create and execute SQL statements at run time. In theory, a standard API can help you write portable applications that are independent of any database product. Of course, in practice things are not that simple. In this section, we go over the SAG CLI and some of its more famous mutants: ODBC and the X/Open SQL CLI.

The X/Open SAG CLI

In 1988, 44 database vendors created a consortium called the *SQL Access Group (SAG)*, which was to provide a unified standard for remote database access. The original goal of the SAG charter founders—Tandem and Digital—was to accelerate the pace of remote SQL standard development and put in place a multivendor SQL solution that would allow any SQL client to talk to any SQL server. Tandem and Digital were very interested in an open set of multivendor front-end tools for enabling their SQL databases. So they drove the SAG effort, which resulted in one of the industry's most successful "open standards."[1]

SAG focused its efforts on two separate undertakings: 1) An interoperability standard that allows any database client to talk to any database server "at the wire" by using common message formats and protocols, and 2) An SQL *Call Level Interface (CLI)* that defines a common API set for multivendor databases. This section focuses on the SAG CLI; we will return to the SAG interoperability standard in the middleware section.

The *SAG SQL CLI* is a vendor-independent set of APIs for SQL databases; it can be used by applications without requiring an SQL precompiler. In theory, an SQL CLI lets you access any database through the same programming interface. Currently, the SAG CLI only supports *dynamic SQL* and provides functions that correspond to the SQL-89 specification. SAG provides common SQL semantics (and syntax), codifies the SQL data types, and provides common error handling and reporting. SAG defines a common set of system catalogs including the table structures they use. SAG's connection management service allows SQL clients to specify connections to remote database servers. The three connection commands defined by SAG—CONNECT, SET CONNECTION, and DISCONNECT—are now part of the SQL-92 standard.

The SAG APIs allow you to connect to a database through a local *driver* (3 calls), prepare SQL requests (5 calls), execute the requests (2 calls), retrieve the results (7 calls), terminate a statement (3 calls), and terminate a connection (3 calls). In December 1994, SAG turned over its finished CLI to X/Open. So X/Open is now the official "guardian" of the SAG CLI, which is now called the *X/Open CLI*, to differentiate it from Microsoft's ODBC and other SAG imitations. The forthcoming SQL3 CLI is based on the X/Open CLI, with some extensions.

Figure 11-8 shows an IBM-supplied DB2 CLI driver; it conforms to the X/Open API (with some extensions) and supports DOS, Windows, OS/2, and AIX clients. The

---

[1] The early efforts of Jim Gray (then associated with Tandem Computers, and now with Microsoft) and of Jeri Edwards (your coauthor) led to the formation of the SAG consortium.

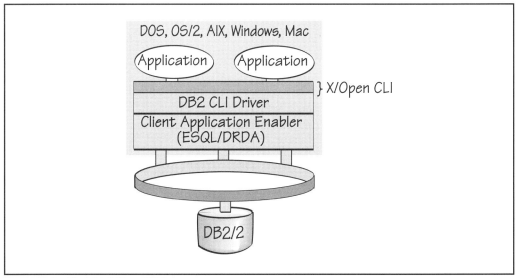

Figure 11-8. The DB2 X/Open CLI Driver.

DB2 CLI driver translates CLI calls to the native ESQL/DRDA calls supported by DB2. Note that the IBM X/Open CLI is largely compliant with the Microsoft ODBC standard.   However, it does not use the Microsoft OBDC manager and its multi-tiered driver architecture (see next section).[2]

The Microsoft ODBC CLI

ODBC has started the process of commoditization of databases, and nine out of 10 DBMS vendors don't like that.

> — *Kingsley Idehen, President*
> *OpenLink*
> *(October, 1995)*

Microsoft's *Open Database Connectivity (ODBC)* Windows API standard for SQL is an extended version of the SAG CLI. In August 1992, Microsoft released the ODBC 1.0 SDK; it was to be the shrink-wrapped answer for database access under Windows.   Since then, ODBC has gone cross-platform.   Visigenic received the

---

[2] The DB2 implementation of the X/Open CLI also introduces new features that are not in X/Open or ODBC. For example, it supports BLOBs and provides better control over transaction isolation. So always keep an eye on the extensions; they will come back to haunt you if you need true portability.

exclusive license from Microsoft to provide ODBC SDKs on non-Windows plat-forms. In addition to Visigenic, third parties—such as Intersolv (*Q+E Software*) and OpenLink—are offering ODBC driver suites on Windows, Windows 95, Windows NT, OS/2, Mac, and Unixes that run against a variety of database servers.

ODBC 1.0 was slow and buggy; it was limited to the Windows platform and lacked the documentation and code examples necessary to educate developers. In April 1994, Microsoft shipped the ODBC 2.0 SDK, which fixed many of the problems with the previous driver manager. In December 1994, the first 32-bit drivers were shipped. ODBC 3.0—announced in February 1995—promises to deliver more function; the SDK is expected to ship in late 1996.[3] Microsoft fully controls the ODBC standard. So the million dollar question is: Will the future ODBC align itself with the SQL3/CLI, or will it become a proprietary OLE-based standard? According to Microsoft, the answer is all of the above. Microsoft promises SQL3 support, yet it announced OLE/DB as the future ODBC replacement.

ODBC 2.0 defines about 61 API calls that fall into three conformance levels:

■ *Core* provides 23 base calls that let you connect to a database, execute SQL statements, fetch results, commit and rollback transactions, handle exceptions, and terminate the connection.

■ *Level 1* provides an additional 19 calls that let you retrieve information from a database catalog, fetch large objects (BLOBs), and deal with driver-specific functions.

■ *Level 2* provides yet another additional 19 calls that let you retrieve data using cursors; it supports both forward and backward scrolling.

Applications are responsible for making sure that an ODBC driver supports a conformance level (see next Briefing box). Note that the X/Open CLI includes ODBC's Core and some of the Level 1 and Level 2 functions. It also includes SQL descriptors that are not in ODBC. The X/Open CLI does not include the ODBC functions that support Microsoft applications—such as SQL Server, Access, and Excel.

Most database server vendors—including Microsoft, IBM, Oracle, Sybase, Tandem, CA/Ingres, and Informix—now support the ODBC 2.X API in addition to their native SQL APIs. They also include ODBC drivers for their respective servers (see Figure 11-9). The problem is that ODBC always seems to play second fiddle to the native interfaces on the client and server sides. For example, Oracle supports

---

[3] ODBC 3.0 adds 300 pages to the existing specification. It introduces 20 new function calls and supports Unicode. ODBC 3.0 will also return more information on approximately 40 new items; it will introduce an SQLDA-like descriptor for dynamic SQL.

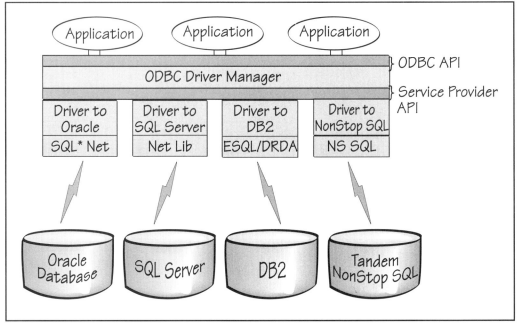

Figure 11-9. The ODBC Components.

ODBC as an optional API, but its native CLI is the *Oracle Call-Level Interface (OCI)*. IBM's DB2 family supports ODBC (with extensions) and the X/Open CLI (with extensions), but its native protocol is ESQL/DRDA. Sybase supports ODBC as an optional API, but its native CLI is the *Sybase Open Client*. Informix has no native CLI; it plans to support an extension of ODBC. Microsoft's SQL Server 6.X is, of course, the exception; it uses ODBC as its native protocol.

The other problem is that server vendors add their own proprietary extensions to the server driver and to the ODBC CLI (for example, most vendors extend ODBC to support stored procedures). If you really must have a portable ODBC solution, your best bet is to require CLIs and drivers from a third party that specializes in ODBC middleware—for example, Intersolv, OpenLink, and Visigenic (see next Briefing box).

Most of us will, hopefully, never encounter an ODBC API call in our working lives. However, many of us will use ODBC via a decision-support tool that calls on the CLI to get to the database functions it needs. If you must program ODBC, it's best to do it using a visual tool like *Visual Basic*, *Delphi*, or *VisualAge*. If you find tools too wimpy for your taste, then you may want to consider programming to ODBC class libraries—such as those provided by Microsoft's *Visual C++*, Intersolv's *DataDirect ODBC/ClassLib*, and Rogue Wave's *Dbtools.h++*. Finally, a chosen few hard-core programmers will be asked to write ODBC driver code for a particular database (see the next Briefing box). If you're one of those chosen few, then your choice of tools are: 1) Microsoft's *ODBC SDK*, 2) PageAhead's *Simba Engine*, and 3) Syware's *Dr. DeeBee ODBC Driver Kit*.

ODBC has many drawbacks. The most serious one is that the specification is controlled by Microsoft, and it is constantly evolving. Its future is also uncertain, given Microsoft's current commitment to OLE/DB, which introduces a different programming paradigm—it is object-based rather than procedural. ODBC drivers are also difficult to build and maintain. The current drivers have different ODBC conformance levels, which are not well documented. The ODBC layers introduce a lot of overhead (especially for SQL updates and inserts), and they are never as fast as the native APIs (see the next Soapbox on page 189). Note that for simple read-only functions, the ODBC 2.X drivers are now within 10% of native driver performance—a great improvement over ODBC 1.0.

FYI

What's a Database Driver?

Briefing

The driver is key to unlocking the mysteries of the target DBMS.

> — **Paul Reed, Consultant**
> **(April, 1996)**

CLIs require the use of intelligent database drivers that accept a CLI call and translate it into the native database server's access language. With the proper driver, any data source application can function as a CLI-server and can be accessed by the front-end tools and client programs that use the CLI. The CLI requires a driver for each database to which it connects. Each driver must be written for a specific server using the server's access methods and network transport stack.

Microsoft's ODBC provides a *driver manager* that routes an ODBC CLI-call to a particular driver (see Figure 11-10). The driver manager talks to the driver through an ODBC-defined *Service Provider Interface (SPI)*. IDAPI—another SAG mutant—goes a step further by providing a networked SPI-like interface, which allows the drivers to reside on a "gateway" machine. This can be very helpful in situations where multiple client workstations need to access multiple servers, each requiring a separate driver. All the driver combinations can reside on a single "gateway" server instead of on every client machine. Note that IDAPI started out life as ODBC's biggest competitor, but it was late to market. It is now used only by Borland in its database products—including *Paradox*, *dBASE*, and the *Borland Database Engine (BDE)*. As promised by its champions, IDAPI is several times faster than ODBC, but that doesn't matter—it lost the API war.

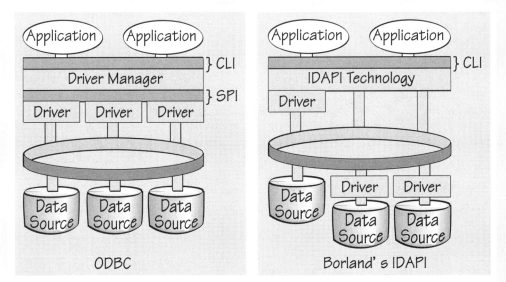

Figure 11-10. Drivers: ODBC Versus IDAPI.

ODBC drivers are usually obtained from database and front-end tool vendors. They are also bundled with some client/server applications that require them. Some database server companies are bundling ODBC drivers with their databases and not charging more for it. Drivers may also be purchased from a new breed of "middleware for middleware" companies. For example, Intersolv's *Q+E Software* provides a suite of drivers for more than 35 database servers. Database vendors are not interested in doing drivers unless they must. As a result, some vendors, such as Oracle, Informix, and Gupta, are directly referring customers who need drivers to Visigenic or Intersolv. However, purchasing drivers from a third party introduces one more complication in an already complicated loop. On the other hand, "middleware for middleware" vendors may find themselves becoming the single point of support and contact for federated database integration using CLIs. ☐

CLI Versus ESQL

Table 11-1 compares the CLI and ESQL capabilities. In general, today's crop of SQL CLIs are flexible but slow. You can only use them for decision-support systems. Higher performance systems will require the use of either stored procedures or static embedded SQL. A CLI, like ODBC, may cheat and let you invoke a vendor-specific stored procedure using pass-throughs (you specify the stored procedure name and server as parameters in the EXECUTE SQL API call). X/Open will eventually specify a CLI stored procedure call based on SQL3. But don't hold your breath waiting. In any case, CLIs are still too slow when compared to the performance of native APIs. And as long as vendors don't implement the CLI natively (see the next Soapbox), this will remain the case.

Table 11-1. The X/Open CLI Versus ISO ESQL

Feature	X/Open SQL Call-Level Interface (CLI)	ISO SQL-92 Embedded SQL (ESQL)
Requires target database to be known ahead of time	No	Yes
Supports static SQL	No (future)	Yes
Supports dynamic SQL	Yes	Yes
Supports stored procedures	No (future)	No (future)
Uses the SQL declarative model	No	Yes
Applications must be precompiled and bound to database server	No	Yes
Easy to program	No	Yes
Tool-friendly	Yes	No
Easy to debug	Yes	No
Easy to package	Yes	No

Soapbox

Which CLI?

The average corporation has eight databases today, and I'd rather have one common client/server language everyone can speak.

— *David Waller, Director, Intersolv*
(October, 1995)

Use native (direct) APIs whenever possible. Standard APIs like ODBC should be considered as a last resort...not the first.

— *Richard Finkelstein*

The reason Finkelstein doesn't like "standard" CLIs is that they require too many levels of translations before they reach the native APIs. Any type of layering scheme requires release-level synchronizations between the different components, which all come from different vendors. As can be expected, vendors will first support their native API sets and then worry about the "standard CLIs." This means the CLIs will not be synchronized with the latest releases of the database engines and drivers. In addition, the CLI approach on top of database drivers adds layers of complexity. For example, debug is far more complicated. You can expect a lot more fingerpointing between vendors when the NOS, API libraries, database drivers, native OSs, and database engines all have to be in sync for things to work.

But the million dollar question is: Why can't vendors—like Oracle, Sybase, and IBM—make the X/Open CLI the "native API" of their respective databases? The answer is that each database engine offers a unique set of extensions to native SQL; these extensions require a different set of APIs to invoke their services. Will vendors ever offer a non-extended version of SQL? Of course not—they're out there trying to differentiate their product! So by definition, the common CLI will always be a "least common denominator" approach that is not optimized for a particular database. Database vendors are not likely to reveal their future "extended plans" to standards bodies, so common CLIs will always trail behind the SQL engine's native API capabilities. And forget portability because even the "standard CLIs" have escape clauses (or pass-throughs) that defeat that goal. The bottom line is that any program that takes advantage of the advanced capabilities of a database engine will not be database-neutral. So much for standards! ❏

What About the Proprietary SQL Languages?

Both the CLI and ESQL approaches let you use your favorite procedural language for writing code. The alternative is letting the SQL vendors introduce new procedural languages for SQL. This is precisely the approach taken by the two leading database vendors: Sybase and Oracle.[4] Sybase requires that you use its proprietary *Transact-SQL* language; Oracle gives you a choice between standard ESQL precompilers or *PL/SQL*, Oracle's own proprietary language.

The benefits of using a vendor-specific proprietary language is that, in theory, all your SQL programs (including the procedural logic) will automatically port to all the platforms these vendors support; you don't have to concern yourself with

---

[4] This approach is not limited to Oracle and Sybase. Ingres provides its proprietary *Ingres/4GL* and Informix supports its own *Stored Procedure Language (SPL)*.

precompilers and compilers for each platform. But be careful—this is not always the case. The price you pay is vendor lock-in. It's the classic trade-off.

The following is a brief description of two vendor-specific SQL programming environments and what they can do for you:

■ ***Sybase Transact-SQL*** supports a vendor-specific SQL dialect, which, prior to Sybase 10, did not even support cursors and many of the standard SQL-92 features. However, Transact-SQL includes powerful proprietary extensions that let you create stored procedures, triggers, and rules. *System stored procedures* are used to supplement the server management commands. You can delay for up to 24 hours with the *WAITFOR* option. The language supports conditional logic and the declaration and initialization of variables. Error handling in Transact-SQL is cumbersome because the programmer must check the error status after each SQL statement; there is no provision for calling exception handlers automatically when an error occurs.

■ ***Oracle PL/SQL*** also supports a modified SQL dialect that is based on the SQL-92 standard. You can use PL/SQL in triggers, stored procedures, or as blocks of SQL statements sent to the server to be executed all at once so as to reduce network traffic. You can use PL/SQL within a host language, such as C or COBOL, or from within one of Oracle's client tools, such as *Power Objects*. PL/SQL provides conditional logic and lets you assign values to variables. In addition, it supports event-driven error handlers; you can use the standard error handler or override it with one you supply. Oracle7 allows you to group PL/SQL procedures within *Stored Packages*. Packages are managed using the regular SQL DDL statements (CREATE, ALTER, and DROP). Objects within a package can be *visible*, which means that they are callable from outside the package, or *hidden*, which means they can only be called from within the package.

In summary, the success of SQL has opened up a plethora of non-standard languages. You'll have to make the decision of which one fits your needs best. You also have the choice of using a standard procedural language with an SQL precompiler. Some database servers, like DB2/2, let you write stored procedures using any language that creates a DLL and supports an SQL precompiler.

OPEN SQL GATEWAYS

In this section, we look at "open SQL gateways" that translate the SQL calls into an industry-standard common *Format and Protocol (FAP)*. The FAP provides the common protocol between the client and the server. As we explained earlier in this chapter, the gateway acts as the broker that translates client API calls into the FAP format, transports them, and then maps them to the appropriate server calls (and vice versa). The open gateway must provide (or support) a standard SQL interface

(CLI or ESQL). It must also be able to locate remote servers and provide catalog services without requiring an intermediary database server. Finally, it must provide tools for creating the server side of the gateway.

We will look at the three contending architectures (or products) for common gateways: ISO/SAG *Remote Data Access (RDA)*, IBM's *Distributed Relational Data Access (DRDA)*, and IBI's *EDA/SQL*—an open gateway that currently supports more than 50 database server platforms. Gateways are a temporary fix until vendors agree on a common FAP and implement it *natively* on their servers. So we will look at which of the contending FAPs has the best chance of becoming this common standard.

RDA and DRDA: More Than Just Gateways

Briefing

DRDA and RDA are more than just gateway protocols. They both provide end-to-end architectures for creating true federated distributed databases. Most gateways simply pass an SQL statement to a remote database system, generally treating each SQL statement as a separate transaction. DRDA and RDA aim at supporting multisite transactions (though RDA isn't quite there yet). Some gateways handle the character conversion but don't have all the sophisticated features provided by DRDA and RDA for creating common data representations. Gateways typically link two locations; DRDA and RDA are built to support data backbones (with multiple entry and exit points). ❑

IBI EDA/SQL

Enterprise Data Access/SQL (EDA/SQL), from Information Builders, Inc. (IBI), is a family of open gateway products that uses SQL to access over 50 relational and non-relational database servers—an industry record. In addition, IBI has developed, with Microsoft, an ODBC driver for EDA/SQL gateway servers. EDA/SQL is a continuation of IBI's 10-year experience in developing gateway code primarily for read-only query access. IBI does not provide a database server; the company is focusing on the "glue" business.

Figure 11-11 shows the EDA/SQL components. Here's what they do:

■ *API/SQL* is another "common" CLI that uses SQL-89 as the standard database access language. API/SQL will pass-through SQL calls that it does not recognize.

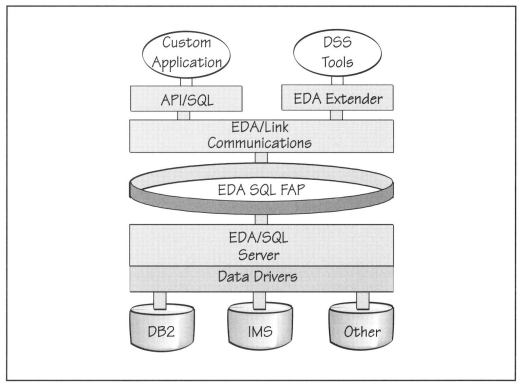

Figure 11-11. The EDA/SQL Gateway Components.

The calls can be issued asynchronously—meaning the client application does not have to block waiting for the call to complete. Clients can query the status of any pending requests. The API/SQL also provides an RPC call that can be used to invoke CICS transactions or user-written procedures. API/SQL is available on DOS, Windows, Windows 95, OS/2, OS/400, AIX, Solaris, VAX/VMS, HP-UX, MVS, VM, Wang/VS, and Macintosh.

■ ***EDA/Extenders*** are utilities that allow API/SQL calls to be issued from within existing products that support some form of dynamic SQL. You can think of the extenders as "redirectors" of SQL calls. Of course, the calls get redirected to API/SQL, which then routes them through the gateway network. Extenders are provided for many popular applications—such as Lotus 1-2-3—and for database front-end tools that work with popular databases (relational or non-relational). Many popular client tools are being delivered "EDA-enabled" out of the box.

■ ***EDA/Link*** supports over 12 communication protocols—including NetBIOS, Named Pipes, SNA, TCP/IP, and DECnet. EDA/Link provides password verification and authentication, and handles message format translations. It lets you create communications profiles using pop-up menus. The stacks it supports vary with different client/server configurations.

■ ***EDA/Server*** is a multithreaded catcher that typically resides on the target database server machine. It receives client requests and translates them into server-specific commands. If the target database is relational, it passes the ANSI-compliant SQL directly to the *EDA/Data Driver*. If the target database is not relational, SQL requests are passed through the *Universal SQL Translator*, which maps the SQL syntax of the incoming request into the data manipulation language that is specific to that server's driver. EDA/Server also handles security, authentication, statistics gathering, and some system management. EDA/Servers are available for every known database server. In addition, IBI provides an EDA/SQL "Transaction Server" for CICS and IMS using EDA/SQL RPCs.

■ ***EDA/Data Drivers*** provide access to data in over 50 different formats. These drivers take care of any variations in syntax, schema, data types, catalog naming conventions, and data representation. A specific data driver must be installed for each data source you need to access.

As a parting note, EDA/SQL is an excellent piece of middleware for decision support systems and data extractions. However, it does not provide the robust transactional support needed for production-type database access. Its FAP is not a candidate for replacing existing vendor-specific middleware. Let's look at RDA and DRDA alternatives to understand why this is the case.

ISO/SAG RDA

RDA has suffered from lack of commercial database vendor support...We really won't know the status of RDA until after voting on it sometime in 1996.

> — Joe Celko, Member
> SQL Standards Committee
> (November, 1995)

The ISO RDA is an emerging standard for universal data access; it is based on the little-used OSI stack. One of SAG's original goals was to port (and extend) the RDA FAP to the TCP/IP protocol. RDA provides functionality that is equivalent to the SQL-89 and SQL-92 (entry) specifications. RDA is *not* very tolerant of SQL deviations. The server will reject any SQL command that does not conform to an RDA-defined SQL subset. However, SAG may allow some cheating with pass-through commands.

The current version of RDA only supports dynamic SQL. RDA allows a client to be connected to more than one database server at a time, but it does not support a two-phase commit protocol to synchronize updates on multiple databases. An RDA client may issue asynchronous requests to a server whenever it desires; it does not have to wait for pending requests to complete.

RDA defines a set of SQL catalog tables that are based on the SQL-92 standard; it does not tolerate any catalog deviations. RDA returns error codes using the SQL-92 SQLSTATE return codes. It also supports the SQL-92 subset of SQLCODE return values. All other return codes are rejected. RDA supports a *repetition count* mechanism that lets any operation be repeated one or more times—for example, multirow fetches. Each repetition may use a different set of inputs.

RDA requires that all data exchanged between the client and the server be converted to a common "canonical" format. This means that all data is converted twice—once by the sender and once by the receiver. The benefit is that everybody needs to learn only one common conversion format. The disadvantage is that multiple conversions may result in the loss of data precision and can impact performance, especially when both the client and server use the same protocol.

RDA uses the ISO *Abstract Syntax Notation One (ASN.1)* to define the messages and then encodes (or tags) their contents using the ISO *Basic Encoding Rules (BER)*. BER uses a type/length/value tagging scheme to convey a value. Each data item must be tagged individually, so if a query generates a result set of 20,000 rows, you must tag each field in each of the 20,000 rows—that's a lot of tagging overhead.

What's coming next? RDA is working on defining a two-phase commit protocol that's based on the *ISO Transaction Processing (ISO TP)* standard. It's also waiting on the final SQL3 specifications for stored procedures before it can incorporate them into RDA. The committee is looking at providing static SQL support along similar lines to DRDA packages. The committee is close to passing *RDA Amendment 1*, which extends RDA support to SQL-92 features.

So what's wrong with this picture? Not much, except that RDA is dying because of lack of vendor interest. The major database companies are not implementing it. RDA's only support appears to come from small middleware companies. Joe Celko believes that RDA's fate will be decided sometime in 1996.

IBM DRDA

IBM's long-term distributed database strategy is known as the *Distributed Relational Database Architecture*, or simply *DRDA*. IBM is promoting DRDA as the standard for federated database interoperability. A number of influential database and gateway vendors—including Oracle, Sybase, Micro Decisionware, IBI, Informix, XDB, Ingres, Borland, Cincom, Progress, Novell, and Gupta—now support DRDA. DRDA is the glue that ties the DB2 family together.

DRDA's goal is to provide an interoperability standard for fully distributed hetero-geneous relational database environments. To do that, DRDA defines the protocols (or FAPs) for database client-to-server and server-to-server interactions. In DRDA terminology, a client is called an *Application Requester (AR)*, and a database server is an *Application Server (AS)*. The AR-to-AS protocol is used for the typical client/server interactions. The AR-to-AR protocol synchronizes transactions that span across multiple SQL servers; it also used to route SQL commands from server to server.

Figure 11-12 shows the four levels of database transactions defined by DRDA:

■ *Remote request* means one SQL command to one database. This is used mostly for issuing queries among dissimilar systems.

■ *Remote unit of work* means many SQL commands to one database. This is your typical client-to-single-server transaction. The client can connect to one database server at a time, issue multiple SQL commands against that server's database, issue a commit to make the work permanent, and then switch over to another database server to start a subsequent unit of work.

■ *Distributed unit of work* means many SQL commands to many databases but each command goes to one database. This is your typical multiserver transac-tion. DRDA handles the multisite synchronization, security, and data integrity functions (two-phase commit). It locates remote data sites and coordinates

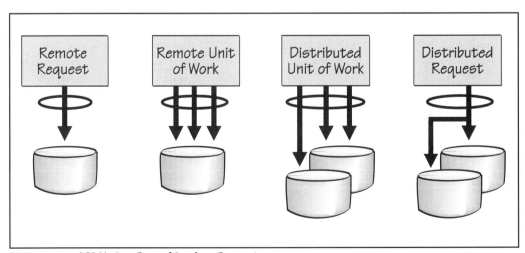

Figure 11-12. DRDA's Four Types of Database Transactions.

requests (including the update of data) at several locations in a single transaction.

■ ***Distributed request*** means many SQL commands to many databases, but each command can execute against multiple databases. With this capability, DRDA can service single requests that span multiple sites, such as a *multisite JOIN*. It can also distribute a single query across multiple servers to improve performance through parallelism.

DRDA Features

DRDA works great if everybody complies with the server's SQL syntax and semantics. But in a heterogeneous world, IS organizations might have to wait a very long time for such compliance.

> — *David Stodder, Editor-in-chief*
> *Database Programming and Design*
> *(October, 1995)*

What type of additional functions does DRDA provide? It mainly handles the thorny network and code portability issues, including:

■ ***SQL Message Content and Exchange Protocol:*** DRDA handles the negotiations between clients and servers for supported server attributes. It only does message translations when needed. There is no concept of a canonical message format; instead, it is a "receiver makes it right" protocol. This means that if data needs to be converted, it is only done once. And no conversion is done if a client and server use the same formats. DRDA takes care of dissimilar data representations, catalog structures, and command syntax conversions. DRDA does not tag every field in every row in a multirow result set. Instead, it creates a single descriptor for the entire result set. All these features help reduce network traffic and improve performance.

■ ***Transport Stack Independence:*** DRDA supports the MPTN interface, which means that it can run on top of APPC/APPN or TCP/IP (the two protocols currently supported by AnyNet) for client/server communications. DRDA handles data blocking, security, authentication, server routing, and generates alerts for both network and database failures.

■ ***Multiplatform Program Preparation:*** DRDA supports under-the-cover, multiplatform program preparation. A program is created locally; its output can be distributed to multiple servers using a remote BIND utility. The BIND process produces executable SQL code (called packages or plans) on the servers.

■ *Static or Dynamic SQL Support:* A DRDA client can invoke the SQL statements on the server one at a time by identifying a package and the statement within it. In addition to dynamic SQL, packages make it possible to execute precompiled static SQL statements on the servers (including support for cursors).

■ *Common Diagnostics:* DRDA returns status information upon completion of each SQL command. DRDA provides a standard set of return codes in the SQLSTATE field (based on the SQL-92 standard). Database specific return codes are still provided in the SQLCODE field. IBM's OS/2 based DataHub product provides an integrated system management approach to DRDA databases. It performs database management tasks across multiple sites. It can trace a transaction through the database network and provide status.

■ *Common SQL Syntax:* DRDA recommends using a subset of SQL-92 for application portability across platforms. DRDA also supports target-specific SQL commands for situations when it is more efficient to use SQL extensions. In other words, if the client knows that a server supports certain SQL commands, it can issue the calls and DRDA will convey them to the server. Who says you can't have your cake and eat it too?

IBM is licensing both the DRDA specifications and the code to interested parties for a nominal fee. At least six major vendors have licensed the DRDA code. IBM also supports the X/Open CLI on top of DRDA.

CONCLUSION

The success of SQL has opened up a plethora of interface and middleware "choices." You'll have to make the decision on which one fits your needs best. As we see it, SQL (with its extensions) will remain vendor-specific for a long time to come. If you're using SQL databases for mission-critical applications, the "mix and match" of SQL database servers can only spell trouble. You might have to accept some form of vendor lock-in, in return for the convenience of getting more SQL power, better support, platform portability, and finding somebody to blame. The situation is better for decision-support systems and data warehouses. There, you have a much better chance of working with data from mulivendor database platforms. The current SQL federated database middleware can easily support these kinds of "non-mission-critical" applications. More on that in the next chapter.

Chapter 12

Data Warehouses: Information Where You Want It

Inherent in the data warehouse architecture is the idea that operational and decision-support processing are fundamentally different.

— *Vidette Poe (1995)* [1]

This chapter provides an overview of the technology used to create *data warehouses*—one of the most exciting new developments in client/server databases. "Warehouses" provide the foundation technology for creating intelligent clients that look like Danny De Vito's desktop in the movie *Other People's Money*. For those of you who haven't seen this movie, Danny's closest associate was an information-hungry PC that literally lived on real-time data, which it grabbed (or got fed) from multiple sources. Danny's PC would continuously grab data, massage it, and present it in dynamic formats—including trends, animations, simulations, and 3-D business graphics—that were relevant to Danny's interests. Danny, of course, was in love with that PC, which he used to make all his investment decisions

---

[1] Source: Vidette Poe, **Building a Data Warehouse for Decision Support** (Prentice-Hall, 1996).

and lots of money. The poor machine even had to wake him up every morning with an analysis of how his investment portfolio was doing.

WHERE IS THAT OLTP DATA KEPT?

Modern businesses live on data. The total quantity of data on computers currently doubles every five years. With the proliferation of client/server (and multimedia) technology, we expect data to double at least once a year in the future. So who is creating all this data? The answer is modern institutions in the course of conducting their everyday business. The computerized production systems that collect and consume this data are called OLTP systems—these are true data factories that run around the clock.

What Is OLTP?

Database-centered client/server applications fall into two categories: *Decision Support Systems (DSS)* and *Online Transaction Processing (OLTP)*. These two client/server categories provide dramatically different types of business solutions. These differences need to be understood before we can appreciate what data warehouses have to offer.

OLTP systems are used to create applications in all walks of business. These include reservation systems, point-of-sale, tracking systems, inventory control, stockbroker workstations, and manufacturing shop floor control systems. These are typically mission-critical applications that require a 1-3 second response time 100% of the time. The number of clients supported by an OLTP system may vary dramatically throughout the day, week, or year, but the response time must be maintained. OLTP applications also require tight controls over the security and integrity of the database. The reliability and availability of the overall system must be very high. Data must be kept consistent and correct.

In OLTP systems, the client typically interacts with a Transaction Server instead of a Database Server. This interaction is necessary to provide the high performance these applications require. Transaction servers come in two flavors: *OLTP Lite* provided by stored procedures, and *OLTP Heavy* provided by TP Monitors. In either case, the client invokes *remote procedures* that reside on a server. These remote procedures execute as transactions against the server's database (more on this in Part 5). OLTP applications require code to be written for both the client component and for the server transactions. The communication overhead in OLTP applications is kept to a minimum. The client interaction with the transaction server is typically limited to short, structured exchanges. The exchange consists of a single request/reply as opposed to multiple SQL message exchanges.

Is Client/Server Creating New Islands of OLTP?

In the old days, OLTP applications ran on expensive mainframes that stored massive amounts of data, provided minimum downtime, and were the pride of the enterprise and the MIS shops. Today, the top-of-the-line OLTP applications—such as airline reservations, banking, stock markets, airport control towers, and hospitals—still run on expensive superservers and mainframes, and MIS shops still control them. However, today any department with enough budget to buy a few PCs, hook them on a client/server LAN, and hire a programmer (or consultant) can create its *own* OLTP application. Software packages are also becoming available off-the-shelf. In other words, database-centric client/server technology has lowered the barriers of entry for creating private or department-owned OLTP systems. These systems are giving the departments total autonomy and control over the applications they create and the data they gather. At the extreme, an entire OLTP system can run on a single-user desktop database; all the data collected can be kept private (in other words, outside the reach of the enterprise). We all know how easy it is to create ad hoc database systems on stand-alone PCs using spreadsheets and simple database tools.

In general, all the data collected by an OLTP system is of direct use to the application and people that are creating this data. They understand exactly what this data means. And they know how to use it to solve their immediate day-to-day production problems. The application typically provides a sophisticated graphical interface to view and manipulate the data with transactional controls. The members of the organization understand how the data is structured. They can create sophisticated built-in reports and manipulate the data for their production uses.

What happens if somebody outside the direct OLTP group needs this data? How do they know what data is available? Where do they find it? How do they access it? What format will it be in? And, what will it mean? The last thing the OLTP people want is to give outsiders access to their precious production systems. These outsiders often don't really know what they want, and they may be issuing long ad hoc queries that can slow down the entire production system, corrupt the data, and create deadlocks.

In the old days, the outsiders could ask their MIS representatives to deal with their MIS counterparts that controlled production data to give them an indication of what data was available and how to get to it. With the proliferation of the private one-person and departmental OLTP solutions, even MIS doesn't know what data is available anymore. The data in the enterprise is fragmented, and we've gone back to islands of data processing. Data ends up being all over the place: on the client that originates it, on the departmental server, on one of many federated servers, or on the enterprise server. There is no integrated view.

One of the great attractions of client/server and PCs is the autonomy they provide. Most of us feel disassociated with enterprise data and would prefer local control of our resources. In many cases, our new-found freedom causes us to withdraw into our own little production turfs and ignore the needs of the larger community. We've created a dichotomy between the departmental (or personal) needs and the needs of the organization or larger community. We've also created a dichotomy between production data and informational data.

So who are these "outsiders" we're trying to keep off our turf? They're the people who comb through data looking for patterns, trends, and informational nuggets that can help them make better decisions. Creating barriers to data is like creating barriers to trade. If they can't get to our data and we can't get to theirs, then everybody loses. Precious data is kept out of the reach of those who may need it most.

INFORMATION AT YOUR FINGERTIPS

How do we preserve the local autonomy of production systems and yet allow access to outsiders? How do we make sure the outsiders don't impact the production systems? What data is made available to those outsiders? What data is kept private within the production system? Who owns the shared data? Who can update it? Should we allow direct access to production data or copy it to another database? How is extracted data maintained and refreshed? We'll answer all these questions in this chapter. But first let's look at the informational needs of these outsiders and understand how decision-support systems differ from OLTP production systems.

Information Hounds

Let's give a name to these "outsiders" who want to consume our information. They range from those with compulsive appetites for data—like the character played by Danny De Vito in the movie *Other People's Money*—to those with occasional needs—such as a student researching a term paper. What shall we call them? How about *decision makers*? Or, would you prefer *information hounds*? Let's settle on *information hounds* because it captures the role millions of us will soon be able to play with database warehouse technology. Anyone with a PC connected to a data warehouse will be able do the same types of things the Danny De Vito character did.

Of course, the first to consume this technology are business people making strategic decisions—pricing and market analysis—that depend on the availability of timely and accurate data. The ability to access information and act on it quickly will become increasingly critical to any company's (or individual's) success. Raw data becomes information when it gets into the hands of someone who can put it in context and use it. The data is the raw ingredient, which makes all this possible. There are many parallels between the manufacturing and distribution of goods and the manufacturing and distribution of information. High impact, high value decision making involves risk. Making decisions using old, incomplete, inconsistent, or invalid data puts a business at a disadvantage versus the competition.

Information is becoming a key component of every product and service. For example, analysts use information to spot the trends and shifts in buying patterns of consumers. Information sleuthing is an iterative process. The sophistication of queries increases as the information hound grasps more of the nuances of the business problem. The hound needs the ability to access information for multiple combinations of "what if" situations.

An example may help explain the value of timely information. An unnamed apparel manufacturer was having problems reconciling the fast-moving fashion season with a distribution system that replenished stock based on what was forecast. The manufacturer decided to adopt a different technique and put in a system that collected daily sales information from the point-of-sale registers. The company also invested in analysis tools for knowledge workers and executives who needed to watch the daily sales. As a result, the manufacturer was able to cut costs by $47 million, resulting in a profit increase of over 25%. So timely information is highly valuable to some people.

What Is a Decision-Support System?

Decision-Support Systems (DSS) are used to analyze data and create reports. They provide the business professional and information hounds with the means to obtain exactly the information they need. A successful decision-support system must provide the user with flexible access to data and the tools to manipulate and present that data in all kinds of report formats. Users should be able to construct elaborate queries, answer "what if" questions, search for correlations in the data, plot the data, and move it into other applications such as spreadsheets and word processor documents. Decision-support systems are not generally time-critical and can tolerate slower response times. Client/Server decision support systems are typically not suitable for mission-critical production environments. They have poor integrity controls and limited multitable access capabilities. Finding information may involve large quantities of data, which means that the level of concurrency control is not very granular; for example, a user may want to view and update an entire table.

Decision-support systems are built using a new generation of screen-layout tools that allow non-programmers to build GUI front-ends and reports by painting, pointing, and clicking. Point-and-click query builders take the work out of formulating the question.

What Is an Executive Information System?

Executive Information Systems (EIS) are even more powerful, easy-to-use, and business-specific than DSS tools. And they're certainly more expensive, which may explain why the "executive" attribute is in the name. In any case, distinctions between EIS and DSS are becoming less clear. The EIS tools have recently expanded their scope and offer a broader range of functions at the enterprise level. Dick Lockert, an information guru, makes a case that the "E" in EIS stands for "Enterprise" instead of "Executive" because these systems now have hundreds of users with many roles such as executive, manager, and business analyst. Some vendors prefer to call them "Everyone's Information Systems" while still charging a small fortune for their tools. If this is not confusing enough, you may often hear these evolving EIS/DSS systems referred to as *Online Analytical Processing (OLAP)* or *Multidimensional Analysis (MDA)* tools. At the upper echelons, they're called *Data Mining* tools or *Intelligent Agents*. If you prefer, let's simply call them the Danny De Vito tools (see next Briefing box).

Regardless of what they're called, these tools are creating a huge market. The IDC market research firm projects a combined EIS and DSS tools marketplace of $1 billion in 1997. These new-breed tools allow information hounds to perform deeper levels of analysis on totally up-to-date, real-time data that is obtained from internal business systems—such as OLTP-driven financial, personnel, and customer information systems—and external data sources—such as Dow Jones and Reuters.

Because the Danny De Vito tools were originally designed for executives, all information is presented in highly visual forms. Extraneous details are filtered out to suit the user's needs. These tools offer unique features—including "hot spot" finders, "slice and dice," "goal seekers," and "drill-downs" to related information. They also provide more mundane features—including graphs, charts, statistical analysis, trends, queries, reports, and project management. The tools specialize in presenting information using visual metaphors that make it easy to navigate and sift through tons of data. Some of the better tools are used to discover late-breaking news on competitors, suppliers, government legislation, market research, economic conditions, or the latest stock market quotes.

Comparing Decision Support and OLTP Systems

As shown in Table 12-1, decision-support applications can be created directly by end-users. Network administrators are still needed to help set up the client/server system, and Database Administrators (DBAs) may help assemble collections of tables, views, and columns that are relevant to the user (the user should then be able to create decision-support applications without further DBA involvement). The design of client/server systems for OLTP is a lot more involved. In OLTP, performance and high availability are kings; if the OLTP system stops, your business stops. Consequently, OLTP systems require a large amount of custom programming effort. We discuss OLTP system requirements in Parts 5.

Table 12-1. Comparing the Programming Effort for Decision Support and OLTP.

Client/Server Application	Client	Server	Messages
Decision Support	Off-the-shelf decision-support tool with end-user scripting. Canned event handlers and communications with the server.	Off-the-shelf database server. Tables usually defined by DBAs as part of a data warehouse.	SQL queries and joins.
OLTP	Custom application. GUI tool lays out screen, but the event handlers and remote procedure calls require programming at the C level.	Custom application. Transaction code must be programmed at the C or COBOL level. The database is off-the-shelf.	Custom function calls are optimized for performance and secure access.

Production Versus Informational Databases

*W*hen an organization is able to examine information over a lengthy period of time, trends become apparent that simply are not observable in current information by itself.

*— W.H. Inmon
(August, 1995)*

Table 12-2 compares the database requirements of OLTP and decision-support systems. We need to understand the differences to get some better insights into what data warehousing can do for information hounds. The key points of difference is that decision-support data needs to be stable at a snapshot in time for reporting purposes. Production databases reflect the up-to-the-minute state of the business in real time. Information hounds typically don't want the data changed so frequently that they can't get the same answer twice in a row. So informational copies may be updated less frequently.

Decision-support data—or *informational data*—is collected from multiple sources; production data is collected by OLTP applications. The raw data that decision support systems extract from production databases is not normally updated directly. However, information hounds have a high requirement to tailor the informational database to their specific needs. This process is called "derived data enhancement." The informational database may contain derived data that records changes over time and summaries. Information hounds are rarely interested in a specific past event. They're always looking at summaries and trends.

Table 12-2. Database Needs: OLTP Versus DSS.

Feature	OLTP Database Needs	Decision-Support Database Needs
Who uses it?	Production workers.	Information hounds.
Timeliness of data	Needs current value of data. Reports cannot be reconstructed.	Needs stable snapshots of time-stamped data. Point in time refresh intervals are controlled by user. Reports can be reconstructed using stable data.
Frequency of data access	Continuous throughout workday. Work-related peaks may occur.	Sporadic.
Data format	Raw captured data. No derived data. Detailed and unsummarized transaction data.	Multiple levels of conversions, filtering, summarization, condensation, and extraction.
Data collection	From single application.	From multiple sources.
Data source known?	Yes, most of it is generated by single application.	No, it comes from different databases.
Timed snapshots or multiple versions	No, continuous data. Single version.	Yes, you can key off a snapshot's date/time. Each snapshot is a version unless you overwrite it during refresh.
Data access pattern	Multiple users updating production database.	Mostly single-user access. Intense usage on an occasional basis. For example, when a report is due.
Can data be updated	Current value is continuously updated.	Read-only, unless you own the replica.
Flexibility of access	Inflexible, access to data via precompiled programs and stored procedures.	Very flexible via a query generator, multitable joins, and OLAP.
Performance	Fast response time is a requirement. Highly automated, repetitive tasks.	Relatively slow.
Data requirements	Well understood. Known prior to construction	Fuzzy and unstable. A lot of detective work and discovery. Subject-oriented data.
Information scope	Finite. Whatever is in the production database.	Data can come from anywhere.
Average number of records accessed	Less than 10 individual records.	100s to 1000s of records in sets.

THE DATA WAREHOUSE

*T*he "data warehouse" in the client/server environment is the repository of data for decision-support processing.

— W.H. Inmon (1993) [2]

Bill Inmon is credited as being the "father of the data warehouse," a concept he started writing about as far back as 1981. Inmon argues that "one cornerstone of client/server applications is the notion of the difference between and separation of operational and decision-support processing." In September 1991, IBM announced its *Information Warehouse* framework, an event that "sparked much interest in the industry." By mid-1994, hundreds of data warehouse products started to ship— including various decision-support tools, Sybase 10's replicated server, Oracle7's replication facility, Teradata, Ingres' Replica Manager, MDI Database Gateway, Red Brick, Prism Solutions' Warehouse Manager, Evolutionary Technologies Extract ToolSuite, Trinzic Corp's InfoPump, and Digital's Data Distributor.

By early 1996, over 90% of large corporations either had adopted or were planning to adopt data warehousing technology. Meta Group predicts that data warehouses will grow into an $8 billon market by 1997, up from $2 billion in 1995. Obviously, all the major database vendors want to own a piece of this huge market. They're being joined by hundreds of new niche players that are vying for smaller pieces of the action via their participation in the various coalitions. The smaller vendors are adeptly providing key pieces of technology such as multivendor replication, data cleansing and purification, multidimensional databases, information and metadata repositories, and tools of every stripe.

In early 1996, we counted over a dozen "integrating" *Data Warehouse Frameworks* from leading vendors—including HP's *OpenWarehouse*, Sybase's *Warehouse Works*, IBM's *Information Warehouse*, Software AG's *Open Data Warehouse Initiative*, Informix's *Data Warehouse*, AT&T's *Enterprise Information Factory*, Prism's *Warehouse Manager*, Red Brick's *PaVER Program*, SAS Institute's *SAS System*, Software AG's *Open Data Warehouse Initiative*, Pyramid's *Smart Warehouse*, and Oracle's *Warehouse Technology Initiative*.

These "frameworks" are nothing more than loose coalitions of vendors that provide a data warehouse solution on a particular database platform (or tool). The framework, at most, defines common metadata and APIs. Of course, the coalitions are formed because no single vendor is able to provide the entire data warehouse solution on its own—large data warehouses are probably the most complex forms of client/server systems in existence. Each partner in the coalition provides one or

---

[2] Source: W.H. Inmon, **Developing Client/Server Applications** (QED, 1993).

more pieces of the data warehousing jigsaw—for example, data extraction, copy management, EIS/DSS tools, information directories, or parallel database engines.

What's a Data Warehouse?

Bill Inmon and vendors like Teradata define a *warehouse* as a separate database for decision support, which typically contains vast amounts of information. Richard Hackathorn defines a *warehouse* as "a collection of data objects that have been inventoried for distribution to a business community."[3] In our own modest definition a warehouse is an active intelligent store of data that can manage and aggregate information from many sources, distribute it where needed, and activate business policies. We hope that one of these definitions will ring a bell for you.

The Elements of Data Warehousing

A *warehouse is a place; warehousing is a process.*

> — *Richard Hackathorn*
> *(May, 1995)*

Data warehousing is too ad hoc and customer-specific to be provided as a single shrink-wrapped solution.[4] Instead, hundreds of vendors provide constituent pieces that contribute to a warehouse solution. We recommend that you pick a vendor framework that bolts all the pieces together (see Chapter 14). Warning: Don't attempt to do it all yourself; you may be able to piece together a solution, but the pieces may not work together.

The first step on the road to data warehousing Nirvana is to understand the constituent elements that make up a solution. Almost all data warehousing systems provide the following four elements (see Figure 12-1):

1. ***The data replication manager*** manages the copying and distribution of data across databases as defined by the information hound. The hound defines the data that needs to be copied, the source and destination platforms, the frequency of updates, and the data transforms. *Refresh* involves copying over the entire data source; *update* only propagates the changes. Everything can be automated or done manually. Data can be obtained from relational or non-relational

---

[3] Source: Richard D. Hackathorn, **Enterprise Database Connectivity** (Wiley, 1993).

[4] You can't generalize in this business. In early 1996, IBM introduced *Visual Warehouse*, a shrink-wrapped data warehousing package for departmental-sized warehouses.

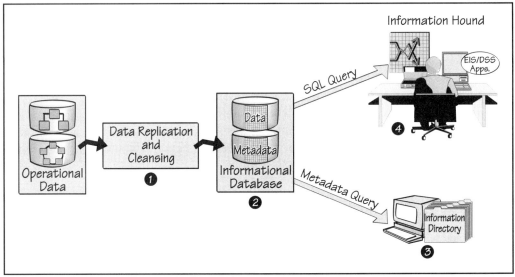

Figure 12-1. The Elements of a Data Warehousing System.

sources. Note that almost all external data is *transformed* and *cleansed* before it's brought into the warehouse. We will be covering data replication in detail in the next sections.

2. **The informational database** is a relational database that organizes and stores copies of data from multiple data sources in a format that meets the needs of information hounds. Think of it as the decision-support server that transforms, aggregates, and adds value to data from various production sources. It also stores *metadata* (or data about data) that describes the contents of the informational database. *System-level metadata* describes the tables, indexes, and source extracts to a database administrator (DBA); *semantic-level metadata* describes the contents of the data to an information hound. The informational database can be a personal database on a PC, a medium-sized database on a local server, or a massively parallel database on an enterprise server. Most of the major SQL database engines can be used as informational databases. We will have more to say on information database engines in the next two chapters.

3. **The information directory** combines the functions of a technical directory, business directory, and information navigator. Its primary purpose is to help the information hound find out what data is available on the different databases, what format it's in, and how to access it. It also helps the DBAs manage the data warehouse. The information directory gets its metadata by discovering which databases are on the network and then querying their metadata repositories. It tries to keep everything up-to-date. Some estimates claim that information hounds in large enterprises spend 80% of their time gathering data and 20% of the time analyzing it. Sometimes the hounds don't even know the names of the

objects they're looking for, where they're located, and how to access them. The information directory helps alleviate these problems by serving as a business directory.

DBAs use the information directory to access system-level metadata, keep track of data sources, data targets, cleanup rules, transformation rules, and details about predefined rules and reports.

Examples of information/metadata directories include Prism's *Directory Manager*, IBM's *DataGuide*, HP's *Information Warehouse Guide*, Minerva's *Infoharvester*, ETI's *Extract and Metadata Exchange*, BrownStone's *Data Dictionary*, Platinum/Reltech's *Data Shopper*, Informatica's *OpenBridge*, and Carleton's *Passport Relational Dictionary*.

4. ***EIS/DSS tool support*** is provided via SQL. Most vendors support ODBC and some other protocol. Some vendors—for example, Red Brick—provide extended SQL dialects for fast queries and joins. The tools are more interested with sequential access of large data quantities than access to a single record. This means that you must tune the table indexes for queries and sequential reads as opposed to updates. The next chapter should give you a feel for what EIS/DSS tools are available and what they can do for you. Note that most data warehouse vendors have alliances with the major EIS/DSS tool vendors.

In summary, data warehousing is the process of automating EIS/DSS systems using the four elements we just described. You must be able to assemble data from different sources, replicate it, cleanse it, store it, catalog it, and then make it available to EIS/DSS tools. The trick is to be able to automate the process and have it run like clockwork.

What's Being Automated?

One major difference between an OLTP system and a data warehouse is the ability to accurately describe the past. OLTP systems are poor at correctly representing a business as of a month or year ago. A good OLTP system is always evolving.

— *Ralph Kimball, Red Brick Founder*
(April, 1996)

Data warehousing is a framework for automating all aspects of the decision-support process. Instead of asking the database administrators (DBAs) what information is available, the information hounds can now directly consult the information directory. Of course, like all good DBAs, the information directory obtains its data definitions from the metadata stored on the various servers.

The hounds simply use the replication manager to perform copies of the data instead of asking the DBAs to do that. The replication manager keeps the informational databases automatically refreshed (or updated) with changes from the source database. If you really want to take automation to the extreme, you may consider using a *workflow manager* to orchestrate the multistep movement of data through the network. For each step of the process—and there can be many steps—the workflow manager knows which tool to invoke and what to do next.

Finally, the informational database is a normal SQL database that replaces all the private schemes that information hounds have used to store copies of their favorite data extracts. Data warehousing makes it easy for the hounds to get to their data and removes the overburdened DBAs from the loop (now they can focus their attention on the OLTP side of the house).

Warehouse Hierarchies: The Datamarts

IT organizations seeking to develop data warehouses will continue to experience greater success developing subject-oriented datamarts than full-scale corporate data warehouses.

— *Meta Group*
(November, 1995)

You can create almost any type of topology with data warehouses. Figure 12-2 shows a multilevel topology that's currently very popular. All data extracts—from production databases—are first applied against an enterprise data warehouse. Once the data gets into the enterprise warehouse, it can then be distributed, as needed, to departmental warehouses, also known as *datamarts*. These datamarts are organized by *subjects* that are of interest to a department; for example, sales data and customers for the West Coast region. There is also a growing interest in *mobile datamarts*. These are personal warehouses that you can load in a laptop and take with you on the road. For example, real-estate brokers could carry a multiple-listing catalog in their laptops. They could then show customers comparative listings during an open house.

So the million-dollar questions for datamart designers are: Why not get the data directly from the production systems? Why go through all these intermediaries? The answer is that you don't want to slow down the production databases with too many data extracts. In addition, it is better to cleanse the data once rather than cleanse it at each datamart. If nothing else, the data will be consistent throughout the enterprise. Finally, there's talk of turning the enterprise data warehouse into an active information database. It's the place where you want to apply rules to data before you distribute it. On the downside, the centralized approach requires

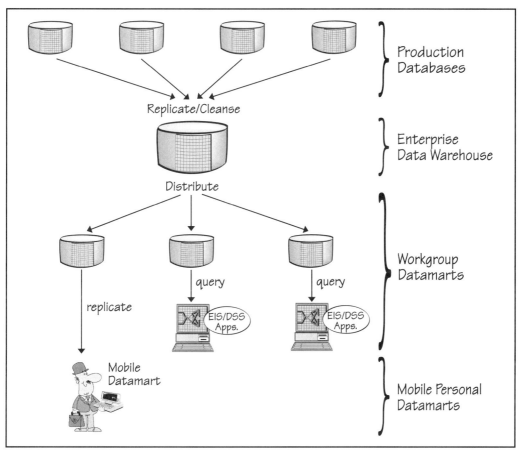

Figure 12-2. The Top-Down Approach to Data Warehousing.

up-front planning and consensus across an organization. It's much easier to spend $20K on a "warehouse in the box" and create your own departmental datamart.[5]

Unfortunately, the "real world" doesn't really work this way. Most organizations typically develop their data warehouses from the bottom up. They start with a small datamart that extracts its data directly from the production databases. If the project succeeds, more datamarts are added incrementally. Soon, you have many isolated datamarts, or the DBAs may try to form a loose federation of datamarts that is collectively called "the data warehouse." The easiest way to do this is to introduce a federated information directory. Finally, some DBAs may succeed in "creating order from chaos" by making a business case for an enterprise data warehouse—

---

[5] Red Brick's new product *Warehouse for Workgroups* is intended for 5 GByte datamarts that service less than 30 users; it sells for between $12K and $30K. IBM's *Visual Warehouse*, the "all-in-one" datamart, sells for between $20K and $33K.

the best justification is that it's needed to keep the production people from going insane.

Replication Versus Direct Access

Applications that can tolerate data that is anywhere from a few hours to a day old are much better candidates for replication.

> — *Glenn Froemming, DBMS Magazine*
> *(March, 1996)*

With the spread of client/server technology and loosely-coupled federated databases, it becomes impractical from many perspectives—performance, security, availability, debt-to-history, and local control—to create a single centralized repository of data. Replicated data management will increasingly be used to remove the capacity, performance, and organizational roadblocks of centralized data access.

Automated copy management—or the management of replicated data—becomes a key technology for sharing data in a federated database environment. Decision-support applications using data warehouses are perfect candidates for replicated data technology. These applications usually tolerate a certain amount of obsolescence—the politically correct term is *volatility*—in their data. Data replication for decision support minimizes the disruption of production systems and allows you to tailor the informational databases to fit your needs.

On the other hand, *direct data access* is required by applications—mostly production OLTP—that cannot tolerate any "volatility" in their data. These applications require "live data" that reflects the state of the business. This type of live data is obtained in distributed situations using one of four approaches:

■ *Using federated databases that support synchronous (or continuous) replication of data*—the target databases must be synchronized within the same transaction boundary as the primary (or source) database. A target database that allows a user to directly update it is called a *replica*. To maintain a single-site update policy, the replica that gets updated becomes the new source database and must immediately propagate its updates. In general, synchronous replicated technology is a risky proposition in federated database environments. It requires support for two-phase commit protocols across heterogeneous databases.

■ *Using a centralized database server*—all the data is kept on one highly-scalable and fault-tolerant server. This solution, if it fits your organizational needs, will give you the least amount of headaches.

■ *Using a single vendor's distributed database multiserver offering—* notice that we did not say multivendor because this technology is still full of holes (see the following Briefing).

■ *Using a TP Monitor to front-end multivendor database servers—*the database servers must support X/Open's XA protocol to be managed by a TP Monitor. As you will find out in Part 5, this technology can be very attractive in many situations.

In summary, there's a need for both kinds of data access: replicated and direct. The issues of direct access are well understood by the industry; many commercial solutions are available. On the other hand, the management of replicated data within a data warehouse framework is opening up exciting new opportunities. As more PCs become multimedia-enabled, we will start seeing federations of informational databases that include the desktop client, where local information is captured and viewed; the local server, which provides overflow storage; and global servers that collectively contain an infinite amount of information and storage. Efficient replication and copy management becomes the glue that ties these new federations of databases together.

 The Distributed Database Model

Briefing

Replication is easier to understand and far easier to implement than two-phase commit protocols.

> — *Gartner Group*
> *(August, 1995)*

Despite vendor claims and widespread wishful thinking among users, replication servers do not rigorously enforce data integrity; they tend to look the other way and patch up the problems later.

> — *John Tibbetts and Barbara Bernstein*
> *(October, 1995)*

Standard *off-the-shelf* commercial distributed database packages will provide, when they fully blossom, transparent access to data on a network. The distributed database keeps track of the location of data on the network, and it will route your requests to the right database nodes, making their location transparent. To be fully distributed, a database server must support multisite updates using a transactional two-phase commit discipline (see Figure 12-3). It should allow

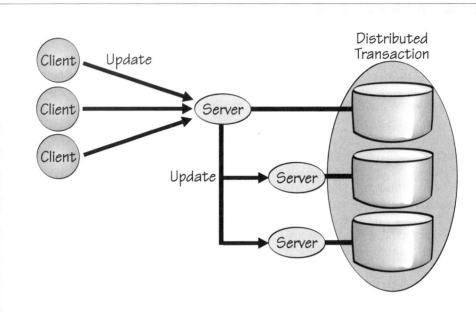

Distributed
Transaction

Client — Update

Client — Server

Client

Update — Server

Server

Figure 12-3. The Distributed Database Model.

you to join data from tables that reside on several machines. It should also *automatically* update data in tables that reside on several machines.

Distributed databases make it easy to write distributed applications without having to first decompose your applications. With *true* distributed databases, the location of the data is completely transparent to the application. The chief advantage of distributed databases is that they allow access to remote data transparently while keeping most of the data local to the applications that actually use it. The disadvantages of distributed databases are:

■ They currently do not work in heterogeneous database environments. As a result, you're locked into a single vendor solution.

■ They poorly encapsulate data and services. You cannot change a local database table if it is being used by other sites.

■ They require too many low-level message exchanges to get work done. Distributed databases exchange messages at the SQL level. This is not as efficient as using stored procedures or RPCs managed by a TP Monitor.

■ They are very slow over long wide-area networks. Two-phase commits are very expensive in terms of messages sent, and it is difficult to join tables located on different computers and achieve good performance.

■ They are very hard to administer. If one machine is not available, all the distributed transactions associated with it cannot execute. In contrast, with replicated databases, you can access data even if one server node is down.

The alternative to distributed databases are *federated* data warehouses, which are more easily adaptable to today's organizational realities. We also believe that eventually millions of desktop machines will come with a standard database. When you start dealing with millions of databases, you're much better off with loose federations that are synchronized using distributed object managers or a new breed of personal TP Monitors—but, now we're talking about the "post-scarcity" client/server scenario. ❏

The Mechanics of Data Replication

For users, replication means data at your service, but for IS, it means finding a solution to the difficult problem of reconciling different versions of the data.

— *David Stodder, Editor-in-chief*
Database Programming and Design
(October, 1995)

It's very common for business people to routinely populate their spreadsheets with data extracted from external sources. The process (see Figure 12-4) consists of the following manual steps: 1) Extract data using a query, 2) Copy the results to a diskette file, 3) Copy the diskette file to the machine with the spreadsheet program, and 4) Import the file into the local database (or spreadsheet). This technique, called *manual extract*, is primitive, labor intensive, and error prone.

Figure 12-4. Getting to the Data Manually.

In this section, we look at the mechanics for the total automation of this extract process (see Figure 12-5). The copy mechanics deal with the following issues: How is the extract specified? How is data from multiple sources blended? Can data be transformed as part of the copy? Who orchestrates the copy process? How is data copied into the informational databases? How are the copies refreshed? How tightly synchronized are the replicas (or extracts) with the source? When can the replicas be updated? What are the transactional boundaries of a copy?

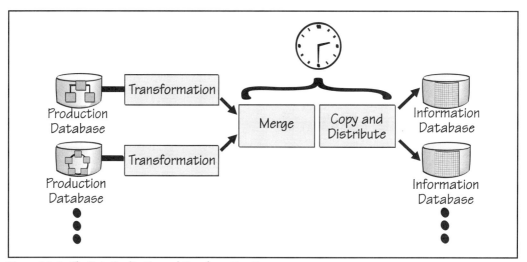

Figure 12-5. The Data Replication and Transformation Process.

Refresh and Updates

The informational databases are populated with data that originates from the various production databases. Typically, the data is copied or extracted using one of two techniques:

- ■ **Refresh** replaces the entire target with data from the source (see Figure 12-6). This works well when you are moving small amounts of data, which have low requirements for frequency of update (that is, the data has low volatility). It is also used for doing initial bulk loads to the target database.

- ■ **Update** only sends the changed data to the target (see Figure 12-7). Updates can be either *synchronous*, which means that the target copy is updated in the same commit scope as the source table, or they can be *asynchronous*, which means that the target table is updated in a separate transaction than the one updating the source. Synchronous updates are useful in production environments for creating replicated databases that provide high availability. Asynchronous updates are useful in data warehousing situations. You get to specify the

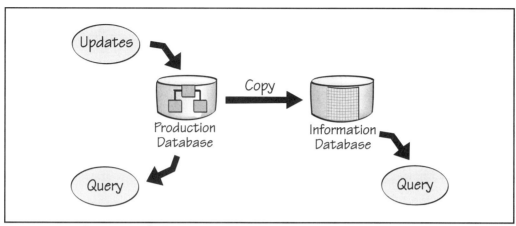

Figure 12-6. Replication via Refresh.

level of synchronization that you want to maintain between the source and the target and the interval of updates. This means that you get to control the level of data obsolescence you can tolerate.

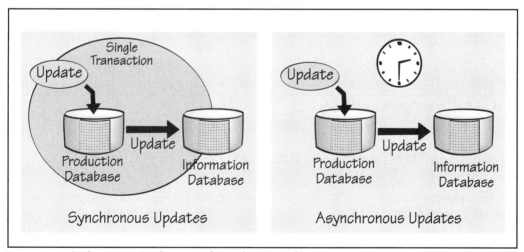

Figure 12-7. Replication via Synchronous and Asynchronous Updates.

Staging the Updates

Some of the warehouse products allow you to finely control the frequency of updates. For example, you can specify the intervals at which you want *asynchronous update* data sent from the source to one or more targets. The changes to the source tables are captured in one or more *staging tables* for subsequent propagation to target tables (see Figure 12-8). At the intervals you specify, all the target databases in the system are updated simultaneously from the staging area.

To be more precise, the *data capture* component takes changed data from the database log and stores it in the *data staging tables* (see Figure 12-8). The *apply* component then takes the data from the staging tables and applies those changes to the target copies.

Staging provides users with a consistent view of the data across the copies. It reduces contention on the production database—the copy tool does not interfere with production applications.

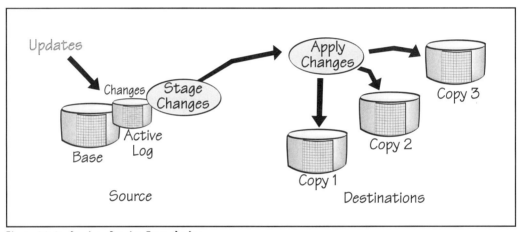

Figure 12-8. Staging: Copying From the Log.

Cleaning and Transforming the Raw Data

As you increase the number of data sources, the complexities involved with a data warehouse increase exponentially.

— *Judith Hurwitz, President*
Hurwitz Consulting
(April, 1996)

One of the attractive features of replicating data in warehouses is that you can control, enhance, and transform the "raw" data before storing it in the target databases. A well-designed warehouse lets you "filter and clean" raw data from production databases and store it in a form that's suitable for your informational needs. In other words, data warehouses are not simply passive collectors of data—they're also in the business of creating value-added data from raw data.

As part of the copy, a warehouse translates data from its original raw formats (which may vary widely) into a single common format that's consistent for the informational application. The related data from multiple sites is combined and merged so that the "copy" becomes a single logical database. During this process, data may also be *enhanced*; that is, empty fields may be filled in or records extended. The data may be timestamped and stored in snapshots that capture a moment in time for historical trend analysis. The copy process also takes care of any data format conversions for different targets.

Some of the more sophisticated warehouses may apply user-defined specialized functions to the data to forecast trends; that is, fill in future values or create on-the-fly video presentations. They will also be able to convert data into formats that are appropriate to the decision support, spreadsheet, and multimedia viewing tools on the client machines. The sky is the limit when it comes to value-added warehousing functions.

Figure 12-9 shows some of the more common functions that you can apply on data extracts:

■ *Subsets* allow you to transmit only the rows and columns that are of interest to your informational applications. You use SQL once to define your subsets to the copy tool, and these subsets will be performed automatically as part of the copy.

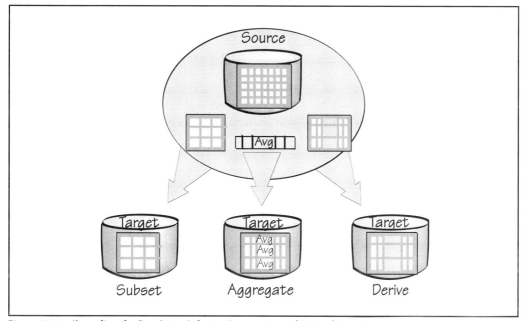

Figure 12-9. Upgrading the Raw Data: Subsets, Aggregates, and Derived Functions.

In addition, different views of the same source data can be delivered to different copy targets. Multitable joins can also be used to define the copy transforms.

■ **Aggregates** allow you to transmit only the aggregations of data such as averages, sums, maximums, and so on. Again, you specify this once using SQL, and the copy tool will perform the aggregate every time a transfer takes place.

■ **Derived functions** allow you to specify data that does not exist but is the result of some calculation (or function) on data that does exist. For example, a new column of data may be defined on the target database that is the sum of two columns on the source database. The new column will automatically get created and updated as part of the automated copy process.

In addition to cleaning and merging the data, these functions can help you reduce the network traffic between the targets and the destinations because you only copy the data you want.

Some of the more sophisticated replication tools let you extract and copy data from non-relational sources such as Lotus Notes, Internet Web Servers, spreadsheets, news feeds, and CICS and IMS databases. Most data warehouses are SQL databases, so the majority of extract tools provide one-way transforms from the foreign data sources into SQL. As you can expect, this involves a significant amount of data cleansing. Most tools provide callbacks that let you apply customized cleansing functions to the data extracts. The data transformations are usually described in the information directory or in a warehouse management tool.

According to Gartner Group, the market for tools that extract, cleanse, and replicate data will grow from $65 million in 1994 to $210 million by 1999. This represents a 26 percent annual growth. Examples of data extraction and replication tools include Carleton's *Passport*, Platinum's *Pipeline*, Legent's *Data Mover*, Sybase's *Replication Server*, Oracle7's *Snapshot*, Praxis's *OmniReplicator*, Ingres's *OpenIngres Replicator*, Software AG's *Entire Transaction Propagator*, Prism's *Warehouse Manager*, ETI's *Extract*, and IBM's *DataJoiner*, *DataPropagator*, and *DataRefresher* tools. Examples of transformation and cleansing tools include Trinzic's *InfoPump*, Apertus Technologies' *Enterprise/Integrator (EI)*, and IBI's *Copy Manager*.

True Replicas

Time is a relative concept in replicated systems, and it is not a concept upon which I would recommend any sort of collision-detection or resolution scheme.

— *Glenn Froemming, DBMS Magazine (April, 1996)*

Replicas are *copies* of data, that you can update (see Figure 12-10). When this happens, the updated replica must find a way to resynchronize its state with the original primary database. Normally, updates only take place on a single designated replica, and the primary server must abstain from doing any non-replica generated changes. So, the site of update shifts from the primary to the replica.

As a result, the replica starts off with a full image of the primary database and sends all subsequent updates to the primary, either continuously or on a periodic basis. The primary database is then in charge of propagating the changes it receives to its target databases using the normal processes. The single-site update constraint may be relaxed by using *check-out* versions of replicated data—a technology that is widely used in Object Databases.

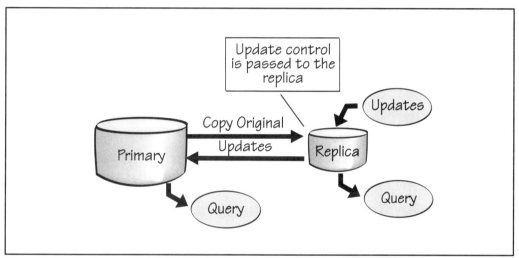

Figure 12-10. Replicas, or When the Copies Become the Master Data.

Ingres implements a database that allows both the master and the replicas to be separately updated and uses a *conflict resolver* to synchronize the data. When the changes in the replica are applied against the master, an *update collision detector* resolves conflicts using one of four user-specified policies: the oldest update has priority, the most recent update has priority, a user-specified action is applied, or all replication is halted. This last approach may be the right thing to do, but can you afford to stop the application completely until someone reconciles the data? You can also specify the winner by location or time interval. More recent entrants in the "update anywhere" derby include ETI's *Extract*, Praxis's *OmniReplicator*, and Oracle's 7.1's *Symmetric Replication* service. Be warned, though, that true replicas can corrupt data.

The Future Warehouses

We move snapshots of the OLTP systems over to the data warehouse as a series of data layers, much like geologic layers. Like geologists, we then dig down through the layers to understand what our business was like at previous points in time.

— Ralph Kimball
(1996) [6]

Data warehouses will pop up everywhere. We expect most personal computer users to have private data warehouses with hot links to information sources all over the globe. We expect large data warehouses to play an important role as data stores for the information highway. The replication technology that was presented in this chapter is an embryonic version of what can be done. In addition to moving tabular data, we'll soon be moving BLOBs of video and sound from the large data warehouses in the sky to our private and departmental warehouses (and vice versa). The EIS/DSS technology will help us distill massive amounts of data into a few visual pieces of information that we can quickly understand and use (see the next chapter). We expect to see personal versions of these currently expensive tools sell in the volume market for $50 (or less). In addition to business information, we expect the warehouses to package tons of information related to personal, educational, and consumer topics. Finally, we expect that object request brokers—such as CORBA and Network OLE—will increasingly be used to integrate the various functional components in a data warehouse; ORBs will let us create more "holistic" warehouses using open middleware.

---

[6] Source: Ralph Kimball, **The Data Warehouse Toolkit** (Wiley, 1996).

Chapter 13

EIS/DSS: From Queries, To OLAP, To Data Mining

---

*T*he whole concept behind decision-support systems is to understand "what if?" rather than report on "what happened." To do this you need a complex understanding of "what has happened."

> — **Dennis Byron**
> **Application Development Trends**
> **(June, 1995)**

*T*here's gold in the data, but we just can't tell how much without exploration.

> — **Don Haderle, Director of Database**
> **IBM**
> **(October, 1995)**

Executive Information Systems (EIS) and *Decision-Support Systems (DSS)* provide the human interface to data warehouses. The better the tools are, the more value we get from our investment in these warehouses. The tools literally bring the information to our fingertips. Not surprisingly, the EIS/DSS tools market is on a high-growth trajectory. The IDC market research firm predicts that the EIS market will climb from \$339 million in 1994 to \$1 billion in 1997.[1] These steep growth numbers are, of course, creating a highly competitive market. Vendors compete by offering products with more functions and ease-of-use. EIS/DSS tools will eventually be priced for volume sales. When this happens, we expect them to become everyday tools—just like today's spreadsheets.

Growth in our business is almost always accompanied by conflicting vendor claims, counter-claims, and an explosion of new acronyms. EIS/DSS is no exception. Figure 13-1 shows the evolution of EIS/DSS tools. As you can see, we've introduced some strange new terminology; it comes with the new territory. The figure should give you the idea that EIS/DSS tools are getting smarter each day (at least they're not standing still). The holy grail of the EIS/DSS tools business is the "hands-off" query. This means that we should eventually be able to sit back and dispatch our personal information agents—armed with search algorithms—on data discovery missions. But we're not quite there, yet. This chapter is an overview of the state of EIS/DSS tools. We start with simple query and analysis tools. We then move to OLAP—an umbrella term for tools that let you view data from multiple perspectives (or dimensions). The next step in the evolutionary ladder is data mining, where the data tells you something about itself; it discovers hidden patterns. Ultimately, there are personal information agents that resemble Danny De Vito's data valet.

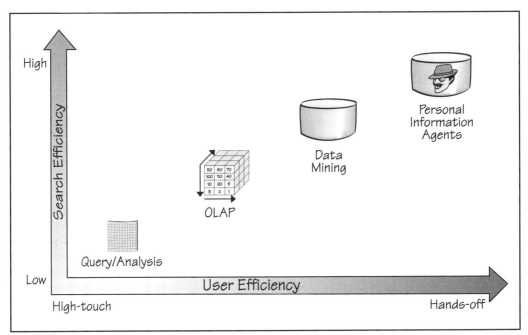

Figure 13-1. The Evolution of EIS/DSS Tools.

---

[1] Note that EIS/DSS is a subset of the data warehouse market.

QUERY/REPORTING TOOLS

Your typical RDBMS query will tell you what, not why.

> — *Christine Comaford, Columnist, PC Week*
> *(February, 1996)*

Query and data analysis tools let you formulate a query without writing a program or learning SQL. You point-and-click to generate the SELECT statements and the search criteria (the WHERE clause). The tool then displays the results in some understandable form—usually a table. Most query tools provide common business graphics—including bar charts, pie charts, histograms, and line graphs—to let you chart the data that's pulled in by a query. Most tools let you run the query and fill in a form or spreadsheet from the output. Some tools let you run the query and then geographically map the output using a map package. Most tools provide scripting facilities that let you automatically schedule the execution of queries and reports.

The better query tools provide safeguards to prevent you from submitting "runaway queries." These queries return very large result sets. The most common safeguard is for the tool to provide a *query governor* that kills a query if it takes too long to execute or returns an excessive number of rows. Some governors cache large result sets on the server and return it to the client in fixed increments. Others display a dialog that shows you the number of rows that will be returned by a query—if the number is excessive, you should be able to click a "Cancel" button.

Examples of query and data analysis tools include Gupta's *Quest*, Trinzic's *Forest & Trees*, SAS Institute's *SAS System*, IBM's *Visualizer*, Brio's *DataPrism*, Intersolv's *Q+E*, IBI's *Focus*, Software AG's *Esperant*, and Cognos's *Impromptu*.

 Tools for Querying Your BLOBs

Briefing

The latest development in query tools is the *BLOB query*, which lets you search for patterns within the BLOB fields in a database. A BLOB, as you may recall, is a SQL-92 data type that is used as a container for large text documents or multimedia data. The good news is that there are now tools for querying BLOB contents (at least BLOBs that contain pictures). These tools let you tell the DBMS "find all pictures that look like this one."

A BLOB query tool lets you search for images in a data warehouse by color, texture, shape, and position. You can create a visual query by manipulating controls and color wheels. You then specify the area in the target pictures where the search is to be applied. We anticipate that BLOB-based query technology will soon be extended to include audio clips and text. Examples of BLOB-based query tools are IBM's *Ultimedia Manager* and Virage Inc.'s *Query Dialog.* Silicon Graphics has a beta release of a BLOB query tool with 3-D rendering. ☐

OLAP AND MULTIDIMENSIONAL DATA

Think of an OLAP data structure as a Rubik's Cube of data that users can twist and twirl in different ways to work through what-if and what-happened scenarios.

— Lee Thé, Editor, Datamation
(May, 1995)

Online Analytical Processing (OLAP) tools create multidimensional data views on top of ordinary 2-D SQL databases (or using specialized multidimensional databases). OLAP's multidimensional access lets you formulate more sophisticated queries, and then look at the results accordingly. Think of OLAP as a multidimensional spreadsheet with multiple axes. For example, you could have a product database that you access via multiple dimensions such as time, region, customer, store, price, and sales. The idea is to let you explore data using different dimensions. OLAP lets you ask the following question: What are the sales—by product, by store, and by month?

OLAP's multidimensional model makes it easier to visualize data. Instead of navigating through multiple tables and rows, you look at data through multidimensional views. Relational/OLAP tools provide this function by introducing a layer of abstraction on top of SQL databases that hides the physical structure of normalized relational tables. Instead, you get to see multidimensional views of that same data. It's like magic. Figure 13-2 shows the difference between relational and multidimensional views. In the example, using OLAP you could analyze the Hawaii tourist industry by island, week, promotions, hotel category, car rentals, promotions, GNP, and so on. OLAP obviously provides a more intuitive way to look at data, especially if you used a spreadsheet's pivoting feature.

The OLAP model comfortably handles data in ten or less dimensions. Beyond this, servers fail from index overload. In addition, our brains may also fail from n-dimensional visual overload. The OLAP tool vendors are split into three camps:

■ **Relational OLAP tools**. These are OLAP client tools that create multidimensional views by extracting data from ordinary SQL databases. These tools simulate multidimensional visualizations using sophisticated indexing, caching,

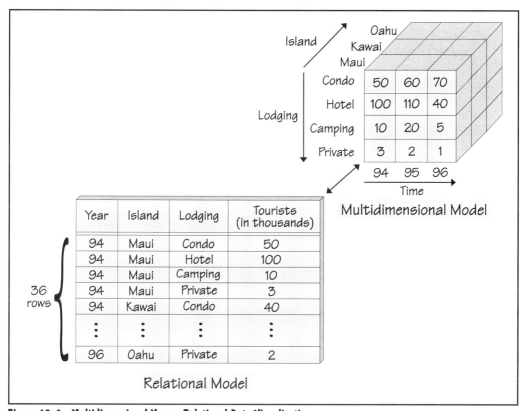

Figure 13-2. Multidimensional Versus Relational Data Visualizations.

and metadata techniques. Tools in this category include Brio's *DataPivot*, Business Objects' *Mercury*, Cognos' *PowerPlay*, Andyne's *Pablo*, Dimensional Insight's *CrossTarget*, MicroStrategy's *DSS/Agent*, and Stanford Technology Group's *MetaCube* family.[2]

■ *OLAP-savvy SQL servers*. The vendors in this camp offer specialized SQL databases that are optimized for running OLAP-savvy queries. The specialized SQL database vendors obtain performance gains by using special indexing techniques, parallel joins, OLAP-savvy SQL generators, and SQL query extensions that help the database engine optimize the query. Vendors in this category include Red Brick's *Red Brick Warehouse* and MicroStrategy's *DSS/Server*.

■ *Multidimensional DBMSs (MDBMSs)*. Rather than storing data as keyed records in tables, MDBMS provide specialized database engines to store data in arrays along related dimensions called *hypercubes*. Most MDBMSs use index-

---

[2] Acquisitions are common occurrences in the tumultuous OLAP market; for example, Stanford Technologies was recently acquired by Informix.

ing-intensive schemes to optimize access to these cubes. MDBMS vendors typically provide OLAP client tools that are optimized for their engines—there are no standards for MDBMS data access. OLAP/MDBMS tools include Arbor's *Essbase*, Kenan's *Accumate*, Pilot's *Lightship Server*, Sinper's *TM/1*, Oracle/IRI's *Express*, Dimensional Insight's *CrossTarget/Diver*, SAS *OLAP++*, Information Advantage's *DecisionSuite Server*, and Holistic System's *Holos*. Commshare's *Commander OLAP* is a front-end tool that uses the Essbase MDBMS engine.

As you can see, you're faced with quite a few OLAP implementation choices, which is normal at this stage for a hot new technology. In the next Soapbox, we speculate on how this technology may evolve.

OLAP: To RDBMS or to MDBMS?

Soapbox

The problem is that under the covers, most OLAP servers are extracting data from a two-dimensional DBMS and populating a multidimensional data cube.

> — *Christine Comaford, Columnist*
> *PC Week*
> *(February, 1996)*

Everyone agrees that OLAP is wonderful. But the million dollar question is: Do you need an MDBMS to get the full benefits of OLAP? Or, can you get them with your trusty old RDBMS? The proponents of MDBMS make the case that you need a change. They make the following arguments:

■ **MDBMS saves you money.** In theory, MDBMSs require less disk space because they use sparse matrices to store data in any number of dimensions, and they often relate the data using an embedded calculation language. Consequently, MDBMSs make better use of the underlying hardware by providing software that is fully optimized for OLAP. In contrast, the RDBMS vendors take the brute force approach by throwing costly massively parallel hardware at the problem—for example, Tandem Himalaya, IBM SP2, and AT&T GIS 3600 (i.e., Teradata).

■ **MDBMS queries are an order of magnitude faster.** MDBMS vendors will show you benchmark results that will make you salivate.

■ **Oracle cried uncle when it bought an MDBMS company.** In June 1995, Oracle purchased IRI—the maker of *Express MDB*—for $300 million. The proponents of MDBMS consider the purchase to be an admission—by the market leader—that MDBMSs are better suited for OLAP than RDBMSs.

Of course, none of these arguments carry much weight in the RDBMS camp. They will quickly point out that:

- **MDBMS data has to be loaded before you can do a query.** MDBMS queries slow down considerably if you first have to load a gigabyte of data from an RDBMS source (the warehouse).

- **MDBMSs are not standardized.** There are no MDBMS standards today.

- **MDBMSs lack a server architecture.** Almost all MDBMSs are built as single user systems. They don't have a multiuser server infrastructure and the corresponding client/server middleware.

- **MDBMSs are not suitable for ad hoc queries.** They only work with predefined hypercubes.

- **RDBMSs are introducing new query smarts.** RDBMSs were traditionally tuned for OLTP, where the average transaction consists of a few database calls. However, because of the dramatic growth in warehousing, DBMS vendors are in a race to introduce better query capabilities. Their databases must now be able to handle queries that issue hundreds of database calls, some of which may need to scan many gigabytes of data.

The DBMS vendors claim they can now meet these new challenges. For example, IBM shipped with DB2 V2 a new cost-based query optimizer based on its "Starburst" research. Sybase augmented System 11 with *Sybase IQ*, which introduces a low-overhead bitmap indexing structure that makes it affordable to fully index an entire database. And Oracle will ship bitmap indexing and a new parallel query optimizer with Oracle7.3 in 1996. If these products don't do it for you, there is always Red Brick.

So who is right? It's obviously not a black and white issue. Both the MDBMS and RDBMS vendors will plug the holes in their products and do whatever it takes to ride the OLAP wave. However, as the Object Database (ODBMS) vendors bitterly discovered, RDBMSs are "king of the hill" and will not be easily displaced by superior technology alone. The next best thing is to co-opt them via coexistence. For example, MDBMSs can become add-ons that play within the DBMS framework. But, you can see how this is playing itself out in the IRI/Oracle marriage; Oracle is in the process of subsuming the MDBMS. If Oracle succeeds, an MDBMS will become nothing more than a new *multidimensional* data type within an RDBMS. ❑

Data Mining

Data mining lets the power of computers do the work of sifting through your vast data stores. Tireless and relentless searching can find the tiny nugget of gold in a mountain of data slag.

> — *Edmund X. DeJesus, Senior Editor*
> *BYTE Magazine*
> *(October, 1995)*

Data-mining tools help you sift through vast quantities of information looking for valuable patterns in the data. A pattern may be as simple as the realization that 80% of male diaper buyers also buy beer. Data mining is the process of discovering unsuspected patterns. Some early data mining pioneers are reporting 1000% return on investment. For example, a department-store chain discovered that shoplifting of batteries, film, and midpriced pens was costing it $60,000 a month. Consequently, these items were moved to more visible store locations, saving the chain over $700,000 annually.

Data mining looks for patterns and groupings that you may have overlooked in your own analysis of a set of data. The tool typically performs a "fuzzy" search, with little or no guidance from an end user. In data mining, the tool does the discovery and tells you something, instead of you asking it a question. In contrast, query tools and OLAP return records that satisfy a query that you must first formulate. Instead of responding to low-level queries, data mining tools deal with fuzzy searches. They don't assume that you know exactly what you're seeking. Most tools use the following search methods:

■ *Associations* look for patterns where the presence of something implies the presence of something else. For example: "Scuba gear buyers are good candidates for Australian vacations."

■ *Sequential patterns* look for chronological occurrences. For example: "When the price of stock X goes up by 10%, the price of stock Y goes down by 15% a week later."

■ *Clusterings* look for groupings and high-level classifications. For example: "Over 70% of undecided voters have incomes of over $60,000, age brackets between 40 and 50, and live in XYZ neighborhood."

The output of the discovery process is often represented in the form of *if-then* rules; for example:

```
If
   Age = 42; and
   Car_Make = Volvo; and
   No_of_Children < 3
Then
   Mailorder_Response = 15%
```

Data mining tools are beginning to be used in many industries. Health researchers use them to discover patterns affecting the success of back surgery. Banks use them to detect credit card fraud and predict which customers are likely to change their credit card affiliations. Attorneys use them to select juries and to analyze voting patterns of Supreme Court justices. Stockbrokers use them to identify stock movements and trading patterns. Insurance companies use them to identify risky customers and behavior patterns. As you can see from these examples, data mining is the ultimate "Big Brother" tool, but it can also be put to good uses.

Data mining tools are still in their pioneer days. Examples of these pioneering data mining tools are ATTAR's *Data Analyser*, Software AG's *NetMap*, A.C. Nielsen's *Spotlight*, and IntelligenceWare's *IDIS*. In addition, IBM is working with select customers on a data mining product called *DataDiscovery*; Pilot Software is beta testing a data mining add-in for its *LightShip* product, which it plans to ship in mid-96.

Personal Information Agents

Agents are mobile applications that are launched on data warehouses to perform specific queries or to search for patterns in data. Most agents are rules-based alerting programs that say, "If this happens, do that." Because agents are ad hoc and scripted, they should not be turned loose on production systems. You should use them to discover unsuspected occurrences within a data warehouse environment. The agents should alert you when something unusual happens. Agenting capabilities are finding their way in today's OLAP and query tools. Examples include Comshare's *Commander OLAP with Detect and Alert*, Trinzic's *Forest & Trees*, Brio's *BrioQuery*, and Information Advantage's *DecisionSuite InfoAlert*.

Conclusion

With the increasing complexity of today's society, the information we can obtain through data mining can be dramatically more valuable than any other asset.

— Dr. Kamran Parsaye, CEO
Information Discovery
(April, 1996)

EIS/DSS tools, OLAP, and multidimensional databases are the hot new technologies of data warehousing. Startups are coming and going, and the market has yet to settle. The best we could do in this chapter was to provide you with a framework for looking at these new technologies; it's a good first step toward understanding what these technologies can do for you. It's still too early to pick winners—the fun is just starting.

Chapter 14

Database: Meet the Players

We have seen much change in the DBMS market, and we believe there will continue to be major changes through the turn of the century. We expect the big vendors to get bigger, additional smaller niche players to fall by the wayside, some of the larger vendors to have problems, and even some new vendors to emerge.

— *Gartner Group*
(February, 1995)

We've been dropping names of database products right and left in the last few chapters without formally introducing you to the players. We wanted to first give you a flavor for the technology before introducing the products. In this chapter, we provide a snapshot of the database market and discuss the current trends. Then we formally introduce the key players most of whom are already household names.

THE DATABASE CLIENT/SERVER MARKET

According to IDC, the SQL database market revenues for 1995 were $5.9 billion and still growing at a rate of 30% per year. Less than 10% of the world's data is stored in relational databases, so there's a lot of growth opportunity ahead. With their new support for BLOBs and object extensions, relational databases are becoming suitable stores for faxes, images, fingerprints, HTML files, spreadsheets, movies, soundclips, e-mail messages, and others. All SQL database applications on Net-Ware, OS/2, and Windows NT follow the client/server model. New database applications on Unix, OS/400s, and mainframes are evenly split between those that use the multiuser terminal model and those that use the client/server model.

TRENDS

At age seventeen, the relational database industry is still in its teens. New developments in this rapid-growth industry are a way of life. The trend toward online data access is unstoppable. DBMSs can now store enormous quantities of online data; EIS/DSS tools make it easy to access this data. Here's a snapshot of the major movements that we're seeing in this industry:

- *SQL databases as portable operating systems*. SQL database engines are becoming portable server environments. They do much more than just manage data—they provide almost complete server environments. All the major SQL vendors, except Microsoft, provide portable server environments that run on multiple platforms—including Unixes, OS/2, NT, NetWare, and mainframes. In addition to managing ordinary data, the environments are now expanding into multimedia, fingerprints, images, sound, video, and multidimensional data. The environments come with their own procedural logic—including stored procedures, triggers, rules, alerts, assertions, and user-defined abstract data types. The environments also include highly non-standard but fully portable crossplatform 4GLs and tools.

- *SQL databases from laptops to teraflops*. SQL database vendors are expanding beyond their departmental server niche and moving into two new areas: 1) Desktops and laptops, where they're replacing the Paradoxes, FoxPros, and XBase engines, thus becoming Trojan horses for production-strength SQL servers; and 2) Massively parallel databases, where they're competing head-on with traditional mainframes to become the new enterprise servers.

- *SQL databases as data warehouses*. SQL databases are expanding beyond their traditional OLTP and departmental decision-support functions to uncharted new territories such as the lucrative data warehousing market.

- *SQL data replicated everywhere*. For early SQL practitioners, redundant data was a sin. Elaborate normalization schemes were created to cut down on wasted duplication and to rationalize the data. Today, the new religion is called *replication*. With the cost of storage devices hitting new lows, you can now carry an entire data warehouse in your laptop. You simply replicate data to wherever you need it. For SQL databases, it's good-bye to the age of scarcity.

■ ***SQL databases discover the Web***. For SQL database vendors, the World Wide Web is potentially the land of milk and honey. They want to capitalize on the opportunity to make SQL data seamlessly available to millions of information-hungry Web surfers. The challenge is to create a commercial infrastructure to charge for these billions of new accesses.

Of course, database vendors can't cover every niche, which is why there are niche players. The predominant niches are *Object Databases (ODBMSs)*, with 1995 revenues of approximately $150 million (and growing at 50%). The niche players will have a strong market in complex online information delivery, especially for the Web. Examples of these systems include document and image content searches, BLOB management, time series, and anything that requires complex data types.

THE PLAYERS

Figure 14-1 shows how the database pie was divided in 1994. Note that the chart did not include Microsoft in 1994. However, IDC estimates that Microsoft became a major player in 1995, with total database revenues of $435 million.[1] Also note that the IBM numbers include both IMS and DB2 revenues—IMS is a hierarchical database. Computer Associates became a major player after it acquired Ingres.

Gartner Group predicts that by the year 2000, the "Big Five" database vendors will be IBM, Informix, Microsoft, Oracle, and Sybase.[2] The second tier will include

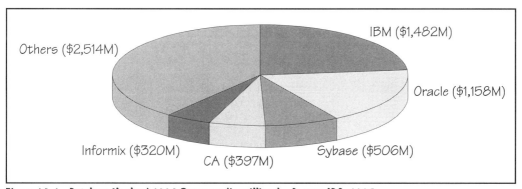

Figure 14-1. Database Vendors' 1994 Revenues (in millions). Source: IDC, 1995.

---

[1] Microsoft's $435 million in database sales breaks down into: $85 million for SQL Server, $300 million for Access, and $85 million for Visual FoxPro.

[2] Source: Gartner Group, "The Future of Databases" (August 9, 1995).

Computer Associates, because of Ingres; Progress Software, because of its vertical market penetration; and Tandem's NonStop SQL, because it has better than 99% scalability when moving from 16 to 64 processors. Gartner's year 2000 predictions seem to indicate that the database market will consolidate around today's winners. The remaining sections look at what these vendors offer today.

Oracle

Oracle continued to carve out mindshare in 1995 by offering its *Oracle7.1* database across more than 90 platforms (60 of which are Unixes). Oracle provides a very consistent environment across all these platforms—from tools, to administration interfaces, to the Data Definition Language (DDL) and SQL directory. Oracle takes advantage of SMP on NetWare, OS/2, NT, AIX, and SCO. On the high-end, it supports massively parallel databases on specialized hardware such as IBM's SP2 (loosely-coupled RS/6000s) and AT&T's GIS 3600 (also known as Teradata). On the low-end, Oracle announced its *Personal Oracle7* and *Oracle7 Workgroup Server*.

Oracle now supports a parallel query optimizer, bidirectional data replication, and distributed database features. Oracle7 supports BLOBs, stored procedures, and triggers. *Oracle7.3*—introduced in early 1996—improves data warehousing performance and provides new media and text add-ons; it also includes a built-in HTTP server and a better authentication mechanism. The add-on options include an e-mail server, OLAP, and a video server.

Oracle8—expected in 1997—will support object extensions based on SQL 3. It will also include *Project Sedona*—a "component server" that supports CORBA, OLE, SQL 3, and Java objects. Sedona is a 3-tier client/server object architecture. The Sedona server components—or business objects—will be able to serve clients on either CORBA or OLE object brokers; the objects will store their state in the Oracle8 database. Sedona will include a component repository and a visual development tool.

IBM's DB2 Family

IBM revamped its relational database family in 1995 with the introduction of *DB2 2.1*—also known as "Common Server." This is the portable version of DB2 that runs on OS/2, NT, AIX, HP-UX, Solaris, and other Unixes. The Common Server DB2 supports advanced object extensions, ODBC, CLI, triggers, BLOBs, SMP (where available), and an advanced cost-based query optimizer. The mainframe and AS/400 versions of DB2—not currently part of the DB2 Common Server code base—were also upgraded to support more parallelism, a smarter query optimizer, and stored procedures.

In 1995, IBM also introduced *DB2 Parallel Edition for SP2*—a shared-nothing parallel database server. At the low-end, IBM is now offering the Lotus *Approach* SQL database with it's Basic-like scripting features, wizards, and easy-to-use front-end. In addition, DB2 for OS/2 is selling about 200,000 copies per year.

Informix

Informix is the fastest growing database company in the Unix market, with annual database license sales growing at 50%. Informix started out as a department server for value added resellers (VARs) with a low-end product called *Standard Edition*. In the last two years, the company shifted its focus to the high-end of the database market by rearchitecting the core database for parallelism. They wrote 800,000 lines of new code. The result was Informix 7.1, which supports clustered SMP. In early 1996, Informix introduced a massively parallel database product—*Informix 8.0 XPS*—that runs on IBM SP2, AT&T GIS 3600, and the ICL/Fujitsu Goldrush.

Informix supports stored procedures, triggers, BLOBs, and the typical SQL paraphernalia. Its forte is OLTP. However, with its newfound scalability Informix is now in a good position to effectively compete in the lucrative data warehousing market.

Sybase

Sybase was back in business in late 1995 with the shipment of *System 11*. The previous release of the product—*System 10*—was a market failure. It performed poorly and could not scale past four machines. Consequently, Sybase locked itself out of the lucrative SMP market. Worse, its customers voted against the system by not upgrading to it. Now all of this is changing with System 11, which is getting excellent reviews for its SMP prowess. The product currently runs on DEC Unix, HP-UX, AIX, Solaris, and Windows NT. System 11 scales on the high-end with *Sybase MPP*, which serves as a high-end informational database engine on massively parallel hardware—including AT&T GIS 3600, IBM SP2, and Sun SPARC-servers.

Sybase pioneered stored procedures and triggers. It supports BLOBs and many avant-garde SQL features. With its new System 11, the company is moving into data warehousing in addition to its traditional OLTP stomping ground. Sybase recently went on an acquisition binge. It acquired both PowerSoft and the Watcom database engine, which it renamed *SQL Anywhere*. It will use this slim but powerful desktop database to establish a presence in the low-end of the market. Sybase is also expanding into the middleware business and is adding MOM capabilities to its SQL databases.

Microsoft

Microsoft is fast becoming a strategic player in the database market. The company fields its flagship *SQL Server* in the high-end and the high-volume *Access* on the desktop. Microsoft's entry in the "serious" database market was a catalyst for driving down the prices of competitive products. Microsoft is the only database vendor that does not aspire to run its engine on every platform—they only do Windows and Windows NT.

In 1994, Microsoft broke up with Sybase and took over the development of MS SQL Server. In September 1995, Microsoft introduced *SQL Server 6.0*—a low-cost, robust server that fixed many of the deficiencies of their previous product, SQL Server 4.2. Even though the new product still has the Sybase look and feel, Microsoft says that it has changed about 60% of the code.

According to benchmarks run by PC Week Labs, the new product is about 12% faster than the old one and slightly more SMP-scalable. The new SQL Server is tightly integrated with NT's SMP engine, system management, and administration. Microsoft now has an improved cost-based query optimizer. In addition, Microsoft's version of Transact SQL is now SQL-92 compliant and supports scrollable cursors. A key feature of SQL Server 6.0 is its new easy-to-use replication service. It introduces a publish-and-subscribe metaphor—the source database publishes rows and tables, and then holds them until SQL Server copies them to the subscribers.

SQL Server 6.5—now in beta—provides substantial new additions. It includes a new *Web Assistant* that helps you specify queries; it will then generate HTML documents for you. You can automatically run these queries at regular intervals to generate Web pages "on-the-fly." The new release introduces two new extended SQL commands—*Cube* and *Rollup*—that can be useful in data warehousing situations. They generate result sets that only contain aggregates, such as running totals. In addition, SQL Server 6.5 extends data replication to include subscribers from Microsoft Access, Oracle, DB2, and other ODBC-compliant databases (the replication is one-way only). Another new feature is *row-level locking*, which SQL Server needed to stay on par with its competitors. The most important new feature is the *Distributed Transaction Coordinator (DTC)*. It is a built-in TP Monitor that uses OLE TP to coordinate transactions, which can span across more than one SQL Server.[3]

So what makes Microsoft—a relative latecomer—such a formidable force in the database market? We can think of four good reasons: 1) High-volume desktop products like *Access* drag sales of SQL Server—the two million copies of Access can

---

[3] DTC hides the nastiness of two-phase commit programming. The transaction objects can be initiated either by client applications or from within SQL Server stored procedures.

serve as client front-ends for SQL Server; 2) SQL Server is packaged with Micro-soft's *BackOffice*—it is perceived to be the database server of choice for Microsoft's immensely popular "front-office" suite; 3) SQL Server is priced to kill; and 4) SQL Server is highly-integrated with NT and perceived as being the database of choice for that platform.

Significant Others: NonStop SQL, Illustra, and MATISSE

Tandem's linear scalability to over 20,000 TPC-C's demonstrates the power of shared-nothing, parallel architectures.

— Meta Group
(February, 1995)

In addition to the "Big Five," you should keep an eye three avant-garde databases: Tandem's *NonStop SQL*, Informix's *Illustra*, and ADB's *MATISSE*. Here's why:

■ **Tandem's NonStop SQL** pioneered parallel SQL databases and shared-nothing, massively parallel architectures. Tandem is a strong player in the high-end OLTP market, and it is now doing very well in the massively parallel data warehousing market. In addition to parallelism, Tandem gives you fault-tolerance for free. It also provides close to linear scalability across thousands of processors using the new *ServerNet* bus.

■ **Illustra** is the company that pioneered object extensions on top of normal SQL database engines. Illustra's *DataBlades* extend SQL databases with new complex data types—for example, time series, text, image, 2D spatial, and 3D spatial. Illustra lets you store sets of objects in a single column and provides an extended SQL syntax to reference these objects. Illustra's success is forcing the major database vendors to reveal their "object hand." For example, IBM's new DB2 now includes object extensions that are similar to Illustra's DataBlades. Oracle also promises to add an object layer on top of its DBMS in its forthcoming *Oracle8*.

When Informix decided it didn't have a viable object/relational product, it solved its problem by buying one. On December 20, 1995 it acquired Illustra for $385 million—Santa was good to Illustra. Informix is now integrating Illustra's DataBlade technology into the Informix engine. The new Informix/Illustra database—called the *Universal Server*—is expected in 1997, or whenever the 1.5 million lines of Informix relational code are combined with 1 million lines of Illustra "object/relational" code.

■ *MATISSE* is an object/relational database that really scales. The MATISSE engine is uniquely tuned to support large BLOBs. It can handle up to 2^{64} gigabyte-sized objects and stream them at almost native disk speeds. The engine is also a screamer when running ordinary SQL TPC-C benchmarks. So you can have an object database that does SQL and BLOBs too. This unique combination makes MATISSE a very good embedded database for the Web.[4]

In addition to the three we picked, hundreds of innovative products are seeking their niches in the very lucrative online database market. The explosion of the new media types—especially on the Web—is creating a lot of new opportunity. Of course, the "Big Five" cannot overhaul their engines overnight to support the new data types—they must first meet the needs of their installed base. As a result, they're acquiring niche players left and right to fill the holes. In the race to be king of the database hill, anything goes.

---

[4] Warning: One of your authors is a senior executive at ADB MATISSE. However, she swears that it's all true.

Chapter 15

Data Warehouses: Prism, IBM, and Sybase

Data warehouses will become strategic imperatives, not luxuries, for most organizations.

— *Gartner Group*
(August, 1995)

With over 15 data warehouse "frameworks" and 100 commercial products to choose from, which do you cover in a product chapter? The three frameworks we picked are: Prism's *Warehouse Manager*, IBM's *Information Warehouse*, and Sybase's *Warehouse Works*.[1] Prism was founded by W.H. Inmon, "the father of data warehousing." It provides a database-secular product with hot features. IBM introduced the first data warehouse framework in 1991 and shipped the first complete line of data warehouse products in 1993. In late 1995, IBM introduced two innovative warehousing products: *DataJoiner* and *Visual Warehouse*. Finally, Sybase represents a stripped-down, fully-tuned data warehouse product offering.

---

[1] Frameworks is an overloaded term. In this case, it means a collection of products and their common protocols.

We picked these frameworks because we are familiar with the products and also because they're a representative sample of what's currently available. We hope you can live with our selection. We are in no way implying that these are the best products on the market—the technology is much too fluid for such endorsements.

PRISM WAREHOUSE MANAGER

It is necessary to approach the data warehouse holistically, treating it as a whole and seeing all the obstacles rather than analyzing it piece by piece.

> — *William H. Inmon, Prism Technology*
> *(March, 1995)*

Prism provides all the data warehousing pieces except for the database engine and EIS/DSS tools. Instead of providing a SQL database, Prism runs on everyone else's engine—including IBM's *DB2 family*, Tandem's *NonStop SQL*, Red Brick's *Red Brick Warehouse*, Sybase's *Sybase 10*, Microsoft's *SQL Server*, Oracle's *Oracle V7.1*, and AT&T's *Teradata*. Instead of providing EIS/DSS tools, Prism lets you plug-and-play any ODBC-compliant tool. Prism likes to do joint bids with Business Objects, Inc., an EIS/DSS tool provider.

Figure 15-1 shows the constituents of the Prism Warehouse Manager framework. The three pieces that Prism provides are the *Warehouse Manager*, *Changed Data Capture*, and *Directory Manager*. The rest of the solution is provided by Prism third parties—including the database informational database and EIS/DSS tools. Of course, Prism makes sure that the pieces work together (Prism offers a wide range of on-site consulting services to help you with your system integration).

■ ***Warehouse Manager*** extracts operational data from a wide selection of databases (see Figure 15-1), integrates the data from the various sources, and then transforms and loads the integrated data into a target database. The Warehouse Manager lets you define the mappings between the sources and their targets using a point-and-click graphical user interface that runs on Windows or OS/2. Prism generates the underlying code for moving the data. It also automatically creates and manages metadata about the extracted data. Prism interacts with multivendor relational database engines using SQL-92; it automatically generates COBOL code for the extraction and transformation programs.

■ ***Changed Data Capture*** refreshes the data warehouse after you first load it. The program captures changes in the source data and applies them to the target. The changed data can be asynchronously applied to the target at intervals that you define.

Chapter 15. Data Warehouses: Prism, IBM, and Sybase

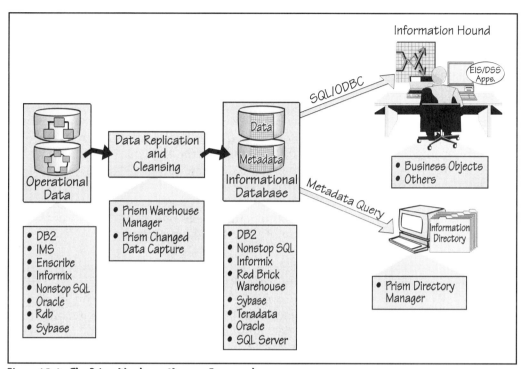

Figure 15-1. The Prism Warehouse Manager Framework.

■ *Directory Manager* keeps track of both technical and business metadata. It also provides a client front-end (OS/2 or Unix) that lets you navigate the metadata and create customized views of metadata objects using familiar business terms. The directory answers these questions: How do I find the subject I need? What is the original source of the data? How were these derivations created? What queries do I use to access this data? The technical views contain physical descriptions of the metadata such as table descriptions, attributes, and mappings. Prism stores its metadata in the informational database. The Directory Manager lets you import and export metadata using the *CASE Data Interchange Format (CDIF)*. Directory Manager V2—introduced in early 1996—provides direct links to HP's *Intelligent Warehouse*, MicroStrategy's *DSS Agent*, and others.

Prism—founded in 1991—is a purebred data warehousing company. It currently employs over 100 people. Prism's strength is that it gives customers total freedom of database platform choice. You get to choose the database platform that best meets your needs. Its main weakness is the lack of an integrated systems management tool.

IBM'S INFORMATION WAREHOUSE

IBM's *Information Warehouse* is closest to providing an integrated top-to-bottom data warehousing solution. The IBM solution includes the informational database, replication and copy management tools, an information catalog, a self-contained datamart, EIS/DSS tools, and an integrated systems management tool. IBM also provides a workflow engine that lets you further automate the warehousing process and integrate it with the rest of the enterprise. IBM publishes the APIs to its various data warehousing tools—including EIS/DSS, replication, information directory, and system management. As a result, it helped create a market for third-party tools that operate within the IBM framework.

Figure 15-2 shows the various IBM products that make up the IBM data warehousing solution. Here's a brief description of what these products do:

■ *DataPropagator Relational* provides replication with aggregation and data cleansing among the DB2 family—including DB2 on OS/2, MVS, AIX, VM, OS/400, HP-UX, Solaris, and Windows NT. The target warehouse can subscribe to updates or full refreshes and also pick the time when it wants them applied. DataPropagator has a unique two-part architecture that consists of: 1) a *staging* component, which executes at the source data site; and 2) an *apply* component, which either executes at the source or target site. The staging area is simply a relational database log (or a queue) of changes to the source data; it can be

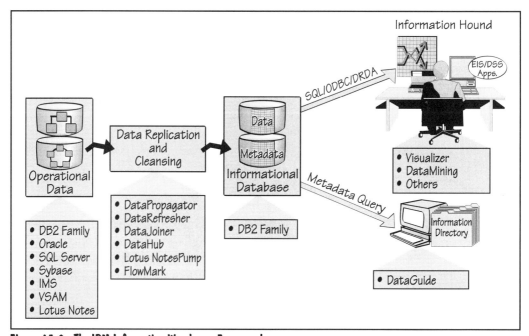

Figure 15-2. The IBM Information Warehouse Framework.

populated from different data sources (see following bullets). The apply component pulls the changes from the staging area to the target at user-defined intervals. Apply can transform the staged data before it is copied using aggregations, joins, or any SQL operation.

■ *DataPropagator NonRelational* extracts IMS data and brings it into DataPropagator's staging area. DataPropagator then replicates the data from the staging area to its subscribers—the target warehouses.

■ *DataRefresher* extracts VSAM and flat file data and brings it into DataPropagator's staging area. DataPropagator then replicates the data from the staging area to target warehouse subscribers.

■ *DataJoiner* transparently accesses and joins data from a variety of relational and non-relational sources—including Sybase, Oracle, SQL Server, DB2 family products, IMS, VSAM, and any ODBC-compliant data source. The extracted data is brought into DataPropagator's staging area for replication to target warehouse subscribers.

■ *Lotus NotesPump* extracts data from Notes databases and then brings it into DataPropagator's staging area for replication to target warehouse subscribers.

■ *DataHub* is an OS/2 product that provides a single point of management for a data warehouse. In addition to letting you manage the replication of data, DataHub provides a uniform "drag-and-drop" environment for managing heterogeneous databases—mostly the multiplatform DB2 family. You can display database objects, manage authorizations, and run database utilities. The tool provides a scheduler for automating the execution of tasks at specific times. With the release of Version 2, a DataHub node can participate in global management by generating SNMP alerts on behalf of the resources that it manages.

■ *FlowMark* is a workflow management product that lets you further automate your warehouse by managing the execution of multi-stepped warehouse processes. For example, you could use FlowMark to perform the following tasks: 1) schedule a multisource data capture, 2) copy the results to a warehouse, 3) run a set of OLAP queries, 4) format a report, and 5) e-mail the results to a distribution list.

■ *DB2 family* products provide the SQL engine for the informational database. DB2 runs on multiple platforms—including OS/2, NT, various Unixes, OS/400, and mainframes. DB2 on AIX and DB2 on MVS now provide support for parallel queries and joins. These two functions should help accelerate searches in large data warehouse environments. When your warehouse gets past a certain size, you either need a massively parallel SQL database or a specialized multidimensional database engine to run OLAP-intensive queries.

- **DataGuide** provides an information directory that lets you discover what data is available. DBAs can drill-down into the technical views of the metadata. Information hounds see a normal directory of business objects. Once you locate a business object, you can launch it by selecting the start function; DataGuide automatically maintains associations between data objects and the programs that manipulate them. IBM defines a format for importing and exporting metadata to and from DataGuide. IBM currently provides metadata bridges for a variety of products—including Oracle, Sybase, Bachman DBA, and Microsoft Excel.

- **Visualizer** is IBM's premier EIS/DSS product. Other IBM EIS/DSS products include the venerable *Application System (AS)*, *Query Management Facility (QMF)*, and the object-based *Data Interpretation System (DIS)*—the old Metaphor system. IBM is also working with select customers on *DataDiscovery*, an advanced Data Mining product. The good news is that IBM's data warehouse is really EIS/DSS tool-neutral. The warehouse can be accessed by any EIS/DSS tool that supports any one of these four SQL APIs: EDA/SQL's CLI, ODBC, X/Open CLI, and DRDA's ESQL. IBM encourages an open DSS and EIS tool strategy around these APIs and has made alliances with the major tool vendors. IBM's framework does not preclude an information hound from directly accessing a production database. In contrast, purists like Inmon feel that decision-support applications should only be able to access the informational database.

In addition to these products, IBM provides an "all-in-one" datamart called the *Visual Warehouse*. The product runs on OS/2 and AIX. You can use it to build data warehouses that contain up to 50 GBytes of data and support up to 30 concurrent users. The Visual Warehouse includes a database (DB2 for OS/2 or AIX), an information directory, a data replicator, and an EIS/DSS tool (IBM's Visualizer). The replicator can extract (with refresh) data from multiple sources—including the DB2 family, IMS, VSAM, Oracle, Sybase, and flat files. Visual Warehouse supports the architected Information Warehouse interfaces, which means that it supports most EIS/DSS tools and can extract its metadata from DataGuide and other metadata sources.

In summary, IBM's Information Warehouse is a very complete data warehousing solution, with published APIs for data replication, metadata extracts, and EIS/DSS tool access. So what's wrong this picture? Not much. IBM's Information Warehouse is really a good match if you're in the market for a DB2-centric warehouse. Even though it's extremely powerful and versatile, IBM's replication solution does not currently support update anywhere or synchronous updates. Finally, the IBM Information Warehouse—like most IBM software products—suffers from the "stealth effect." This means that the products exist but because of insufficient marketing, no one seems to be aware of them.

SYBASE WAREHOUSE WORKS

Companies are going to build bigger and bigger warehouses. We're looking at 600-800 GBytes of data with a few customers talking about growing to multiple Terabytes.

> — *Mark Hoffman, CEO*
> *Sybase*
> *(November, 1995)*

Sybase *Warehouse Works* is another example of a database-specific warehousing framework. In this case, the SQL database engine of choice is Sybase System 11—introduced in October 1995, as a high-performance upgrade to System 10. System 11's *Sybase MPP* engine is optimized for parallel queries and runs on parallel hardware platforms such as AT&T's GIS 3600 and IBM's SP2. Sybase—the world's sixth largest software company—considers data warehousing to be one of its three primary markets. To improve its position in the data warehousing market, Sybase recently acquired a diverse set of companies—including Micro Decisionware, Inc. (MDI) for database connectivity, Express Technologies for query acceleration, PowerBuilder for tools, and Complex Architectures for middleware.

In October 1995, Sybase outlined its *Warehouse Works* alliance program that includes published APIs and partner programs with more than 50 vendors. Examples are Dun & Bradstreet's Information Systems, EDS, Price Waterhouse Consulting, Prism, Trinzic, and key EIS/DSS tool vendors—including Pilot, Arbor, MicroStrategy, ETI, Brio, Holistic, and Business Objects.

Figure 15-3 shows the core products that make up the Sybase data warehousing solution. Here's a brief description of what these products do:

- *Sybase Replication Server 11* uses a *replication agent* to read the transaction log of a Sybase database and, at periodic intervals set by a DBA, replicates these changes to the target System 11 warehouse. Sybase recently introduced a replication agent for Oracle. It is also working on a replication agent for its low-end *SQL Anywhere* database—previously known as the Watcom database.

- *Sybase/Legent DB2 replication agent* captures data from a DB2 database and passes it to the Sybase Replicator.

- *Sybase Enterprise Connect*—previously known as the MDI gateway—extracts and transforms data from a variety of databases—including DB2 family, IMS, CICS, and Teradata. MDI transforms data types between systems and provides hooks for data cleansing.

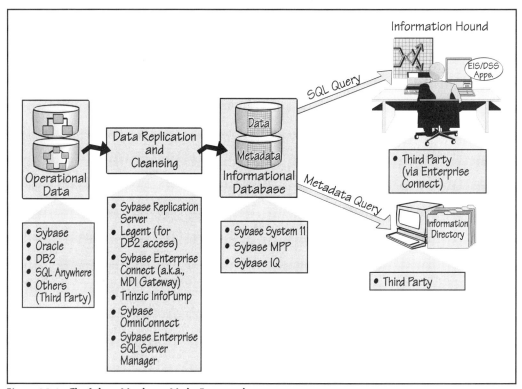

Figure 15-3. The Sybase Warehouse Works Framework.

- *Trinzic InfoPump* was recently integrated with the Sybase Replication Server to provide bulk transfers and data cleansing. InfoPump provides a scripting language that lets you define data transformations as part of bulk transfer process. The scripts are typically invoked by triggers when data changes.

- *Sybase Enterprise SQL Server Manager* is Sybase's latest distributed systems management tool; it includes a replicated server manager. A GUI console lets you track replication objects, monitor performance, test network connections, and act on alerts. Sybase incorporated Tivoli-based management protocols in its tool, which makes it open to third parties.

- *Sybase System 11* provides the low-end informational database engine on uniprocessors and SMP machines. The product currently runs on DEC Unix, HP-UX, AIX, Solaris, and Windows NT.

- *Sybase MPP* serves as a high-end informational database engine on massively parallel hardware—including AT&T GIS 3600, IBM SP2, and Sun SPARCservers.

■ **Sybase IQ** augments the database's query optimizer with advanced indexing capabilities optimized for ad hoc searching. Sybase claims that ad hoc queries with IQ are an order of magnitude faster. IQ uses a low-overhead bitwise indexing structure that makes it affordable to fully index your entire database. The idea is that you never have to do a linear table scan once you have everything fully indexed. Also you don't have to worry about predefining the paths of the query to the search engine.

There's Still Money To Be Made in Database

Soapbox

Data warehousing is clearly an explosive market, and 1995 is the first year that showed any kind of substantial revenue within that market.

> — Dennis McEvoy, VP Products Group
> Sybase
> (October, 1995)

This concludes our conceptual introduction of SQL Database servers. It was a long tour, which is to be expected from a technology that accounts for the majority of client/server applications that are in production today. Database technology is still in its prime. SQL database servers are becoming commodity items and are now learning how to coexist in federated database arrangements. Mission-critical database systems will continue to be sold in packages that superbly integrate scalable fault-tolerant hardware with software. The new areas of growth will be in the mass markets for database-oriented products. What does it mean to put a data warehouse inside each desktop and mobile laptop? Who will keep these warehouses fed with continuous real-time information? How will data warehouses play on the Web? What tools will help us digest all this information in real time?

Yes, there are still fortunes to be made in database technology. Database companies—including Sybase, Oracle, Gupta, Informix, Tandem, IBM San Jose, and Ingres—are transforming Silicon Valley (where your authors live) into "Database Valley." And they did it all with some relational and SQL technology from IBM research. We predict (this is, after all, a Soapbox) that the marriage of "data warehouses" and "information highways" will create opportunities in database that dwarf anything we've seen so far. So the best is yet to come. And we certainly expect our valley to be called Database Valley by the end of the decade. ❑

Part 5
Client/Server
Transaction
Processing

An Introduction to Part 5

TP Monitors, together with 3-tier client/server development, are one of the hottest IT technology items. In 1996, 55% of business critical applications will use a TP Monitor.

— *Jim Johnson, Chairman*
Standish Group
(May, 1996)

So what did you Martians think of the new California gold country? Oh, you want to start panning for SQL gold. Yes, it's a great business—but they do have earthquakes in California. And we have some other great opportunities to show you. For example, Part 5 is about transaction processing and TP Monitors, another important area of new client/server opportunity. Why? Because client/server computing can't live on shared data alone. The programs that operate on that data are just as important. To create effective client/server solutions, we need the software equivalent of a symphony conductor. That's the guy who waves the little wand to orchestrate all the musical instruments so that they play together.

So where is this client/server software conductor? What little wand can be used to orchestrate programs that don't even know about each other? How do we get these programs to act in unison when it takes tons of NOS and middleware just to get them to talk to each other? We've got news for you: The software conductor exists, and it is called a *TP Monitor*. The wand these software conductors use are called *transactions*. Using these transactions, a TP Monitor can get pieces of software that don't know anything about each other to act in total unison.

No, we're not selling snake oil. TP Monitors have solid credentials—they've been used for many years to keep the biggest of "Big Iron" running. In the mainframe world, a TP Monitor is sold with every database. The folks there discovered that without that conductor, they just had some very "inactive" data. If they needed TP Monitors on these single-vendor mainframes, we need them even more on client/server networks where every piece of software only knows how to play its own tune.

Without a conductor, don't expect any client/server music. Yes, an occasional Jazz ensemble may spontaneously create music, but it's becoming the exception. We're being deluged with new software every day, and we can't just depend on good luck and Jazz. We need to hire a software conductor for the network. And eventually, every desktop will have a personal software conductor.

So get your tuxedos out—we're going to the symphony. What? You didn't bring them? No problem. The TP Monitor people are not very formal these days; they, too, have discovered sneakers. The plan for Part 5 is to first explore *transactions*. Transactions are to TP Monitors what SQL is to relational databases—it's the commodity that brings it all together. You'll discover that transactions come in all types: flat, chained, nested, long-lived, and sagas. But all transactions have one

thing in common: They have ACID properties. What's that? We'll tell you soon. It's good stuff. Eventually, all our software will be ACID-ized.

With transactions in the bag, we're ready for TP Monitors. What do they do? What do the new client/server models look like? What kind of standards do they follow? We'll answer all these questions and more. You'll discover that the conductor may save you enough money to more than pay for itself. What a business! The SQL database servers are making gold—the TP Monitors help you save enough so that some of that gold gets diverted your way. Does this mean you don't move to California? We're not sure yet. The database people are making moves that suggest they may want to keep all the gold in their valley. They've invented something called *TP-Lite*—or "miniconductors" for their databases. You've already encountered some elements of TP-Lite: stored procedures, triggers, and SQL transactions. We'll go over the TP-Lite versus TP-Heavy "miniwar." Do you still have your helmets from the OS wars?

Chapter 16

The Magic of Transactions

The idea of distributed systems without transaction management is like a society without contract law. One does not necessarily want the laws, but one does need a way to resolve matters when disputes occur. Nowhere is this more applicable than in the PC and client/server worlds.

— Jim Gray (May, 1993)[1]

Transactions are more than just business events: They've become an application design philosophy that guarantees robustness in distributed systems. Under the control of a TP Monitor, a transaction can be managed from its point of origin—typically on the client—across one or more servers, and then back to the originating client. When a transaction ends, all the parties involved are in agreement as to whether it succeeded or failed. The transaction becomes the contract that binds the client to one or more servers.

In this chapter, we first go over the so-called ACID properties that make transactions such desirable commodities in client/server computing. We then explain the *flat*

---

[1] Source: Jim Gray, "Where is Transaction Processing Headed?" **OTM Spectrum Reports**.

transaction, which is the workhorse of all the commercial transaction systems—including TP Monitors, Database Managers, transactional file systems, and message queues. The flat transaction is not without its shortcomings; we look at these in some detail and suggest some workarounds. Finally, we go over some of the proposed alternatives to the flat transaction including sagas, chained transactions, and nested transactions.

THE ACID PROPERTIES

Transactions are a way to make ACID operations a general commodity.

— **Gray and Reuter (1993)** [2]

A transaction is a collection of actions embued with ACID properties. In this case, ACID—a term coined by Andreas Reuter in 1983—stands for Atomicity, Consistency, Isolation, and Durability. Here's what it means:

- ■ *Atomicity* means that a transaction is an indivisible unit of work: All of its actions succeed or they all fail; it's an all-or-nothing proposition. The actions under the transaction's umbrella may include the message queues, updates to a database, and the display of results on the client's screen. Atomicity is defined from the perspective of the consumer of the transaction.

- ■ *Consistency* means that after a transaction executes, it must leave the system in a correct state or it must abort. If the transaction cannot achieve a stable end state, it must return the system to its initial state.

- ■ *Isolation* means that a transaction's behavior is not affected by other transactions that execute concurrently. The transaction must serialize all accesses to shared resources and guarantee that concurrent programs will not corrupt each other's operations. A multiuser program running under transaction protection must behave exactly as it would in a single-user environment. The changes to shared resources that a transaction makes must not become visible outside the transaction until it commits. Again, this is how the consumer of the transaction sees it.

- ■ *Durability* means that a transaction's effects are permanent after it commits. Its changes should survive system failures. The term "persistent" is a synonym for "durable."

---

[2] Source: Jim Gray and Andreas Reuter, **Transaction Processing Concepts and Techniques** (Morgan Kaufmann, 1993). This 1000-page book is the Bible of transaction processing. It gives some great insights into the motivation behind transaction processing written by two of the original gurus who have pioneered this field.

A transaction becomes the fundamental unit of recovery, consistency, and concurrency in a client/server system. Why is that important? Take a simple debit-credit banking operation. You'd like to see all credit made to *your* account succeed. Any losses would be unacceptable (of course, any unexpected credits are always welcome). This means you're relying on the application to provide the integrity expected in a real-life business transaction. The application, in turn, relies on the underlying system—usually the TP Monitor—to help achieve this level of transactional integrity. The programmer should not have to develop tons of code that reinvents the transaction wheel.

A more subtle point is that all the participating programs must adhere to the transactional discipline because a single faulty program can corrupt an entire system. A transaction that unknowingly uses corrupted initial data—produced by a non-transactional program—builds on top of a corrupt foundation.

In an ideal world, *all* client/server programs are written as transactions. ACID is like motherhood and apple pie. It's necessary—and you can't have too much of it. OK, enough preaching. Let's take a look at how software transactions model their business counterparts.

TRANSACTION MODELS

When should a transaction start? When should it end and have its effects made accessible to the outside world? What are appropriate units of recovery in case of failures? Can computer transactions mirror their real-world counterparts? To answer these questions, we will look at the *flat transaction*, go over its shortcomings, and take a quick peek at the proposed extensions.

So What's a Flat Transaction?

Flat transactions are the workhorses of the current generation of transactional systems. They're called flat because all the work done within a transaction's boundaries is at the same level (see shaded area in Figure 16-1).

The transaction starts with *begin_transaction* and ends with either a *commit_transaction* or *abort_transaction*. It's an all-or-nothing proposition—there's no way to commit or abort *parts* of a flat transaction. All the actions are indivisible, which is what we wanted in the first place. Table 16-1 compares the commands used in different TP Monitors to delineate the transaction boundaries.

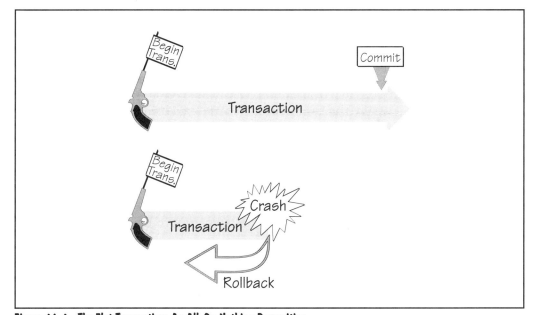

Figure 16-1. The Flat Transaction: An All-Or-Nothing Proposition.

Table 16-1. Comparing Flat Transaction Delimiters for Major TP Monitors (Adapted from OTM Spectrum Reports; February, 1993).

System	Transaction Delimiter		
	Start	**Commit**	**Abort**
Tuxedo	TPBEGIN	TPCOMMIT	TPABORT
Top End	tx_begin	tx_commit	tx_rollback
Encina RPC	transaction	onCommit	onAbort
X/Open	tx_begin	tx_commit	tx_rollback
OSI TP	C-BEGIN	C-COMMIT	C-ROLLBACK
Tandem RSC	Begin_Transaction	End_Transaction	Abort_Transaction
CICS	SYNCPOINT	SYNCPOINT	SYNCPOINT or ROLLBACK

We Like Our Transactions Flat

Soapbox

The major virtue of the flat transaction is its *simplicity* and the ease with which it provides the ACID features. Thousands of commercial applications were created using the very simple concept of a flat transaction. Historically, the flat transaction was first developed for banking applications—it provides an excellent fit for modeling short activities.

But as the transactional discipline begins to permeate all facets of computing, we're discovering that the flat transaction model does not provide the best fit in all environments. Millions of lines of code have been written to compensate for its shortcomings. The model is particularly weak when it comes to handling business transactions that span over long periods of time—days or even months. It's somewhat weak in the area of batch jobs. And it's a nuisance in situations that require partial rollbacks without throwing away an entire transaction's work—the rigid "all-or-nothing" application of the ACID principle gets in the way.

For political reasons, flat transactions using two-phase commits are usually not allowed to cross intercorporate boundaries—asynchronous MOM may be the preferred approach in such situations. With MOMs, you lose end-to-end ACID protection in return for relaxing the strict lockstep synchronization imposed by a global two-phase commit protocol. We're also experiencing difficulties with the flat model in client/server environments where client "think time" is part of the transaction loop. There are workarounds for each of these problems, but they require writing some custom code. Wouldn't it be nice if we could extend the transaction model to automatically take care of all these situations for us?

It turns out that computer scientists everywhere are frantically searching for a "unified theory" of transactions that covers all the complex real-life situations and yet still maintains the ACID properties and the simplicity of the flat model. As a result, the academic literature is flooded with new transaction models that have esoteric-sounding names like Sagas, Chained, Promises, ConTracts, Check-Revalidate, Long-Lived, Multilevel, Migrating, Shopping Cart, and Anarchic and Non-Anarchic Nested Transactions.

With the exception of Non-Anarchic Nested Transactions—implemented in Transarc's *Encina*—none of these esoterics have found their way into commercial products. They make great reading and are always very clever. However, it's turning out not to be easy to extend the transactional model and still do ACID simply. And the jury is still out when it comes to nested transactions—they may be too difficult to manage in normal commercial applications.

At the risk of sounding too conservative, we still feel there's a lot of life left in venerable flat transactions. They can be used "as is" in over 90% of commercial client/server applications. And writing a *little* bit of code around them doesn't particularly bother us—at least we can get them to do exactly what's needed. We feel (remember, this is a Soapbox) it's more important to keep pushing the flat transaction discipline into every known program so that they can all participate in TP-Monitor coordinated transactions.

Transactions are here to help simplify our applications and give us better control over the environment in which they run. Some of the proposed extensions may create more problems than they solve. In any case, as Gray and Reuter point out, "No matter which extensions prove to be the most important and useful in the future, flat transactions will be at the core of all the mechanisms required to make these more powerful models work. Most of the commercial databases and TP Monitors implement the flat transaction model." ❏

Baby Stepping With Flat Transactions

A typical flat transaction does not last more than two or three seconds to avoid monopolizing critical system resources such as database locks. As a result, OLTP client/server programs are divided into short transactions that execute back-to-back to produce results (see Figure 16-2). We call this effect transaction *baby stepping*—or getting work done by moving in "baby steps" from one stable state to the next.[3] For example, you could implement a complex multistep workflow as a sequence of flat transactions that are either conversational or queued.

---

[3] The term "baby step" is adapted from the movie, *What About Bob?* Richard Dreyfus played the role of a psychiatrist who advocated baby stepping as a cure-all.

Figure 16-2. Back-to-Back Flat Transactions.

The Distributed Flat Transaction

Can a flat transaction run on multiple sites and update resources located within multiple resource managers? Yes. Even though a high level of parallelism may be involved, as far as the programmer is concerned, it's still just a flat transaction (see Figure 16-3). The programmer is not aware of the considerable amount of "under-the-cover" activity that's required to make the multisite transaction appear flat. The transaction must travel across multiple sites to get to the resources it needs. Each

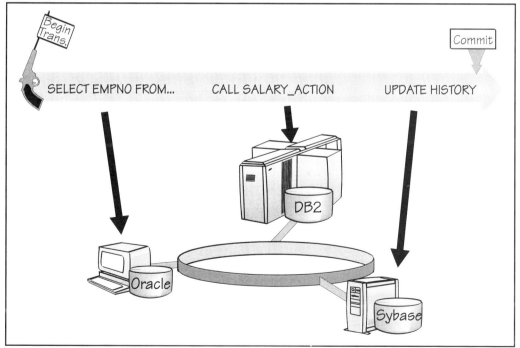

Figure 16-3. A Multisite Distributed Flat Transaction.

site's TP Monitor must manage its local piece of the transaction. Within a site, the TP Monitor coordinates the transactions with the local ACID subsystems and resource managers—including database managers, queue managers, and message transports. For example, the TP Monitor will ensure that when a database gets updated, a message gets delivered, and an entry is made in a workflow queue. Either all of these actions will occur (exactly once) or none will. In addition, one of the TP Monitors must coordinate the actions of all its fellow TP Monitors. This is all done using a *two-phase commit* protocol, which coordinates the transaction's commit or abort across multiple sites (see the following Details box).

What's a Two-Phase Commit Protocol?

Details

The *two-phase commit* protocol is used to synchronize updates on different machines so that they either all fail or all succeed. This is done by centralizing the decision to commit but giving each participant the right of veto. It's like a Christian marriage: You're given one last chance to back out of the transaction when you're at the altar. If none of the parties present object, the marriage takes place.

It should come as no surprise by now that each commercial implementation introduces its own variation of the two-phase commit protocol. As usual, they don't interoperate. And, of course, there are standards bodies that are trying to make it all work together. In December 1992—after a five-year development cycle—ISO published its *OSI TP* standard that defines very *rigidly* how a two-phase commit is to be implemented (see Figure 16-4). Let's go over the mechanics of this protocol:

1. *In the first phase of a commit*, the *commit manager* node—also known as the *root node* or the *transaction coordinator*—sends *prepare-to-commit* commands to all the *subordinate* nodes that were directly asked to participate in the transaction. The subordinates may have spawned pieces of the transaction on other nodes (or resource managers) to which they must propagate the prepare-to-commit command. It becomes a transaction tree, with the coordinator at the root.

2. *The first phase of the commit terminates* when the root node receives *ready-to-commit* signals from all its direct subordinate nodes that participate in the transaction. This means that the transaction has executed successfully so far on all the nodes and they're now ready to do a final commit. The root node logs that fact in a safe place (this information is used to recover from a root node failure).

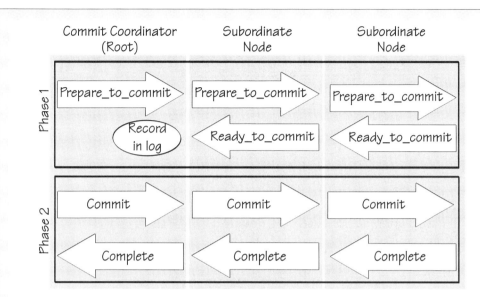

Figure 16-4. The Mechanics of the OSI TP Two-Phase Commit.

3. ***The second phase of the commit starts*** after the root node makes the decision to *commit* the transaction—based on the unanimous yes vote. It tells its subordinates to commit. They, in turn, tell their subordinates to do the same, and the order ripples down the tree.

4. ***The second phase of the commit terminates*** when all the nodes involved have safely committed their part of the transaction and made it durable. The root receives all the confirmations and can tell its client that the transaction completed. It can then relax until the next transaction.

5. ***The two-phase commit aborts*** if any of the participants return a *refuse* indication, meaning that their part of the transaction failed. In that case, the root node tells all its subordinates to perform a rollback. And they, in turn, do the same for their subordinates.

The X/Open XA specification defines a set of APIs that work with the underlying OSI TP protocol. To participate in an XA-defined two-phase commit, TP Monitors and resource managers (like databases and message queues) must map their private two-phase commit protocols to the XA commands. They must also be willing to let somebody else drive the transaction—something they're not accustomed to doing. The XA specification allows participants to withdraw from further participation in the global transaction during Phase 1 if they do not have to update resources. In XA, a TP Monitor can use a one-phase commit if it is dealing with a single resource manager. We'll have a lot more to say about XA in the next chapter.

In early 1996, most TP Monitors could easily handle transactions that spanned across one hundred two-phase commit engines. However, the two-phase commit protocol is by no means perfect. Here are some of its more serious limitations:

- **Performance overhead**, which is introduced by all the message exchanges. The protocol has no way of discerning valuable transactions that need this kind of protection from the more tolerant transactions that don't need protection. It generates messages for all transactions, even read-only ones.

- **Hazard windows**, where certain failures can be a problem. For example, if the root node crashes after the first phase of the commit, the subordinates may be left in disarray. Who cleans up this mess? There are always workarounds, but it's a tricky business. It helps if you have in your system some fault-tolerant hardware that is coordinating the transaction.

A number of suggestions were introduced on how to improve the two-phase commit protocol—including single-phase commits, read-only optimizations, overlapped transactions, implicit prepares, and delegated commits. We don't expect to see any of these proposals in the standard soon. However, the *delegated commit* proposal is of practical interest in client/server applications. It means that a transaction originating from an unreliable platform—such as a cellular notebook—can delegate the commit coordination to an alternate node. Most of today's TP Monitors don't allow their clients to coordinate transactions. They prefer to do it for them. "Delegated commit" makes the process more democratic. ❏

The Limitations of the Flat Transaction

The "all-or-nothing" characteristic of flat transactions is both a virtue and a vice.

— Gray and Reuter

So when does the all-or-nothing nature of the flat transaction become a liability? Mostly, in situations that require more flexibility than the all-or-nothing approach. The following are examples of business transactions that require a more flexible approach:

- **Compound business transactions that need to be partially rolled back.** The classical example is a complex trip that includes travel arrangements, hotel reservations, and a car rental (see Figure 16-5). What happens if you simply want to cancel the car reservation but preserve the rest of the reservations? You can't do that within a flat transaction—the entire reservation is rolled back. It's an all-or-nothing proposition. This means you must give up the hotel and plane

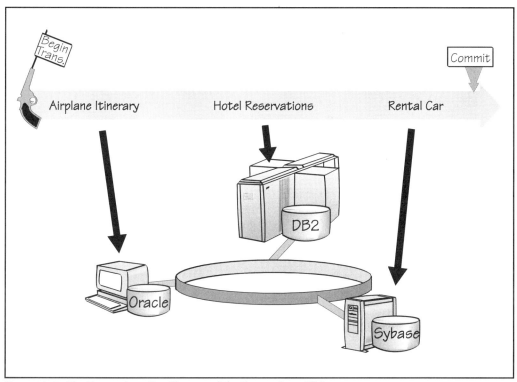

Figure 16-5. Flat Transactions: One Change and You Have to Start All Over.

reservations just to get rid of the car—a real nuisance. The hotel/car reservation problem is used to justify the need for nested or chained transactions. But flat transaction advocates could make a case that the hotel/car transaction should be broken down into separate hotel and car transactions. In other words, use multiple flat transactions to simulate the compound one.

■ ***Business transactions with humans in the loop.*** This is a classical GUI client/server transaction where a set of choices are presented to the user on a screen, and the server must wait for the decision. In the meantime, locks are held for those records that are on the tube. What happens if an operator that's viewing some airline seats decides to go to lunch? How long are the seats locked out? If it's executed as a single flat transaction, the seats will be held as long as that user is thinking or eating. Nobody else can get to those seats. This is obviously not a very good way to run a business. The solution is to split the reservation into two transactions: a query transaction that displays the available seats, and a reservation transaction that performs the actual reservation (see Figure 16-6). Of course, the existence of the seats must be revalidated before the update. If the seat is gone, the user must be notified. These extra steps mean more work for the programmer.

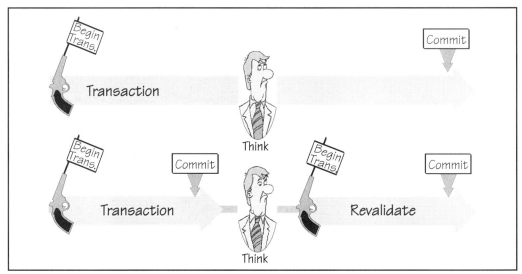

Figure 16-6. Keep the Human Out of the Loop by Creating Two Flat Transactions.

■ *Business transactions that span long periods of time.* These are your typical engineering Computer-Aided Design (CAD) transactions that may require CAD-managed components to be worked on for days and passed from engineer to engineer (see Figure 16-7). The CAD transaction must be able to suspend itself and resume after shutdowns, preserve ongoing work across shutdowns, and know where it left off and what needs to be done next. In essence, it becomes a workflow manager. Obviously, flat transactions must be augmented by a workflow program to handle such long-lived work. This is an area where alternative transactional models—including object database check-in check-out transactions, replica management, versioning, and workflow—look very promising.

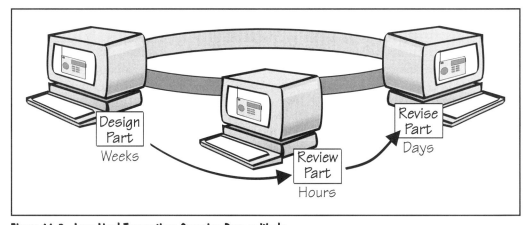

Figure 16-7. Long-Lived Transactions Spanning Days or Weeks.

■ *Business transactions with a lot of bulk.* The classical problem here is: How do you handle one million record updates under transactional control (see Figure 16-8)? Must the entire transaction be rolled back if a failure occurs after record 999,999 is updated? Yes, it's all-or-nothing if you're using a single flat transaction to do the million updates. On the other hand, if you make each update a separate transaction, it is much slower—a million separate commits are required—and where do you restart after the failure? This is an area where syncpoints or chained transactions have been proposed as a solution. But the solution may slow you down because it introduces more commits and maybe some restart code. We think you may be better off restarting an occasional flat transaction than going with the alternatives. After all, how often can a bulk transaction fail?

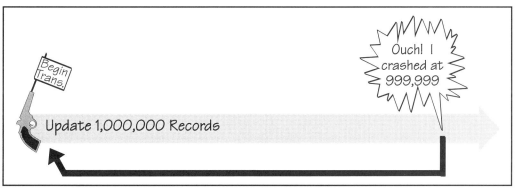

Figure 16-8. Flat Transaction: It Failed—Restart That Million Update Job.

■ *Business transactions that span across companies or the Internet.* The problem here is a political one. Very few companies will allow an external TP Monitor (or database) to synchronize in real time a transaction on their systems using a two-phase commit. The more politically correct solution may be to conduct an intercompany exchange using loosely coupled transactional message queues. A MOM solution allows organizations to split the unit of work into many transactions that can be executed asynchronously, processed on different machines, and coordinated by independent TP Monitors within each company (see Figure 16-9). You lose instantaneous consistency, but you're able to maintain arm's length controls between companies. From a software perspective, we ended up breaking a single two-phase commit flat transaction into three independent flat transactions that execute on company A's TP Monitor, MOM, and company B's TP Monitor. The MOM transaction ensures that the transaction has safely made it from company A's computer to company B's computer. We're assuming that MOM provides a durable queue that gives you the "D" in ACID at commit time.

In summary, most of the flat transaction's problems come from the rigidity (and interlock) imposed by the all-or-nothing discipline in situations that require more flexibility. You can work around most of these problems by breaking down transac-

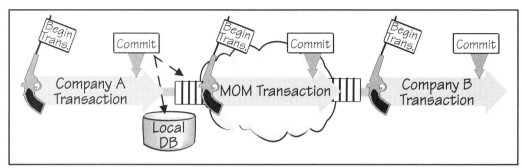

Figure 16-9. Flat Transactions: Using MOM for Intercompany Transactions.

tions into smaller units and developing the control code that synchronizes the several smaller transactions. It's a trade-off: You can write one long transaction that can fail in a big way, or several smaller ones that fail in smaller ways. The designer, as usual, must perform a balancing act.

The Alternatives: Chained and Nested Transactions

Most of the proposed alternatives to the flat transaction are based on mechanisms that extend the flow of control beyond the linear unit of work. Two of the most obvious ways to extend the flow of control are by chaining units of work in linear sequences of "mini" transactions—the chained transaction or Saga—or by creating some kind of nested hierarchy of work—the nested transaction. Each of these two basic approaches have many refinements.

The solution to the long-lived transaction requires some form of control flow language for describing activities that evolve in time. This is more or less the model proposed in some of the more recent research literature under names such as *ConTracts*, *Migrating Transactions*, and *Shopping Cart Transactions*. None of these models are available in commercial applications. We feel that the best commercial solutions available today for long-lived transactions are in workflow managers and object databases, which we cover in Parts 6 and 7. So we will defer this discussion until then.

Syncpoints, Chained Transactions, and Sagas

The chained transaction, as the name implies, introduces some form of linear control for sequencing through transactions. The simplest form of chaining is to use *syncpoints*—also known as savepoints—within a flat transaction that allow periodic saves of accumulated work (see Figure 16-10). What makes a syncpoint different from a commit? The syncpoint lets you roll back work and still maintain a live transaction. In contrast, a commit ends a transaction. Syncpoints also give

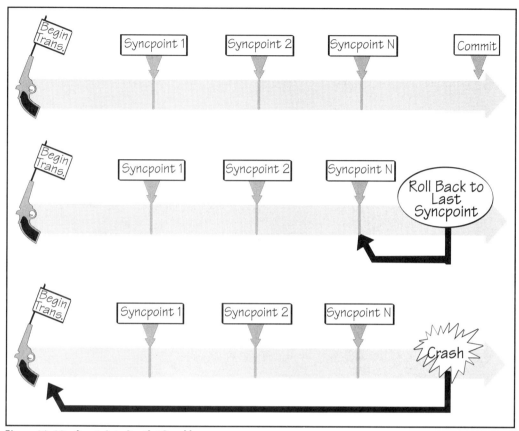

Figure 16-10. Syncpoints Are Not Durable.

you better granularity of control over what you save and undo. You can divide the transaction into a series of activities that can be rolled back individually. But the big difference is that the commit is durable while the syncpoint is volatile. If the system crashes during a transaction, all data accumulated in syncpoints is lost.

Chained transactions are a variation of syncpoints that make the accumulated work durable. They allow you to commit work while staying within the transaction, so you don't have to give up your locks and resources. A commit gives you the "D" in ACID without terminating the transaction (see Figure 16-11). But what you lose is the ability to roll back an entire chain's worth of work. There's no free lunch.

Sagas extend the chained transactions to let you roll back the entire chain, if you require it (see Figure 16-12). They do that by maintaining a chain of compensating transactions. You still get the crash resistance of the intermediate commits, but you have the choice of rolling back the entire chain under program control. This lets

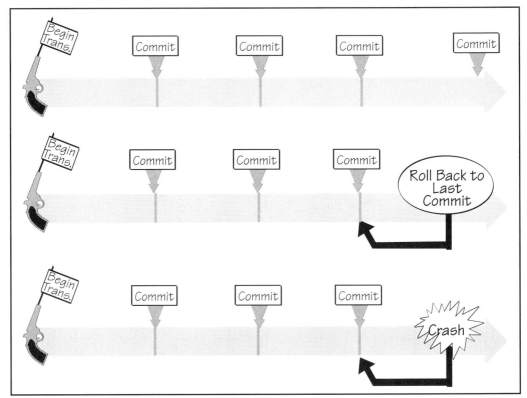

Figure 16-11. Chained Transactions: Commits Are Durable.

you treat the entire chain as an atomic unit of work. You can now have your cake, and eat it, too.[4]

Nested Transactions

Nested Transactions provide the ability to define transactions within other transactions. They do that by breaking a transaction into hierarchies of "subtransactions," (very much like a program is made up of procedures). The main transaction starts the subtransactions, which behave as dependent transactions. A subtransaction can also start its own subtransactions, making the entire structure very recursive (see Figure 16-13).

Each subtransaction can issue a commit or rollback for its designated pieces of work. When a subtransaction commits, its results are only accessible to the parent

---

[4] The term "Saga" was first suggested by Bruce Lindsay of IBM Almaden Research. The concept was fully developed by Hector Garcia-Molina and K. Salem in 1987.

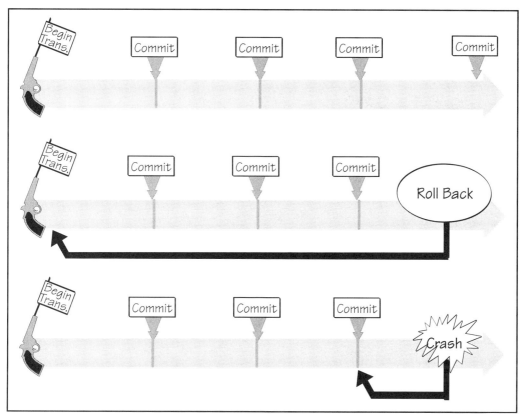

Figure 16-12. Sagas: Commits Are Durable but Can Be Rolled Back.

that spawned it. A subtransaction's commit becomes permanent after it issues a local commit and all its ancestors commit. If a parent transaction does a rollback, all its descendent transactions are rolled back, regardless of whether they issued local commits.

The main benefit of nesting is that a failure in a subtransaction can be trapped and retried using an alternative method, still allowing the main transaction to succeed. Nesting helps programmers write more granular transactions. The only commercial implementation of nested transactions we know of is the Encina TP Monitor. Encina's Transactional C (or C++) allows you to declare the nesting directly in your code where it starts resembling regular procedure invocations. In some cases, nesting may be overkill; it creates more problems than solutions. Of course, now that the Encina TP Monitor is on the market, you can decide for yourself.

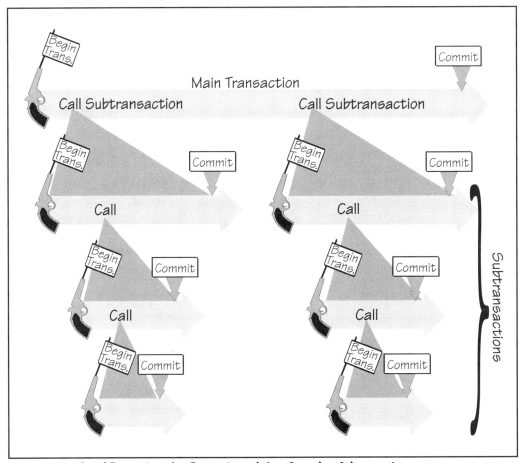

Figure 16-13. Nested Transactions: One Transaction and Many Dependent Subtransactions.

Conclusion

Transactions are important because they give ordinary programs ACID qualities without writing a line of messy code. All you need to do is say begin and end transaction—and suddenly the magic appears. In the next chapter, we explain how the magic wand of TP Monitors provides the robust mechanisms that keep these transactions running under all sorts of conditions. We also noted that transactions are now being used to represent more complex business activities. Eventually, our transactions will be extended beyond their flat origins to cover some of these more complex business activities. The more pressing need is to permeate the simple flat transactions into all our client/server programs and "ACIDify" them. ACID is the best antidote to the inherent complexity in distributed systems.

Chapter 17

TP Monitors: Managing Client/Server Transactions

TP Monitors make a silk purse out of a sow's ear—they turn mundane operating systems into fast, highly reliable transaction engines.

— *Jeri Edwards, Director*
Transaction Processing Development
Tandem Computers

TP Monitors specialize in managing transactions from their point of origin—typically on the client—across one or more servers, and then back to the originating client. When a transaction ends, the TP Monitor ensures that all the systems involved in the transaction are left in a consistent state. In addition, TP Monitors know how to run transactions, route them across systems, load-balance their execution, and restart them after failures.

One of the great appeals of a TP Monitor is that it is the overseer of all aspects of a distributed transaction, regardless of the systems or resource managers used. A TP Monitor can manage resources on a single server or multiple servers, and it can cooperate with other TP Monitors in federated arrangements. Future TP Monitors may reside on every client machine to bring desktop resources—such as the user interface, local data warehouses, or personal agents—within a distributed transaction's reach.

In this chapter, we explain in some detail what TP Monitors are and what functions they perform. We go over X/Open's model for how TP Monitors interact with other resource managers in an open environment. We conclude with a list of benefits that TP Monitors provide. We felt this list was needed because the benefits of TP Monitors are not well understood in the PC LAN and Unix worlds. TP Monitors are either treated with awe and left to the "High Priests" of computer science, or they are dismissed as antiques. Neither is true. TP Monitors are fun to program, and they create transactional magic on ordinary client/server networks. But enough talk; this isn't a Soapbox.

TP MONITORS

TP Monitors first appeared on mainframes to provide robust run-time environments that could support large-scale OLTP applications—airline and hotel reservations, banking, automatic teller machines, credit authorization systems, and stock-brokerage systems. Since then, OLTP has spread to almost every type of business application—including hospitals, manufacturing, point-of-sales retail systems, automated gas pumps, and telephone directory services. TP Monitors provide whatever services are required to keep these OLTP applications running in the style they're accustomed to: highly reactive, available, and well-managed. With OLTP moving to client/server platforms, a new breed of TP Monitors is emerging to help make the new environment hospitable to mission-critical applications.

What's a TP Monitor?

It should come as no surprise that our industry has no commonly accepted definition of a TP Monitor. We'll use Jeri Edwards' definition of a TP Monitor as "an operating system for transaction processing." This definition captures the essence of a TP Monitor. So what does an operating system for transaction processing do in life? How does it interface with the rest of the world? What services does it provide? We'll answer all these questions. In a nutshell, a TP Monitor does two things extremely well:

- **Process management** includes starting server processes, funneling work to them, monitoring their execution, and balancing their workloads.

- **Transaction management** means that it guarantees the ACID properties to all programs that run under its protection.

TP Monitors and OSs: The Great Funneling Act

TP Monitors were originally introduced to run classes of applications that could service hundreds and sometimes thousands of clients (think of an airline reservation application). If each of these thousands of clients were given all the resources it needed on a server—typically a communication connection, half a MByte of memory, one or two processes, and a dozen open file handles—even the largest mainframe server would fall on its knees (see Figure 17-1). Luckily, not all the clients require service at the same time. However, when they do require it, they want their service *immediately*. We're told that the humans on the other end have a "tolerance for waiting" of two seconds or less. TP Monitors provide an operating system—on top of existing OSs—that connects in real time these thousands of impatient humans with a pool of shared server processes.

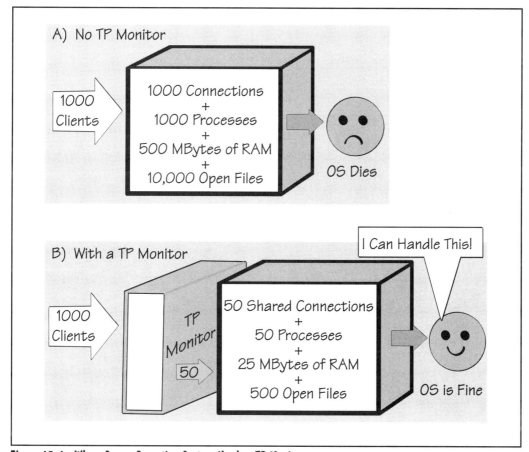

Figure 17-1. Why a Server Operating System Needs a TP Monitor.

How Is the Great Funneling Act Performed?

The "funneling act" is part of what a TP Monitor must do to manage the server side of a user-written OLTP application. In PC environments, the server side of the OLTP application is typically packaged as a DLL that contains a number of related functions. The TP Monitor assigns the execution of the DLL functions to *server classes*, which are pools of prestarted application processes or threads, waiting for work. Each process or thread in a server class is capable of doing the work. The TP Monitor balances the workload between them. Each application can have one or more server classes. (Note: these are not classes in the object-oriented sense of the word.)

When a client sends a service request, the TP Monitor hands it to an available process in the server class pool (see Figure 17-2). The server process dynamically links to the DLL function called by the client, invokes it, oversees its execution, and returns the results to the client. After that completes, the server process can be reused by another client. The operating system keeps the already loaded DLLs in memory, where they can be shared across processes. It doesn't get better!

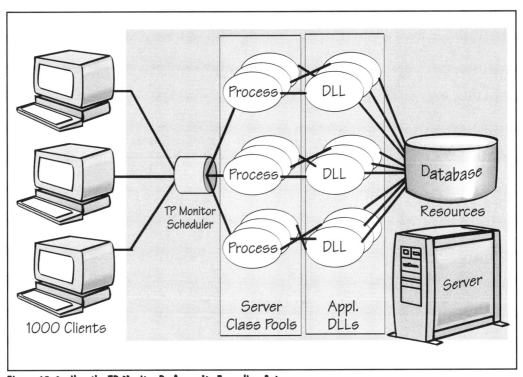

Figure 17-2. How the TP Monitor Performs Its Funneling Act.

In essence, the TP Monitor removes the process-per-client requirement by funneling incoming client requests to shared server processes. If the number of incoming client requests exceeds the number of processes in a server class, the TP Monitor may dynamically start new ones—this is called *load balancing*. The more sophisticated TP Monitors can distribute the process load across multiple CPUs in SMP or MPP environments. Part of the load balancing act involves managing the priorities of the incoming requests. The TP Monitor does that by running some high-priority server classes and dynamically assigning them to the VIP clients.

Typically, short-running and high-priority functions are packaged in high-priority server classes. Batch and low-priority functions are assigned to low-priority server classes. You can also partition server classes by application type, desired response time, the resources they manage, fault-tolerance requirements, and client/server interaction modes—including queued, conversational, or RPC. In addition to providing dynamic load balancing, most TP Monitors let you manually control how many processes or threads are available to each process class.

In their load-balancing capacity, TP Monitors play the role of a client/server *traffic cop*. They route client requests to pools of application processes spread across multiple servers some of which consist of multiple processors in SMP or MPP configurations.

TP Monitors and Transaction Management

*S*ystems involving thousands of clients and hundreds of services have lots of moving parts. Change is constant, and TP Monitors manage it "on-the-fly."

> — *Jim Gray and Jeri Edwards*
> **BYTE Magazine**
> **(April, 1995)[1]**

The transaction discipline was introduced in the early TP Monitors to ensure the robustness of multiuser applications that ran on the servers. These applications had to be bullet-proof and highly reliable if they were going to serve thousands of users in "bet-your-business" situations. TP Monitors were developed from the ground up as operating systems for transactions. The unit of management, execution, and recovery was the ordinary transaction and the programs that invoked them. The job of a TP Monitor is to guarantee the ACID properties while maintaining high transaction throughput. To do that, it must manage the execution, distribution, and synchronization of transaction *workloads*.

---

[1] Source: Jim Gray and Jeri Edwards, "Scale Up with TP Monitors" **BYTE** (April, 1995).

With TP Monitors, the application programmers don't have to concern themselves with issues like concurrency, failures, broken connections, load balancing, and the synchronization of resources across multiple nodes. All this is made transparent to them—very much like an operating system makes the hardware transparent to ordinary programs. Simply put, TP Monitors provide the run-time engines for running transactions—they do that on top of ordinary hardware and operating systems. They also provide a framework for running your server applications.

TP Monitor Client/Server Interaction Types

Ordinary operating systems must understand the nature of the jobs and resources they manage. This is also true for TP Monitors—they must provide an optimized environment for the execution of the transactions that run under their control. This means they must load the server programs, dynamically assign incoming client requests to server processes, recover from failures, return the replies to the clients, and make sure high-priority traffic gets through first.

So what kind of assumptions do TP Monitors make about their client/server transaction interaction types? They typically fall into one of four categories: conversational, RPC, queued, and batch (see Figure 17-3). The batch transactions typically run in low-priority mode. RPC and conversational transactions usually involve a human user that requires immediate attention; they run in high-priority mode. MOM-based queued transactions can be of either type.

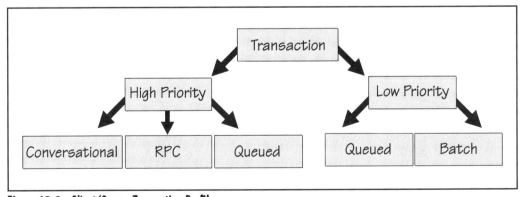

Figure 17-3. Client/Server Transaction Profiles.

In addition, TP Monitors must be prepared to communicate with all the resource managers on which the transaction executes—whether they're on the same machine or across a network. When the resource managers are across networks, the TP Monitor synchronizes the transaction with the remote TP Monitors using a two-phase commit.

Transactional RPCs, Queues, and Conversations

On the surface, transactional client/server exchanges appear to use the traditional NOS communication models: queues, RPCs, and conversational peer-to-peer communications. This is not so. They're using highly augmented versions of these traditional communication mechanisms. However, most of the value-added elements are made transparent to the programmer—they look like ordinary exchanges bracketed by start and end transaction calls. The transactional versions augment the familiar NOS exchanges with the following value-added extensions:

■ They piggyback *transactional delimiters* that allow a client to specify the begin-transaction and end-transaction boundaries. The actual commit mechanics are usually *delegated* to one of the server TP Monitors because the client is assumed to be unreliable.

■ They introduce—under-the-cover—a three-way exchange between a client, server, and TP Monitor (the transaction manager). A new transaction is assigned a unique ID by the coordinating TP Monitor. All subsequent message exchanges between the participants are tagged with that transaction ID. The message exchanges allow the TP Monitor to keep track of what Jim Gray calls the "dynamically expanding web" of resource managers participating in a distributed transaction. TP Monitors need that information to coordinate the two-phase commit with all the participants in a transaction.

■ They embed transaction state information within each of the messages exchanged. This information helps the TP Monitor identify the state of the distributed transaction and figure out what to do next.

■ They allow a TP Monitor to enforce *exactly-once* semantics—this means that the message only gets executed once.

■ They guarantee that a server process is at the receiving end of the message. Traditional RPCs and MOMs do not worry about this kind of stuff—they assume that a program will "automagically" appear on the receiving end.

■ They provide server routing based on server classes, server loads, automatic fail-over, and other factors.

As you can see, there's a lot more going on here than a simple RPC or MOM exchange. The literature calls these enhanced services *Transactional RPC (TRPC), Transactional Queues*, and *Transactional Conversations*. The distinguishing factor is that all resource managers and processes invoked through these calls become part of the transaction. The TP Monitor is informed of any service calls; it uses that information to orchestrate the actions of all the participants, enforce their ACID behavior, and make them act as part of a transaction. In contrast, traditional RPCs, messages, and queue invocations are between separate programs that are not bound by a transaction discipline. Table 17-1 summarizes the differences between transactional communication mechanisms and their traditional NOS equivalents.

Table 17-1. Transactional Versus Non-Transactional Communications.

Feature	Traditional MOM, RPC, and Conversations	Transactional MOM, RPC, and Conversations
Who participates?	Loosely-coupled client/server programs.	Transactionally bound client/server and server/server programs. The message invocation causes the recipient program to join the transaction.
Commit synchronization	No	Yes
Only-once semantics	No	Yes
Server management on the recipient node	No. It's just a delivery mechanism.	Yes. The process that receives the message is started, load-balanced, monitored, and tracked as part of the transaction.
Load balancing	Using the directory services. The first server to register becomes a hotspot. No dynamic load balancing is provided.	Using the TP Monitor's sophisticated load-balancing algorithms. Can spread work across multiple SMP machines and dynamically add more processes to cover hotspots of activity.
Supervised exchanges	No. Exchanges are simply between the client and the server. The exchanges are transient. No crash recovery or error management is provided. You're on your own.	The TP Monitor supervises the entire exchange, restarts communication links, redirects messages to an alternate server process if the first one gets hung, performs retries, and provides persistent queues and crash-recovery.

Examples of commercial implementations of a TRPC include the Encina Transactional RPC and the CICS External Call Interface (ECI). Examples of conversational transactional interfaces include Tuxedo's ATMI, Tandem's RSC, and APPC's Syncpoint features. MQSeries is an example of a transactional implementation of an "open" MOM queue. Some TP Monitors also include their own bundled versions of recoverable queues—in Encina's case it is RQS, and in Tuxedo it is /Q; CICS uses transient queues.

Three-Tier Client/Server, TP Monitor Style

Soapbox

TP Monitors insulate the application from the RDBMS and make it easier to substitute one RDBMS for another. This will limit database vendors' ability to lock their customers. It effectively relegates their products to the status of interchangeable commodities.

— *Summit Strategies*
Report 6 (November, 1995)

TP Monitors are an example (but not the only one) of a 3-tier client/server architecture. Remember, we belong to the school that defines a 3-tier distributed application as consisting of: 1) the GUI front-end, 2) the application logic, and 3) the back-end resource managers. Examples of resource managers include SQL databases, hierarchical databases, file systems, document stores, message queues, HTML stores, legacy applications, and other back-end services.

TP Monitors fit this 3-tier model because they manage the application processes independently from the database or the GUI front-end. TP Monitors provide an extra tier that separates client front-ends from the resource managers (see Figure 17-4).

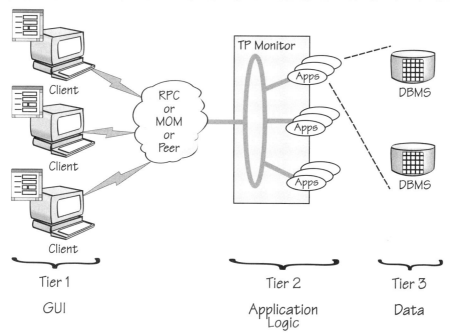

Figure 17-4. Three-Tier Client/Server, TP Monitor Style.

By breaking this direct connection, TP Monitors control all the traffic that links hundreds (or thousands) of clients with application programs and the back-end resources. TP Monitors ensure that the transactions are completed accurately, provide load balancing, and improve the overall system performance. More importantly, TP Monitors make your processes independent of any resource manager. They let you work with any back-end resource.

In a nutshell, TP Monitors treat processes as first-class citizens. They have a separate existence outside the database or GUI. This means that you can distribute processes across machines and networks to wherever it makes the most sense. In contrast, with database client/server, the application is either buried deep inside the bowels of a front-end tool (the fat client) or deep inside the bowels of a database in the form of stored procedures (the fat server). The database model does not treat processes as independent first-class citizens. So even though stored procedures have a 3-tier veneer, their packaging is the epitome of 2-tier.

As we explain later in the book, the 3-tier approach is the only one that makes sense in an intergalactic, multiserver world. But keep in mind that TP Monitors are just one way to implement 3-tier client/server solutions. We will show you other approaches as we progress throughout the book. As usual, you get to pick the style that best suits your needs. ❏

TRANSACTION MANAGEMENT STANDARDS: X/OPEN DTP AND OSI-TP

TP Monitors need standards because they're the ultimate glue software. The applications they coordinate could be running on different platforms with access to different databases and resource managers. These applications are most likely developed using different tools. And they have absolutely no knowledge of each other. The only way to make these disparate pieces come together is through "open standards" that specify how a TP Monitor interfaces to resource managers, to other TP Monitors, and to its clients.

Most of the standards activity around TP Monitors comes from two sources: the International Standard Organization (ISO)—the OSI-CCR and OSI-TP specifications—and X/Open's *Distributed Transaction Processing (DTP)* specifications. The ISO-OSI standards specify the message protocols (i.e., FAPs) that allow TP Monitors to interoperate. The OSI-TP specification, which we covered in the last chapter, is the most important of these standards; it defines, among other things, the two-phase commit protocol. X/Open has taken the lead in defining the APIs within a general framework for transaction processing. Together, X/Open DTP and OSI-TP form the foundations for "open transaction management." This section covers the X/Open DTP.

The X/Open DTP Reference Model—Vintage 1991

*T*he X/Open DTP model is a software architecture that allows multiple application programs to share resources provided by multiple resource managers, and allows their work to be coordinated into global transactions.

> — X/Open, DTP Reference V2
> (December, 1993)

In 1991, the X/Open XTP group published the *Transaction Processing Reference Model*, which has achieved wide acceptance in the industry. The primary purpose of this model is to define the components of a transaction-based system and to locate the interfaces between them. The 1991 model defined three components: application programs, transaction managers, and resource managers (see Figure 17-5). In X/Open's definition:

■ A *resource manager* is any piece of software that manages shared resources— for example, a database manager, a persistent queue, or transactional file system—and allows the updates to its resources to be externally coordinated via a two-phase commit protocol.

■ A *transaction manager* is the component that coordinates and controls the resource managers. The transaction manager and resource manager communicate via X/Open's *XA interface* published in 1991. The transaction manager use xa_* API calls to interact with the resource managers; the resource managers use ax_* API calls to interact with the transaction manager. For example, the transaction manager issues an xa_start to tell a resource manager to join a new transaction. It issues $xa\_prepare$, xa_commit, and $xa\_rollback$ to tell a resource manager to perform a two-phase commit. And it issues xa_end to tell the resource manager to leave this transaction. XA defines some additional calls for performing the recovery of "in-doubt" transactions. In the reverse direction, a resource manager issues an ax_reg call to register its presence dynamically with the transaction manager.[2]

■ An *application program* uses the general APIs supplied by a resource manager (for example, SQL), but it issues the transaction bracketing calls directly to the transaction manager via X/Open's *TX interface* published in 1992. An application calls tx_begin to start a transaction, tx_commit to commit it, $tx\_rollback$ to abort it, and $tx\_set\_transaction\_controls$ to set the chaining mode. Transactions can be chained or unchained (the default mode). The tx_info call returns

---

[2] X/Open allows resource managers to become associated with a global transaction only after the application directly calls them. They use the ax_reg call to dynamically register their presence.

information about the global context of a transaction. You should note that in the X/Open model, the application decides when it wants to participate in a transaction. The TX interface drives the XA interface when managing a global transaction. In theory, this allows an application to be developed independently of the TP Monitor target environment.

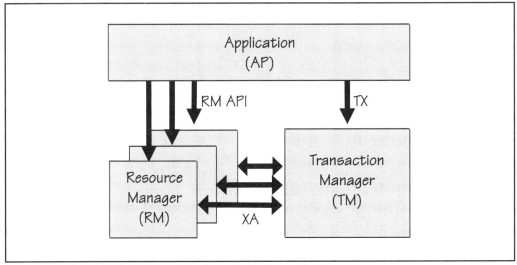

Figure 17-5. The X/Open 1991 Transaction Processing Reference Model.

The 1991 X/Open model only deals with programs talking to their local resource and transaction managers. The transaction can only execute within a single transaction manager's domain. It does not cover how an application requests resources that are on remote nodes and how these remote nodes join the transaction.

The X/Open DTP Reference Model—Vintage 1994

In 1994, X/Open issued Version 2 of its Distributed Transaction Reference Model. This version adds a fourth component to the model: the *communication resource manager*. This component controls communications between distributed applications (see Figure 17-6). X/Open also defined a superset of XA called *XA+* that defines the interface between the communication resource managers and the transaction manager. This interface lets the transaction manager know which remote resource managers the transaction is visiting. It also supports global transaction information flows across transaction manager domains. XA+ is still an X/Open snapshot; it will eventually supersede XA.

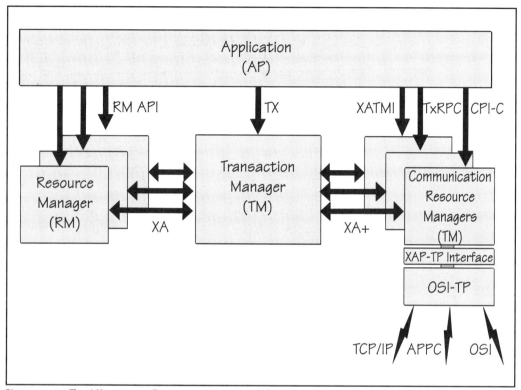

Figure 17-6. The X/Open 1994 Transaction Processing Reference Model.

At the application level, X/Open is in the process of defining *three* interfaces between applications and communication resource managers:

■ **TxRPC** is a transactional version of the DCE RPC. An RPC call can either have *transaction-mandatory* or *transaction-optional* attributes that are specified through the IDL. The underlying mechanism for TxRPC is a technology from Digital called *Remote Task Invocation (RTI)* that uses OSI-TP to do the two-phase commit (also see the following Soapbox).

■ **CPI-C V2** is a peer-to-peer conversational interface based on CPI-C and APPC. An IBM-led working group is in the process of extending CPI-C to support OSI-TP semantics.

■ **XATMI** is a client/server conversational interface based on Tuxedo's *Application/Transaction Management Interface (ATMI)*. The interface allows you to issue a single request/response using the *tpcall* API. Or you can use it in general conversation mode through the *tpconnect, tpsend, tprecv* calls.

The target upper-layer protocol for each of these APIs is the OSI-TP FAP. Below the OSI-TP FAP, communication resource managers can support multiple transport protocols—including TCP/IP, OSI, and APPC. Of course, proprietary protocols may be used between homogeneous transaction manager domains. The use of OSI-TP is mandatory for communications between heterogeneous transaction manager domains. In theory, we should be able to achieve some level of multivendor interoperability (this is, after all, the idea behind all these standards). However, X/Open does not address the relationship between the different communication APIs—for example, it says nothing about an XATMI application being able to exchange messages with a CPI-C application via the X/Open specified communication resource managers.

Figure 17-7 shows how a global transaction exchange may be conducted. The application on the left node interacts with the remote resource via its communications resource manager. The transaction manager on the node where the request originates acts as the commit coordinator using the services of the communications resource manager. The commit coordinator is the *root* transaction monitor and the remote monitor is a *subordinate*.

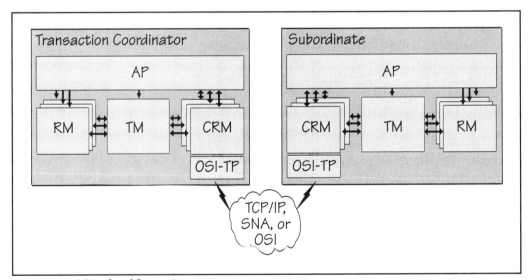

Figure 17-7. A Distributed Transaction.

Of course, more than two nodes can participate in an exchange. Global transactions that operate across distributed transaction managers are managed using trees of transaction manager relationships (see Figure 17-8). The example shows B to be the *superior* to both C and D, but it is a *subordinate* of A, which acts as the commit coordinator. During the two-phase commit, the superior manages the commitment coordination of its subordinates and reports the results up the chain.

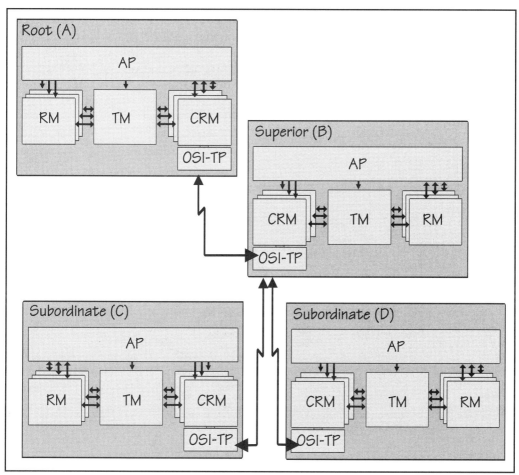

Figure 17-8. A Global Transaction Tree Structure.

Why Three Interface Standards?

Soapbox

So why do we need three interfaces at the application level? Wouldn't a single API make more sense from the portability and interoperability perspectives? We think so, but the "official" X/Open line is that they each bring their own rich set of interapplication communication paradigms. A more likely explanation is that the committee put together a specification that would make its three warring contingents—DCE, CICS, and Tuxedo—happy. This is how most standards are born!

By the way, there's more coming. X/Open is currently looking at adding a message queuing interface. Three base proposals were submitted for consideration: MQI (IBM), /Q (Tuxedo), and RQS (Encina). In addition, there's OSI-MQ. So perhaps we may get four more "standard" interfaces that will make everybody else on the committee happy. And a glaring omission is that nobody's defined a thin client interface that can issue a "delegated commit" and then let the closest TP Monitor take it over from there. This could also lead to a few more interfaces! Note: In mid-1994, X/Open decided to cease work on the three incompatible CRM options; it will wait for the marketplace to pick the winner. ❑

What the Transaction Standards Do Not Address

The X/Open standard does *not* address many issues that are of practical importance to TP Monitors; for example:

■ Process management—including starting processes, registering processes, balancing workloads among processes, and so on.
■ Configuration, installation, and monitoring of transaction processing systems.
■ Security.
■ Naming and directory services.
■ System management and operator interfaces.
■ Fault-tolerance.
■ Desktop originated transactions. At a minimum, X/Open should address the issue of thin clients and delegated commits.

The X/Open model *does* address a very small but important subset of a TP Monitor: The transaction interfaces and how transactions are declared. However, it does not address the inner core: *transaction processing*. Yet, we need to standardize a lot of this inner core so that federated TP Monitors can become a reality.

Alternatives to the Standards

The alternative is to standardize on a single vendor's TP Monitor platform— preferably one that runs on many OSs and interoperates with a wide variety of resource managers. For example, IBM offers a "CICS on everything" solution; it provides CICS on MVS, AIX, HP-UX, OS/2, OS/400, and NT. Tuxedo runs on 36 Unix platforms, NT, and Tandem Computers' highly-scalable Pathway environment. IBM and Transarc are also porting Encina to as many platforms as money and time permits.

The benefits provided by this single-vendor approach are:

■ You can pick and choose and even "mix-and-match" resource managers (such as databases). You can do that because most TP Monitors and database managers now support XA and XA+ interfaces.

■ Your applications are easier to manage because you're dealing with a single point of management.

■ Your applications are easier to port (on your TP vendor's other supported OS/hardware platforms) because you get a large number of portable API calls. Your applications can take advantage of a much larger number of services than those provided in a least common denominator portability approach.

The negatives of this single-vendor approach are:

■ Your applications are not portable across TP Monitor platforms.
■ Your applications may not interoperate with other TP Monitors.
■ You're locked into a single vendor TP Monitor solution.

It's the typical Catch-22 of client/server computing: single vendor lock-in with peace of mind, or multivendor openness but waiting for up-to-date standards and broader functionality. Independence Technologies recently developed a product called *iTRAN* that can help you out of the Catch-22; *iTRAN* provides a TP-neutral toolkit that works with CICS, Encina, Top End, and Tuxedo. The iTRAN libraries work with a variety of C++ compilers and desktop tools. They make TP Monitors services resemble local procedure calls or method invocations. Of course, the downside is that you have an iTRAN API lock-in. In this business, you always seem to trade one lock-in for another.

DO YOU NEED A TP MONITOR?

A *word of congratulations to the OLTP community is in order: We can now glue most any systems together.*

— *Alfred Spector, CEO, Transarc*
(September, 1995)

Because TP Monitors may be unfamiliar to many of our readers, we will go over a list of benefits that TP Monitors offer to client/server applications. Even though TP Monitors were originally introduced to serve very large "mission-critical" applications, the new versions are well-suited for handling client/server applications that span from a few nodes to thousands of nodes. Eventually, we believe that a TP Monitor component will reside on every workstation that's connected to a network—not just servers.

Here's a list of benefits that can be obtained from using the current crop of client/server oriented TP Monitors:

- *Client/Server application development framework.* Increasingly, visual tool vendors are directly supporting RPCs and making the TP Monitor transparent to the developers. IDL-defined RPCs are easier to integrate with front-end tools than proprietary stored procedures. On the server side, TP Monitors provide general-purpose server shells (server classes) that run your RPCs. The TP Monitor introduces an event-driven programming style on servers by letting you associate RPCs (event handlers) with server events. In addition, the TP Monitor run-time environment enforces the ACID discipline without requiring any specialized code other than begin/end transaction. You can think of a TP Monitor as providing a pre-built *framework* that helps you build, run, and administer a client/server application (you don't start from ground zero). TP Monitors—augmented with open vendor GUI tools—provide an excellent platform for developing robust, high-performing, client/server applications quickly.

- *Firewalls of protection.* In a client/server world, it is important to protect yourself from everything that can go wrong in the distributed environment. TP Monitors implement "firewalls" between applications and resource managers and between applications themselves. TP Monitors support tightly-coupled firewalls such as two-phase commits or loosely-coupled firewalls such as those provided by transactional queues. The unit of protection is the ACID transaction.

- *High availability.* TP Monitors are designed to work around all types of failures. The permeation of ACID principles throughout all components helps create self-healing systems. TP Monitors are always aware of the status the client/server resources under their control. With ACID, you can detect a failure exactly where it happens. If a hardware failure occurs, the TP Monitor can then restart the failed process or switch over to a process on another node. Architectures with no single point of failure are achievable.

■ ***Load balancing.*** TP Monitors specialize in process management and support both static and dynamic load balancing techniques. TP Monitors support the prioritization of requests and can *dynamically* replicate server processes on the same server node or on different nodes. In the static case, a pool of server classes may be scheduled to handle certain peak loads (for example, between work shifts) and then scaled down to support other job mixes during the day. The TP Monitor's load balancing software is an excellent match for today's new breed of SMP (and MPP) server hardware.

■ ***MOM integration.*** TP Monitors complement MOMs very well. Together they can provide support for long-lived transactions and workflow type of applications. TP Monitors can act as the transaction coordinator for work that is exchanged through transactional queues. The queued events can trigger server processes managed by the TP Monitor.

■ ***Scalabilty of function.*** TP Monitors encourage you to create modular reusable procedures that encapsulate resource managers. With a TP Monitor, you export the function call and not the data itself. This means that you can keep adding new function calls and let the TP Monitor distribute that function over multiple servers. TP Monitors allow you to create highly complex applications by just adding more procedures. The TP Monitor guarantees that procedures that know nothing about each other will work together in ACID unison. In addition, the TP Monitor lets you mix resource managers, so you can always start with one resource manager and then move to another one while preserving your investments in the function calls. All functions—even legacy ones—join the TP Monitor managed pool of reusable procedures. In other words, TP Monitors let you add heterogenous server resources anywhere without altering the existing application architecture. The Standish Group calls this "matrix scalability."

■ ***Reduced system cost.*** With TP Monitors you can save money. According to the Standish Group, TP Monitors may result in total system cost savings of greater than 30%—depending on system scale—over a more database-centric approach. In addition, the Standish Group research shows that significant "development time" savings—up to 40% or 50%—can be achieved. In addition, the funneling effect of TP Monitors can result in large savings in the acquisition of resource managers. This is because database vendors charge by the number of active users; funneling cuts down on that number, which equates to lower license fees. For example, the Standish Group estimates that with a TP Monitor you can save 62% on a 128-user Oracle system. TP Monitors, with their load balancing, also provide better performance using the same system resources; this means that you can run your application on less expensive hardware. Finally, TP Monitors don't lock you into a vendor-specific database solution, which makes the acquisition process more competitive and adds to cost savings (instead, they lock you into a TP Monitor single vendor solution).

So when should you use a TP Monitor? Standish Group recommends that you use a TP Monitor for any client/server application that has over 100 clients, processes five or more TPC-C type transactions per minute, uses three or more servers, and/or uses two or more databases. Bobby Cameron of Forrester Research prefers using a TP Monitor as a middleware traffic cop (almost like a CORBA ORB).

Your authors recommend that you use a TP Monitor for all your client/server applications. It will put you in the habit of writing 3-tier client/server applications, which is goodness in our book. And it prepares you for the world of CORBA ORBs—the final destination. Now that some of the popular client/server tools have added support for TP Monitors, you can't use the excuse that they're too difficult to program. And if you believe Standish, they save you money in the long run, so cost should not be an issue. We continue this discussion in the next chapter.

Chapter 18

TP-Lite or TP-Heavy?

The database companies want to control the application space through the use of their proprietary database stored procedures. By controlling the application space, they control the customer.

> — *Jim Johnson, Chairman, Standish Group*
> *(April, 1995)*

TP Monitors are proprietary environments. It is a bit silly to suggest that their use provides independence.

> — *Bobby Cameron, Forrester Research*
> *(April, 1995)*

You may recall from Part 4 that the SQL database managers are also in the business of managing transactions across their own resources. Some database-centric advocates argue that database transactions with stored procedures is all that's needed in the area of transaction management. They call their approach *TP-Lite*.

In contrast to database managers, TP Monitors extend the notion of transactions to *all* resources, not just data-centric ones. TP Monitors track the execution of functions on a single server or across servers on the network—their approach is called *TP-Heavy*. We will go over the current industry debate between TP-Lite and TP-Heavy. As Jim Gray puts it, "Your problems aren't over by just embracing the concept of RPC or even TP-Lite."

And while these two TP camps are debating, the majority of the PC-centric (and Unix) client/server world is *TP-Less*. There is very little awareness in the PC world today of what transaction management is and why it's even needed. However, transaction management is second nature to most IS people who are "downsizing" from mainframe environments. These folks won't deploy an OLTP application on PC LANs without some kind of TP Monitor. As a result, they're creating demand for a new breed of LAN-based TP Monitors. The Standish Group calculated that the total revenue from TP Monitors was $17.2 billion in 1995 and is expected to reach $20 billion in 1997. These numbers say that the OLTP market represents a huge opportunity for client/server systems.

In this chapter, we cover the TP-Lite versus TP-Heavy debate. It's important to understand what's missing from database-centric transaction processing. And, of course, there will be a Soapbox that tells you our side of that debate. Again Jim Gray is right: "TP is where the money is: both literally (most banks are TP systems) and figuratively (CICS has generated more revenues than any other piece of software)." So it may be worth exploring which type of TP system—Lite or Heavy—is best for client/server needs.

THE ORIGINS OF TP-LITE

My transaction hopes are pinned on the impact of the distribution of processing—when it is realized that data is not everything and that process is just as important.

— Jim Gray

In the good old days of mainframes, the divisions were clear: Database servers focused on managing data, while TP Monitors focused on managing processes and applications. The two sides stayed out of each other's turf and kept improving on what they did best. It was a classical win/win situation where everybody prospered. This happy coexistence came to an end in 1986, when Sybase became the first database vendor to integrate components of the TP Monitor inside the database engine.

Sybase Breaks the Truce

How did Sybase do it? You may recall from Part 4 that Sybase funnels all client requests into a multithreaded, single-process server. It's an N-to-1 funnel. This may be called a case of *funnel overkill* because the database and user applications share the same address space—a sure invitation for disaster.

But Sybase did not stop with funneling; it also became the first database vendor to introduce stored procedures and triggers—two functions that definitely belong on the procedural side of the house. With its new architecture, Sybase became the uncontested champion of the database benchmarking wars. Of course, most database vendors were quick to follow suit. By now, most of them provide some level of funneling and support for stored procedures in their database engines. Application developers and tool vendors were quick to exploit the benefits of stored procedures, and the *TP-Lite* client/server architecture was born.

Given the popularity of database servers on PC LANs, does this mean TP Monitors are dead? Are they just an anachronism from the mainframe days? Is TP-Lite integrated with database the new platform of choice for application servers and OLTP? The answers to all these questions must, of course, be no; we didn't write an entire part on TP Monitors for nothing. So let's first review the facts in a cool, analytical manner. Then we'll jump on the Soapbox and throw in some opinions about where all this is heading.

What Is TP-Lite?

TP-Lite is simply the integration of TP Monitor functions in the database engines. Currently, only a few of the TP Monitor functions are integrated—including function shipping, some level of funneling, single-function transaction management, and RPC-like calls. It is not clear if the database vendors plan to reinvent the wheel and develop all the missing TP Monitor functions in TP-Lite. There's still a long list of unimplemented functions; the TP Monitor people have a ten-year headstart.

What Is TP-Heavy?

TP-Heavy are TP Monitors as defined in this chapter. The new generation of *TP-Heavy* products for client/server LANs includes CICS, Encina, Tuxedo, Tandem's Pathway, Top End, and Digital's ACMS. All these TP Monitors support the client/server architecture and allow PCs to initiate some very complex multiserver transactions from the desktop. All these products are supported by open visual builder tools that let you create the front-end separately from the back-end.

TP-Heavy includes all the functions defined in this chapter—including process management, load balancing, global transaction synchronization, interfaces to multiple resource managers, and error recovery.

TP-LITE VERSUS TP-HEAVY

TP-Lite systems may not solve all the world's problems, but they solve many simple ones. According to Ziph's law: most problems are simple.

> — Jim Gray, High Performance
> Transaction Workshop (September, 1993)

We won't have an OLTP environment manufactured by a single vendor (TP-Lite), but rather an OLTP environment that includes a mosaic of services (TP-Heavy). I think TP-Heavy will win.

> — Alfred Spector, High Performance
> Transaction Workshop (September, 1993)

The competition between TP-Lite and TP-Heavy is painfully unequal. It's like comparing a Harley-Davidson motorcycle with a bicycle. TP-Lite can best be defined by what it lacks, which is a long list of functions. In a nutshell, TP-Lite functions don't execute under global transaction control, there is no global supervisor, and the process management environment is very primitive. TP-Lite server functions only work with a single resource manager (the local database), and they don't support any form of ACID nesting. Like a bicycle, these functions are perfect fits for certain environments. But you should realize what you're missing because you'll rarely see it mentioned in the database marketing literature.

TP-Lite Versus TP-Heavy: Scope of the Commit

A *TP-Lite* stored procedure is written in a database-vendor proprietary procedural language—PL/SQL, Transact SQL, and so on—and is stored in the database. A stored procedure is a transactional unit, but it can't participate with other transactional units in a global transaction. It can't call another transaction and have it execute within the same transaction boundary. As shown in Figure 18-1, if stored procedure A dies after invoking stored procedure B, A's work will automatically get rolled back while B's work is committed for posterity. This is a violation of the ACID all-or-nothing proposition. This limitation causes you to write large transactions that put everything within the scope of the commit. It doesn't help the cause of modularization or writing reusable functions.

In contrast, *TP-Heavy* procedures are written using standard procedural languages. They can easily provide all-or-nothing protection in situations like the one shown in the right-hand side of Figure 18-1. For TP-Heavy, dealing with global transactions is second nature.

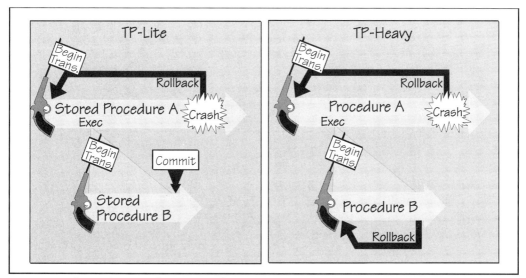

Figure 18-1. TP-Lite Versus TP-Heavy: Scope of the Commit.

TP-Lite Versus TP-Heavy: Managing Heterogeneous Resources

RDBMSs do not support the notion of a global transaction that encompasses more than one program.

> — *Richard Finkelstein, President*
> *Performance Computing*
> *(November, 1995)*

A *TP-Lite* stored procedure can only commit transaction resources that are on the vendor's database or resource manager (see Figure 18-2). It cannot synchronize or commit work that is on a foreign—local or non-local—database or resource manager. In contrast, *TP-Heavy* procedures can easily handle ACID updates on multiple heterogeneous resource managers within the scope of a single transaction.

Note that some database vendors (i.e., TP-Lite) can extend two-phase commit to multiple databases—usually their own. Oracle7's *Open Gateway* even lets you manage the two-phase commit across heterogeneous XA-compliant databases.

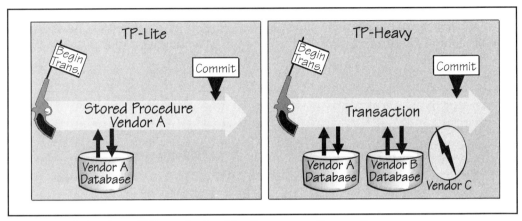

Figure 18-2. TP-Lite Versus TP-Heavy: Synchronizing Heterogeneous Resource Managers.

However, the catch is that gateways are built on the assumption that a stored procedure within a single database is the entire application (and also the point of origin of the transaction). Gateways do not allow multiple applications (or stored procedures) to participate in a transaction. Gateways also lock you into a database vendor's proprietary TP-Lite (or stored procedure) environment. On the other hand, TP-Heavy really makes your applications resource-neutral.

TP-Lite Versus TP-Heavy: Process Management

A *TP-Lite* stored procedure gets invoked, executed under ACID protection (within a single-phase commit), and *may* then be cached in memory for future reuse. That's about it. In contrast, *TP-Heavy* processes are prestarted and managed as server classes (see Figure 18-3). If the load on a server class gets too heavy, more

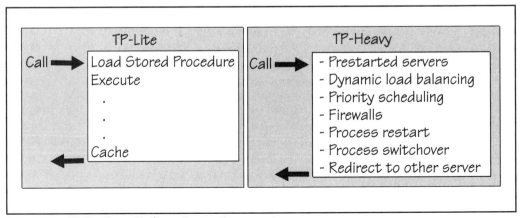

Figure 18-3. TP-Lite Versus TP-Heavy: Process Management.

processes are automatically started. Server classes support priorities and other class-of-service attributes. Server processes have firewalls around them so that the programs that run within them don't interfere with each other. If a server class process dies, it is restarted or the transaction can be reassigned to another server process in that class. The entire environment runs under the constant supervision of the TP Monitor. The server class concept helps the TP Monitor understand what class of service is required by the user for a particular group of functions. It's an intelligently managed environment.

TP-Lite Versus TP-Heavy: Client/Server Invocations

The *TP-Lite* stored procedure invocation is extremely non-standard. Vendors provide their own proprietary RPC invocation mechanism. The RPCs are not defined using an IDL. And they're not integrated with global directory, security, and authentication services. The communications links are not automatically restarted, and they're not under transaction protection. In addition, TP-Lite does not support MOM or conversational exchanges.

In contrast, the *TP-Heavy* environment is very open to different communication styles (see Figure 18-4). The RPC can use DCE as its base. You can easily integrate MOM transactional queues into the global transaction. Most TP Monitor vendors also support APPC/CPI-C for peer-to-peer communications.

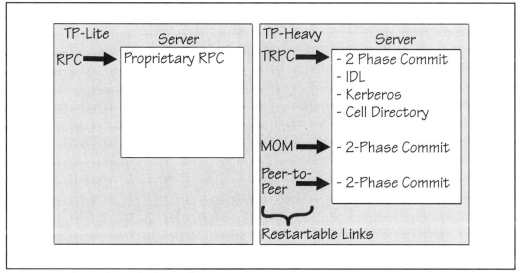

Figure 18-4. TP-Lite Versus TP-Heavy: Client/Server Invocation.

TP-Lite Versus TP-Heavy: Performance

TP-Lite stored procedures are much faster than networked static or dynamic SQL because they cut down on network traffic. However, they don't perform as well as TP-Heavy managed procedures, especially under heavy loads. Most stored procedures dynamically interpret each SQL statement for each transaction and then recreate the access plan. In addition, most stored procedures are written using interpreted 4GLs, which are slow. Virtually all standardized database benchmarks are executed with a TP Monitor managing the application services in front of a database. In December 1995, 23 out of the top 25 TPC-C database benchmark scores were obtained using TP Monitors.[1] The exception is Microsoft; it was able to obtain good benchmarking results on *SQL Server* by directly optimizing to NT's SMP scheduling. However, Microsoft is building a TP Monitor into the next release of SQL Server, so this should tell you something.

TP Monitors also save you money by being more efficient and requiring less hardware. Essentially, the TP Monitor offloads the database server by multiplexing client requests. It acts as a funnel on top of whatever funnel the database may have already put in place. In addition, the TP Monitor's precompiled (and prebound) application code runs more efficiently than the interpreted stored procedures.

Let's see how this can help even the "over-funneled" Sybase server. In the example shown in Figure 18-5, instead of seeing 1000 clients, a Sybase multithreaded server is made to think it's dealing with 50 clients. The Sybase database server sees a reduced number of database clients, and acts more responsively as a result. The same story applies to other vendors' databases, some more than others.

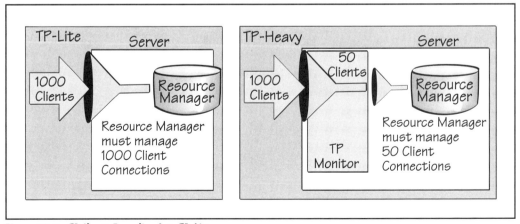

Figure 18-5. TP-Heavy Funneling Into TP-Lite.

---

[1] Source: FT Systems (December, 1995)

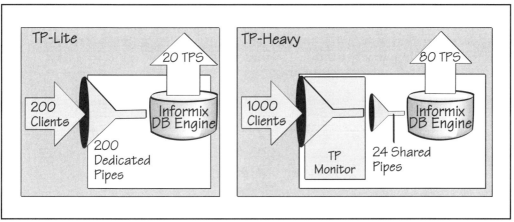

Figure 18-6. How TP-Heavy Helps the Performance of TP-Lite (Source: Unisys Corporation).

Figure 18-6 shows you how dramatic some of these numbers can be—the benchmarks were run on the same hardware with an Informix database engine (with and without a TP Monitor). In addition, significant cost savings can be achieved because fewer database resources are needed to support a given workload (the Informix example makes the point).

Conclusion

If I had to do an application that had a lot of processing, I'd use a distributed TP Monitor.

> — *Ed Wood, VP of Interoperability*
> *Sybase*
> *(August, 1995)*

TP-Lite has turned out to be as complex as TP-Heavy once it is forced to move out from beneath the protection of the simple single server (with a small number of clients) environment where it originally took root.

> — *Charles Brett, Senior Editor*
> *Middleware Spectrum*
> *(September, 1995)*

TP-Heavy products were created to meet the process management requirements of mission-critical OLTP environments. They tend to be very robust and have excellent system management facilities. TP-Lite products are newcomers in the area of process management and haven't had time to develop mature field-tested products.

It takes years of product incubation to develop the right facilities in areas such as online distribution of new processes, remote debugging, built-in statistics, administration tools, and automatic switchovers during failures (and later reconciliations). See the Soapbox below for a stronger opinion.

So Is It TP-Lite or TP-Heavy?

Soapbox

TP-Lite or TP-Heavy? Most likely neither. The debate about the need for a TP Monitor is only interesting in the short term, since today's transactional infrastructures are inappropriate for supporting business process reengineering.

> — *Gartner Group*
> *(November 22, 1993)*

The attributes that made TP-lite so profoundly dominant are about to become the same attributes that cause it to take a second seat to a rebirth of TP-heavy, disguised as object systems.

> — *Mohsen Al-Ghosein, TP Architect*
> *Microsoft*
> *(September, 1995)*

Rome wasn't built overnight and neither were TP Monitors. And as far as we can see, TP Monitors have a huge head start over TP-Lite in the area of process management. TP-Lite doesn't even come close to managing environments where a transaction spans across machines or resource managers (the so-called multi-domain transactions). TP-Heavy provides global management and allows multi-vendor resource managers (including databases) to plug into the system; it gives us choice. You can then depend on TP-Heavy to make the "mosaic" whole. In contrast, TP-Lite provides an entry-level, single-domain, single-database solution for transaction processing.

So TP-Lite, like a bicycle, is quite useful in situations where you're dealing with a single vendor database and a small to medium number of users. And, as bicycles teach us the joy of being on wheels, TP-Lite will teach thousands of programmers the joy of transaction processing. TP-Lite is ideal in entry-level situations because it's less complex; you only have to deal with one server component: the database. The TP-Lite vendors also understand how to market to the client/server world—a very important advantage.

However, TP-Heavy technology is extremely important to the future of client/server computing. Think about what you could do with a Harley-Davidson instead of a bicycle. TP Monitors let us mix together components in all sorts of wild combinations; at the same time, they guarantee that everything comes together like clockwork. In other words, TP Monitors let us do the mix-and-match that is the forte of an open client/server world. Unfortunately, the TP Monitor vendors are having a very hard time selling this message. They still use a lot of antique terminology that sounds very foreign to the PC LAN culture.

TP-Heavy vendors should focus on putting a "friendly" version of a TP Monitor on every desktop and in every 32-bit operating system. Gartner (see previous quote) would like to see transaction processing move to the next phase and start worrying about workflow—the topic of Part 6. We wholeheartedly agree. Microsoft's Mohsen Al-Ghosein thinks transaction processing should move to objects. We fully agree with him, too (although we suspect he means OLE objects—our bias is towards CORBA objects). But given the current mindset of the TP-Heavy vendors, we'll be lucky just to get a TP Monitor on an occasional PC or Unix LAN server. They don't have the volume channels or the right packaging for their products, and they can't get beyond their "selling to MIS" origins. Yet MIS and the rest of us can greatly benefit if every PC on the network were ACID-ized. Wouldn't it be nice if every PC could participate in a global transaction? We believe that most exchanges in the "post-scarcity future" will be in the form of global transactions.

As you will see in the next chapter, open TP Monitors are starting to radically improve the OLTP image. They managed to gain a solid toe-hold in the client/server market by popularizing 3-tiered applications, as well as introducing GUI tools and flexible middleware such as MOMs and event brokers. However, they are nowhere near capturing the hearts and minds of the client/server mainstream. There is still not enough mass marketing and too much "CICS-speak" left in the products. People still believe that you have to be a high priest of computer science to deal with TP Monitors (and transactions in general).

Later in the book (after we explore a few more concepts), we will tell you why we believe that distributed objects are the answer. In a nutshell, objects can subsume the functions provided by TP Monitors, groupware, and Internet servers. And, they have the right shape to put a transaction manager in every PC. Yes, the future belongs to function shipping and 3-tiered client/server, but this vision will be realized using "TP Objects" and CORBA middleware. Remember, this is a Soapbox and you're getting an extra-strong dose of opinion at this early stage. ❏

Chapter 19

TP Monitors: Meet the Players

TP Monitors are like the Rolling Stones—been around for a long time, but still drawing large crowds.

— **David Linthicum, CSC Consulting**
(July, 1995)

Like the Rolling Stones, TP Monitors are being rediscovered by a new generation of technologists. And like the Rolling Stones, TP Monitors are continuously reinventing themselves. This chapter gives you a snapshot of the TP Monitor market, goes over the current trends, and then introduces the key players. Of course, we will not be throwing reference manuals at you describing all the products. At this stage, it's more important for you to understand how commercial TP Monitors are lining up, where they are going, and what they can do for you. The good (and bad) news is that there are only a few major players to cover: AT&T GIS's *Top End*, Transarc/IBM's *Encina*, IBM's *CICS family*, and BEA's *Tuxedo*. We will also cover Tandem's *Pathway*—a massively parallel TP Monitor engine that runs other people's TP Monitors as guests.

TP MONITOR MARKET OVERVIEW

Today, 90% of all mission-critical transaction processing is done through one of the more than 100,000 currently installed TP Monitors.

— *Jim Johnson, Chairman*
Standish Group
(April, 1995)

According to the Standish Group, TP Monitor software revenues for 1995 were $1.186 billion. In the same year, the total TP Monitor-related systems sales—including hardware and tools—topped $17 billion. Today, 90% of all TP Monitor applications are implemented on high-end systems such as IBM's *CICS on MVS*, IBM's *IMS/TP,* and Tandem Computer's *Pathway.* However, a new generation of "open" TP Monitors has entered the market—including *Encina, Top End, Tuxedo,* and *CICS client/server.* These products run on multiple operating systems and are mostly client/server-based (as opposed to terminal-based). According to Standish, Open TP Monitor sales experienced 382% growth from 1993 to 1994. Standish expects these products to account for over one-third of all TP Monitor sales by 1998 (see Figure 19-1).

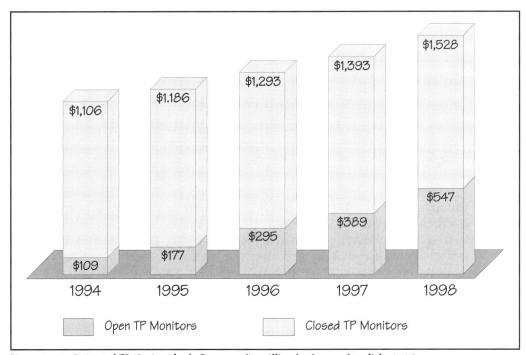

Figure 19-1. Estimated TP Monitor Yearly Revenues (in millions). Source: Standish, 1995.

TRENDS

TP Monitors are competing with objects to become the application server platform of choice for 3-tier client/server computing—the fastest growing segment of the client/server market. In addition, TP Monitors are going after new sources of transactions such as the Internet, Intranets, and server-to-server electronic commerce. Again, they will face strong competition from CORBA objects in all these areas. Here's a snapshot of the major movements that we're seeing in the TP Monitor industry:

■ ***TP Monitors become portable application server environments***. TP Monitors can now run across most major server operating systems. Consequently, they provide portable server application environments. You write your 3-tier application once and port it to the server environments of your choice.

■ ***TP Monitors become universal traffic cops***. In addition to supporting their traditional clients, TP Monitors now intercept and route calls from other types of clients—including Lotus Notes, the Internet, and MOM.

■ ***TP Monitors become resource brokers***. In addition to SQL databases, TP Monitors now support all kinds of back-end resource managers—including a multiplicity of file systems, hierarchical databases, persistent queues, image stores, HTML repositories, and Lotus Notes document databases.

■ ***TP Monitors discover client/server tools***. In addition to their venerable COBOL workbenches, TP Monitors are teaming up with popular client/server tools—including Sybase's *Powersoft*, Four Season Software's *SuperNOVA 4GL*, JYACC's *Jam 7 4GL*, Borland's *Delphi*, Digitalk *Parts*, Gupta's *Centura*, and IBM's *VisualAge*. It's getting to the point that you can access TP Monitor services from any tool which supports DLLs—for example, *Visual Basic*. A new generation of 3-tier client/server tools also support TP Monitors—including *Dynasty, Open Horizon, Forte, Magna, Unify Vision*, and IBM's *VisualGen*. TP Monitor vendors learned this lesson: Without equivalent tools, programmers will not convert from 2-tier to 3-tier development.

■ ***TP Monitors meet objects***. Most TP Monitors now provide C++ class libraries to access their services. Some TP Monitors let CORBA clients call their services using CORBA IDL-defined interfaces. In addition, some TP Monitors are implementing interfaces to the CORBA-defined *Object Transaction Service*. This will let TP Monitor-managed applications participate in global transactions with CORBA objects. We explain what this all means in Part 7.

The good news for TP Monitors is that they're very well situated to go after the fast-growing 3-tier client/server market. The 3-tier market is expected to grow to 20% of total client/server applications in 1997 (up from 5% today). The bad news is that TP Monitors are being sandwiched between two very popular competing technologies: database stored procedures at the low end and CORBA distributed objects at the intergalactic level. TP Monitor vendors may discover that the fastest way to succeed is to "morph" into CORBA object request brokers. We will have more to say about this morphing in Part 7, after we introduce CORBA objects.

THE PLAYERS

Figure 19-2 shows how the TP Monitor pie was divided in 1995. Note that CICS and IMS/TP sales account for over 60% of TP Monitor sales. Microsoft is expected to become a major TP Monitor player in 1997 with OLE/TP; it currently does not even show up on the radar screen. Microsoft's approach is to build TP hooks into all its products and the operating system. Consequently, there will be many new sources of transactions, as well as new types of resource managers that can participate in global transactions. This may translate into increased sales for TP Monitors and for their future CORBA and OLE competitors.

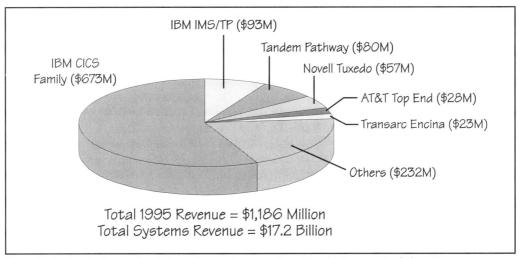

Figure 19-2. TP Monitor Vendors Estimated 1995 Revenues (in millions). Source: Standish, 1995.

Standish Group predicts that by the year 1997, the "Big Four" TP Monitors will be IBM's *CICS*, BEA's *Tuxedo*, Transarc's *Encina*, and AT&T GIS's *Top End*. We believe that this group may also include a future OLE-based TP Monitor product from Microsoft and a follow-on to Tandem's *Pathway*. In the remaining sections, we look at what these vendors offer today.

IBM's CICS

IBM continued to carve out mindshare in 1995 by offering CICS across more platforms. In late 1995, it introduced *CICS for NT*—a clone of the OS/2 version. IBM also introduced a newer version of *CICS for AIX* that takes advantage of SP2 MPP (according to IBM, the new version offers ten-fold performance improvement over the previous version). So the latest roundup of CICS server offerings from IBM includes CICS for MVS, OS/400, OS/2, NT, and AIX. In addition to IBM, several other vendors provide CICS servers on Unix—including HP's *CICS for HP 9000*, Digital's *CICS for OSF/1*, Tandem's *Parallel CICS* personality, Bull's *Unikix*, MicroFocus's *CICS Option*, and VISystems' *VIS/TP.*

In 1995, IBM also introduced a "universal CICS client" that runs on OS/2, Windows, Mac, and DOS. With the new CICS client capability, IBM now offers a consistent client/server TP Monitor solution across a wide variety of client and server platforms. CICS clients and servers communicate using a transactional RPC called the *External Call Interface (ECI)*. First introduced in 1993 with *CICS for OS/2*, ECI provides a thin client environment that lets you directly invoke CICS programs over a variety of transports—including NetBIOS, TCP/IP, APPC, and IPX/SPX. Some tools—for example, VisualAge and Easel—now support the ECI from within their environments. This means that you do not have to directly code to the API.

As an added option, CICS clients can emulate terminals using the *External Presentation Interface (EPI)*. Yes, terminals are still alive and well in many TP Monitor shops. At the other extreme, CICS supports the DCE-based Encina Transactional RPC on some of its Unix platforms. Note that the new version of *CICS for AIX* reduces some of DCE's complexities by not requiring the security and name servers to be installed on single-domain servers.

In late 1995, IBM delivered a *CICS Internet Gateway.* This lets Web users access CICS applications via the Internet's *Common Gateway Interface* (see Figure 19-3). We explain the CGI in Part 8. IBM is also providing a *Lotus Notes CICS Gateway* that lets Notes clients access CICS applications via either a CICS client running on a Notes server, or an *MQSeries* MOM connection. We explain Lotus Notes in Part 6.

IBM is also providing a *CICS to SOM* gateway. SOM is IBM's CORBA-compliant Object Request Broker (ORB). The idea is to let CORBA clients invoke CICS applications and let CICS clients invoke CORBA business objects. IBM plans to provide this service using a two-way CORBA/ECI gateway. For CICS clients, IBM will wrap a SOM-compliant C++ interface around its two procedural APIs—ECI and EPI. The gateway should let you describe CICS applications using the CORBA *Interface Definition Language (IDL)*. We explain CORBA in Part 7.

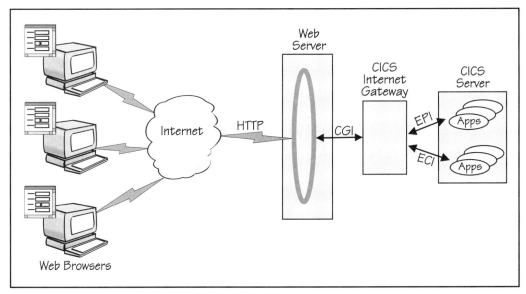

Figure 19-3. TP Monitor Meets Web: The CICS Internet Gateway.

Finally, in 1995, IBM radically changed the CICS pricing structure; it no longer uses a systems-based pricing schedule. Instead, pricing is now based on the number of registered users. Entry-level pricing for 10 users costs $3,500, which makes CICS more affordable to low-end users.

BEA/Novell's Tuxedo

Tuxedo is one of the only technologies that lets people build distributed applications that are OS-agnostic.

*— Sheldon Laube, CTO, Novell
(September, 1995)*

BEA/Novell's Tuxedo, originally from Unix Systems Lab (USL) provides a TP Monitor environment that runs on more than 36 Unix platforms—including HP-UX, AT&T GIS, AIX, Solaris, and OSF/1. Tuxedo provides client support on DOS, Unix, OS/2, and Mac OS. In addition, in 1995, Tandem shipped a parallel Tuxedo "personality" on top of its Pathway TP Monitor. Depending on the source, Tuxedo currently owns between 25% and 32% of the Unix TP Monitor market; it's down from 50% in 1992. [1] However, Tuxedo's revenues still grew by a healthy 140% in 1995.

---

[1] Source: Summit Strategies, **Report 6**, 1995.

In 1995, Novell finally decided to pull Tuxedo out of its Unix closet and position it as a key middleware technology for tying Windows NT, Unix, OS/2, and mainframe systems into NetWare networks. In late 1995, Novell started shipping *Tuxedo 6.1*, which runs on Unixes, NetWare, and NT. However, with the demise of Novell's SuperNOS—in late 1995—some industry observers were predicting that Tuxedo was heading for the auction block. They were right. In February 1996, Novell turned control of the non-NetWare development and distribution responsibility for Tuxedo to BEA Systems—a well-funded California start-up.[2]

Tuxedo 6.1 breaks new grounds by introducing the following features:

■ *NetWare Directory Service (NDS) Integration*. Novell offers an adjunct gateway product called *NetWare TransactionLink* that only runs on NetWare servers. It lets NetWare clients use NDS to access Tuxedo applications in addition to their existing NLM file, print, and e-mail services. You should be able to click on objects in an NDS tree to run applications on remote Tuxedo servers. Eventually, Novell plans to replace Tuxedo's namespace with NDS to provide a common directory that lets clients seamlessly access Tuxedo applications and NetWare resources. Note that NDS is currently only available on NetWare. So don't hold your breath waiting for this grand unification to take place.

■ *Graphical Application Manager*. Tuxedo 6.1 includes a Motif-based utility— called the *Application Manager*—that lets you manage and administer remote Tuxedo servers. The utility can monitor applications and provide statistics on performance in an SNMP Management Information Base (MIB). If there's a bottleneck, the software can reconfigure parameters "on-the-fly" and tune for load balancing and priority scheduling.

■ *SNMP Support*. Tuxedo 6.1 provides an SNMP agent and MIB. This means that popular enterprise management frameworks—such as HP's *OpenView* and IBM's *SystemView*—can remotely access the information collected by Tuxedo's *Application Manager*.

■ *Publish-and-Subscribe Event Brokering*. Tuxedo now provides an *Event-Broker* that mediates between publishers of events and subscribers. The broker automatically notifies subscribers when an event that affects them occurs—for example, when a stock price exceeds a threshold. With Tuxedo you can register the actions it should take when an event occurs. You should be able to trigger a series of processing steps across multiple applications in response to pre-

---

[2] BEA is not your ordinary start-up. Its goal is to become the "transaction company." Its entire business case is built around building and integrating TP Monitors. In addition to Tuxedo, BEA acquired the VISystems' CICS on Unix engine and the two leading suppliers of enterprise-level Tuxedo services Information Management Company (IMC) and Independence Technologies, Inc (ITI).

specified events. Tuxedo also lets you transfer data to subscribers as part of the event. On the receiving end, Tuxedo lets subscribers filter events based on wildcards. The advantage of letting a TP Monitor serve as the event manager is that it combines transactional reliability with event management.

In addition, *Tuxedo 6.1* supports dynamic data routing, which transparently routes queries to appropriate data repositories and allows administrators to change routing rules "on-the-fly." *Tuxedo 6.1* also provides new security features based on access control lists (ACLs). It lets you control the access to Tuxedo's queues, applications, and RPCs. The security system is also integrated with the event manager. For example, an ACL violation can trigger an event that sends a message to your top security sleuth.

The Tuxedo System 6.1 runtime sells for $395 per user. The developer version of Tuxedo sells for $2,395.

Transarc/IBM's Encina

Transarc's Encina was designed from the ground up as a postmodern TP Monitor based on OSF's DCE. In mid-1994, IBM acquired Transarc and now owns two TP Monitors: CICS and Encina. Encina 2.0 started shipping in late 1995 on top of DCE 1.1. By mid-1996, Encina 2.0 should be available on nearly ten operating systems—including OS/2, NT, HP-UX, AIX, Solaris, and OSF/1. The servers support eight resource managers—including Oracle, Sybase, DB2, and Informix. Encina clients will talk to their servers using a "lightweight" DCE client that provides a transactional RPC on top of TCP/IP and APPC stacks.

Transarc claims that performance improvements of up to 30% can be achieved using Encina 2.0—most of these improvements are attributed to DCE 1.1. Encina always used DCE as its underlying plumbing. DCE provides security and naming across networks as well as threads, distributed time, and a Distributed File System (DFS). Encina supports transactions across multiple resource managers—including SQL databases, ISAM, and Encina's own *Recoverable Queuing Service (RQS)* and *Structured File System (SFS)*. SFS extends DCE's DFS with support for nested transactions.

Encina 2.0 includes C++ class libraries that let you build transaction processing applications using the *Encina++* development framework. *Encina++* masks some of DCE's complexities from the developer. For example, it automatically establishes DCE security mechanisms and object-location services without additional programming on your part. Encina 2.0 also provides interfaces to the CORBA *Object Transaction Service*.

Encina 2.0 comes with the *Encina Console*—a GUI-based management interface that lets you configure and monitor the distributed application environment. For example, you can use the console to manage Encina and non-Encina resources—including recoverable queues, distributed file systems, peer-to-peer communications gateways, application servers, and external databases. Encina also supports the SNMP management protocol.

Since it acquired Transarc, IBM has repackaged *CICS for AIX* to include components of the Encina transaction processing engine. While some analysts speculated that IBM might give up Encina or CICS (or vice versa), it seems the company is still developing both products. IBM believes that each product attracts a different kind of customer. Encina is the better choice for users that have an intimate knowledge of how distributed systems work and intend to build an application using DCE. CICS is a less complicated choice for the 300,000 application programmers (mostly on mainframes) that are familiar with its APIs. Encina typically sells for $5,500 per server and $150 per client.

AT&T's Top End

Top End from NCR—now AT&T GIS—is a high-end TP Monitor for Unix SVR4 platforms. It supports MPP platforms such as AT&T's GIS 3600; it also works on ordinary Unix OSs such as AIX, Solaris, and HP-UX. In 1995, AT&T shipped Top End for NT—its first non-Unix platform. Top End uses XA to interface to database managers such as Oracle, Sybase, Teradata, and Informix. Developers can configure their Top End applications for either high availability or performance.

AT&T rarely sells a Top End system directly to MIS. Instead, most Top End systems are sold as part of an integrated vertical business solution. AT&T has defined a number of vertical frameworks for different target markets—including retail, inventory management, branch banking, communications, and call centers. A large number of Top End monitors are embedded in AT&T's voice and phone message management systems.

In 1995, AT&T introduced *Tempo*—an application development environment for Top End. *Tempo* lets you create Top End front-ends using Powersoft's *PowerBuilder*; and back-ends using Four Season Software's *SuperNOVA 4GL* server-based tools. *Tempo* provides the glue that lets you associate Top End server applications with PowerBuilder client events. *SuperNOVA* generates server code for a variety of database managers—including Informix, Oracle, Sybase, CA-Ingres, and Teradata.

Also in 1995, AT&T added *Recoverable Transaction Queueing (RTQ)* to the Top End TP middleware. Previously, Top End was the only TP Monitor that did not support a transactional MOM service. The turmoil in AT&T's GIS division makes it difficult to speculate on Top End's future direction. Top End is a pricey system that sells for around $600 per user. However, remember that most Top End solutions are bundled; AT&T does not go out of its way to sell TP Monitors directly to MIS.

Microsoft's Component Coordinator

We look at the world's most demanding transaction-processing systems and we ask ourselves: What does it take to make PCs or networks of PCs suitable for those tasks?

> — Bill Gates, Chairman
> Microsoft
> (January, 1995)

Microsoft will challenge the established TP vendors for control of new, emerging forms of distributed production work.

> — Gartner Group
> (January, 1995)

Even though Microsoft is not currently a player in the TP Monitor market, it has hired some top OLTP talent. In 1995, Microsoft issued a preliminary specification for *OLE/Transactions*. The OLE specification is in direct competition with the CORBA *Object Transaction Service (OTS)*. However, it leaves no doubt that Microsoft believes that the future of software is with 3-tier architectures and OLE-based objects. Transactions provide the glue that makes it all work in unison.

Microsoft plans to become a major player in the transaction market by adopting a bottom-up approach to transaction processing. First it plans to freely incorporate OLE-based transaction managers and logs with all its key software—including file systems, SQL Server, Excel, Access, Exchange, and the Internet Information Server (IIS). Next, it will provide a *Component Coordinator* that combines the function of an enterprise ORB and a TP Monitor. The coordinator will coordinate OLE objects and other resources across an enterprise using ACID principles. In its final version—due in 1997—the coordinator will support MOM interactions as well as RPC-like object invocations. We expect to see a reduced version of the Component Coordinator in *SQL Server 6.5* (expected in late 1996). It's a distributed transaction coordinator that supports two-phase commit and the XA standard. While this version of the coordinator does not support OLE Automation, it does include an OLE/TP API that gives C++ programmers access to transaction programming functions.

Tandem's Pathway

Tandem's *Pathway* is a high-end TP Monitor for loosely-coupled MPP systems. Pathway, which accounts for about 10% of the TP Monitor market, underwent some radical transformations over the last few years. In 1993, Pathway added support for a client/server architecture using a proprietary transactional RPC called *RSC*. RSC provides a thin RPC that runs on every client platform—including DOS, OS/2, Windows, NT, Mac, and almost every known flavor of Unix. By 1995, more than 70% of new Pathway applications were based on the client/server model. Pathway boasts of some of the largest known client/server applications (some support over 17,000 clients).

But there's even more to the *Pathway* story. In 1994, Tandem introduced a "multiple-personality" architecture on top of its core transaction engine. This means that Pathway can run other people's TP Monitor APIs in addition to its own. In 1995, Tandem shipped a parallel Tuxedo personality on top of Pathway. In 1996, Tandem expects to ship a parallel CICS personality, an Internet Commerce Server personality, and an IBM SOM-based CORBA personality. A TP Monitor application running on any of the personalities can invoke application services on any other personality—the TP Monitor engine acts as one big switch. In addition, the TP Monitor can dynamically load balance the processes to run on thousands of loosely-coupled processors. If any processor fails, the TP Monitor provides automatic switchover.[3]

CONCLUSION

As you can see, TP Monitors have come a long way. TP Monitor vendors have successfully created a need for their products in the 3-tier client/server application space. In addition, TP Monitors are constantly reinventing themselves and finding new uses for their services. Database vendors will continue to push back on TP Monitors and 3-tier applications in general.

The biggest challenge for TP Monitors will come from the CORBA ORB vendors. CORBA ORBs provide the ideal middleware for running distributed components that can play in all three tiers. In addition, TP Monitors are starting to discover objects but they're still playing in the CORBA periphery. In other words, they look at CORBA as just another client; objects are just a way to package class libraries.

As you will later discover, CORBA is a lot more than just another way to issue an RPC. CORBA provides the best open middleware platform on which TP Monitors

---

[3] Warning: If this sounds too glowing, it's because one of your authors managed the development of the Pathway product line during the last four years. However, she claims that it all works as advertised.

can build their services. Of course, TP Monitor vendors will claim that they already own the 3-tier space and that their middleware is just fine. So can there be a convergence? You'll have to wait until Part 7 to get an answer. As you can see, we're trying to generate some suspense.

Part 6

Client/Server

Groupware

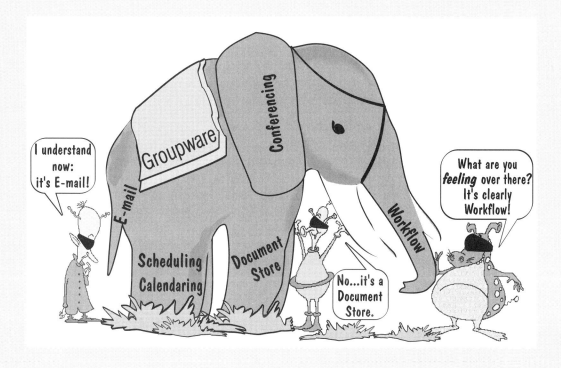

An Introduction to Part 6

If you buy into the motto that diversity is the spice of life, then groupware is for you.

— *Joe Paone, Internetwork*
(October, 1995)

Well, if you Martians think that ACID transactions and TP Monitors were fun, wait until you see groupware. Oh, by the way, we have an Earthling game for you to play—its called the blind men and the elephant. We're going to put some blindfolds on you and let you guess what groupware is. The winner gets a night on the town. Are you ready?

OK, so what's groupware? Martian number one says "it's e-mail." Martian number two thinks it's a multimedia "document store." And Martian number three says they're both wrong: "it's clearly workflow." Do we have any more takers? Does anybody think it's got something to do with electronic conferencing? How about group calendaring and scheduling? As you can see from the cartoon, the groupware elephant is all of the above. OK, so you all won a night on the town. Do you need a party guide? We have a volunteer.

Part 6 is about this amorphous client/server category called groupware; it's amorphous because it's so new, and we don't yet fully understand its potential. The groupware proponents claim that their technology allows us to create new classes of client/server applications that are unlike anything we've seen on mainframes or minis. It does that by enabling the people-to-people elements in client/server communications. The PC revolution was built around *personal* computing; groupware may create an analogous software revolution around *interpersonal* computing. Yes, of course it includes Martians. Is groupware lucrative? IBM must think so—it paid $3.5 billion to acquire Lotus Notes, the premier groupware product. Anytime someone writes a $3.5 billion check for a technology, we should take notice. So where is Groupware Valley? You Martians are always one step ahead of us.

We'll start by defining groupware. (Don't laugh: we really *can* do it.) We then go over what makes groupware different from SQL databases and TP Monitors. Next, we explore the constituent technologies that make up groupware—including multimedia document processing, workflow, e-mail, conferencing, and group calendaring and scheduling. However, with groupware, the whole is more than the sum of the parts, so we need to explore where that synergy comes from. We conclude with *Lotus Notes* and its closest competitors—including Netscape's *Collabra Share*, Microsoft's *Exchange*, and Novell's *GroupWise XTD*.

Chapter 20

Client/Server Groupware

Groupware is what you make it.

— Karl Wong, Dataquest
(December, 1995)

Client/server groupware is a collection of technologies that allow us to represent complex processes that center around collaborative human activities. It builds on five foundation technologies: multimedia document management, workflow, e-mail, conferencing, and scheduling. Groupware is not another downsized mainframe technology; it's a genuinely new form of computing. It provides an excellent example of how you can use client/server technology to extend the computing envelope into uncharted territory. Of course, this also means that groupware doesn't neatly fit into predefined software categories. So we'll have some explaining to do.

Our plan for this chapter is to first define groupware and the problems it solves. We'll then place groupware in the client/server model we've been building throughout this book. This won't be easy—groupware is an elusive concept that's continuously redefining its role as well as its relationship to the more established technologies. In addition, no single groupware product incorporates all the technology pieces—although Lotus Notes comes pretty close. After we get a working definition, we'll look at the foundation technologies and how groupware combines the pieces within a client/server setting.

WHY IS GROUPWARE IMPORTANT?

People don't talk about operating systems; they simply assume they're there. Eventually, groupware will evolve the same way.

— *Esther Dyson, Editor, Release 1.0*

The Workgroup Technologies market research firm believes the groupware market will grow to almost $6.5 billion in 1998 from $2.3 billion in 1995. The fastest growing segments will be e-mail, workflow, and groupware implementation services. Lotus Notes—an amorphous groupware product that escapes definition—has sold more than 5 million licenses to 7,000 companies. Lotus predicts that Notes will run on 20 million seats by the year end 1997. According to Dataquest, revenues from Notes will shoot to $1.2 billion in 1998 from $261 million in 1994. This translates to a compound annual growth rate of 52%.[1] Input Research Institute predicts that Notes product and service revenues will top $4 billion in 1999. Lotus estimates that for every dollar in Notes sales, resellers make another $7 or $8 in application design, systems administration, and training.

So what's causing all this sudden interest in groupware? According to David Coleman, editor of the newsletter "GroupTalk," the rapid growth is occurring because groupware can transform a company by changing the way people communicate with each other and, as a result, change the business processes. For example, you can use groupware to automate customer service and make a company more responsive. Groupware also has the potential to flatten organizations and remove layers of bureaucracy (see the following Soapbox).

Groupware allows direct contributors—wherever they may be—to collaborate on a job using client/server networks. We anticipate the growth of "virtual corporations" that get formed by unaffiliated groups of people to collaborate on a particular project. Groupware helps manage (and track) the product through its various phases; it also allows the contributors to exchange ideas and synchronize their work. It keeps track of the "collective memory" of the group.

Groupware, in many cases, allows departments to develop and deploy their own applications. Anyone who can create a simple spreadsheet can learn how to create a Lotus Notes application—few programming skills are required. The ability for

---

[1] These figures—compiled before the IBM acquisition of Lotus—do not include the sizeable mini-industry that has developed around Notes.

departments to develop and create their own client/server groupware applications is leading to phenomenal returns on investment. For example, a study of 65 Notes users by IDC in 1994 revealed that return on investment ranged from 16% to 1,666% on a median investment of $100,000. More than half showed returns greater than 100%, and a quarter showed returns of more than 200%. Because of these extraordinary numbers, IDC repeated the study with a different set of users and obtained similar results. The groupware phenomenon—like spreadsheets or Macintosh hypercards—is self-feeding. The difference is that groupware is a self-feeding client/server application; it is networked and interpersonal. Most groupware products also support open APIs that allow third parties (and IS shops) to add new functions on top of the foundation.

Soapbox

Groupware and Reengineering

Are we investing in groupware to infuse the organization with collaborative energy? Or are we investing primarily to staunch the bleeding?

— *Michael Schrage, Fellow*
MIT Sloan School

Bureaucracy in most organizations is very resilient; it will take a lot more than groupware to eliminate it. In fact, groupware can be misused to automate bureaucracy and make it more permanent. The current "reengineering" movement thinks it has found the problem: We've been applying Ford's assembly-line processes to business operations. We need to rethink the way we work—that is, reengineer the process. We wish them luck. Hopefully, they'll leave a few jobs behind after the reengineering.

The reengineering movement asserts that throwing technology into a poorly performing process won't help. We agree; nobody can quarrel with the fact that it doesn't make sense to automate a process that shouldn't be there in the first place. However, groupware is a secular technology; it can automate any type of process, including bad ones. You can use it to automate inefficient processes and make them more "efficiently inefficient." Or you can automate the reengineered structures and shoot to attain the order of magnitude improvements the Gurus promote. But we'll probably see a great deal of misuse of the technology until people learn this lesson. It's a lot more effort to rethink the way we work than to throw a shrink-wrapped package of groupware at it. Groupware vendors will make the same amount of revenue either way, but the value of their products to the companies that buy it will be radically different. ❑

WHAT IS GROUPWARE?

If you were to put twelve groupware experts in a room, you would get twenty definitions.

— David Coleman

In a contest for the most fuzzily defined client/server software category, "groupware" would be the hands down winner. Over 500 products call themselves groupware. So let's cut the suspense and propose the following working definition: "Groupware is software that supports the creation, flow, and tracking of non-structured information in direct support of collaborative group activity."

There are other terms used as synonyms for groupware—collaborative computing, workgroup computing, and the academic sounding "computer-supported cooperative working." Groupware is the easiest of these terms to remember; vendors like the way it sounds because of the "ware" attached to it. So groupware it is.

Our definition implies that groupware is involved in the management of both information and activities. The "million dollar" question is: What makes groupware different from database managers and TP Monitors? For a change, we have some ready and straightforward answers.

How Is Groupware Different From SQL Databases?

Using an RDBMS to support documents is like teaching an elephant to fly.

— Frank Ingari, VP Marketing, Lotus
(February, 1993)

The relational databases we covered in Part 4 deal with highly structured data that is accessed using SQL. They are excellent for managing applications that require high concurrency controls—including locking and isolation features—that are needed for immediate updates. They also provide excellent ad hoc query facilities. In contrast, groupware deals with highly unstructured data—including text, image, graphics, faxes, mail, and bulletin boards. Groupware provides the tools to capture this data at the point of entry and organize it in a nebulous thing called a *document*. You can think of a document as the container of diverse types of information. The document is to a workgroup what a table is to a SQL database: It's a basic unit of management. Groupware helps end users create document databases. It can move these documents via electronic mail and database replicas. And it provides everything you need to query, manage, and navigate through document databases. Documents are the currency of groupware.

Using OLE, OpenDoc, or native editors, groupware lets you view the components of the documents by launching the tools that created them in the first place. This means that if the document contains an image, movie, or sound clip, the groupware software will find it for you and let you view it. But can't we do that kind of stuff using SQL database BLOBs? Not quite. (See the following Soapbox.) SQL databases are great for providing access to structured data that's organized in table formats, but when it comes to multimedia and non-structured data, they're almost hopeless. Groupware-style document management fills this gap very well.

What About BLOBs?

Soapbox

In their current form, BLOBs are a lousy tool for handling advanced data types. They buy little or no leverage over storing data in a flat file. The RDBMS acts as little more than a very expensive flat file server.

— Wayne Duquaine
Sybase

A BLOB, at least in a SQL database, is nothing more than up to four GBytes of uninterpreted binary data. All the rich semantic information is buried in the binary headers that the SQL database ignores. The headers describe the various sub-types and components that make up the BLOB—including the data type (image, voice, text, and so on), the compression type, and the various indexes. The SQL database throws back at the application all the navigation tasks that are required to move through the BLOB's components.

SQL does not specify a self-describing data standard for BLOBs. Determining what's in the BLOB has to be reinvented by each application. GUI tools are left blind and clueless as to what each BLOB contains and how it should be processed. When it comes to BLOBs and multimedia, a SQL database is just a glorified and expensive file server with no value added. In contrast, the groupware document servers have made great strides toward providing some kind of a multimedia, client/server solution. Note that some SQL database vendors now provide proprietary object extensions that let you manipulate BLOB-like data types—including images, fingerprints, files, and e-mail messages. As SQL databases become more object-oriented, they will give the document databases a run for their money. ❏

How Is Groupware Different From TP Monitors?

The TP Monitors we covered in Part 5 deal with management of transaction processes across client/server networks. So how do they compare with groupware? When it comes to document stores, TP Monitors can complement groupware software very well. The TP Monitor treats the document store like any other resource manager. If it supports a two-phase commit, the TP Monitor will gladly coordinate a distributed transaction that includes the document store. However, TP Monitors and groupware compete in the area of workflow. We believe that the groupware workflow is a much more developed technology than the TP Monitor long-lived transaction (but it's less protected).

The current workflow model—and groupware in general—is not transaction-oriented in the ACID sense. Groupware is good at reflecting the changing states of information over time, but it does not do very well when it comes to reflecting the current state of the data in real time. For example, groupware does not use two-phase commits to synchronize distributed changes across resource managers. It would be nice if TP Monitors and groupware combined efforts to infuse workflow with ACID properties (if it can be done). We cover workflow later in this chapter.

THE COMPONENTS OF GROUPWARE

As we said earlier, groupware builds on five foundation technologies: multimedia document management, workflow, e-mail, conferencing, and scheduling (see Figure 20-1). Groupware achieves its magic by combining these technologies and creating new synergy. The technology for multimedia document management and workflow comes from electronic document imaging systems; e-mail and scheduling come from office automation; and conferencing is native to groupware. Before we

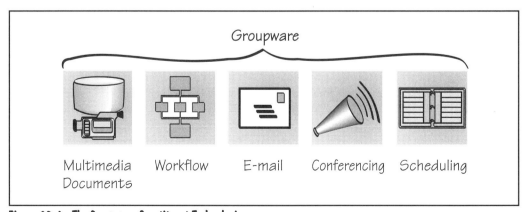

Figure 20-1. The Groupware Constituent Technologies.

get into groupware proper, let's quickly review what these component technologies have to offer.

From Electronic Imaging To Multimedia Document Management

Groupware document management technology has its roots in electronic imaging. If we want to be purists, electronic imaging is just another form of special-purpose groupware. Of course, electronic imaging people—who have created a huge multi-billion dollar industry—can make the claim that groupware is just an imaging spin-off. In either case, we need to look at electronic imaging because it's an important client/server industry that is a precursor to groupware.

Electronic imaging started small. In the 1960s many businesses replaced large information paper warehouses with microfilm and computer-aided retrieval systems. By the mid-1980s, the appearance of PCs, LANs, scanners, compression boards, and optical disk juke-boxes allowed the automation of image storage as well as the data-centered tracking systems that locate those images. The new technologies made the online storage and display of images economical. In some applications, the cost savings associated with reduced staff and faster online access to documents (in seconds rather than days) justified the incremental expense for the new client/server systems. It costs $25,000 to fill a four-drawer paper file cabinet and $2,160 annually to maintain it. More importantly, 3 percent of paper is lost; the average cost to recover a document is $120. It is estimated that 3 billion paper documents are buried in US businesses alone; it's those kind of numbers that gave birth to the electronic imaging industry.

Electronic Imaging Client/Server Architecture

Electronic imaging systems are inherently database-oriented, client/server applications (see Figure 20-2). The client PCs capture and manipulate the images; they serve as front-ends to the data stored in image servers. The client PC typically does the following:

■ The scanner attached to the client's PC digitizes the image through a process similar to that of a fax machine. (Not so coincidentally, fax machines sometimes serve as remote scanners.)

■ After being digitized, the image is displayed and checked for quality; it is rescanned if necessary.

■ While the image is displayed, information is extracted from it by an operator who enters the data in the fields of a GUI form. At a minimum, the document is assigned a simple index and identification code so that it can be retrieved later.

More sophisticated (and costly) applications automate the extraction of information from the image into the GUI form using intelligent character recognition or bar-code readers.

■ A software or hardware coprocessor compresses the images and then sends them to the server where they get stored.

■ The client can always access the documents in the server and visually display them. An image can be reviewed, printed, faxed, annotated with red lines or electronic notes, and so on.

The server side of an imaging application manages a shared database of images. Image servers typically store all the structured information in an SQL database; the document itself (i.e., the BLOB) is stored in a file server. Large image servers can handle 200,000 documents or more per day. Images are big. The average compressed digitized image weighs in at about 75 to 100 KBytes, but images can be as large as 2.5 MBytes for medical X-rays and engineering drawings. Consequently, many imaging applications may require terabytes of online storage.

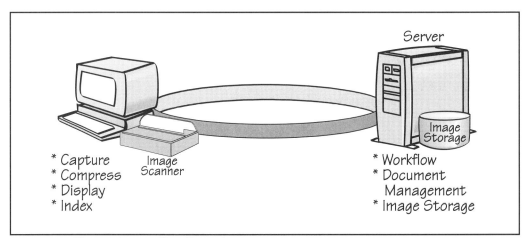

Figure 20-2. Electronic Imaging Client/Server Systems.

The image servers manage the workflow, security, image indexing (or metadata), and the pointers to the file systems where the BLOBs are physically stored. Here are some of their key functions:

■ Servers manage electronic renditions of file cabinets, which contain drawers and folders comprising documents. A document comprises a series of multimedia pages.

■ Workflow automates the movement of documents by moving them from one business operation to the next according to customer-defined rules and routes.

The image server uses rules to control the routing, which may be based on document content, age, priority, workload balancing, external events, the day you need a document, database triggers, and other user-defined criteria.

■ User profiles and work queues are created and maintained on the server to specify the type of work users receive.

■ Reporting facilities allow managers to monitor the volume and types of work-in-process in the system, and to note its progress.

■ Documents are stored on various media; the server moves them around to optimize the delicate trade-off between storage cost and performance.

Groupware Multimedia Document Management

The groupware document management paradigm is a generalization of the electronic imaging file cabinet. For example, the basic unit of storage in groupware, such as Lotus Notes, is the *document*. A Notes document has an extremely flexible structure; it can be tagged with properties such as *client*, *region*, and *subject*. A Notes document can have any number of BLOB-like *attachments* (or embedded objects). Notes supports a multimedia document architecture, which means that it can handle multiple data types—including text, images, graphics, voice clips, and video.

Related collections of Notes documents are stored in *databases* that can then be indexed and retrieved by any of the documents' properties, or by the actual contents of the documents. Notes also supports full-text indexing. In addition, Notes created its own document database technology from scratch; unlike the image vendors, it does not build on top of existing file and SQL database servers. We're dealing with a *new* groupware-specific, document-centric, and multimedia-enabled database technology.

Workflow: What Is It? Where Does It Come From?

Imagine submitting a home mortgage application and having it go through in a matter of hours. Workflow is the "up and coming" client/server technology that can be used to automatically route events (and work) from one program to the next in structured or unstructured client/server environments (see Figure 20-3). The "classical" workflow paradigm is a river that carries the flow of work from port to port and along the way value gets added. Workflow defines the operations that must be visited along the way and what needs to be done when exceptions occur. The

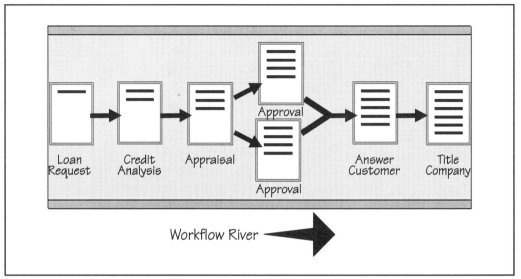

Figure 20-3. The Workflow River.

original work item may be merged with other work, transformed, or routed to another workflow. It's quite a dynamic environment. Some workflows may be fuzzy and not understood very well; others are deterministic and highly repetitive. In all cases, these workflows are there to help us collaborate in getting work done.

To appreciate what workflow is all about, you must understand its origins. Workflow technology has its historical roots firmly planted in the world of image management and computer-integrated manufacturing technology. FileNet Corporation—an imaging vendor—was a pioneer of this technology in 1984. FileNet and other electronic imaging companies—including ViewStar, Sigma, Wang, and IBM's Image-Plus—discovered that workflow could be used to automate the high-volume, formerly paper-based processes (see Figure 20-4).

Workflow is especially applicable to "paper factories," meaning large offices that routinely process documents representing business transactions (for example, loans, claims processing, and tax returns). Paper to these factories is what raw material is to manufacturing: "grist for the mill" that produces the organization's product. When the paper became an electronic image, workflow automated the movement of documents from one image processing operation to the next. Both the workflow controller and the work are electronic renditions of real-life factory constructs.

The imaging workflow systems are costly, rigid, centralized, and typically require a highly skilled IS professional to do the design and integration. These systems tend to be proprietary and cannot interface well with other applications. On the positive

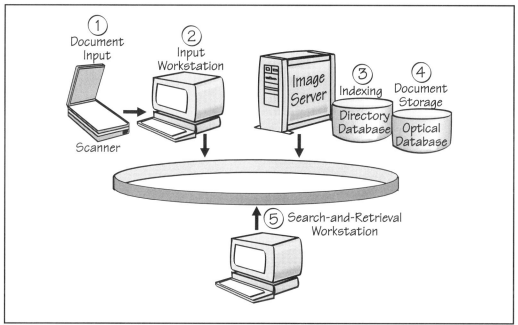

Figure 20-4. Workflow in Electronic Imaging Systems.

side, they can handle very large workloads and have excellent built-in security and version controls. They are very good at scheduling document-related tasks and tracking them to completion. The cost of such systems start at $5,000 per seat.

The New Workflow Systems

Groupware introduces a new breed of client/server workflow software for the masses. The new workflow packages go beyond their imaging counterparts in the following areas:

■ **Support for ad hoc user needs.** The new workflow packages address both structured and unstructured process automation needs. They can automate well-understood processes as well as more nebulous ones.

■ **Low-cost.** The new workflow packages sell at PC software prices—expect to pay between $100 to $500 per seat.

■ **Integration with other applications.** The new workflow packages can integrate with existing applications by either spawning a process or sending them some type of message-based event notification when their intervention is needed (using DDE, OLE, e-mail, and so on). Applications can also call the workflow manager to participate in or initiate a workflow process.

- ■ ***Programming with visual metaphors.*** The new workflow packages support drag-and-drop iconic manipulations for creating workflows and defining business rules. They typically provide tools for designing forms (or importing them from a GUI Builder), designing sequential or conditional routes, and scripting languages to specify the business logic. The routes and workflow definitions are sometimes stored in SQL databases. Templates are provided to help jump start the creation of a workflow application.

- ■ ***Integration with e-mail, MOM, or RPC.*** The new workflow packages use loosely coupled forms of communication, such as e-mail or MOM message queues, to inform humans or programs that their intervention is required. Action Technologies, for example, defines a set of message formats that can be conveyed using all the popular mail transports. These formats are used to convey, capture, or initiate workflow commands and actions. Action also supports the transmission of workflow commands using DDE, Named Pipes, RPCs, and peer-to-peer protocols.

- ■ ***Provide facilities for tracking work-in-progress.*** Most of the packages allow you to query the status of work-in-progress and what stage of the workflow it's in. Some of the better packages help you identify inefficiencies in the routes and bottlenecks.

- ■ ***Provide users with tools to complete an action.*** In addition to notifying users that an action is required, some of the better tools provide users with help panels that tell them how to complete an action and sometimes even the tools to perform the requested action. The user may also be able to obtain information about where the task fits in the overall process.

- ■ ***Provide APIs that let developers customize workflow services.*** This feature is currently very vendor-specific. However, the standards for workflow APIs are now being defined by the Workflow Coalition (see next section).

The heart of a workflow system is the server that receives requests and events from the various client workstations and interprets them according to a user-defined workflow. The client agents are programmed to execute the repetitive parts of a user-defined script. The workflow server acts as a clearinghouse that determines what needs to be done next based on the global state of the system (and the rules). It usually maintains a database that dynamically tracks the work-in-progress and contains instructions (and rules) for what needs to be done at a given instance of a workflow process.

Workflow Models

The three R's of workflow are: Routes, Rules, and Roles.

— *Ronni T. Marshak, Editor*
Workgroup Computing Report

The workflow software must create electronic renditions of real-world collaborative activity. The "real world," however, covers a wide spectrum of activities—from tax return processing to co-authoring a paper. These activities differ radically in their structure, number of users, flow of control, and process predictability. Almost any workflow can be represented using raw code; however, the trick is to minimize custom development using shrink-wrapped workflow models. The workflow packages must be able to visually define who does "what, when, and to what"; parallel routes; logic for dynamically determining routes at run time; and the exceptions to any rules. It must take into account Ronni Marshak's three R's: routes, rules, and roles.

- ■ **Routes** define the paths along which the object moves. They also include definitions of the objects—documents, forms, events, electronic containers and parts, messages, and so on—that are to be routed.

- ■ **Rules** define what information is routed and to whom. Rules define both the conditions the workflow must meet to traverse to the next step and how to handle exceptions: "If the loan is over $100,000, send it to the supervisor or else send it to the next hop."

- ■ **Roles** define job functions independently of the people who do it. For example, the "supervisor" role can be handled by users "Mary" and "Jeri." Any one of these people can do the job; just put the job on the next available supervisor's queue.

Groupware packages must provide the three R's for automating well-defined applications, which is called *process-oriented workflow*. And they must provide them for the more spontaneous type of applications, called *ad hoc workflow*. Here's the differences between the two models:

- ■ **Process-oriented workflows** are used to automate business systems that have definable, repetitive, and well-understood policies and procedures. For example, a mortgage loan is an understood business process that goes through a prescribed set of procedures. Loans are processed in the same way every day. The routing of the work is automatic and requires very little user involvement. It's like taking a train. This type of workflow is a natural candidate for TP Monitor initiated Sagas or long-lived transactions.

- *Ad hoc workflow* deals with short-lived and unstructured work processes. They can involve task forces of people working on a common problem. Consider a short-duration project with a deadline. The workflow is used to assign roles, track and route work-in-progress, monitor deadlines, and track who got what and when. It's an excellent tool for tracking work among people who are physically dispersed. This type of workflow is like driving a car. The navigation is driver-centric, but you need road signs and a map to figure out where you're going. The driver also needs to know the set of options available at every turn. Ad hoc workflow is used for incremental automation—leaving anything the system can't handle to humans. It takes full advantage of desktop power to help humans navigate through the country roads.

Workflow Routes

Modern workflow packages support the same type of topologies that are common in human communications (see Figure 20-5). Typically, these packages let you specify a route that defines the set operations a unit-of-work traverses. They also let you define rules that specify acceptance conditions for moving from one operation to the next. You can create sequential routes, parallel routes (alternate paths), routes with feedback loops (for example, rework), circular routes, wheel-spoked routes, and fully interconnected routes. The first four routes are used in process-oriented workflows, while the last two are used in more ad hoc workflows.

Workflow Splits and Joins

Workflow objects can go off on different routes and then merge back into a single route at a "rendezvous" point. In addition, a workflow object can be split into multiple parts and merged back into a single part as it moves down the workflow river (see Figure 20-6). This is done using splits and joins, as explained in the following examples:

- *And-Splits* are used to explode an object into many parts. For example, a set of chips on a wafer is tracked as a group until the chips are split; each then goes their own way.

- *Or-Splits* are used to peel off a few parts from a group. For example, a few chips may be split off the wafer for random testing; they rejoin the group later using an Or-Join.

- *Or-Joins* allow certain members to rejoin the group. For example, in a manufacturing line, a defective part can go to a rework operation; it can then rejoin the group when it's fixed using an Or-Join.

■ ***And-Joins*** are rendezvous points that are used to group together objects so that they move in a route as a group. For example, you can use an And-Join to package many units into a container that can be shipped as a unit.

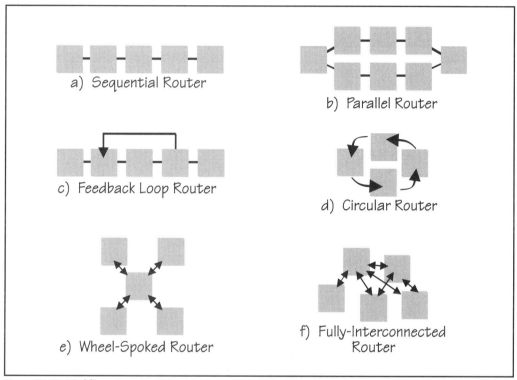

a) Sequential Router

b) Parallel Router

c) Feedback Loop Router

d) Circular Router

e) Wheel-Spoked Router

f) Fully-Interconnected Router

Figure 20-5. Workflows Come in All Patterns.

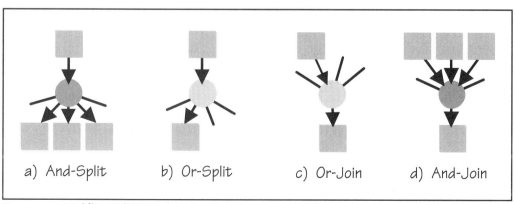

a) And-Split   b) Or-Split   c) Or-Join   d) And-Join

Figure 20-6. Workflow: Splitting and Joining Work.

The Action Workflow Model

Briefing

Action Technologies' *Action Workflow*—an innovative ad hoc workflow product—is based on research by Terry Winograd and Fernando Flores on how people communicate to make an action happen. Action identifies for each unit of work in a workflow the *performer* who is doing the actual work for a *customer* (meaning the person for whom the work is being done). Each step in the workflow involves a negotiation loop between a customer and a performer (see Figure 20-7). At the end of each step, the conditions must be fulfilled to have a satisfied customer.

According to the Action Technologies methodology, every action in a workflow consists of four phases in which customers and performers coordinate with each other (see Figure 20-8):

1. ***Preparation*** is when the customer prepares to ask for something—often, for example, by filling out a form.

2. ***Negotiation*** is when the customer and performer agree on the work to be done and on the conditions of satisfaction—that is, they determine *exactly* what must be done to complete this job to the satisfaction of the customer.

3. ***Performance*** is the phase in which the actual job is done. After completion, the performer reports to the customer on how the mission was accomplished.

4. ***Acceptance*** of a job or task is not considered complete until the customer signs off and expresses satisfaction to the performer.

At any phase, there may be additional actions, such as clarifications, further negotiations, and changes of commitments by the participants.

The Action Technologies approach does more than just coordinate between tasks: It helps specify the client/server contract and does it all very recursively. The entire application is a client/server task that gets broken down recursively into subtasks as defined by the workflow. The application is a series of "who is getting what done for whom" steps and the conditions of satisfaction. Action provides a set of visual tools to help capture the negotiation semantics and automatically generates the scripts from them.

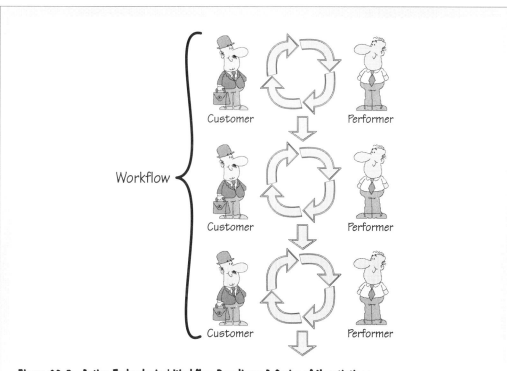

Figure 20-7. Action Technologies' Workflow Paradigm: A Series of Negotiations.

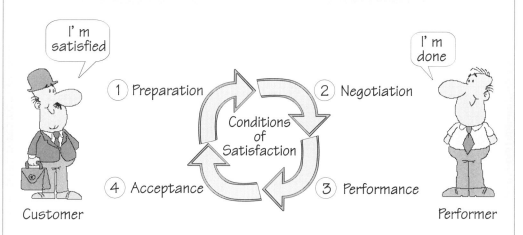

Figure 20-8. Action Technologies' Workflow: The Negotiation Details.

Workflow: Meet the Players

We've literally built a whole business around the confusion and interest generated by workflow. Many users have no idea what the technology is.

> — *Tom Koulopoulos, President*
> *Delphi Consulting*
> *(September, 1995)*

Workflow is currently a very hot technology. Delphi Consulting estimates that spending on workflow reached the $1 billion mark in 1995, up from $722 million in 1994. BIS Strategic Decisions estimates that the total number of workflow seats could reach 5.8 million by 1998—representing a $3 billion market—up from 514,000 seats in 1994.

Over 100 vendors are now competing in the workflow market, and they're frequent targets of acquisitions. For example, BancTec recently acquired Recognition International, Wang acquired Sigma, and FileNet bought Watermark. The workflow market is still in flux; there is no clear leader. According to Delphi, in 1994 these five products accounted for over 40% of the workflow market: FileNet's *Workflo* (17%), ViewStar's *ViewStar* (7%), IBM's *FlowMark* (6%), Recognition International's *Floware* (6%), and Wang's *Open Workflow* (5%). Note that the majority of the "top five" are imaging vendors.

Some of the more innovative workflow packages come from small vendors who have less than 5% of the market share each. Many of these vendors offer workflow products around Lotus Notes—including Lotus itself, Quality Decision Management's *At Work*, Action Technologies' *ActionWorkflow Builder for Notes*, and Reach Software's *WorkMAN*. Some of the up-and-coming products include XSoft's *InConcert*, Digital's *TeamRoute*, and Delrina's *Formflow*. Finally, Microsoft views workflow as an extension of the e-mail system; Action Technologies is partnering with Microsoft to add workflow features to *Windows 95* and a future version of *Exchange*.

Software vendors are now offering workflow as part of their packaged applications. For example, SAP built a workflow engine from scratch for its *R/3 Release 3.0*, and Oracle developed its own workflow software for its new *SmartClient 10* application software suite. In contrast, PeopleSoft is licensing its workflow engine from third parties—including Action Technologies, Delrina, and IBM/Lotus. System vendors are also workflow enabling their applications via third-party licensing. For example, the Action workflow engine is being embedded in products from Sybase, Saros, Verity, Platinum, and LaserData. And, Novell is licensing FileNet's *Ensemble* workflow engine for inclusion in its *Groupwise* messaging system.

The Workflow Coalition

The *Workflow Management Coalition (WfMC)* was founded in August 1993 as a non-profit international body for the development and promotion of workflow standards. Its membership is open to all parties interested or involved in the creation, analysis, or deployment of workflow management systems. In 1996, WfMC had over 150 members—including all the key workflow vendors and leading system integrators.

In January 1995, WfMC published a glossary of workflow-related terms—a first step toward creating a common vocabulary for the industry. The end goal is to create a language for specifying workflow *processes* that a variety of workflow *engines* can interpret and instantiate. According to WfMC, a workflow process consists of a collection of *activities*. An activity is a logical step that contributes toward the completion of a workflow process; it is executed by a *tool*, which is an application outside the workflow system. Figure 20-9 shows how the pieces of the workflow jigsaw come together in WfMC's conceptual framework.

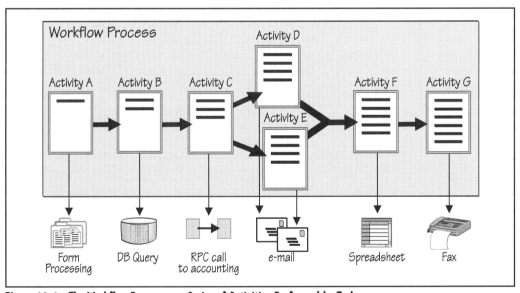

Figure 20-9. The Workflow Process as a Series of Activities Performed by Tools.

The long-term goal of WfMC is to define a set of APIs that client applications and tools can use to invoke and define workflow functions and to control a workflow engine. WfMC is also working on an interoperability protocol that lets multivendor workflow engines communicate. In December 1995, WfMC published its first set of APIs called the *Workflow Client API*. This API is used by workflow client applications to invoke the services of multivendor workflow engines.

The new Workflow Client API makes it possible for an application to request work from a variety of workflow products and construct a single worklist for the user. This means you don't have to deal with multiple desktop windows for each workflow product your organization uses. The APIs will help create standards-based workflow systems such as insurance claims or factory automation software.

The Workflow Client API consists of 56 function calls divided into four broad categories (see Figure 20-10):

- **Connection functions** consist of 2 API calls that let you connect to a workflow engine and disconnect when you're done.

- **Process control and status** consists of 23 API calls that let you query a process definition, read and update the current state, create a process instance, start the process, and obtain process status.

- **Activity control and status** consists of 13 API calls that let you query an activity, read and update its attributes and state, and obtain its current status.

- **Administration and worklist control** consists of 18 API calls that let you query a worklist, manipulate the work items it contains, and manage the execution of processes and activities.

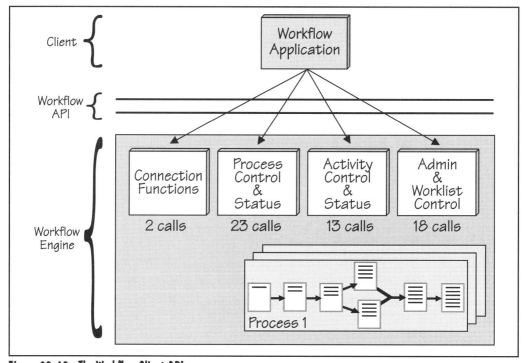

Figure 20-10. The Workflow Client API.

The Workflow Client API does not address security, locking, process integrity, user interfaces, roles, and defining ad hoc activities. Despite these shortcomings, the Workflow Client API provides a giant first step toward standardizing diverse workflow engines that have their roots in imaging, e-mail, and ad hoc workflows. WfMC members that are implementing the specification include Action Technologies, Computron, CSE Systems, Fujitsu, IBM, ICL, Integrated Work, Lion GmbH, Recognition International, SAP, Siemens Nixdorf, Staffware, Telstra Applied Technologies, and Xsoft.

Workflow: The Bottom Line

Workflow helps bring the information to the people who can act on it. It coordinates existing software and tracks the processes to make sure the work gets done by the right people. Workflow by itself cannot do too much; but with other software—such as e-mail, databases, and desktop productivity tools—it can create some dynamite combinations.

The Electronic Mail Component

The notion that a proprietary network can exist in the Internet era is gone.

> — *Larry Moore, Lotus VP*
> *(March, 1996)*

For many organizations, all the groupware they need may be an e-mail package that's closely tied to group calendaring and scheduling features. Of course, groupware allows you to do much more with electronic mail; it uses it to extend the client/server reach. Why is e-mail so important to groupware? Because it matches the way people work. You can use e-mail to send something to others without making a real-time connection; the recipients don't have to respond to senders until they're ready to do so. In addition, it's one of the easiest ways for electronic processes to communicate with humans. And it's ubiquitous.

According to Karl Wong of Dataquest, there are approximately 60 million corporate e-mail mailboxes in the world. Of these, 35 million are LAN based; the remainder are on host systems and public systems. In addition, there are 12 to 15 million Internet mail users. These numbers add up to between 72 and 75 million active e-mail users in early 1996. Mail-enabled groupware applications can take advantage of this very extensive mail infrastructure to send and receive information and communicate directly with users—electronic mail is one of the most hassle-free forms of distributed interactions. Most electronic mailboxes will soon be globally interconnected through mail backbones and gateways. E-mail front-ends are not the only way to send messages. Mail APIs, such as VIM and MAPI, are designed to let any application work with the mail messaging infrastructure.

The Electronic Mail Infrastructure

The infrastructure required to create ubiquitous mail backbones is coming into place. There is a crucial distinction between the mail application—the front-end—and the mail infrastructure—the back-end. Ideally, the front-end and back-end should communicate along client/server lines—this is what Lotus Notes 4.0 does today (see Figure 20-11). The older LAN-based e-mail packages bundle the front-end and the back-end in the same process and use a file server on the LAN for the mail store. This is the approach used by Lotus cc:Mail, the most popular e-mail product in the industry. Most PC LAN e-mail products follow the cc:Mail file server approach, but that's changing. For example, Lotus redesigned cc:Mail along

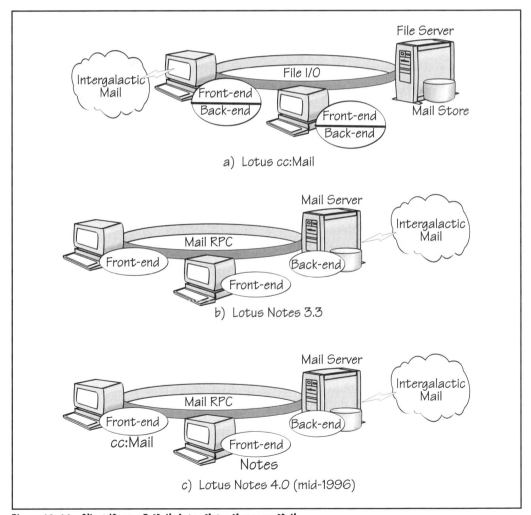

Figure 20-11. Client/Server E-Mail: Lotus Notes Versus cc:Mail.

client/server lines. Both cc:Mail and Notes currently share the same back-end mail server. Microsoft and Novell are also migrating their popular e-mail products—Microsoft Mail and Novell Groupwise—to the client/server model.

However, it takes more than cc:Mail or Notes to create an intergalactic mail infrastructure. How do you connect cc:Mail or Notes to other mail networks? You need to hook into a server-to-server *mail backbone*. There are two ways to do that:

- **Gateways**—you'll need one gateway for each different e-mail system you need to access. But this could quickly turn into a management nightmare. Gateways also limit some functions like the capability to search for an address. They're also poor at providing synchronized directory management services, efficient message routing, global system management, and so on.

- **Mail backbone**—you'll need one gateway to the backbone, period. But the question is: Which backbone? The contenders are the *X.400* international standard, Novell's *Message Handling Service (MHS)*, and the Internet's *Simple Message Transport Protocol (SMTP)* mail service. The pendulum seems to be swinging in X.400's favor—it is much simpler and less expensive than it once was (see the following Details box). The Internet SMTP is also very popular. Of course, MHS, SMTP, and X.400 backbones will most likely be interconnected via gateways. So all the backbones may win.

The separation of mail functions along client/server lines will facilitate the creation of front-end clients that are totally independent of the back-end mail engines. We'll now look at the mail API standards that will help make all of this happen.

X.400 Mail Backbones

Details

The X.400 mail protocol is finally hitting the critical mass as the common mail backbone for the industry. It has been adopted by all the major public service providers across the world. Most e-mail vendors—including Lotus, Microsoft, HP, IBM, and SoftSwitch—are coming out with X.400 products. Several large vendors—such as IBM, Tandem, and Digital—use X.400 as a way to link their messaging systems. An X.400 version of Lotus Notes and cc:Mail should be available by the time you read this book—it will give X.400 a friendly look on all platforms. X.400 provides the following features:

- **Support for BLOB exchanges.** X.400 defines a way to exchange images, fax, and other binary attachments to messages.

- ***Electronic Data Interchange (EDI) support***. EDI defines the contents and structures of messages that are used in electronic business exchanges (for example, invoices, billing forms, and so on). X.400 consolidates both e-mail and EDI on the same backbones. It maintains audit trails of EDI exchanges as required by the X.435 EDI standard.

- ***Support for distributed directories***. The X.500 standard, developed as part of the X.400 1988 specification, defines how a single system image is provided using directories that are distributed over multiple nodes.

- ***Security***. X.400 adheres to the X.509 security standard that specifies the mechanisms for password identification, digital signatures, encryption, and audit trails.

- ***Mail API***. The X.400 Common Mail Calls (CMC) API combines subsets of MAPI and VIM, and it has been adopted as a "compromise" API by both parties. We'll have more to say about that in the mail API section.

Clearly X.400 offers a secure, standards-based approach to creating electronic mail backbones. ❑

The E-Mail APIs: VIM, MAPI, and CMC

A new hot area in our industry is *mail-enabled applications*. The primary purpose of these applications is not mail, but they still need to access mail services. Most groupware products fall into that category. E-mail becomes just another form of client/server middleware. *Electronic Data Interchange (EDI)* is becoming an important source of mail-enabled business transactions (see previous Details box). Personal agents will be making extensive use of EDI to pay your bills and do your electronic shopping. And e-mail by itself supports the exchange of faxes, files, BLOBs, documents, and workflow events at an application-to-application level. It's a powerful form of middleware that may already be in place in an organization (in that case, it's free and ready to be exploited). One of the main advantages of using e-mail over lower-level APIs—like NetBIOS or RPC—is the store-and-forward capability that's built into the mail system.

An application becomes mail-enabled by using e-mail APIs that allow programs to directly access mail transport services, mail directories, and message stores (see Figure 20-12). These used to be the *private domain* of mail vendors. The newly-exposed APIs are making it easy for developers to mail-enable their applications without becoming e-mail experts. What kind of functions can we expect from an open e-mail API that can work across multiple mail transports?

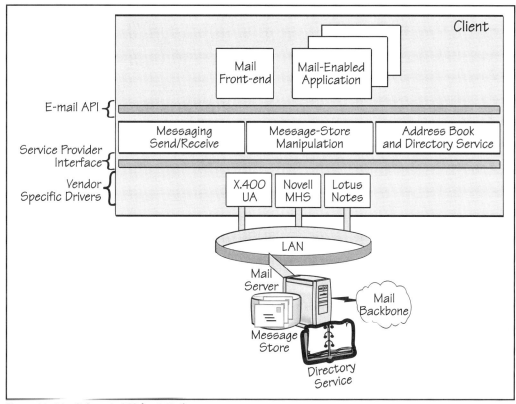

Figure 20-12. A Generic API for E-Mail.

The following is a composite of functions provided by the three leading contenders for the "common" mail API:

- **_Simple messaging services._** These are functions for addressing, sending, and receiving a mail message—including files and enclosures. An optional user interface is provided for logon, addressing the mail, and text entry.

- **_Message store manipulation._** This includes opening and reading messages delivered to a message store, saving messages, deleting messages, navigating through the contents of the store, searching for messages, and moving messages across containers. The message store can be external to the mail package. For example, a message store could be an SQL database, a Lotus Notes document database, or an Object Database. The same APIs should work across all stores. Message stores contain a wealth of information that is of interest to groupware applications. We expect to see a lot of exciting developments in this area.

- **_Address book and directory services._** An address book is a collection of individual or group recipients; it's really a bunch of distribution lists. Address books can be personal (cached on the local system) or part of a global directory. The API should let you read and write directory information as well as navigate through hierarchies of address books. You should be able to add or remove groups or members from address books and search through them.

■ **Mail object manipulation.** The APIs should let you access the subcomponents of a mail object. For example, a message may consist of heading fields and various data items.

■ **Authentication and security services.** This includes APIs that let an application log on to the mail system and authenticate its users.

■ **Service provider interface.** This interface allows service providers to supply their own back-end services to the front-end mail APIs. For example, a Lotus Notes mail server is accessed through the proprietary Lotus RPC. We've already encountered the concept of the service provider interface in the ODBC section in Part 4. The service provider interface creates an open environment for the providers of mail services; it doesn't do much for the developers of mail-enabled applications.

The separation of the mail front-end from the back-end allows a single API set to work with multiple mail back-ends. In addition, different vendors can offer their own specialized plug-in services (for example, message stores). So what is the common API set that gives us access to all this mail server power?

Surprise! The e-mail industry has more than one common, open API set. Remember, we *always* get to choose from more than one standard. In the case of e-mail, we started with five standards, but we're now down to three: VIM, MAPI, and CMC. In addition, both Novell and Lotus currently support MAPI and CMC in addition to VIM. So we may end up with one common standard—MAPI.

■ **Vendor Independent Messaging (VIM)** is an interface that is jointly backed by Lotus, Apple, IBM, Borland, MCI, Oracle, WordPerfect, and Novell. VIM was designed from the ground up as a cross-platform interface. VIM consists of 55 API calls—10 are optional—that support simple mail, message store, and address book services. VIM also provides a *Simple Mail Interface (SMI)* that consists of two calls: SMISendMail and SMISendDocuments. The main strength of VIM is its cross-platform support and the vendors who are behind it. Its main weakness is that it does not provide a Service Provider Interface (SPI).

■ **Messaging API (MAPI)** is Microsoft's WOSA offering for e-mail. MAPI started out as a Windows first client API—it's a Windows DLL that works primarily with Microsoft Mail back-ends. MAPI is now supported by virtually every vendor. The MAPI front-end APIs are written to the Windows *Mail Spooler*. Mail server providers can redirect the Mail Spooler calls to their back-end services using the

MAPI SPI. Simple MAPI consists of 12 API calls that provide simple mail, message store, and address book services. *Extended MAPI*—a technology that is partially implemented in Windows 95—supports 100 API calls that allow applications to handle large numbers of messages, filter through mail, manage message stores, and access complex addressing information. Extended MAPI exposes the SPI to the application. There are three types of SPIs: Transport, Address Book, and Message Store. MAPI's strength is its virtual universality.

■ ***Common Mail Calls (CMC)*** is the X.400 API Association (XAPIA) interface. It was published in June 1993 as part of a negotiated truce in the mail API wars—both the VIM and MAPI camp endorse it. Microsoft and Lotus provide a free DLL library for CMC. CMC consists of 10 API calls—a subset of the VIM and MAPI calls (see Figure 20-13). It does not include the Extended VIM or Extended MAPI functionality. CMC only does simple mail. It is a poor man's e-mail API.

The e-mail API wars are over: it appears that MAPI won. Microsoft is now shifting its attention to the merger of e-mail with workflow. In October 1995, it announced the *MAPI Workflow Framework*—a preliminary specification for allowing workflow engines and messaging systems to interoperate. The framework will allow e-mail users to start a workflow process, learn its status, and keep track of workflow tasks in an in-box. Microsoft has discussed the framework with the Workflow Management Coalition (it's work-in-progress).

So the good news is that we now have a universal mail API that could potentially become workflow-enabled. It will make it easier to mix-and-match multivendor mail clients with servers. For example, Lotus Notes 4.0 can now act as a mail server for

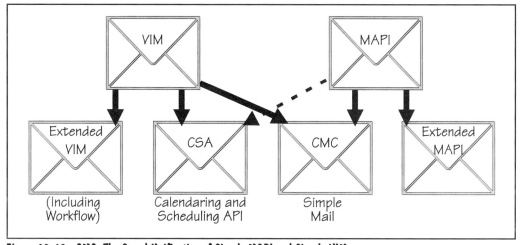

Figure 20-13. CMC: The Grand Unification of Simple MAPI and Simple VIM.

MAPI-based Microsoft Mail clients. The bad news is that Microsoft controls this key API.

Scheduling and Calendaring

Scheduling is a native groupware technology. There's extensive innovation behind the electronic scheduling of meetings, sharing calendars and "to do" lists, and all that good stuff. Scheduling was designed from the ground up on a solid client/server foundation. The client front-ends make excellent use of GUI facilities; the servers use background tasks, shared data, and triggers to manage and schedule group events. Now, imagine what could happen if we combine this scheduling and calendaring technology with workflow managers, e-mail, and multimedia document stores. This could result in some dynamite combinations of groupware. A workflow manager would be able to automatically add a meeting to the calendars of all the participants, schedule a meeting room, and send them reminder notices. Or, a workflow manager could consult group calendars to discover who is on vacation and route (or re-route) work accordingly.

So how do we get to the services provided by the scheduling and calendaring servers? Using APIs and client/server exchanges, of course. But which APIs? The good news is that the XAPIA standards association recently defined the *Calendaring and Scheduling API (CSA)*, which lets you programmatically access an underlying group scheduling system. This API is on its way to becoming an all-time favorite for personal agents.

Conferencing

Conferencing, or "electronic meetings," is another native groupware technology. Millions of PC users are now discovering the wonders of conferencing through electronic bulletin boards on CompuServe, America Online, Prodigy, and Internet. We can divide client/server conferencing technology into two types: realtime and anytime.

Realtime Conferencing

Realtime conferences allow groups to interactively collaborate on a joint project using instantly refreshed document replicas, electronic whiteboards, different-colored cursors with the initials of each participant, and a designated chairperson that controls access to the shared document. Participants can speak on their microphones and see each other in video windows on their computer screens. Eventually—when we get the cheap bandwidth—we will be able to augment these conferences with movie clips. Lotus makes the *RealTime Notes* conferencing package available at no cost in Notes clients. IBM will also bundle it with OS/2 Warp and selected IBM PCs. This makes conferencing technology extremely affordable for the first time.

Anytime Conferencing

Anytime conferences allow people to participate in group discussions when and where they want. You can join the discussion, add your own two cents, and leave at anytime. And because you can jump into an ongoing discussion at anytime, you can see the entire discussion in context. This flexible environment helps articulate spontaneous groups around a topic of interest—customer support, operating system advocacy, shared problems, and project tracking. The medium is open and democratic. Everyone gets the opportunity to express themselves—ideas are never lost.

Using replicas, the system makes all the contributions available to all participants in close to realtime. The contributions then become part of the group memory—they are stored for posterity in the document databases that manage this wealth of shared information. As these conferences flourish and multiply, tools are provided for viewing and navigating through the mazes of information they contain. Conferences provide one more technology that helps articulate the "group" in groupware. Electronic meeting environments provide an almost bottomless set of opportunities for client/server technology. We're just seeing the tip of the iceberg.

GROUPWARE: BRINGING IT ALL TOGETHER

Our groupware technology can serve to alienate and isolate people, or it can serve to forge a community. It is our choice.

— *Carol Anne Ogdin*
Deep Woods Technology

This chapter dealt with many of the emerging technologies that form a new genre of client/server software called "groupware." What's new is the synergy gained by bringing the pieces together on client/server networks. Groupware supports the asynchronous distribution of information to groups. It's a flexible technology that can adapt to the way people do business in both structured and ad hoc settings. The e-mail foundation helps bring humans into the loop. The information that is collected and distributed can be highly unstructured and rich with meaning. Workflow allows the creation of highly intelligent "routing clouds" that deliver information to the points where it can be processed. It also creates what Forrester calls "value-added rivers," as information moves from one point to the next along an intelligent route.

Groupware: Is It Just Hype?

Soapbox

In the future, any application that isn't groupware-enabled will run the risk of being an island in a sea of global communications. Groupware will bring together individuals, agents, processes, businesses, and corporations.

— *Karl Wong, Dataquest*
(December, 1995)

Like every new client/server technology, groupware is getting its share of high-decibel marketing hype. What makes it worse is that any multiuser piece of software can be called "groupware." All client/server software deals with group communications in some form or another. Even though we carefully defined the constituent technologies in groupware, there is still a tremendous amount of fuzziness associated with the term. You can't find two people—even from Lotus—that can give you a common definition of Lotus Notes; yet Notes is selling like hot cakes. So it must be fulfilling some need somewhere.

Groupware is a moving target. Groupware applications are constantly expanding into new territory as a result of changes in the technology. For example, groupware is now moving into two new areas: the Internet and telephony. We cover the Internet in Part 8. Telephony APIs—such as Microsoft's *TAPI* and the competing Novell/AT&T *TSAPI*—let you telephone-enable groupware applications. This means that your groupware applications will be able to answer, place, screen, and route telephone calls. The telephony APIs also let you route messages, manage voice-mail, and integrate voice, fax, and e-mail into one cohesive system. In a sense, a groupware application can now add to its repertoire of functions almost everything a modern PBX can do today. According to Dataquest, PC-based telephony systems are expected to grow by 2,000% to $2.8 billion in 1998, from $154 million in 1994. So welcome to another high-growth area.

We believe that any new technology will be fuzzy at first. The trick is to sort out reality from marketing hype, and then understand what we can do with the technology. In the case of groupware, the opportunity is in creating client/server applications—unlike any we've ever seen—using multimedia document databases, e-mail, workflow, conferencing, calendaring, and scheduling technology. The groupware industry is creating the common interfaces between these disparate pieces. All we need to do is learn how to use them and perhaps even integrate them with database warehouses, the Internet, and distributed object technology. □

Chapter 21

Groupware: Meet the Players

Most large organizations will do their evaluations this year and start rolling out a system next year. This is going to be a very fast war.

— *Tom Austin, Gartner Group*
(March, 1996)

Groupware is a fast-growing industry that's in a state of tremendous flux. For many years, groupware was synonymous with Lotus Notes. In early 1996, there's still no groupware product that's as comprehensive as Notes. However, we expect Notes to face strong competition from three new products: Novell's *GroupWise XTD*, Netscape's *Collabra Share*, and Microsoft's *Exchange*. These products are all backed by companies with strong mindshare and market presence. And all three products will eventually try to match Notes' comprehensive all-in-one groupware offering.

This chapter starts out by giving you a quick snapshot of the groupware market and the key trends within that industry. Then we look at Notes 4.0 in some detail—it's the product that sets the bar for all groupware vendors, so it's the product competitors must beat. We then briefly cover Lotus Notes' potential competitors—

GroupWise XTD, Collabra Share, and Exchange. We end with a Soapbox about where we think this is all going.

GROUPWARE MARKET OVERVIEW

As we mentioned in the last chapter, groupware was a $2.3 billion industry in 1995, and it's heading towards $6.5 billion in 1998. The lion's share of revenues went to the vendors of e-mail, workflow, Lotus Notes, and to system integrators. Notes, the industry's leading all-in-one groupware package, is closely aligned with Lotus' *cc:Mail*—the industry's leading LAN-based e-mail system, with over 8.3 million seats in 1995. Two of Notes' top three competitors are also closely aligned with popular LAN-based e-mail packages. Exchange includes *Microsoft Mail*, which had an installed base of over 7 million in late 1995. GroupWise XTD includes Novell's popular *GroupWise* mail product, which had an installed base of over 5 million in late 1995. Collabra Share is the exception; it works on top of other people's e-mail systems, but does not have one of its own.

So, excluding Collabra, we can say that the leading LAN-based e-mail vendors are turning into all-in-one groupware vendors. Collabra is depending on the Internet and other e-mail vendors to provide the missing pieces; it will provide an all-in-one groupware offering by integrating the pieces. Collabra is an important player because of its Netscape connection. It may provide a pure Internet-based alternative for doing groupware.

TRENDS

Notes is still the product that's defining the groupware industry. And the competing e-mail vendors are still trying to field a credible alternative to Notes. The news is that after missing so many schedules, the Notes competitors are finally starting to ship product. The other news is that the groupware industry is facing new challenges on many fronts—from SQL database vendors with their new data warehousing facilities, from the exploding Internet with its document publishing and conferencing facilities, and from CORBA Object Request Brokers. Here's a snapshot of the major movements that we're seeing in the groupware industry:

■ *Groupware vendors are embracing the Web*. The Web, with its open document standards—including document browsers, firewalls, the pervasive HTML/HTTP publishing standards, and the SMTP/MIME e-mail backbone—is the most formidable competitor groupware vendors are currently facing. Some pundits have gone as far as claiming that the Web has made Lotus Notes irrelevant. This is obviously not true. Instead, groupware vendors are in the best position to provide industrial strength technology for the Web—including scalable document databases, mission-critical mail backbones, security, server-to-server document replication, support for mobile users, workflow, and system management. Without exception, all the major groupware vendors have decided not to fight the Web; instead, they will join it. They are now in the process of recreating their groupware offerings on top of open Web standards.

■ *Groupware is now mission-critical ready.* Lotus Notes 4.0 is the first product to provide a truly robust, scalable, and OS-independent groupware infrastructure. The product now includes important backbone features such as dynamic routing, replication, pass-through servers, thread-based background routing, security, and global system management. Notes 4.0 has set a new bar for the robust features you should expect from a groupware server. We expect that its "big three" competitors will follow suit with products that are just as robust and mission-critical. So the good news is that groupware has finally moved from the experimental stage to the production stage.

■ *Groupware is expanding into new areas*. If they succeed in subsuming the Internet, the groupware vendors will be in a good position to subsume other forms of client/server—including database and TP Monitors. Groupware is also moving into new areas such as telephony. Finally, groupware's workflow and agent-based mail systems are strong candidates for managing business processes across an enterprise.

■ *Groupware is becoming tool-friendly.* Like TP Monitors and SQL databases, the groupware industry discovered that it takes great tools to win the hearts of client/server software developers. You can now create groupware applications that incorporate data from both document stores and SQL databases using popular client/server tools—including *Delphi*, *Visual Basic*, *PowerBuilder*, *SQL Windows*, and *VisualAge*. However, we do not know of any 3-tier client/server groupware tools—for example, a tool that lets you create workflows in the middle tier.

Groupware has come a long way. However, the technology is still handicapped by its lack of support for ACID transactions. Groupware also suffers from being a monolithic technology that is not well-suited for dealing with distributed components. In other words, groupware lacks the component middleware foundation of a distributed object bus, such as CORBA. However, groupware technology is here today, and you can use it to create some very exciting client/server applications— especially on the Internet and Intranets.

LOTUS NOTES 4.0

Lotus Notes—now in its fourth release—is the premier client/server groupware product in the industry. Even though Notes has been in the field for over three years and has sold over 5 million seats, it still remains a mystery to the vast majority of

PC users. It's even a mystery to its competitors. Some call it a "cute bulletin board," others label it "glorified e-mail," and some SQL purists pooh-pooh it as—Heaven forbid—an "unstructured database." In reality, Notes is a multifaceted, client/server groupware product. And as we know from the last chapter, it is hard to define groupware in 25 words or less. The secret of a good groupware package is that it creates a whole that is *much* more than the sum of the parts. Notes does this very well.

So What Is Lotus Notes?

Version 1 of Notes was about conferencing, version 2 was about information sharing, version 3 was about workflow, and version 4 is about inter-enterprise applications.

> — **David Marshak, VP**
> **Seybold**
> **(May, 1995)**

Lotus Notes allows groups of users to interact and share information that can be of a highly unstructured nature. Its client/server application development and run-time environment provide the following functions (see Figure 21-1):

- *A document database server* stores and manages multiuser client access to semi-structured data—including text, images, audio, and video. Release 4 supports up to 1000 concurrent Notes clients using 32-bit SMP server platforms (this is an order of magnitude greater than Release 3).

- *An e-mail server* manages multiuser client access to mail. Notes comes with a mail backbone infrastructure; X.400 is available as an optional component. Release 4 fully integrates X.400 and Internet SMTP/MIME backbone options.

- *A backbone server/server infrastructure* supports both mail-routing and database replication. The replication mechanism synchronizes copies of the same database, which can reside on multiple server (or client) machines. Release 4 now supports a new *server passthrough* feature; it lets you dial into one Notes server and reach any other server to which you are authorized. Passthrough also lets you access multiple databases on multiple servers at the same time.

- *A GUI client environment* presents views of the document databases and provides an electronic mail front-end. Users can navigate through the databases and their document contents. Views are stored queries that act as filters for the information in the databases. The e-mail front-end is just a specialized view of a mail database. Notes can attach GUI forms (private or public) to the various databases used for data entry. Release 4 introduced the new *Notes Mail* client; it supports a flexible three-pane user interface that integrates cc:Mail, Web browsing, and the traditional Notes client. It also provides a universal in-box that can accept all types of mail, faxes, and forms.

- **Distributed services** include electronic signatures, security and access control lists, database administration services, system management, and an X.500 based global namespace.

- **Application development tools** include: 1) a GUI forms generator; 2) tools and templates for creating databases; 3) a primitive scripting language consisting of *formulas*; and 4) an open API set—including the Notes API, VIM, MAPI, and ODBC. Release 4 supports *Intelligent Agents*. These are scripted Notes applications that you can use to automate repetitive tasks—including database replication, data-handling, the in-box actions, and messaging services. Release 4 also introduces *LotusScript 3.0*—a cross-platform, BASIC-like, object-oriented programming language. In addition, you can write Notes applications using many popular third-party client/server tools—including *Delphi*, *SQLWindows*, *PowerBuilder*, *New Era*, *VisualAge*, *Notes ViP*, and *Visual Basic* (via the Lotus-provided *HiTest* VBXs).

All Notes communications—client/server and server/server—are done using a proprietary RPC. Notes supports client/server drivers for NetBEUI, TPC/IP, IPX/SPX, and AppleTalk stacks. Optional APPC and X.25 drivers are available for server to server communications.

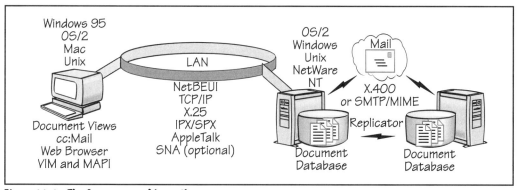

Figure 21-1. The Components of Lotus Notes.

The Multimedia Document Database

Ray Ozzie—founder of Iris Associates, the company that developed the original Notes under contract to Lotus—describes the foundation of the Notes architecture as a "database engine for semi-structured and unstructured information." Ozzie's model of a database is more akin to computer conferencing than Online Transaction Processing (OLTP). The Notes database was designed as a vehicle for gathering and disseminating all types of information; it was not meant to be a "database of record" that reflects the real-time state of the business. In this respect, Notes is more like a data warehouse, except that the data tends to be highly eclectic. Another way of putting it is that Ray Ozzie was more interested in adding and capturing real-time information than providing synchronized access to shared data for updates. You'll get a better feel for this after we explain the Lotus Notes replication model.

The primary commodity in a Notes system is a semi-structured, multimedia *document* that can contain a variety of data types—including voice, BLOBs, video, and multifont text (see Figure 21-2). A Notes system organizes, stores, replicates, and provides shared access to documents. Related collections of Notes documents are stored in a *database*, which you can index and retrieve by any of the documents' properties, or by the actual contents of the documents. Notes supports full-text indexing and searching. A Notes *document* consists of a set of fields, also known as *properties*; each has a name, type, and value. For example, you can tag a Notes document with properties such as *client*, *region*, and *subject*. The regions can contain any number of BLOB-like *attachments* (or embedded files). Embedded files are managed and organized as part of a Notes document.

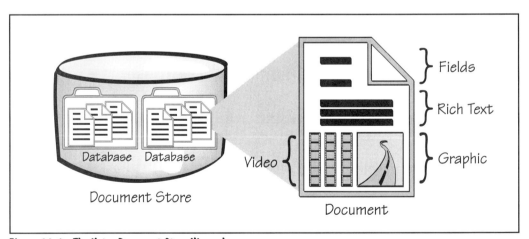

Figure 21-2. The Notes Document Store Hierarchy.

Notes Release 4 lets you create truly gigantic databases. Here are some of the new capabilities they advertise:

- **Object stores can be of unlimited size.** An administrator allocates maximum object store sizes in up to 4 GByte chunks—called *segments*. Notes will automatically span data across multiple segments and physical storage boundaries.

■ ***Databases can have an unlimited number of documents.*** Notes stores an entire database in a single file (or object store). A Notes application typically consists of many databases that are organized by topic.

Again, the Notes concept of a database is more akin to conferencing (data is organized by topic) rather than relational DBMSs (all data is organized in a single database consisting of multiple tables).

Notes Database Replication

Like data warehouses, Notes allows you to replicate databases across servers (and clients). Unlike the warehouses we covered in Part 4, Notes has no notion of a master database—it uses replicas. The *replicator* is responsible for bidirectionally adding, deleting, or updating documents among all *replicas* of the database. Notes uses replication as a means to disseminate (or broadcast) information across geographically distributed locations.

The Notes replicator supports both full and partial replication and has a tunable level of consistency based on the desired frequency of replication. Notes time-stamps all new and edited (or updated) documents that are known to have replicas. Unattended servers can dial each other up, compare notes, and swap changes at times configured by an administrator. You can also store replicas on client worksta-tions and initiate swaps from there.

Notes Release 3 introduced *background replication*, which allows Notes laptop clients to continue working in Notes while replication is taking place in the background. Laptop users will find replication to be very helpful for on-the-road activity. You copy a Notes database, work on it, and then swap changes with the server when you can make a connection (see Figure 21-3). *Selective replication* limits the sections in documents that get replicated. You can choose not to replicate binary attachments to save on local disk space. You can also limit the size of each document to be replicated (for example, the first 200 characters). Or, you can choose to only replicate unread messages from your boss or messages that are labeled urgent. Notes Release 4 provides *field-based replication* that gives you even more fine-grained control over the replication process. You can now replicate selective fields within a document. This new option lets you transmit only the updated fields within a changed document. With earlier versions, you had to wait for Notes to replicate all of a document's fields, even if only one field had been modified.

This loosely synchronized style of information update is adequate for most confer-encing applications, but it is a far cry from the synchronous two-phase commit updates used in OLTP applications. So how are concurrent updates handled? Prior to Notes Release 3, if two users simultaneously updated a server-based document,

Figure 21-3. Replicated Databases Can Be Used on the Road.

the first save was accepted and the next save was notified that it was overwriting someone else's changes. The decision of whether or not to overwrite the data was left to the user (not a very comforting thought if you were the first user). Notes Release 3 (and later) introduce a versioning capability that lets an edited document become a response to the original document. Or, the last updated version can become the main document, with all previous versions displayed as responses.

Versioning does not guarantee that the last version is the most accurate, and it cannot merge changes into a single copy of the data. So even Release 4 of Notes is not a suitable technology for OLTP database applications or applications that require high concurrency controls involving immediate updates. However, versioning eliminates the loss of data through concurrent updates or through replication. It's quite useful for its intended use: document-centric groupware applications—an area that OLTP doesn't even touch.

How to Build a Notes Application

You typically create a new Notes *database* by using one of the Lotus-provided templates and customizing it. A database is simply a new file; it can be given an identifying icon, a title, help panels, and a *policy document* that explains what it's all about. You use *forms* to enter information or view information in a database. To create a form, you can start with one of the pre-existing forms and modify it using the GUI editor. Forms provide data entry fields, text fields, and graphic areas where pictures or other sources of multimedia data can be pasted (or attached). Lotus provides a macro language—it's like 1-2-3 spreadsheet formulas—that allows you to associate commands with specific events and actions. In addition, you can use *LotusScript* to write your event handlers. And, in the future, you will be able to write your Notes event handlers using the Java language. The forms you create are associated with the database. You can designate them as either *public*, which means they're available to all client applications that have access to the database; or you can make them *private*, which means only the creator can use them.

Views are stored queries that display the contents of a database or of a particular document. You use them for navigation and for the filtering of information— examples are display documents less than one month old "by region" or "by salesperson." The view will display the list of documents in a tabular or outline format. Any database has one or more views that the designer creates for easy access to information. Users also can create *private* views to provide a listing or access criteria that the database designer didn't anticipate.

On the client side, a user has a *workspace*—a notebook-like visual that organizes databases by topics (see Figure 21-4). A notebook consists of six color-coded workpages; each has a folder-like tab that identifies a category into which you want to organize your databases. Each workpage can contain from zero to hundreds of

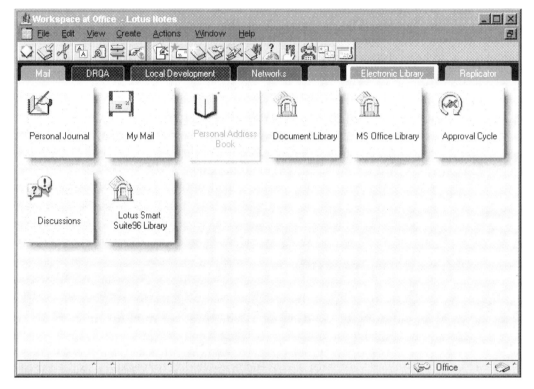

Figure 21-4. The Notes Client Workspace: An Organizer of Databases.

databases. Each database is represented by an icon and a title. You must associate a new database to a workpage. You double-click on it to open it and then work with its views. Notes lets you open multiple databases and gives each its own window. However, you still can't join documents from different databases into a single view. But you can create hypertext links from any document in any database to any other database. Release 4 provides a three-pane display for navigating and viewing the contents of a database. The *navigator pane* lets you navigate the database contents in outline format. The *view pane* displays the contents of a view or folder. The *preview pane* displays the details of a highlighted document without opening it.

The process of creating a new Notes client/server application and tailoring forms and views can take less than an hour. It's that simple. For the more adventurous, the Notes *formula macro language* provides about 200 functions to control almost everything from field input validation to database queries and document routing. The even more adventurous can use *LotusScript* or program directly to the Notes API. You can associate a *prompt* command with any event to display a dialog box that prompts users to enter data or to select an entry from a listbox. Notes provides *periodic macros* that you can use to launch macros or scripts at a specific time interval or as a result of a particular action or condition—for example, when a document is deleted. This is the Notes equivalent of a trigger.

The Lotus Notes API

Notes also provides a C++ programming API, which developers can use to store and retrieve Notes documents. It also gives you broad access to many of the features of the Notes user interface. The API allows you to:

- Create or delete databases.
- Read, write, and modify any document and any field in the document.
- Create and use database views.
- Control database access with access control lists.
- Gather and report server performance statistics and register new workstations and servers.
- Write custom tasks that you can add to the Notes server software and specify the schedule under which the custom task executes.
- Create, read, and run Notes macros using the API.
- Perform full-text searches using the new search-engine.
- Issue calls to restrict what documents get exchanged during replication.
- Obtain the list of names and address books in use locally or on a server.
- Issue mail gateway calls.

In addition, Notes supports both the VIM and MAPI e-mail client APIs. It also supports ODBC for SQL database access.

Notes and SQL Databases

An external database API based on DataLens drivers is available free of charge. It lets Notes users access data stored in external databases using Notes' keywords and lookup capabilities. The foreign data can be displayed in Notes fields. In addition, Lotus provides a relational database interface that supports the ODBC CLI. The ODBC driver allows programmers to write SQL queries that can be translated into Notes queries. It provides the capability to bring Notes data into a relational database. Figure 21-5 shows the bidirectional Notes/SQL capability.

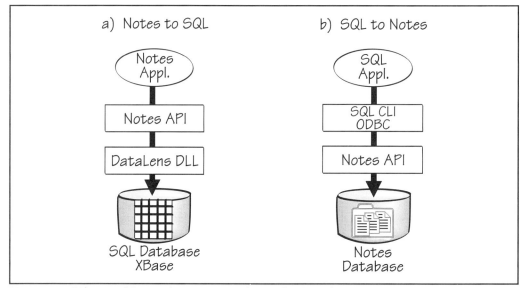

Figure 21-5. Bidirectional Data Exchanges Between Notes and SQL Databases.

Notes E-Mail

We want to enhance Notes as the place to live on the network.

— *Jim Manzi, ex-CEO*
Lotus

From a client workstation's perspective, e-mail is just another Notes database that contains a collection of mail documents. The procedures to read incoming mail, sort through mail, or create a mail document are the same ones used to create and read documents in any Notes database. You simply use forms and views that are tailored to your mail documents. Of course, one of the differences is that the mail documents you create will be sent to someone else's mailbox. Notes provides visual indicators to let you know that you have incoming mail. You then open the database and read it. Ray Ozzie's design seems to be very consistent.

The Notes e-mail server is open. If you don't like the Notes Mail front-end, you can use the VIM or MAPI APIs to create your own. Or you can simply use VIM or MAPI to mail-enable your applications using the Notes server as a back-end. With Release 4, cc:Mail clients are able to use the Notes Mail server. So what kind of services does a Notes Mail server provide? It provides mail backbone functions with the following features:

- *Routing optimization.* The techniques include outbound message prioritization and dynamic adaptive route selection based on link costs.

- *Separate router threads.* All server-to-server communications are handled by separate transfer threads. Threads allow multiple concurrent transfers to occur on different backbone routes. In addition, threads prevent large mail messages from delaying other server tasks.

- *Delivery failure notification.* Senders can be notified when delivery isn't possible (including the reasons).

- *X.500 namespace support.* Notes supports the full X.500-compliant hierarchical naming as its native means of identifying *users* within the system. This makes it straightforward for Notes directories to interoperate at the naming level with other X.500-compliant systems. It avoids naming conflict headaches.

- *Mail gateways and directory services.* Notes provides e-mail gateways to the most popular e-mail networks, including X.400, SMTP, cc:Mail, MHS, PROFS, Exchange, VinesMail, Fax, VAXmail, and SoftSwitch (see Figure 21-6).

- *Electronic signatures.* Notes uses the RSA public key cryptography for all aspects of Notes security, including encryption. (In Part 3, we explained that RSA was good for electronic signatures, but very slow when it came to general encryption.) If you sign a message, it takes Notes a few seconds longer to send it because it must generate an RSA electronic signature. If it takes a few seconds just to encrypt a name, how long does it take to encrypt a medium-sized document?

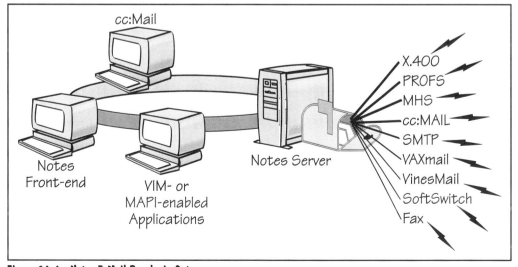

Figure 21-6. Notes E-Mail Reach via Gateways.

■ *Open client support.* Notes Release 4 supports both VIM and MAPI calls, which means that Notes users can select their mail clients independently from the server.

As we explained in the last chapter, the Notes 4.0 mail engine serves both Notes and cc:Mail front-ends. Notes provides a true client/server e-mail architecture. The clients and servers communicate via RPC. VIM and MAPI provide the call-level interface on the client side.

Notes and the Web

Notes is so complex and monolithic...it's a very IBM-like product. It will be interesting to see if there is a future for it in these open network environments, where people are looking for more flexible systems.

> — Marc Andreessen, VP
> Netscape
> (December, 1995)

The most complete Internet strategy for corporations I've heard so far is Lotus'. That's for the simple reason that Lotus has the best product to marry to the Internet—Notes.

> — John Dodge, Editor
> PC Week
> (December, 1995)

In December 1995, Lotus took a giant step toward merging Notes 4.0 with the World Wide Web and other Internet standards (see Figure 21-7). The new Notes Mail client includes an embedded Web browser that lets you access Notes and HTML documents via URLs. In addition, Lotus bundled the *InterNotes* server—previously priced at $2,995—with the Notes 4.0 server. InterNotes is a bidirectional Notes/Web document converter. It lets you Web-enable a Notes server, which means you can store HTML documents in a Notes database. In the other direction, it lets you convert existing Notes documents, views, and forms into HTML. In mid-1996, Lotus will ship a completely Internet-integrated HTTP Notes server on all standard Notes server platforms; the bundle will also include the *Verity* search engine.[1] Lotus will also Java-enable its Notes forms and servers.

---

[1] Notes servers sell for $495 on single processor systems. Notes Mail client sells for $69 (down from $155 in Release 3).

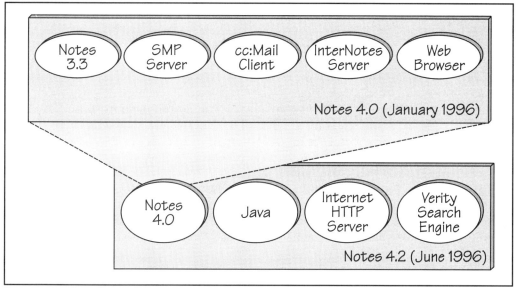

Figure 21-7. The Evolution of Notes to an Internet Server.

If all this terminology sounds confusing, please bear with us. We cover the Web in gory detail in Part 8. The point we're making here is that the groupware vendors are embracing the Internet big time. Notes is positioning itself as the Internet server of choice. It will use its multiplatform and scalable server technology to provide mission-critical Internet and Intranet databases. Lotus has a head start over competing Internet server vendors with Notes' replication technology, robust messaging middleware, security, workflow, conferencing, systems management, and application development environment. All Lotus had to do was embrace the Internet standards and then augment them with Notes capabilities. It seems to be doing both (also see next Soapbox).

Notes Systems Management

Lotus *NotesView* is a graphical management utility that lets you manage an enterprise-wide Notes environment from a single management station. The package lets you control any Notes Server and monitor the health of a Notes backbone network. The utility displays an entire mail-routing topology, including routes to and from selected servers. It also shows you the replication topology, including the replication maps of specific databases. NotesView provides real-time statistics on mail volume, number of pending or dead messages, replication time, low-level packet traffic, router loads, and so on. It can also serve as a proxy management station in an enterprise management hierarchy by supporting the SNMP management protocol and the new *Mail And Directories MANagement (MADMAN)* MIB. We will have more to say on SNMP and MIBs in Part 9.

How Revolutionary Is Notes?

Soapbox

Notes is a very exciting product that makes you want to jump in and create client/server applications just for the fun of it. Notes databases tend to proliferate like rabbits. Once you get the hang of them, they're contagious. With Release 4, Notes starts to address the client/server needs of mobile users and intergalactic enterprises. You can carry your Notes databases in a laptop or have them replicated to the far corners of the universe. Lotus is also doing more to open up the Notes environment at the API level so that ISVs and IS programmers can jump in and provide add-ons. So in many ways, Lotus Notes may be a "killer app" that does for client/server what Lotus 1-2-3 did for PCs and DOS.

We like Notes and highly recommend it for certain classes of applications. But it's important to understand what it can and cannot do. Notes is a very good fit for applications that collect multimedia information, perform very few updates, and need to be integrated with e-mail. But Notes is not very good at handling applications that deal with structured data, are query intensive, and require multiuser updates with high levels of integrity. Notes does not handle transactions well; it does not even know how to spell ACID. These types of applications are best handled by TP Monitors, data warehouses, transactional MOMs, and SQL and object databases. ❑

NOVELL'S GROUPWISE XTD

Novell has a lot of the pieces, and a few of them are very well-integrated.

> — *David Marshak, VP*
> *Seybold*
> *(May, 1995)*

Someone once remarked that Novell's *GroupWise* went through more name changes than an ex-con. It's true. The product—originally named *WordPerfect Office*—became *WordPerfect Symmetry* in May 1994 to avoid confusion with Microsoft Office. In July 1994, Novell acquired WordPerfect and renamed the product *GroupWise*. In September 1994, *GroupWise 4.1* was released on multiple platforms. In 1996, the client/server version of the product was renamed *Group-Wise XTD*.

In January 1996, Novell sold its WordPerfect division to Corel, but it kept the very successful GroupWise product. By year-end 1995, the product had sold over 5 million copies, making it the third-most popular LAN e-mail package after *Lotus cc:Mail* and *Microsoft Mail*. GroupWise grew by 128% over the past year, and is the fastest growing product that Novell has at the moment. The product was declared to be a key piece of infrastructure in Novell's latest strategy, called the "Smart Global Network." Novell's intent is to leverage the large installed base of NetWare networks and provide a common platform for administering both the network and groupware applications.

So what is GroupWise? Novell calls it "a messaging application." In its current incarnation, it is an e-mail product with groupware add-on functions. GroupWise is an integrated package that includes e-mail, calendaring, scheduling, task management, Internet messages, and faxes. It supports what Novell calls "rules-based messaging"—it lets you associate actions to incoming and outgoing e-mail messages. All of GroupWise's functions run under a common user interface.

GroupWise client software runs on Windows, DOS, Macintosh, OS/2, HP-UX, AIX, SCO, DG-UX, Solaris, SunOS and Unix SVR4. The server groupware engine software runs on numerous Unix variants, NetWare, and OS/2. In addition, the Windows client supports simple MAPI, while the Mac client supports AOCE and AppleScript. On the server side, Novell provides gateways to almost every known e-mail messaging backbone system.

In December 1994, Novell signed an agreement with Collabra to integrate collaborative discussion software within the GroupWise product. Later in 1995, Novell signed a similar agreement with FileNet to provide workflow support for Group-Wise. The next move for GroupWise is *GroupWise XTD*, which should be available by the time you read this book. GroupWise XTD offers server-to-server and server-to-client replication, workflow, and some electronic forms and document management capabilities. GroupWise XTD does message replication instead of database replication.

GroupWise XTD features a *universal in-box* that lets you access all types of incoming messages in one place—including e-mail, schedule requests, delegated tasks, voice mail, faxes, and electronic forms. The in-box profiles and manages information in the same way, regardless of data type. You should be able to sort, route, copy and delegate a voice message exactly like you would with an e-mail message. It frees you from having to piece together information from separate applications or locations. In addition, XTD will provide a *replicated folder* capability that lets teams share applications, information, and in-box items. You should be able to share information related to a particular topic or project. In

Part 6. Client/Server Groupware

January 1996, Novell announced *WebAccess*—an add-on product that lets you access your GroupWise in-box using any Web browser.

The XTD *universal out-box* lets you track messages and retract them if they're unopened. You can see if your messages have been received, opened, deleted, or delegated. GroupWise XTD is a modular offering; it will let you purchase *a la carte* just the functions that you need (see Figure 21-8). If Novell succeeds in delivering on all of its promises, GroupWise XTD may provide the first real competition to Lotus Notes.

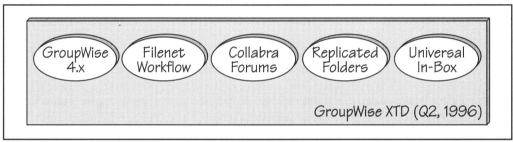

Figure 21-8. GroupWise XTD: An Integrated Groupware Offering.

NETSCAPE'S COLLABRA SHARE

UseNet is a wild and wooly place...We need to take Internet conferencing to the next level.

> — *Eric Hahn, CEO*
> *Collabra*
> *(October, 1995)*

When Netscape acquired Collabra in November 1995, there was a perception that Internet-based Groupware is right around the corner. In reality, Collabra Share 2.0 is not a full-featured groupware environment like Lotus Notes. It's more like a bulletin board add-on that works on top of existing e-mail systems—they must be enabled for either MAPI or VIM. Collabra lets you create discussion groups—called forums—using ordinary e-mail instead of a document database. Note that Collabra's discussion group features are based on a proprietary protocol—called the *Collaborative Object Store*—instead of the Internet's *Network News Transport Protocol*.

In Collabra, if you want to start a new message thread or reply to an existing message, you simply click on the appropriate button in the toolbar to invoke a message form. You typically post a message to a forum. Collabra also provides a "Post and Notify" feature that lets you both post a message and send a copy of the posting as an e-mail message to specific users. You access all messages by viewing threads in individual conferences. Collabra lists conference topics in chronological order. It indents all responding messages directly underneath a topic, clearly marking messages that you haven't yet read.

Collabra provides powerful search and sort tools that let you quickly find the information you're after in the various forums. You can sort messages in a forum by author, title, date, size, or relevance. The *Search Assistant* lets you enter phrases, multiple terms, or wild cards. You can restrict searches to the body, title, or author of documents. In addition, you can combine search terms using boolean and proximity operators.

The Collabra *Replication Agent* lets you replicate entire forums across multiple servers, but it does not provide Lotus-like filters or field-based replication. Collabra does not support bidirectional replication because all replication is done via e-mail. However, only the creators can edit forum postings. Consequently, it is easy to ensure that all servers have identical copies of a forum. Collabra lets you schedule replication times for each forum individually, but you're still constrained by your e-mail system's message propagation time.

Collabra is a client/server system. The clients run on Windows, and the servers run on NT. As you can see, Collabra is really an e-mail-based conferencing system that will somehow be incorporated in future releases of Netscape Navigator client browsers and Netscape servers. Collabra alone is not a Lotus replacement. Even Collabra Share 2.1—the first product to come out of the union between Netscape and Collabra—does not do enough to harness the power of the Web. The product simply adds connections to Web sites and newsgroup postings from within Collabra forums. It also lets you launch the Netscape browser via an icon in Collabra Share's tool bar.

However, both Collabra and Netscape have endorsed Java as their development and scripting environment. Consequently, we may see a future Collabra/Netscape, Web-based groupware offering augmented with a Java Internet development environment. This can potentially lead to a very potent combination.

MICROSOFT'S EXCHANGE

Where Lotus views the world as one big business process, Microsoft sees it as one big mail system. Microsoft is about where Lotus was with the second generation of Notes.

— *David Marshak, VP*
Seybold
(May, 1995)

Microsoft's long-delayed Exchange product—it finally shipped in mid-1996—is a client/server messaging system. Exchange provides server-based e-mail, fax, and voice mail integration capabilities to Microsoft Mail clients. The server code only runs on Windows NT. Exchange will also integrate group scheduling, electronic forms, and business productivity applications under one unified user interface. Exchange is an integral part of Microsoft's BackOffice. Consequently, it builds on top of NT's common infrastructure for security, user authorization, and network administration. For example, Exchange lets you modify a user's profile directly from within the NT *User Manager Utility.*

Originally billed as a "Notes killer," Exchange—in its latest incarnation—is closer in function to Collabra than to Lotus Notes (see Figure 21-9). Like Collabra, Exchange provides public folders for group discussions on top of a mail-centric system. In contrast, Notes provides a groupware application development environment on top of a shared document database.

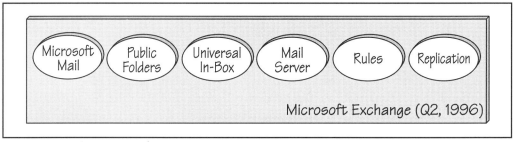

Figure 21-9. Exchange: Microsoft's Next Generation Mail Server.

If you're one of the 7 million users of Microsoft Mail, you will feel right at home in Exchange. You can think of Exchange as a client/server version of Microsoft Mail. Exchange replaces Mail's shared folders with a new *public folder* facility that runs on servers. Clients that have access to these public folders can now post messages directly to the folder instead of sending them to a particular user or group of users. This means that you can use these public folders to create public forums where groups of users can create and respond to postings. Exchange keeps track of the message threads in the public folders and displays them in a tree-like configuration within the forum window. This lets you see how the messages in a public folder relate to each other.

In addition, Exchange provides a "publish and subscribe" service on top of its public folders. For example, it lets you subscribe to a public folder and then receive automatic notifications whenever anyone posts a message to that folder. A built-in form designer lets you create custom forms for posting messages. You can also create forms using Visual Basic.

Like GroupWise and cc:Mail, Exchange provides a "universal in-box" that lets you collect e-mail, faxes, and messages from public folders. You will be able to filter messages, sort them, and create multiple views of your message folders. For example, you should be able to sort messages by topic, date, sender, or by the special contents of a custom field. You will also be able to define rules (or actions) that are invoked when a message is received. These rules—called *AutoAssistants*—execute on the server.

Like Collabra and GroupWise, Exchange supports server-to-server replication using e-mail. In contrast, Notes uses a specialized RPC to speed up the replication process and improve its robustness. Unlike Notes, Exchange won't let you replicate databases to remote clients, which can be a problem for mobile users. Exchange is now seen as primarily a way to synchronize e-mail communications. It is not seen as a replacement for Notes. Instead, it's more like Microsoft's next-generation e-mail system.

Is Groupware Still Synonymous With Notes?

Soapbox

The next casualties of the Web will be workgroup applications, such as Lotus Notes and Microsoft Exchange. IBM and Microsoft are, for once, in the same position—making the same mistake.

> — *Charles Ferguson, President, Vermeer
> (November, 1995)*

Instead of wiping out the need for applications like Notes, the Web will in many cases only increase the need for them, and that's the dynamic that drove Netscape to acquire Collabra.

> — *Jamie Lewis, President, Burton Group
> (October, 1995)*

Now that Lotus has embraced the Web in a big way, the Internet is no longer a threat to Notes. On the contrary, the Internet and Intranets may become important sources of new revenues for groupware vendors. Lotus Notes provides ideal technology for supporting document databases—the stuff the Internet is made from. Notes servers crate a database paradigm on top of ordinary files. It is an order of magnitude better than dealing with billions of raw files.

In 1996, there is still no groupware product that matches Notes' comprehensive cross-platform strengths and scalability. Without Notes, you end up putting together a set of disparate groupware services on your own. In the long run, the alternative that poses the most threat to Notes is Microsoft's Exchange because it is bundled with BackOffice.

Exchange will prove irresistible to companies that standardize on Windows NT and Microsoft suites. The million dollar question is: Will these companies use Exchange as their e-mail package and use Notes for groupware? Or, will they use Exchange to provide their total groupware solution? Even if they make the latter choice, Lotus has a huge head start over Exchange even on the NT platform. It will take a long time for Microsoft to match Notes' mobile and mission-critical infrastructure. Of course, Notes will not stand still in the meantime—it can only get stronger with its new Web-integrated features.

So it looks like Notes has an almost invincible grip on the groupware market. We say "almost" because we believe that in the long run, the biggest threat to Notes will come from ORB-based distributed components and objects. Some enterprising company will eventually recreate the Notes functionality using a CORBA object bus. When this happens, Notes will become an antique. CORBA is a much better backbone bus than Notes because it was designed from the start to support distributed components and transactions.

Lotus may decide to jump on the CORBA bandwagon and build the next generation of Notes using SOM—IBM's cross-platform CORBA ORB. If this happens, Notes may have a long and happy life ahead of it. So far, IBM and Lotus have only created gateways between Notes and key IBM products—including DB2, CICS, ImagePlus, MQSeries, and IBM Internet servers. These gateways were not built using SOM. We believe it's only a matter of time before the Notes architects discover SOM. Meanwhile, their competitors at Microsoft are using Network OLE as the backbone ORB for all the Microsoft suite products. So the future of groupware is going to be objects. The question is: Whose objects? ❏

Part 7
Client/Server With
Distributed Objects

An Introduction to Part 7

Living with both CORBA and OLE is likely to be the game plan for the foreseeable future.

— *Mark Betz, Director of Objects*
Block Financial
(March, 1996)

So did you all enjoy that night on the town? Oh, you want to play elephant and blind men again? We can't afford it—you Martians party too hard. But, we have a great new adventure ahead of us, and it's going to be fun. We're going to explore the uncharted territory of distributed objects. No, we're not talking about *Unidentified Flying Objects (UFOs)*—that's Martian stuff. Sorry, that was rude: Of course you Martians are not objects and, yes, you have identities. What we're dealing with here are computer objects. Do they fly? Yes, some do over wireless networks. And, we know of roaming objects that live on networks and their brokers who organize communities of objects. Yes, it's another new frontier, and there may be a pot of gold there, too. Are you all packed and ready for another adventure?

Part 7 is about distributed objects. The word *distributed* is important because it means we're dealing with objects that participate in client/server relationships with other objects. More plumbing? Yes, but this is supposed to be the "mother of all plumbing." Objects can do everything we've covered in this book, and supposedly *they do it better.* Here's why:

- **Objects** themselves are an amazing combination of data and function, with magical properties like polymorphism, inheritance, and encapsulation. This magic works wonders in distributed environments.

- **Object brokers** provide the ultimate distributed system. They allow objects to dynamically discover each other and interact across machines and operating systems.

- **Object services** allow us to create, manage, name, move, copy, store, and restore objects.

- **Object TP Monitors** may emerge as the most powerful and flexible transaction managers yet. Objects and transactions are a dynamite combination.

- **Object groupware** may change the way we interact. The new groupware will be built using roaming objects, intelligent event managers, and object replication services.

- **Object databases** provide the ultimate management system for BLOBs, documents, and almost any type of information—especially new information types.

- *Object Web* technology provides the foundation for the next generation of the Internet and Intranets, as described in Part 8.

- *Object linking* technology allows us to create highly flexible webs among programs that don't know about each other. The webs emanate out of ordinary looking desktop documents.

- *Object frameworks* promise to revolutionize the way we build our distributed systems. They provide flexible, customizable, prefabricated software sub-systems.

Objects—packaged as components—may provide the ultimate infrastructure for building client/server systems. We say "may" because success depends on more than just great technology. What products are available? Are the major players lined up behind the technology? Are the key standards in place?

We think you Martians will love this distributed object stuff. It has all the elements of a new gold rush. But first we must clearly understand what makes this 20-year-old technology finally ready for prime time. The answer is CORBA. You'll

An Introduction to Part 7

have to read the ORB chapter to discover what's behind CORBA magic. Complementing CORBA are distributed object services, compound document technology (OpenDoc), and object databases. But CORBA is not the only game in town. As we go to press, Microsoft is getting ready to ship its own ORB, which it calls *Distributed Component Object Model (DCOM)*, or *Network OLE*. As usual, the competition will be quite exciting. So pack up; we have an interesting journey ahead of us. Pack lots of trail mix and energy bars—you'll need it all. And yes, it's new frontier country. So bring along all your exploration gear, and let's hope we don't lose any of you in those uncharted and potentially treacherous mountain passes and ravines.[1]

---

[1] Note: Part 7 is derived from our 600-page book, **The Essential Distributed Objects Survival Guide** (Wiley, 1996). We include this material to make this Survival Guide stand on its own and to provide you with the background information you'll need for Part 8.

Chapter 22

Distributed Objects and Components

An object is a living, breathing blob of intelligence that knows how to act in a given situation.

— *Steve Jobs*

By now, anybody associated with computers knows that objects are wonderful—we simply can't live without them. Smalltalk can be used to create GUI front-ends, C++ is the only way to write code, and the literature is full of articles on the wonders of encapsulation, multiple inheritance, and polymorphism. But what can these things do on a client/server network? Where do objects fit in a world dominated by SQL databases, TP Monitors, and Lotus Notes? What happens when we stray away from the cozy single-address space of a program and try to get objects to talk across a network? What happens to inheritance in a world of federated operating systems separated by networks? In a nutshell, we need to understand how object technology can be *extended* to deal with the complex issues that are inherent in creating robust, single-image, client/server systems.

The purpose of the next few chapters is to describe exactly what objects can do for client/server systems. The key word is *systems*—or how objects work together across machine and network boundaries to create client/server solutions. We're not going to rehash the marvels of Object-Oriented Programming (OOP), Smalltalk, and C++ because we assume you've heard about them all before. We're moving on to the next step: distributed objects. We strongly believe that this is the area where objects will realize their greatest potential; in the process, they will become the new "mainstream computing model." We also believe that the Internet and Intranets need distributed objects to fullfil their intergalactic promise—more on that in Part 8. Finally, we believe that without a strong distributed object foundation, the management of client/server systems is a lost cause—more on that in Part 9. In this chapter, we cover distributed objects and components. This is the background information you'll need to understand the CORBA, OLE, and OpenDoc chapters.

WHAT DISTRIBUTED OBJECTS PROMISE

Just as databases were at the center of the design of the applications of the '70s and '80s, components are at the center of design of the application of the '90s and the next century.

> — **David Vaskevitch, Director of Enterprise Microsoft**
> **(1995)**[1]

Object technology radically alters the way software systems are developed. The promise is compelling: We will be able to put together complex client/server information systems by simply assembling and extending reusable software components. Any of the objects may be modified or replaced without affecting the rest of the components in the system or how they interact. The components may be shipped as collections of class libraries preassembled in *frameworks*, where all the pieces are known to work together to perform a specific task. Components will revolutionize the way we create client/server systems. They promise to provide the ultimate in mix-and-match capabilities.

The Benefits of Distributed Objects

Distributed object technology is extremely well-suited for creating flexible client/server systems because the data and business logic are encapsulated within objects, allowing them to be located anywhere within a distributed system. The granularity of distribution is greatly improved. Distributed objects have the inherent potential to allow granular components of software to plug-and-play, interoperate across networks, run on different platforms, coexist with legacy applications through object wrappers, roam on networks, and manage themselves and the resources they

---

[1]   Source: David Vaskevitch, **Client/Server Strategies, 2nd Edition** (IDG, 1995).

control. Objects are inherently self-managing entities. Objects should allow us to manage very complex systems by broadcasting instructions and alarms. Each receiving object will react differently to the message based on its object type.

Why This Sudden Interest in Distributed Objects?

Object technology has the ability to revolutionize client/server computing because it makes software easier and faster to develop for programmers, easier to use for users, and easier to manage for system administrators.

> — *Ronald Weissman, Director*
> *NeXT*

We still need to answer this question: Why is there a renewed interest in the 20-year-old object technology? The technology is now ripe. And we can't build the type of applications we need with any other technology. Also, our industry has now created the foundation for a distributed object infrastructure that includes an object software bus and the technology for components that can plug-and-play on this bus. Monolithic applications are monolithic because they're built as a whole. The object bus and component infrastructure make it unnecessary to build information systems from scratch. They let us create whole applications from parts.

However, distributed objects (and components) by themselves are not enough to get us there. They need to be packaged as components that can play together in *suites*. These suites combine the best in client/server and distributed object technology. They allow us to "build to order" entire information systems by assembling off-the-shelf object components. We will be able to assemble—in record time— highly flexible client/server applications tailored to a customer's needs. The components may be shipped in preassembled suites, where all the pieces are known to work together to perform a specific task. We anticipate that components and the client/server suites that integrate them will create vast new opportunities for ISVs, system integrators, and in-house IS developers.

For objects to be successful, they must reside in open client/server environments and learn how to "plug-and-play" across networks and operating systems. In theory, object technology is well-suited for creating client/server systems because the data and business logic are encapsulated within objects, allowing them to be located anywhere within a distributed system. The *granularity* of distribution is greatly improved. Objects can easily mask the platform-specific elements and make the pieces appear to interoperate seamlessly.

Object-oriented client/server applications can afford to be much more flexible than traditional vertical applications—frameworks allow end-users to mix-and-match components without making the distributed application *less* robust. Distributed objects allow granular components of software to plug-and-play, interoperate across networks, run on different platforms, coexist with legacy applications through object wrappers, roam on networks (for example, Java Applets), and manage themselves and the resources they control. In addition, objects have this unique property of separating their interfaces from the implementation. This means that you can use object interfaces to wrapper your existing applications and make them look like ordinary objects. So you don't have to toss away these old applications as you would have to do with other forms of middleware. Figure 22-1 shows some of these benefits. What more could we want?

FROM DISTRIBUTED OBJECTS TO COMPONENTS

A classical object—of the C++ or Smalltalk variety—is a blob of intelligence that encapsulates code and data. Classical objects provide wonderful code reuse facilities via inheritance and encapsulation. However, these classical objects only live within a single program. Only the language compiler that creates the objects knows of their existence. The outside world doesn't know about these objects and has no way to access them. They're literally buried in the bowels of a program.

In contrast, a *distributed object* is a blob of intelligence that can live anywhere on a network. Distributed objects are packaged as independent pieces of code that can be accessed by remote clients via method invocations. The language and compiler used to create distributed server objects are totally transparent to their clients. Clients don't need to know where the distributed object resides or what operating system it executes on; it can be on the same machine or on a machine that sits across an intergalactic network. Distributed objects are smart pieces of software that can message each other transparently anywhere in the world. Distributed objects can interrogate each other—"tell me what you do." Distributed objects are very dynamic—they come and go and move around.

Components: The Grand Prize of Objects

When we talk about distributed objects, we're really talking about independent software *components*. These are smart pieces of software that can play in different networks, operating systems, and tool palettes. A component is an object that's not bound to a particular program, computer language, or implementation. Objects built as components provide the right "shapes" for distributed applications. They are the optimal building blocks for creating the next generation of distributed systems.

Distributed objects are, by definition, components because of the way they are packaged. In distributed object systems, the unit of work and distribution is a

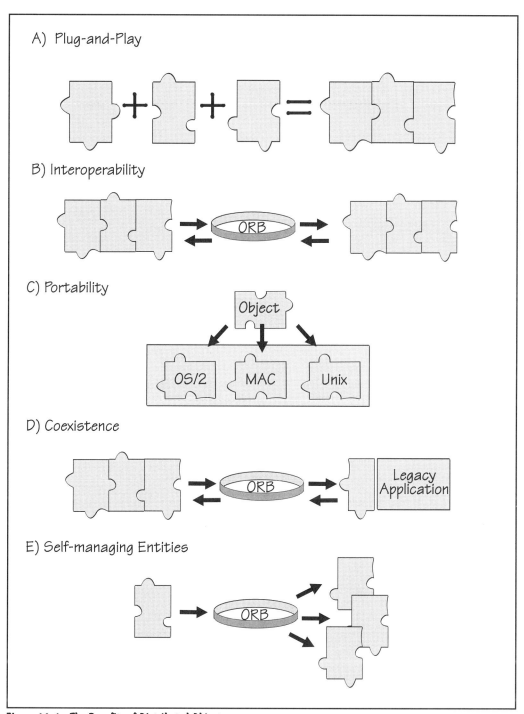

Figure 22-1. The Benefits of Distributed Objects.

component. The distributed object infrastructure makes it easier for components to be more autonomous, self-managing, and collaborative.

Component technology—in all its forms—promises to radically alter the way software systems are developed. For example, distributed objects allow us to put together complex client/server information systems by simply assembling and extending components. The goal of object components is to provide software users and developers the same levels of plug-and-play application interoperability that are available to consumers and manufacturers of electronic parts or custom integrated circuits.

The Driving Force Behind Components

The component revolution is being driven from the desktop, where vendors are realizing that to be profitable, they must quickly rearchitect their existing applications and suites into components. Today's desktop applications are monolithic and bloated. They contain every possible feature you might use—whether or not you really want them. Most of us use less than 10% of an application's features—the rest of the features simply add complexity and bulk. We must wait—it seems forever—to get the new features we really need in the form of new upgrades or replacements. This is because vendors must bring forward all the hundreds of product features with every new release, leading to long and costly development cycles. Vendors take the "shotgun" approach because they don't know which features you need; they try to be all things to all people.

These feature-heavy, bloated, monolithic applications are very costly for vendors to upgrade and maintain. Each change challenges the fragile integrity of the monolith and requires long regression test cycles (and resources). Maintaining these applications is no picnic either. The smaller *Independent Software Vendors (ISVs)* face these same problems but even more acutely. They have much more limited resources to throw at them.

To give you an idea of the magnitude of the problem, consider that it took WordPerfect just under 14 developer years to upgrade their product from version 3 to version 4. However, it took 250 developer years to move the same product from version 5 to version 6. If things continue at this rate, it could cost them as many as 4,464 developer years to move the product to version 8. Microsoft is experiencing the same phenomenon. For example, the size of Excel went from 4 MBytes in 1990, to over 16 MBytes today. Microsoft is looking at OLE components to improve the situation. Lotus has a similar story. It shipped 1-2-3 on one floppy in 1982; today, 1-2-3 requires 11 MBytes of disk space to install. Lotus is looking at both OLE and OpenDoc to fix the problem.

Components to the Rescue

Objects have been freed from the shackles of a particular language or platform. Programmers have been liberated from the confines of one compiler or family of class libraries. Objects can be everywhere, working together and delivering a new world of opportunity to the next generation of systems architectures.

> — *Martin Anderson, Chairman*
> *Integrated Objects*
> *(June, 1995)*

Object-oriented programming has long been advanced as a solution to the problems we just described. However, objects by themselves do not provide an infrastructure through which software created by different vendors can interact with one another within the same address space—much less across address spaces, networks, and operating systems. The solution is to augment classical objects with a standard component infrastructure.

OpenDoc and OLE are currently the leading component standards for the desktop; CORBA provides a component standard for the enterprise. CORBA and OpenDoc complement each other—OpenDoc uses CORBA as its object bus. These new component standards will change the economics of software development. Monolithic applications—both on the desktop and in the enterprise—will be replaced with component suites. Here's how this new technology will affect you:

- *Power users* will find it second nature to assemble their own personalized applications using off-the-shelf components. They will use scripts to tie the parts together and customize their behavior.

- *Small developers and ISVs* will find that components reduce expenses and lower the barriers to entry in the software market. They can create individual components with the knowledge that they will integrate smoothly with existing software created by larger development shops—they do not have to reinvent all the functions around them. They can get fine-grained integration instead of today's "Band-Aid" integration. In addition, they get faster time to market because the bulk of an application is already there.

- *Large developers, IS shops, and system integrators* will use suites of components to create (or assemble) enterprise-wide client/server applications in record time. Typically, about 80% of the function they need will be available as off-the-shelf components. The remaining 20% is the value-added they provide. The resulting client/server systems may be less complex to test because of the high reliability of the pretested components. The fact that many components are black boxes reduces the overall complexity of the development

process. Components—especially of the CORBA variety—will be architected to work together in intergalactic client/server networks.

■ *Marketing People* will use components to assemble applications that target specific markets (for example, "Word for Legal Firms"). Instead of selling monster suites—packed with everything but the kitchen sink—at rock-bottom prices, they will be able to provide their consumers with what they really need. Increased customization and more malleable products will create new market segments. Consumers will not be at the mercy of the long product release cycles to get new functions. They can buy add-on functions—in the form of components—when they need it.

In summary, components reduce application complexity, development cost, and time-to-market. They also improve software reusability, maintainability, platform independence, and client/server distribution. Finally, components provide more freedom of choice and flexibility.

When Can We Expect These Components?

The transition to component-based software will change the way we buy and build systems and what it means to be a software engineer.

> — *Dave Thomas, President*
> *Object Technology International*
> *(March, 1995)*

By 1997, most new software will be developed (or assembled) using components. According to *Strategic Focus*, 25% of developers are already building component software today. This number climbs abruptly to include 61% of all developers by 1997.[2] This means that almost two out of three developers will have adopted the component approach (see Figure 22-2).

If this forecast is correct, then the software industry is now at the same point where the hardware industry was about 23 years ago. At that time, the first integrated circuits (ICs) were developed to package discrete functions into hardware. ICs were wired together on boards to provide more complex functions. These boards were eventually miniaturized into ICs. These new and more powerful ICs were wired together on new boards, and so on. We should experience the same spiral with software. A component is what Brad Cox calls a *software IC*. *Frameworks* are the boards into which we plug these components. The object bus provides the backplane. Families of software ICs that play together are called *suites*. You should be

---

[2] Source: **Strategic Focus** (January, 1995).

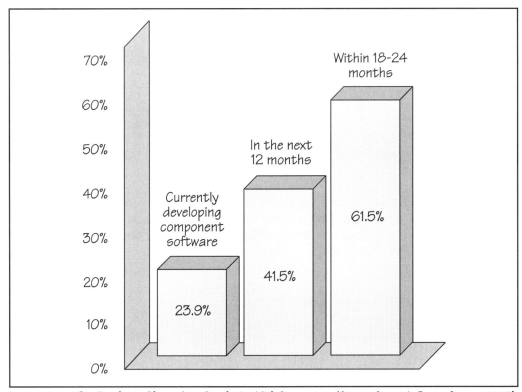

Figure 22-2. When Developers Plan to Start Developing With Components (Source: Strategic Focus, January 1995).

able to purchase your software ICs—or components—through standard part catalogs. According to Gartner Group, components will foster the emergence of three new markets: 1) the component market itself, 2) a market for component assembly tools, and 3) a market for custom applications developed using components.[3]

Why Didn't It Happen Sooner?

So, the million-dollar question is: Why didn't this happen any sooner? Why did we have to wait 23 years to follow the footsteps of our cousins, the hardware engineers? Yes, it's true that for almost 23 years, the software industry has been talking about reuse, objects, and methodologies that would get us out of the crises of the day. The difference this time is that we have two standards to choose from: OpenDoc/CORBA and OLE/DCOM. Without standards, you cannot have components. So, it didn't happen sooner because our industry did not have the right component infrastructure or standards. We now have both.

---

[3] Source: **Gartner Group**, "Object Orientation for the Rest of Us" (March, 1995).

So, What Exactly Is a Component?

A component is a piece of software small enough to create and maintain, big enough to deploy and support, and with standard interfaces for interoperability.

> — *Jed Harris, ex-President*
> *CI Labs*
> *(January, 1995)*

Components interoperate using language-neutral, client/server interaction models. Unlike traditional objects, components can interoperate across languages, tools, operating systems, and networks. But components are also object-like in the sense that they support inheritance, polymorphism, and encapsulation. Note that some components—Ivar Jacobson calls them *black box* components—cannot be extended through inheritance. OLE components fall into the black box category. However, both CORBA and OpenDoc components support inheritance. As a result, they let you build either white box or black box components. A *white box* component is a component that behaves like a classical object.

Because components mean different things to different people, we will define the functions a *minimal* component must provide. In the next section, we expand our definition to include features that supercomponents must provide. Our definition of a component is a composite of what CORBA, OpenDoc, Java, and OLE provide. Most of the earlier definitions of components were based on wish lists. Now that we have standards, we can use them to derive a definition. So, a minimalist component has the following properties:

- ■ *It is a marketable entity.* A component is a self-contained, shrink-wrapped, binary piece of software that you can typically purchase in the open market.

- ■ *It is not a complete application.* A component can be combined with other components to form a complete application. It is designed to perform a limited set of tasks within an application domain. Components can be fine-grained objects such as a C++ size object; medium-grained objects such as a GUI control; or coarse-grained objects such as a Java applet.

- ■ *It can be used in unpredictable combinations.* Like real-world objects, a component can be used in ways that were totally unanticipated by the original developer. Typically, components can be combined with other components of the same family—called suites—using plug-and-play.

- ■ *It has a well-specified interface.* Like a classical object, a component can only be manipulated through its interface. This is how the component exposes its function to the outside world. A CORBA/OpenDoc component also provides an *Interface Definition Language (IDL)* that you can use to invoke the component or inherit and override its functions. Note that the component's object-like interface is separate from its implementation. A component can be implemented using objects, procedural code, or by encapsulating existing code.

■ *It is an interoperable object.* A component can be invoked as an object across address spaces, networks, languages, operating systems, and tools. It is a system-independent software entity.[4]

■ *It is an extended object.* Components are *bona fide* objects in the sense that they support encapsulation, inheritance, and polymorphism. However, components must also provide all the features associated with a shrink-wrapped standalone object. These features will be discussed in the next section.

In summary, a component is a reusable, self-contained piece of software that is independent of any application.

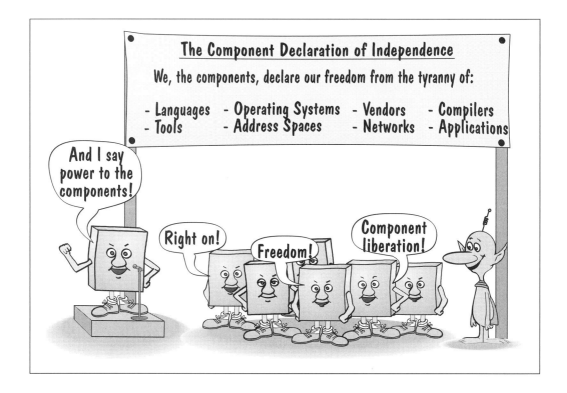

---

[4] The term "interoperable object" was first coined by Ray Valdes in a special issue of **Dr. Dobb's Journal** on "Interoperable Objects" (January, 1995).

So, What Is a Supercomponent?

If the components come with a bad reputation, no one will use them. Therefore, components must be of an extraordinary quality. They need to be well-tested, efficient, and well-documented...The component should invite reuse.

> — Ivar Jacobson, Author
> Object-Oriented Software Engineering
> (Addison-Wesley, 1993)

Supercomponents are components with added smarts. The smarts are needed for creating autonomous, loosely-coupled, shrink-wrapped objects that can roam across machines and live on networks. Consequently, components need to provide the type of facilities that you associate with independent networked entities, including:

■ *Security*—a component must protect itself and its resources from outside threats. It must authenticate itself to its clients, and vice versa. It must provide access controls. And it must keep audit trails of its use.

■ *Licensing*—a component must be able to enforce licensing policies including per-usage licensing and metering. It is important to reward component vendors for the use of their components.

■ *Versioning*—a component must provide some form of version control. It must make sure its clients are using the right version.

■ *Life cycle management*—a component must manage its creation, destruction, and archival. It must also be able to clone itself, externalize its contents, and move from one location to the next.

■ *Support for open tool palettes*—a component must allow itself to be imported within a standard tool palette. An example is a tool palette that supports OLE OCXs or OpenDoc parts. A component that abides by an open palette's rules can be assembled with other components using drag-and-drop and other visual assembly techniques.

■ *Event notification*—a component must be able to notify interested parties when something of interest happens to it.

■ *Configuration and property management*—a component must provide an interface to let you configure its properties and scripts.

■ **Scripting**—a component must permit its interface to be controlled via scripting languages. This means the interface must be self-describing and support late-binding.

■ **Metadata and introspection**—a component must provide, on request, information about itself. This includes a description of its interfaces, attributes, and the suites it supports.

■ **Transaction control and locking**—a component must transactionally protect its resources and cooperate with other components to provide all or nothing integrity. In addition, it must provide locks to serialize access to shared resources.

■ **Persistence**—a component must be able to save its state in a persistent store and later restore it.

■ **Relationships**—a component must be able to form dynamic or permanent associations with other components. For example, a component can contain other components.

■ **Ease of use**—a component must provide a limited number of operations to encourage use and reuse. In other words, the level of abstraction must be as high as possible to make the component inviting to use.

■ **Self-testing**—a component must be self-testing. You should be able to run component-provided diagnostics to do problem determination.

■ **Semantic messaging**—a component must be able to understand the vocabulary of the particular suites and domain-specific extensions it supports.

■ **Self-installing**—a component must be able to install itself and automatically register its factory with the operating system or component registry. The component must also be able to remove itself from disk when asked to do so.

This list should give you a pretty good idea of the level of quality and functionality we expect from our components. The good news is that both OpenDoc/CORBA and OLE/DCOM already provide quite a few of these functions. Typical OpenDoc/CORBA implementations let you add this behavior to ordinary components via mixins at build time. Some CORBA implementations—for example, SOM—even let you insert this system behavior into binary components at run time. OLE lets you add the behavior at build time by composing components that consist of multiple interfaces; an outer component can then call the appropriate interfaces via a reuse technique called *aggregation*.

Business Objects: The Ultimate Components

Components will help users focus on tasks, not tools, just as a well-stocked kitchen lets you focus on preparing and enjoying great food and not on the brand of your ingredients.

— Dave LeFevre, Novell
(January, 1995)

Distributed objects are by definition components. The distributed object infrastructure is really a component infrastructure. Programmers can easily get things to collaborate by writing code for the two sides of the collaboration. The trick, however, is to get components that have no previous knowledge of each other to do the same. To get to this point, you need standards that set the rules of engagement for different component interaction boundaries. Together, these different interaction boundaries define a distributed component *infrastructure*.

At the most basic level, a component infrastructure provides an object bus—the *Object Request Broker (ORB)*—that lets components interoperate across address spaces, languages, operating systems, and networks. The bus also provides mechanisms that let components exchange metadata and discover each other. At the next level, the infrastructure augments the bus with add-on *system-level services* that help you create supersmart components. Examples of these services include licensing, security, version control, persistence, suite negotiation, semantic messaging, scripting, and transactions.

The ultimate goal is to let you create components that behave like *business objects*. These are components that model their real-world counterparts in some application-level domain. They typically perform specific business functions—for example, a customer, car, or hotel. You can group these business objects into visual suites that sit on a desktop but have underlying client/server webs.

So the ultimate Nirvana in the client/server components business are supersmart business object components that do more than just interoperate—they collaborate at the semantic level to get a job done. For example, roaming agents on a global network must be able to collaborate to conduct negotiations with their fellow agents. Agents are examples of business objects. The infrastructure provides application-level collaboration standards in the form of *application frameworks*. These frameworks enforce the rules of engagement between independent components and allow them to collaborate in suites.

Figure 22-3 shows the evolution of components from interoperability to collaboration. This evolution corresponds to the service boundaries of the component infrastructure. The component bus gives you simple interoperability; the system services give you supersmart components; and the application frameworks provide the application-level semantics for components to collaborate in suites.

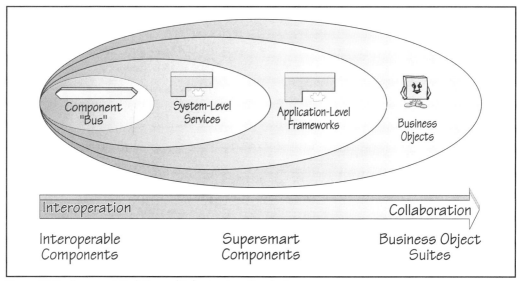

Figure 22-3. Component Evolution and Infrastructure Boundaries.

3-TIER CLIENT/SERVER, OBJECT-STYLE

Cooperative Business Objects (CBOs) are real things. Like other real things, they can be mixed and matched to suit user requirements—with no developer intervention necessary. You take an entity-like thing such as a customer and that's what you deliver—a customer object all by itself. You get a whole customer and nothing but the customer ready to run and use!

> — *Oliver Sims, Author*
> *Business Objects*
> *(McGraw-Hill, 1994)*

Business objects are ideal for creating scalable 3-tier client/server solutions because they are inherently decomposable. A business object is not a monolithic piece of code. Instead, it is more like a Lego of cooperating parts that you break apart and then reassemble along 3-tier client/server lines (see Figure 22-4). The first tier represents the visual aspects of the business object—one or more visual objects may each provide a different view. These visual objects typically live on the client. In the middle tier are server objects that represent the persistent data and the business logic functions. In the third tier are existing databases and legacy server applications. The partitioning of business objects is very dynamic. You should be able to decide where to host the different parts at run time.

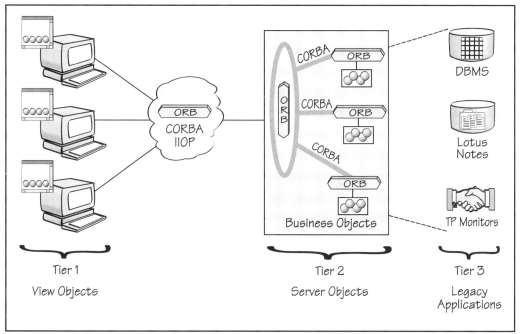

Figure 22-4. 3-Tiered Client/Server, Object-Style.

Middle-tier server objects interact with their clients (the view objects) and implement the logic of the business object. They can extract their persistent state from multiple data sources—for example, SQL Databases, HTML files, Lotus Notes, and TP Monitors. The server object provides an integrated model of the disparate data sources and back-end applications. Clients interact with business objects that naturally correspond to domain entities. They do not have to concern themselves with the hodgepodge of functions, stored procedures, and databases that live in the third tier. The business object hides all this nastiness.

The server object can cache the data it extracts on a local object database for fast subsequent access; or it may choose to directly update the third-tier data sources with fresh views from the object state. Clients must never directly interact with third-tier data sources. These sources must be totally encapsulated and abstracted by the middle-tier server objects. For example, you should be able to swap a database for another without impacting the clients.

The clients typically interact with the middle-tier server objects via an ORB. In addition, middle-tier objects can communicate with each other via a server ORB that they can use to balance loads, orchestrate distributed transactions, and exchange business events. This makes ORB-based business objects very scalable. Finally, server objects communicate with the third tier using traditional middleware. We will have a lot more to say about business objects in the next few chapters.

CONCLUSION

Everybody can resonate with objects—managers, 3 year olds, and superprogrammers. Object-oriented technology appeals to all these different camps.

> — *Jim Gray*
> *(February, 1995)*

Distributed components—modelled as business objects—are an excellent fit for 3-tier client/server architectures. They provide scalable and flexible solutions for intergalactic client/server environments and for the Internet and Intranets. Business objects can be naturally decomposed and split across multiple tiers to meet an application's needs. They are self-describing and self-managing blobs of intelligence that you can move around and execute where it makes the most sense. Most importantly, business objects are evolutionary—they don't force you to throw away your existing server applications and start from scratch. You can encapsulate what you already have and incrementally add new intelligence, one component at a time. The next few chapters describe the CORBA/OpenDoc and OLE/DCOM distributed component infrastructures that enable much of this magic.

Chapter 23

CORBA: From ORBs To Business Objects

---

*O*rb—*A jeweled globe surmounted by a cross that is part of a sovereign's regalia and that symbolizes monarchical power and justice.*

— **American Heritage Dictionary**

ORB—Putting down some pavement on the dirt road called distributed computing.

— **Chris Stone, President of OMG**

The *Common Object Request Broker Architecture (CORBA)* is the most important (and ambitious) middleware project ever undertaken by our industry. It is the product of a consortium—called the Object Management Group (OMG)—that includes over 650 companies representing the entire spectrum of the computer industry. The notable exception is Microsoft, which has its own competing object bus called the *Distributed Component Object Model (DCOM)*. For the rest of our industry, the next generation of middleware is CORBA. The CORBA object bus defines the shape of the components that live within it and how they interoperate. Consequently, by choosing an open bus, the industry is also choosing to create an open playing field for components.

What makes CORBA so important is that it defines middleware that has the potential of subsuming every other form of existing client/server middleware. In other words, CORBA uses objects as a unifying metaphor for bringing to the bus existing applications. At the same time, it provides a solid foundation for a component-based future. The magic of CORBA is that the entire system is self-describing. In addition, the specification of a service is always separated from the implementation. This lets you incorporate existing systems within the bus.

CORBA was designed to allow intelligent components to discover each other and interoperate on an object bus. However, CORBA goes beyond just interoperability. It also specifies an extensive set of bus-related services for creating and deleting objects, accessing them by name, storing them in persistent stores, externalizing their states, and defining ad hoc relationships between them.

CORBA lets you create an ordinary object and then make it transactional, secure, lockable, and persistent by making the object multiply-inherit from the appropriate services. This means that you can design an ordinary component to provide its regular function, and then insert the right middleware mix when you build it or create it at run time. So, welcome to the age of flexible "made to order" middleware. There is nothing like it for any other form of client/server computing.

This chapter is about the CORBA object bus and the object system services that extend the bus. We start with an overview of CORBA and what it does for intelligent components. We then cover the CORBA object model and the architecture that ties it all together. Finally, we will put the whole thing in a familiar client/server perspective. As you will see, some key distributed object pieces are still lacking. So we will also look at what's brewing in the upcoming OMG specifications.

DISTRIBUTED OBJECTS, CORBA-STYLE

Standards are more important for distributed objects than for any other technology in any other industry. Objects from one company must be able to communicate and cooperate with objects from other companies.

— *Roger Sessions, Author*
Object Persistence
(Prentice-Hall, 1996)

Perhaps the secret to OMG's success is that it creates interface specifications, not code. The interfaces it specifies are always derived from demonstrated technology submitted by member companies. The specifications are written in a neutral *Interface Definition Language (IDL)* that defines a component's boundaries— that is, its contractual interfaces with potential clients. Components written to IDL should be portable across languages, tools, operating systems, and networks. And with the adoption of the CORBA 2.0 specification in December 1994, these components should be able to interoperate across multivendor CORBA object brokers.

What Is a CORBA Distributed Object?

CORBA objects are blobs of intelligence that can live anywhere on a network. They are packaged as binary components that remote clients can access via method invocations. Both the language and compiler used to create server objects are totally transparent to clients. Clients don't need to know where the distributed object resides or what operating system it executes on. It can be in the same process or on a machine that sits across an intergalactic network. In addition, clients don't need to know how the server object is implemented. For example, a server object could be implemented as a set of C++ classes, or it could be implemented with a million lines of existing COBOL code—the client doesn't know the difference. What the client needs to know is the interface its server object publishes. This interface serves as a binding contract between clients and servers.

Everything Is in IDL

OMG IDL is the best standard notation language available for defining component boundaries. It provides a universal notation for specifying APIs. IDL supports library function interfaces just as well as distributed objects across a network.

> — *Tom Mowbray et al., Authors*
> *The Essential CORBA*
> *(Wiley, 1995)*

As we said earlier, OMG uses *Interface Definition Language (IDL)* contracts to specify a component's boundaries and its contractual interfaces with potential clients. The OMG IDL is purely declarative. This means that it provides no implementation details. You can use IDL to define APIs concisely, and it covers important issues such as error handling. IDL-specified methods can be written in and invoked from any language that provides CORBA bindings—currently, C, C++, Ada, and Smalltalk (COBOL, Java, and Objective C are in the works). Programmers deal with CORBA objects using native language constructs. IDL provides operating system and programming language independent interfaces to all the services and components that reside on a CORBA bus. It allows client and server objects written in different languages to interoperate (see Figure 23-1).

You can use the OMG IDL to specify a component's attributes, the parent classes it inherits from, the exceptions it raises, the typed events it emits, and the methods its

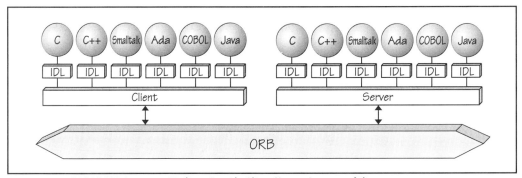

Figure 23-1. CORBA IDL Language Bindings Provide Client/Server Interoperability.

interface supports—including the input and output parameters and their data types. The IDL grammar is a subset of C++ with additional keywords to support distributed concepts; it also fully supports standard C++ preprocessing features and pragmas.

The ambitious goal of CORBA is to "IDL-ize" all client/server middleware and all components that live on an ORB. OMG hopes to achieve this goal by following two steps: 1) it will turn everything into nails, and 2) it will give everyone a hammer.

■ The "nail" is the CORBA IDL. It allows component providers to specify in a standard definition language the interface and structure of the objects they provide. An IDL-defined contract binds the providers of distributed object services to their clients. For one object to request something from another object, it must know the target object's interface. The CORBA *Interface Repository* contains the definitions of all these interfaces. It contains the metadata that lets components discover each other dynamically at run time. This makes CORBA a self-describing system.

■ The "hammer" includes the set of distributed services OMG providers will supply. These services will determine which objects are on the network, which methods they provide, and which object interface adapters they support. The location of the object should be transparent to the client and object implementation. It should not matter whether the object is in the same process or across the world.

Does this all sound familiar? It should. We're describing the "object wave" of client/server computing; this time it's between cooperating objects as opposed to cooperating processes. The goal of this new wave is to create multivendor, multiOS, multilanguage "legoware" using objects. Vendors such as Sun, HP, IBM, Digital, Tandem, and NCR are all using CORBA as their standard IDL-defined interface into the object highway. The IDL is the contract that brings it all together.

CORBA Components: From System Objects To Business Objects

Objects can vary tremendously in size and number. They can represent everything down to the hardware or all the way up to entire design applications. How can we decide what should be an object?

> — Erich Gamma et al., Authors
> Design Patterns
> (Addison Wesley, 1994)

Notice that we've been using the terms "components" and "distributed objects" interchangeably. CORBA distributed objects are, by definition, components because of the way they are packaged. In distributed object systems, the unit of work and distribution is a component. The CORBA distributed object infrastructure makes it easier for components to be more autonomous, self-managing, and collaborative. This undertaking is much more ambitious than anything attempted by competing forms of middleware. CORBA's distributed object technology allows us to put together complex client/server information systems by simply assembling and extending components. You can modify objects without affecting the rest of the components in the system or how they interact. A client/server application becomes a collection of collaborating components.

The ultimate "Nirvana" in the client/server components business are supersmart components that do more than just interoperate—they collaborate at the semantic level to get a job done. Programmers can easily get things to collaborate by writing code for the two sides of the collaboration. The trick, however, is to get components that have no previous knowledge of each other to do the same. To get to that point, you need standards that set the rules of engagement for different component interaction boundaries.

OMG'S OBJECT MANAGEMENT ARCHITECTURE

In the fall of 1990, the OMG first published the *Object Management Architecture Guide (OMA Guide)*. It was revised in September 1992. The details of the Common Facilities were added in January 1995. Figure 23-2 shows the four main elements of the architecture: 1) *Object Request Broker (ORB)* defines the CORBA object bus; 2) *Common Object Services* define the system-level object frameworks that extend the bus; 3) *Common Facilities* define horizontal and vertical application frameworks that are used directly by business objects; and 4) *Application*

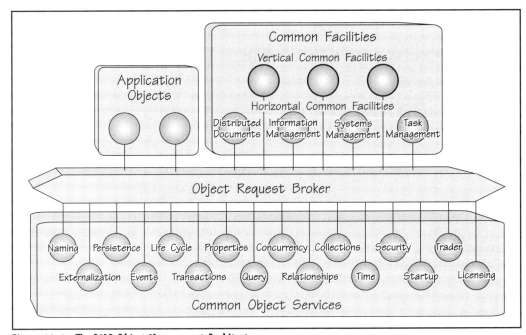

Figure 23-2. The OMG Object Management Architecture.

Objects are the business objects and applications—they are the ultimate consumers of the CORBA infrastructure. This section provides a top-level view of the four elements that make up the CORBA infrastructure.

The Object Request Broker (ORB)

CORBA puts any required middleware where it belongs: out of sight and out of mind.

— John Kador, BYTE Magazine
(April, 1996)

The *Object Request Broker (ORB)* is the object bus. It lets objects transparently make requests to—and receive responses from—other objects located locally or remotely. The client is not aware of the mechanisms used to communicate with, activate, or store the server objects. The CORBA 1.1 specifications—introduced in 1991—only specified the IDL, language bindings, and APIs for interfacing to the ORB. So, you could write portable programs that could run on top of the nearly dozen CORBA-compliant ORBs on the market (especially on the client side). CORBA 2.0 specifies interoperability across vendor ORBs.

A CORBA ORB provides a very rich set of distributed middleware services. The ORB lets objects discover each other at run time and invoke each other's services. An ORB is much more sophisticated than alternative forms of client/server middleware—including traditional Remote Procedure Calls (RPCs), Message-Oriented Middleware (MOM), database stored procedures, and peer-to-peer services. In theory, CORBA is the best client/server middleware ever defined. In practice, CORBA is only as good as the products that implement it.

To give you an idea of why CORBA ORBs make such great client/server middleware, we offer the following "short" list of benefits that every CORBA ORB provides:

■ **Static and dynamic method invocations.** A CORBA ORB lets you either statically define your method invocations at compile time, or it lets you dynamically discover them at run time. So you either get strong type checking at compile time or maximum flexibility associated with late (or run-time) binding. Most other forms of middleware only support static bindings.

■ **High-level language bindings.** A CORBA ORB lets you invoke methods on server objects using your high-level language of choice—currently C, C++, Ada, and Smalltalk. It doesn't matter what language server objects are written in. CORBA separates interface from implementation and provides language-neutral data types that make it possible to call objects across language and operating system boundaries. In contrast, other types of middleware typically provide low-level, language-specific, API libraries. And they don't separate implementation from specification—the API is tightly bound to the implementation, which makes it very sensitive to changes.

■ **Self-describing system.** CORBA provides run-time metadata for describing every server interface known to the system. Every CORBA ORB must support an *Interface Repository* that contains real-time information describing the functions a server provides and their parameters. The clients use metadata to discover how to invoke services at run time. It also helps tools generate code "on-the-fly." The metadata is generated automatically either by an IDL-language precompiler or by compilers that know how to generate IDL directly from an OO language. For example, the MetaWare C++ compiler generates IDL directly from C++ class definitions (it also directly writes that information in the Interface Repository). To the best of our knowledge, no other form of client/server middleware provides this type of run-time metadata and language-independent definitions of all its services. As you will discover later in this chapter, business objects and components require all the late binding flexibility they can get.

■ **Local/remote transparency.** An ORB can run in standalone mode on a laptop, or it can be interconnected to every other ORB in the universe (using CORBA 2.0's inter-ORB services). An ORB can broker interobject calls within a single process, multiple processes running within the same machine, or multiple processes running across networks and operating systems. This is all done in a manner that's transparent to your objects. Note that the ORB can broker among fine-grained objects—like C++ classes—as well as more coarse-grained objects. In general, a CORBA client/server programmer does not have to be concerned with transports, server locations, object activation, byte ordering across dissimilar platforms, or target operating systems—CORBA makes it all transparent.

■ **Built-in security and transactions.** The ORB includes context information in its messages to handle security and transactions across machine and ORB boundaries.

■ **Polymorphic messaging.** In contrast to other forms of middleware, an ORB does not simply invoke a remote function—it invokes a function on a target object. This means that the same function call will have different effects, depending on the object that receives it. For example, a *configure_yourself* method invocation behaves differently when applied to a database object versus a printer object (also see following Briefing box).

Of course, CORBA also has its share of shortcomings. We explore all these shortcomings in a soapbox at the end of this chapter entitled *Is This "The Year of the ORB"?*

ORB Versus RPC

Briefing

Brokers of all types—stock brokers as well as object brokers—exact a price for their services.

— Bill Andreas, Chief Architect
HyperDesk

So how are ORB method invocations different from RPCs? The mechanisms are very similar, but there are some important differences. With an RPC, you call a specific function (the data is separate). In contrast, with an ORB, you're calling a method within a *specific* object. Different object classes may respond to the same method invocation differently through the magic of polymorphism. Because each object manages its own private instance data, the method is implemented on that *specific* instance data (see Figure 23-3).

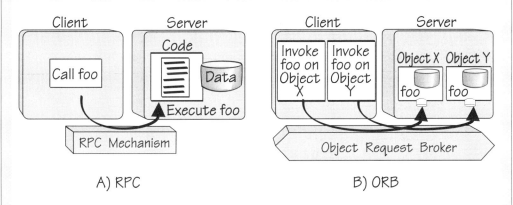

Figure 23-3. ORBs Versus RPC.

ORB method invocations have "scalpel-like" precision. The call gets to a *specific* object that controls *specific* data, and then implements the function in its own *class-specific* way. In contrast, RPC calls have no specificity—all the functions with the same name get implemented the same way. There's no differentiated service here.

Of course, some ORBs are built on top of an RPC service, so you end up paying a performance penalty for this "refined" level of service. It's worth every penny if you're taking advantage of new levels of distributed granularity provided by objects. Otherwise, you just bought yourself another layer of middleware—with all the costs and headaches that come with it. Note that within a single address space, ORBs are now targeting method resolution performance equivalent to C++ virtual function invocations (for example, this is SOM 3.0's target). If they achieve this low overhead, you will be able to use ORBs for very small-grained objects as well as the larger ones. ☐

The Anatomy of a CORBA 2.0 ORB

A request broker mediates interactions between client applications needing services and server applications capable of providing them.

— Richard Adler, Coordinated Computing
(April, 1995)

A CORBA 2.0 *Object Request Broker (ORB)* is the middleware that establishes the client/server relationships between objects. Using an ORB, a client object can transparently invoke a method on a server object, which can be on the same machine or across a network. The ORB intercepts the call and is responsible for finding an object that can implement the request, pass it the parameters, invoke its method, and return the results. The client does not have to be aware of where the object is located, its programming language, its operating system, or any other system aspects that are not part of an object's interface. It is very important to note that the client/server roles are only used to coordinate the interactions between two objects. Objects on the ORB can act as either client or server, depending on the occasion.

Figure 23-4 shows the client and server sides of a CORBA ORB. The light areas are new to CORBA 2.0. Even though there are many boxes, it's not as complicated as it appears to be. The key is to understand that CORBA, like SQL, provides both static and dynamic interfaces to its services. This happened because the OMG received

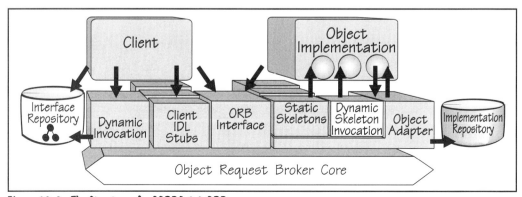

Figure 23-4. The Structure of a CORBA 2.0 ORB.

two strong submissions to its original ORB *Request For Proposal (RFP)*: one from HyperDesk and Digital based on a dynamic API, and one from Sun and HP based on static APIs. The OMG told the two groups to come back with a single RFP that combined both features. The result was CORBA. The "Common" in CORBA stands for this two-API proposal, which makes a lot of sense because it gives us both static and dynamic APIs.

Let's first go over what CORBA does on the client side:

- *The client IDL stubs* provide the static interfaces to object services. These precompiled stubs define how clients invoke corresponding services on the servers. From a client's perspective, the stub acts like a local call—it is a local *proxy* for a remote server object. The services are defined using IDL, and both client and server stubs are generated by the IDL compiler. A client must have an IDL stub for each interface it uses on the server. The stub includes code to perform *marshaling*. This means that it encodes and decodes the operation and its parameters into flattened message formats that it can send to the server. It also includes header files that enable you to invoke the method on the server from a higher-level language (like C, C++, Java, or Smalltalk) without worrying about the underlying protocols or issues such as data marshaling. You simply invoke a method from within your program to obtain a remote service.

- *The Dynamic Invocation Interface (DII)* lets you discover methods to be invoked at run time. CORBA defines standard APIs for looking up the metadata that defines the server interface, generating the parameters, issuing the remote call, and getting back the results.

- *The Interface Repository APIs* allow you to obtain and modify the descriptions of all the registered component interfaces, the methods they support, and the parameters they require. CORBA calls these descriptions *method signatures*. The *Interface Repository* is a run-time distributed database that contains machine-readable versions of the IDL-defined interfaces. Think of it as a dynamic metadata repository for ORBs. The APIs allow components to dynamically access, store, and update metadata information. This pervasive use of metadata allows every component that lives on the ORB to have self-describing interfaces. The ORB itself is a self-describing bus (see next Briefing box).

- *The ORB Interface* consists of a few APIs to local services that may be of interest to an application. For example, CORBA provides APIs to convert an object reference to a string, and vice versa. These calls can be very useful if you need to store and communicate object references.

The support for both static and dynamic client/server invocations—as well as the Interface Repository—gives CORBA a leg up over competing middleware. Static invocations are easier to program, faster, and self-documenting. Dynamic invoca-

FYI

CORBA 2.0 Global Repository IDs

Briefing

With CORBA 2.0, ORBs provide global identifiers—called *Repository IDs*—to uniquely and globally identify a component and its interface across multivendor ORBs and repositories. The Repository IDs are system-generated, unique strings that are used to maintain consistency in the naming conventions used across repositories—no name collisions are allowed. Repository IDs are generated via *pragmas* in IDL. The pragma specifies whether to generate them via DCE *Universal Unique Identifiers (UUIDs)* or via a user-supplied unique prefix appended to IDL-scoped names. The Repository ID itself is a string consisting of a three-level name hierarchy. ❏

tions provide maximum flexibility, but they are difficult to program; they are very useful for tools that discover services at run time.

The server side cannot tell the difference between a static or dynamic invocation; they both have the same message semantics. In both cases, the ORB locates a server object adapter, transmits the parameters, and transfers control to the object implementation through the server IDL stub (or skeleton). Here's what CORBA elements do on the server side of Figure 23-4:

■ The **Server IDL Stubs** (OMG calls them *skeletons*) provide static interfaces to each service exported by the server. These stubs, like the ones on the client, are created using an IDL compiler.

■ The **Dynamic Skeleton Interface (DSI)**—introduced in CORBA 2.0—provides a run-time binding mechanism for servers that need to handle incoming method calls for components that do not have IDL-based compiled skeletons (or stubs). The Dynamic Skeleton looks at parameter values in an incoming message to figure out who it's for—that is, the target object and method. In contrast, normal compiled skeletons are defined for a particular object class and expect a method implementation for each IDL-defined method. Dynamic Skeletons are very useful for implementing generic bridges between ORBs. They can also be used by interpreters and scripting languages to dynamically generate object implementations. The DSI is the server equivalent of a DII. It can receive either static or dynamic client invocations.

■ The **Object Adapter** sits on top of the ORB's core communication services and accepts requests for service on behalf of the server's objects. It provides the run-time environment for instantiating server objects, passing requests to them, and assigning them object IDs—CORBA calls the IDs *object references*. The Object Adapter also registers the classes it supports and their run-time instances (i.e., objects) with the *Implementation Repository*. CORBA specifies that each ORB must support a standard adapter called the *Basic Object Adapter (BOA)*. Servers may support more than one object adapter.

- The **Implementation Repository** provides a run-time repository of information about the classes a server supports, the objects that are instantiated, and their IDs. It also serves as a common place to store additional information associated with the implementation of ORBs. Examples include trace information, audit trails, security, and other administrative data.

- The **ORB Interface** consists of a few APIs to local services that are identical to those provided on the client side.

This concludes our panoramic overview of the ORB components and their interfaces.

CORBA 2.0: THE INTERGALACTIC ORB

CORBA 1.1 was only concerned with creating portable object applications; the implementation of the ORB core was left as an "exercise for the vendors." The result was some level of component portability, but not interoperability. CORBA 2.0 added interoperability by specifying a mandatory *Internet Inter-ORB Protocol (IIOP)*. The IIOP is basically TCP/IP with some CORBA-defined message exchanges that serve as a common backbone protocol. Every ORB that calls itself CORBA-compliant must either implement IIOP natively or provide a "half-bridge" to it. Note: It's called a half-bridge because IIOP is the "standard" CORBA backbone. So any proprietary ORB can connect with the universe of ORBs by translating requests to and from the IIOP backbone.

In addition to IIOP, CORBA supports *Environment-Specific Inter-ORB Protocols (ESIOPs)* for "out-of-the-box" interoperation over specific networks. CORBA 2.0 specifies DCE as the first of many optional ESIOPs (pronounced "E-SOPs"). The DCE ESIOP provides a robust environment for mission-critical ORBs (see next Soapbox). The DCE ESIOP is supported in HP's *ORB Plus* and Digital's *ObjectBroker*; it will eventually be supported in IBM's *SOM*.

You can use inter-ORB bridges and IIOPs to create very flexible topologies via federations of ORBs. Figure 23-5 shows an IIOP backbone with various proprietary ORBs feeding into it via half-bridges. Note the presence of the DCE ESIOP. You can segment ORBs into domains based on administrative needs, vendor ORB implementations, network protocols, traffic loads, types of service, and security concerns. Policies on either side of the fence may conflict, so you can create firewalls around the backbone ORB via half-bridges. CORBA 2.0 promotes diversity and gives you total mix-and-match flexibility, as long as you use IIOP for your global backbone.

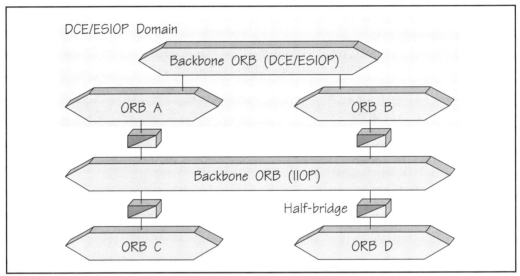

Figure 23-5. An Intergalactic Federation of Multivendor ORBs.

Is It CORBA Versus DCE?

Soapbox

CORBA did not build on anything from DCE; they are reinventing the wheel.

> — *David Chappell, Keynote Speaker*
> *DCE Developer's Conference*
> *(April, 1995)*

Many of us believed that, ultimately, CORBA would build on top of DCE. We never dreamed that inter-ORB backbones would be built on anything but DCE. The choice of IIOP as the inter-ORB protocol was extremely traumatic for us DCE supporters. We felt that the DCE/ESIOP should have gotten, at the very least, equal billing with IIOP; it should have been a mandatory part of CORBA 2.0. Well, we didn't win this vote. So is DCE really on a collision course with CORBA? Should the DCE camp focus its energy on object DCE, provide an OO IDL for DCE, and forget CORBA? Or better yet, why not just use Microsoft's DCOM/OLE as the object foundation for DCE and completely forget CORBA?

Before answering these questions, we have a confession to make: We've grown to like IIOP over the last year. Yes, we like the idea of using the Internet as a backbone for ORBs. IIOP will eventually transform the Internet into a CORBA bus; it's a nice evolutionary migration plan (see Part 8 for more details). IIOP is also a lightweight, easy-to-install ORB. Consequently, it's ideal for the Small Office Home Office (SOHO) market. So hats off to the people that brought us IIOP (sorry we didn't see the light earlier).

So what about DCE? Well, it's there. IBM, Digital, and HP will support it on their ORBs. And you can still use the DCE/ESIOP to create your ORB backbones. DCE will interoperate very nicely with IIOP because both sides follow the CORBA object model. So we can have our cake and eat it too: the Internet and secure industrial-strength ORBs.

Creating a new object model on top of DCE—as some have suggested—is totally ridiculous. The world needs another object model like it needs a hole in its head. DCE is just a fancy RPC with security and directory services. To create an object model on top of this RPC would require an effort of the same magnitude as CORBA. OSF can't repeat this enormous undertaking. Can you imagine recreating the dynamic invocations, Interface Repository, object adapters, and the various CORBA services—including transactions, events, relationships, security, persistence, query, and so on? CORBA is the collective product of the best minds in the object industry. It has an almost insurmountable head-start in distributed objects.

Is OLE the DCE Killer App?

Microsoft's strategy towards standards is like the Trojan horse. Believers welcomed Microsoft into the community believing that it would help DCE survive. Once in, however, it will alter the standard so that it is proprietary, all but killing the open version of DCE.

— Gartner Group
(January, 1995)

But life isn't that simple. There's a company with very deep pockets that is trying to create a distributed object bus—of CORBA magnitude—on top of DCE. We're talking about Microsoft, which is becoming the great hope of the DCE avant-garde. Never mind the fact that Microsoft is creating a closed standard that's a far cry from the open systems idealism that drove the early DCE work. It doesn't seem to matter. Microsoft has the resources to attempt to recreate CORBA single-handedly on top of DCE. And this is the great hope of the purists that don't want their DCE to play second fiddle to IIOP or any other protocol. Of course, Microsoft is at least two years behind CORBA in its distributed objects quest. So the DCE purists can either wait for Microsoft to catch up, or they can learn how to coexist with IIOP.

DCE needs CORBA, and CORBA needs DCE. DCE enhances CORBA with a mission-critical RPC infrastructure. CORBA enhances DCE with an open platform for objects. There's nothing wrong with bridges to IIOP—as long as both sides of the bridge use the same CORBA 2.0 object model. So even though we dearly love IIOP, we also believe that DCE/ESIOP is also crucial to CORBA's success. CORBA needs the two. The magic of OMG is that it was able to synthesize competing technologies. For example, the OMG merged two warring submissions to give us both static and dynamic invocations. The CORBA 2.0 merger of DCE and IIOP falls into the same category—it gives us two complementary technologies for ORBs. So let's make the best out of this situation and move on to the more important things—like business objects. ❑

CORBA OBJECT SERVICES

CORBA *object services* are collections of system-level services packaged with IDL-specified interfaces. You can think of object services as augmenting and complementing the functionality of the ORB. You use them to create a component, name it, and introduce it into the environment. By mid-1996, OMG has defined standards for thirteen object services:

■ The *Life Cycle Service* defines operations for creating, copying, moving, and deleting components on the bus.

■ The *Persistence Service* provides a single interface for storing components persistently on a variety of storage servers—including Object Databases (ODBMSs), Relational Databases (RDBMSs), and simple files.

■ The *Naming Service* allows components on the bus to locate other components by name; it also supports federated naming contexts. The service allows objects to be bound to existing network directories or naming contexts—including ISO's X.500, OSF's DCE, and Sun's NIS+.

■ The *Event Service* allows components on the bus to dynamically register or unregister their interest in specific events. The service defines a well-known object called an *event channel* that collects and distributes events among components that know nothing of each other.

■ The *Concurrency Control Service* provides a lock manager that can obtain locks on behalf of either transactions or threads.

■ The *Transaction Service* provides two-phase commit coordination among recoverable components using either flat or nested transactions.

■ The **Relationship Service** provides a way to create dynamic associations (or links) between components that know nothing of each other. It also provides mechanisms for traversing the links that group these components. You can use the service to enforce referential integrity constraints, track containment relationships, and for any type of linkage among components.

■ The **Externalization Service** provides a standard way for getting data into and out of a component using a stream-like mechanism.

■ The **Query Service** provides query operations for objects. It's a superset of SQL based on the upcoming *SQL3* specification and the Object Database Management Group's (ODMG) *Object Query Language (OQL)*.

■ The **Licensing Service** provides operations for metering the use of components to ensure fair compensation for their use. The service supports any model of usage control at any point in a component's life cycle. It supports charging per session, per node, per instance creation, and per site.

■ The **Properties Service** provides operations to let you associate named values (or properties) with any component. Using this service, you can dynamically associate properties with a component's state—for example, a title or a date.

■ The **Time Service** provides interfaces for synchronizing time in a distributed object environment. It also provides operations for defining and managing time-triggered events.

■ The **Security Service** provides a complete framework for distributed object security. It supports authentication, access control lists, confidentiality, and non-repudiation. It also manages the delegation of credentials between objects (see next Briefing box).

Three more services—trader, collections, and startup—should be available by the end of 1996. The *Trader* service is a Yellow Pages for objects; it allows objects to publicize their services and bid for jobs. The *Collections* service provides CORBA interfaces to generically create and manipulate the most common collections. Finally, the *Startup* service will enable requests to automatically start up when an ORB is invoked. All these services enrich a component's behavior and provide the robust environment in which it can safely live and play.

Figure 23-6 shows the *Request For Proposal (RFP)* schedules that OMG is using to develop the object service specifications. OMG RFPs are requests for a technology. They result in responses from members on how to implement a particular standard. Members must base their responses on existing products or products that are in development (some proof of concept is needed). Usually an RFP is met by merging the responses obtained from several organizations. From the time the

OMG issues an RFP, it takes about 12 to 16 months to obtain a working standard. As you can see, the OMG has almost completed the work on its object services and ORB specifications. The action is now shifting to the Common Facilities and Business Objects.

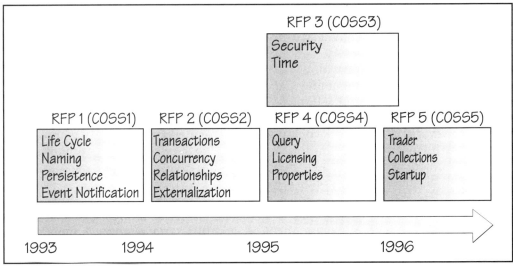

Figure 23-6. The OMG Road Map for Delivering Object Services.

Are Distributed Objects Less Secure?

FYI

Briefing

Distributed objects face all the security problems of traditional client/server systems—and more. As we explained in Part 3, the client/server environment introduces new security threats beyond those found in traditional time-shared systems. In a client/server system, you can't trust any of the client operating systems on the network to protect the server's resources from unauthorized access. And even if the client machines were totally secure, the network itself is highly accessible. You can never trust information in transit. Sniffer devices can easily record traffic between machines and introduce forgeries and Trojan horses into the system. This means the servers must find new ways to protect themselves without creating a fortress mentality that upsets users. In addition to these threats, distributed objects must also be concerned with the following added complications:

- **Distributed objects can play both client and server roles**. In a traditional client/server architecture, it is clear who is a client and who is a server. Typically, you can trust servers, but not clients. For example, a client trusts its database server, but the reverse is not true. In distributed object systems, you cannot clearly distinguish between clients and servers. These are just alternate roles that a single object can play.

- **Distributed objects evolve continually.** When you interact with an object, you're only seeing the tip of the iceberg. You may be seeing a "facade" object that delegates parts of its implementation to other objects; these delegates may be dynamically composed at run time. Also, because of subclassing, the implementations of an object may change over time without the original programmer ever knowing or caring.

- **Distributed objects interactions are not well understood**. Because of encapsulation, you cannot fully understand all the interactions that take place between the objects you invoke. There is too much "behind the scenes" activity.

- **Distributed object interactions are less predictable**. Because distributed objects are more flexible and granular than other forms of client/server systems, they may interact in more ad hoc ways. This is a strength of the distributed object model, but it's also a security risk.

- **Distributed objects are polymorphic**. Objects are flexible; it is easy to replace one object on the ORB with another that abides by the same interfaces. This makes it a dream situation for Trojan horses; they can impersonate legitimate objects and thus cause all kinds of havoc.

- **Distributed objects can scale without limit.** Because every object can be a server, we may end up with millions of servers on the ORB. How do we manage access rights for millions of servers?

- **Distributed objects are very dynamic.** A distributed object environment is inherently anarchistic. Objects come and go. They get created dynamically and self-destruct when they're no longer being used. This dynamism is, of course, a great strength of objects, but it could also be a security nightmare.

To maintain a single system illusion, every trusted user (and object) must be given transparent access to all other objects. How is this done when every PC poses a potential threat to network security? Will system administrators be condemned to spend their working lives granting access level rights to objects— one at a time—for each individual object on each server across the enterprise? The good news is that many of these problems can be solved by moving the security implementation into the CORBA ORB itself.

The ORB can manage security for a range of systems—from trusted domains (within a single process or machine) to intergalactic inter-ORB situations. Components that are not responsible for enforcing their own security are easier to develop, administer, and port across environments. In addition, moving security inside the ORB can minimize the performance overhead. The CORBA Security Service—adopted by OMG in March, 1996—addresses *all* of these requirements; it's probably the most comprehensive client/server security standard in existence. ❏

Object Services: Build-to-Order Middleware

You should note that CORBA object services provide a unique approach for creating *build-to-order* middleware. It's unlike anything classical client/server systems provide today. With CORBA, component providers can develop their objects without any concern for system services. Then, depending on what the customer's needs are, the developer (or system integrator) can mix the original component with any combination of CORBA services to create the needed function. They do this by subclassing the original class, and then mixing it with the required object service classes via multiple inheritance. It's all done via IDL—no source code is needed. For example, you may develop a component called "car" and create a concurrent, persistent, and transactional version of car by multiply inheriting from the corresponding services.

In addition, some ORB vendors will take advantage of their metaclass CORBA extensions to let you create your mixins at object-creation time. A *metaclass* is a class that is also a run-time object. For example, IBM's SOM extends CORBA by treating classes as first-class objects. This means that you can create and customize new classes at run time. Object factories can use these metaclass facilities to compose a class at run time based on a client's request. You can create made-to-order classes by multiply inheriting from existing object services. For example, the factory can take an ordinary component such as a "car" and make it transactional, lockable, and secure by multiply inheriting from existing object service classes. This approach is the ultimate form of made-to-order middleware. The beauty is that the original component provider may have known nothing about transactions, security, or locking. These services are dynamically added to the component at factory creation time based on the client's requirements.

If you don't like multiple inheritance, some ORB implementations let you add methods "on-the-fly" to existing classes. In particular, you can add *before* and *after* callbacks that are triggered before and after any ordinary method executes. You can use these before and after calls to call any of the existing CORBA services—or, for that matter, anything that lives on an ORB. You can even attach scripts to before/after triggers. For example, you can use a *before* trigger to obtain a lock from the concurrency service; you use the *after* trigger to release the lock.

By combining metaclass technology with CORBA services, you will be able to create "customize at the last minute" middleware environments for running particular components. It demonstrates the ultimate flexibility of objects. Most component developers will probably take a more conservative approach and create their mixins at compile time or via a tool at build time. In either case, it's still a lot more flexible than anything you can do with today's client/server middleware.

CORBA COMMON FACILITIES

Common Facilities are collections of IDL-defined components that provide services of direct use to application objects. Think of them as the next step up in the semantic hierarchy. The two categories of common facilities—*horizontal* and *vertical*—define rules of engagement that business components need to effectively collaborate. To give you a feel for where things stand, in October 1994 the OMG issued the Common Facilities *Request for Proposal 1 (RFP1)* to obtain technology submissions for compound documents. In March 1996, OMG adopted OpenDoc as its compound document technology. It calls it the *Distributed Document Component Facility (DDCF)*. DDCF specifies presentation services for components and a document interchange standard based on OpenDoc's Bento.

The Common Facilities that are currently under construction include mobile agents, data interchange, business object frameworks, and internationalization. Like the highway system, Common Facilities are an unending project. The work will continue until CORBA defines IDL interfaces for every distributed service we know of today, as well as ones that are yet to be invented. When this happens, CORBA will provide IDL-interfaces for virtually every distributed service we know today (many will be IDL-ized versions of existing middleware).

CORBA BUSINESS OBJECTS

A business object is a representation of a thing active in the business domain, including at least its business name and definition, attributes, behavior, relationship, and constraints. A business object may represent, for example, a person, place, or concept.

— OMG, *Business Object Task Force*

Business objects provide a natural way for describing application-independent concepts such as customer, order, competitor, money, payment, car, and patient. They encourage a view of software that transcends tools, applications, databases, and other system concepts. The ultimate promise of object technology and components is to provide these medium-grained components that behave more like "the real world does." Of course, somebody must first define the rules of engagement for these components to play, which is where the OMG comes into the picture.

According to OMG's *Business Object Task Force*, a business object is an application-level component you can use in unpredictable combinations. A business object is, by definition, independent of any single application. Post-monolithic applications will consist of suites of business objects—the application simply provides the environment to execute these business objects. In other words, a business object is a component that represents a "recognizable" everyday life entity. In contrast, system-level objects represent entities that make sense only to information systems and programmers—they're not something an end-user recognizes.

In a high-rise building, everyone's ceiling is someone else's floor until you get to the penthouse. Then the sky is your ceiling. You may think of the business object as the penthouse of components. According to the OMG definition, these top-level objects are recognizable to the end-user of a system. The size of the object maps to "business" things like cars or tax forms. The word business is used in a very loose sense. A business object is a self-contained *deliverable* that has a user interface, state, and knows how to cooperate with other separately developed business objects to perform a desired task.

Cooperating Business Objects

A *group of business objects can form an information system only if they become a system and interact with each other.*

— Rob Príns, CYCLADE Consultants
(June, 1995)

Business objects will be used to design systems that mimic the business processes they support. In the real world, business events are seldom isolated to a single business object. Instead, they typically involve clusters of objects. To mimic their real-world counterparts, business objects must be able to communicate with each other at a semantic level. You can capture and describe these object interactions using most of the popular design methodology tools—including Ivar Jacobson's *use cases*, Ian Graham's *task scripts*, Grady Booch's *interaction diagrams*, and Jim Rumbaugh's *event trace* diagrams. All these methodologies use some form of scenario diagrams to show who does what to whom and when. These scenarios can document the full impact of specific business events.

Business objects must have late and flexible binding and well-defined interfaces so that they can be implemented independently. A business object must be capable of

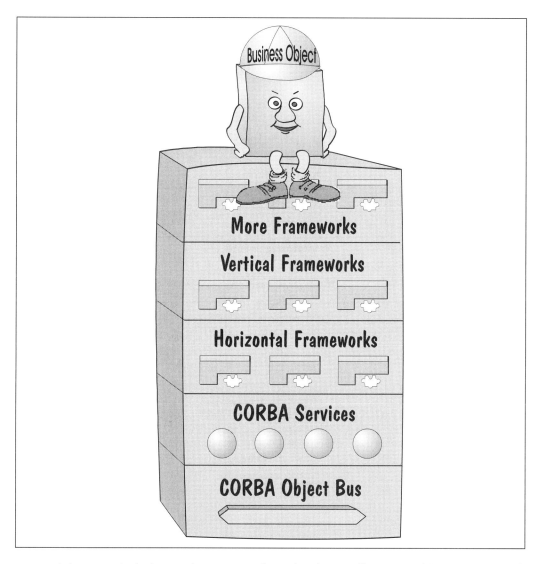

recognizing events in its environment, changing its attributes, and interacting with other business objects. Like any CORBA object, a business object exposes its interfaces to its clients via IDL and communicates with other objects using the ORB.

Figure 23-7 shows a suite of four business objects that are part of a car reservation system: *customer*, *invoice*, *car*, and *car lot*. Note that *car lot* is a business object that contains other business objects—cars. Clearly, these four business objects have some agreed upon semantics for communicating with each other to perform business transactions. Under the cover, they could use the CORBA Object Transaction Service to synchronize their actions. They also know how to share a single window to display their views seamlessly.

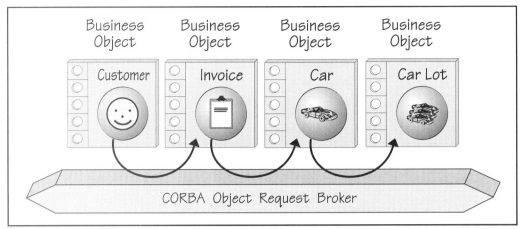

Figure 23-7. A Car Reservation System Using Cooperating Business Objects.

So how is this different from a traditional application? With very little work, you can reuse some of these business objects in another application context. For example, a car sales program could reuse most of these objects, especially if they were designed to work with more than one semantic suite. For example, the car, customer, and invoice objects could support multiple views to handle different business situations. In the extreme, the business objects could be specialized through inheritance to take into account the particularities of the car sales business. As you'll see in the next section, a business object is not a monolithic entity. It is factored internally into a set of cooperating objects that can react to different business situations. Business objects are highly flexible.

The Anatomy of a CORBA Business Object

Business objects directly represent the model of the enterprise, and this model becomes part of the information system. Every person, place, thing, event, transaction, or process in the business can be represented by an active object in the information system.

> — **Cory Casanave, OMG Director**
> **(June, 1995)**

An OMG business object is a variation of the *Model/View/Controller (MVC)* paradigm. MVC is an object design pattern used to build interfaces in Smalltalk and in almost every GUI class library. MVC consists of three kinds of objects. The *model* represents the application object and its encapsulated data. The *view* represents the object visually on the screen. And the *controller* defines the way the user interface reacts to user input and GUI events.

In the OMG model, a business object also consists of three kinds of objects (see Figure 23-8):

- **Business objects** encapsulate the storage, metadata, concurrency, and business rules associated with an active business entity. They also define how the object reacts to changes in the views or model.

- **Business process objects** encapsulate the business logic at the enterprise level. In traditional *Model-View-Controller* systems, the controller is in charge of the process. In the OMG model, short-lived process functions are handled by the business object. Long-lived processes that involve other business objects are handled by the business process object—it's a specialization of the business object that handles long-lived processes and the environment at large. For example, it knows how to handle a workflow or long-lived transaction. The process object typically acts as the glue that unites the other objects. For example, it defines how the object reacts to a change in the environment. This type of change may be caused by the execution of a business transaction or by an incoming message from another business object. Note that some business objects may be entirely process-oriented and not associated with specific data or presentations.

- **Presentation objects** represent the object visually to the user. Each business object can have multiple presentations for multiple purposes. The presentations communicate directly with the business object to display data on the screen. And sometimes they communicate directly with the process object. The OMG also recognizes that there are non-visual interfaces to business objects.

A typical business object component consists of a business object, one or more presentation objects, and a process object. Note that these entities act as a body.

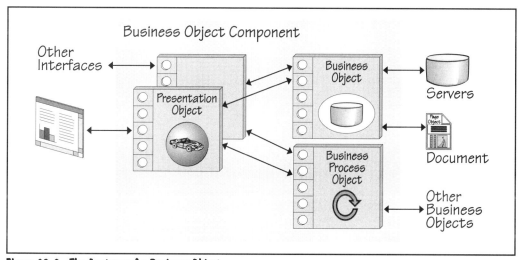

Figure 23-8. The Anatomy of a Business Object.

The underlying division of labor between the various objects is transparent to the users and clients of the business object. A business object also interacts with other servers and system-level objects but, again, in a totally encapsulated manner. The user only sees the *aggregate* business object. And clients of the object only deal with IDL-defined interfaces that are exposed by the aggregate business object. As we go to press, OMG has issued an RFP for *Common Business Objects* and a *Business Object Facility*. The facility will provide a framework for business objects to exchange semantic information and agree on the rules of engagement. We expect this framework to be fleshed out by early 1997.

The Anatomy of a Client/Server Business Object

Typically, a business object—like a car—may have different presentation objects spread across multiple clients. The business object and the process object may reside in one or more servers. The beauty of a CORBA-based architecture is that all the constituent objects have IDL-defined interfaces and can run on ORBs (see Figure 23-9). So it does not matter if the constituent objects run on the same machine or on different machines (ORBs provide local/remote transparency). As far as clients are concerned, they're still dealing with a single business object component, even though it may be factored into objects running in different machines. A well-designed business object builds on the CORBA services. For example, you can use the concurrency and transaction services to maintain the integrity of the business object's state. The ORB gives you these services for free, so you might as well use them.

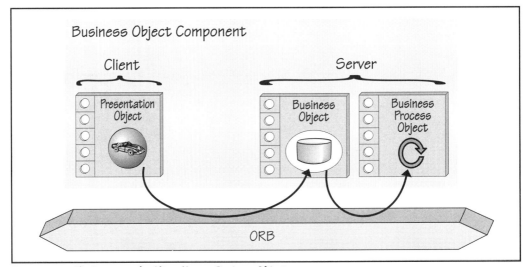

Figure 23-9. The Anatomy of a Client/Server Business Object.

CORBA: Meet the Players

The CORBA market is still in its infancy. Everyone is still trying to figure out how to use these ORBs. Industrial strength CORBA 2.0 ORBs are starting to dribble in. By the end of 1996, all the major ORB vendors will have introduced CORBA 2.0 versions of their ORBs (see the next Soapbox). At this stage of the game, it's still too early to pick winners. The ORB vendors fall into two camps: the major system vendors and innovative software startups.

ORBs from major system vendors include Digital's *ObjectBroker*, which now runs on over 20 platforms; IBM's *SOM 3.0*, which supports eight CORBA object services, including transactions; Sun's *NEO* and *JOE*, with their excellent Internet and Java support (see Part 8); and HP's *ORB Plus*, with its mission-critical DCE support.

ORBs from software startups include Expersoft's *PowerBroker* with its enterprise ORB features; Iona's *Orbix*, which holds the world record for multiplatform ORB support; and PostModern's *BlackWidow*, which is the first CORBA 2.0 Java ORBlet.

This list of ORB vendors is by no means complete. In addition, the CORBA world also includes literally hundreds of products that build on top of ORB middleware—including client/server tools, publish-and-subscribe systems, component repositories, ODBMSs, and system management platforms. The CORBA market will start to explode in 1997 (see the next Soapbox).

Is This "The Year of the ORB"?

Soapbox

The fact that CORBA is a standard that people are using today dwarfs any potential shortcoming it may possess.

> — W. Roelandts, Manager
> HP's General Computer Systems
> (April, 1995)

In the early 1980s, a favorite industry pundit game was to predict the "Year of the LAN." After many false starts (and predictions), the year of the LAN finally arrived in 1986. It was the year when LANs were everywhere. This was also the year when pundits stopped talking about LANs—they had become a given. In this Soapbox, wc want to talk about the "Year of the ORB." The question is really this: When will ORBs be ready for prime time? In our "fearless" forecast, we declare *1997 to be the year of the ORB*. We believe that by early 1997, ORBs

will become ubiquitous. And we won't be talking about them any more. Read on to find out why.

The best way to support this prediction is to first look at what's missing from CORBA; when can we expect the missing pieces; and what, if any, are the showstoppers for the technology. We also have a surprise in the bag; it will prove beyond doubt that 1997 is the year of the ORB. The good news on the CORBA front is that our list of shortcomings is much shorter this time than the one we put together for the previous edition of this book. But there's still some bad news on the CORBA front:

■ *Commercial ORBs are slow and inefficient.* This first generation of CORBA ORBs is totally unsuited for mission-critical client/server environments. Most of today's ORBs don't perform any garbage collection, load-balancing or concurrency control. None of the CORBA servers on the market can deal with millions of fine-grained objects—they just don't scale. In addition, there are no fault-tolerant servers for ORBs. Note that objects are inherently very scalable and can easily be replicated to provide fault tolerance. The problem is that on the server side, existing commercial ORBs are not on par with TP Monitors, ODBMSs, or even RDBMSs—they're not mature server products.

■ *Where's MOM?* MOM stands for *Message-Oriented Middleware*. It provides asynchronous message queues on both the client and server sides. MOM allows clients and servers to function at their own designated times and speeds without necessarily being simultaneously active. ORBs must provide MOM services to support mobile users and to facilitate communications in heterogeneous environments. The OMG Common Facilities task force is currently working on a MOM RFP to introduce messaging and queuing classes into CORBA.

■ ***The server code is not very portable.*** The CORBA specification does not sufficiently define all the interfaces required to write portable server code. In contrast, the specification to write fully portable clients is complete. OMG is aware of this shortcoming and is starting to work on a solution.

■ ***Standard CORBA does not support metaclasses.*** The ability to treat classes as first-class objects is very important for business objects and customizable middleware. We went over some of the miracles that meta-classes can perform in the Object Services section. The run-time flexibility provided by metaclasses is an absolute necessity for business objects. It would be nice to see OMG standardize on the SOM metaclasses (or something equivalent) to create a level playing field for all vendors. Currently, SOM-based CORBA vendors have an edge over their competitors because of SOM's support for metaclasses. The bad news is that these SOM metaclass implementations are not portable across CORBA ORBs, which is a real shame.

■ ***IDL needs to support semantic-level extensions.*** The OMG IDL needs to provide extensions for semantic message structures. The idea is that components should be able to interact with each other at the semantic level. CORBA IDL should provide "glue" to deal with mismatches between what a client component expects and what a server component provides. In other words, a flexible self-describing form of messaging is needed. The Business Object Task Force is starting to resolve these issues.

Are any of these items showstoppers? The only major showstopper is the first item on our list—the lack of robust commercial implementations. The rest of the issues are also important, and also need solutions. But without robust server implementations, ORBs will never be able to displace other forms of client/server middleware or application environments. In our opinion, OMG has created a nice set of standards (with the noted deficiencies). The ball is now in the vendors' court. They must deliver commercial implementations that are robust enough to satisfy the client/server mainstream. The first truly robust ORBs will probably be delivered by TP Monitor vendors. We predict that the next generation of TP Monitors will be called ORBs. You should note that TP Monitor vendors helped define the CORBA Object Transaction Service. They are very aware of the synergy between ORBs and classical transaction processing environments.

So are ORBs ready for prime time? They're getting there. You can use the current generation of ORBs in homogeneous environments to develop a better understanding of distributed object technology and encapsulate some of your key legacy applications with object wrappers. The current ORBs will help you create and manage a consistent set of distributed interfaces to all your important networked applications, tools, utilities, and medium-grained objects. The ORB becomes the "great integrator." However, heterogeneous, object-oriented production applications with fine-grained distributed objects will come later. How much later?

We predict we will get these functions by late-1996, when CORBA 2.0-compliant ORBs hit the market. Typically, products lag standards by about 16 months. The relevant CORBA 2.0 standards—including the transactions and concurrency services—were passed in December 1994. So our late 1996 assumption may be right on target. By then, we expect to see a new generation of ORBs with built-in, CORBA-compliant transaction services. These are the ORBs that will ultimately revolutionize the way we do client/server computing.

There's More To This Story

Is our forecast built entirely on the delivery of robust technology by CORBA ORB vendors? Not really—that would be too foolish. There's another wild card on the horizon that will greatly accelerate the penetration of CORBA ORBs—it's called OLE. As you may recall, OLE is part of Windows 95. As a result, it is practically free. When Windows NT 4.0 ships in late 1996, OLE will be extended across networks. In other words, it will become an ORB. It's also a high-volume ORB that will compete head-on with CORBA. To meet the competition from OLE, we expect that over the next few years CORBA vendors will be bundling their ORBs with mass volume desktops—such as OS/2 Warp, Windows 95, and Macintosh. In fact, this is precisely what the OpenDoc consortium is planning to do. In addition, we expect Java versions of CORBA ORBs to be bundled with Web browsers (more on this in Part 8).

As a result, we anticipate that sometime in 1997, industrial-strength CORBA ORBs will become ubiquitously available—they will be part of every shipping OS/2 Warp and Macintosh. In addition, IBM and CI Labs plan to make Open-Doc/CORBA available on Windows through some form of contamination (free downloads, preloads, and other "free" distribution programs). You can't beat free. So yes, 1997 will be the year of the ORB. If it does not happen by then, it's good-bye CORBA. It means that OLE would have won the battle for the ORB. So by 1997, the world will either be fully populated with OLE ORBs or CORBA ORBs (or, in the worst case, by both). ❑

Chapter 24

Compound Documents: The Client Framework

The real lure of this compound document technology is component software. It promises the ability to "roll your own" application by simply placing components together in a standard document that knows how to handle them.

> — David Linthicum
> Open Computing
> (January, 1995)

By 1997, compound documents will become the dominant framework for deploying components on the desktop and across the enterprise via the Internet and Intranets. They will provide the mass channel for selling millions of components. The "document" metaphor may be the breakthrough we've been awaiting. It provides an intuitive way to group related objects, display them seamlessly in a window, store them in a shared file, and ship them across networks to other desktops or to servers. In addition, the document maintains persistent client/server links that let these embedded components extract data from servers anywhere in the enterprise. So the document becomes the universal client—the ultimate front-end to servers. In fact, servers can ship compound documents directly to their clients to create storefronts for their services. It's like shipping Mosaic on steroids. This chapter covers the fundamentals of compound documents. In the next two chapters we introduce the real products—including OpenDoc and OLE.

COMPOUND DOCUMENTS: WHY ALL THE FUSS?

A *compound document* is nothing more than a metaphor for organizing collections of components—both visually and through containment relationships. It's an integration *framework* for visual components. The document is essentially a collection site for components and data that can come from a variety of sources. Because documents are so familiar, they create a very natural paradigm for the large-scale introduction of objects "for the masses." For most users, their first interaction with objects will be through these compound documents.

The Borderless Desktop

Compound documents are "places" where components live. The desktop itself is in the process of becoming a giant compound document that integrates in a "borderless" manner applications and operating system services. Did we have too much espresso? Perhaps, but if you think about it, OLE is an integral part of Windows 95. And OpenDoc will be shipped with every copy of OS/2 Warp and Macintosh. Both OpenDoc and OLE are frameworks for creating compound documents and managing components that live within these documents. Eventually, every object that appears on a desktop—in Windows, OS/2 Warp, or Mac—will be a component. Most of these components will be able to contain other components.

So the modern desktop simply becomes a giant container of components some of which are containers of other components, and so on. Components can be moved via drag-and-drop from the desktop to any visual container (and vice versa) to fit a user's needs for working "space." But isn't that the same as moving files into desktop folders? Yes, except that the visual components that are being moved around are more intelligent than anything that lives on today's desktops. In addition, they know how to collaborate with other components to share visual real estate and storage. Instead of seeing boxes within boxes, you will see something that looks more like a visual tapestry. It's really a self-organizing tapestry made up of intelligent components.

Documents Come in All Shapes

A compound document is primarily a visual container of components. With newer compound document technologies—such as OpenDoc—these components can have irregular shapes. With irregular shapes, we can create container/component combinations that are bounded only by the imagination. For example, it's easy to imagine containers that look like airplane bodies, stadiums, garden plots, cities, shopping malls, and so on. You will be able to create applications by dragging components from palettes and dropping them into containers. It's just like a game of *SimCity*, except that each of these components is live and can directly interact with a user (see Figure 24-1). The beauty is that these components can be supplied by different vendors that know nothing of each other. Note that containers themselves are also components—they too can be embedded inside other components. So everything is very recursive.

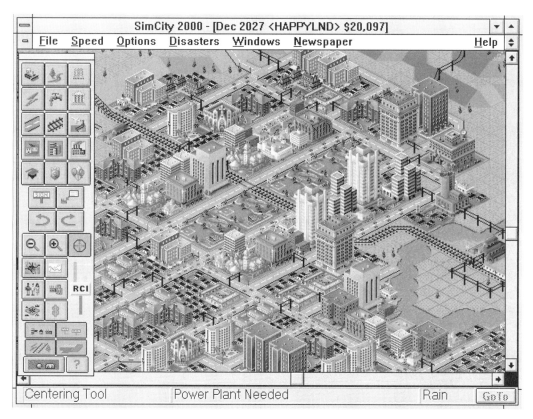

Figure 24-1. If SimCity Were a Compound Document.

A Home for All Data Types

Compound document data is more than the vanilla text of spreadsheets and paper documents. Data can be anything—including movies, sounds, animation, controls, networked calendars, and virtual folders. Each new kind of medium that is developed—video, sound, animation, simulation, and so on—can be represented by a component in a document. Database access components can feed visual information to users and to other components. For example, using scripts you can feed the data to a spell-checker component or a data-trend analysis component. Of course, all these components must have agreed upon data structures.

Compound documents can accept new kinds of data at run time because the data content is managed by the component that owns the data. In contrast, a traditional application restricts the types of data that can go into a document to the data types that are known by the application at compile time. If a new type of content becomes available, the application has no way to incorporate it into a document. You must modify and recompile a traditional application to incorporate new data types.

In-Place Editing

Switching among visual components within a document or across documents is much less intrusive than switching between conventional applications. You can immediately edit any content *in-place* without having to launch and execute different applications to create and assemble data. In-place editing allows the component to bring its editing tools to the container—including menus, toolbars, adornments, and small child windows. Instead of the user going to the program that manipulates data, the program comes to the container.

You no longer need to manually manage the various file formats that make up a compound document—all the pieces are now held in one place. The software that manipulates the document is hidden. You're manipulating parts of a document instead of switching between applications. The compound document either contains the data for its components or maintains links to data that's stored elsewhere. So you never have to visually leave the document—everything is right there.

Mobile Documents

By 1997 enterprise business documents will become the primary paradigm for capturing corporate information, challenging the dominance of record-oriented data. Compound document technology will become the overall framework for managing various non-record oriented information.

— Meta Group

Compound documents make it easier for developers to share storage for their separately developed components. And they make it easier for users to exchange documents. Documents can be printed, edited, shared, viewed, annotated, and circulated for review. You can pull data into the documents from several sources using client/server relationships. You can use a compound document to route work from one machine to the next. The routed document can contain data for the work-in-process, the user interface elements, and scripts that make the document intelligent. When the document lands on a workstation, an embedded script can log on the user and show the portions of the document that match the user's capabilities. A script can also decide where a document goes next.

THE COMPOUND DOCUMENT FRAMEWORK

The whole point of a compound document is to be able to mix the types of content, and to create the boundaries that sort out where one kind of content ends and another begins. This must all be done without the parts losing either their identities or boundaries.

— *Kurt Piersol, OpenDoc Architect*
Apple Computers

The compound document framework provides the protocols that let the component managing a document communicate with the components that own objects within the document. The protocols must also let these components effectively share resources such as a document file or a window on the screen. The trick is to make these protocols general enough to allow independently developed components, with no prior knowledge of each other, to discover each other and collaborate at run time.

Figure 24-2 shows the constituent technologies of a compound document framework. Notice that the framework builds on top of an existing object bus and core

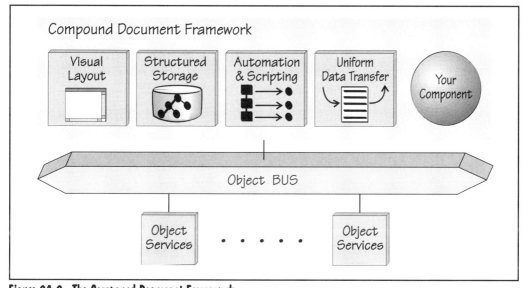

Figure 24-2. The Compound Document Framework.

object services. It provides four value-added services to its components: *visual layout, structured storage, scripting/automation*, and *uniform data transfer*. This section provides a brief introduction to these technologies. We cover them more extensively in the product chapters.

Document Layout

The *document layout* service defines the rules of engagement that allow independently developed components to share the container's window. Using the container as the mediator, components must cooperate to produce a seamless-looking document for the end-user. Remember, the word "document" is used in the SimCity sense. Containers activate the components that are embedded within a document and allocate to each a piece of the visual real estate. The components display their data in the area they're given and interact with the user.

Containers distribute events to their components and notify them when anything of interest happens within their surroundings. The container also arbitrates the use of shared resources—for example, a shared menu bar. A container must be able to accept a component that's dropped within its boundaries and figure out what to do with it. Embedded components negotiate with their containers for additional screen real estate if they need it.

Structured Storage

A traditional document is a monolithic block of data—inside a file—controlled by a single application. In contrast, a compound document consists of many smaller blocks of content data; each block is controlled by its own software component. The compound document provides the protocols that keep the components from corrupting the common document in which they live.

Compound documents must be able to partition a single file into storage compartments that can be allocated to individual components. Each component gets to store whatever data it wants within its storage. They're called compound documents because they can hold different kinds of data. When a compound document is first opened, it knows how to find and activate the components that manipulate the data. A component, in this case, is the data plus the code that manipulates the data. The container never touches or manipulates data that belongs to its embedded components.

Structured storage is the technology that creates a "file system within a file" by providing a layer of indirection on top of existing file systems. Each component is given a directory-like structure to organize and describe the contents of its storage; the data itself is stored in streams. These streams must be able to accommodate tiny records as well as giant BLOBs of data—for example, a full-feature movie like *Gone With The Wind.*

The data in a compound document can come from a variety of sources, including foreign components and SQL databases. The container provides the appropriate hooks to activate the foreign components that are associated with the separate data elements. It does this by directly embedding the foreign data within a document or by maintaining pointers—or *links*—in the document to the external data sources. In either case, the document is still editable by various applications; each sees its data in native format.

Scripting and Automation

The interconnection and specialization of application-level components are now referred to as scripting...Of course, scripting is programming, but we don't want to tell all those end-users that they've actually been programming, do we?

> — *Dave Thomas, President*
> *Object Technology International*
> *(March, 1995)*

Scripting—also called *automation*—is a major feature of the compound document component model. Scripts allow users to customize their applications. In compound document situations, they allow power users and scripters to create custom relationships between components in the document using standard document-editing facilities. Scripts allow programmers and system integrators to create client/server relationships that use the document metaphor for client front-ends. They also let you create smart documents.

Attached scripts can let a document track each time it is read or written. The document can notify its owners via e-mail each time their document is read. The script can also control what's being displayed in a document based on a user's authority. The script could request a password, validate digital signatures, and consult with an authentication server and a capabilities database before letting you see parts of the document. A smart document can adjust itself to your tastes. Scripts can also dynamically pull in content; for example, you could use a script to query a data warehouse to pull in data.

Scripts and compound documents complement each other very nicely. The document houses various scripts and invokes them when certain events fire—for example, when you open or close a document. In return, scripts protect the document and provide the intelligence that makes it self-sufficient. The result of marrying these two technologies are intelligent, self-managing documents. You can also use this technology to create mobile components that roam over networks and do all kinds of useful work. For the first time, we have off-the-shelf technology that lets us create and deploy collections of truly self-sufficient objects. A compound document can contain a component's state, data, intelligence, and user interface.

Uniform Data Transfer

Compound documents must be able to exchange data and components with their surroundings. *Uniform data transfer* provides a single data interchange mechanism that you can use with a variety of protocols—including clipboard, cut-and-paste, drag-and-drop, and linking. The uniform data transfer mechanism must be capable of exchanging traditional data content as well as entire components—including components that are embedded within them. You can think of this as a form of "deep" copy or move.

FYI

How Does It all Come Together?

Briefing

*P*lanning and construction will be guided by a process which allows the whole to emerge gradually from local acts...based on a communal pattern language that forms the basis for a shared agreement in the community.

> — Christopher Alexander et al., Authors
> The Oregon Experiment
> (Oxford, 1975)

Existing systems will not be replaced wholesale with object components. They'll be augmented gradually. If you already made the move to client/server, the transition to components will be smooth—the object bus is just another level of client/server middleware. Objects are simply the next level of evolution in the client/server ladder. Here are some of the steps you can take to prepare yourself for the object component phase of client/server:

■ **Think parts.** Carve out components from existing applications. At one extreme, an entire monolithic application can be encapsulated with CORBA IDL interfaces and treated as one giant part. At the other extreme, the entire application gets scrapped and recreated as collaborative parts. To get the maximum benefits of part reuse and modularity, you will need to decompose your applications into smaller parts, but you can get there gradually.

■ *Think compound documents on the client side.* Start by reorganizing your front-end applications into task-specific *places*. Decide on the business objects, things, and people that will live in these places. Next, create (or purchase) components that match these entities. Then decide which data is going to be embedded in the document and which will be accessed via links. Which functions will your users tinker with via scripts? Make sure to expose these functions. The *place*—built as a compound document container—is the heart of the client application. Places are mobile. They can be stored on servers and shipped to clients over the Internet or Intranets.

■ *Think CORBA on the server side.* Encapsulate all existing services on the network with CORBA IDL-wrappers. Use the CORBA Interface Repository and Naming Service to keep track of all the functions your servers export. Objects are additive, so start with what you have and add new components whenever you want. These pieces must be built from the start on top of an enterprise-wide distributed object infrastructure such as CORBA IIOP over the Internet or Intranets.

■ *Think script.* Increasingly, scripts will become the predominant paradigm for orchestrating intercomponent collaborations on both the client and the server and between clients and servers. Design your components for scriptability—ensure that your components expose a set of actions and attributes that can be invoked, configured, and modified at run time.

■ *Think resell.* Use the emerging component distribution channels to resell some of your parts and suites in the open parts market. If you're an IS shop, reselling components should help you recover some of your costs. It also encourages your programmers to create smaller, nimbler, and more competitive pieces of software that play in an open component bus like an IIOP Intranet.

■ *Think suites.* Take advantage of the component bus to break applications into components, and use suites as the integration mechanism. New applications should be architected as parts and suites—from desktop to enterprise server components.

■ *Think frameworks.* Use frameworks and object-oriented tools to build your new parts. Why build anything from scratch if you can avoid it?

Eventually all new applications will be assembled from component parts and suites, and then purchased through part catalogs. Part vendors and system integrators will use the catalogs as their main distribution channel. Customers will be able to browse, test drive, and purchase their parts online. Entire multiplatform client/server systems will be created on demand in a matter of days. ❏

CONCLUSION

Compound documents provide a framework and visual metaphor for organizing components. They provide negotiation protocols through which embedded components merge their user interface elements into the container's window space and share a document file. Embedded scripts add intelligence to the document and protect it from threats. Because the desktop operating systems themselves are becoming compound document frameworks, they will provide a mass market for components that play by the new rules of engagement. Remember, these rules of engagement are over and above those provided by the underlying object bus and services. Compound documents introduce a higher level of collaboration.

Compound documents are particularly attractive because they provide a powerful metaphor for integrating components. Compound document frameworks let you visualize the components, store them in a common file, exchange them via data transfers, and extend them using scripts and automation. In addition, everything is built on an object bus that allows these components to play in intergalactic networks and to be packaged in language-independent dynamic libraries.

Of course, the price of living within a framework is that you must accept the constraints (and rules of engagement) that it imposes to accrue the benefits. It's an all-or-nothing proposition. The constraints imposed by a compound document framework include its protocols for sharing a common file, negotiating for visual real estate, and exchanging information with the outside world. Components are no longer free-standing. They live within the document. And they also use the container as an intermediary to receive events, share resources, and communicate with each other. In return, components achieve higher levels of visual collaboration and can be distributed via mass market channels. It's a classic trade-off.

Compound documents are also a key technology for enterprise client/server systems and for the Internet and Intranets. Servers can ship flexible front-ends (for example, a storefront) for their services using compound documents. In addition, you can use compound documents to package and ship across networks all types of self-contained components—including roaming agents, mobile components, and workflow. We call this technology *shippable places*. So welcome to this brave new world. We cover *OpenDoc* and *OLE*—the two *de facto* standards for compound documents—in the next two chapters. We cover shippable places in Part 8.

Chapter 25

The OpenDoc Component Model

In March 1996, OMG adopted OpenDoc as the basis for its compound document technology. This means that CORBA now has a consistent architecture for both the client and the server. In addition, OpenDoc makes it possible for CORBA clients and servers to exchange components via mobile document containers. OpenDoc enables CORBA to get into the mobile object business in a big way. It also makes it possible for CORBA to play on both the client and server sides of the Internet and Intranets. So the news is that CORBA is no longer just middleware and server technology; it can now play on clients as well. This chapter gives you a bird's eye view of OpenDoc and how it plays in the CORBA world. It also explains the OpenDoc compound document model.

PARTS: COMPONENTS, OPENDOC-STYLE

OpenDoc is a component software architecture implemented as a set of cross-platform classes and services. The component model is a pure rendition of the compound document paradigm. Components in the OpenDoc world are called *parts*. Parts live within compound documents. You can't have free-floating OpenDoc components. All OpenDoc components must be associated with a compound document. An OpenDoc part consists of data stored in compound documents—including text, graphics, spreadsheets, and video—plus a *part editor* that manipulates this data. An OpenDoc document is a user-organized collection of parts.

OpenDoc defines the rules of engagement for parts to coexist in compound documents and to share visual real estate. It also provides an elaborate scripting model that lets parts collaborate via scripts. The OpenDoc runtime—packaged as IDL-defined CORBA classes—provides a cross-language and cross-platform compound document environment.

If you come from the world of CORBA, an OpenDoc part is nothing more than a CORBA object with desktop smarts. OpenDoc extends the CORBA ORB to the desktop. Parts within a desktop can use a CORBA ORB to collaborate with other desktop parts and to access server objects wherever they reside. The ORB provides transparent access to remote components and CORBA services such as security, transactions, and naming. But before we get into these client/server collaborations, let's first go over the OpenDoc component model and see how it complements and extends CORBA.

OPENDOC'S CONSTITUENT TECHNOLOGIES

OpenDoc is similar to OLE in its intent but offers more features, support for object messaging across networks, a more elegant user interface convention, and support for multiple platforms. OpenDoc components can also interoperate with OLE components.

— *John R. Rymer, Editor*
Distributed Computing Monitor
(January, 1995)

The *Component Integration Lab (CI Labs)* is a nonprofit consortium whose purpose is to provide common technology and services to enable "an open, distributed component software platform through a vendor-neutral process." CI Labs' membership includes Adobe, Apple, IBM, Justsystem, Lotus, Novell, OMG, and Oracle. OpenDoc is the first distributed component technology to be offered by CI Labs.

OpenDoc uses the familiar document metaphor for visually organizing components on the desktop. OpenDoc parts are medium-grained objects. Jed Harris, ex-President of CI Labs, defines an OpenDoc *part* as a piece of software "small enough to create and maintain, big enough to deploy and support, and with standard interfaces for interoperability." Parts can represent almost any type of data—including text, movies, sound clips, clocks, calendars, spreadsheets, and data types that haven't yet been invented. All these parts are concurrently active within the same document, which is why they're sometimes called "living, breathing documents" or, to be less dramatic, just "compound documents."

OpenDoc defines the rules of engagement for parts to: 1) seamlessly share screen real estate within a window; 2) store their data within a single container file; 3) exchange information with other parts via links, clipboards, and drag-and-drop; 4) coordinate their actions via scripts, semantic events, and CORBA method invocations; and 5) interoperate with other desktop component models—for example, OLE and Java applets. Figure 25-1 shows OpenDoc's constituent technologies and how they relate. The CORBA-compliant *System Object Model (SOM)* is from IBM. The rest of the technologies—including *Bento*, *Uniform Data Transfer*, *Compound Document Management*, and the *Open Scripting Architecture (OSA)*—are from Apple. In addition, IBM is distributing *ComponentGlue*, an interface and library that provides seamless interoperability between OLE and OpenDoc for Windows. In addition, IBM is working on *Arabica*—a portable version of OpenDoc written entirely in Java.

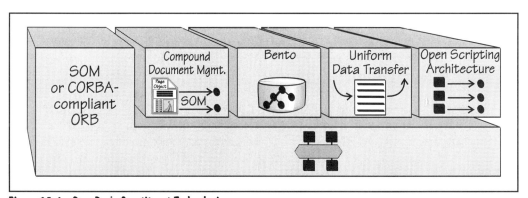

Figure 25-1. OpenDoc's Constituent Technologies.

SOM

SOM provides local and remote interoperability for OpenDoc parts (or components). SOM is a language-independent, CORBA-compliant ORB that lets objects communicate in a single address space or across address spaces on the same machine or across networks. Because SOM is included with every OpenDoc runtime, a part developer can access any service on any CORBA-compliant ORB. This literally opens up a universe of possibilities.

SOM is also a component packaging technology. It allows OpenDoc developers to package their parts in binary format and ship them as DLLs. SOM's support for multiple inheritance—both implementation and interface—makes it possible for developers to derive new OpenDoc parts from existing ones. They do this by subclassing an existing OpenDoc part via CORBA IDL, and then either reusing or overriding the method implementations delivered in the DLL binaries. In addition, SOM allows developers to add methods to existing parts without impacting the programs that use them.

Bento

Bento—named after Japanese plates with compartments for different foods—defines a container format that you can use in files, network streams, clipboards, and so on. A Bento file container allows applications to store and retrieve collections of objects in a single structured file, along with their references—or links—to other objects.

The Bento container format is platform neutral; it can store any type of data. In a Bento document, each object has a persistent ID that moves with it from system to system. Bento also supports references between objects in different documents. If there are several drafts of a document, Bento only stores the incremental changes. This makes it easy to maintain different versions of the same document.

The Bento design is optimized for document interchanges. A Bento container is an excellent carrier for exchanging compound documents between applications running on different platforms. You can also use Bento to move groups of objects with their attached scripts, which makes it a very good foundation technology for mobile components.

Uniform Data Transfer

The OpenDoc storage APIs provide *Uniform Data Transfer* across and within applications. The same method invocations used for document storage can also be used to transfer data and parts via drag-and-drop, copy and paste, and linking. The data can be represented in a variety of formats. OpenDoc lets you move entire parts and the parts they embed in one operation. In addition to data transfer, linking adds notification calls that dynamically refresh the transferred information.

Compound Document Management

Compound Document Management defines the protocols that allow parts to share a visual space and coordinate their use of shared resources such as keyboard entries, menus, and the selection focus. *Parts* are the fundamental building blocks in OpenDoc. Every document has a top-level (or root) part in which all other parts are embedded. A part can contain other parts. *Frames* are areas of the display that represent a part. They also represent the part in the negotiations for space during the layout of a document.

Parts are associated with *part editors*. These are the active elements that handle the part's data and interact with the user. An OpenDoc component is the combination of the part editor and its data. You can select at run time an editor that will work with a particular part type. OpenDoc encourages vendors to provide part viewers that can be freely distributed with a document. The viewer lets you display the part but not alter the contents.

Open Scripting Architecture

The *Open Scripting Architecture (OSA)* is an extension of the Macintosh's *Apple Events*. OSA lets parts expose their contents via semantic events that any OSA-compliant scripting language can invoke. The commands sent via these semantic events operate on an *object specifier* that identifies in a natural manner objects the user sees on a screen (or within some other context). And because we're dealing with objects, the commands are polymorphic. For example, "next" can mean the next cell or the next word, depending on the type of part that receives the command. Note that an object specifier describes things the user sees. This description gets translated by OSA into the actual object reference.

A scriptable part must be prepared to provide at run time the list of objects it contains and the operations it supports. OpenDoc can deliver event messages from the scripting system to the parts. Scripting lets you coordinate the interaction between parts. OpenDoc also lets you attach scripts to semantic events. This makes an OpenDoc part "tinkerable," which means that a user-written script can be triggered when a semantic event fires. By intercepting the event, the script can modify the part's behavior.

In addition, OpenDoc parts can be designed to be *recordable*. In this case, the part editor intercepts every incoming action, converts it into a semantic event, and then resends the event to itself—this is called a *bottleneck*. You can use bottlenecks to check for attached scripts and to record all events. The recorded events can be converted to your preferred OSA scripting language and replayed at a later time.

OpenDoc: Looks Are Everything

Soapbox

Comparing OpenDoc with OLE/DCOM is like comparing a modern human with a Neanderthal. If you were to dress a Neanderthal in a suit and stand back, the two might even look the same. But you would have to look much closer if one was going to help run your business.

— *Cliff Reeves*
(January, 1995)

Are all compound document models equal? Not really—some are better engineered than others. But as we all know, you don't buy a house because it has great plumbing. You buy it because of the way it looks. In the case of OpenDoc, the plumbing is first class—the combination of CORBA, OSA's semantic events, and Bento allows you to perform new client/server feats. And luckily for OpenDoc, it can also let you create some great-looking parts.

So what are the key visual features that differentiate OpenDoc? For starters, it was built for *in-place* editing. This means that you can edit any visible part within a document—no matter how deeply embedded it is—with a single-click activation. You don't have to first activate the surrounding parts. In-place editing creates a seamless editing experience; it lets you move very naturally from part to part within a document. It's the next generation of Object-Oriented User Interfaces (OOUIs).

With OpenDoc, the distinction between a part and a document is purposely blurred. For example, if you drag an icon representing a closed document from the desktop (or a palette) into an open document, a copy of the transferred document immediately becomes an embedded part. Likewise, if you drag a part (or frame) from an embedded document and drop it on the desktop, a copy of that part immediately becomes a separate document represented by an icon.

Another important visual feature in OpenDoc's repertoire is the support of irregularly shaped parts. This means that not all parts must be rectangular. Irregular parts help reinforce the seamless look. You can create parts that look more like their real-life counterparts. The parts seamlessly fit together and give the appearance they were all created by the same application. For example, a container part could be shaped like an airplane body—a highly irregular shape—and populated with other irregularly shaped parts that represent passengers, crew, and luggage. Other examples of irregular container parts are donut-shaped stadiums, cruise-ship floor plans, office layouts, and garden plots. You can fill all these containers with interesting looking parts.

So, perhaps it is this pretty face that will differentiate OpenDoc from OLE with end-users, not its great client/server plumbing. Of course, we're more interested in the plumbing capabilities of OpenDoc than in its pretty face. After all, this is a book about client/server computing. ❑

COMPONENTGLUE: OPENDOC BECOMES OLE AND VICE VERSA

OpenDoc is the "rest of the world's" response to Microsoft's OLE. It even encapsulates its archenemy, OLE.

— *David Linthicum, Open Computing*
(January, 1995)

OpenDoc was designed from the very start with OLE compatibility in mind. IBM's *ComponentGlue* provides a bidirectional gateway between OpenDoc and OLE. This means that an OpenDoc container sees an OLE object as an OpenDoc part, and vice versa. The ComponentGlue translation layer provides a direct map between OLE and OpenDoc compound document APIs. When you write to the OpenDoc APIs, you automatically get an OLE container/server that runs on NT and Windows 95.

ComponentGlue lets an OpenDoc document contain both parts and OLE objects, and vice versa. Within such documents, a user can drag-and-drop, cut and paste, and even link data between OLE and OpenDoc components. Parts and OLE objects can exchange data using the same drag-and-drop, clipboard, and link facilities. OpenDoc parts and OLE documents can share the same Bento file containers or Windows *DocFiles*. Further, ComponentGlue maps between OLE's automation services and OpenDoc's semantic events. This means you can control both OLE and OpenDoc components with scripts written in either OLE-compliant or OSA-compliant scripting languages.

In contrast to ordinary CORBA/OLE gateways that only provide communication mappings, ComponentGlue provides a deep translation layer between OLE and OpenDoc. It provides full two-way compatibility between OLE objects and OpenDoc parts. It lets OpenDoc parts appear as OLE objects to the Windows Registry; and OLE objects—including ActiveXs—appear as OpenDoc parts to the OpenDoc binder. With ComponentGlue, you can embed OpenDoc parts in OLE documents, and you can embed OLE objects in OpenDoc documents.

CI Labs claims that OpenDoc with ComponentGlue makes it easier to develop OLE containers and servers—including OCXs and ActiveXs. And Microsoft provides its seal of Windows 95 approval to OLE components developed using OpenDoc. Note that IBM only provides ComponentGlue on Windows and the Mac. However, the technology is part of the OpenDoc architecture and can be adapted to other platforms. In theory, ComponentGlue could let users view (but not edit) OLE objects embedded within an OpenDoc document on platforms that do not have native Microsoft OLE support, such as OS/2 or Unix. In practice, it remains to be seen.

WHAT OPENDOC DOES FOR CLIENT/SERVER SYSTEMS

OpenDoc component technology introduces new opportunities for the creation of client/server systems. OpenDoc brings the CORBA bus into the desktop, making it the hub of all interprogram communications. You can use the same object model to connect enterprise objects as well as medium-grained visual objects that reside on a common desktop. It's all very consistent. It now becomes possible to repackage monolithic desktop applications into parts that can plug-and-play together on the same desktop or across the network.

Client/Server, OpenDoc-Style

From a client/server viewpoint, an OpenDoc document acts as a central integration point for multiple sources of data that reside on different servers (see Figure 25-2). Parts can be linked to corporate databases, workflow managers, image repositories, e-mail, or the local spreadsheet. The document is the client/server application. It

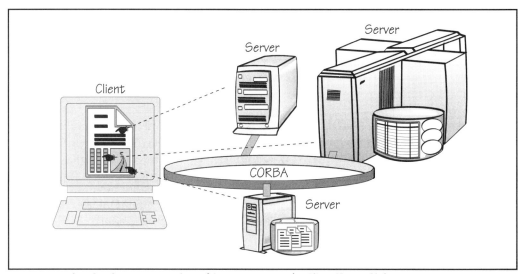

Figure 25-2. OpenDoc Document as a Central Integration Point for Client/Server Links.

acts as a repository of client/server relationships or "links" to external data sources and remote functions. End-users can assemble these applications by simply opening an OpenDoc container document and dragging parts into it. They can lay out live parts within a visual document just like we do today with page layout programs. Creating an application becomes a paste and layout job—no programming is required. Power users, IS shops, and system integrators can create more sophisticated client/server systems by writing OpenDoc scripts that orchestrate complex interpart collaborations.

It's easy to imagine other metaphors for visual containers into which parts can be dragged, dropped, rearranged, and manipulated to suit a user's needs. Examples of OpenDoc containers are business forms, airplanes, database front-ends, floor plans, desktops, garden plots, and any visual representation that you can use as a container of parts. We anticipate that software providers will provide "designer containers" to complement the parts business; parts and containers will work together "hand in glove." For example, an airline container can be populated with parts representing seats, passengers, crew, luggage, and so on.

Live OpenDoc documents can be saved, shipped across networks to different platforms, and reopened later with the same client/server links. Remember that we're talking about live multimedia documents with application intelligence and links to external data sources. You can move these roaming compound documents—via a workflow manager—from place to place to reflect a business process within and across enterprises.

In summary, OpenDoc will encourage new levels of direct manipulation on the desktop. End-users will be able to create custom applications by choosing a container and populating it with active parts that live on the desktop or on servers anywhere on the network. Imagine being able to access multiple data sources and business objects through multiple client/server connections from within a single visual container or document. Kurt Piersol, the Apple Computers OpenDoc architect, calls it "an entire information system in a document."

How OpenDoc Enhances CORBA

OpenDoc introduces component enhancements over and above what CORBA provides today, including:

- **_Reference counts_**. OpenDoc objects maintain counts of who is using them. This helps the system release memory when components are no longer in use.

- **_Named extension suites_**. OpenDoc allows components to create named suites of services called _extensions_. A client can ask a component if it supports a particular named suite of functions and obtain a reference to it—extensions are objects. These extensions allow groups of parts to act like a suite. For example, a part can support an "airline reservation" extension. All the parts that belong to the airline reservation extension will share common semantics, protocols, and metadata that are registered with CI Labs. OpenDoc extensions will form the basis for collaborative desktops consisting of "very smart" parts that act like horizontal suites, vertical suites, or client/server suites.

■ *Component versioning*. SOM provides proprietary extensions to the CORBA IDL for keeping track of major and minor versions. Because OpenDoc part editors are packaged using SOM, they can keep track of their version/release numbers. In addition, you can use Bento drafts to provide versioning on a document's data.

■ *Property editors*. OpenDoc provides GUI interfaces—property dialog boxes or notebooks—for updating a component's properties and scripts at run time. This allows components to be inspected and modified by power users and system integrators.

■ *Semantic messaging*. OpenDoc's OSA complements the CORBA messaging model by introducing a vocabulary of verbs and object specifiers that let clients manipulate the contents of server parts at the semantic level. It's a form of dynamic messaging. The messages are created "on-the-fly" at run time. However, unlike CORBA's dynamic method invocations, you do not invoke a method on an object reference on the server. Instead, the semantic message contains an *object specifier* that describes in human terms what the user sees—meaning the content objects on the screen. The messaging system resolves these "content descriptions" into target objects—ones that have unique object references. OpenDoc's semantic messaging provides the basis for language-independent scripting. It is also a general purpose client/server semantic messaging system that can be used by all types of business objects and smart components. Semantic messages are grouped into named suites that are, of course, tracked by CI Labs.

■ *Scriptable components*. OpenDoc's parts are scriptable. This allows end-users and system integrators to quickly assemble ensembles of components and integrate them using scripts. Scripts make it easy to combine components from different sources into custom solutions.

OPENDOC: MEET THE PLAYERS

CI Labs was given the mandate to make the OpenDoc source code available to the industry. The idea was to create an open playing field for desktop component software by placing all the relevant standards and the associated plumbing in the public domain. CI Labs relies on its sponsors to distribute the OpenDoc runtimes across multiple platforms. The OpenDoc runtimes are freely available from Apple on Mac and IBM on OS/2, Windows 95, and AIX. IBM plans to ship OpenDoc with every copy of OS/2 Warp. Apple will ship it with every Mac. In addition, IBM will distribute OpenDoc on Windows through a "contamination" process. This means that IBM will make OpenDoc freely available on bulletin boards, preload it on PCs running Windows, and make the runtime freely available to part distributors. Note that OLE 2 is distributed in the same manner on Windows 3.1. So it looks like the OpenDoc camp will do everything they can to make OpenDoc as ubiquitous as OLE but on more platforms.

CONCLUSION

OpenDoc is present tense. And about time, too. Give it a serious look.

> — *Peter Coffee, Columnist*
> *PC Week*
> *(March, 1996)*

OpenDoc is a good piece of compound document technology that complements CORBA very nicely. The marriage of OpenDoc and CORBA will let us create a new generation of client/server systems based on components. Servers will be able to ship to their clients Bento documents loaded with components. These components will provide customized front-ends to services anywhere on the intergalactic network. With OpenDoc's support of irregular shapes, these client front-ends are only limited by the imagination.

However, it takes more than good technology for OpenDoc to succeed. CI Labs and its partners must also: 1) create a very strong parts business—this includes channels for selling parts around an architecture that defines part suites for every known industry; 2) provide superior OpenDoc tools for creating and assembling parts that run on multiple platforms (see Soapbox); and 3) define an architecture and the semantic events for client/server enterprise parts (i.e., distributed OpenDoc). CI Labs must drive all these efforts to provide an open playing field. If these conditions are met, CI Labs and its member companies may be able to contain OLE on the Windows desktop. And even there, they may be able to encapsulate OLE behind a layer of OpenDoc ComponentGlue. If they don't meet the challenge, OLE may win the battle for desktop components. Microsoft will then use the desktop as a springboard to win client/server components and the enterprise object bus.

Soapbox

Questions To Ask Your OpenDoc Providers

For you to succeed with OpenDoc, the system and part vendors must provide an infrastructure for parts and the right application tools. Here's a set of questions to ask your favorite OpenDoc vendor:

■ How will OpenDoc handle cross-platform parts? How will common rendering be done across Windows, OS/2, Mac, and Unixes? Which scripting language should I use across these platforms?

■ What cross-platform tools are available for part construction and assembly? Will these tools support OpenDoc parts in their palettes? Will they support OLE OCXs? Will they support component partitioning across client/server boundaries? Will they support server components on CORBA ORBs?

■ How will the parts be distributed, certified, and maintained? Who will certify part suites—including client/server suites? Who do I call when a part breaks? Who do I call when a suite of multivendor parts doesn't perform as advertised?

■ Who do I call when an OpenDoc-wrapped OLE component doesn't perform: Microsoft or CI Labs? ❑

Chapter 26

OLE/DCOM: The Other Component Bus

> *M*any years from now, a Charles Darwin of computerdom might look back and wonder how the Microsoft Windows APIs evolved into an object-oriented operating system.
>
> — Kraig Brockschmidt, Author
> Inside OLE 2, Second Edition
> (Microsoft Press, 1995)

If CORBA is the industry's leading standard for distributed components, then Microsoft's *Object Linking and Embedding (OLE)* is the *de facto* "other standard." What makes OLE so important? Microsoft. Everything it is doing and will do is based on OLE. Windows itself is morphing into OLE. Or, if you prefer, OLE is the object-oriented foundation of Windows. By the time Cairo ships, all of Windows will be OLE. So what does this have to do with distributed objects? It may come as a surprise, but OLE is built on top of an ORB called the *Distributed Component Object Model (DCOM)*. Even though DCOM is currently a single machine ORB, Microsoft plans to carry DCOM—and most of today's OLE—to NT 4.0 and Cairo. OLE and DCOM will provide the basis for Microsoft's future distributed computing environment. Windows 95 will participate as a client.

OLE FOR THE ENTERPRISE

Microsoft is saying some pretty wild stuff about how they understand the enterprise and how OLE will be usable for production work.

> — Roy Schulte, Gartner Group
> (May, 1995)

In May 1995, Microsoft announced an "OLE everything" strategy for the enterprise. Over the next few years, Microsoft plans to deliver *OLE DB*, *OLE Transactions*, *OLE Team Development*, and *Network OLE* (also known as DCOM). Even highly successful Microsoft "standards" like ODBC are being tossed out in favor of OLE DB. Microsoft has already released specifications for these new OLE interfaces. Products incorporating these extensions will start rolling out in late 1996.

Microsoft sees the "enterprise" as a key market in the next few years. The company roughly has four areas of focus: Desktop, Home, Information Highway, and Enterprise. Microsoft foresees a world with 300,000,000 PCs. This leads them to conclude that there will be a market for at least 30,000,000 servers. Thus the enterprise market is not seen as fundamentally different from other markets in which they have entered and prospered. In their words, "it is high volume, high profit, and fun." Finally, OLE and DCOM provide the foundation technology for Microsoft's Object Web and Internet product offerings (more on this in Part 8).

WHAT IS OLE?

The first thing you must know about OLE is that its name—"Object Linking and Embedding"—is misleading. OLE is more than just a compound document technology—it's a complete environment for components that competes head-on with CORBA and OpenDoc. Like CORBA, OLE is building a set of common services that allow these components to collaborate intelligently. Like CORBA, OLE covers the entire component spectrum—from fine-grained objects to coarse-grained existing applications. Unlike CORBA, OLE does not currently address the needs of distributed components—it's a big hole that will take a some time to fill. OLE will evolve in two directions: 1) compound documents will provide the framework for the visual components that live on the desktop; and 2) DCOM will provide the distributed object bus and services.

OLE: A Short History

In 1990, Microsoft introduced the OLE 1 technology as its basic strategy for integrating multiple applications and multimedia data types within a compound document framework. OLE 1 was a clumsy and slow protocol built on top of DDE.

When an application was launched from within a compound document, it was given its own window, and the data it needed was copied into its address space. There was no way for the application to directly access the document.

OLE 2, introduced in 1993, fixed many of these shortcomings with a new object-encapsulation technology called the *Component Object Model (COM)*. All of OLE 2 is built on top of COM—it's the heart of OLE. OLE 2 grew beyond the boundaries of compound documents into a much more generic object service architecture. The lion's share of OLE still belongs to compound documents. In late 1994, Microsoft added a new custom control architecture—also known as OCX—to the compound document model. An OCX is the OLE version of a generic part that plugs into the compound document framework.

In early 1996, Microsoft announced *ActiveXs*, which are minimalist OLE objects for the Internet. OLE's new *component categories* define the interfaces an ActiveX supports. In March 1996, Microsoft released the first distributed version of DCOM as part of the NT 4.0 early beta; the final product is expected to ship by late 1996.

In late 1996, *OLE TP* will make its first product appearance as *SQL Server 6.5's* new *Distributed Transaction Coordinator*. However, the best of OLE TP is yet to come; it is called the *Component Coordinator* (the code name is Viper). The product is in early alpha as we go to press. It is a TP Monitor for components that also supports long-lived transactions. Viper appears to be the OLE kingpin for the enterprise; it could eventually provide the scalability and robust intercomponent coordination that OLE sorely lacks.

OLE Is OLE

*Y*ou may have noticed that OLE is no longer given a version number.

— *Kraig Brockschmidt, Author*
Inside OLE 2, Second Edition
(Microsoft Press, 1995)

According to Microsoft's Kraig Brockschmidt, OLE will no longer be given a version number. The reason for this change is that the name OLE 2 implies that there will be an OLE 3. This is not the case any more. According to Kraig, "new features and technologies can be added to OLE within the existing framework." For example, OCXs were released a year after the original release of OLE 2, but OLE was not given a new version number—although some people now call it OLE 2.1. New OLE interfaces will simply be buried within new releases of Windows or new releases of Microsoft's Visual C++.

What this means is that OLE is not a separate product—it is the Windows operating system. Windows will evolve into a giant collection of OLE interfaces, with DCOM

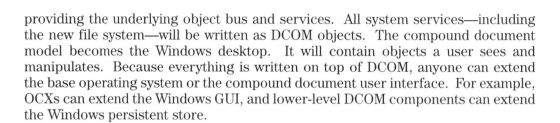

providing the underlying object bus and services. All system services—including the new file system—will be written as DCOM objects. The compound document model becomes the Windows desktop. It will contain objects a user sees and manipulates. Because everything is written on top of DCOM, anyone can extend the base operating system or the compound document user interface. For example, OCXs can extend the Windows GUI, and lower-level DCOM components can extend the Windows persistent store.

OLE: Interfaces Everywhere

OLE consists of a number of "interfaces" as well as Win32-style APIs. OLE interfaces are similar in concept to CORBA's—they define a set of related functions. An *interface* defines a contract between components. An OLE component can support one or more interfaces. DCOM provides an interface negotiation protocol that lets clients acquire pointers—at run time—to the interfaces a component supports. Programmers can write their own interfaces using DCOM's *Interface Definition Language (IDL)*. DCOM also provides an *Object Description Language (ODL)* for describing these interfaces to a *Type Library*. This is the DCOM equivalent of a CORBA Interface Repository. Clients can discover dynamically which interfaces an object supports and what parameters they require. Like CORBA, DCOM provides both static and dynamic method invocations.

As we go to press, OLE consists of about 100 interfaces—each one supports on the average about six member functions. In addition, the OLE/DCOM library provides about 120 Win32-style APIs. This means that OLE introduces about 720 new function calls (over and above Win32). Some of these interfaces are simply abstract classes with no implementation. They only define the interface contract. The component implementor must provide the code that implements the interface. This can be quite a bit of work. Microsoft provides tools to help alleviate some of the burden. In addition to the Microsoft-defined interfaces, you can create your own interfaces—OLE calls them *custom* interfaces. You can also provide components that replace the ones Microsoft ships, as long as you match their interface contracts.

So, What Is an OLE Component?

An OLE component is defined by a *class* that implements one or more interfaces and a *class factory*—this is the interface that knows how to produce a component instance of that class. Unlike an OpenDoc part, an OLE component is not a predefined, self-contained unit. All OpenDoc parts have the same basic interfaces, but they can also support extensions. In contrast, an OLE component is a group of interfaces. It requires many interfaces to make an OLE component reach the same level of sophistication as an OpenDoc part.

In late 1994, Microsoft introduced *custom controls* (or OCXs) that have a set of predefined interfaces (a la OpenDoc part). An OCX is a well-defined, medium-grained component that is packaged like an OpenDoc part. However, OCXs still lack some of the function in OpenDoc parts. For example, an OCX cannot embed other parts—OLE containers do that. So an OCX is a set of contracts between an OLE visual component and its container. Of course, these contracts must be implemented by the OCX provider.

Like CORBA, OLE supports components of all sizes: fine-grained, medium-grained, and large-grained. An ActiveX is a minimalist component; an OCX is a medium-grained component. OLE containers are large-grained, application-size components.

OLE'S CONSTITUENT TECHNOLOGIES

Like OpenDoc, OLE uses the familiar document metaphor for visually organizing components on the desktop. Like OpenDoc, OLE defines the rules of engagement for OCXs and other visual components to share screen real estate within a single window and to store their data within a single container file. Like OpenDoc, OLE provides interfaces that let components exchange information with other components via links, the clipboard, and drag-and-drop. And like OpenDoc, OLE provides automation support that lets components coordinate their actions via automation scripts.

Figure 26-1 shows OLE's constituent technologies and how they relate. Notice that the figure is almost a replica of the one you saw in the OpenDoc chapter, but the names of the technologies have changed. The object bus is DCOM instead of SOM/CORBA. Structured storage is provided by compound files instead of Bento. OLE has its own model for doing automation and scripting. Even the uniform data transfer models are different. And, as you would expect, OLE and OpenDoc have very different compound document design points—OLE does not currently support irregular shaped parts, and it has limited in-place editing. As a result, OLE components don't look as if they're all part of the same application—they lack the

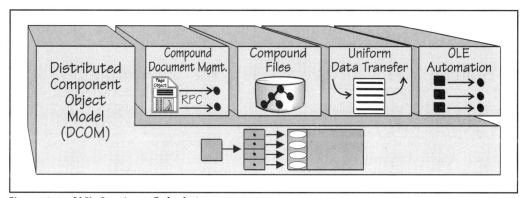

Figure 26-1. OLE's Constituent Technologies.

visual continuity OpenDoc provides. In this chapter, we provide a brief overview of OLE's constituent technologies.

The Distributed Component Object Model (DCOM)

DCOM is a first step toward distributed objects, but it attempts to reinvent many of the mechanisms successfully addressed by CORBA...Unfortunately, DCOM represents a major fragmentation of distributed object technology.

> — Dr. Thomas Mowbray, Principal Scientist
> MITRE

But one might certainly argue that having a single, financially strong leader that owns the standard is more likely to ensure that it is clear-cut and not a product of committee think.

> — David Sarna, Columnist
> Datamation

DCOM specifies interfaces between component objects within a single application or between applications. DCOM, like CORBA, separates the interface from the implementation. Like CORBA, it provides APIs for dynamically discovering the interfaces an object exports and how to load and invoke them. Like CORBA, DCOM requires that all shared code be declared using object interfaces (Microsoft even provides two proprietary interface languages: the IDL and the ODL).

Unlike CORBA, DCOM's object model does not support multiple inheritance. Instead, a DCOM component can support multiple interfaces. DCOM uses the multiple interface capability to provide reuse through a technique called *aggregation*. It's a fancy name for a component that encapsulates the services of other components. Clients call the encapsulating component, which in turn calls the contained component (or puts it directly in touch with the client). What all this means is that the DCOM environment is inherently flat. "Inheritance" is achieved through a web of pointers that link or aggregate different interfaces.

DCOM defines interfaces for object factories and provides a rudimentary component licensing mechanism. It also provides a local directory service based on the Windows Registry. A DCOM client asks for the services of a component by passing a unique *Class Identifier (CLSID)*. Then the DCOM *Service Control Manager (SCM)*—also known as "Scum"—locates a server using the Registry and tells it to create an instance of that component by invoking the class factory interface.

Scum—with help from DCOM—is responsible for locating out-of-process and remote objects, and then starting them (see Figure 26-2). If the object is in-process, the caller is the client itself. Otherwise, the caller is a *stub object* provided by DCOM that picks up the remote procedure call from the *proxy* in the client process and turns it into an interface call to the server object. Clients and servers always communicate using some in-process or local code (again, see Figure 26-2). The DCOM proxy and stub mechanism is very similar to the way CORBA implements local/remote transparency using static stubs on the client side and interface skeletons on the server side.

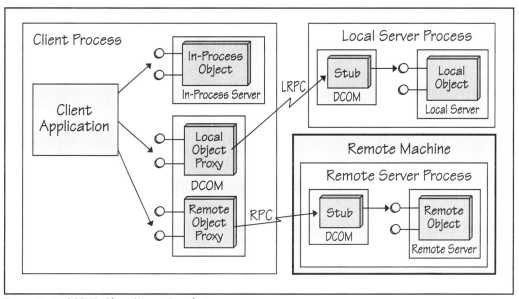

Figure 26-2. DCOM's Client/Server Boundaries.

Finally, DCOM requires that every OLE component implement the **IUnknown** interface. This interface is used by clients to discover at run time the interfaces a component provides and then connect with them. **IUnknown** also defines two methods that help components do garbage collection via reference counting. The two methods—*AddRef* and *Release*—let components increment and decrement a reference counter every time a client connects to an interface or releases it. When the reference count of a component goes to zero, you can safely delete it from memory—this is DCOM's version of component life cycle management. Figure 26-3 shows the anatomy of a DCOM (or ActiveX) component.

OLE's Automation and Scripting Services

OLE's Automation and Scripting services allow *server* components to be controlled by automation clients (also called automation *controllers*). An automation controller is typically driven by a scripting language or from a tool such as Visual Basic. Automation is based on OLE's dynamic invocation facilities called *dispatchable*

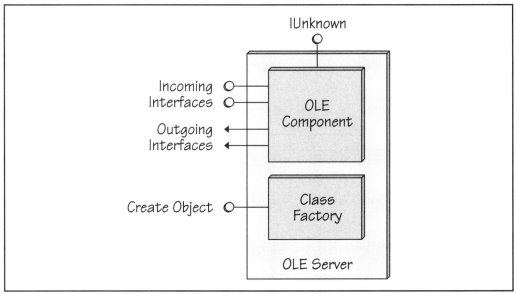

Figure 26-3. The Anatomy of a DCOM Component.

interfaces. Like CORBA's dynamic method invocations, OLE's dynamic dispatch allows a client to invoke a method or manipulate a property through a late-binding mechanism. A dispatch ID is passed to an *invoke* method that resolves which method to call at run time.

Of course, automation clients must discover at run time what interfaces an automation server provides. This includes the methods an interface supports and the types of parameters that are required by each method. It also includes the properties a component exposes to its clients. Clients can obtain all this information at run time from *Type Libraries*—the OLE equivalent of a CORBA Interface Repository. How is this information entered in Type Libraries in the first place? You create it using an Object Definition Language (ODL) file that describes the interfaces.

OLE's Uniform Data Transfer

Like OpenDoc, OLE provides a generalized intercomponent data transfer mechanism that can be used in a wide range of situations and across a variety of media. Data can be exchanged using protocols such as the clipboard, drag-and-drop, links, or compound documents. The exchanged data can be dragged and then pasted or dropped into the same document, a different document, or a different application. The actual data transfer can take place over shared memory or using storage files. Asynchronous notifications can be sent to a linked client when source data changes. OLE's uniform data transfer provides a single interface for transferring data that works with multiple protocols.

OLE's Structured Storage and Persistence Services

OLE's Structured Storage System provides a file system within a file. The current implementation of this architecture is called *compound files* (previously known as *DocFiles*). Compound files introduce a layer of indirection on top of existing file systems. With Cairo, compound files will become the actual file system. Compound files break a file into a collection of *storages* (or directories) and *streams* (or raw data values). You can use this internal directory system to organize the contents of a document. OLE allows components to control their own storage in the compound document. The directories describe the streams; the hierarchical structure makes it easy for OLE objects to navigate within the document. Compound files provide some rudimentary transaction facilities for committing information to storages or restoring their previous states.

OLE also provides a set of interfaces that allow a client to communicate with a *persistent* object. These interfaces define the capabilities of a persistent object. At one end, a persistent object may know nothing about structured storage; it only knows how to store and manipulate its state in a regular file. At the other end, an object knows how to navigate the storages of a compound file. In the middle are objects that only know how to manipulate a single stream. In OLE, the client creates an object and then hands it a persistent store that contains state information. The object then initializes its state by reading the storage object. The client can also ask the object to write its state to storage.

OLE provides a persistent naming service called *monikers*. A moniker is an intelligent name that can be bound to some persistent data. All monikers have the same interface, but they can have different binding algorithms to find the data that's associated with a name. The binding algorithm is defined by the Class ID that implements the moniker. For example, monikers can serve as aliases (or nicknames) for a remote file, an item within a file, or a SQL query that extracts data from a relational database.

OLE's Compound Document Service

When you think of OLE, probably the first thing that comes to mind is compound documents.

— Chris Weiland et al.
Windows Tech Journal

OLE's compound document service defines the interfaces between a *container* application and the *server* components that it controls. In this case, a server is a visual component that "serves" a container. The container/server interfaces define protocols for activating the servers and editing their contents "in-place" within the container's window. The container applications manage storage and the window for displaying a compound document's data. Each server component controls its own data. You can use the container/server relationship to visually integrate data of different formats, such as bitmaps or sound clips. The server data is *embedded* if it is stored within the container's compound document. It is *linked* if it is stored in another container's file.

OCXs are a special kind of server. They combine OLE automation and compound document technology to create very flexible container/server relationships. OCXs are embedded servers that support in-place editing. More importantly, OCXs use automation to expose their methods and properties to their containers. The containers also use automation to receive event notifications from OCXs whenever anything of interest happens. In addition, a container maintains *ambient* properties that inform OCXs of their surroundings. OCXs can use this information to blend with the document and other OCXs. The container, of course, exposes its ambient properties using automation.

CONCLUSION

It's clear that Microsoft is creating an entire distributed object foundation around OLE and DCOM. OLE is an integral part of Windows 95. You just can't ignore it. In distributed objects, DCOM is about two years behind CORBA. Even on the desktop, OLE's compound document technology is not as good as OpenDoc's—one problem is that Microsoft has too much "legacy" code to accommodate on existing interfaces. Objects are really a new paradigm. It will be very costly for Microsoft to break down its existing monolithic application code base into medium-grained components. The move to components will be much less costly for vendors that do not have a large legacy code base to protect.

The best OMG and Microsoft can do—short of having Microsoft give up DCOM for CORBA, or vice versa—is to create a single two-way gateway specification between CORBA and DCOM. So OMG, with help from Microsoft, is currently specifying two gateway standards between CORBA and DCOM: one that targets local DCOM, and a later one that targets distributed DCOM.

Interoperability between OLE's non-distributed DCOM and CORBA is a snap—implementations are available from IBM, Iona, Candle, Visual Edge and Digital. Eventually DCOM and CORBA will interoperate. But because they have dissimilar object models, the components will never be able to fully collaborate across object environments. Each model will have its own rules of engagement. Component providers will most likely have to choose between OpenDoc/CORBA versus OLE/DCOM. It won't be an easy decision.

Part 8

Client/Server

and the Internet

An Introduction to Part 8

The Web may be sparking the last gold rush of the millennium.

> — *Tom Halfhill, Senior Editor*
> *BYTE Magazine*
> *(March, 1996)*

For the Internet specifically, we were quite aware that something very significant was going on, but I don't think anyone expected it to become so popular so quickly.

> — *Bill Gates, Chairman*
> *Microsoft*
> *(April, 1996)*

Do you Martians still have gold rush fever? This part is about client/server with the World Wide Web, which promises to be "the last gold rush of the millennium." If nothing else, it's the last gold rush we cover in this book. In case you haven't noticed yet, the Web is the hottest topic on our planet. There's no place to hide from it. It's everywhere—in the movies, on the billboards, in the tabloids, and on late night TV. It's our planet's last great technological frontier and our brightest hope for the future. It's a virtual world—free of hunger and disease. It's the fastest way to make a billion dollars.

So what does this all have to do with client/server? Everything. For starters, the Web is the world's largest client/server application. It's the first application that brings client/server to the masses. And it is the first client/server application of intergalactic proportions. Yes, you will be able to interact with Michael Jackson's avatar. What's an avatar? It's your electronic persona on the Web. The Web is creating *habitats* inhabited by avatars. Welcome to the brave new *virtual worlds*.

But the Web is more than fun, games, and avatars; it's also big business. The patrons of the Web—meaning those who are paying for the free goodies—are the stock market and our largest corporations. These patrons look at the Web and see Intranets and electronic commerce. *Intranets* allow them to rebuild their private corporate networks using Web client/server technology. *Electronic commerce* is about turning the Web into the world's largest shopping mall; it's a new frontier for commerce of all sorts. The stock market looks at the Web and sees one thing— money. So it keeps the stocks going up. It's a self-feeding frenzy.

So when will this bubble burst? It won't, if the Web fulfills its promises. Right now, all we're getting are "cool" Web pages and lots of hype and noise. To become the world's largest shopping mall, the Web needs to build on a solid client/server foundation. We will make the case that the Web infrastructure needs to blend with distributed objects to fulfill its intergalactic destiny. Objects let us create more realistic virtual worlds called *shippable places*. Places are containers of components that can be shipped from the server to the clients to create a new generation of mobile Web-based client/server applications.

Part 8 covers the Web from a client/server perspective. We start with today's hyperlinked Web. We look at the client/server technology behind the Web pages and the hypertext links. Then we go over the extensions that are being used to make the Web more interactive—that is, to make it behave more like a typical client/server system. These extensions include HTML forms and tables on the client side and the CGI protocol on the server side. CGI is being used to attach any type of server to the Web, but it's just a Band-Aid; it does not provide a long-term solution. We also look at the security extensions for the Web—including firewalls, certificates, and secured protocols such as SSL and S-HTTP. These acronyms will become perfectly clear by the time you finish reading this part.

The heart of Part 8 is the Object Web. We believe that the Web is moving to objects in a big way. Java is just the first step in this progression. The Object Web chapters cover Java in depth. Then we look at how ORBs—such as CORBA and Network OLE—extend Java for interobject communications. We also look at how compound documents will be used as containers of Web components that can be directly manipulated in-place. The containers can also be used to ship places (or virtual worlds) from the servers to the clients. The Object Web is a 3-tier client/server architecture that combines the best of two worlds—ORBs and the Web. The Object Web will also be a great incubator of components built using Java, OLE, and OpenDoc—it's the closest thing to component heaven.

We conclude Part 8 with a market and product overview. It's your guide to the gold. Before you start on this trek, it's important to understand that life on the Internet is measured in dog years, not human years. This means that Internet technology moves very rapidly. The Internet seems to transform itself every two years. We're currently entering the Java phase of the Internet moving to the Object Web. So wear your seat belts tight because this will be a fast-moving ride with lots of bumps. We hope you'll have fun.

Chapter 27

Web Client/Server: The Hypertext Era

The Web will drive the client/server reengineering revolution. This will be an industrial revolution whose scope makes the PC industry of the early 1980s seem like a small family business by comparison.

*— Charles Ferguson, Chairman
Vermeer
(November, 1995)*

Over the last five years, the Internet grew from a private sandbox for university researchers to a client/server application of intergalactic proportions. The "killer application" that brought the Internet into the public consciousness is the *World Wide Web*—the Web, for short. It's the world's most widely deployed client/server application. The Web consists of over 100,000 connected servers supporting 500,000 home pages and 15 million users (growing at the rate of 1 million per month). As we go to press, the size of the Web is doubling every 53 days, with 3,000 new sites added daily. Instead of dealing with thousands of individual servers, users experience the Net as a huge virtual disk crammed with every form of information, which is all available at the click of a mouse. The world becomes one big *hyperlinked* document.

In late 1993, the Mosaic graphical Web browser introduced the first true client/server application environment on top of the Internet. This was the birth of Web-style client/server. This new model of client/server consists of thin, portable, "universal" clients that talk to superfat servers. Web client/server does certain things very well; for example, electronic publishing, personal bulletin boards, document sharing, and discussion groups. In 1995, the Web technology was extended to support slightly more interactive client/server applications through the use of HTML forms and the CGI server protocol. In addition, Netscape and others introduced new protocols to make the Web more secure. Examples of these new protocols include *Secure Sockets Layer (SSL)*, *Secure HTTP (S-HTTP)*, and all types of firewalls.

The Web as we know it today is not the fabled Information Highway—"the mother of all client/server systems." To achieve this lofty goal, we need cheap abundant bandwidth and a marriage of the Web with distributed object technology. Java is the first step in this direction. Figure 27-1 shows the progression of Web technologies. In 1994, the Web was mainly a giant—and very trendy—unidirectional medium for publishing and broadcasting electronic documents. In late 1995, the Web became a more interactive client/server application platform; the *Common Gateway Interface (CGI)* is now being used to access every known server environment.

In 1996, the Web finally discovered objects. Java is the first step toward creating a client/server *Object Web*. Is there life after Java? This may come as a surprise, but

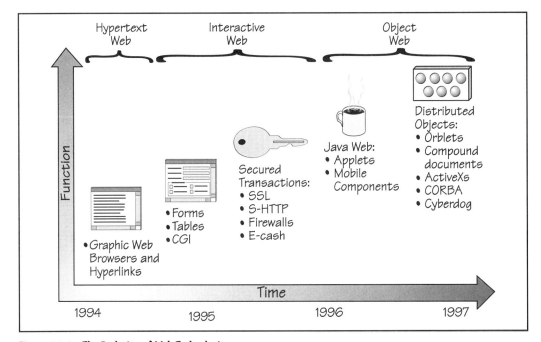

Figure 27-1. The Evolution of Web Technologies.

the answer is yes. Java is a necessary but not sufficient step toward creating an Object Web. The next step requires even more object caffeine. We're talking about blending Java with a distributed object infrastructure; your cup of Java will soon include CORBA ORBlets, OLE COMlets, and compound document frameworks such as OLE and OpenDoc. We hope you like your coffee strong.

Is there anything left unsaid about the Internet? Could the computer press, tabloids, local dailies, and national magazines have missed anything? We think so, which is why we're about to embark on a five-chapter tour that covers the Web from a client/server perspective.

This chapter starts the tour by covering the hypertext era of the Web; it introduces the foundation client/server technologies on which the Web is built—including HTML, HTTP, and Web browsers. Chapter 28, "Web Client/Server: The Interactive Era," introduces the interactive Web technologies—including forms, CGI, and the security protocols that are needed for Web-based electronic commerce. Chapter 29, "Web Client/Server: The Java Object Era," introduces the Java Web. Chapter 30, "Web Client/Server: The Distributed Object Era," covers the Object Web beyond Java; it's about the marriage of Java with distributed component technologies such as CORBA, OLE, and OpenDoc. Finally, Chapter 31, "Web Client/Server: Meet the Players," concludes the tour with an overview of the Web client/server market.

CLIENT/SERVER, WEB STYLE

The Internet is the world's largest experiment in anarchy.

— *Eric Schmidt, CTO, Sun*
(October, 1995)

The Web builds client/server order on top of what Sun's Eric Schmidt calls, "the world's largest experiment in anarchy." In its enormously popular first incarnation, the Web is simply a global hypertext system. *Hypertext* is a software mechanism that links documents to other related documents on the same machine or across networks. The linked document can itself contain links to other documents, and this can go on forever. A link can also point to other external resources such as image files, sound clips, or executable programs. The Web could eventually link every document produced on this planet.

The beauty of the Web is in its simplicity. The Web client/server model achieves its intergalactic reach by using highly portable protocols on top of TCP/IP. Portability, platform-independence, and content-independence are emphasized at every level—they're the mantras of the Web architects. So what makes hundreds of thousands of distributed servers behave like a single application? This magic is created by introducing four new technologies on top of the existing Internet infrastructure: graphical Web browsers, the HTTP RPC, HTML-tagged documents, and the URL global naming convention. We will explain what all this means in the next sections.

The Web Protocols: How They Play Together

At the moment, 99% of the Web is static publishing, where you put out pages and they don't change.

> — *Steve Jobs, CEO*
> *NeXT*
> *(August, 1995)*

The first generation Web applications were mostly read-only and static, which means that they were simple. By dealing with read-only documents, Web designers were able to avoid the thorny issues of distributed multiserver application design—such as security, transactions, and synchronized updates. A Web server simply returns documents when clients ask for them by name.

Because it is so simple and useful, the Web was able to mushroom. Although most of us don't think of the Web in this way, it has become the most visible demonstration of the power of intergalactic client/server computing today. The first generation Web applications are built on the following technologies and protocols:

- ■ ***The Internet is the global backbone***. The Web achieves its global reach by using the Internet as its backbone. The Internet is the world's largest public network. It consists of over 30,000 interconnected networks that span across 70 countries. These networks extend deep inside corporations as well as people's homes. The number of networks is expected to double each year. The beauty of the Web is that its application protocols are Internet-ready—they run on top of TCP/IP. In less than two years, the Web has become the graphical face of the Internet. Today, more than half of the 30 million people that access the Internet use the Web as their front-end. The Web subsumes most of the existing Internet application protocols—including the *Simple Mail Transfer Protocol (SMTP)*, *Telnet*, *File Transfer Protocol (FTP)*, *Network News Transfer Protocol (NNTP)*, and *Gopher*.

- ■ ***The Internet is the private backbone***. The Web model of client/server encourages the creation of private corporate networks—called *Intranets*—using existing Internet and Web technology. The idea is that the same interfaces, protocols, and networking infrastructure can be used for both public and private networks. The private Webs exist behind secure Internet *firewalls*. You could even set up an Intranet on the public Internet using secured communication links such as SSL or S-HTTP. We cover these protocols in the next chapter.

■ ***URLs are used to globally name and access all Web resources***. The *Unified Resource Locator (URL)* protocol provides a consistent intergalactic naming scheme to identify all Web resources—including documents, images, sound clips, and programs. URLs fully describe where a resource lives and how to get to it. URLs support the newer Web protocols—such as HTTP—as well as older Internet protocols such as FTP, Gopher, WAIS, and News.

■ ***HTTP is used to retrieve URL-named resources***. The Web provides an RPC-like protocol—called the *Hypertext Transfer Protocol (HTTP)*—for accessing resources that live in URL space. HTTP is a stateless RPC that 1) establishes a client/server connection, 2) transmits and receives parameters including a returned file, and 3) breaks the client/server connection. HTTP clients and servers use the Internet's MIME data representations to describe (and negotiate) the contents of messages.

■ ***HTML is used to embed hyperlinks and to describe the logical structure of Web documents.*** The *Hypertext Markup Language (HTML)* is the lingua franca of Web documents. The Web is a gigantic collection of HTML documents linked together to form the world's largest file server. A Web document—or *page*—is a plain ASCII text file with embedded HTML commands. The HTML commands—also known as *tags*—are used to describe the structure of a document, provide font and graphics information, and define hyperlinks to other Web pages and Internet resources. HTML documents live in HTTP servers—also known as *Web servers*. The beauty of HTML is that it is simple and portable. In addition, server programs can easily generate HTML-tagged text files in response to client requests.

■ ***Web browsers are universal clients***. A Web browser is a minimalist client that interprets information it receives from a server, and displays it graphically to a user. The client is simply there to interpret the server's commands and render the contents of an HTML page to a user. Web browsers—like those from Netscape and Spyglass—are primarily interpreters of HTML commands. The browser executes the HTML commands to properly display text and images on a specific GUI platform; it also navigates from one page to another using the embedded hypertext links. HTTP servers produce platform-independent content that clients can then request. A server does not know a PC client from a Mac client—all Web clients are created equal in the eyes of their Web servers. Browsers are there to take care of all the platform-specific details.

So this is the Web client/server story in a nutshell. The devil is in the details, which we cover next. If you don't care about the details then just read the next section and move on. You'll at least know the names of the key protocols and client/server pieces. This alone should make you quite dangerous.

Your First Web Client/Server Interaction

The model we see emerging is a universal client, able to navigate the local network or the Internet and to go to any application at any point in time.

> — Marc Andreessen, VP
> Netscape
> (September, 1995)

Figure 27-2 shows how the Web client and server pieces play together:

1. ***You select a target URL***. A Web client/server interaction starts when you specify a target URL from within your Web browser. You do this by either clicking on a hypertext link, picking a URL off a list, or by explicitly typing in the URL (this is typically your last resort).

2. ***Browser sends an HTTP request to server***. The browser takes the URL you specified, embeds it inside an HTTP request, and then sends it to the target server.

3. ***Server comes to life and processes the request***. On the receiving side, the HTTP server is spinning in a loop, waiting for requests to arrive on its well-known port (the default port is 80 for HTTP). The incoming request causes a socket connection to be established between the client and the server. The server receives the client's message, finds the requested HTML file, ships it back to the client along with some status information, and then closes the connection.

4. ***Browser interprets the HTML commands and displays the page contents***. The browser displays a status indicator while waiting to receive the requested URL. When it finally receives the URL, the browser looks at the type. If it's an HTML file, it interprets the tags and displays the contents in its window. Otherwise, it invokes a *helper* application that's associated with a particular resource type and hands it the returned file. The helper displays the contents in its own window or in an agreed upon area within the browser's window. For example, most browsers don't know what to do with a video file, so they hand it to a video player—the helper—which then plays the movie in a separate window.

This primitive client/server interaction accounts for over 90% of today's Web transactions. In the next chapter, we go over the CGI protocols and browser forms and explain how they extend the basic model. But before moving to the next

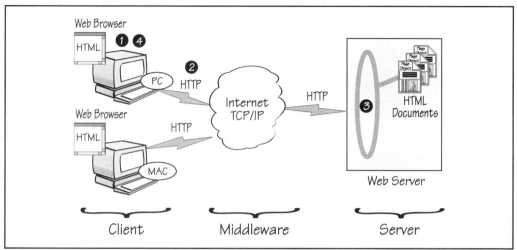

Figure 27-2. A Web Client/Server Interaction.

chapter, we must first cover the details of the URL, HTTP, and HTML protocols. You must understand how these protocols work before you tackle CGI, forms, Internet security, and Web objects.

SO WHAT EXACTLY IS A URL?

Information wants to be free—free of platform, output destination, formatting instructions, proprietary file formats, and physical location.

> — *Art Fuller, Data Based Advisor*
> *(June, 1995)*

A URL provides a general-purpose naming scheme for specifying Internet resources using a string of printable ASCII characters. The printable characters enable you to send URLs in mail messages, print them on your business card, or display them on billboards. A typical URL consists of four parts (see Figure 27-3):

■ ***The protocol scheme*** tells the Web browser which Internet protocol to use when accessing a resource on a server. In addition to HTTP, URL supports all major Internet protocols—including Gopher, FTP, News, Mailto, and WAIS. *HTTP* is the Web's native protocol; it points to Web pages and server programs. *Gopher* is a precursor to the Web; it displays information on servers as a hierarchy of menus. *FTP* is oldest Internet protocol for retrieving files. *News* is a discussion group protocol that lets you specify a newsgroup or article. *Mailto* lets you send mail to a designated e-mail address. *WAIS* lets you specify the domain name of a target database to be searched as well as a list of search criteria. Of course, the protocol scheme that you choose will directly affect the interpretation of path information within the URL.

■ **The server name** is usually an Internet host domain name that identifies the site on which the server is running. Note that you can also use numeric IP addresses and include an optional user name or password. However, numeric IP addresses are hard to remember. Also, putting a password in a URL is not a secure way to access a resource.

■ **The port number** identifies a program that runs on a particular server. You explicitly specify a port number after a server name using a colon (:) as the separator. If you do not specify a port number, the browser will direct the call to a well-known port. For example, HTTP resources are on port 80, Gopher uses port 70, FTP files are on port 21, and so on.

■ **The path to a target resource** starts with the forward slash after the host and port number. The interpretation of this field varies depending on the resource you access. The most common representation consists of a set of directory paths that lead to a particular file.

As you will see in the next chapter, you can also use URLs to specify specialized server functions. For example, you can specify a search by appending to the end of a URL a question mark followed by a query string. You can only do this with servers that support this function—currently, this means HTTP, Gopher, and WAIS.

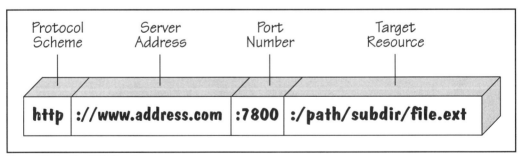

Figure 27-3. The URL Structure.

THE WORLD'S SHORTEST HTML TUTORIAL

Personal Web pages are the '90s equivalent of home video, except that you don't have to visit someone else's house to fall asleep—you can do so in the comfort of your own home.

— *Ray Valdes, Senior Editor*
Dr. Dobb's Journal
(September, 1995)

HTML is an elaborate protocol, and we can't possibly cover it completely in the next few pages. So short of writing another book, we will hit on some of the highlights of HTML to give you a feeling for what it does. We also cover some of HTML's more advanced features in the next two chapters—including the form extensions for data entry and the new Java applet tags.

If you get a sinking feeling in the next few sections that HTML—to quote from Yogi Berra—is "like deja vu all over again," you're probably right. The technology is definitely late 70s retro. HTML is rooted in the ISO SGML standard, which has been around for quite some time. However, bear in mind that retro is a small price to pay to achieve universality. HTML was designed to be fully portable across every conceivable GUI, operating system, CPU architecture, and file system. You can print and view HTML documents on machines that have barebone displays; it's truly a minimalist protocol.

How To Mark Up Text in HTML

An HTML document is an ordinary text file whose appearance is controlled by magical tags that are embedded within the text. Whenever you want to highlight some text—for example, an italicized word or a link to another page—you place either a single tag or a pair of tags around it. *Tags* are non-case-sensitive commands surrounded by angle brackets. A tag pair consists of a command, then some text, and finally the inverse command—represented as the command with a slash in front of it. The first tag in the command pair applies the command while the second tag turns it off. This means that the command only applies to the text enclosed within tag pairs.

Figure 27-4 shows some of the more common HTML text markup tags and the output they produce on a typical Web browser. Note that we use the <BR> tag to force line breaks.

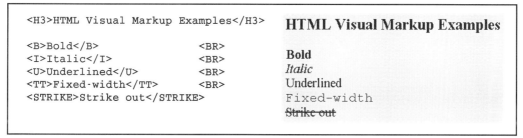

Figure 27-4. HTML: Visual Markup Examples.

The General Structure of an HTML Document

Right now, people just want to connect easily. Once that's accomplished, they'll see that content is what it's about.

> — Christine Comaford, Columnist
> PC Week
> (March, 1996)

Figure 27-5 shows the structure of an HTML document. The structure primarily is there to help a browser understand how a document is organized. A well-structured HTML document begins with <HTML> and ends with </HTML>. In addition, every HTML document should have a header section at the top, bracketed by <HEAD> and </HEAD> tags, and a body section bracketed by <BODY> and </BODY> tags. The header contains information that describes the contents of the body, its title, URL, and whether the document is searchable. A Web browser displays the text marked off by <TITLE> and </TITLE> tags in the title bar of its window. This is also the text that describes the document in a user's hotlist (or *bookmark* list).

The <BODY> and </BODY> tags contain the portion of the document that you see displayed within the client area of a Web browser's window. This is where you view an HTML document's contents. HTML lets you further structure a document's body using a hierarchy of headings that can be nested up to six levels deep. You specify the headings in descending order using the tags <H1> through <H6>. When a Web browser encounters a heading tag, it terminates the current paragraph and displays the heading text using a left-aligned visually distinct font. Figure 27-6 shows a screen capture of a particular Web browser's rendition of the HTML in Figure 27-5.

```
<HTML>
  <HEAD>
    <TITLE>My Document</TITLE>
  </HEAD>
  <BODY>
      <H1>This is an H1 Heading</H1>
      <H2>This is an H2 Heading</H2>
      <H3>This is an H3 Heading</H3>
      <H4>This is an H4 Heading</H4>
      <H5>This is an H5 Heading</H5>
      <H6>This is an H6 Heading</H6>
  </BODY>
</HTML>
```

Figure 27-5. HTML for My Document.

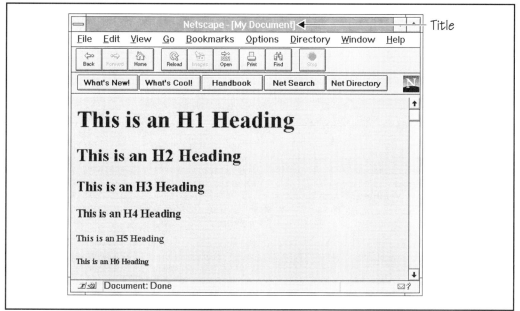

Figure 27-6. A Web Browser's Rendition of My Document's HTML.

How To Structure the Flow of Text in an HTML Document

You typically break the text within a document into paragraphs that you place under various headings. You use the <P> tag to indicate a new paragraph; <HR> to draw a horizontal line; and <PRE> to introduce a block of preformatted style text—such as a program listing or a table. Note that <P> and <HR> are singleton tags—they do not require </P> or </HR> pairs.

Figure 27-7 is an example of an HTML document that uses the <P>, <HR>, and <PRE> tags. Figure 27-8 shows how this document is rendered by a typical Web browser. Notice that all the text between <P> tags is reflowed by the Web browser to fit the window size, fonts, and general shape of the document. Most Web browsers use one line height's worth of white space to set each paragraph apart from the next. The horizontal rule is drawn with some amount of white space above and below it. You should use horizontal rules whenever possible. They help create a uniform appearance and are also much more efficient to transfer over the network than a bitmap or a line's worth of underscore characters.

Finally, note that the text marked off by <PRE> and </PRE> is not very attractive, but it respects the layout we specified in the HTML. We basically told the browser that the <PRE> text is off limits. Consequently, the browser can't reflow the text, make it pretty, or use an attractive proportional font to display it. Instead, it displays the text "as is," using a nonproportional font that maintains the white space, tabs, carriage returns, and strings of ASCII spaces. <PRE> tags are the only way to present tabular information on browsers that do not support HTML 3's table tags. We cover table tags in the next chapter.

```
<HTML>
<HEAD>
<TITLE>The Essential Distributed Objects Survival Guide</title>
<BODY>
<H1>Zog is Back</H1>
<P>Zog, the lovable, green, perpetually perplexed Martian, has returned,
this time to explore the world of distributed objects.  This new Survival
Guide by Bob Orfali, Dan Harkey, and Jeri Edwards provides a
comprehensive coverage of the big three object/component technologies:
CORBA, COM/OLE, and OpenDoc.  Here's a snapshot of the Table of Contents:

<PRE>
Part 1. Client/Server With Distributed Objects           42 pages
Part 2. CORBA: The Distributed Object Bus               174 pages
Part 3. Frameworks for Business Objects and Components  122 pages
Part 4. OpenDoc Under the Hood                           86 pages
Part 5. OLE/COM Under the Hood                          108 pages
Part 6. Component Nirvana: Client/Server With Parts      72 pages
<HR>
</PRE>
</BODY>
</HTML>
```

Figure 27-7. HTML for "The Essential Distributed Objects."

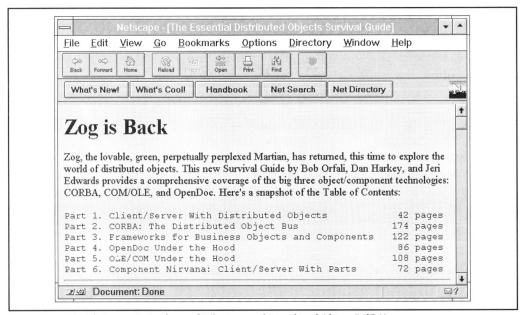

Figure 27-8. A Web Browser's Rendition of "The Essential Distributed Objects" HTML.

HTML Lists

HTML lets you specify a variety of list format types in your text—including unordered lists using the <UL> tag; ordered lists using the <OL> tag; definition lists using the <DL> tag; directory lists using the <DIR> tag; and menus using the <MENU> tag. You can also nest lists within lists. Most Web browsers display unordered lists using a hierarchy of differently shaped and colored bullets. Figure 27-9 shows the HTML for ordered and unordered lists and how they are displayed by a typical Web browser.

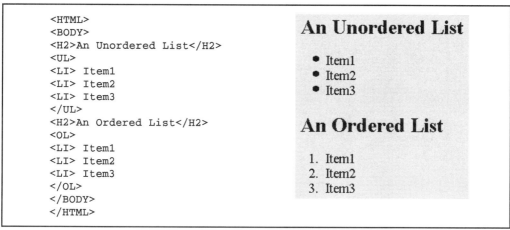

Figure 27-9. HTML Lists.

Embedding Images in Documents

Today, you can't have a "cool" Web page without embedding one or more in-line images within your text. In fact, some say that cool graphics is probably the main reason why the Web exploded out of nowhere in 1994 and eclipsed its text-only predecessors—for example, Gophers. You embed an image in your documents with the <IMG> tag. This tag includes an attribute—called SRC—that contains the URL of the external picture file or the name of a local file. For example, <IMG SRC= "zog.gif">. Attributes only appear in the first tag of tag-pair; they provide additional directives to the browser. Most Web browsers support the 8-bit GIF format that displays images in 256 colors. A few support the "true color" 24-bit JPEG format. JPEG can display up to 16 million colors, if your hardware supports it.

Second-generation Web browsers—such as Netscape Navigator—use background threads to retrieve graphics. This lets you scroll through the text of a document or jump to another document before the browser fully downloads the graphic elements. The browser must merge the images into the displayed text using the layout rules that you specify with the optional ALIGN parameter. The default alignment is BOTTOM, which means that the image aligns with the bottom of the text. Figure 27-10 shows the "cool" version of the Distributed Objects page. All we did is insert <IMG SRC= "zog.gif" ALIGN=RIGHT> after the <P> tag. This tells the Web browser to flow the text around Zog's image, on the left-hand side.

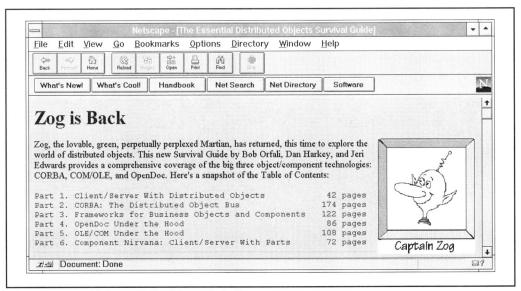

Figure 27-10. A Web Browser's Rendition of Zog's Picture.

Hyperlinks

In our opinion, what really made the Web explode out of nowhere are hyperlinks. They provide the hooks that let you transparently navigate from server to server by simply clicking the mouse. You hyperlink your document to other documents or to other locations in the same document using a pair of *anchor* tags that look like this: <A HREF="Target URL"> This is a hot link</A>.

You insert between the <A> and </A> tags the text that the user can click on to jump to the linked page. Most browsers highlight and underline the text to make it stand out. In addition to text, you can also place an <IMG> tag to hotspot an in-line graphic. The "very cool" hotspots—or visual links—combine text with graphics.

The HREF—or reference attribute—specifies the target document. You can specify the URL in one of three ways: 1) *Absolute*, which means it contains the full hostname and filename of the target document; 2) *Relative*, which means that the target's hostname and starting directory for the path are the same as the document containing the anchor tag; and 3) *Local*, which means that the file resides on the client machine, not on the Web server.

HTML links also let you point to other anchors within an HTML file. This means that you can hotlink not just to a file, but also to a specific point within a file. You do this by adding the name of the anchor after the filename separated by a pound sign "#". For example, the tag <A HREF="HTTP://host/target.html#mymarker> will transfer you to mymarker. Of course, you must first create mymarker in the target file by using an anchor tag with a NAME attribute. For example, <A NAME=mymarker">Text</A>. Figure 27-11 shows such a link.

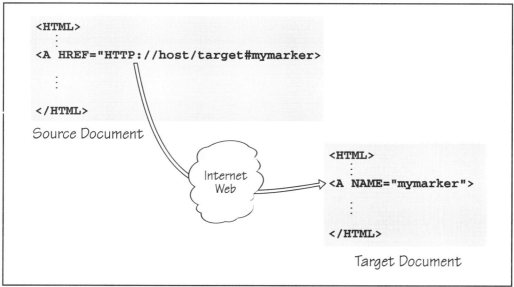

Figure 27-11. Hyperlinking to an Anchor Point Within a Target Document.

HTML Versions

There are several different versions of HTML, and you should know a little bit about them. HTML is defined by a working group of the *Internet Engineering Task Force (IETF)* and by an industry consortium called *W3C*.[1] There are several versions of HTML. The first version—called HTML 1.0—has been on the market for a couple of years. The current standard is HTML 2.0, which offers minor improvements on HTML 1.0. HTML 3.0 (originally known as HTML+), provides substantial improvements over HTML 2.0. However, according to W3C, we should not expect to see a new HTML 3.0 standard—or even HTML 2.1—anytime soon. Instead, W3C will issue piecemeal standards for different new features such as tables, applets, frames, and active objects.

---

[1] The World Wide Web Consortium (W3C) is headed by Tim Berners-Lee. It includes over 100 Web vendor companies. The purpose of W3C is to accelerate the production of Web standards.

HTTP

The *Hypertext Transfer Protocol (HTTP)* has been in use on the Web since 1990. The first version of HTTP—referred to as HTTP/0.9—was a simple protocol for raw data transfer across the Internet. HTTP/1.0—now in its sixth release—improved the protocol by introducing self-describing messages using a variant of the Internet Mail's MIME protocol.

In November 1995, the original authors of HTTP—Tim Berners-Lee, Roy Fielding, and Henrik Frystyk Nielsen—released a draft version of HTTP/1.1. This new version is backwards-compatible with HTTP/1.0, but includes more stringent requirements to ensure that its features are implemented reliably. Further on the horizon is HTTP-NG, which promises to evolve HTTP 1.X into a more efficient protocol. This chapter covers the HTTP basics. We cover some of the more advanced features in the next two chapters.

So What Exactly Is HTTP?

As we mentioned earlier, HTTP is the Web's RPC on top of TCP/IP. It is used to access and retrieve URL-named resources. The HTTP RPC is stateless. The client establishes a connection to the remote server, then issues a request. The server then processes the request, returns a response, and closes the connection. A client—typically a Web browser—requests a hypertext page, then issues a sequence of separate requests to retrieve any images referenced in the document. Once the client has retrieved the images, the user will typically click on a hypertext link and move to another document. Note that HTTP sets up a new connection for each request. The client must wait for a response before sending out a new request.

HTTP is a simple protocol because it does one thing at a time, which makes it easy to implement. This is the good news. The bad news is that HTTP is an inefficient protocol. It must establish a separate TCP connection for every request, which creates a lot of unnecessary overhead. For example, it costs HTTP six distinct connections to access a document containing five inline images—one to retrieve the document, and five to retrieve the individual images. So, HTTP does not let you issue multiple requests in parallel over the same session. As you would expect, the Web architects opted for simplicity over performance.

HTTP Data Representations

An important feature of HTTP is that it lets you pass self-describing data over the RPC. The protocol allows Web browsers to inform their server about the data representations they can understand. Clients and servers must negotiate their data representations every time a connection is made. This adds to the connection overhead. Why don't the servers keep track of their clients' attributes? Remember, HTTP servers are stateless, which means they have no recollection of previous client connections. HTTP's statelessness works well in simple client/server environments. It allows servers to function very efficiently. They pick up connections, fulfill the request, and quickly drop the connection. Note, however, that state is needed in all but the simplest client/server interactions. So this can be a problem with the current HTTP protocol. There are some very clumsy workarounds to this problem that we cover in the next chapter.

So What Does an HTTP Request Look Like?

An HTTP client/server interaction consists of a single request/reply interchange. Figure 27-12 shows the syntax of an HTTP request. It consists of a *request line*, one or more optional *request header fields*, and an optional *entity body*. The lines

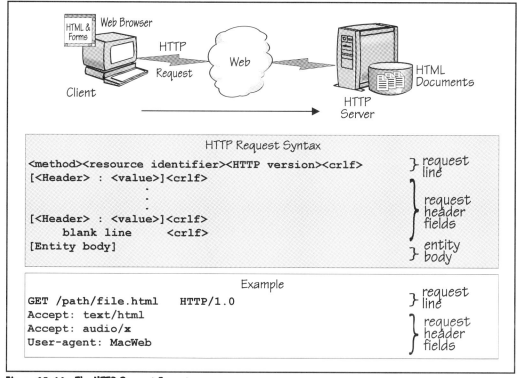

Figure 27-12. The HTTP Request Format.

are separated by a carriage-return/line-feed (crlf). The entity body is preceded by a blank line. Here are the details:

- *The request line* consists of three text fields, separated by white spaces. The first field specifies the method—or command—to be applied to a server resource. The most common method is GET, which asks the server to send a copy of the resource to the client. We cover the rest of the HTTP methods in the next details box. The second field specifies the name of the target resource; it's the URL stripped of the protocol and server domain name. The third field identifies the protocol version used by the client; for example, HTTP/1.0.

- *The request header fields* pass additional information about the request, and about the client itself, to the server. The fields act like RPC parameters. Each header field consists of a name, followed by a colon (:) and the field value. The order in which you transmit the header fields is not significant.

- *The entity body* is sometimes used by clients to pass bulk information to the server.

The bottom of Figure 27-12 is an example of an archetypical HTTP GET request—the client requests a file called file.html from the server. The first *accept* header field tells the server that the client knows how to handle text HTML files. The second accept field tells the server that the client can also handle all audio formats. Finally, the *user-agent* field lets the server know that the client is a MacWeb browser. So, the various accepts tell the server which data types the client can handle; user-agent gives the implementation name of the client. We list all the HTTP header fields in the next Details box.

HTTP At-A-Glance

Details

If you ever take a close look at the HTTP specification, you'll find all sorts of things that haven't really been implemented yet. The current crop of servers really don't do it justice.

— John Labovitz, O'Reilly

HTTP Methods

As you can see from Table 27-1, HTTP is not standing still. It is evolving into a more mature client/server protocol, at least when it comes to the methods it supports. HTTP/1.1 supports 13 methods versus 3 for HTTP/1.0. The most widely implemented methods remain GET and POST. We have already covered GET in this chapter. We will cover POST in the next chapter.

Table 27-1. HTTP Methods at a Glance.

Method	HTTP/1.0	HTTP/1.1	Method Description
GET	Y	Y	Retrieve the specified URL.
HEAD	Y	Y	Identical to GET, except that the server does not return the document in the response; it only returns the response headers. Clients use it to obtain resource metadata or to test the validity of hypertext links.
POST	Y	Y	Send this data to the specified URL.
PUT	N	Y	Store this data in the specified URL, replacing the old contents.
PATCH	N	Y	Similar to PUT, except that it contains a list of differences between the original version of the URL and the desired contents after the method is applied.
COPY	N	Y	Copy the resource identified by the URL to the specified location(s).
MOVE	N	Y	Move the resource indicated by the URL to the specified location(s). This method is equivalent to a COPY/DELETE.
DELETE	N	Y	Delete the resource identified by the URL.
LINK	N	Y	Establish one or more link relationships between the resource identified by the URL and other resources.
UNLINK	N	Y	Remove one or more link relationships from the specified URL.
TRACE	N	Y	Echo back whatever is received from the client in the entity body of the response.
OPTIONS	N	Y	Requests information about the communication options available on the request/response chain for the specified URL. It allows clients to determine the capabilities of a server without retrieving a resource.
WRAPPED	N	Y	Allows request(s) to be wrapped together and possibly encrypted to improve the security and/or privacy of the request. The destination server must unwrap the message and feed it to the appropriate handler.

HTTP Header Fields

We list the HTTP header fields in Tables 27-2 through 27-5. Again, note that HTTP is evolving very rapidly. HTTP/1.1 supports over 41 header fields versus 17 for HTTP/1.0. To help you wade through all this information, we divide the header fields into four categories: 1) *general headers*, which you can include within both request and response messages; 2) *request headers*, which can only appear within request messages; 3) *response headers*, which can only appear within response messages; and 4) *entity headers*, which can appear within requests or responses. The entity headers describe the contents of the message data; for example, a document that a server returns or form data that a client sends. We cover forms in the next chapter.

HTTP General Headers

Table 27-2. HTTP General Headers.

Header	HTTP/1.0	HTTP/1.1	Description
Cache-Control	N	Y	Contains request/response caching directives.
Connection	N	Y	Contains information that may not be forwarded to gateways.
Date	Y	Y	Contains date and time the message was originated.
Forwarded	N	Y	Contains information used by gateways to trace intermediate steps and avoid request loops.
Keep-Alive	N	Y	Contains diagnostic information.
MIME-Version	Y	Y	Contains the MIME version used to encode the message.
Pragma	Y	Y	Contains implementation directives (for example, no-cache).
Upgrade	N	Y	Lists additional communication protocols a client supports and would like to use if the server agrees.

HTTP Request Headers

Table 27-3. HTTP Request Headers.

Header	HTTP/1.0	HTTP/1.1	Description
Accept	N	Y	Lists acceptable MIME type/subtype contents.

Table 27-3. HTTP Request Headers. (Continued)

Header	HTTP/1.0	HTTP/1.1	Description
Accept-Chars	N	Y	Lists acceptable character sets.
Accept-Encoding	N	Y	Lists acceptable encodings such as compress and zip.
Accept-Language	N	Y	Lists acceptable natural languages.
Authorization	Y	Y	Passes user authentication and encryption schemes.
From	Y	Y	Contains user's Internet e-mail address.
Host	N	Y	Contains name of target host.
If-Modified-Since	Y	Y	Contains a date/time used by GET to conditionally download documents.
Proxy-Authorization	N	Y	Allows clients to present their identity to a proxy.
Refer	Y	Y	URL of document from which this request originated.
Unless	N	Y	Lists header conditions that must be met before a method is applied to a resource.
User-Agent	Y	Y	Provides client browser information.

HTTP Response Headers

Table 27-4. HTTP Response Headers.

Header	HTTP/1.0	HTTP/1.1	Description
Location	Y	Y	Returns the exact location of the resource.
Proxy-Authenticate	N	Y	Returns the encryption/authorization scheme used in this session.
Public	N	Y	Lists all the non-standard methods supported by a server.
Retry-After	N	Y	Indicates (in seconds) when to retry a service.
Server	Y	Y	Returns information about the software used on server.
WWW-Authenticate	Y	Y	Returns encryption/authorization scheme the server wants to use for all its Web interactions.

HTTP Entity Headers

Table 27-5. HTTP Entity Headers.

Header	HTTP/1.0	HTTP/1.1	Description
Allow	Y	Y	Lists methods supported by the URL resource.
Content-Encoding	Y	Y	Specifies encoding of reply such as compress and zip.
Content-Language	N	Y	Specifies natural language of reply (for example, French).
Content-Length	Y	Y	Length in bytes of entity body.
Content-Type	Y	Y	MIME content type of reply.
Content-Version	N	Y	Contains a resource version number.
Derived-From	N	Y	Identifies the previous version of the resource.
Expires	Y	Y	Contains date/time after which document is stale.
Last-Modified	Y	Y	Contains date/time when the resource was last modified.
Link	N	Y	Contains document link information.
Title	N	Y	Contains the document title.
Transfer-Encoding	N	Y	Identifies a transformation applied to the document (or message body).
URL-Header	N	Y	Contains the resource name part of the URL.

So What Does an HTTP Response Look Like?

Figure 27-12 shows the syntax of an HTTP response. It consists of a *response header line*, one or more optional *response header fields*, and an optional *entity body*. The lines are separated by a carriage-return/line-feed (crlf). The entity body must be preceded by a blank line. Here are the details:

■ ***The response header line*** returns the HTTP version, the status of the response, and an explanation of the returned status.

■ ***The response header fields*** return information that describe the server's attributes and the returned HTML document to the client. Each header field consists of a name, followed by a colon (:) and the field value. The order in which the server returns the header fields is not significant.

■ *The entity body* typically contains an HTML document that a client has requested.

The bottom of Figure 27-13 shows a typical server's response to a GET request. The result code 200 indicates that the request was successful. The *server* header field identifies the server as a NCSA/1.3. The *MIME-version* field indicates that the server supports MIME 1.0 (see next Details box). The *content-type* field describes the returned object as being a text/HTML document. The *content-length* field indicates the document length. This is followed by the HTML document itself—the object of the request. The server sends the requested data and then drops the TCP/IP connection. That's all there is to it. Congratulations, you're now a bona fide HTTP expert.

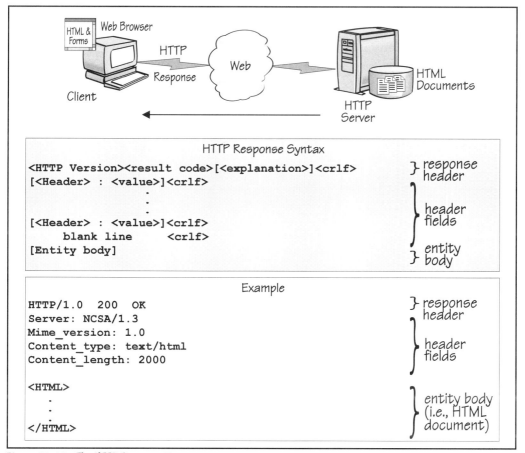

Figure 27-13. The HTTP Response Format.

HTTP and MIME

Details

HTTP borrows heavily from the *Internet Mail* (RFC 822) and the *Multipurpose Internet Mail Extensions (MIME)* (RFC 1521), which provides extensible mechanisms for transmitting multimedia e-mail. In case you're interested, RFC 822 deals mostly with the headers that appear at the top of your Internet Mail, but it does very little to describe the contents of the mail. MIME supplements RFC 822 by specifying additional headers that describe what sorts of data the message body contains. For example, MIME defines several headers that are used to specify if a message consists of multiple parts and how these parts are separated. A MIME header uses the familiar format "content-type: type/subtype" as in "content-type: text/html." MIME currently supports seven data types—including plain text; audio; video; still images; message, which can point to an external message; multipart messages in which each part can have a different type; and application-specific data. Each MIME type can also have subtypes.

It should come as no surprise that HTTP's content-type headers are very MIME-like. However, HTTP itself is not a MIME-compliant application. HTTP's RPC-like performance requirements differ substantially from those of Internet Mail. Consequently, the HTTP architects chose not to obey the constraints imposed by RFC 822 and MIME for mail transport. But even though HTTP is not MIME-compliant, you can include a *MIME-version* header field in a message to indicate what version of the MIME protocol was used to construct the message content-type headers. ❏

Conclusion

In five minutes on the Web, you suddenly understand Marshall McLuhan. The Web implodes the planet and places it on your desk. In a stroke, all the world is hypertext.

— *Art Fuller, Data Based Advisor*

This concludes our whirlwind tour of the technologies that form the basis for the hypertext era of Web client/server. This relatively simple technology lets us very effectively construct interconnected webs of hyperlinked nodes that mirror the distributed nature of information. The webs are malleable, easy to restructure, and can support arbitrary complex collections of documents. In the next chapter, we explore how the Web technology—HTTP and HTML—is being extended to provide better client/server interactivity.

Chapter 28

Web Client/Server: The Interactive Era

---

*W*eb technology isn't just a way to publish electronic documents. It's also a way to build networked applications that work within and across corporate boundaries. But it isn't yet a client/server developer's dream.

— *Jon Udell, Executive Editor*
BYTE Magazine
(October, 1995)

In the hypertext era, the only way you could interact with Web servers was by clicking on hyperlinks to surf between documents. However, in the middle of 1995, the Web began to go through a subtle transformation from a passive browsing medium into a more interactive client/server medium. So what triggered this transformation? The usual suspects, of course—market demand and the availability of new technology. We will spare you the "Web market explosion" story because you can get it from the headline stories in your local paper, the six o'clock news, or from your neighborhood barber. Instead, we will focus on the less glamorous extensions of HTML and HTTP that have made all this possible, including everything you ever wanted to know about forms, tables, CGI, "cgi-bin" programs, and S-HTTP.

3-TIER CLIENT/SERVER, WEB-STYLE

The Navigator is more like a 3270 terminal than anything else, with the big difference being that you don't just use that terminal to access one mainframe.

— Marc Andreessen, VP
Netscape
(September, 1995)

Web browsers are the modern renditions of yesterday's 3270 terminals. Yes, we're going back into the future. But where are the 3270 "fill-out forms?" These are the computer equivalents of the paper forms that we fill out every day of our life. It so happens that the Web is teeming with forms. They're everywhere. In case you haven't seen one, a *Web form* is an HTML page with one or more data entry fields and a mandatory "Submit" button. You click on the Submit button to send the form's data contents to a Web server. This causes the browser to collect all the inputs from the form, stuff them inside an HTTP message, and then invoke either an HTTP GET or POST method on the server side.

On the receiving end, the typical Web server does not know what to do with a form—it's not your ordinary HTML document. So the server simply turns around and invokes the program or resource named in the URL and tells it to take care of the request. The server passes the method request and its parameters to the back-end program using a protocol called the *Common Gateway Interface (CGI)*.

The back-end program executes the request and returns the results in HTML format to the Web server using the CGI protocol. The Web server treats the results like a normal document that it returns to the client. So, in a sense, the Web server acts as a conduit between the Web client and a back-end program that does the actual work. Figure 28-1 shows the elements of this new 3-tier client/server architecture, Web-style. The first tier is a Web browser that supports interactive forms; the second tier is a vanilla HTTP server augmented with CGI programs; and the third tier consists of traditional back-end servers.

In addition to forms, Netscape pioneered the concept of HTML *tables*. These are new tags that let a browser display multirow information—for example, query results received from a server—inside a graphic table widget. Many popular browsers now support the Netscape table tags. As we go to press, W3C and the IETF have published a draft document that specifies table extensions for HTML 2. Luckily, the draft is backward compatible with the Netscape extensions.

The CGI technology makes it possible for Internet clients to update databases on back-end servers. In fact, updates and inserts are at the heart of online electronic commerce. However, most online service providers will not let you update their databases without some form of iron-clad client/server security. This is where

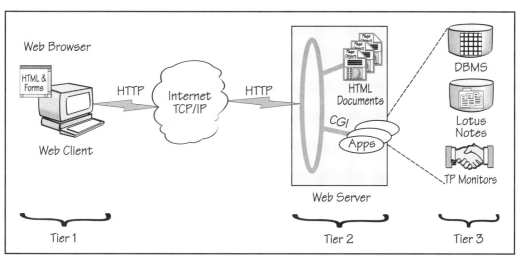

Figure 28-1. 3-Tier Client/Server, Web-Style.

protocols like *Secure Sockets Layer (SSL)*, *Secure HTTP (S-HTTP)*, and Internet firewalls come into the picture. They provide one more technology that's needed to turn the Internet into the world's largest shopping mall.

Software vendors are using the technology we just described to connect Web browsers to virtually every form of client/server system—including SQL databases, TP Monitors, groupware servers, MOM queues, e-mail backbones, distributed object brokers, and so on. All these systems now provide gateways that accept CGI requests. And they all provide *transformers* to dynamically map their data into HTML so that it can be displayed within Web browsers. In other words, the servers build a Web page "on-the-fly" to display their results.

As they said in the movie *Field of Dreams*, "If you build it they will come." In the case of the Web, they built the universal client and then the servers all came. Unfortunately, as you will soon discover, these servers live on the other side of a bottleneck called CGI.

HTML 2.0'S WEB-BASED FORMS

HTML is slowly becoming an application programming interface.

> — **Bill Machrone, VP of Technology**
> **Ziff-Davis**
> **(November, 1995)**

In September 1995, W3C published the HTML 2.0 specification, which includes *forms* that let you embed within your documents text-entry fields, radio boxes, selection lists, check boxes, and buttons. Forms are used to gather information for a CGI-based server application. Figure 28-2 shows a very useful example of a form that you can use to order pizza via the Web. It's not very pretty—most Web forms aren't—but it will do the job, especially if you're hungry. You can use forms for surveys, data entry, placing and tracking orders, database queries, and every imaginable Web transaction.

Figure 28-2. A Form Example: Pizza Hut's World Famous http://www.pizzahut.com/

Creating a form is a three-step process. First, you must create the HTML for the input form. Second, you must write the server CGI application that acts on the data from the input form. Finally, you must design the reply document a user sees after submitting the form; the HTML for the reply document is dynamically generated by the CGI program. A reply document can be very simple or quite elaborate. A simple reply may say, "We received your request; thank you very much." An elaborate reply may return thousands of table rows from an SQL database; you may have to generate an HTML table "on-the-fly" to display the results in a row-column format.

The Form Tag

A form begins with <FORM> and ends with </FORM>. By convention, you visually separate the FORM contents from the rest of an HTML document with a horizontal line (or HR tag). A document can contain one or more forms, but they can't be nested within each other.

The <FORM> tag has two mandatory attributes: METHOD and ACTION. The METHOD can be either an HTTP GET or POST; it specifies how the data entered in the various fields of the form is transmitted to the CGI server application. The ACTION attribute specifies the URL to which you send the form's contents; it must be the name of a server CGI program (or script) that can process the form's data. Here's an example of a FORM tag:

```
<FORM METHOD="POST" ACTION="HTTP://www.mylab.org/cgi-bin/sampleform">
```

So what is *cgi-bin*? It's the name of a special executable directory where CGI programs reside. This directory is usually under the direct control of a webmaster—you don't want the average user tampering with programs on your server. The /cgi-bin/ directory in a URL indicates to a Web server that the incoming HTTP request is for a CGI program. In this example, the URL causes the server to invoke—via the CGI protocol—an external program called *sampleform*.

The Form Interface Elements

You can have anything inside a form except another form. HTML 2.0 defines new tags for creating interface elements that you can place anywhere within a form to interact with a user. Figure 28-3 is a screen shot of a form that uses most of these interface elements; Figure 28-4 shows the HTML tags we used to generate this form. HTML defines three types of interface elements: input fields, text areas, and selection fields. Let's go over the details of what they each do.

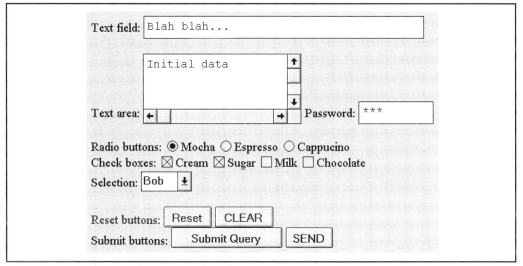

Figure 28-3. Sample Form: The Major Interface Elements.

```
<FORM METHOD="POST" ACTION="HTTP://www.mylab.org/cgi-bin/sampleform">

Text field:<INPUT TYPE="text" NAME="name" SIZE=40 Value ="Blah blah...">

<P>Text area: <TEXTAREA NAME="textarea" ROWS=3 COLS=20>Initial data
             </TEXTAREA>

Password: <INPUT TYPE="password"  NAME="password"  SIZE=10 VALUE="Mom">

<P>Radio buttons:   <INPUT TYPE="radio" name="myrb"
                     VALUE="Mocha" CHECKED>Mocha
                    <INPUT TYPE="radio" name="myrb"
                     VALUE="Espresso">Espresso
                    <INPUT TYPE="radio" name="myrb" VALUE="Cap">Cappucino

<BR>Check boxes:    <INPUT TYPE="checkbox" name="mycb"
                     VALUE=Cream CHECKED>Cream
                    <INPUT TYPE="checkbox" name="mycb"
                     VALUE=Sugar CHECKED>Sugar
                    <INPUT TYPE="checkbox" name="mycb" VALUE=Milk>Milk
                    <INPUT TYPE="checkbox" name="mycb"
                     VALUE=Chocolate>Chocolate

<BR>Selection:      <SELECT NAME="myauthor">
                    <OPTION SELECTED>Bob<OPTION>Dan
                    <OPTION>Jeri
                    </SELECT>

<P>Reset buttons:   <INPUT TYPE="reset">
                    <INPUT TYPE="reset"  VALUE="CLEAR">

<BR>Submit buttons:<INPUT TYPE="submit">
                    <INPUT TYPE="submit"  VALUE="SEND">

</FORM>
```

Figure 28-4. The HTML for the Sample Form.

INPUT Fields

You use input fields to enter and capture data. You can specify eight types of inputs with the HTML tag:

```
<INPUT TYPE="field-type" NAME="Name of field" VALUE="default value">
```

The TYPE property lets you specify an input type, which can be either text, password, hidden, checkbox, radio, reset, submit, or image. The NAME and VALUE properties create the name/value pairs that you submit to the server application. NAME specifies the symbolic name of the variable; it is not the displayed name. VALUE contains the actual data. In our example, most of the fields have default values.

You can override these defaults while interacting with the form. Let's go over the details:

- **_Text_** is the default input field; it lets you enter a single line of text data. You can specify the maximum number of characters in the field via the optional MAX-LENGTH attribute.

- **_Password_** is a text entry field that echoes asterisks (*) when you type a value into it.

- **_Hidden_** is a field that does not appear on the form; it may contain a default value that you send to the server application.

- **_Checkbox_** is a toggle field that is either checked or unchecked. You can have a set of checkboxes with the same name. The browser ignores unchecked boxes; it sends the checked items to the server as name/value pairs.

- **_Radio_** displays a group of radio buttons. All the radio buttons have the same name, and only one button can be checked. This means that a group of radio buttons only returns a single value to the server.

- **_Reset_** displays a pushbutton of type "reset." You click on the reset button to clear the contents of a form and restore its default values. You can display any words you want inside a reset button using the VALUE property. If you do not specify a NAME property, the value will not be returned to the server application.

- **_Submit_** displays a pushbutton of type "submit." When you click on submit, the browser collects the data from all the fields in a form, pairs each data item with a name, and then posts the name/value pairs to the server application. Each form must have exactly one field of type submit. HTML does not support multiple submit buttons—that is, one for each task. If you put multiple submit buttons in a form, they will all return the same thing. The FORM tag can only post the form's contents to a single server application. You can display any words you want inside a submit button using the VALUE property. If you do not specify a NAME property, the VALUE will not be returned to the server.

- **_Image_** is a special submit type; it displays a picture instead of a button. You submit the form by clicking on the image.

Now that you know what these input fields do, you may want to review the HTML in Figure 28-4. Hopefully, it will make more sense this time around.

The SELECT Field

A SELECT tag lets you create a dropdown list box from which a user picks one or more items (or options). The selected items become the values associated with the

SELECT tag's NAME attribute. If you pick more than one item, the browser will generate a "name/value" pair for each item you pick. The syntax for the SELECT tag is:

```
<SELECT NAME="Name of field" SIZE ="N" MULTIPLE>
<Option>choice 1
<Option>choice 2
        .
<Option>choice N
</SELECT>
```

You include the optional attribute MULTIPLE after the NAME string to specify multiple selections. The optional SIZE attribute lets you specify the number of visible items. In general, option menus are a good substitute for radio buttons. You can recover some space on a form by replacing radio buttons with option menus; it's a much more efficient use of space within a form's real estate.

The TEXTAREA Field

The TEXTAREA tag lets you create multiline data entry fields. In contrast, the INPUT type allows for only single-line text input. So a text area is simply a two-dimensional text box. The syntax for the TEXTAREA tag is:

```
<TEXTAREA NAME= "Name of field" ROWS="Visible rows" COLS="Visible columns">
  Default Text goes here
      .
      .
</TEXTAREA>
```

The TEXTAREA attributes, ROWS and COLS, let you specify the number of visible rows and columns in the text area. This is the field's visible dimension specified in character units. Most Web browsers let you scroll the text beyond these limits; they typically render the field's contents in a fixed-width font. You can optionally place some initial text between the TEXTAREA start and end tags. This lets you put some words in your user's mouth when the form is first displayed. Note that there is no way to specify a maximum size on entered text. A user can literally type in text forever, and there's nothing you can do to stop it.

HTML 3.0 Tables

The table tag is a very useful HTML extension that is now supported in most browsers. With the exception of a few enhancements, the tables these browsers implement are as described in the HTML 2.0 extension. In a Web client/server context, tables allow a CGI program to dynamically format the result of searches in a row/column grid format. So it is useful to give you a quick overview of how to create these tables in HTML.

A table begins with the <TABLE> tag and ends with </TABLE>. You must enclose the table elements with the surrounding <TABLE> tag pairs. HTML 3.0 currently defines four tags for creating table elements:

■ **<TR>..</TR>** defines a single table row. The number of rows in a table is exactly specified by how many of these tags it contains.

■ **<TD>..</TD>** defines a single *data cell* within a table row. A cell may contain any of the HTML tags normally present in the body of an HTML document.

■ **<TH>..</TH>** defines a header cell within a table row. A header cell is identical to a data cell in all respects, except that the text it contains is bold and centered (the default).

■ **<CAPTION>..</CAPTION>** lets you add captions to your tables. A caption can either appear at the bottom or at the top of a table; the default is top. Captions are always horizontally centered with respect to the table.

A picture is worth a thousand words, so let's put together some HTML to demonstrate tables in action. Figures 28-5 and 28-7 show the HTML for the same data content using two different table layouts; Figures 28-6 and 28-8 show how these two tables are rendered by a Web browser. Note how easy it is to give the table a new look by simply playing with the layout of the headers. The COLSPAN attribute can appear in any table cell; it specifies the number of table columns this cell should span.

```
<TABLE BORDER>
 <TR><TH>Month</TH><TH>Maui</TH>
     <TH>Kawai</TH><TH>Big Island</TH><TH>Wakiki</TH>
 </TR>
 <TR><TD>January</TD><TD>9,400</TD><TD>2,100</TD>
     <TD>3,200</TD><TD>30,900</TD>
 </TR>
 <TR><TD>February</TD><TD>8,210</TD>
     <TD>1,450</TD><TD>2,640</TD><TD>24,550</TD>
 </TR>
 <TR><TD>March</TD><TD>11,234</TD><TD>2,410</TD>
     <TD>3,560</TD><TD>31,100</TD>
 </TR>
<CAPTION ALIGN="Bottom">Hawaii Hotel Occupancy for <B>Q1, 1997</B>.
</TABLE>
```

Figure 28-5. HTML Table 1 Example.

Month	Maui	Kawai	Big Island	Wakiki
January	9,400	2,100	3,200	30,900
February	8,210	1,450	2,640	24,550
March	11,234	2,410	3,560	31,100

Hawaii Hotel Occupancy for **Q1, 1997**.

Figure 28-6. How a Typical Web Browser Renders the Table 1 Example.

```
<TABLE BORDER>
<TR><TH></TH><TH COLSPAN=4>Hawaii Hotel Occupancy: <B>Q1, 1997</B></TH>
</TR>
<TR><TH></TH><TH>Maui</TH><TH>Kawai</TH>
    <TH>Big Island</TH><TH>Wakiki</TH>
</TR>
<TR><TH>January</TH><TD>9,400</TD><TD>2,100</TD>
    <TD>3,200</TD><TD>30,900</TD>
</TR>
<TR><TH>February</TH><TD>8,210</TD><TD>1,450</TD>
    <TD>2,640</TD><TD>24,550</TD>
</TR>
<TR><TH>March</TH><TD>11,234</TD><TD>2,410</TD>
    <TD>3,560</TD><TD>31,100</TD>
</TR>
</TABLE>
```

Figure 28-7. HTML Table 2 Example.

	Hawaii Hotel Occupancy: Q1, 1997			
	Maui	**Kawai**	**Big Island**	**Wakiki**
January	9,400	2,100	3,200	30,900
February	8,210	1,450	2,640	24,550
March	11,234	2,410	3,560	31,100

Figure 28-8. How a Typical Web Browser Renders the Table 2 Example.

CGI: THE SERVER SIDE OF THE WEB

So how is a form's data passed to a program that hangs off an HTTP server? It gets passed using an end-to-end client/server protocol that includes both HTTP and CGI. The best way to explain the dynamics of the protocol is to walk you through a POST method invocation. As we explain later, you should avoid at all cost using GET even though it is the default method for submitting forms.

A CGI Scenario

Figure 28-9 shows how the client and server programs play together to process a form's request. Here's the step-by-step explanation of this interaction:

1. ***User clicks on the form's "submit" button***. This causes the Web browser to collect the data within the form, and then assemble it into one long string of *name/value* pairs each separated by an ampersand (&). The browser translates spaces within the data into plus (+) symbols. Yes, it's not very pretty.

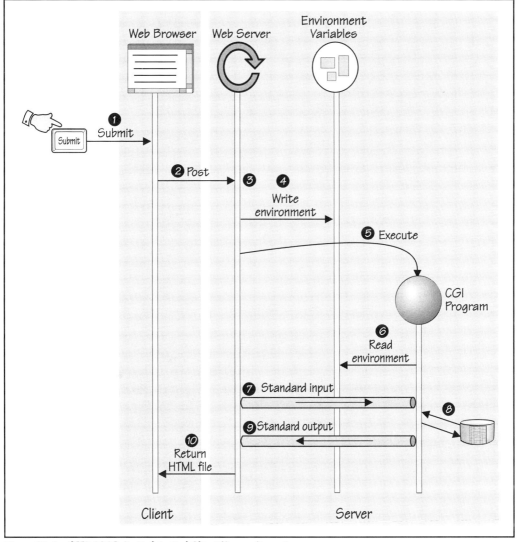

Figure 28-9. HTTP POST: An End-to-End Client/Server Scenario.

2. ***The Web Browser invokes a POST HTTP method***. This is an ordinary HTTP request that specifies a POST method, the URL of the target program in the "cgi-bin" directory, and the typical HTTP headers. The message body—HTTP calls it the "entity"—contains the form's data. This is the string: *name=value&name=value&...*

3. ***The HTTP server receives the method invocation via a socket connection***. The server parses the message and discovers that it's a POST for the "cgi-bin" program. So it starts a CGI interaction.

4. ***The HTTP server sets up the environment variables***. The CGI protocol uses *environment variables* as a shared bulletin board for communicating information between the HTTP server and the CGI program. The server typically provides the following environmental information: *server_name*, *request_method*, *path_info*, *script_name*, *content_type*, and *content_length*.

5. ***The HTTP server starts a CGI program***. The HTTP server executes an instance of the CGI program specified in the URL; it's typically in the "cgi-bin" directory.

6. ***The CGI program reads the environment variables***. In this case, the program discovers by reading the environment variables that it is responding to a POST.

7. ***The CGI program receives the message body via the standard input pipe (stdin)***. Remember, the message body contains the famous string of *name=value* items separated by ampersands (&). The *content_length* environment variable tells the program how much data is in the string. The CGI program parses the string contents to retrieve the form data. It uses the *content_length* environment variable to determine how many characters to read in from the standard input pipe. Cheer up, we're half way there.

8. ***The CGI program does some work***. Typically, a CGI program interacts with some back-end resource—like a DBMS or transaction program—to service the form's request. The CGI program must then format the results in HTML or some other acceptable MIME type. This information goes into the HTTP response entity, which really is the body of the message. Your program can also choose to provide all the information that goes into the HTTP response headers. The HTTP server will then send the reply "as is" to the client. Why would you do this? Because it removes the extra overhead of having the HTTP server parse the output to create the response headers. Programs whose names begin with "nph-" indicate that they do not require HTTP server assistance; CGI calls them *nonparsed header programs (nph)*.

9. ***The CGI program returns the results via the standard output pipe (stdout)***. The program pipes back the results to the HTTP server via its standard

output. The HTTP server receives the results on its standard input. This concludes the CGI interaction.

10. ***The HTTP server returns the results to the Web browser.*** The HTTP server can either append some response headers to the information it receives from the CGI program, or it sends it "as is" if it's an nph program.

As you can see, a CGI program is executed in real time; it gets the information and then builds a dynamic Web page to satisfy a client's request. CGI makes the Web more dynamic. In contrast, a plain HTML document is static, which means the text file does not change. CGI may be clumsy, but it does allow us to interface Web clients to general-purpose back-end services as well as to Internet search utilities such as *Yahoo!* and *InfoSeek*. You can even stretch CGI to its limits to create generalpurpose client/server programs like the Federal Express package-tracking Web page.

FYI

Windows CGI

Briefing

The Windows CGI 1.1 specification—introduced by Robert Denny—is a Windows-friendly version of the CGI protocol. Denny hopes that it will be standardized on Windows-based HTTP servers. In this scheme, the HTTP server uses the *WinExec* call to launch the CGI program. Instead of using environment variables and the standard input/output, Windows CGI uses a set of files to exchange information. It's still a very crude protocol, but it may be easier for people who like to deal with files instead of standard input/output and environment variables. ❏

CGI and State

So how does CGI maintain information from one form to the next? Well, it doesn't. As we explained earlier, the protocol is totally stateless. The server forgets everything after it hands over a reply to the client. However, the nice thing about the Internet is that there is always some "kludge" that you can use to work around problems. In this case, the kludge is to use *hidden* fields within a form to maintain state on the client side.

Hidden fields are basically invisible; they contain values that are not displayed within a form. They are used to store information a user enters and resubmit that information in subsequent forms without having the user reenter it or even be aware that the information is being passed around. In other words, the hidden fields act as variables that maintain state between form submissions. So how does this information get passed from one form to another? It gets passed through the CGI program.

Figure 28-10 shows an electronic transaction that requires multiple form submissions, which lead to an electronic payment. The first set of forms lets you pick the merchandise that you place on your electronic shopping cart. The next form requests a delivery address and time. The last form presents you with the bill and requests some form of payment.

How is the state of this transaction maintained across form invocations? Here's how: The CGI program processes a form and then presents you with the next form; this continues until you make your final payment or abort the transaction. The trick here is that the CGI program uses invisible fields to store information from the previous forms in the next form. For example, it writes inside the invisible fields the goods you selected in the previous forms. You never see the contents of these hidden fields. You never know they're there, unless you view the document's HTML. However, when you submit the form, all these hidden fields are passed right back to the CGI program along with any new data.

So, in essence, the CGI program stores the state of the transaction in the forms it sends back to the client instead of storing it in its own memory. What do you think of this workaround? We did warn you that it was going to be a real work of art.

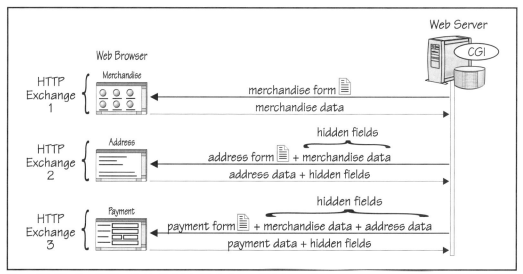

Figure 28-10. How Hidden Fields Maintain State Across Web Invocations.

Stay Away From GETs

Warning

Even though GET is the default HTTP method for submitting a form's contents, we strongly recommend that you *always* use POST instead. The best way to understand why is to look at an end-to-end GET interaction. On the client side, GET causes the set of "name=value" contents of the form to be appended to the URL after a separating question mark (?). In contrast, POST appends the contents to the body of the HTML message.

On the receiving side, GET causes the HTTP server to parse the URL and insert the entire string of name/value pairs that follow the question mark (?) into the *query-string* environment variable. The server is really fooled into thinking that it received a query. The CGI program reads the *query-string* environment variable to obtain the contents of the form.

So what's wrong with this picture? It's deadly. Here's why: Most operating systems limit their environment variables to between 256 and 1024 characters *total*. This means that any data that exceeds this maximum size will either be truncated or cause the operating system to blow up. As we explained earlier, there's no way to limit the amount of data from a multiline input field. For this reason, you should always use POST with forms; don't even think of using GET. ❏

WEB SECURITY

*T*he Internet has long fought a battle to maintain security of resources in the face of unlimited access from the outside world.

— Michael Goulde, Seybold Analyst
(January, 1996)

Security is a critical factor in the establishment and acceptance of commercial applications on the Web. For example, if you are using a home banking service, you want to be assured that your client/server interactions are both confidential and untampered with. In addition, both you and your bank must be able to verify each other's identity and to produce auditable records of your transactions.

Security on the Web is a two-sided affair that involves both the client (the browser) and the server. They each have a role to play. Currently, most of the Web security technology is focused on solving four immediate problems that are standing in the way of widespread electronic commerce:

- **Encryption:** You don't want to send your password, credit card number, electronic cash, and other sensitive messages in the clear (i.e., plain text). Who knows what "sniffing" devices may be lurking on the wide open intergalactic backbone?

- **Authentication:** Are you really who you claim to be, and vice versa? Both the client and the server must prove their identity to a trusted third party before they can start a secure session. On the Internet, the clients must prove their identity; so must the servers. The last thing you want is to send your credit card to a Trojan horse masquerading as the real server.

- **Firewalls:** How do you protect your private Intranets from the Internet hordes? This typically involves creating some kind of gateway (or buffer) between the Intranet and the Internet.

- **Non-repudiation:** This means uncontestable proof that a document (or message) was really originated by you and only you. This requires some form of unforgeable *electronic signature* that can stand in a court of law.

Currently, the Web supports two security protocols: Netscape's *Secure Sockets Layer (SSL)* and EIT's *Secure HTTP (S-HTTP)*. SSL is important because it is supported by the most popular browser on the Web: Netscape Navigator. S-HTTP is a more complete solution; it is supported by Spry Mosaic and NCSA Mosaic browsers, as well as other Mosaic clones. In many ways the SSL and S-HTTP protocols complement each other. And they both support public key encryption to encrypt data, authenticate users, and provide non-repudiation via electronic signatures. Most servers will end up supporting both protocols.

SSL

As the name implies, *Secure Sockets Layer (SSL)* is a secured socket connection. SSL implements a security-enhanced version of sockets that provides transaction security at the transport level. You can think of SSL as providing a security layer between the TCP/IP transport and sockets. In other words, SSL provides a secured communications link without involving the applications that invoke it; for example, the existence of SSL is transparent to e-mail or HTTP. In Netscape's implementation, HTTP servers that implement SSL must run on socket address 443 instead of the standard 80.

The SSL protocol provides: 1) private client/server interactions using encryption, 2) server authentication, and 3) reliable client/server exhanges via message integrity checks that detect tampering. When a client and server first start communicating, they agree on an SSL protocol version, select the cryptographic algorithms, optionally authenticate each other, and use public-key encryption techniques to generate shared secrets.

The SSL *handshake protocol* must first be completed before an application can transmit or receive its first byte of data. The handshake protocol is like a dance that allows the client and server to authenticate each other and to negotiate an encryption algorithm. An SSL session may include multiple secure connections; in addition, you can have multiple simultaneous sessions. The encryption established between a client and a server remains valid over the multiple connections.

SSL uses public key authentication and encryption technology developed by RSA Data Security, Inc. Netscape *Navigator's* export implementation of SSL—U.S. government approved—uses a 40-bit key RC4 stream encryption algorithm; it would take a dedicated 64-MIP computer over a year to break this encryption. The 128-bit domestic version provides many more orders of protection.

Netscape's Navigator and Commerce Server deliver server authentication using signed *digital certificates* issued by trusted third parties known as *certificate authorities*. A digital certificate verifies the connection between a server's public key and the server's identification (just as a driver's license verifies the connection between your photograph and your personal identification). Cryptographic checks, using digital signatures, ensure that information within a certificate can be trusted. The forthcoming Netscape Navigator 3.0 will also provide client certification.

The Netscape Navigator identifies secure documents in several ways. First, you are able to tell whether a document comes from a secure server by looking at the URL. If the URL begins with *https://*, then the document comes from a secure server. You'll always be warned if a secure URL is redirected to an insecure location, or if you're submitting a secure form to an insecure location.

The second way you can verify the security of a document is by examining the security icon in the bottom-left corner of the Netscape Navigator window or the colorbar across the top of the content area (see Figure 28-11). The icon consists of a doorkey on a blue background to show secure documents and a broken doorkey on a gray background to show insecure documents. The colorbar across the top of the content area is blue for secure and gray for insecure.

The third way you are made aware of security is through notification dialogs. For example, the Netscape browser informs you via notification dialog boxes when you enter or leave a secure space, view a secure document that contains insecure information, or use an insecure submission process. The dialog boxes typically display the encryption type, which protects the document and provides information about the certificate that backs the document. The certification request process requires that each server administrator supply an e-mail address and certain identifying information about the certifying authority (see next Details box).

Security
Color Bar

Security Icon

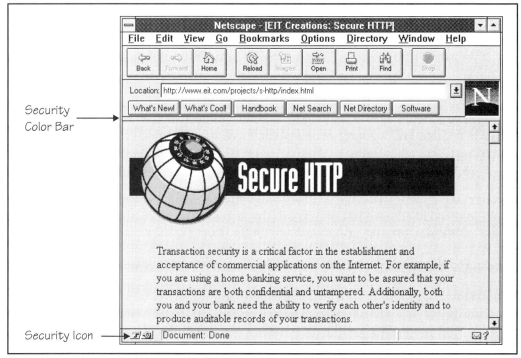

Figure 28-11. Netscape Navigator Security Cues.

 FYI

The Security Toll Booth

Briefing

How do clients know that a server's public key is valid? What keeps an imposter server from sending you its public key instead? The answer is the "trusted" certificate authority that signs the public key. To use its security features, Netscape Commerce Server requires a digitally signed certificate. Without a certificate, the server will operate in a non-secured mode. Netscape will only authenticate a server that has a key, which is either signed by: 1) Netscape, which the public can't get; or 2) VeriSign—an RSA spin-off company. VeriSign will sign your keys and provide you with a digital certificate for a fee, provided you meet some conditions.

To obtain a key from VeriSign, you must first submit a *certificate request* along with $290 for the first server and $95 for each additional server. The request must provide information about you and your company. If VeriSign is happy with all the information you provide, they will e-mail you a signed certificate that's good for a year; it costs another $75 per server to renew the license each year. You can then install on your server the signed, valid certificate to enable security. Of course, you'll need to take the usual precautions to maintain the integrity of the signed certificate and your private key.

Certificates are protected by public and private key pairs linked by a cryptographic algorithm. These keys have the ability to encrypt and decrypt information. No one else's keys can decipher messages to you encrypted with your public key. And no one else's keys can be used to pose as you by sending messages encrypted with your private key.

According to Netscape, this rather contorted approval process was put in place to "protect you, your organization, and the certificate authority." In addition to making money for RSA/VeriSign, security certificates issued by trusted third parties help solve the following problem: How do we issue for our servers the equivalent of the PIN numbers or driver licenses that uniquely identify us? The solution, in this case, was to introduce an authority—VeriSign—that could vouch for the server's public/private key pair.

Yes, there is a toll to pay for using a secure road. Welcome to the security toll booth. The good news is that VeriSign will soon be facing competition from the U.S. Postal Service. Yes, there is good money to be made in this certificate business. The next big opportunity is to issue digital certificates to the millions of client machines. This will allow a client and server to mutually authenticate each other's identity before initiating an electronic transaction. ❏

S-HTTP

S-HTTP is a security-enhanced variant of HTTP that was developed by EIT. A fully functional reference implementation of an S-HTTP client and server was released by EIT to members of CommerceNet in the fall of 1994. A commercial implementation of S-HTTP is available from Terisa Systems, which was co-founded by EIT and RSA Data Security in 1994. Terisa produces a security toolkit software product that allows software developers to integrate S-HTTP into their Web clients and servers.

S-HTTP adds application-level encryption and security on top of ordinary sockets-based communications. The client and server communicate over an ordinary HTTP session and then negotiate their security requirements; they use a MIME-like protocol to encrypt the contents of their messages.

S-HTTP provides the following security features: 1) it authenticates both clients and servers, 2) it checks for server certificate revocations, 3) it supports certificate chaining and certificate hierarchies, 4) it supports digital signatures that attest to a message's authenticity, 5) it allows an application to negotiate the security levels it needs, and 6) it provides secured communications through existing corporate firewalls.

Like SSL, S-HTTP incorporates public key cryptography from RSA. In addition, it supports traditional shared-secret (password) and Kerberos-based security systems. Like SSL, HTTP also provides security at a document level—each document may be marked as private and/or signed by the sender.

In summary, S-HTTP provides many of the security services that are needed for electronic commerce—including encryption, authentication, message integrity, and non-repudiation.

Are SSL and S-HTTP Mutually Exclusive?

S-HTTP and SSL approach the problem of security from two different perspectives. S-HTTP marks individual documents as private or signed. In contrast, SSL ensures that the channel of communication between two parties is private and authenticated. SSL layers security beneath application protocols, while S-HTTP adds message-based security on top of HTTP.

An outstanding concern in the market has been the development of two different security approaches—S-HTTP and SSL—that were unable to interoperate with each other. The good news is that SSL and S-HTTP are not mutually exclusive. They can easily coexist in a very complementary fashion by layering S-HTTP on top of SSL (see Figure 28-12). Consequently, we can get much better security than either approach provides on its own. Is this overkill? Absolutely not. You can never have enough security on the Internet.

The other good news is that in late 1995, Netscape, IBM, America Online, and CompuServe acquired a stake in Terisa Systems. As a result of this great coming together, Terisa now offers a toolkit that supports both S-HTTP and SSL. So it looks like we may get interoperable Internet security after all.

However, there still remains a dark horse on the horizon—Microsoft. In September 1995, Microsoft published its own security specification called *Private Communications Technology (PCT)*. PCT competes head-on with SSL 2.0—Microsoft claims that PCT "enhances" SSL by separating the authentication from encryption functions. Fortunately, Microsoft plans to support both SSL and PCT in its forthcoming Internet products. In addition, PCT uses the same record formats as SSL, which means that a future convergence is not out of the question.

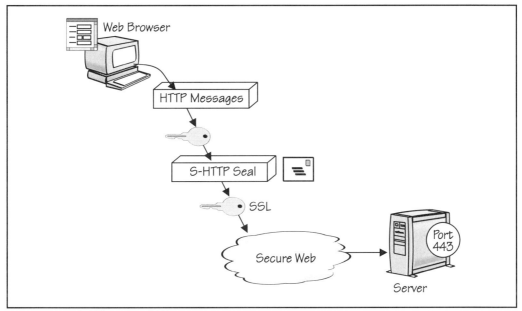

Figure 28-12. S-HTTP on Top of SSL.

Firewalls: The Network Border Patrol

A firewall is a gatekeeper computer that sits between the Internet and your private network. It protects the private network by filtering traffic to and from the Internet based on policies that you define. You use the firewall to define who can get on to your network and when. In theory, you should also be able to use a firewall to prevent the unauthorized export of proprietary information from your private network to the Internet.

A firewall typically provides two network interfaces—one connects to the internal protected network, and the other connects to the external, unprotected network (see Figure 28-13). The firewall provides a single chokepoint where you can impose access controls and audit network traffic. There are, generally speaking, two types of firewalls: *packet-filtering routers* and *proxy-based application gateways*.

Packet-Filtering Firewalls

A packet filter is a mechanism that provides a basic level of network security at the IP level. Packet filters are typically implemented in routers. They are configured using complex tables to indicate what communications protocols are allowed into

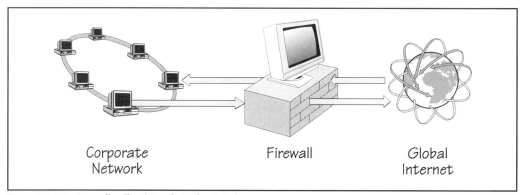

| Corporate | Firewall | Global |
| Network | | Internet |

Figure 28-13. Firewalls: The Network Border Patrol.

and out of a particular network. Packet filters drop, reject, or permit packets based on destination IP address, source IP address, and application port numbers.

Packet filters do not maintain context or understand the application they're dealing with. They make their decisions purely by looking at the IP header of the current packet, and then interpreting the rules they were programmed to follow. Crackers can exploit this lack of general information to spoof IP packets past the router; for example, they can mimic the IP addresses of trusted machines. Networks that rely solely on packet filtering technology are less secure from the outset than those guarded by proxy-based firewalls. And because packet-filtering solutions are more complex to maintain, they are also more susceptible to security breaches. It is difficult to tell what holes you may have left open.

Proxy Firewalls

Proxy firewalls—also known as *application* firewalls—are the most secure form of firewall. They run a small number of programs—called *proxies*—that can be secured and trusted. All incoming Internet traffic is funneled to the appropriate proxy gateway for mail, HTTP, FTP, Gopher, and so on. The proxies then transfer the incoming information to the internal network, based on access rights of individual users. Because the proxy is an application, it makes its decisions based on context, authorization, and authentication rules instead of IP addresses. This means that the firewall operates at the highest level of the protocol stack. This lets you implement security policies based on a richer set of defensive measures.

Proxies are relays between the Internet and the private network. The proxy's firewall address is the only one visible to the outside world. Consequently, the IP addresses on your internal network are totally invisible to the outside world. Outsiders must authenticate themselves to the appropriate proxy application. The proxy will not forward any packets that contain a final destination address on the internal network. Many proxies require that end-users set up their application programs to point to the proxy. *Transparent proxies*, on the other hand, are completely transparent to end-users—they don't even realize that they're using a proxy.

Some firewalls combine router and proxy techniques to provide more security. Figure 28-14 shows a popular firewall combination that runs proxies on a "bastion host" and uses a router to block all traffic to and from the Internet, except for the bastion host. The router is configured to only allow traffic from the bastion host's IP to get into the inner sanctum. This means that computers on both sides of the firewall can only communicate via the proxies on the bastion machine; all other traffic is blocked. It is very easy to configure such a router. So this is one way to sleep better at night.

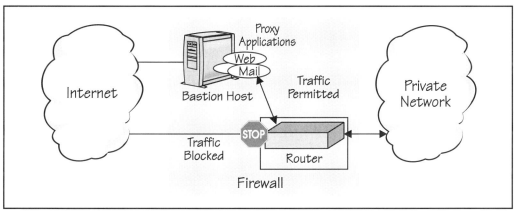

Figure 28-14. Firewall Combo: Proxies and Routers.

Electronic Payments

Banks and merchants are not stampeding toward the Internet because it is so much fun; they're doing it because of economics. The cost of a teller-driven transaction is about $2. In contrast, the cost of an electronic transaction is less than 15 cents. The world's first bank on the Internet—*Security First*—opened its digital doors in October 1995 (see Figure 28-15). Many banks now allow customers to use the Web to pay bills electronically, balance their checkbooks, and submit applications for loans.

Most banks are creating their electronic payment infrastructure on top of SSL and S-HTTP (see next Soapbox). However, there is no reason why all cash transactions must occur within the context of S-HTTP or SSL dialogs. For example, CyberCash lets you use your credit card but conducts the transaction on its own secure channel

Figure 28-15. Security First: The Internet's First Online Bank.

with the bank that issued your credit card. CyberCash uses neither SSL nor S-HTTP, but instead relies on its own encryption; it can do this because it provides the software that runs on both sides of the secure channel. In a sense, CyberCash is simply bypassing the Internet and resorting to a secured private channel to perform the electronic payment. This means that your credit card number never traverses the open Internet. Portland Software's *ZipLock* provides a similar bypass scheme on top of the communications infrastructure built by a major credit-card clearing house.

First Virtual offers yet another private Internet security scheme based on what it calls a *VirtualPIN*. The First Virtual system does not require special hardware, software, or encryption. All you need is ordinary e-mail. The VirtualPIN serves as an alias for your credit card. You can use it to shop on the Web. Your credit card number is never transmitted over the Internet.

To receive a VirtualPIN, you must submit an application to First Virtual that includes a credit card number and an e-mail address. You do this on the phone. Once you have a VirtualPIN, you can use it to purchase goods over the Internet. You use it instead of a credit card number. First Virtual will then send you an e-mail to confirm every purchase you make. If you confirm the sale, your credit card is charged by First Virtual completely off the Internet. Figure 28-16 shows the 3-way dialog that results in a VirtualPIN purchase.

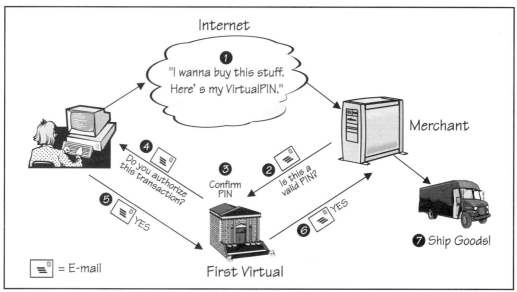

Figure 28-16. First Virtual Uses PINs and E-mail to Confirm Electronic Transactions.

So where is the Internet equivalent of cold hard cash? What is the equivalent of anonymous dollar bills that maintain our privacy when we shop? Digicash, a Netherlands startup, provides such a system on top of SSL/S-HTTP; it is based on a denomination called *e-cash*. You can withdraw money from your account in the bank in the form of e-cash bills. These are long strings of digits encoded with the verifying signatures and appropriate monetary denominations ($1, $5, $10, $20, and so on). These bills cannot be traced to your account if you do not authorize it. You can carry these e-cash bills in your electronic wallet and use them for anonymous purchases. The wallet is also a visual object that displays how much cash you've got on hand. Note that with e-cash, you can't buy on credit; you must have a wallet full of e-cash to make a purchase.

In addition, the IETF is working on an EDI-MIME specification that will enable companies to exchange invoices on the Internet. The public Internet becomes a substitute for the *Value-Added Networks (VANs)* on which vendors and their suppliers now conduct *Electronic Data Interchange (EDI)*; the Gartner Group estimates that over 150,000 companies worldwide conduct business with EDI. EDI-MIME defines a common method for sending EDI documents over the Net. So how are these messages made secure? In addition to SSL and S-HTTP, there are at least two standards-based security options for MIME. The first is the *MIME Object Security Services (Moss)*, formerly known as *Privacy Enhanced Mail*. The second is Phil Zimmermann's *Pretty Good Privacy (PGP)*.[1] Both offer encryption, authentication, and privacy features.

Visa or Mastercard?

Soapbox

This is ridiculous.

— Tim Vernel, Internet Sporting Goods Merchant

Before you send payments or your credit card all over the Web, you'll want someone to cover you in case of fraud. This is where Visa and Mastercard come into the picture. Until recently, they were each supporting a different standard for electronic payment. The Mastercard standard—called the *Secure Electronic Payment Protocol (SEPP)*—is also backed by Netscape, RSA, IBM, and CyberCash (Netscape calls it *Secure Courier*). The Visa standard—called the *Secure Transaction Technology (STT)*—is also backed by Microsoft, Spyglass, RSA, and Internet Shopping. The good news is that Visa and Mastercard have agreed to work on a common solution called *Secure Electronic Transaction (SET)*. And they may all end up backing the *Joint Electronic Payments Initiative (JEPI)* announced by W3C and CommerceNet in April of 1996. JEPI seeks to achieve compatibility among the different electronic payment schemes—including e-cash, e-checks and electronic credit cards. If this happens, the merchants on the Internet will be spared the inconvenience of having to deal with multiple payment systems. This is one war we can do without. ❑

THE INTERNET AND INTRANETS

Internal corporate applications are the biggest opportunity and the fastest growth area.

— Mike Homer, VP of Marketing
Netscape
(October, 1995)

The Web client/server technology is also being used on private networks called *Intranets*. These are internal corporate networks that are developed using Web

---

[1] PGP is an unlicensed implementation of RSA that is distributed as Freeware by Phil Zimmermann; the code is freely available on the Internet. ViaCrypt will sell you a licensed version of PGP.

client/server technology. Intranets are either standalone enterprise networks or they sit on the other side of a firewall. An Intranet simply leverages the public technology on which the Web is built. Intranets may become the new corporate backbones. Netscape reports that Intranets account for over 70% of its server sales.

To Intranet or Not To Intranet

In 1996, client/server application implementors building mission-critical, internal applications have little need for Internet-derived technology for anything other than support-role purposes.

> — *Gartner Group*
> *(December 28, 1995)*

It is natural for corporations that have already standardized on TCP/IP to add support for HTTP to their client/server backbones. HTTP lets you use very inexpensive Web client and server software. Web browsers are very familiar to users, run on multiple client platforms, and are practically free. Web servers are also relatively inexpensive. They provide gateways to every known server platform, which makes them a hub for gathering and distributing information.

Web client/server tools are also turning the Web into a client/server application development platform for the masses. These masses include corporate developers who are now able to use Internet technology in their own internally-developed client/server applications. However, make sure to read about the caveats in the next chapter before joining the "the Internet is the system" bandwagon. At best, the current Web is an infrastructure under construction. The stateless HTTP/CGI protocol may be fine for simple queries and for browsing information. However, it falls short when it comes to creating rich, mission-critical, scalable, enterprise-wide client/server applications.

Intranets Versus Corporate LANs

A few short years ago, it seemed as if LANs would expand into intergalactic backbones. Now it seems that the Internet is the intergalactic backbone; LANs are just extensions of the Internet. In some circles, corporate LANs are seen as very fast private extensions of the Internet—in other words, they're just Intranets. You can interconnect geographically distributed Intranets via the Internet backbone (using firewalls).

Intranets—built on top of LANs and fast corporate WANs—may lead to the prolif-eration of low-cost "Web terminals" in corporations. LAN-speed Intranets provide the high bandwidth that Web terminals require. Of course, PCs will not go away, as some pundits have claimed.

Table 28-1 compares the current state of the Web with traditional client/server environments. Obviously, the Web does certain things very well. But in its current form, the Web is not the savior that will free corporate IS from its client/server woes. As we explain in the next chapter, the Web needs to be supplemented by a distributed object and component infrastructure before it can play that role.

Table 28-1. Web Client/Server Versus Traditional Client/Server.

Application Characteristic	Web Client/Server	Traditional Client/Server
Number of clients per application	10,000,000+	Less than 10,000
Number of servers per application	100,000+	Less than 10
Geography	Global	Campus-based with some wide-area access
Access	Open	Highly secure
Content	Semi-static	Very dynamic
Transactional updates	Very infrequent	Pervasive
Usage	Electronic publishing and form-based queries	Line of business
Development effort	Small	Large
Robustness	Low	High
Persistent Connections	No	Yes

CONCLUSION

In this very long chapter, we covered the fundamentals of the Web's interactive client/server technology—including CGI, HTTP, tables, forms, and security. This detailed discussion should give you an appreciation of what limits exist in the current Web model, at least from a client/server perspective. The Web is truly a minimalist client/server architecture; it can be used to create very portable solutions. However, the current Web model must be augmented with some form of object-request-broker middleware before it can serve as an intergalactic client/server foundation. We will have a lot more to say about this in the next two chapters.

Chapter 29

Web Client/Server: The Java Object Era

> *The Internet is the killer application that will accelerate object usage; it has transformed objects into a mass-market opportunity that is attracting the best and brightest developers from around the world.*
>
> — **Donald DePalma, Forrester Research**
> **(February, 1996)**

The current Web is not the "Information Highway." For the Web to achieve this vision, it must be augmented with a distributed object infrastructure. In other words, we need the "Object Web." Java is the first step in this direction. However, Java is not enough; it needs to be complemented with a distributed object infrastructure, which is the topic of the next chapter.

In this chapter, we explain how the new "Java Web" is coming into place. We start with client/server, Java-style—or how the new applet model is changing the nature of client/server interactions on the Web. Next we provide a high-level overview of *mobile code systems*; we look at Java's mobile code system features. Then we go over the Java language and system services; we look at Java as a minimalist operating system. We conclude with the Java component model.

515

JAVA AND HOTJAVA

Java blows Bill Gates's lock and destroys his model of a shrink-wrapped software program that runs only on his platform.

> — Scott McNealy, CEO, Sun
> (December, 1995)

Unless you spent the last year hiding in a cave, chances are you've heard of Java—the new object-oriented programming language from Sun. Java is more than a C++ derived language; it's also a portable operating system environment. In addition, Java lets you write portable components that can be distributed on the Web. One key part of the Java environment is *HotJava*, which is a special Web browser that can interpret Java-generated code. HotJava was developed by Sun to showcase the capabilities of the Java programming language. Both Netscape and Spyglass have adopted features of HotJava. By the time you read this book, all the key browsers on the market will provide HotJava-like capabilities.

So Is There Anything Java Can't Do?

Most of us have a vision for Java; the reality will be clear in a few months.

> — Christine Comaford, Columnist, PC Week
> (April, 1996)

So is there anything Java can't do? It turns out, quite a bit. First, Java by itself is not an ORB; it does not provide a distributed object bus. Java needs CORBA-like facilities to talk to existing applications across a network and for Java components to communicate with each other. The good news is that Sun and other CORBA vendors are in the process of creating CORBA-compliant Java ORBs. Second, the current Java does not provide a compound document framework a la OLE or OpenDoc. Again, there is ongoing work to support OLE and OpenDoc from within Java. Third, Java does not provide CORBA-like distributed component services. As you would expect, Sun and others are making sure that all CORBA services are available from within the Java environment.

In addition, Java needs better client/server tools, compilers, and all the things you would expect from a mature development environment. The good news is that the Java tools market is exploding. By the time you read this, you'll be able to get top-of-the-line Java client/server tools from Borland, Symantec, Sybase/PowerBuilder, JavaSoft, IBM, Microsoft, and many others (see Figure 29-1). We will spend the rest of this section explaining the Java language, the portable Java operating system environment, and the component facilities.

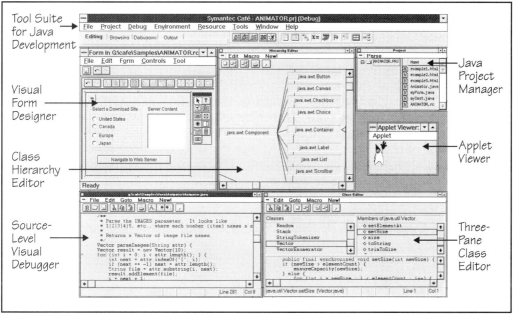

Figure 29-1. Symantec's Cafe: The First Java Visual Builder.

Web Client/Server, Java-Style

If you build the client side of an application in Java, then launching a client app becomes just switching to a page. Installing is trivial—just put it on a Web server. And there are no ports, just one version of the application.

— *James Gosling, Java Creator*
(September, 1995)

Java introduces an entirely new model of client/server interaction for the Web. It lets us write small component-like programs called *applets* that can be downloaded into a browser that is Java-compatible. Applets allow us to distribute executable content across the Web along with data. Figure 29-2 shows a Web client/server interaction scenario that includes a Java applet. Here are the steps:

1. ***Request the applet***. A Web browser requests a Java applet when it encounters the new HTML <APPLET> tag. The tag's attributes include the name of the program—the *class* filename. The program typically resides on the same server from which the HTML page originates.

2. ***Receive the applet***.   The browser initiates a separate TCP/IP session to download each applet it encounters within a Web page. The browser treats the Java applet like any other HTML object (for instance, an external image).

3. ***Load and execute the applet***. The browser loads the applet into the client's memory, and then executes it. Typically the applet will create some kind of dynamic visual effect within the area of the page that is assigned to it. The <APPLET> tag attributes specify the size of the region the applet will own. This is the piece of real estate within a page that belongs to the applet. The applet paints the contents of its region, chooses the background color and fonts, and handles all the keyboard and mouse events. Note that the applet's region doesn't visually integrate with the rest of the page. It's really a poor man's compound document architecture.

4. ***Discard the applet***. The browser deletes the applet from memory when it exits the Web page.

As you can see from this scenario, Java applets allow us to create highly interactive Web pages that have locally executable content.   These applets introduce an unparalleled degree of flexibility. They allow the client to execute snippets of code (the applets), while the server becomes a warehouse of programs, data, and HTML pages.

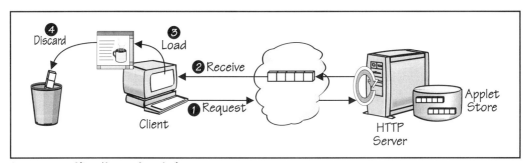

Figure 29-2. Client/Server, Java-Style.

Java's Mobile Code System

*T*here are a lot of mechanisms in Java to let you sort of transparently move behavior around; it's about building applications that can rove around the network in a safe way.

> — *James Gosling, Java Creator*
> *(March, 1996)*

In addition to exchanging traditional content—such as text, graphics, audio, and video—Java lets Web applications exchange *mobile code*. Java is a mobile code system. Other examples of mobile code systems are *Safe-Tcl*, Colusa's *Omniware*, and General Magic's *Telescript*. Microsoft may also provide a portable version of its *Visual Basic Script (VB Script)* engine.[1]

Mobile code systems provide the foundation technology for *mobile agents*. They let you distribute code (and data) across clients and servers. Mobile objects—Java calls them *applets*—are self-contained pieces of executable code. Like traditional software, mobile code consists of a sequence of executable instructions. Unlike traditional software, mobile code is dynamically loaded and executed by standalone programs such as Web browsers and servers.

At a minimum, mobile code must be portable and safe. As users browse the Web, they will be downloading and executing hundreds of these executable code modules, so it is crucial that you should be able to precisely control each module's access to host resources. Here's a short list of the services you should expect from a mobile code system:

- *A safe environment for executing mobile code*. You should be able to precisely control an applet's environment—including its access to memory, system calls, and server function calls.

- *Platform-independent services*. The system must provide cross-platform memory management, threads, synchronization, communications, and GUI services—including a compound document framework. The applets must execute on top of a variety of operating systems and hardware platforms.

- *Life cycle control*. The system must provide a run-time environment for loading, unloading, and executing the code.

- *Applet distribution*. The system must provide facilities for moving applets across the network. It must guarantee that the code is not tampered with when in transit. It must also certify the applet and authenticate the identities of both clients and servers. In other words, you must do whatever you can to prevent mobile code from becoming a conduit for viruses.

In essence, mobile code lets you write an application once and then run it anywhere. The network becomes the distribution vehicle for software applications. Mobile code systems slash software distribution costs and allow you to reach millions of customers instantly via global networks. Mobile code means that you do not have to deal with issues like porting and end-user installation.

---

[1] Microsoft acquired Colusa in March, 1996.

The Magic of Bytecodes

Java delivers the goods right into the heart of Microsoft territory and breaks their lock on the desktop.

— Dr. Jeff Sutherland, Homepage.Journal
(March, 1996)

Like all mobile code systems, Java delivers both portability and safety. A Java *applet* is a portable unit of mobile code. Java achieves portability by compiling applets to the *Java Virtual Machine*, which is modeled after a virtual RISC processor's instructions. These primitive instructions are called *bytecodes*. Bytecodes bring the compiled instructions to the lowest level possible without making them machine dependent. The Java language puts a stake in the ground by specifying the size of its basic data types and the behavior of its arithmetic operators. Your programs are the same on every platform—there are no data type incompatibilities across hardware and software architectures.

Bytecodes make Java a partially compiled language. Creating the bytecodes is about 80% of the compilation work; the last 20% is performed by the Java run time. So you can think of Java as being 80% compiled and 20% interpreted. This 80/20 mix seems to provide excellent code portability; the bytecode abstraction was designed to transport code efficiently across multiple hardware and software platforms.

Of course, there's no free lunch. In this case, you're trading off performance for portability—the Java interpreted code is about fifteen times slower than native compiled code. Java also supports regular compilers as well as *just-in-time* compilers, which can generate code that runs at C++ native speeds.

The Java Verifier

Figure 29-3 shows the steps you must follow to create and execute a Java applet. First, you run your applet through a Java virtual machine compiler to create the bytecodes and store them on a server. Your bytecodes will be copied to a target client machine when a browser requests your applet. As soon as the bytecodes reach the target machine, they're run through a Java *verifier*, which is highly suspicious of any code it receives.

The verifier runs the bytecodes through a gauntlet of tests. It looks for things like forged pointers, access violations, parameter type mismatches, and stack overflows. In a sense, the verifier acts as a gatekeeper; it ensures that the code it receives from both local and remote sources is safe. No code is allowed to execute without passing the verifier's tests. If the verifier is satisfied that everything's OK, it hands over the bytecodes to the class loader.

The *class loader* typically hands the bytecodes to an *interpreter*. This is the run-time element that executes the Java instructions on the target machine. The interpreter can proceed with the execution without checking anything because it knows that the code it received was sanitized. It can run at full speed without compromising reliability.

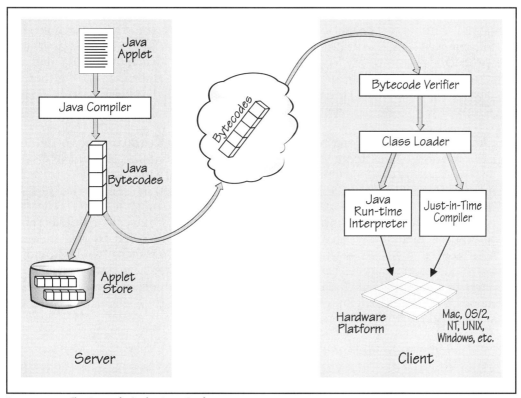

Figure 29-3. The Bytecode Cycle: From Production to Execution.

However, even at "full speed," an interpreter is still an order of magnitude slower than native compiled code. So the Java designers are now trying to improve the situation with *just-in-time* compiler techniques, which means translating an entire applet into native code prior to executing it. This may add some overhead during the translation process, but it allows the resulting code to run at close to native speeds.

Java's Defense System

Microsoft has always had a very casual attitude about security and viruses. All their systems are just designed to host viruses. I mean, it's like a petri dish with the best culture you could buy.

— James Gosling, Java Creator
(March, 1996)

Importing code across the network is potentially an open invitation to all sorts of problems. Without the proper checks, Java applets can become a breeding ground for computer viruses. Java starts with the assumption that you can't trust anything, and proceeds accordingly. The environment provides five interlocking defense mechanisms or defense perimeters: 1) the Java language itself, 2) the verifier, 3) the Java bytecode loader, 4) the access control lists, and 5) the Java browser. Here's a quick overview of Java's defense perimeters:

■ *The Java language defense perimeter.* One of Java's primary lines of defense is its memory allocation and reference model. The *memory layout* decisions are not made by the Java language compiler, as they are in C and C++. Instead, memory layout is deferred to run time. In addition, Java does not support "pointers" in the traditional C and C++ sense—meaning memory cells that contain the addresses of other memory cells. Instead, the Java compiled code references memory via symbolic "names" that are resolved to real memory addresses at run time by the Java interpreter. Together, these two late-binding mechanisms ensure that crackers can't infer the physical memory layout of a class by looking at its declaration. Java's memory allocation and referencing model is completely opaque to them. There's no way for them to go behind the scenes and forge pointers to memory.

■ *The verifier's defense perimeter.* As we described in the previous section, imported Java code fragments are subjected to a battery of checks by the verifier before they're allowed to run on the target platform. The verifier protects the Java run-time environment from a range of external threats—including hostile compilers, code tamperers, and faulty bytecodes.

■ *The class loader's defense perimeter.* The loader partitions the set of Java classes into separate *namespaces*. A class can only access objects that are within its namespace. Java creates one namespace for classes that come from the local file system, and a separate namespace for each network source. When a class is imported from across the network, it is placed into the private namespace associated with its origin. When a class references another class, Java first searches the namespace of the local system (built-in classes), and then it searches the namespace of the referencing class. Note that Java resolves all symbols at load time. Each class referenced by an applet is loaded in the browser, and all the symbolic references and class inheritance relationships are resolved at this time.

■ ***The access control lists' defense perimeter.*** Java uses access control lists to provide additional levels of security on top of its already secured language and run-time base. For example, the file access primitives implement access control lists. This lets you control read and write access to files by imported code (or code invoked by imported code). The defaults for these access control lists are very restrictive. If an attempt is made by a piece of imported code to access a file to which you did not grant access, a dialog box pops up to let the user decide if this specific access can proceed.

■ ***The Java browser's defense perimeter.*** HotJava browsers let you set the security mode using a properties dialog box. The strictest level of security is *none*—meaning the applets cannot access the network. *Applet host* mode allows applets to access data only on the home server from which they originate (see Figure 29-4). *Firewall* mode allows applets from outside the firewall to only access resources that are outside the firewall. Finally, *unrestricted* mode allows applets to connect to any host on the Internet.

Sun is also working on an *applet certification* scheme that uses public key technology to certify that an applet comes from a reputed source. The idea is to place fewer restrictions on these "certified" bytecode fragments.

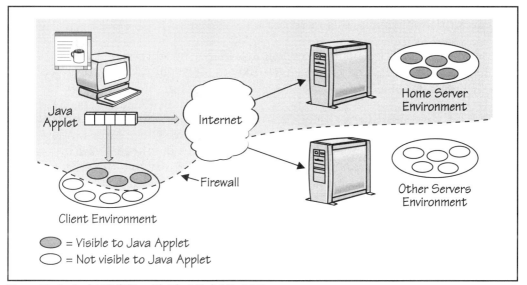

Figure 29-4. Applet Visibility with "Host Mode" Restriction.

In summary, Java surrounds its applets with various levels of protection. It controls all access to client resources and remote server processes. In theory, Java lets you construct applications that can't be invaded from outside and are secure from intrusion by unauthorized code attempting to get behind the scenes and create viruses or invade file systems. Of course, it is still too early to declare victory.

The Java Language

Java is C plus-plus-minus-minus.

> — *Bill Joy, Cofounder*
> *Sun*
> *(December, 1995)*

Sun describes the Java language as "simple, object-oriented, distributed, interpreted, robust, secure, architecture-neutral, portable, multithreaded, and dynamic." So what is left for us to say? Well, we still haven't covered the multithreaded and object-oriented aspects of the language.

Unlike C++, Java only supports a single inheritance model for object class implementations. However, it supports multiple inheritance at the interface level. A Java *interface* is very much like CORBA IDL; it specifies a class's interface contracts without getting into the implementation. A Java class may implement one or more interfaces as well as adding its own functions. However, because Java lacks multiple implementation inheritance, you must reimplement the interface's functionality in each class that implements this interface.

Java addresses the C++ naming collision problem by introducing a namespace concept called *packages*. A package—like modules in CORBA IDL—collects related classes into named packages.

Unlike C++, Java provides automatic garbage collection. You do not need to worry about destroying objects via destructors. This means you can instantiate new objects without worrying about memory leaks. Java's multithreaded features are also very useful—they make it much easier to provide portable thread-safe code. Exception-handling is built into Java; the documentation for a method must indicate the exceptions it throws. In general, Java is a C++ programmer's delight. It keeps the good in C++ and throws away the ugly. Our only complaint is the loss of multiple implementation inheritance; we happen to like mixins.

APPLETS: COMPONENTS, JAVA-STYLE

In the pre-Java world, a Web page is essentially a piece of paper. In the Java world, a browser becomes a framework.

> — *James Gosling, VP*
> *JavaSoft*
> *(September, 1995)*

You can run Java applications as standalone programs or as applets invoked by a browser. Technically, an applet is a piece of code that inherits its behavior from the Java *Applet* class, which it then extends with new function. An applet is not a complete application. It's really a component that runs within a browser's environment. In this case, the browser acts as a framework for running Java components—or applets.

So what type of component framework services do browsers provide? While a Java browser falls short of being an OLE or OpenDoc container, it does provide three useful services to its applets. First, the browser fully controls the applet's life cycle. Second, it supplies the applet with attribute information from the APPLET tag. And third, it serves as the main program or process within which the applet executes—it provides the *main* function. Let's quickly go over the first two services.

Applet Life Cycle Management

A Web browser manages all phases of an applet's life cycle. Remember, the browser first downloads the applet and then runs it within its environment. The browser is also kind enough to inform the applet of key events that happen during its life cycle. The Java *Applet* and *Runnable* interface defines the methods that a browser invokes on an applet during its life cycle (see Figure 29-5). Most Java applets implement code that reacts to these method invocations.

The browser invokes *Init* after it loads the applet in memory. It invokes *Start* to tell the applet it should do whatever it has to do before running. *Paint* tells the applet to display its contents. *Stop* and *Destroy* tell the applet to kill all its threads, stop executing, and release all resources. This happens when the browser replaces the Web page that contains the applet with another page. In summary, the browser owns the applet; it provides it with a running environment that includes life cycle management.

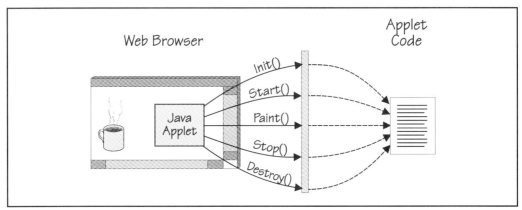

Figure 29-5. Applet Life-Cycle Management.

The HTML Applet Tag

Live objects is our term for things like Java applets and inlined viewers embedded in HTML documents.

— Marc Andreessen, VP
Netscape
(December, 1995)

A Java applet's main role in life is to provide live content to Web pages displayed in a Java-enabled browser. In contrast, a Java application can run without a Web browser. You use the APPLET HTML tag to place an applet in a Web page and describe its attributes and environment (also see the next Background box). The tag tells the browser where to find the applet to download. Java provides a set of methods that an applet uses to obtain information about its environment—including the embedded tag attributes and their values.

The APPLET tag provides the essential information that connects the Web browser to the embedded applet. It also lets you specify key attribute information; you can use these attributes to configure an applet and control its behavior without having to write a line of code. A well-designed applet will provide as many attributes as is needed to let you control its behavior via HTML.

The APPLET tag contains the required attributes CODE, WIDTH, and HEIGHT; it also contains optional attributes such as CODEBASE and ALIGN. The CODE attribute specifies the file that contains the applet's bytecode. This file is normally in the same directory as the document-URL. However, you can use the optional CODEBASE attribute to specify a different location. The WIDTH and HEIGHT attributes specify the area within an HTML page that belongs to the applet. You can use the optional ALIGN attribute to tell the browser where you want it to place the applet (it's a relative placement). Here's an example of the APPLET tag:

```
<APPLET
CODE=Hello.class
CODEBASE="applets/myapps"
WIDTH=300
HEIGHT=200   ALIGN=Left>
<PARAM NAME=Parm1   VALUE="Java is cool">
<PARAM NAME=Parm2   VALUE="Is there life without Java?">
</APPLET>
```

The PARAM attributes are specific to each applet. Each applet can define as many parameters as it needs. You must provide a PARAM tag for each parameter you want to pass to the applet via HTML; each tag contains a name/value pair. An applet can access any parameter—by name—by invoking the Java method *getParameter*.

FYI

Active Objects: HTML 3.0's INSERT Tag

Briefing

The ubiquitous APPLET tag is just one of several non-standard approaches that let you insert active objects inside an HTML document. Other approaches include Netscape's EMBED tag for compound document embedding and Microsoft's DYNSRC attribute for video and audio. In addition, HTML 2.0 provides an IMG tag for inserting media into HTML documents. Each of these proposed solutions attacks the problem from a slightly different perspective, and on the surface they appear to be very different.

In December 1995, W3C Director Tim Berners-Lee announced a convergence agreement for "active objects" that had the support of Sun, Netscape, Microsoft, Spyglass, and IBM. It appears that these companies have agreed to support a new active object tag called INSERT. This universal tag will be used to insert almost any object within HTML—including HTML images, Java applets, OLE components, OpenDoc parts, media handlers, and a wide range of plug-ins.

As we go to press, the new tag is still being drafted. Like the APPLET tag, INSERT lets you specify persistent data as well as properties and parameters that you can use to initialize active objects placed within HTML documents. You can specify the location of the code for the object in several ways: using the object's unique ID (UUID) via a URL, or by specifying the combination of class name and a network address. This simple example demonstrates how INSERT is used to specify a Java applet:

```
<INSERT
 CLASSID="Java:NervousText.class"
 CODE="http://java.acme.com/applets/NervousText.class"
 WIDTH=300  HEIGHT=200  ALIGN=Left>
 <PARAM NAME=text  VALUE="This is the Applet Viewer">
</INSERT>
```

This next example shows how INSERT is used to specify an OLE control (or ActiveX) for a clock:

```
<INSERT
 ID=clock1
 CLASSID="uuid:{663C8FEF-1EF9-11CF-A3DB-080036F12502}"
 TYPE="application/x-oleobject"
 CODE="http://www.foo.bar/test.stm"
 DATA="http://www.acme.com/ole/clock.stm"
 WIDTH=300  HEIGHT=200  ALIGN=Left
</INSERT>
```

The ID attribute allows other controls on the same page to locate the clock. The DATA attribute points to a persistent stream that you can use to initialize the object's state. The CODE attribute points to a file that contains the code for this object. Note that if a global OLE directory is present, then the CLASSID may be all you need to locate the code. In the case of OLE, the CLASSID is a DCE UUID. In the case of CORBA objects, it's a global identifier. The prefix is used to identify the object system. Again, we warn you that the semantics of the INSERT tag are still "under construction" as we go to press. ❏

IS JAVA REALLY AN OPERATING SYSTEM IN DISGUISE?

We will have a simple OS, component-based small applications, and live content.

— *Eric Schmidt, CTO, Sun*
(February, 1996)

Yes, Java is a new operating system, at least for Internet client machines. Figure 29-6 shows Sun's vision of the ultimate Java Internet client machine. Starting from the bottom are RISC chips that natively execute Java bytecodes. Sun's Java processor family will consist of three lines: *PicoJAVA*, *MicroJAVA*, and *UltraJAVA*. The processors will vary in price/performance and application capability.

Sun expects to sample PicoJAVA chips in early 1997; they will be priced at around $25. Eric Schmidt—Sun's chief technical officer—estimates that Java chips could run 50 times faster than current implementations. If this performance is achieved, Java will become an extremely popular Internet appliance machine. The *Java Virtual Machine* specification is available on Java's home page. Consequently, we should expect other vendors to bring their own Java RISC chips to market.

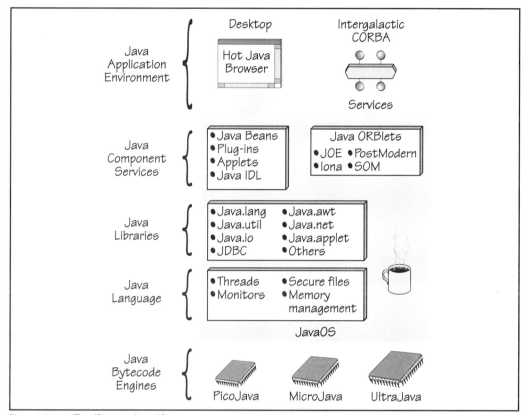

Figure 29-6. The Ultimate Java Client.

The next layer up is the Java "operating system." It consists of the Java language, the Java libraries, JDBC, and ORBs. As we explained earlier, the Java language proper provides powerful run-time services—including threads, monitors, memory management, security, access controls, and so on. In February 1996, Sun announced *Kona*—a barebones operating system based on Java. Kona will provide multithreading and built-in networking, but it won't have a file system or support virtual memory.

The Java Libraries

The *Java libraries* extend the language; they provide a portable environment for writing thread-safe Java applications. The libraries consist of six Java packages that implement hundreds of classes. Here's a brief description of what these packages offer:

■ ***Java.lang*** provides classes that support basic Java objects and native types. You should always import this package into your code. This is where you'll find implementations of the root class hierarchy, threads, exceptions, primitive data types, and a variety of other primitive classes.

■ ***Java.io*** provides classes that support reading and writing streams, files, and pipes. This is where you'll find the Java equivalent of the familiar C standard I/O library.

■ ***Java.net*** provides classes that support network programming—including sockets, telnet interfaces, HTTP, and URLs.

■ ***Java.util*** provides a collection of utility classes that encapsulate data structures such as: dictionaries, hash tables, stacks, dates, strings, and others.

■ ***Java.awt*** is an *abstract windowing toolkit (awt)*. It provides a portable GUI layer for writing applications that you can move from one windowing system to another. The library contains classes for basic user interface elements—including events, frame containers, and widgets. The current awt provides a least common denominator GUI environment with a minimalist set of controls.

■ ***Java.applet*** is a subclass of awt that supports animation and audio.

Together, all these layers provide a portable application environment for Java developers. In the Sun vision, the Java client is an extendable Web browser written in Java—for example, Sun's HotJava browser and similar applications. The browser should be able to extend itself via Java applets that it can download over the Web. This means that the client environment will be able to dynamically renew itself to meet new needs.[2]

Java Database Connection (JDBC)

In March 1996, Sun published the initial specification for the *Java Database Connection (JDBC)*; it was jointly developed with Oracle, Sybase, Informix, and others. JDBC is a set of Java classes that provide an ODBC-like interface to SQL databases. Like ODBC, JDBC uses a driver manager to automatically load the right JDBC driver to talk to a given database (see Figure 29-7).

Unlike ODBC, JDBC must pay close attention to mobile code issues. For example, a JDBC driver must prevent an *untrusted applet* from accessing databases outside its home machine—meaning the machine from which the applet originates. Likewise, a driver that is downloaded as an applet can only be allowed to access its home database. Of course, applets and drivers can get around these limitations by

---

[2] At its JavaOne conference in May 1996, SunSoft formally announced a ROM-able *JavaOS*. It also announced *Java Beans*—a component architecture for Java; details were sketchy. In addition, it announced a ton of Java extensions including 3-D graphics, telephony, animation, and CORBA extensions. Finally, it announced *Servlets*, which are Java applets that run within a server environment. SunSoft's Java server environment is called *Jeaves*.

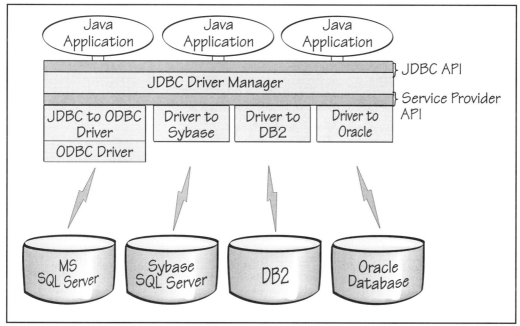

Figure 29-7. The Java Database Connection (JDBC).

convincing the Java loader that they are trustworthy; for example, by presenting certificates that authenticate them.

So how does an applet find its JDBC driver? It does this using the following URL-based naming scheme: *jdbc:<subprotocol><domain name>*. For example, the URL to access "MyJavaDB" via a JDBC-to-ODBC bridge might look like this:

```
jdbc:odbc://www.bob.com/MyJavaDB
```

In this example, the subprotocol is "odbc" and the hostname is "www.bob.com." You can also use this scheme to provide a level of indirection in database names. You do this by specifying a naming service as the subprotocol. Here's an example of a URL that does this:

```
jdbc:dcenaming:MyJavaDB
```

In this example, the URL specifies that the DCE naming service is used to resolve the database name "MyJavaDB" into a global name that connects to the database. JDBC recommends that you provide a *pseudo-driver* that looks up names via a networked name server. It then uses the information to locate the real driver and pass it the connection information.

We expect the JDBC specification to be completed by the time you read this. Sun will bundle a JDBC driver manager with future releases of Java; it will also provide a JDBC-to-ODBC bridge. We expect that JDBC might eventually become an even more important database API standard than ODBC or OLE/DB.

Note that the ODMG—with help from SunSoft—is also working on Java bindings for ODBMSs. These bindings will give you the most direct path to store your Java objects; you can totally bypass SQL.

Java and CORBA: JOE, PostModern, and Iona

In addition to HotJava, Sun is developing the *Java Object Environment (JOE)*, which is a portable CORBA ORB written entirely in Java. Because of its small footprint, JOE can be downloaded on demand or it can be bundled with the Java run-time environment. JOE will allow any Java applet to seamlessly access any CORBA service on an intergalactic ORB. Sun is not the only vendor that is working on a Java ORB. By the time you read this, Java ORBs will also be available from PostModern and Iona.

PostModern's *BlackWidow* currently implements the client and server sides of a CORBA 2.0 ORB in less than 100 KBytes of Java bytecode. This small size makes it an ideal *ORBlet*—which means an ORB that you can download on-demand like any other Java applet. We will have a lot more to say about Java and ORBs in the next chapter.

CONCLUSION

I think people are only beginning to understand what networks really mean.

> — **James Gosling, Java Creator**
> **(March, 1996)**

The bottom line is that Java provides a simpler and newer way to develop, manage, and deploy client/server applications. You can access the latest version of an application by simply clicking on the mouse. You can distribute an application to millions of clients by putting it on a Web server. Distribution is immediate. And you don't have to concern yourself with installation and updates.

Java is also good for servers. It lets you write mobile server code that you can use in very flexible arrangements. For example, servers can transmit applets to other servers to look for information. Executable software can move to where its needed most. Java provides a flexible, just-in-time execution environment on servers as well as on clients. So does this mean that we've finally reached client/server Nirvana? No, we're not quite there yet. The next chapter explains why.

Chapter 30

Web Client/Server: The Distributed Object Era

---

*W*eb technology and distributed object technology are naturally complementary. We want to ensure that OMG and W3C work together to define a common future.

> — *Tim Berners-Lee, Director*
> *W3C*
> *(February, 1996)*

Java is the first step toward creating an Object Web, but it is still not enough. Java needs to be augmented with a distributed object infrastructure, which is where OMG's CORBA comes into the picture. As we go to press, Java-based CORBA ORBs were announced by PostModern, Sun, and Iona.

The Object Web also needs a compound document framework such as OLE or OpenDoc. Compound documents with Java will allow us to create *shippable places*. A place is an ensemble of visual components; it's a shippable OLE or OpenDoc container filled with components. You will typically store places on servers. You will be able to download your favorite places using ordinary HTTP commands. You can then interact with a place by simply clicking on the visual components it contains. The contents of a place are dynamic—you can edit everything "in-place."

Compound documents will also be used to create the next generation Web browsers. Today's Web browser is a monolithic application. Helper applications and inline plug-ins provide primitive "brute force" approaches for extending them. The next generation Web browsers will consist of components that are seamlessly contained and displayed within compound documents. Apple's *Cyberdog* and Microsoft's *Explorer 3.X* are the best examples of this new browser technology.

Finally, *Web business objects* provide a component environment for encapsulating server functions. They are the object version of a 3-tier client/server architecture. NeXT's *WebObjects* is the first commercial implementation of this technology. WebObjects currently work with regular HTML front-ends. The objects encapsulate back-end services in a very scalable fashion.

In this chapter, we explain how the new Object Web is coming into place. We first explain how CORBA extends Java, HTTP, and CGI. Then we cover the new Java ORBs. Finally, we explain how compound documents and shippable places provide the mortar that binds it all together.

JAVA MEETS CORBA

*T*he real future for Java is in the integration with CORBA.

> — *Michael Goulde, Seybold Analyst*
> *(January, 1996)*

Java clearly introduces a new model of distributed application development for the Web. It makes the Web clients smarter and more interactive. Java extends the Web past its text and image origins; it allows developers to create platform-independent client applications for mass distribution over the Internet. However, as you may have noticed, Java does little to improve the server side of the equation. The server is able to distribute some of its function to the client in the form of applets that it controls, but it is still primarily an HTTP/CGI server engine.

As you may recall from the last chapter, CGI is a slow, cumbersome, and stateless protocol. It is not a good match for object-oriented Java clients. In a sense, the Web server lives in the middle ages while the clients are postmodern. Some server vendors are trying to extend CGI with proprietary server APIs. Examples of such attempts include Netscape's *NSAPI*, Microsoft's *ISAPI*, NeXT's *WebObjects frame-work*, and Oracle's *WebServer API*. If this trend continues, we may end up with a totally non-standard server Web.

Sun's *JOE*—and the joint OMG/W3C work—is an attempt to reverse this trend. The idea is to create an open Web server environment based on CORBA. This makes a lot of sense because CORBA is a distributed object bus built with open standards;

it was designed from the start to support intergalactic client/server systems. This section explains how Java clients and CORBA ORBs complement each other. We also review some of the pioneering work that shows how the Web and CORBA play together. Finally, we look at the OLE alternative.

Java Clients and CORBA ORBs

Currently, most Java applications have been standalone demos, but the real value of Java is when you build a portable front-end to much larger transactional systems. And the standard environment for object transactional systems is CORBA.

> — *Larry Podmolik*
> *Strategic Technology Resources*
> *(February, 1996)*

Sun—the creator of Java—was one of the six founding members of OMG. Consequently, Sun's client/server vision has always been "distributed objects everywhere." In September 1995, Sun announced NEO—a 3-tier client/server architecture that brings together Java, CORBA objects, and the Web. The NEO acronym does not stand for anything in particular. The NEO product includes: 1) the NEOnet CORBA ORB (previously known as DOE), 2) the Java and OpenStep client environments, 3) the *Solstice* distributed systems management framework, and 4) client/server development tools and programmer workbenches. In January 1996, Sun announced JOE—a portable version of the NEOnet ORB written entirely in Java (also see the next Briefing box). In Sun's view, you can use the NEO Web for all client/server application development—including departments, Intranets, and the Internet.

FYI

PostModern's Java ORBlet

Briefing

PostModern's *BlackWidow* won the distinction of being the first Java ORBlet on the market. With BlackWidow, an ordinary Java applet can directly invoke methods on CORBA objects using the IIOP protocol over the Internet. The applet totally bypasses CGI and HTTP; the client and the server establish a direct communication link using the ORB. You can load the client-side BlackWidow Java applet into any commercial Java-enabled browser and execute it. The applets can even use SSL secured communications if the browser supports it.

> BlackWidow clients can invoke a wide variety of IDL-defined operations on the server. In contrast, HTTP clients are restricted to a limited set of operations. BlackWidow server applications are regular CORBA objects. Consequently, they are available on a permanent basis. There is no need to go through the overhead of spawning a CGI script for every invocation. Note that any CORBA 2.0 compliant client can perform invocations on a BlackWidow server.
>
> To create CORBA-compliant Web clients and servers, you must first define the functions a server object exposes using IDL. Then you run your IDL through the BlackWidow precompiler. The precompiler generates skeleton code for the server objects in C++ or Java; it also generates Java stubs for the client side. You must, of course, fill out the skeletons with the application logic. The BlackWidow ORB was implemented in less than 100 KBytes of Java bytecodes. Consequently, you can easily download it to the client machine if it's not already there. ❏

In addition to Sun, other members of the OMG began to realize the potential of marrying CORBA with the Java Web. In late 1995, OMG started a joint study with the W3C consortium on how to integrate CORBA IIOP with HTTP and Java. The OMG is also using a fast-track process to develop Java language bindings for CORBA. In addition, some OMG members—such as the ANSA European consortium—are already quite far along in their investigation of how CORBA and the Internet play together (also see the next Soapbox). As a result of all this work, a new *Object Web* model is starting to emerge along the lines shown in Figure 30-1.

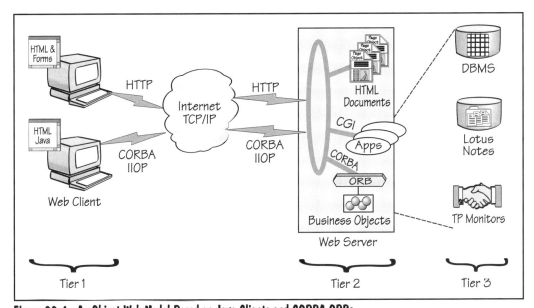

Figure 30-1. An Object Web Model Based on Java Clients and CORBA ORBs.

The figure shows a 3-tier client/server application model that consists of: 1) Java clients in the first tier, 2) CORBA business objects in the middle tier, and 3) traditional servers in the third tier. The CORBA business objects provide the application logic and encapsulate existing database, TP Monitor, and groupware servers. So the CORBA business objects replace CGI applications in the middle tier, which is good.

In addition, the Java client can directly communicate with a CORBA object using the Java ORB. This means that CORBA replaces the HTTP/CGI as the middleware layer for object-to-object communications, which is also very good. Like HTTP, CORBA's IIOP uses the Internet as its backbone. This means that both IIOP and HTTP can run on the same networks. HTTP is used to download Web pages, applets, and images; CORBA is used for Java client-to-server communications. So we have an evolutionary solution that does not disrupt existing Web applications. Also note that Java clients cannot communicate across processes today. CORBA also solves this problem.

CORBA Meets Internet

Soapbox

We know of three approaches to merge CORBA IIOP with HTTP/CGI. The first approach, taken by Digital's *Web Broker*, is to write a CGI-to-CORBA gateway. This approach is extremely evolutionary, but it does not solve the CGI bottleneck and it does not extend Java with a distributed object infrastructure. The second approach is to provide HTTP-to-IIOP bidirectional gateways and to write a CORBA HTTP server that services HTTP requests. This is the approach taken by ANSA. If done right, it would allow CORBA to totally replace HTTP in older environments and to directly extend Java in newer environments. The third approach is the live-and-let-live environment that we described in the previous section (see Figure 30-1).

In our opinion, the third approach is the most pragmatic one. It's also the easiest one to implement and deploy. On the server side, you simply provide a CORBA IIOP server next to the existing HTTP server. On the client side, you must provide a CORBA ORB. This can be done by either downloading a Java ORBlet from the server, or by incorporating a Java ORB with the Web browser. We like the third approach because it lets both CORBA/IIOP and HTTP happily coexist over the same backbone. You only use CORBA IIOP to support the new Java client/server interactions; HTTP continues to service HTML documents and the legacy CGI applications. ❏

What CORBA Does for the Web

Competition for future control of the Internet infrastructure is just beginning.

— *Gartner Group*
(January, 1996)

Augmenting the Web infrastructure with CORBA provides three immediate benefits: 1) It gets rid of the CGI bottleneck on the server; 2) It provides a scalable and robust server-to-server Web infrastructure; and 3) It extends Java with a distributed object infrastructure. We briefly explain what this means:

■ *CORBA avoids the CGI bottleneck.* It allows clients to directly invoke methods on a server. The client passes the parameters directly using precompiled stubs, or it generates them "on-the-fly" using CORBA's dynamic invocation services. In either case, the server receives the call directly via a precompiled stub. You can invoke any IDL-defined method on the server, not just the ones defined by HTTP. In addition, you can pass any typed parameter, instead of just strings. This means there's very little client/server overhead, especially when compared with HTTP/CGI. With CGI, you must start a new instance of a program every time an applet invokes a method on a server; with CORBA, you don't. In addition, CGI does not maintain state between client invocations; CORBA does.

■ *CORBA provides a scalable server-to-server infrastructure.* Pools of server business objects can communicate using the CORBA ORB. These objects can run on multiple servers to provide load-balancing for incoming client requests. The ORB can dispatch the request to the first available object and add more objects as the demand increases. CORBA allows the server objects to act in unison using transaction boundaries and related CORBA services. In contrast, a CGI application is a bottleneck because it must respond to thousands of incoming requests; it has no way to distribute the load across multiple processes or processors.

■ *CORBA extends Java with a distributed object infrastructure*. Currently, Java applets cannot communicate across address spaces using remote method invocations. This means that there is no easy way for a Java applet to invoke a method on a remote object. CORBA allows Java applets to communicate with other objects written in different languages across address spaces and networks. In addition, CORBA provides a rich set of distributed object services that augment Java—including metadata, transactions, security, naming, trader, and persistence.

Table 30-1 summarizes the differences between today's Java-to-CGI client/server approach and a solution based on CORBA's IIOP protocol. CORBA was designed from the start to provide powerful 3-tier client/server solutions. In contrast, client/server interactions were wedged into HTTP and CGI; it's more of an after-thought. CORBA naturally extends Java's object model for distributed environments. CORBA also makes it easier to split Java applets into components that can be distributed along client/server lines. This means that the client side of the applet can remain small, which reduces the download time.

Table 30-1. Java Clients With CORBA IIOP Versus HTTP-CGI.

Feature	Java With CORBA ORB	Java With HTTP-CGI
State preservation across invocations	Yes	No
IDL and Interface Repository	Yes	No
Metadata support	Yes	No
Dynamic invocations	Yes	No
Transactions	Yes	No
Security	Yes	Yes
Rich object services	Yes	No
Server/server infrastructure	Yes	No
Client/client infrastructure	Yes	No
Server scalability	Yes	No
IDL-Defined Methods	Yes	No

This highly uneven comparison clearly demonstrates why the Java Web needs CORBA. However, CORBA is not the only object model to extend the Web. There are at least two other serious contenders—NeXT's *WebObjects* and OLE-based *ActiveXs*. The OLE alternative will eventually include both an object request broker—DCOM—and a compound document framework.

NeXT's WebObjects

NeXT's WebObjects takes an evolutionary path to distributing objects on the Internet. It does this by introducing objects on the server side while maintaining the CGI/HTTP client/server architecture. A WebObject is an Objective C object; it communicates with other WebObjects using the Objective C distributed object infrastructure. A special WebObject called the *distributor* accepts CGI requests; it then dispatches them to other WebObjects that do the actual work. The WebObjects can be distributed across machines, which helps with scalability and load-balancing issues. Like other business objects, WebObjects run the application logic and extract their data from database stores and legacy servers.

Developers typically store the persistent state of the WebObject in relational databases such as Oracle and Sybase. Unlike CGI applications, WebObjects provide extensive state-management facilities to help developers manage variables across client invocations. For example, you can declare variables to be valid for a particular client across HTTP invocations. Like other CGI applications, WebObjects dynamically generate Web pages in response to a client's request. A new WEB-OBJECT tag is required to specify the dynamic pages. This non-standard HTML tag is also used to specify the variables and actions that are passed to a WebObject.

Are WebObjects the Answer?

Soapbox

The most important thing right now is to let the Web accumulate users and establish ubiquity until it's so entrenched that even Microsoft can't own it, and then let's add the cool stuff. I am a little worried that the microcosmic lust for perfection will give Microsoft the time it needs to own the Web.

— Steve Jobs, CEO, NeXT
(January, 1996)

So what's wrong with WebObjects? Nothing, if you are willing to settle for a nice evolutionary solution. You get server objects on top of the existing HTTP infrastructure. The problem is that you're not leveraging the power of Java objects on the client. The WebObject server bus does not extend to the client. You still use HTTP for your client/server communications. In addition, WebObjects requires a new HTTP tag to express the client/server interaction semantics. You never get a completely free lunch in this business.

Now for the real Soapbox stuff. We've always maintained that the world could, at most, tolerate two distributed object buses—CORBA and DCOM/OLE. We do not think there's room for a third object bus—in this case, Objective C. Of course, like everyone else in the object world, we have a soft spot for the excellent features that are in Objective C and OpenStep. But we've always said that NeXT should adopt CORBA as their distributed object bus. So, are WebObjects the answer? Yes, if you need a quick solution that does not require Java on the client. However, it's not the architecture we would pick for building a long-term Object Web. To be fair, Steve Jobs makes it clear that in this Web business we can't afford the "microcosmic lust for perfection." But it doesn't hurt to try. ❏

COMPOUND DOCUMENTS AND THE OBJECT WEB

We need a secure, platform-independent, extensible, component-based dynamic environment that is easy to maintain and will give us the reuse we crave. And we haven't had it ... until Java.

> — *Christine Comaford, Columnist*
> *PC Week*
> *(January, 1996)*

Java and CORBA are not enough. The Object Web must also be augmented with compound documents. Why? Because compound documents can literally provide magic on the Web, especially when combined with Java. Compound document frameworks—like OLE and OpenDoc—provide two key technologies: 1) a visual component foundation for creating open Web browsers, and 2) the container technology for distributing, caching, and storing groups of related components and their data—meaning *shippable places*. In the remainder of this section, we first explain what these compound document technologies do for the Web. We also offer two architectural scenarios on how OpenDoc and OLE can play in the Object Web.[1]

Compound Documents as Open Web Browsers

Imagine a Web browser built entirely from components. In addition, imagine that the Web browser itself is a visual container of components. This means that it's a component that also lets you embed other components. For example, the Web browser can be built as an OpenDoc or OLE container. So what can you do with such a thing?

For starters, this new kind of browser can provide an integrated visual experience unlike anything you've seen to date. Components and Java applets will be able to seamlessly share the visual real estate within a browser's window. You will be able to edit the contents of any component in-place regardless of how deeply embedded it is within other components. You will also be able to drag and drop components within the browser as well as between the browser and the surrounding desktop. This means that you should be able to embed components within other components and then move them around at will across documents, desktops, and networks.

---

[1] It costs over $100 million to develop a compound document infrastructure like OpenDoc or OLE. It is highly unlikely that browser vendors will be able to recreate all this technology from scratch. So we expect browser vendors to ally themselves with one of the two contending component infrastructures.

In today's browsers, components own a static rectangular area within a page. In a compound document browser, components can take any shape, and you can move them around and embed them at will. You should be able to resize components within a browser, zoom in on their contents, and visually rearrange the contents of the page in any way you want. The components will automatically share the document's menu, clipboard, and palette. Everything will look very seamless.

Unlike today's browsers, the visual components will be able to interact with each other in many unpredictable ways. For example, you'll be able to drag a URL and drop it on a button to create an active pushbutton. You'll be able to shop by dragging merchandise and dropping it in an electronic shopping cart. You'll pay with e-cash that you pull out of an electronic wallet and drop on an invoice. And you will be able to drag an electronic signature and drop it on a message to seal a deal. The imagination is really at the controls in terms of what you can do with this marriage of Internet technology and components.

Compound Documents Versus HTML Plug-Ins

Compound documents provide a well-defined, open, and extendable architecture for plug-ins. In contrast, today's Web browsers are built in a monolithic fashion; they're "hardwired" to support every Internet protocol and data format. If the browser does not understand a data type, it fires off a separate *helper* application to deal with the unknown data. However, the continuity of the browsing experience is lost by launching a separate application that displays in a separate window.

Java applets and Netscape *plug-ins* are a way to bridge the gap between the monolithic applications of today and the component "suites" of tomorrow. They both provide some form of *in-line rendering*, which means that they can display their contents within a Web browser's window. However, they both suffer from the limitations of having to operate from within the confines of a monolithic browser.

Plug-ins and Java applets can only display their visual contents within a preassigned rectangular area. You cannot move plug-ins around at will—you can't drag them and then drop them on another object to perform a task. In addition, you cannot freely embed other components or applets within a plug-in. Plug-ins only under-stand the rules of the browser they were designed to extend; they don't know what to do if they're moved to another document or to the surrounding desktop. Netscape's *frames* stretch HTML's visual capabilities to the limit. They let you display multiple scrollable panels within a single page, each with its own distinct URL. In addition, frames can be resized.

The Desktop Is the Browser

The next generation Internet browser will consist of a set of components and the compound document *containers* in which they play. In addition to Web pages, you'll be able to download containers of components called *shippable places*. So where do I find one of these component-based Web browsers? It turns out that both the OLE and OpenDoc camps are developing component suites and frameworks for the Internet.

The OpenDoc suite—called *Cyberdog*—is the most advanced of the two (see the next Briefing box). Cyberdog is an extendable suite of OpenDoc parts and containers for the Internet. The OLE suite—called *Sweeper*—is a component toolkit for creating Internet applications; it builds on top of an OLE document extension called *DocObjects*. This is a visual container that looks like the Office 95 three-ring binder. Microsoft's *Internet Explorer 3.X*—code named *Striker*—will be built entirely from OLE components.

Both OLE and OpenDoc will eventually provide component wrappers for Java applets and Netscape plug-ins. This means that you will be able to embed Java applets and Netscape plug-ins inside either OpenDoc or OLE containers. So the bottom line is that today we have three contending container technologies for the Internet—OLE, OpenDoc, and HTML. OLE and OpenDoc were built from day one as component containers. HTML was not. HTML is, at best, a poor man's container. It will take a lot more work to bring it to par with either OLE or OpenDoc. However, HTML owns the Internet today. So the million dollar question is: Which container technology will own the Internet tomorrow? We will answer this question in a later soapbox (see the Soapbox—*Which Object Web?*—on page 549).

FYI

So What Is Cyberdog?

Briefing

*T*he browser is going to be so successful there won't be a browser—it will be part of the operating system.

— **Mike Zisman, CEO of Lotus Division**
IBM
(January, 1996)

Cyberdog—from Apple—is the code name for an Internet access framework based on OpenDoc. It's a collection of OpenDoc parts that work together to offer

Internet access. The framework allows the independently developed OpenDoc parts to behave like a cohesive visual application. Cyberdog provides common components that can be used "as is" or extended by part providers. The common glue includes the Cyberdog *Notebook* part, which lets you store your favorite Internet places in a hierarchical notebook. The *Log* part remembers where you've roamed and provides a notebook view of the sites you visited. You can use OpenDoc's drag-and-drop facilities to drag URLs from the Notebook (or the Log) to a browser window, and vice versa.

The heart of Cyberdog is the *PathFinder* part, which contains buttons that launch other OpenDoc Internet parts (see Figure 30-2). You can seamlessly access any Internet service by simply clicking on its button. All "dog-savvy" parts share the common Notebook and Log and act like a single application. You do not experience context switches as you switch between parts. In addition, multiple parts can be active at the same time.

Cyberdog also provides a MIME-conformant *Mail* part. You can create an e-mail message by styling some text into which you can drag-and-drop any type of visual content—including URLs that act as active links, not text addresses. You then send the mail message—including the embedded URLs—to other Cyberdog users (see Figure 30-3). Cyberdog mail agents use the MIME message headers to filter incoming mail—based on various user-specified criteria—before delivering them to the appropriate in-trays.

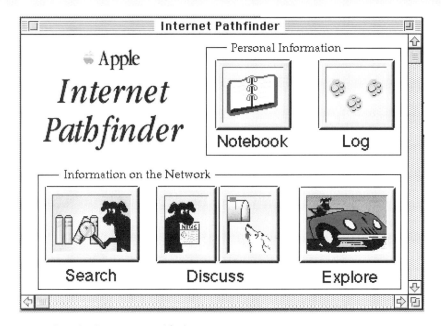

Figure 30-2. The Cyberdog Internet Pathfinder Container Part.

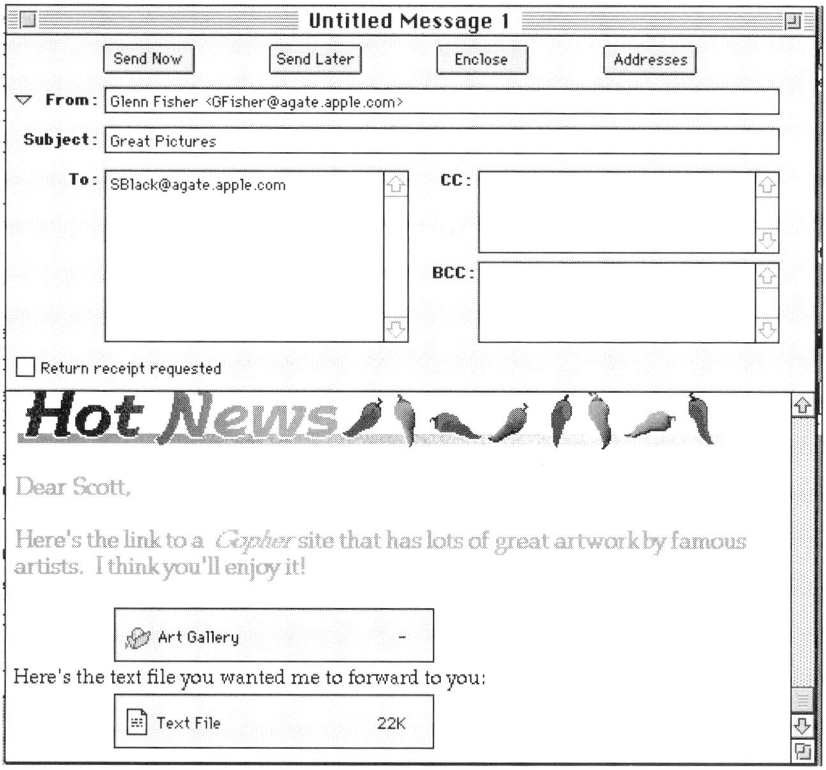

Figure 30-3. The Cyberdog Mail Part.

Cyberdog parts work with any OpenDoc container application. This means that you can drag parts and drop them on the desktop, and vice versa. You can ship parts in e-mail containers. Finally, you can embed Cyberdog parts in any OpenDoc application to make it Internet-aware. The Cyberdog parts work the same way no matter what container you use.

With Cyberdog, a URL is a first-class part. You can drag-and-drop URLs across containers, Web browsers, and the desktop. You can even drop them on a *Cyberbutton* part to create links to other Web resources. For example, you can drag Cyberbutton stationery from the OpenDoc palette, drop a bitmap icon on it to customize the button's visual appearance, and then make the button live by dropping a URL on the icon. You can create as many of these custom buttons as you like, place them within a mail message or Web page, and then distribute them via e-mail to the rest of the world.

The Cyberdog browser part supports all of HTML 2.0 and most HTML 3.0 extensions. The Cyberdog engineers plan to provide wrappers for Java applets and Netscape plug-ins so that they can be treated like any other OpenDoc component. The final release will also support SSL. Cyberdog is freely available from Apple's Web site (http://cyberdog.apple.com); the final version will be bundled with Macintosh computers and Mac OS releases.

So how does Cyberdog achieve its magic? It turns out that everything in Cyberdog is derived from four OpenDoc part extensions: *CyberItem* provides an object-wrapper for URLs; *CyberStream* downloads bytes from somewhere; *CyberExtension* makes regular OpenDoc parts "dog-savvy" by providing access to the Notebook and Log; and *CyberService* represents servers. These extensions serve as the Cyberdog framework; they provide everything you need to create dog-savvy parts. Welcome to the world of componentized browsers. ❏

Compound Documents as Portable Component Stores

Today most Web pages are simply files that get transmitted out of the file system or the Web server and sent down the wire to the client. But increasingly, as information becomes more rich and more finely honed, you want to pull that information from other sources. Over time, I think most information that gets sent over the Internet will not come out of file systems, but will come out of some structured stores.

> — Paul Maritz, Group VP
> Microsoft
> (December, 1995)

One of the key pieces of a compound document technology are the portable *structured files* they provide to store and distribute components. The two best-known examples of such containers are OpenDoc's *Bento* file system and OLE's *compound files* (also known as *DocFiles*). Both systems provide a "file system within a file." They both let components store their data in self-describing, navigatable data streams. So what can these structured containers do for the Object Web?

Simply put, structured containers allow us to store multiple components in a single document, move them as a single unit across networks, cache them where it makes most sense, and store them in document databases. The component store also becomes a unit of defense for an entire set of components. For example, OpenDoc's Bento lets you selectively encrypt a set of components. Finally, the containers can also persistently store a document's context and act accordingly. For example, you can store in a Bento file—along with a set of components—a user's preferences, login state, and the most current visual layout of the document. Bento also lets you store the previous snapshots of the documents in the form of drafts.

In summary, components need component stores so that you can move them around the Web at will. Structured containers are lightweight, shippable, object databases that were designed specifically to store, manage, and transport components. We can think of hundreds of ways these structured component containers can be used to create a smarter Object Web. The next section looks at one such example—*shippable places*.

So, What Is a Shippable Place?

*U*sers will live in their browsers? Ridiculous. Browsers will live inside our applications. We won't even realize they are there.

— Jesse Berst, PC Week
(December, 1995)

A *place* is a visual ensemble of related components. A *shippable place* is a mobile container of components; it's a place that can be shipped over the Net. Today's user interfaces are centered around a primitive place that represents a desktop. In contrast, shippable places let you interact with multiple places that represent collaborative environments based on real-world models. A place is a mini *virtual world*. For example, we can have places for 12-year olds, lawyers, or accountants. A place is typically used to display components that represent people and things. For example, places can represent meeting rooms, libraries, offices, homes, stadiums, shopping malls, museums, parks, and auditoriums. *People* live, work, shop, and visit these places. *Things* are tools that help us communicate, interact, and work within these places.

A place is implemented as a collection of components stored in a structured file container. You assemble a place by dragging components and dropping them within a visual container, which you then store in a structured file. You should be able to connect to a place via its URL and then download it just like any ordinary Web page. Of course, a place will have a digital signature that guarantees it came from a trusted server. The client will also have to authenticate itself before it can use the downloaded place.

Once the place is secured on your desktop, it will serve as a visual front-end for all kinds of specialized Internet services and business objects. The components within a place will typically communicate with their back-end counterparts using an ORB. A place is a dynamic assembly of ever-changing data, video feeds, and other live content.

You will probably keep the place on your desktop for weeks or months at a time, occasionally refreshing it with a newer version. The place is really one of many alternate desktops. You can also customize a place to reflect your preferences and needs. So, a place is a mobile document that you will store and access over time. In contrast, a Web page is more transient; it comes and then goes. With Web pages screen updates are wholesale page replacements, which destroy a user's context. In addition, there is no easy way for servers to tell clients that something has changed. Places fix these problems; they provide an anchor on the client that servers can call.

The Future Web Client

The operating system shell and the Internet browser will be one and the same.

> — *Bill Gates, Chairman*
> *Microsoft*
> *(April, 1996)*

Figure 30-4 shows three client models for the Web. In the first model, the browser is the desktop; it assumes that people live within their browsers. This is the current Netscape model of the world. In the second model, everything on the desktop is Web-enabled; the idea is that you will be able to access the Web from within any application or component without starting a browser. This is the Cyberdog model of the world; Microsoft will also support this model in Windows 97. The third model is shippable places; it lets you access the Web from within your places. A place can have multiple concurrent sessions with Web object servers. In addition, multiple places can be concurrently active on the same desktop. The Object Web may end up supporting all three models.

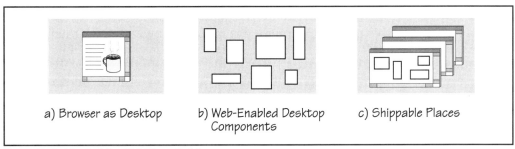

a) Browser as Desktop   b) Web-Enabled Desktop Components   c) Shippable Places

Figure 30-4. The Evolving Web Client Model.

In summary, compound document frameworks—like OpenDoc and OLE—were built to transport and display components. They will now allow us to display Web pages made up of components. And they will componentize the Web browser itself. Compound documents will allow us to create, assemble, and distribute an infinite variety of dynamic Web content. Both OpenDoc and OLE will support distributed components on top of their respective ORBs—CORBA and DCOM. The next section speculates on how the pieces may play together in a CORBA or OLE Object Web (also see the next Soapbox).

Which Object Web?

Soapbox

Instead of having OpenDoc containers, or OLE containers, or whatever they're going to be called, you're going to have HTML documents containing all these different types of things: Java objects, Macromedia Director files, different types of audio formats, video formats, portable document formats—just about everything.

> — Marc Andreessen, VP, Netscape
> (December, 1995)

Microsoft has built an infrastructure for client/server computing on the corporate Intranet that will take years to create in Java.

> — Dr. Jeff Sutherland, VP of Objects
> VMARK Software (March, 1996)

The bottom line is that Java alone cannot deliver a 3-tier client/server Object Web. Java needs to be augmented with an ORB and some form of compound document framework. It takes all three to create an Object Web. We do not agree with Marc Andreessen that HTML can evolve overnight into a compound document architecture; it will cost him another two years and over $100 million to recreate the features that are currently in OLE and OpenDoc. Marc can't afford to wait two years—Microsoft won't let him. We expect Microsoft to have all three pieces in late 1996 when Network OLE ships. Microsoft also has great tools and a loyal following of Windows/OLE developers (over a million strong).

The Java camp will have CORBA ORBlets before Network OLE ships. However, it must also provide an integrated compound document architecture in order to effectively compete with Microsoft. This is where OpenDoc and Cyberdog come into the picture. OpenDoc is multiplatform and vendor-neutral; its specifications are controlled by CI Labs and OMG. It is not inconceivable for CI Labs and OMG to put the Internet versions of CORBA and OpenDoc in the custody of W3C—the multivendor consortium that controls the Internet standards. We do not expect Microsoft to ever put the OLE specification in the custody of W3C.

So it looks like we're heading for another major war. This one will be fought for the control of the Object Web. Microsoft will deploy DCOM, OLE DocObjects, and VB Script. If it gets its act together, the Internet crowd will deploy Java, CORBA, and OpenDoc; it will also provide bridges to OLE ActiveXs. Can this war be avoided? Yes, if one of two things happen: 1) Microsoft hands over the custody of the OLE, DCOM, and Windows specifications to W3C; or 2) the Internet community fails to provide a unified Object Web solution based on open standards. Which do you think is more likely? □

THE DCOM/OLE OBJECT WEB

For Microsoft, OLE is the plumbing. And the way OLE components talk to each other is OLE and distributed OLE or Network OLE. Period. For us there is no other mechanism.

— *Roger Heinen, Senior VP of Development*
Microsoft (January, 1996)

Figure 30-5 is a rendition of the Microsoft Object Web—Microsoft calls it the *Active Internet Platform (AIP)*. It is, of course, a 3-tier client/server architecture. The first tier belongs to the client. In this case, the client belongs to *Sweeper's* OLE-based client components and services. Clients will be able to access the Internet via componentized browsers—such as the *Internet Explorer 3.X*. In addition to ordinary HTML pages, the browser will be able to play *DocObject* titles—also known as *ActiveX documents* (see next Briefing box).[2] A title is a three-ring binder document that contain pages. A page can contain OLE ActiveXs, Java applets, Visual Basic applets, and regular HTML content. DocObjects can play within browsers or any frame window (see next Briefing box). In addition,

---

[2] The entire Microsoft product line is being made DocObject-aware. For example, Microsoft Excel, Word, and all Office products are DocObjects. You will be able to plug these applications into a Microsoft browser frame, but they're too fat to ship over the net.

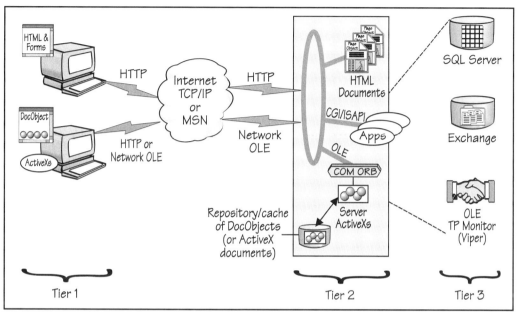

Figure 30-5. The Microsoft Object Web.

DocObjects can play inside other OLE containers; for example, the desktop. So, in theory, a title is a shippable place. It is also a unit of distribution and caching.

So how will Microsoft ensure that titles and their embedded ActiveXs are "safe"? Where are the Java-like language defenses and mobile-code safeguards? Microsoft's approach is to rely on *digital signatures* instead of the language to ensure component safety. To achieve its goal, Microsoft has signed up VeriSign to issue digital signatures for components—yes, more certificates. A VeriSign certificate will ensure that a component has not been tampered with after it leaves the hands of its creator.

You will be able to create OLE document titles using the *Microsoft Internet Studio*. Like Visual Basic, it is a drag-and-drop tool for assembling and laying out components within pages and binders. Once you create a document title, you should be able to upload it to an Internet server by pressing a button; Microsoft calls it "push-button publishing." The documents will be transported using *Internet Files*, which is Microsoft's "cool" name for OLE compound files. You will be able to glue together the ActiveXs via Visual Basic or Java scripts; Microsoft is creating a tool code-named *Jakarta* to support Java within the Internet Studio framework.

The second client/server tier consists of Microsoft's *Internet Information Server (IIS)*, previously known as Gibraltar. IIS is bundled with NT Server, which means that it is practically free. In addition to supporting ordinary HTML files, IIS will serve as a repository and cache for OLE document titles. IIS tracks a document (or title) by assigning it a globally unique ID (or GUID); it maps GUIDs to URLs using

OLE *monikers*, which is a fancy term for a rudimentary naming service (see next Details box).

What's an Async Moniker?

Details

Sweeper introduces a new kind of moniker called *async moniker*. Browsers use it to download files using separate background threads. The moniker notifies the browser via a callback when it completes the download. This is called "lazy loading." The idea is to let the browser interact with a user even while downloading large objects from the net. The *URL moniker* is an implementation of the async moniker; it is used to encapsulate Internet URLs. Note that OLE's URL monikers borrow heavily from a similar construct in Cyberdog. ❑

IIS will also provide an application framework for running OLE-based business objects. This framework will allow client components—including ActiveXs, Java applets, and VB applets—to invoke server business objects via the Network OLE ORB (also known as DCOM). Business objects will also be able to interact with each other using the OLE ORB. They interact with legacy applications via IIS-supplied APIs for CGI, ODBC, and ISAPI.

The third tier consists of Microsoft's BackOffice, and any server application that can be accessed using ISAPI or ODBC. Eventually, Microsoft intends to provide an OLE-based TP Monitor—called the *Component Coordinator*—to orchestrate transactions across different resource managers. When this happens, the business objects will become transactional. Of course, a TP Monitor also provides load-balancing and scalability. In addition, Microsoft's Cairo will provide an ODBMS for managing and accessing BLOBs and other forms of rich data. To top it all, Microsoft will provide tools for assembling 3-tier client/server Object Web applications. The tools will help you construct (or assemble) both the client and server sides of the Object Web equation.

In summary, Microsoft has put together a very compelling Object Web story. Are there any caveats? Without turning this section into a soapbox, there appear to be three problems with this story: 1) IIS is NT-centric, 2) Network OLE is a proprietary and unproven ORB, and 3) the OLE compound document architecture is proprietary. If you don't mind proprietary and NT-centric, then this is a very good story. However, it is difficult for us to see how Microsoft's closed standards will be reconciled with the Web's open culture. But let's face it, the Microsoft challenge will force the W3C to accelerate its timetable for an open Object Web architecture, which we discuss in the next section.

What Are DocObjects and ActiveXs?

Briefing

DocObjects are OLE documents that can act as their own containers. Microsoft originally developed them for Office 95, where they are used to lump documents, spreadsheets, and PowerPoint slides into a single three-ring binder. You can save, view, print, copy, or move the entire binder as a single entity. DocObjects are now being repositioned as mobile OLE containers of components for the Internet.

DocObjects provide a standard way for traditional applications to plug themselves into a Microsoft Web browser's window frame. In addition, they're being groomed to become general-purpose containers of components. A DocObject page can contain lightweight OCXs—or *ActiveXs*—as well as other component types. In contrast to a simple compound document container, the DocObject binder knows how to handle pagination, headers, footers, title pages, views, and other visual constructs.

The DocObject is a compound document container, so it provides its own storage and it becomes a unit of storage management. For our OLE techie readers, DocObjects introduce three new OLE interfaces: **IOleDocument** and **IOleDocumentView** on the component (or OLE Server) side, and **IOleDocumentSite** on the container side.

Microsoft would like to see its DocObject titles populated with its newest *OCX 96* controls—the new marketing term is *ActiveX components*. These new controls are stripped down OLE OCXs that have fewer mandatory OLE interfaces to support. Technically speaking, the control is simply required to be a self-registering DCOM object; it must implement OLE's **IUnknown** and **IClassFactory** interface and whatever interfaces it needs to perform its functions. So the control is freed of all the extra OLE baggage. In theory, these slimmed down controls may end up being about 1/3 the size of current OCXs, which means they should be faster to download over the Internet.

Microsoft is also developing a standard set of *component categories* and their descriptions. By not requiring any particular interfaces, ActiveXs are free to do whatever they please; Microsoft has effectively relaxed the OLE control requirement to nothing. This places an extra burden on OLE containers, which are now expected to dynamically discover the interfaces an ActiveX supports. OLE's new component categories provide a way for controls to tell their containers what they do. As you'd expect, Microsoft defines an *InternetAware* category—these are controls that load their data via asynchronous monikers. Each ActiveX component will be represented in the OLE registry with a *Category ID*.

> Microsoft is partnering with NetManage to implement a suite of core Internet components that you will be able to insert into any application to add Internet or Web connectivity. By the time you read this, there should be a full line of ActiveX components—including *ActiveMovie*, *ActiveAudio*, and *ActiveVRML*. These are the OLE-control equivalents of Cyberdog parts and Netscape plug-ins. As we go to press, over 100 vendors are developing ActiveX Internet components. You can develop ActiveX components using the Microsoft *ActiveX Development Kit* and *Visual C++ version 4.1*'s new MFC classes. ❑

THE CORBA OBJECT WEB

*B*y integrating the WWW, Java, and CORBA, customers will have a powerful set of technologies for developing and deploying distributed object applications over the global Internet.

> — *Michael Goulde, Seybold Analyst*
> *(January, 1996)*

Figure 30-6 is a rendition of the open Object Web. The picture is very similar to Microsoft's Object Web, except that all the technologies are based on open standards.[3] The open Object Web is also a 3-tier client/server architecture. As usual, the first tier belongs to the client. In this case, the client belongs to Java components, ORBlets, OpenDoc compound documents, and shippable places.

Clients will be able to access the Internet via componentized browsers; for example, Cyberdog or a future version of Netscape. In addition to ordinary HTML pages, the browser will be able to play OpenDoc titles. A title is a shippable place; it will be able to contain ActiveXs, OpenDoc parts, Java applets, and regular HTML content. Titles will be played within browsers as well as within other containers; for example, an OpenDoc or OLE-enabled desktop. Remember, OpenDoc parts can play in OLE containers; they can also contain OLE OCXs and ActiveXs. So, in theory, everything can play within everything else.

The second tier will be provided by any server that can service both HTTP and CORBA clients. This combination is supported on almost every server platform—including Unixes, NT, OS/2, NetWare, Mac, OS/400, MVS, and Tandem Nonstop Kernel. CORBA objects act as a middle tier; they encapsulate the application's business logic. They interact with client components via a Java ORBlet or any regular CORBA ORB that can run IIOP over the Internet. Of course, the CORBA

---

[3] Open is an overloaded term. In this case, "open" means technology that is not controlled by a single vendor. CORBA, OpenDoc, and the Web are open because they are controlled by a multivendor consortia—namely, OMG, CI Labs, and W3C/IETF.

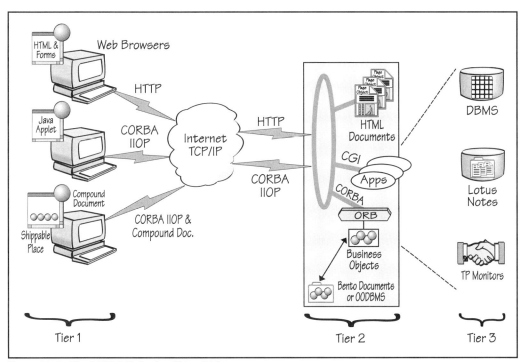

Figure 30-6. The CORBA/Cyberdog Object Web.

objects on the server can interact with each other using a CORBA ORB. They can also talk to existing server applications in the third tier using SQL or any other form of middleware. The third tier is almost anything a CORBA object can talk to. This includes TP Monitors, MOMs, DBMSs, ODBMSs, Lotus Notes, and e-mail.

In a CORBA/OpenDoc Object Web, the second tier also acts as a store of component titles and shippable places. These can be stored in shippable *Bento* files that are managed by an ODBMS or DBMS. ODBMSs are better suited for the task. An ODBMS can treat a Bento file as just another user-defined data type; an SQL database must support object extenders to provide the same kind of service. An ODBMS could transparently cache active Bento files in memory. So when a client requests a shippable place or component Web page, the ODBMS can service the request almost instantaneously by shipping a Bento file that's in-memory. The advantage of using Bento as a portable structured file is that it can run on multiple operating systems; it was designed to be a portable component store.

So as you can see, the "open camp" also has great technology for creating an Object Web. But what are the caveats? The main caveat is that it takes a great amount of intervendor cooperation to pull all these technologies together. Because we have such strong opinions on this subject, we will continue this discussion in the next Soapbox.

The Lemming Effect

Soapbox

Microsoft is hard-core about the Internet. Very hard-core.

> — *Bill Gates, Chairman*
> *Microsoft*
> *(December, 1995)*

Microsoft's main Internet strategy is to "extend" HTML in a Java-like style to launch the company's proprietary OLE-based Internet infrastructure.

> — *Gartner Group*
> *(January, 1996)*

Microsoft has been unwavering in its component vision. The company has spent the last few years retooling itself around the DCOM ORB and the OLE component technology. Now Microsoft is applying all this technology towards creating an Object Web. Microsoft will create everything it does on the Web on top of its distributed component infrastructure.

In contrast, Microsoft's competitors all seem to have a piece of the object puzzle, but none have it all. So it will take some serious intervendor collaboration to weave together a cohesive set of open Object Web products and tools. At a minimum, they must be as cohesive as Microsoft's offerings.

Unfortunately, some of Microsoft's competitors currently feel they're ahead of the game and can win on their own. We call this the "lemming effect." What this means is that without a solid object foundation, each competitor is going to jump off the cliff at a different point. For example, without a solid compound document infrastructure, Netscape will eventually fail against Microsoft. We can say the same for Sun's Java, Lotus Notes, and Oracle. None of these technologies can stand up on their own against Microsoft's Object Web. Unless these companies work together to create an open Object Web quickly, Microsoft is destined to become the next Microsoft. ❑

Chapter 31

Web Client/Server:
Meet the Players

---

*T*wo years ago the Internet was an emerging fad. Now it's a tsunami and vendors are scrambling to accommodate it.

> — *Jamie Lewis, President*
> *Burton Group*
> *(December, 1995)*

The computer industry is once again recreating itself. The Internet is a giant tsunami that will not leave anything untouched in its path. It is redefining the client/server envelope and reshuffling the cards. As you can imagine, the Internet will create more than its fair share of new instant winners and losers in the computer industry. And nobody knows for sure where the Internet market will lead.

It would be sheer lunacy for us to predict what the Internet client/server landscape will look like in the next two years. For example, server companies—like Sun, IBM, and Oracle—may use Java to regain the desktop from Microsoft. Or, Microsoft may use the OLE Object Web to become the new enterprise server company; it may then wipe the existing server companies from the face of the Earth. In between, there are fortunes to be made in Internet commerce, multimedia databases, security, firewalls, authoring tools, mobile agents, avatars, and virtual worlds. Beyond the basic plumbing, there are even greater fortunes to be made by providers of online content and goods—including entertainment, education, and commercial services.

One thing we can say for sure is that the Internet client/server race is turning out to be quite complex, with lots of contestants all vying for a lead within numerous market niches. This chapter starts out by giving you a quick snapshot of the Internet client/server market. We then bravely forecast some of the key trends. How big is the prize? What markets are emerging? Next, we pick our favorites in the Web client/server sweepstakes. Where is Jimmy the Greek when we need him? We conclude with the obligatory Soapbox about where we think all this is going. Note that this chapter only focuses on the client/server aspects of the Internet; extending the coverage beyond this limit would be too suicidal—even for us.

INTERNET MARKET OVERVIEW

The Internet is basically a stack, and there are different amounts of opportunity at each level in the stack.

— *Bill Gates, Chairman*
Microsoft
(April, 1996)

The Internet means different things to different folks; it's become the umbrella name for multiple emerging subindustries. Figure 31-1 divides the Internet industry into six major segments:

■ ***Internet equipment providers.*** This includes the manufacturers of backbone routers, Internet access equipment, and server computers.

■ ***Internet service providers (ISPs).*** This includes traditional bandwidth providers such as PSI, UUNet, Netcom, BBN Planet, and @Home. It also includes providers of consumer online services such as America Online (AOL), Microsoft Network (MSN), Prodigy, and CompuServe; these vendors are fiercely counterattacking the traditional ISPs to get their share of the Internet market. Finally, the telephone and cable-TV companies have also entered the fray; they are vying for a share of the high bandwidth sweepstakes.

■ ***Internet client/server software.*** This includes browsers, server software, security, and tools—the software we covered in the last three chapters. It includes software used for both the Internet and Intranets. Note that we do not include in this list related server software—including ORBs, RDBMSs, ODBMSs, Data Warehouses, Infobases, TP Monitors, and groupware. These related server

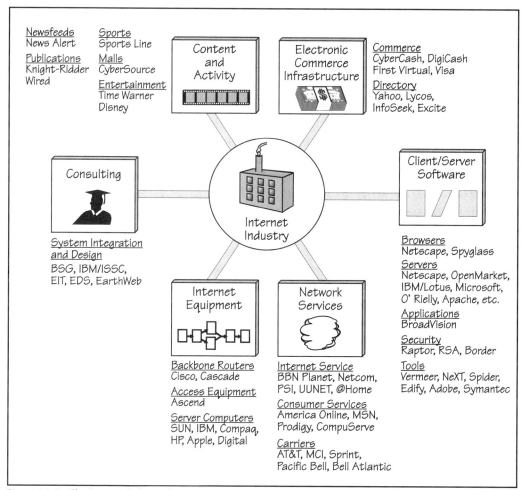

Figure 31-1. The Internet Industry Segments.

markets were covered in previous parts of this book; including them here would be double-counting.

■ *Internet Electronic Commerce Infrastructure.* This includes e-cash, electronic credit and debit cards, online banks, and anything that helps facilitate electronic commerce. This category also includes directory services and search engines that help you find things; for example, Yahoo! and InfoSeek. We also include in this category electronic shopping frameworks; for example, Broadvision, Electric Communities, and OpenMarket.

■ *Internet content and activity.* This includes electronic newsfeeds, sports, malls, publications, entertainment, and other forms of content. Ultimately, this is what Internet client/server is all about—fun, games, education, and business.

■ *Internet consulting.* This includes traditional systems integrators that will be called in to create corporate Intranets. It also includes a new breed of Internet consultant; for example, graphic designers and online advertisement and Internet presence-building agencies.

The six categories we just described closely match those used by *Hambrecht and Quist Research* in their ground-breaking market study called *The Internet— Webbing The Information Economy* (September 22, 1995). So we can use their projections to describe the size of the total Internet market and each of its segments.

According to Hambrecht and Quist, the Internet was a $1.18 billion market in 1995; Figure 31-2 shows how the pie is divided between each of the six market categories. It looks like the people making the money are currently the hardware vendors and ISP providers. In spite of all the hype, Web client/server software is a mere $260 million blip on the Internet radar screen. Note that the study does not include the $1 billion that corporations spent developing their Web pages in 1995; it seems that creating Web pages falls in the "labor of love" category.

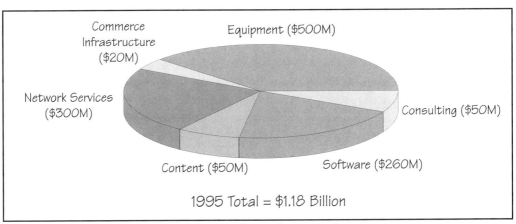

Figure 31-2. The Internet Market in 1995. (Source: Hambrecht and Quist)

Hambrecht and Quist forecast that the Internet will become a $23.2 billion market by the year 2000 (see Figure 31-3). The biggest growth will be in Internet content; it is expected to expand from the current $100 million to over $10 billion by the end of the decade. The second growth area is network services; it is expected to grow to $5 billion by the year 2000, which represents a 76% compound annual growth rate (CAGR). Finally, the Internet client/server software market is also headed for good times; it is expected grow to $5 billion, which is a 73% CAGR.

The numbers in the Hambrecht and Quist forecast explain why the investment community is so strongly behind the Internet; they believe it will become a $23.2 billion business by the year 2000. The projected growth rates are astronomical.

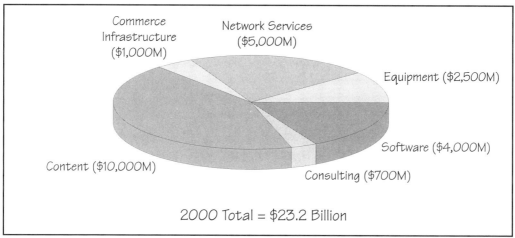

Figure 31-3. The Projected Internet Market in 2000. (Source: Hambrecht and Quist)

But nevertheless, the numbers seem to match the extraordinary valuation the stock market places on anything that has to do with the Internet.

Is the bubble going to burst? We don't know. Pundits have been predicting the "death of the Internet" almost every year since the mid-70s. It certainly hasn't happened yet. We feel quite comfortable with the assumptions behind the Hambrecht and Quist forecast. If anything, they may be a bit too conservative. We also believe that many of today's Internet superstars may not be around in the year 2000. Revolutions tend to eat their own children; the Internet is no exception.

TRENDS

Client/server is a total system. You might shift the center of gravity and say, "I'll give away clients and make money on servers," or you can shift and say, "I'm going to charge for clients and give away servers."

— *Jim Clark, Chairman*
Netscape
(October, 1995)

The Hambrecht and Quist study identifies e-mail as the predominant application on today's Internet (see Figure 31-4). It also forecasts that the Web will have 200 million users in the year 2000—a truly phenomenal number. If we had to place our bets, e-mail will be subsumed by the Web long before the year 2000; it will become just another Web application. So the real questions are: How will the Web expand to 200 million users? What will a Web with 200 million users look like? Who will get us there? And, how will it happen?

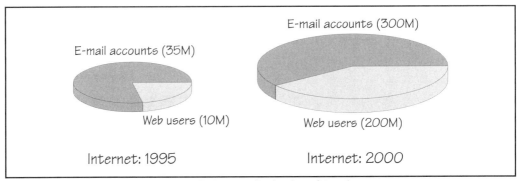

E-mail accounts (300M)

E-mail accounts (35M)

Web users (10M)

Web users (200M)

Internet: 1995

Internet: 2000

Figure 31-4. Internet Usage: E-mail vs. Web. (Source: Hambrecht and Quist)

There are no sure answers to these questions. The Web seems to recreate itself every two years. At this rate, by the year 2000, the Web will have gone through two more transformations. An Object Web could quite possibly subsume every other form of client/server computing. So here's a snapshot of the major movements that we anticipate in the near-term evolution of the Web:

■ *Distributed objects and components will be everywhere*. The Web will recreate itself on top of a distributed object bus; the two top contenders for the bus are CORBA and Network OLE. HTML will morph into a true compound document container; the two contenders for this role are OpenDoc's Bento and OLE's compound files. Finally, Web pages will simply become containers of live components. The three contending component camps are CORBA-enabled Java components, CORBA-enabled OpenDoc parts, and OLE ActiveXs. The component wars will be fought at the tool level; for example, Symantec's Java-based *Cafe* versus Microsoft's OLE-based *Internet Studio*. It would make a lot of sense for the Java and OpenDoc camps to merge—they have complementary component infrastructures. In summary, the component world war is just starting; the grand prize is the Internet.

■ *Intranets will extend the reach of corporate networks*. Corporations are migrating from private networks to Intranets. This means that private networks will layer on top of Internet technology. The Intranets are the first step towards opening up the corporate network. We anticipate that corporations will take advantage of the common Internet technology to link up with their suppliers, customers, and business partners. Instead of hiding behind firewalls, corporations will increasingly use the Internet's wide-area security mechanisms— including SSL, S-HTTP, and public keys—to reach out to the world at large. In contrast, today's corporate networks are primarily closed systems.

■ *Web transactions will create vast new markets.* The Web lowers barriers to entry and stimulates new forms of competition; you don't have to be a giant retail chain to compete on the Web. The irrelevance of size will recreate many of our existing distribution channels. Retailers will become wholesalers, and manufacturers will become distributors. The Internet will restructure the way industries deliver service; for example, what does it mean to be a bank in an online world? In addition, the Web will generate new types of online goods and services; examples include travel guides, interactive education, art exhibits, and multiserver games. It's just a matter of time before the Web turns into the world's largest shopping mall and games arcade. We expect the Web to generate trillions of new electronic transactions each year. In addition, the Web will become your *information utility*—just as important to you as electricity and the telephone. You won't be able to function in the modern world without it.

■ ***The Web will generate demand for millions of skinny Internet PCs.*** Yes, there will be a huge demand for lightweight Java machines. These $500 Web machines will download applets and mobile objects on demand to perform a task. And, of course, they will be easier to use, maintain, and upgrade than current PCs. They will be used by millions of users who can't afford, comprehend, or deal with the cost of ownership of a full-blown PC. The Web PCs (or Java machines) will become as ubiquitous as the telephone. Components and shippable places will become the primary software distribution mechanisms in this new environment. Java machines can potentially outflank Microsoft Windows in many new environments.

■ ***The Web will also generate demand for millions of fat client/server machines.*** Yes, there will also be demand for millions of ordinary PCs that act as both clients and personal Web servers. You will be able to publish Web pages faster than you can send electronic mail today. So your Web server will act as your electronic proxy (or avatar) to the world at large. You will existentially define yourself by your Web presence: "I'm on the Web; therefore, I am."

■ ***The Web will expand into new client/server areas***. In the client/server technology world, you either subsume other technologies or get subsumed. We believe that an Object Web is an ideal architecture for subsuming all existing forms of client/server computing—including database, TP Monitors, and groupware. Of course, if the Web does not evolve beyond CGI, it will simply become one more client type for the existing client/server models.

■ ***Mobile containers will be everywhere.*** The Web is about to create an explosion in mobile BLOBs, applets, and components that run within "containers." If you think about it, our current file systems and databases will not be able to deal with this new explosion of interlinked BLOBs. The trick is to use scalable Object Databases (ODBMSs) to track relationships between objects and the relationships between objects and their containers. Mobile containers or structured files will be used to ship groups of related objects and BLOBs to any destination on the World Wide Web. A shippable place is an example of a visual container of components.

The Web promises to unleash a wellspring of entrepreneurial activity around client/server components. This new software distribution model will accelerate the shift toward components and applets; it will attract millions of small developers. It's only a matter of time before these developers supply the "killer applets" that will bring the masses to the Web. We will see killer applets for home shopping, electronic banking, entertainment, education, and many activities still to be invented.

Remember, the magic number was 200 million users by the year 2000. 20 million of us are already on the Web. We will soon be joined by 100 million people with PCs today that are not yet on the Web. But where will the next 80 million come from? This is where the $500 Web PC comes into the picture; it's the low-priced "volkscomputer" that will open up the Web to the masses. If we build it, they will hopefully come.

So where are the showstoppers in this rosy picture? Three immediately come to mind: bandwidth, more bandwidth, and a million applets. It's obvious that the Web cannot become an information utility for the masses without low-cost abundant bandwidth. The ultimate fate of the client/server Web may depend on the adoption rate of technologies like ISDN, ATM, and cable modems. In addition to bandwidth, the Web must recreate all of client/server computing using mobile components. This is obviously a very tall order; it will take millions of Java-programmer-years to get us there. In summary, the Web needs abundant bandwidth and applets to maintain its current feeding frenzy.

MEET THE PLAYERS

It's a war, a world war.

> — *Mary McCaffrey, Internet World*
> *(March, 1996)*

Thousands of small start-ups will make their fortunes by providing new Web content, special-purpose software, infobases, and innovative services. In addition, a few million of us will make a good living on the Web selling wares, components, applets, and services; it's a giant online flea market. So there are fortunes to be made at the application level. However, we anticipate that the lion's share of the Web client/server middleware revenues will end up in the pockets of the usual suspects—Netscape, Sun, Microsoft, Lotus/IBM, Apple, and Oracle.

Netscape and Apple have mindshare. The rest have that, plus deep pockets and a strong client/server technology base on which to build. Deep pockets are very important because much of the Web client/server infrastructure is given away. Even though the Web crowd expects everything to be free, we all know that there is no such thing as a perpetual "free lunch." Someone must eventually pay for all these goodies. In the case of the Web, money comes from two sources: 1) the stock market, and 2) corporations that buy Intranet and Internet technology. The stock market is fickle; it will continue investing in the Web only if it sees revenues at the end of the tunnel. So that leaves us with the corporate Intranets. In the short term, large corporations will pay for the Web infrastructure. In the long run, the Web will pay for itself by becoming the world's largest shopping mall.

Being Cool Just Isn't Enough

The good news is that corporations are expected to spend over $5 billion on Intranets in 1997. Most corporations are, of course, not starting from ground zero with client/server technology, which means they will expect the Web to fit within their existing infrastructures. This means that the Web technology must be able to seamlessly interface with existing databases, TP Monitors, NOSs, groupware, and system management platforms. Corporations also expect their systems to be robust and mission-critical. This means that the Web players with the most mature client/server technologies are in the best position to win. Just being "cool" won't be good enough.

Someone once said that sorting through Internet client/server product offerings is a bit like trying to describe a passing bullet train. It's an intensively competitive market in which vendor strategies and alliances change almost daily. To get the latest information, turn to the six o'clock news or read about it in the tabloids. In the next few sections, we give you a snapshot of what the top Web client/server vendors are offering today.

Netscape

1995 may be looked back on as the end of the Windows era and the beginning of the networked era that Netscape exemplifies...Netscape intends to make Navigator both the de facto operating system and "office suite" of cyberspace.

— Peter Lewis, New York Times
(November, 1995)

Netscape is one of the shining Internet stars. In less than a year, it went from nothing to a company valued at $2 billion. Netscape currently owns the browser market; its *Navigator 2.0* was the first browser to support Java applets, SSL security, frames, and plug-ins. Navigator 2.0 is more than a browser; it's an Internet client suite. It handles e-mail, threaded discussion groups, FTP, gopher, chat, and so on. It's also a platform on which you can build live online applications. In April 1996, Netscape shipped a beta of *Navigator 3.0*; it supports VRML, multimedia, and client-side digital certificates—you won't have to enter your password every time you visit a secured site. So Navigator is a product that doesn't stand still. It has a six month technology lead over its primary competitors: Spyglass Mosaic and the Microsoft Web Explorer.

The much awaited *Netscape Navigator Gold* provides point-and-click Web author-ing and push-button publishing from within Navigator itself—you never leave the browser. Gold lets you directly edit the page you're viewing within your browser. Of course, it supports all the Netscape extensions and it lets you instantly add hyperlinks by dragging bookmarked sites to the document you're creating. Gold also provides point-and-click administration of Web servers. At the high end of the tools market, Netscape offers *LiveWire Pro*—a professional visual development environment with built-in connectivity to most leading databases—including Infor-mix, Oracle, Sybase, Illustra, and Microsoft.

As we go to press, Netscape owns about 17% of the Internet server market; it holds third place after NCSA (28%) and Apache (27%). However, the company owns a much bigger percentage of the lucrative Intranet server market. *FastTrack* is Netscape's low-entry server offering; it is an easy-to-install, self-configuring, low-cost Web server that supports the Java and JavaScript programming languages. FastTack is bundled with Navigator Gold and sells for $295; it sells for $495 when bundled with LiveWire Pro.

In March 1996, Netscape announced *SuiteSpot*. This is an integrated suite of server offerings that includes: 1) *Enterprise Server*—a secure, high-performance, and scalable Web server; 2) *Mail Server*—an HTML-based SMTP mail server; 3) *News Server*—a discussion group server; 4) *Catalog Server*—a directory server that helps you find people and documents on Intranets; and 5) *Proxy Server*—a server that caches frequently accessed Internet documents inside the corporate firewall. SuiteSpot runs on a variety of Unixes and on Windows NT. The entire suite—with LiveWire included—sells for $3,995. You can also purchase the pieces "a la carte" for about a $1,000 each. Netscape also plans to introduce a *Certificate Server* by the end of 1996.

Netscape's strategy is to weaken Microsoft's grip on the client market by minimizing the importance of the operating system; it is also using plug-ins to wrest the control of the client API from Microsoft. Netscape is also well-positioned on the server side, with its integrated server suite and its new directory and naming services.[1]

---

[1] The Netscape directory uses the *Lightweight Directory Access Protocol (LDAP)*—it's a lightweight version of the X.500 DAP protocol for the Internet. Like DAP, LDAP provides interoperability services between directories. In addition to Netscape, it is supported by Novell, Banyan, Microsoft, and IBM.

Netscape has the support of 14,000 ISVs. It has also developed excellent distribution channels by signing up over 1,000s VARs. The list includes industry giants— such as SGI, HP, Sun, IBM, Novell, Digital, AT&T, Apple, and MCI. In addition to the obligatory browser, many of these VARs are licensing Netscape server products.

So what are Netscape's weaknesses? At the technical level, Netscape does not have a good Object Web story. It must quickly develop an alliance with the CORBA and OpenDoc camps to counter the Microsoft object juggernaut.[2] Netscape could make CORBA ubiquitous by shipping an ORBlet with every browser. It could also use CORBA to integrate its server suite. Of course, OpenDoc is a natural candidate for creating a component-based Netscape browser and for a shippable places offering.

At the business level, Netscape is fighting a nasty price war with Microsoft. However, Netscape was able to counter Microsoft's bundling of the *Internet Information Server (IIS)* with NT by offering a richer suite of server products— including the directory and naming services. But to stay ahead of the game, Netscape needs to include a scalable, high-performance object store with its Web server. It must do this to counter Microsoft's tight integration of IIS with NT's file system.

Sun and JavaSoft

It's no accident that the most vocal advocates for "thin client" devices are companies like Oracle, Sun, and IBM, who'd love to see a world where servers become the high-growth platform.

— *Soft-Letter*
(February, 1996)

Sun helped create the Internet, but now the Internet is redefining Sun. About 20% of Sun servers in operation are now Intranet or Internet servers; Sun expects that number to grow to 80% by 1998. In other words, the Internet may become Sun's core business. As the owner of Java, Sun is in an excellent position to obtain a toe-hold on the client side with its Internet Java PCs.

Most importantly, Sun has a strong 3-tiered Object Web story. It includes downloading Java applets on the client that can then talk to CORBA business objects (NEO) via a Java ORBlet (JOE). NEO is a very strong server platform that includes multithreaded server objects, a scalable CORBA ORB, business object development

---

[2] In May 1996, Marc Andreessen announced Netscape's support of OpenDoc at the Apple World-Wide Developer's Conference (WWDC).

tools, and the Solstice system management platform. NEO uses the *Persistence* class libraries to provide object interfaces to the major DBMSs and ODBMs.

Sun's position as a hardware vendor provides both strengths and weaknesses. On the plus side, Sun can provide a complete line of bundled Internet hardware/software combinations—including low-cost Java machines, 3-D graphics workstations, routers, firewalls, and superservers.

On the negative side, Sun is perceived to be a Solaris-first hardware vendor; it does not project the image of a crossplatform software solution provider. The creation of *JavaSoft* as an independent software subsidiary may help change this perception; it may also help Sun generate huge software revenues from multiplatform Java component sales.

Sun's other weakness is the lack of a compound document and shippable-place architecture. This considerably weakens Sun's position as an independent component provider. Because of OLE's market thrust, compound documents are becoming an important part of the middleware substrate; they cannot be ignored. Sun can acquire this technology—on a CORBA platform—by joining the OpenDoc camp.

Microsoft

Microsoft has one thing nobody else has. They can give everything away free for the next 20 years.

> — *Eric Schmidt, CTO*
> *Sun*
> *(February, 1996)*

Until December 1995, Microsoft appeared to be suffering from an uncharacteristic lack of clarity as it confronted the Internet. Perhaps it was hoping that MSN would replace the Internet in one fell swoop. Of course, this did not happen; MSN was a market failure by Microsoft standards. As a result, Microsoft decided that it could not continue to ignore the Internet. Its new Trojan Horse strategy seems to be to embrace the Internet and its standards so as to morph them into OLE. Microsoft can do this by adding hundreds of proprietary extensions.

In March 1996, Microsoft announced ActiveXs and its new OLE Internet thrust. This time, hundreds of ISVs jumped on the Microsoft Internet bandwagon. As we explained in the last chapter, Microsoft has a very consistent Object Web story. If the Internet crowd does not get its Object Web act together soon, the Web may simply morph into OLE.

Did we have too much espresso? Not really. As Sun's Eric Schmidt points out, Microsoft has the deepest pockets in our industry. It can afford to bundle anything it wants with either Windows 95 on the client or NT on the server. The bundling of IIS with NT made Microsoft an instant player in the Web server market. Microsoft's *Internet Explorer 3.X* will be totally integrated within Windows 97. In addition, Microsoft was able to coax both CompuServe and America Online into bundling the Explorer with their packages. All this free bundling may give Netscape a run for its money on the client side.

Microsoft plans to integrate IIS with its *BackOffice* suite—including Exchange, SQL Server, and its forthcoming OLE-based TP Monitor. In late 1996, Microsoft plans to introduce a BackOffice proxy server (or firewall), a merchant server, and a media server. MSN is being repositioned as a "for-pay" Web service. In addition, Microsoft *Office* applications—including Excel, Word, and PowerPoint—will be Internet-enabled with add-ons that let them interact directly with IIS. Microsoft is also bundling the *Internet Assistant*—a low-end HTML publishing tool—with Word. Finally, Microsoft also supports the Internet via an impressive family of tools that includes the *Internet Studio*, *Visual Basic*, *Visual C++*, *Jakarta*, and the recently acquired *Vermeer*; these tools were described in the last chapter.

The bottom line is that Microsoft is a formidable player on the Internet, especially for Windows-only shops. Microsoft brings to the equation a complete Object Web story. Microsoft's main weakness is that the story does not play well on non-Windows platforms. The Web is too diverse to become a Windows-only shop. So this is Microsoft's Achilles' heel. However, for the Microsoft "Windows everywhere" crowd, this may not be perceived to be a weakness. For them, the Internet simply becomes another Windows extension for which Microsoft sets the standards.

Apple

Our vision is to make the Internet as friendly as the Mac is today.

> — *Larry Tessler, Chief-Scientist*
> *Apple*
> *(May, 1996)*

Mac users have a disproportionately strong presence on the Web; they may account for almost 20% of the Web client population. While the current Mac is not the world's best Web server platform, it is very friendly and gentle; for example, Apple's *Workgroup Server* is a good Web server for small businesses that don't anticipate thousands of hits a day. Apple may become a major Web server player when its microkernel-based Mac OS—code-named *Copland*—ships in 1997. In the meantime, it's the client software that makes the Mac shine on the Web.

Apple views the Web as a key software and hardware initiative. Its strategy is to extend the Mac's friendliness to the Web. To get there, Apple will make the Web an inherent part of Copland using Cyberdog. Internet access becomes part of the OS. Apple is counting on OpenDoc's seamless visual experience to provide "a killer user interface" to the Internet; it will feel like a video arcade game. People will buy Macs just to get the best Internet multimedia experience.

As a hardware vendor, Apple is well-positioned to enter the Internet PC sweepstakes with *Pippin*—a low-cost system architecture based on the Power Mac. Apple and Bandai recently demonstrated a Pippin Web machine that may sell for under $500. All Pippin titles run from a CD-ROM. You can turn Pippin into a Web client by supplying a CD with a Java-enabled browser; there is no software to install or maintain. Perhaps Santa will bring you a Pippin Cyberdog next Christmas. In summary, Apple is another visionary force on the Web; it may give Netscape and Microsoft a run for the money on the client side.

IBM/Lotus

A *Web browser on every desktop and a Notes server in every data center. This is an extremely aggressive "get market share" strategy. It would not have been possible if Lotus had not "acquired a parent" (IBM) with deep pockets.*

> — *Gartner Group*
> *(January, 1996)*

We explained what Notes brings to the Internet in Part 6. Notes makes a very good Web server; its document database technology is miles ahead of its competitors. Notes offers customers a proven approach to Web application development; it brings to the Web advanced features—including database replication, built-in security, SMP scalability, strong search engines, database navigation facilities, enhanced e-mail, and systems management. Notes also runs on multiple client and server platforms. Its client/server platform is familiar to thousands of ISVs and corporate developers. The product is well-supported and has excellent distribution channels. In addition, Notes is integrated with the rest of the IBM server products—including CICS, DB2, MQSeries, and SOM. Notes on the Web is currently a very good solution.

Like Microsoft, IBM is "very hard-core" about the Internet; it has become the center-piece of its client/server thrust. IBM will be offering bundled Internet server suites as part of its "Eagle" initiative. These suites will run on OS/2, AIX, Windows NT, and other server platforms. They will provide a single point of installation, support, and system management. The *NetCommerce Server* will include every conceivable Web service—including proxies and firewalls, electronic commerce services, security (SSL, S-HTTP, and SET), digital certificates, and system management. You will be able to use IBM's *VisualAge* tool to visually assemble Web client and server applications. IBM/Tivoli's *net.TME* will provide object-based system management for these Internet applications.

In addition to products, IBM has the system integration expertise, wide-area networking experience, and enterprise client/server know-how that makes it very credible with IS shops. This means that IBM is in an excellent position to become a "one-stop shop" for Intranet client/server solutions.

IBM is also in a good position to build and distribute an Internet PC or Java machine. There are also rumors that the company is developing Java versions of OpenDoc and SOM to take full advantage of a Java OS. IBM has tons of new technologies in its development labs, but getting them out of the door is another story.[3]

So, are there showstoppers? Not in the very short term, but there are some clouds on the horizon. Lotus Notes gives IBM a formidable head start in the Intranet race. However, Notes must quickly evolve into an Object Web architecture to meet the Microsoft challenge. This architecture must be built on top of CORBA and OpenDoc, not OLE. We say this because there is no way Lotus can "out-OLE" Microsoft; it does not control the DCOM/OLE standard.[4] Lotus' best bet is to rebuild the Notes client/server engine using IBM's SOM and OpenDoc. So, IBM has all the pieces it needs to win today's Intranet, but can it deliver tomorrow's Object Web? Can IBM create a winning solution that brings together Notes, SOM, and OpenDoc?

Oracle

The Web server is just part of the database if you're Oracle, and just part of the operating system if you're Microsoft.

— **Brian O'Connell, Technologic Partners**
(February, 1996)

Oracle is very serious about the Intranet client/server business; it's the first database vendor to support a full line of Web products called the *WebSystem*. The line includes *WebServer, PowerBrowser,* and a commerce server. In addition, Oracle has created a separate consulting group dedicated to the Internet. And as everyone knows, Oracle Chairman Larry Ellison is very excited about the diskless Internet PC business.

---

[3] In May 1996, IBM announced *Arabica*—an OpenDoc runtime written entirely in Java.
[4] Like everyone else, Notes must still provide connectivity with OLE.

Oracle's approach to the Internet is very database-centric. *WebServer* provides end-to-end security by integrating SSL and S-HTTP with database security. Instead of supporting CGI, WebServer uses a proprietary API called the *Oracle Web Request Broker*. This API links directly into the Oracle database services; it maintains state information so that clients don't have to connect to the DBMS every time they issue an SQL request. The WebServer also offers an integrated Java run-time environment with extensions for Oracle7; the idea is that you can now create server-side Java applets. WebServer will eventually run on most server platforms. The first releases run on NT and Solaris; they sell for $2,945.

With sales of $3.5 billion, Oracle is the world's second-largest software company. Oracle could become a major supplier of Intranet crossplatform server software— a game it plays well. On the negative side, Oracle lacks a clear Object Web strategy. It has an excellent component tool—*PowerObjects*—but no distributed object or compound document infrastructure. With a good Object Web story, Oracle could become a formidable supplier of Web Intranet software.

CONCLUSION

There are more people on the Net every day than watch CNN. The number of households that can log on is about the same as the number of black-and-white televisions in 1950, and we expect the same explosion in growth.

> — *Dennis Tsu, Director of Internet SunSoft (March, 1996)*

To use Dennis Tsu's analogy, if today's HTTP Web is black-and-white TV, then the Object Web is color TV. We're starting to see some of that color with Java, but the best is yet to come. It will take the Object Web to create the kind of content that will bring the masses to the Internet; it will also do wonders for the Intranet crowd. So does it ever stop? Not really. We did tell you that life on the Web is measured in dog years. Now you understand why.

Part 9
Distributed System Management

Before DSM

After DSM

Well, maybe in a few years...

An Introduction to Part 9

Our ability to build complex networking infrastructures and applications usually outstrips our ability to manage them.

— **John McConnell**
(1996)[1]

You Martians have so far been getting the scenic tour of client/server computing. You've seen all the cool stuff—objects, groupware, database, and NOSs. But there's also a seamy side to client/server—the nasty little secrets that are normally kept out of the grand tour circuit. So what are these nasty little secrets? In a nutshell, the first generation client/server applications were "systems from Hell" when it came to keeping them up and running. These client/server projects were either single-vendor based or kept very small until we could figure out the kinks. Many of the early "Kamikazes" who attempted to build large scale open systems often fell prey to the technology; some never returned to talk about it. We call this nasty secret "client/server burnout."

So what is the cause of client/server burnout? The root cause is that we all got the scenic tour and fell in love with the promise of client/server. However, no one ever told us that we were *totally* on our own after we unwrapped the glossy packages from the different vendors. There was no single number to call when something went wrong. Yes, the different vendors gave us some rudimentary tools to manage their products, but these tools did nothing to help us manage the *sum of the products*. When something went wrong, it was always "the other vendor's fault."

We were left in the great "no-vendor's-land" of client/server, trying to make our systems work or face losing our jobs. Many of us burned the midnight oil trying to learn how to read the bits and bytes that flew over the network using Sniffers and other protocol analyzers. These early tools were real lifesavers—without them, we would have been totally blind. However, this is not the answer. We can't expect every client/server installation to have its resident TCP/IP, SQL, and object guru.

OK, you want us to get to the point—enough of this early "pioneer" talk. But we have news for you: We're *still* in the pioneer days of client/server. The *Distributed System Management (DSM)* technology—the topic of Part 9—*may* be the cure to client/server burnout. We say "may" because DSM products are just coming out of the labs; most are still untested in the battlefield. In addition, the success of a DSM platform depends on how easy it is for third-party tools to "snap into" it. And that won't happen overnight. So the good news is that there is a cure: DSM platforms. The bad news is that DSM platforms are in their infancy; you may have to pack a Sniffer back to Mars and be prepared to look at some bits and bytes.

---

[1] Source: John McConnell, **Managing Client/Server Environments** (Prentice-Hall, 1996).

An Introduction to Part 9

Part 9 starts out by going over DSM platforms and what they can do for you today. Next, we spend time going over DSM standards and middleware. DSMs can only succeed by creating an open platform based on standards. Standards allow management applications to "plug-and-play" into the DSM frameworks and access their agents anywhere in the intergalactic client/server universe. As usual, there are many standards from which you can choose. We will review the Internet, OSI, and CORBA-based standards for system management; they're also called the neoclassical and postmodern standards. So welcome to the seamy side of client/server. We hope that this won't be a Conrad-like journey into the "Heart of Darkness."

Chapter 32

Client/Server Distributed System Management

Now that my applications have moved off the mainframe, how am I going to manage this mess?

— **Anonymous MIS Manager**

The mere existence of a problem is no proof of the existence of a solution.

— **Yiddish proverb**

Client/Server has applied a giant chainsaw to centralized systems, slicing them into small pieces and scattering them all over the network. Then along came "open systems," which sliced up the software even further so that each piece comes from a different vendor. How do we manage the pieces? Management and support issues are the Achilles' heel of client/server computing. Even though the benefits of client/server systems are real—lower hardware and software costs, more flexible systems, easier to use front-ends—we're discovering that administration and support is far more costly than for centralized systems. Client/server computing disperses applications across multiple systems on a network and creates daunting problems for all types of administrators concerned with keeping these systems running. The gap is widening between what users expect and what the support organization can deliver. It obviously doesn't make economic sense to ship a database and network administrator with every new client/server application that we deploy. So the rapidly escalating support burden of client/server systems must be brought under control, or the entire edifice may crumble.[1]

Are we in a no-win situation like the one described by the Yiddish proverb? Is there a solution to the problem of distributed system management in multivendor client/server environments? Until *very* recently, client/server management tools and products were totally inadequate for dealing with the complexities of distributed environments—they were always far less developed than their mainframe counterparts. You had to be a total masochist (or suicidal) to deploy a client/server solution in intergalactic environments. Departmental-sized solutions had slightly better success rates because somebody local was willing to put in the long hours of "volunteer" work. The first generation of client/server systems were mostly a "labor of love" by people who were willing to put in long hours to gain control over their local computing environment.

Fortunately, the situation may be turning around. Some very creative solutions to systems management are starting to come on the market. Most of them use client/server technology to help manage client/server systems. It's very recursive in that sense. Vendors of all sizes have finally come to the realization that no single system management product (or suite) can solve all the world's problems. The new trend is for vendors to create products that plug-and-play in one of the "open" distributed system management platforms—including HP's *OpenView*, Sun's *Solstice Enterprise Manager*, IBM's *OpenView* family, and Tivoli's *TME*.

These open management platforms can exchange management information with almost anything that lives on the network—including low-level devices, system software, and user applications—using standard protocols such as SNMP, CMIP, and DMI. The distinction between the network management and system management disciplines is quickly fading. Object-oriented user interfaces are providing single views of the managed environment; management information databases are providing common views of the managed data. Finally, management platforms can interoperate in all sorts of flexible arrangements, ranging from peer-to-peer to complex manager-of-manager relationships. This chapter answers some of the questions related to distributed management: Why the chaos? What needs to be managed? Next we explain the popular manager/agent paradigm for solving the world's problems. Then we look at the management platforms that house these managers and the applications that launch their services. Finally, we take a quick look at the services that management platforms and applications must provide.

---

1 Tom Furey, IBM's General Manager of Client/Server, estimates that "for every dollar you spend on client/server hardware and software, you'll spend five in maintenance, integration, and consulting."

NEW WORLD DISORDER

In many large companies the network control center room seems as complex as the bridge deck of the starship Enterprise. Many systems are linked into the control center, but few are integrated...As a result, operations staff must be rocket scientists to integrate fault, performance, configuration, and other information gleaned from multiple management systems.

— *Gartner Group*
(March, 1993)

System management is, of course, much more complex in distributed environments—especially heterogeneous ones. Unlike past generations of computers, client/server systems consist of three logically integrated but physically dispersed types of components: computer nodes, networks, and applications. The health of the system is dependent on the individual health of its component parts, as well as their interrelationships. All the problems associated with managing a typical computer system exist, and they are exacerbated by a substantial set of problems unique to the network itself.

Ironically, the multivendor diversity that's inherent in client/server solutions is also the primary obstacle to effective and affordable system management. You save money by buying components "a la carte," but you must turn around and spend what you just saved (and often more), making these components "whole" again. The

great variety of vendors, networks, software packages, and system configurations make each client/server system different from the last one. And, until quite recently, vendors' management tools were customized for their own set of products and were generally targeted at the workgroup or departmental level.

As a result, client/server control centers in large organizations *do* look like the bridge deck of the starship *Enterprise*. So who takes care of the correlation between the different management platforms? The operators, of course. They must learn a different set of commands for each user interface and product. And they must continuously correlate information—such as fault, configuration, and performance—from the different management consoles. Because each system has its own separate management database, it's not unusual for the same information to be re-keyed multiple times. A single error may cause hundreds of different messages to flash on all the different consoles at the same time. In many cases, functions may overlap leading to more confusion. The first generation client/server systems were much too complex to manage—even in limited configurations with only a few vendors involved.

DEALING WITH CHAOS AND LEARNING TO LOVE IT

Sometimes the most vexing questions have simple answers: Distributed applications need distributed management.

> — **James Herman, VP**
> **Northeast Consulting Resources, Inc.**

In the early 90's, the industry began to realize that multiplying incomplete tools by multiple vendors created an unmanageable mess that threatened to derail the entire client/server movement. Something had to be done fast; the industry met that challenge and introduced many innovations very quickly. In the last few years, *three* generations of management architectures were introduced in rapid succession: *Manager of Managers, Distributed System Management (DSM)*, and *Open DSM* platforms (see Figure 32-1). We cover these architectures in the rest of this section.

Manager of Managers

IBM's NetView was one of the first attempts to solve the problems of distributed system management at the enterprise level. NetView introduced the concept of *Manager of Managers*, which made it possible for a "mainframe in the sky" to oversee an entire enterprise. The idea was to create a single system image using a three-level hierarchy of management elements: low-level *entry points* that collect

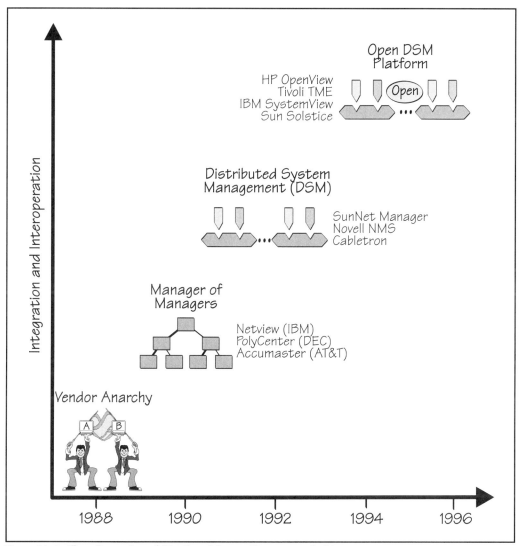

Figure 32-1. Three Generations of Distributed System Management Architectures.

management information and send it upward; middle-manager *service points* that act on some of the information and send the rest upward; and *focal points* at the top that maintain a central database of management information and present a unified view of all the distributed resources. NetView/PC—the first *service point* product introduced by IBM—also served as a gateway that could convert management information from non-SNA devices into a format the mainframe focal points could understand using the SNA Network Management Vector Transport (NMVT).

It didn't take long for Digital and AT&T to introduce their own Manager of Managers: *PolyCenter Framework* and *Accumaster Integrator*. Each product was based on a proprietary distributed management architecture. So the race was on between IBM, Digital, and AT&T to see who would be the first to manage the entire universe. It quickly became apparent that no one vendor—not even IBM, Digital, or AT&T—could possibly anticipate all the customer needs and requirements for a manager-of-managers product. There was just too much diversity for any one vendor to absorb—it was a huge and costly undertaking. IBM, Digital, and AT&T must have come to that same conclusion because they're now among the strongest proponents of open management platforms.

Distributed System Management Platforms

The next step in the evolution of management systems was the *Distributed System Management (DSM)* platform approach pioneered by Sun Microsystem's *SunNet Manager*, Cabletron's *Spectrum*, and Novell's *NetWare Manager System (NMS)*. These systems introduced two innovations:

■ **The use of client/server technology in system management.** Instead of a hierarchy of managers, these systems split up management applications along client/server lines. A GUI-based client workstation can work with any management server using RPCs to obtain management information. The servers collect their information from agents all over the network. The client workstation can provide a single view of the LAN by visually integrating management information that resides on multiple servers. Peer-to-peer or manager-of-managers arrangements among servers can manage the back-end data—the architecture is very flexible.

■ **The use of "toaster" platforms.** The new DSM systems pioneered the concept of the "toaster" model that allows management applications to plug into the platform and play. They accomplished that by creating a "barebones" management infrastructure consisting of published APIs, a starter kit of system management middleware, a system management workstation with integrated graphical utilities, and a management database on the server. The infrastructure was designed to entice third-party management application providers to write to the platforms. The success of a platform is measured by the number of applications that it supports, the type of services these applications provide, and how well they integrate with other applications.

The combination of client/server and toaster platforms caused a massive migration by third-party management application developers to the DSM platforms. The flexible client/server architecture provided scalability from entry level LANs to enterprise systems.

Open DSM Platforms

The most recent step in the evolution of distributed management systems is *open DSM platforms*. Simply put, this is a DSM platform model that uses industry standards for its main interfaces. So where do these industry standards come from? The usual places, of course. Here's the list of standard bodies and consortia that *together* provide all the pieces needed to create a working distributed management platform: X/Open for management APIs; DME for conceptual frameworks; OMG for ORBs and object services; OSI and the *Internet Engineering Task Force (IETF)* for specialized middleware; and the *Desktop Management Task Force* for managing the desktop and PC-attached devices. In addition, DSM platforms are starting to use off-the-shelf RDBMSs (or ODBMSs) for storing management data. This means the database and the DSM server code can run on different machines. Think of it as a 3-tier client/server architecture. Actually, DSM management is really a multi-tiered client/server architecture; it supports multiple layers of managers and agent/managers feeding each other.

MANAGER TO AGENTS: WHAT'S GOING ON OUT THERE?

Mirror Worlds are software models of some chunk of reality, some piece of the real world going on outside your window. Oceans of information pour endlessly into the model (through a vast maze of software pipes and hoses): so much information that the model can mimic the reality's every move, moment-by-moment.

— David Gelernter, Author
Mirror Worlds
(Oxford, 1992)

In his fascinating book, **Mirror Worlds**, David Gelernter defines five key ingredients that make up a mirror world: a deep picture that is also a live picture, agents, history, experience, and the basic idea that knits these all together. We found the "mirror world paradigm" to be very applicable to distributed system management. To make sense out of a chaotic distributed environment, we need to be able to grasp the whole and then move selectively into the parts. This is done by creating a mirror world of the client/server environment. Even though Gelernter does not mention it in his book, today's open management platforms provide the most advanced mirror world implementations.

So what does an open management platform do? It manages mulivendor devices and applications on the network, runs management applications, interoperates with other managing stations, provides an integrated user interface of the managed components, and stores management data. How does it do it? By running an elaborate network of agents—it's like the CIA. The agents reside on the different managed entities on the network and report on their status. The management station can "parachute" its software agents anywhere on the network to look after its interests and gather the data it needs. The agents are also capable of executing commands on its behalf.

The agents help the manager create a "mirror world" of the client/server universe to be managed. Each agent monitors one piece of the universe. There could be thousands of agents parachuted throughout the network. They all run simultaneously, never stop to take a break, are always on the lookout for what may go wrong, and are always gathering data that may be of use to some manager. The manager software sifts through the massive amounts of real-time information it collects looking for the nuggets—the trends and patterns as they emerge. It must make sure the operator isn't overwhelmed with data. To do that, it must create a data model of the "chunk of reality" it manages. "Data refineries" must convert the data into useful information. A managing workstation should include either a relational or object database for managing and organizing the information that's collected and to remember past occurrences.

A mirror world isn't a mere information service—it's a *place*. You can stroll around inside the mirror world. To allow you to do that, the managing station uses iconic images to create visual computer representations of "what's going on out there." Multiple views allow you to zoom in, pan around, and roam through the network. You can read the screen like a dashboard when you need to see the status of a system

at a glance, or you can wade through massive amounts of information organized in many views when you need to do some serious detective work. At every level, the display is live; it changes to reflect the changing conditions of the system as you watch. The way things are presented is a very important aspect of system management. Ideally, you should be able to see and control every aspect of a managed system from a single managing workstation. System management has the visual look and feel of an electronic arcade game, but in the background it deals with real agents that collectively control every aspect of a distributed system.

A management platform also provides the middleware needed for communicating with all types of agents. This ranges from simple agents that manage hardware devices (such as routers) to complex agents that chase after objects that roam on networks. The simple agents may be reached using a simple protocol like SNMP; the complex agents may be invoked via an ORB. In between, we have traditional agents for client/server applications that communicate using RPCs and MOM. In summary, distributed system management uses client/server technology to manage client/server systems. It's all very recursive. Mirror worlds are examples of how client/server technology will be used in the years to come. We can get a jump start by understanding the workings of the system management mirror world.

THE COMPONENTS OF AN OPEN DSM PLATFORM

During the past several years, IT organizations have implemented piecemeal DSM solutions.

— *Meta Group*
(September, 1995)

Figure 32-2 shows the main components of an open management platform. It's a composite of the OSI, OSF-DME, UI-Atlas DM, and IBM SystemView conceptual models of distributed management. More importantly, the figure is also a good composite model of commercial open management platforms such as HP's OpenView, IBM's SystemView, and Tivoli. Let's quickly introduce the management components of an open management platform before getting into the details. We start at the top of Figure 32-2 and work our way downward:

■ The **OOUI User Interface** provides visual representations of managed objects. The managing workstation should be able to automatically discover the topology of agents on a network, and then display them in a top view. You can use background maps to indicate the geographic locations of agents. Clicking on an icon representing a managed object displays a view of its current status and options for observing and controlling its state. You should be able to visually define event/action combinations. Query dialogs are provided to let you view

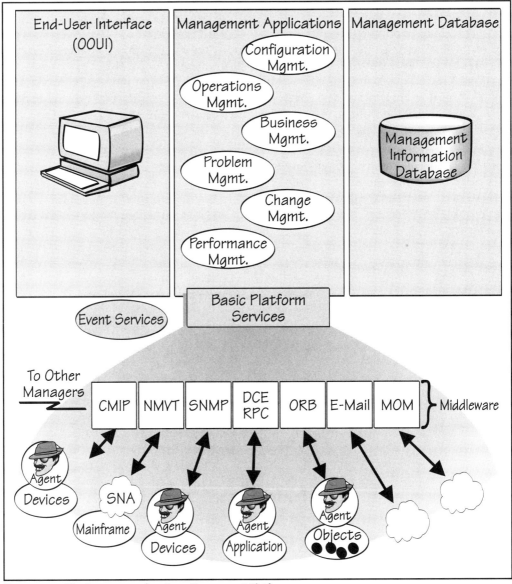

Figure 32-2. The Components of an Open Management Platform.

information in the management database. You can use tree views to traverse information that's stored on any remote agent.

■ The *Management Applications* are typically provided by third parties on top of the management platform's underlying facilities—including the user interface, the management database, the topology discovery services, and the facilities for communicating with remote agents and managed applications. The management applications fall into the following categories: problem management, change management, configuration management, performance management, operations management, and business management.

■ The ***Management Information Database*** is a database of information collected from the agents under the managing workstation's control. It can be implemented using an RDBMS or ODBMS. The database engine may provide active backgound daemons that monitor the historical data for trends and unusual developments. You can use triggers to proactively launch corrective actions. Note that a portion of the real-time management data is maintained by the agents themselves and stored in the local nodes they manage—the MIBs. So in a sense, we're dealing with a distributed database of hierarchical information. The data is spread on MIBs throughout the network. The managing workstation maintains aggregate snapshots of this distributed data. However, the data in the central database is not as up-to-date as the data kept in the remote MIBs (the point of capture).

■ The ***Basic Platform Services*** provide high-level APIs that allow a managing application to communicate with agents, other managing applications, other managing platforms, and with the event management service. These APIs conform to open industry standards.

■ The ***Middleware Stacks*** provide the elaborate communication infrastructure needed by a management workstation and its applications to talk to distributed agents, other management workstations, and operators. A good management platform should support all the industry standards for agent-to-managing-station communications—including SNMP, CMIP, DCE, and CORBA. It should also support legacy management protocols such as SNA NMVT alert packets. E-mail and MOM services are needed for sending asynchronous alerts and notifications to operators. Finally, either SNMPv2, CMIP, RPC, or CORBA may be used for communications between management stations.

In summary, the management platform isolates the managing applications from the distributed environment and provides the common OOUI, database, and event services needed to create a single-system image of client/server management. The managing applications themselves are written by third parties. The more standard the APIs supported by a platform, the easier it is for third parties to port their applications. Of course, the real management work is done by these management applications—the platforms just provide the necessary plumbing and the installed base.

MANAGEMENT APPLICATIONS: COPING WITH DIVERSITY AND COMPLEXITY

With standardized APIs and what we believe will be the convergence to a small number of management platforms, an entirely new market is being created. A major opportunity now exists for the development of best-of-breed management applications.

— *Gartner Group*

Management applications do the real work in distributed system management. They help us answer the following questions: How well is my client/server system performing? What is out there and where? Who is doing what to whom? How do I install new software? What went wrong? How do I fix it? Is everything being backed up? Can my system survive an 8.0 earthquake? In this section, we take a quick look at the categories of system management software that help us answer these questions.

How Well Is My Client/Server System Performing?

Collecting real-time information from various system components in a client/server environment and pinpointing the causes of performance problems can be a real headache for system and database administrators. The management software must be able to collect extensive data, in real time, from different sources in a client/server environment. It must then act on that data or present it in graphical or numerical form for further analysis. You should be able to correlate the performance data with information collected from configuration management tools and proactively identify system bottlenecks.

Performance monitoring tools gather statistical data on resource utilization levels of key components in a client/server system, and then generate alarms when some administrator-defined criteria are not met. Some of the tools may even provide scripting facilities for generating repair actions or doing preventive maintenance. The tools monitor utilization levels on typical resources—including networks, CPUs, disks, memory, file space, processes, server transactions, e-mail, modems, and routers. The better systems use histograms and standard deviations to monitor the response time of servers. Performance monitoring tools maintain a database on the historical performance of the system so that trends can be discovered. You should be able to obtain graphical displays of usage data on any computer, network, or database resource. The tool should be able to automatically collect relevant data over a period of time so that you can analyze resource utilization during peak hours before making hardware capital expenditure decisions.

In 1996, *application performance monitoring* tools are beginning to appear. The first of these tools have focused on monitoring and fine-tuning DBMSs. The DMI and the application MIB are standardizing the parameters an application needs to communicate to a management tool or agent. These standard formats are exactly what is needed for this area of system management to take off. Unfortunately, very few generic tools can be used to automate the corrective actions in the area of performance tuning. In this case, what's needed are tools that automate load balancing in response to varying loads. Some of this is done by specialized system components such as TP Monitors and routers.

What Is Out There and Where?

Inventory management tools, also known as "asset managers," keep track of what programs run on which machines, what levels of software they run, and the like. They also keep track of hardware inventory and maintain a database of inventory information. Most tools can automatically notify you when they detect changes to the hardware and software on the LAN. Some of the more "authoritarian" tools may do more than just report changes; they may automatically revoke and restore files to the parameters that an administrator sets—for example, login files.

In theory, an automated inventory manager should be able to automatically determine all the software, workstations, peripherals, routers, and servers directly attached to the LAN. Unfortunately, most tools require you to key in some data; there is no way to automatically gather information such as the serial number of devices. In addition, it is hard to track all the software that's used on the LAN because no single comprehensive list of software exists. Vendors typically rely on a list from the Software Publisher Association (SPA). This list is updated twice a year and contains only the software from vendors that have paid to have their applications included. Some tools can isolate unknown software by checking the file size and version number, and then making educated guesses as to what the application is.

Configuration management tools can set software parameters and fine-tune complex systems such as relational databases or operating systems. Fortunately, generic software management tools are becoming less scarce. However, hardware configuration tools are still what most people think about in terms of configuration control—they've been around longer. These tools can set device thresholds and tuning parameters. They can also collect configuration information from any managed system via its MIB. You should be able to track changes in the configuration of the client/server environment over time and use that information to perform crucial maintenance and tuning work such as identifying and balancing the load around bottlenecks. For example, a database management tool should be able to monitor database resource utilization, database space fragmentation, application deadlocks, application throughput, computer resources, dead processes, and resource "hogs."

The client/server computing environment is always in flux as new clients and applications log on and off the network. *Topology management tools* keep track of how the network is interconnected, what nodes are out there, and how to best reach them. They make it easy for an administrator to continuously monitor the changes in the client/server environment. The administrator can graphically display crucial information, such as which client is using which server, which database resource resides on which server, and which applications are available on each server.

Who Is Doing What to Whom?

Security tools monitor access to resources and manage who can access what. These tools provide a friendly interface that help you maintain user and group account information as well as access lists and the like. The NOS provides the middleware that does the actual authentication and access protection. The management tool provides the user interface and the environment to manage passwords, run virus scans, and track intruders. The idea is to provide an integrated view of client/server system management. So it makes sense to have the NOS services (such as security and directories) managed through the open system management platform.

How Do I Install New Software?

The number of programs on each individual machine has risen dramatically over the last few years. Administrators have had a hard time managing this explosion; it's one of their top five headaches. *Software distribution and installation tools* let you download, update, track, and deinstall software packages on any networked machine. These packages can include anything from new operating system releases to end-user applications. Most of these tools can track the version number and status of the software. The better tools can perform unattended pushes from the code server to a particular client machine. *Software license management* tools can meter and enforce the use of licensed software. They typically support a wide range of licensing policies. This is an area where proper standards are important.

Users can subscribe to a particular software package and have it automatically delivered and installed on their machine. Of course, this delivery must be coordinated with the license metering application. A typical installation tool is divided into three components: clients or recipients of a delivery, the software package to be distributed, and the delivery schedule. You should be able to create distribution lists of recipients, making it easier to send software updates to a group of users. The delivery can be scheduled for a particular date and time. Clients can also perform installations on their own time—the *pull method.*

You should be able to define software distribution packages and subscription lists using a GUI (or preferably an OOUI). The "management by subscription" approach is used to automatically push the packages to all the subscribers. An OOUI allows you to create a subscription list by simply dragging and dropping individual host icons on a software package. The package typically consists of two component types: the files and directories that make up the software to be distributed, and the name of a program to be executed after the software is copied on each subscriber machine. Adding a new subscriber to a distribution list is just a matter of dragging a new icon and dropping it on the package.

Still missing is a "software vending machine" concept that lets clients browse from a wide selection of applications available on the server and try out an application before they buy. If they want to buy, the system should generate a purchase order, inform the licensing tool that it's OK to use this application, and update the inventory tool.

What Went Wrong? How Do I Fix It?

The number one headache of any administrator is, of course, how to deal with faults. The distributed nature of client/server systems—different transports, OSs, and databases—add several degrees of complexity. Failures can be caused by any single component or from mysterious combinations of conditions. *Fault management and help desk tools* receive alarms, identify the failure, and launch corrective actions. The best tools can combine network, systems, and application-level management views. They help break down walls between database, network, and system management functions, making it easier to correlate failure symptoms. The tool should maintain error logs and issue *trouble tickets* to the people who need to know about the problem.

If an alarm occurs, a tool should be able to perform any combination of the following: send a notification, send an e-mail message, call a beeper, invoke a user-supplied program, update a log file, flash an icon, and pop up an alarm window. The better management systems provide scripting facilities that make it easy to automate the known corrective actions. Some tools provide mechanisms for associating events with actions (event handlers). It's a typical event-driven system—for each failure event, there is an event-handler action script. The event-handler script language should be able to call on other managing applications (for example, the configuration control tool) to perform some corrective action or to gather information on what went wrong. It's also important to provide sophisticated filters for events to narrow down the conditions that require intervention. Finally, the system must have enough smarts to recognize events caused by other events; it should then treat all these events as a single event.

Most tools do a good job of gathering real-time data on device and connection status, but then fall short on tasks like trend analysis, trouble ticketing, and reporting on network elements. The management software should continuously monitor the system for potential problems, and it must be able to automatically launch preventive or corrective actions to resolve problems before they occur. Instead of relying on problem *autopsy* and after-the-fact repair actions, potential problems should be avoided without requiring human interaction. This makes managing client/server systems less tedious and less susceptible to human error.

Can My System Survive an 8.0 Earthquake?

It's not just for disaster recovery anymore. Network backup is becoming part of a storage-management strategy that removes the weak link: you.

— Michael Peterson, PC Magazine

Data on the network is continually growing, leaving the administrator with another big headache: How can you manage this growth within the allocated budget, while keeping the data safe from disasters? Disaster recovery includes everything from scheduling daily backups to maintaining hot-standby sites. *Disaster backup, archive, and recovery tools* can initiate the backup or restore action where the source and destination of the operation can be located anywhere on the network. These tools provide a user interface for scheduling the operations in unattended mode. The backup can be performed on any type of media. The better tools provide *hierarchical storage management* for multiple levels of storage—including memory caches, file servers, and an archive medium such as an optical juke box or tape drives. The tool should allow you to monitor where all the data resides and let you set policies like backup times. The best tools have the ability to learn from access patterns; they have some understanding of how information is related.

Chapter 33

Distributed System Management Standards

As we move to this new distributed client/server relationship, the question is: Are we going to have to put an administrator in each location? At $100,000 a year or so for each person, that gets expensive.

— Gary Falksen, DBA with XES Inc.

This chapter introduces about a dozen distributed management standards and a gaggle of new acronyms. We cover the traditional manager/agent standards—including SNMP, SNMPv2, RMON, RMON-2, XMP, and XOM. We cover a standard for tiny desktop agents—the DMTF's DMI. And we conclude with the CORBA-based system management standards—including Tivoli and DME. Of course, there is a Soapbox that gives you *our* opinion of system management in client/server environments. What would life be without Soapboxes?

Two "standard" network management protocols have been defined: the Internet's SNMP and OSI's CMIP. Both are manager/agent protocols. Each of these protocols is capable of describing management information. The two protocols have much in common (including a confusing similarity in terminology), but they differ in a number of important ways. SNMP's approach is simple and straightforward, while

CMIP's is both more powerful and more complex. The SNMPv2 protocol—first introduced in 1993—is still under construction. It fixes many of the "simple" SNMP's shortcomings, but it cannot be called simple anymore—the specification is now over 400 pages. To isolate developers from the underlying management protocols, X/Open defines the *X/Open Management Protocol (XMP)* API that works on top of either SNMP or CMIP. The other contending standard is based on the use of distributed objects (of the CORBA variety) for system management.

THE INTERNET MANAGEMENT PROTOCOLS

The impact of adding network management to managed nodes must be minimal, reflecting a lowest common denominator.

— **Marshall T. Rose, Chairman**
SNMP Working Group

In 1988, the *Internet Engineering Task Force (IETF)* decided it needed an immediate stopgap solution to system management. The *Simple Network Management Protocol (SNMP)* was created to fill that need. IETF originally planned to pursue a two-track approach: SNMP in the short term, and the OSI *Common Management Information Protocol (CMIP)* in the long term. The OSI CMIP was far too complex for the needs of most devices; SNMP was simple and easy to implement. To help the transition, it was originally intended that the SNMP *Management Information Base (MIB)* and *Structure of Managed Information (SMI)* be subsets of the OSI systems management. Eventually, that requirement was dropped, and each protocol went its own way; but they still retain a lot of common terminology. SNMP is the dominant network management protocol today. However, SNMP has a lot of deficiencies—it cannot meet modern system management needs. SNMPv2, introduced by the IETF in 1993, is intended to remove some of these deficiencies. In the meantime, many large corporations, telephone companies, and governments are committed to the OSI approach.

Defining Management Information: SMI and MIB-II

The Internet and OSI have introduced their own versions of a Data Definition Language for system management; in the process, they've also introduced a lot of strange and confusing terminology. To put it simply, the OSI and Internet people have created a language for defining the structure of the data that's kept on the managed devices. Their language defines a hierarchical (tree-based) database and names the components within the tree. The managing workstation uses this information to request data via a protocol such as SNMP or CMIP. The two protocols use the same type of architecture and terminology; however, CMIP is much richer and more complex than SNMP. CMIP uses richer data structures, more object-oriented data definition techniques, and a more sophisticated protocol for exchanging the data.

Both SNMP and CMIP use object-oriented techniques to describe the information to be managed; each resource to be managed is called a *managed object*. The managed objects can represent anything that needs to be managed—an entire host, a program, or just a variable maintaining a counter of received TCP packets. A *Management Information Base (MIB)* defines a structured collection of managed objects. The *Structure of Management Information (SMI)* defines the model, notations, and naming conventions used to specify managed objects within a particular protocol (such as CMIP or SNMP). If you view the MIB as a database, then the SMI provides the schema.

SMI identifies the data types and the representation of resources within a MIB, as well as the structure of a particular MIB. The ISO *Abstract Syntax Notation One (ASN.1)* is a formal language used to define MIBs for both SNMP and OSI management systems. ASN.1 describes the data independently of the SMI encoding technique used. The Internet's RFC 1155 defines a simple SMI to be used with SNMP MIBs; it only supports a subset of simple data types consisting of scalars and two-dimension arrays of scalars. (In contrast, OSI supports complex data structures and inheritance relationships for data.) An *object identifier* consists of a left-to-right sequence of integers known as subidentifiers. The sequence defines the location of the object within a MIB tree.

RFC 1123 defines MIB-II, which is a superset of MIB-I (RFC 1156). MIB-II adds additional groups of managed objects. Figure 33-1 shows the structure of managed objects that are defined in MIB-II. Objects are defined by their hierarchical location in the tree—for example, the IP object group is 1.3.6.1.2.1.4. New objects are always added "down and to the right." The ten object groups defined by the Internet are essential for either fault or configuration management. All devices that claim to be Internet managed nodes must implement the MIB; however, not all functions need to be present on all nodes. The *group* provides a convenient way to organize management objects according to the functions they provide. All objects within a group must be supported to be MIB-II compliant. For example, an implementation must include all objects within the IP group if it implements the IP protocol. The *experimental* node is used to introduce and debug new Internet-defined object categories before they become official MIB objects. The IETF believes that ideas must be proved in a working environment before they are considered for standardization.

The ten MIB-II object groups are not particularly thrilling. They contain several hundred low-level objects that perform TCP/IP network management functions from the transport layer down. The interesting system management stuff is left to the private MIB extensions.

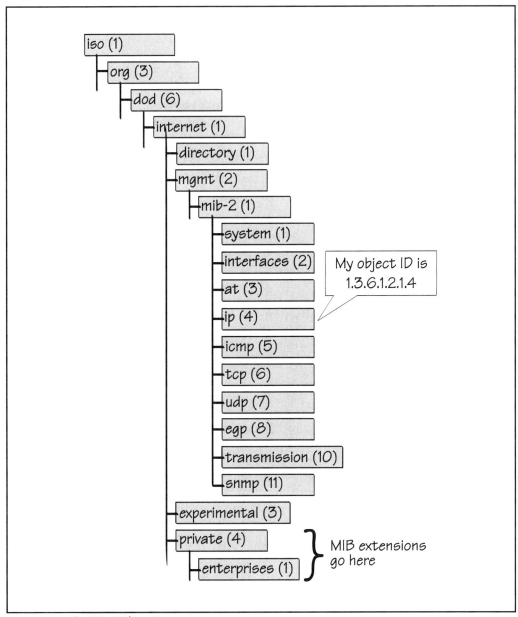

Figure 33-1. The MIB-II Object Groups.

New management objects are typically defined as MIB extensions in the *private* subtree; they allow vendors to create extensions that make their products visible to a managing station. The *enterprises* group is used to allocate *enterprise object IDs* to each vendor that registers for one. Vendors must describe their MIB extensions using formal descriptions—as defined in RFC 1155 or RFC 1212—

inside a text file. Enough information must be provided to allow a managing station to load and compile the vendor-specific MIB definition and add it to the library of managed object descriptions. The managing station can only access information it knows how to ask for. The private MIB extensions are the heart of SNMP and OSI system management, but they're also the areas of greatest confusion. Users must make sure that the management platforms they select can handle the private MIB extensions for their systems. Different management systems are known to produce different results when managing the same MIB data; it's scary stuff.

MIB Tools

Most management platforms provide tools that make MIBs friendly. A MIB is, in essence, a form of hierarchical database that's distributed across managed stations. Like any database, it requires tools that make it accessible. Here are the typical tools that make it easier to work with MIBs:

- A *MIB compiler* takes a file in RFC 1155 format and converts it to a format that can be used by the management station. The compiler is also used to update an existing MIB and add new vendor-specific definitions.

- A *MIB browser* displays the MIB tree in a graphical manner; it allows you to search for objects by groups or attributes. You can refresh instance data from any managed node. The browser should allow you to create aliases for MIB objects (i.e., give them names that you find meaningful). The browser is really nothing but a specialized query tool for MIB databases. It lets you "walk the MIB." Some vendors allow you to overlay the MIB information on maps or on pictures of the objects you're interested in.

- A *MIB report writer* allows you to graphically create reports of the managed data. You can augment these reports with business graphs, maps, and other forms of visual presentation.

MIB tools are typically integrated with other visual management tools. For example, an agent discovery tool can display the location of the agents on the network, and you can use the MIB query tool to browse through the data they contain. You should note that MIBs are not very human-friendly. They were designed to be used by applications, not humans. So it's best to hide their details through graphic display tools.

The Internet's SNMP

The *Simple Network Management Protocol (SNMP)* is the most widely implemented protocol for network management today—it is supported by a constantly growing number of network devices. SNMP, as defined in RFC 1157, is designed to do exactly what its name suggests—it performs relatively simple management of the components in a network. It is used to alter and inspect MIB variables. SNMP is an asynchronous request/response protocol that supports four operations (see Figure 33-2):

■ **GET** is a request issued by a managing station to read the value of a managed object. The get operation is atomic; either all the values are retrieved or none are. SNMP only supports the retrieval of leaf objects in the MIB.

■ **GET-NEXT** is a request made by a managing station to traverse a MIB tree; it reads the value of the "next" managed object in the MIB.

■ **SET** is a request issued by a managing station to modify the value of a managed object. This operation is often not supported because SNMP provides no effective security or ways to control who is allowed to perform SETs. The last thing you need are intruders causing havoc on the network using unprotected SNMP SETs.

■ **TRAP** is a notification from a managed system to a managing station that some unusual event occurred. SNMP traps are very limited; they report one of seven events: cold start, warm start, link down, link up, authentication failure, external gateway neighbor loss, and enterprise specific trap. The traps use unacknowledged datagrams.

SNMP exchanges use TCP/IP's *User Datagram Protocol (UDP)*—this is a very simple, unacknowledged, connectionless protocol. It is also possible to support SNMP over the ISO stack using the connectionless transport system. Most SNMP agents are implemented as TSRs or Daemon background tasks.

SNMP's Limitations

So what are the limitations of SNMP? The list is long; it's a classical tradeoff between simplicity and the complex requirements of modern management systems. Here's a quick summary of SNMP's more blatant shortcomings:

■ ***SNMP is not secure.*** The protocol provides a very trivial form of authentication; it is child's play for an intruder to break into the system. Most network managers do not allow the use of the SET command. This can be very limiting.

■ ***SNMP is inefficient.*** The protocol is not suited for retrieving bulk data; you must send one packet for each packet of information you want returned. SNMP relies on polling, which can swamp a network with traffic. Because the event traps cannot be extended, they cannot be used to create an event-driven

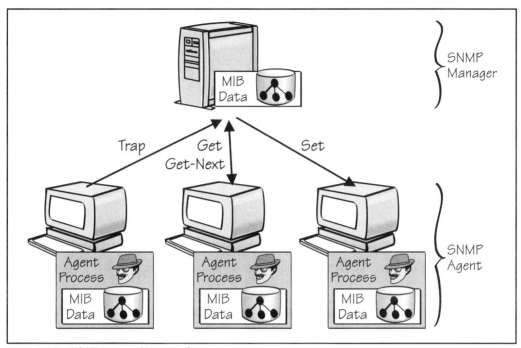

Figure 33-2. SNMP Manager/Agent Exchanges.

environment. The server calls the agent and not the other way round. Polling limits the number of variables that can be monitored by a managing station, which translates into more cost.

■ **SNMP lacks important functions.** The protocol cannot be used to create new instances of MIB variables; it cannot execute management commands; and it does not support manager-to-manager communications.

■ **SNMP is unreliable.** The protocol builds on the UDP, which is an unacknowledged datagram mechanism. The traps are unacknowledged, and the agent cannot be sure they are received by the managing station. The SNMP designers believe that a datagram may have a better chance of reaching its destination under catastrophic conditions (that may be a bit far-fetched).

In summary, SNMP is excellent at its intended task—simple network management. However, it is too limited to handle the more complex functions of systems management.

Stretching SNMP's Limits: The RMON MIB-II Extensions

The *Remote Network-Monitoring (RMON)* standard defined in RFC 1757 is a very significant extension of MIB-II that stretches SNMP to its limits.[1]   The moving forces behind RMON were the network monitor vendors; they needed extensions to SNMP that would allow their equipment to participate in the management of networks. A *network monitor*—for example, Network General's *Sniffer*—is a "promiscuous" device that sits on the network and can capture and view any packet, regardless of who sends it to whom. Clearly, these sniffer-like devices collect a tremendous amount of information that can be very useful to an SNMP managing station. Monitors are the ultimate "secret agent." They're tapped into the network and can see anything that moves on it. So the question is: How does a managing station obtain this massive information using SNMP? The answer is through the RMON MIB-II extensions.

What makes RMON so interesting is that it is the most intelligent entity ever defined by the Internet; it breaks the mold of the simple-minded and brain-dead managed device. A monitor must have enough intelligence to filter and act on the information it collects without directly involving the managing station for every action or swamping the network with massive amounts of bulk data transfers. Through *preemptive monitoring*, the sniffer (or *probe*) continuously runs diagnostics on the network traffic, notifies the managing station when a failure is detected, and provides useful information about the event. This activist style is a far cry from the typical SNMP philosophy that views each managed node as a set of remote MIB-defined variables.

RMON defines the conventions, using MIB-II extensions on standard SNMP, for telling a remote monitor what data to collect. Remember that SNMP does not support imperative commands, and it cannot create new instances of objects. So, RMON does it all via conventions that allow a MIB variable to represent a command and other variables to represent the parameters to the command; it's all very clumsy, but it shows what can be done in desperation. RMON defines a number of new MIB-II objects that represent commands. The monitor executes the command when the managing station writes to these objects using the SNMP SET command. The RMON specification defines how rows are to be added, deleted, or modified in a MIB setting. The bulk of RMON defines nine MIB-II object group extensions that are used to store data and statistics gathered by a monitor (see Figure 33-3).

Each of the nine RMON groups provide a set of control variables that allow a managing workstation to remotely control the operation of a monitor agent. These variables can be seen as state tables that tell the monitor what to collect and how

---

[1] RFC 1757—introduced in February 1995—supersedes RFC 1271; it extends the Ethernet-rooted objects in RFC 1271 to include Token Ring and FDDI.

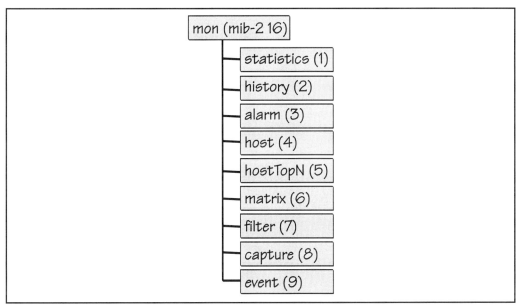

Figure 33-3. The RMON MIB-II Group Extensions.

to handle the events it generates. In a more modern setting, all of this could have been done using RPCs, MOM, or ORB invocations. RMON is a weird data-centric protocol that uses MIB variables to pass instructions, parameters, and control information between a managing station and an agent. It's a "kludge."

Here Comes RMON-2

In August 1995, the RMON-2 MIB draft was submitted to the IETF; it is expected to become a standard by the time you read this. RMON-2 adds new groups on top of RMON. It collects information on the workings of the network layer (or layer three in the OSI model). In contrast, the original RMON only deals with OSI layers one and two. RMON-2 allows management tools to construct end-to-end views of the entire network. In contrast, RMON only deals with single network segments.

With RMON-2, you will be able to get a complete picture of how an entire network functions, not just the individual LAN segments. You will be able to proactively manage your networks and detect culprits that cause network segments to slow down or crash. Note that some vendors have extended RMON-2 to collect information on all seven layers of the OSI model. However, any implementations above layer three are totally non-standard.

RMON-2 is more cost-effective than RMON. You won't have to place probes on each LAN segment to collect information. Instead, probes will be embedded within routers and hubs, where they can collect backbone traffic information. As we go to press, all the major internetworking players are either shipping or have embedded RMON in their routers and switches—including Bay Networks, Cisco, 3Com, and Cabletron. So will this kill the standalone RMON probe industry? We do not think so. These vendors are more likely to become an extinct species because of acquisitions. In March 1996, 3Com acquired Axon Networks for $65 million, just one week after rival Bay Networks paid $33 million for Armon Technologies.

The coming of RMON-2 will further stimulate the already overheated RMON market. IDC predicts that revenues from RMON will increase from $385 million in 1995 to $744 million in 1996 and $2.4 billion in the year 2000. So the future of RMON-2 looks bright.

SNMPv2: What's New?

Nobody thought it would take so long to nail SNMPv2 down. Work has now dragged on for over three and a half years.

> — *Joe Paone, INTERNETWORK*
> *(March, 1996)*

SNMP Version 2 (SNMPv2) has become the Bosnia of standards. It was first introduced in March 1993 by Jeffrey Case, Keith McCloghrie, Marshall Rose, and Steven Waldbusser—the designers of the original SNMP and related Internet management standards. The proposed standard consisted of 12 RFC documents that totaled over 416 pages. SNMPv2 improvements over SNMP included a new security protocol, optional encryption, manager-to-manager communications, bulk data transfer, new SMI data types, new MIB objects, and the ability to add or delete table rows (a la RMON).

In March 1993, the SNMPv2 task force disbanded and vendors started to implement the protocol. Unfortunately, the vendors weren't too happy with some of what they found. They all seemed to agree with the majority of SNMPv2 features, but two areas proved to be overly complex—security and the administrative framework. The SNMPv2 working group was reconvened in December 1994 to fix these two problem areas. However, the group could not agree on a solution, so two competing proposals emerged (see next Soapbox). This section describes the parts of SNMPv2 that are common to all the proposals. Most of these new protocols are finished and have been published.

SNMPv2 Operations

An SNMPv2 node can be both a managing and a managed object. This makes it possible to create manager-of-managers arrangements, and it allows SNMPv2 to share management information with its fellow managers. A *Manager-to-Manager (M2M)* MIB was defined to support this topology. SNMPv2 is a "proper extension" of SNMP.

Here's the list of the old and new operations SNMPv2 proposes (see Figure 33-4):

■ **GET** is identical to SNMP. The only difference is in the way responses are returned. SNMPv2 removes the atomic constraint, meaning that it will return whatever values can be returned—partial results are allowed. In contrast, SNMP either returns all the required variables or it posts an error.

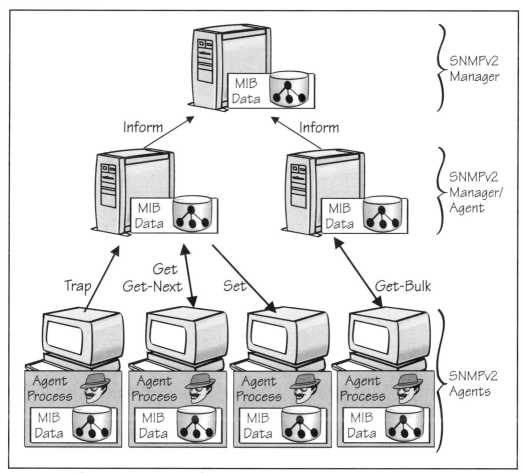

Figure 33-4. SNMPv2: Manager/Agent and Manager/Manager Exchanges.

■ **GET-NEXT** is identical to SNMP, except that the atomic requirement is relaxed.

■ **GET-BULK** is a new command issued by a managing station. It is similar to GET-NEXT. However, instead of just returning the next variable, the agent can return as many successor variables in the MIB tree as will fit in a message.

■ **SET** is identical to SNMP. It is a two-phased operation. The first phase checks that all the variables in the list can be updated; the second phase performs the update. Like SNMP, it's an all-or-nothing proposition.

■ **TRAP** performs a role similar to SNMP, but it uses a different packet format (the SNMP trap header only recognizes a TCP/IP address type; SNMPv2 is more general). And, like SNMP, the trap is unacknowledged.

■ **INFORM** is a new command that's sent by an SNMPv2 manager to another manager. It is used to exchange management information. The messages can be sent to all the manager nodes specified in the M2M MIB or to a particular manager. The M2M MIB allows a superior manager node to define the subordinate events it's interested in.

Like SNMP, SNMPv2 is connectionless; it uses a datagram service. The specification includes mappings to UDP, IPX, AppleTalk, and the OSI connectionless service. It also includes a new data type for high-speed networks and better error return values.

The Great SNMPv2 Stalemate

Soapbox

It's Bosnia. We've got Serbs and Croats.

> — *Marshall Rose, SNMPv2 Co-author*
> *(March, 1996)*

When SNMPv2 access rights and security proved too difficult and cumbersome to implement, the original SNMPv2 working group went back to the mountain and returned with two competing security proposals:

■ ***User-based Security Model (USEC)*** is championed by Marhall Rose and Keith McCloghrie. USEC proposes a simple, minimalist security model. It's an agent-centric design that requires minimum involvement from the management station. Consequently, the security administration is also minimal.

- **SNMPv2* (or "V2 star")** is championed by Jeffrey Case and Steven Waldbusser (who is also the author of RMON-2). SNMPv2* introduces a security framework on top of USEC to make it "more complete." As Case puts it, "USEC has fewer features, but the question is, are there enough features in USEC?" Of course, Case must think the answer is no, which is why he came up with SNMPv2*; it offers multiple authentication and privacy services. In contrast, USEC's Rose thinks that SNMPv2* has the potential to become "the CMIP of the mid-90s—very capable, but extremely complex, large, costly, and ungainly."

As a result of this stalemate, the IETF disbanded the SNMPv2 working group in December 1995 to "let tempers cool down." It will be reconvened later in 1996, if the authors can agree. Both sides are drumming up support to establish "de facto" industry standards before the IETF reconvenes. However, most vendors are waiting on the sidelines for a winner to emerge before implementing products.

In our opinion—this is, after all, a Soapbox—perhaps it's time for the industry to drop all SNMPv2 variants and move on to object-based system management. SNMPv2 has lost its window of opportunity (you will hear more on this in a later Soapbox). Who said system management is not exciting? ❏

THE OSI MANAGEMENT FRAMEWORK

Many of SNMP's deficiencies are addressed by OSI network management. Some, however, see this as a case of the cure being worse than the disease, given the complexity and the size of OSI network management.

— William Stallings, Author
SNMP, SNMPv2, and CMIP
(Addison Wesley, 1993)

OSI distributed system management is defined by over 30 standards. Are you ready for a new dose of acronyms? In the OSI worldview, network management is divided into five application-level components called *System Management Functional Areas (SMFAs)*. These include fault management, accounting management, configuration management, performance management, and security management (see Figure 33-5). SMFAs rely on the services of 13 OSI-defined *System Management Functions (SMFs)*, which can be used by one or more SMFAs. The SMFs rely on the *Common Management Information Services Element (CMISE)*. CMISE is a combination of the protocols defined by the *Common Management Information Services (CMIS)* and the *Common Management Information Protocol (CMIP)*.

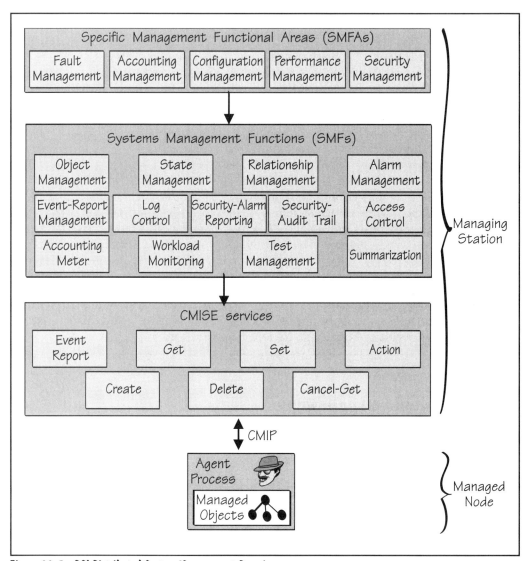

Figure 33-5. OSI Distributed System Management Overview.

CMIP, like SNMP, performs the actual exchanges between a managing station and an agent on the managed system. And like SNMP, it relies on a MIB to understand the capabilities of the managed agents and the data they store. OSI, of course, has its own CMI that defines information using ASN.1 notation; the basic unit of information is an object.

What's an OSI Object—and What Can It Do?

While SNMP was intended to be simple, immediately useful, and quickly deployed, the groups developing OSI management took a different approach. The goal of OSI management is to provide a comprehensive solution to the broad problems of network—and, to some extent, systems—management. Because of its ambitious goals, OSI provides a comprehensive framework for defining *managed objects* borrowing heavily from object-oriented technology. The OSI notation used for describing managed objects is much richer than that used by SNMP. CMIP relies on a series of *templates* for defining managed objects and their attributes. You can specify the following characteristics for each managed object:

■ *Attributes* are variables that represent the data elements in a managed object. Each attribute represents a property of the resource the object represents.

■ *Operations* are the actions that can be performed on the attributes of an object or on the object itself. The actions that can be performed on the object's attributes include *get, replace, set, add,* and *remove members*. The actions that can be performed on the object itself include *create, delete,* and *action*. OSI does not provide the semantics for defining the behavior of an object (i.e., method implementations or inheritance).

■ *Notifications* are events that are emitted by a managed object—for example, when some internal occurrence that affects the state of the object is detected. ISO defines a number of notification types, including the format of the data carried in a CMIP *event-report* and an object ID that uniquely identifies the source. Notification types include various alarms and violations, attribute value changes, object creation and deletion, and object state changes.

■ *Inheritance* is a managed object class that inherits all the characteristics of its parent class. ISO defines a number of object classes that can be used as parent classes for the purposes of inheritance, including an *alarm record, log, system, security alarm reports,* and an *event forwarding discriminator.*

The notation for defining objects is defined in *ISO 10165*; it is also know as **Guidelines for the Definition of Managed Objects (GDMO)**. The notation is commonly referred to as GDMO templates; it is substantially more powerful (and complex) than the simple language for defining SNMP objects. As we explained, ISO objects have a rudimentary level of object-oriented characteristics; in contrast, SNMP MIB objects are just glorified variables in a hierarchical tree. The GDMO is closer in intent to the CORBA IDL. However, CORBA provides much more advanced and comprehensive object semantics.

OSI Management Protocols: CMIP, CMOT, and CMOL

CMIP is really an abbreviation for the (overly) Complex Management Information Protocol.

> — *Marshall T. Rose, Author*
> *The Simple Book*
> *(Prentice Hall, 1991)*

CMIP is the OSI protocol for manager-to-agent and manager-to-manager communications. In sharp contrast to SNMP, *CMIP* is a connection-oriented protocol that runs on top of a complete seven-layer OSI stack. *CMIP over TCP/IP (or CMOT)* provides a skinnier version of CMIP for TCP/IP networks. *CMIP over LLC (or CMOL)* is the skinniest CMIP yet; it was designed by IBM and 3Com to run directly on top of the IEEE 802.2 logical link layer. CMIP is much richer in functionality than its SNMP counterpart. The CMIP protocol provides the following services:

■ **Get** requests data from the agent's management information base. The request may be for a single managed object or a set of managed objects. For each managed object value, one or more of its attributes can be requested.

■ **Event-Report** is a notification sent by an agent to a managing system indicating that some event has occurred. The service can optionally request a confirmation. Five parameters are passed with the notification event to specify the class of object and instance where the event originated, the type of event, the time it was generated, and any user information about the event.

■ **Action** is a request that directs a managed object to perform some particular action. The action is implemented by a procedure that's specified as part of the managed object. The *action-information* parameter, if present, can be used to pass input parameters and other information.

■ **Create** is a request made by a managing system to create a new instance of a managed object class.

■ **Delete** is a request made by a managing system to delete an instance of a managed object class.

All the CMIP services may be optionally performed with confirmation. To specify the context for the management objects of interest, CMIP employs two constructs: *scoping* and *filtering*. Scoping marks a node within the information tree where the search tree starts; filtering is a boolean search expression applied to the attributes of the scoped objects.

TINY AGENTS: THE DESKTOP MANAGEMENT INTERFACE (DMI)

Not a single vendor adapter should be sold without a MIF...MIF everything in sight. MIFing now means users will be a lot less miffed later.

— Jamie Lewis
PC Week

At the other end of the spectrum, an industry consortium called the *Desktop Management Task Force (DMTF)* is defining standards to manage all components on a PC, Mac, or workstation—including hardware, OSs, applications, storage, and peripherals. The DMTF consortium consists of 122 formal members; the leadership includes Compaq, Dell, Digital, HP, IBM, Intel, Microsoft, NEC, Novell, SCO, Symantec, and SunSoft. In October 1993, DMTF released the first version of its *Desktop Management Interface (DMI)*. IBM, Microsoft, and Apple announced they would build DMI into future releases of their OSs. The DMI, however, is independent of protocol, platform, and operating system.

DMI solves a real problem: It makes it practical to manage the 10,000 or so PC components that are on the market. One of the reasons management hasn't proliferated down to PC components through SNMP is *cost*. To be SNMP-compliant, add-in vendors had to create a private MIB, work out the interfaces to SNMP agents, and negotiate with vendors of management platforms to have their MIBs interpreted. In addition, most PCs running DOS and Windows don't have enough RAM to support multiple SNMP agents or their protocol stacks. To compensate, proprietary agents were sometimes placed in adapter cards—for example, Ethernet cards from 3Com or Cabletron. With DMI, component vendors only have to "MIF" their device; DMI does the rest.

DMI support became widespread in 1996. It is being incorporated into the wares of adapter vendors (Intel, Madge, and 3Com), PC manufacturers (AST, Dell, and Apple), and system management vendors (Novell, IBM/Tivoli, and Sun). In addition, DMI is now supported by almost every LAN inventory program on the market—including Frye's *LAN Directory*, McAfee's *LAN Inventory*, and Norton-Lambert's *Administrator for Networks*. Finally, Apple, IBM, Sun, and Ki networks have announced a *common agent technology* that allows DMI-compliant components to be managed by existing SNMP-based management consoles. The common agents map between DMI MIFs and SNMP MIBs. IBM will provide common agents for OS/2, Windows 95, and NT; Apple will provide a common agent for the Mac; and Sun and Ki will provide common agents for Solaris, HP-UX, and other Unixes. Note that Microsoft provides a partial implementation of the DMI standard in the Windows 95 plug-and-play feature. In the future, Microsoft will make the information in the Windows and NT registry available to DMI agents via an OLE interface.

The DMI Architecture

A DMI agent represents a PC and its managed resources to the rest of the world. The DMI interface allows these resources to be managed by SNMP, CMIP, or CORBA-based management applications. Using a concept called "slushware," the DMI agent can load and unload different pieces of code on demand, never taking up more than 6 KBytes. The agent is packaged as a terminate-stay-resident (TSR) program for DOS and as a DLL for Windows and OS/2; it only consumes RAM when activated. The agent loads on demand the code needed to manage a device. After it is loaded, the agent unobtrusively collects information while other applications are running.

The DMI architecture (see Figure 33-6) consists of four elements:

■ The **Component Interface** allows vendors of PC components such as memory boards, CD-ROMS, LAN adapters, and modems to register their devices and interfaces with DMI.

■ The **Service Layer** provides generic agent services. This device-independent layer interfaces to the local MIF database to deal with device-specific issues.

■ The **Management Interface File (MIF)** contains descriptions of the managed devices; it's similar in function to a MIB. The MIF is interpreted by the Service Layer, which uses the information to determine what actions to take on a managed device. The idea is that each of the 10,000 or so PC components will

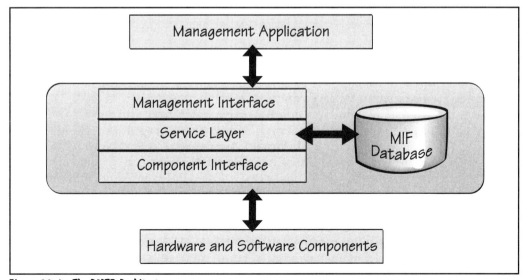

Figure 33-6. The DMTF Architecture.

have a MIF provided by the component vendor. The vendor supplies the MIF, and DMI handles the management.

■ The ***Management Interface*** provides a platform-independent API to the DMI services. The DMI agent can be externally accessed via SNMP, CMIP, or local applications; it provides the protocol to get to the MIFs.

DMI 2.0

In April 1996, DMTF published the *DMI 2.0* specification. It defines a standard way for DMI agents to send management information across a network and ORBs. DMI 2.0 also defines IDL-specified APIs that can be invoked via the DCE RPC. The new DMI allows a component to define events within the MIF; it also defines an interface for setting event filters in the Service Layer. This means management stations will be able to specify the types of events for which they want to receive notifications; they will also be able to set severity thresholds.

One of the more exciting features in DMI 2.0 is its greatly expanded *Software MIF*. This new MIF makes it easier to manage, inventory, install, and uninstall software applications on your PCs, Macs, and workstations. The MIF specifies preinstallation file lists, software IDs and CRC signatures, version numbers, superseded products, installation dependencies, and support information. However, it neither collects real-time information nor maintains relationships between software components that run on both clients and servers. Instead, it focuses on an individual computer system. Even with its shortcomings, the new MIF makes it possible for agents to check your hardware and software environment, install your applications, tell you where to get support, and finally uninstall the programs when you no longer need them. Generally, a software product will ship with one MIF file.[2]

X/OPEN MANAGEMENT STANDARDS

Wherever there are APIs, there's an X/Open standard lurking. So of course there are some X/Open standards for distributed system management calls. The idea is to provide a set of standard management APIs that isolate applications from the underlying management protocols (such as SNMP or CMIP). It's a very strange business we're in—we need standards to isolate us from other standards. X/Open defines two API sets: *XMP* and *XOM* (see Figure 33-7).

---

[2] The IETF is also working on an application MIB that provides more information about the state of a running application as well as describing associations between software modules. However, this MIB is still in its experimental stages.

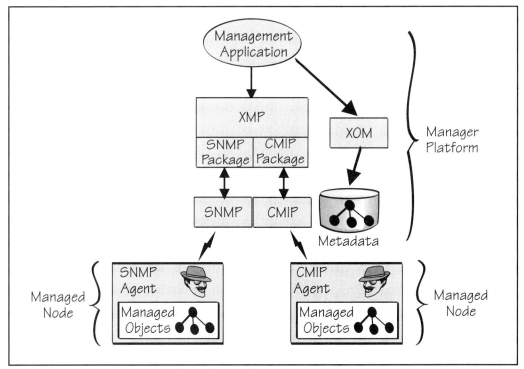

Figure 33-7. X/Open's XOM, XMP, and Metadata Database.

The X/Open XMP API

The *X/Open Management API (XMP)* is derived from an earlier interface called the *Consolidated Management API (CM-API)* from Bull and HP. The XMP API is used for standards-based, process-to-process communications between a managing system and a managed system. XMP defines a set of C API calls that allow access to both SNMP and CMIP. The interface semantics are more like CMIP than SNMP. Because of the differences in the representation of managed data, XMP does not make SNMP or CMIP totally transparent to the application. But as a compromise solution, XMP provides different XOM-based "packages" for use with the different protocols (XOM is explained in the next section). One package is defined for standard SNMP operations, and one is defined for standard CMIP operations.

The X/Open XOM API

XMP relies on another X/Open-defined API called *X/Open Object Manager (XOM)*. The XOM API is used to manipulate the data structures associated with managed objects. The XMP data structures are prepared using XOM API calls. The current version of XOM provides a way to deal with complex ASN.1-defined types in C. Both SNMP and CMIP use ASN.1. XOM is general enough to be used by protocols that are not even related to system management. For example, DCE uses XOM in its Global Directory Services.

To support the more complex CMIP object hierarchies, X/Open includes a *Package Development Kit (PDK)*. The primary component of the PDK is a *metadata compiler*, capable of reading GDMO definitions and producing a package (which is actually a set of C data types). You can then use C structures with XMP and XOM. The metadata compiler populates a local database with information derived from GDMO definitions. The information about CMIP-managed object classes includes their superior and subordinate object classes, the attributes of the class, and whether a given object class supports create and delete requests. You can access the metadata database using normal XMP calls. This process is similar in nature to the CORBA IDL compiler and Interface Repository. But the CORBA architecture is generally much more consistent, and it provides more advanced functions.

THE OSF DME STANDARD

In July 1990, the OSF issued a Request for Technology (RFT) for a *Distributed Management Environment (DME)*, which was to provide a total solution for system and network management in heterogenous multivendor environments. Anyone, OSF member or not, could respond. 25 organizations submitted technologies. In September 1991, OSF announced the winners, which included HP's OpenView, Tivoli's WizDOM, IBM's Data Engine, and Groupe Bull's CMIP and SNMP drivers. In May 1992, OSF published a very comprehensive architecture that combined a traditional network management framework with a postmodern, CORBA-based object framework.

In late 1994, OSF "downsized" its DME effort. Instead of using the Tivoli ORB, OSF now specifies management interfaces to any CORBA-compliant ORB. It appears that OSF is putting most of its efforts in the management of DCE. As a result, open platform vendors are acquiring parts of the DME technology directly from its originators and incorporating them into their products. For example, IBM licensed parts of OpenView from HP, which got incorporated into NetView/6000 and LAN NetView. Digital then licensed NetView from IBM; it is the foundation for *Polycenter NetView*. Finally, IBM acquired Tivoli in early 1996. So Tivoli is now the foundation for IBM's CORBA-based system management platform called *TME 10*.

Despite its retrenchment, the DME system management architecture remains of great interest. DME provides a comprehensive framework for understanding distributed system management in its classical and postmodern approaches. The DME architecture uniquely reconciles these two approaches by using object wrappers and a CORBA-compliant IDL and ORB. This section provides a brief overview of DME's two design points:

- The *Network Management Option (NMO)* takes a classical manager/agent approach to system management.

- The *Object Management Framework (OMF)* provides a postmodern, object-oriented solution based on CORBA.

In addition, DME includes a *Distributed Services* component that provides an infrastructure for services in a distributed environment. It also includes a user interface component.

The DME Network Management Option (NMO)

DME's *Network Management Option (NMO)* provides a traditional management platform for applications that wish to access SNMP and/or CMIP. DME augments the traditional X/Open components with an *Instrumentation Request Broker (IRB);* see Figure 33-8. The IRB provides additional services on top of SNMP or CMIP. These services include the use of the DCE directory services to locate agents on the network, configurable retries, and a gateway service to the future DME CORBA-based management environment. Via the IRB, objects will be able to access SNMP and CMIP managed resources.

The DME Object Management Framework

*O*bject orientation is particularly appropriate for creating network and system management software, where tasks are so varied and complex that no single vendor can hope to undertake more than a small subset.

— Mike Hurwicz, Seybold Analyst
(July, 1995)

DME's *Object Management Framework (OMF)* takes a radically new approach towards unifying network and system management; it builds on CORBA and the OMG services. The DME OMF is composed of multiple objects that cooperate and share information. The new framework goes beyond the traditional manager/object relationship. Instead, an object may at any time take either of two roles: a client requesting a service or a service provider. The DME *I4DL*—an upwardly compatible CORBA IDL with some extensions for event management and installation instructions—is used to describe the interfaces, attributes, and inheritance relationships of any management object. The communication between objects takes place over any

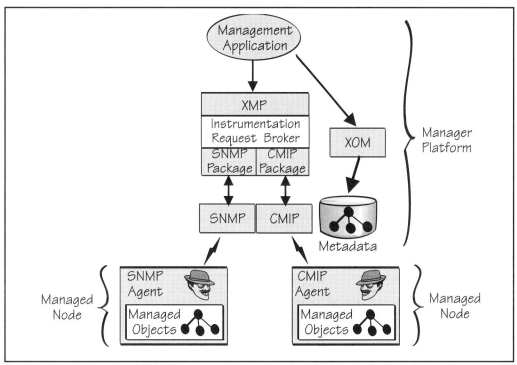

Figure 33-8. DME's Instrumentation Request Broker.

standard CORBA ORB that uses DCE for its core communications (see Figure 33-9). DME calls this DCE-based ORB the *Management Request Broker (MRB)*.

How does the postmodern, object-oriented DME incorporate devices that are managed using traditional protocols such as SNMP and CMIP? The answer is through special DME encapsulators called adapter objects (not to be confused with the CORBA object adapters used on servers). The I4DL is used to encapsulate legacy protocols and bring them to the object world. The adapter object looks like any other IDL-defined object. An application object can invoke operations on the adapter just like it does on any object using the typical remote invocations. Proxy methods invoked on the adapter call XMP to perform SNMP or CMIP functions. The adapter may define a set of operations that emulate the corresponding CMIP or SNMP calls, or it could augment them in some useful ways. For example, a CMIP adapter object might aggregate several CMIP operations on some managed object into one, providing a higher level of abstraction to the legacy object.

In summary, DME's OMF uses objects to encapsulate the implementation of any management resource. You can access a managed object only through an IDL-defined set of interfaces. The combined network and system management is modeled as the communication between objects that represent the resources of the

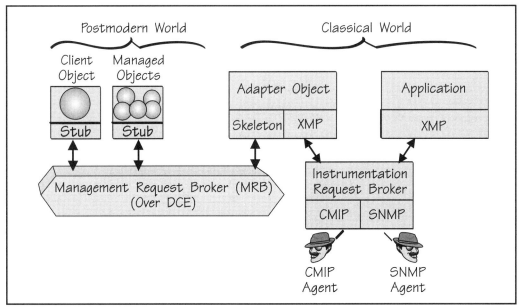

Figure 33-9. The DME Object Management Framework.

system and objects that represent the user interface and managing applications. DME primarily deals with communication between management objects. Object adapters are used to encapsulate standard management protocols—such as SNMP, CMIP, and DCE. The DME Management Request Broker (with the help of the DCE directory services) provides a uniform naming space for all its objects (legacy or postmodern). It knows how to find them and invoke their services. So welcome to the postmodern world of system management with distributed objects. The commercial incarnation of this new architecture is the *Tivoli Management Environment (TME)*, which we cover later in this chapter.

FYI

The New OSF

Briefing

The OSF's new mission is to focus on architecture, subcontracting, and the distribution of standards-based infrastructure software. They no longer have a complete software development organization. The new OSF has adopted a secular approach to the management ORB—any CORBA-compliant ORB will do. When OSF members decided to move to a CORBA-compliant management ORB, they made the decision that OSF should leave the ORB business to OMG. Any CORBA-compliant ORB now qualifies as an MRB. ❑

UI-Atlas Distributed Management Framework

Unix International (UI) was the industry's other Unix consortium; its 270 members defined the requirements for the evolution of distributed software for Unix within an architecture framework called *Atlas*. In July 1991, UI published its *Atlas-Distributed Management (Atlas-DM)* requirements—distributed objects were the key unifying concept. USL elected to implement the first release of Atlas using existing Tivoli technology. The second release, which was due in 1994, was to be CORBA-based. The UI requirements, in the pre-Novell acquisition days, were implemented by USL (or whomever USL contracted out for the job). We're using the past tense because UI was dissolved on December 31, 1993. We still cover Atlas-DM in this section because it's an important architecture that may still end up being implemented in some Unix variants.

Architecturally, UI went even further than OSF's DME in its support of objects—the first release of Atlas didn't even bother with SNMP and CMIP. Atlas-DM, like the postmodern DME, defines management applications as collections of objects that interact with each other and with objects that represent the managed resources. The UI *Management ORB (MORB)* provides transparent access to managed objects across the network (see Figure 33-10). The objects represent generic resources in the distributed environment—including hosts, users, LANs, DBMSs, applications, disks, files, and OSs. A single dynamic API call—the Tivoli *objcall*—is used to invoke methods on objects (all parameters are passed as ASCII character strings). Object references can be passed at run time. In addition, Tivoli allows the

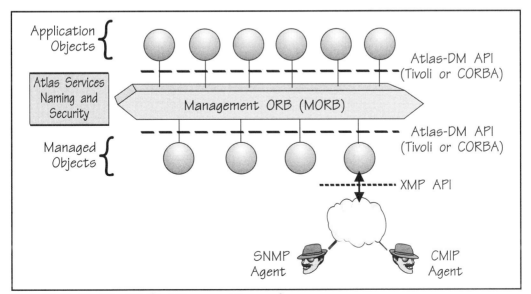

Figure 33-10. The Atlas-DM Object Management Framework.

dynamic discovery of objects and the operations they support. The second release of Atlas-DM would have used CORBA IDL stubs, dynamic method invocations, and a CORBA-compliant ORB. It was going to implement the X/Open XMP API for interfacing to SNMP and CMIP. Of course, Atlas-DM is now history.

So What Is CORBA's System Management Solution?

In 1995, the OMG started to define a CORBA *System Management Facility* that includes interfaces and services for managing, instrumenting, configuring, installing, operating, and repairing distributed object components. For a distributed component to be managed, it must implement IDL-defined management interfaces. The system management framework defines the following interfaces:

■ *Instrumentation*—lets you collect information on a component's workload, responsiveness, throughput, consumption of resources, and so on.

■ *Data collection*—lets you collect information on historical events related to a component. Any component may have a history—meaning a log of events. The data collection interface allows a managing workstation to query that log.

■ *Quality of service*—lets you select the level of service a component provides in areas such as availability, performance, reliability, and recovery.

■ *Security*—lets you manage the security system itself. It is distinct from the CORBA Security Service, which implements the security mechanisms.

■ *Event management*—lets you generate, register, filter, and forward event notifications to management applications. It builds on the CORBA Event Service.

■ *Scheduling*—lets you schedule repetitive tasks and associate event handlers with events. For example, you can schedule the execution of a task when an event fires or a timer pops.

■ *Instance tracking*—lets you associate objects with other managed objects that are subject to common policies.

The most likely candidate technology for these services is X/Open's new *SysMan* standard. SysMan itself is based on the *Tivoli Management Environment (TME)*, which provides a CORBA-based distributed system management framework (see next section). TME 2.0 provides a set of CORBA-based technologies and services to create, maintain, and integrate distributed system management applications.

Tivoli, CORBA, and IBM

*O*ur idea was to build management applications around an ORB instead of network management protocols. So in 1989, we began working on a distributed object framework for managing applications.

> — *Todd Smith, Chief Scientist*
> *Tivoli Systems*
> *(February, 1995)*

Tivoli is a tiny system management company that IBM acquired for a cool $743 million in January of 1996. Why did IBM pay this phenomenal sum to acquire a 300-person company with under $45 million in revenues? Because Tivoli is the best CORBA-based system management framework on the market. The Tivoli framework was exactly what IBM needed to complement its SOM-based suites for system management (also known as Karat and SystemView). The converged SystemView/Tivoli management platform is called *TME 10*; it builds on TME. Tivoli has become the foundation platform on which all IBM system management products will be built.

So what does TME look like? It consists of *Tivoli/Enterprise Console*, *Tivoli Management Framework (TMF)*, and a set of core management services (see Figure 33-11). Tivoli/Enterprise is a desktop management console that collects management events and provides a rules-based technology for automating management operations and event processing. TMF includes basic services for handling user-defined policies, scheduling tasks, instance tracking, instrumentation, and security. TMF also provides a set of system management classes (in the form of mixins) that managed and managing objects can multiple inherit from and customize.

Tivoli has an active OEM program to license TME. Participants include Sybase, Informix, Sun, Unisys, and Siemens-Rolm. Tivoli and IBM will provide TME-based object management services as part of SOM 3.X. Tivoli will be available on all major platforms—including Unixes, NetWare, OS/2, Windows NT, DOS, and Windows. Tivoli is providing adapters to other system management platforms—including OpenView, SunNet Manager, NetView, NetWare Management System, Sybase, and Oracle. Finally, Tivoli is working with JavaSoft (and others) on system management standards for the Internet based on *Tivoli/Net.Commander*. TME is the *de facto* and *de jure* (via X/Open) system management standard for CORBA ORBs. The most OMG can do is ratify the X/Open standard and make it more coherent in certain areas. So, for all practical purposes, systems management for ORBs is mostly here today—it's called Tivoli. Hopefully, IBM's acquisition of Tivoli will bring in the financial and marketing muscle that will accelerate the use of CORBA objects for distributed system management (also see next Soapbox).

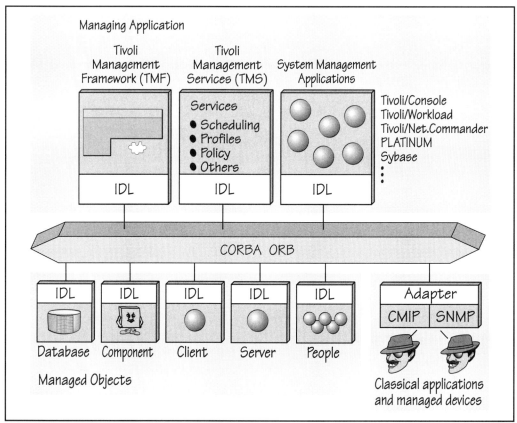

Figure 33-11. The Tivoli Management Environment (TME).

System Management: Why Objects Are the Answer

Soapbox

A network management system is limited by the capabilities of the network management protocol and by the objects used to represent the environment to be managed.

— *William Stallings, Author*
SNMP, SNMPv2, and CMIP
(Addison-Wesley, 1993)

We believe CORBA provides a modern and natural protocol for representing managed entities, defining their services, specifying instance data, and invoking methods via an ORB. You can use the CORBA Interface and Implementation Repositories to discover and dynamically invoke methods on these managed objects at run time. The managed objects can directly call the managing station when they have something significant to report (in contrast, SNMP relies mostly on polling). The CORBA event service is ideal for distributing asynchronous system management events. And the CORBA object services provide a ton of useful functions that would have to be reinvented by SNMP or OSI's CMIP—for example, life cycle, naming, transactions, and persistence. Using CORBA, distributed system management becomes just another service on the ORB. Objects can manage themselves. Management applications provide views on collections of self-managing objects.

The *Simple Network Management Protocol (SNMP)*—today's predominant management protocol—is too limiting for the requirements of total systems management. It needs to be replaced. This means that in the next few years, we'll be experiencing a large migration to more sophisticated management software. The three contenders for replacing SNMP are SNMPv2, OSI's CMIP, and CORBA. All three require more memory and smarter processors than SNMP. So the question is: Which one do you choose? In our opinion, it should be CORBA. SNMPv2 and CMIP are both antiques and incredibly clumsy to program. MIBs are an anachronism in the age of IDL and object persistent stores. They require that management applications interact with a very large number of low-level attributes that they manipulate through *get* and *set*. SNMPv2 does not allow you to register operations on managed objects; CMIP does this very clumsily. We feel the "simple" SNMP was a wonderful, basic protocol that solved many real problems in the age of scarcity and simple network management. But now that we're moving to total systems management, the sooner the world moves away from SNMP, SNMPv2, and CMIP and replaces them with CORBA, the better off system management will be.

Table 33-1 compares the features of SNMP, SNMPv2, CMIP, and CORBA. SNMP and SNMPv2 place a minimum amount of event-emitting logic in the agents so that the managed nodes are simple. The smarts are in the managing station. As a result, traps (or events) are infrequently used, and the managing station must poll the agents to find out what's happening. In contrast, CMIP and CORBA are event driven, which means the agents are smarter; the managing station doesn't have to poll as much. As a result, a CORBA managing station can handle a much larger number of managed objects.

In general, CMIP or CORBA are better suited for the management of large, complex, multivendor networks than SNMP. Of course, SNMP's simplicity allows it to be deployed on more devices, which, in turn, makes it easier to manage large networks. The designers of SNMP understood these trade-offs very well. They opted for the least common denominator approach and were willing to live with the consequences. SNMPv2 makes the same architectural trade-offs as SNMP. Looking at the comparison table, we're not so sure SNMP is still the way to go. Systems management operational costs are just too high—the design point has shifted. We need smarter systems management software that knows how to deal with smarter objects anywhere on the intergalactic network. We believe CORBA is the answer to the distributed systems management nightmare. ❏

Table 33-1. Comparing SNMP, SNMPv2, CMIP, and CORBA Objects.

Feature	SNMP	SNMPv2	CMIP	CORBA Objects
Installed base	Huge	Small	Small	Very small
Managed objects per managing station	Small	Small	Large	Very large
Management model	Manager and agents	Manager and agents	Manager and agents	Communicating objects
View of managed objects	Simple variables organized in MIB trees	Simple variables organized in MIB trees	Objects with inheritance defined in MIBs	Objects with IDL defined inter-faces, attributes, and multiple inheritance
Manager/agent interactions	Polling. Infre-quent traps	Polling. Infre-quent traps	Event driven	Event driven
Explicit manager to agent command invocations	No	No	Yes	Yes
Security	No	Perhaps	Yes	Yes
Manager-to-manager exchanges	No	Yes	Yes	Yes
Bulk transfers	No	Yes	Yes	Yes
Create/delete managed objects	No	No (but can add table rows)	Yes	Yes
Communication model	Datagram	Datagram	Session-based	ORB
Standards body	Internet	Internet	ISO	OMG, X/Open
Approximate memory requirements (KBytes)	40-200	200-500	300-1000	64-2000

System Management: Meet The Players

Figure 33-12 is a Gartner Group projection of where the market for network and system management software is heading. Clearly, the trend is toward distributed system management. Three groups of system manager vendors will be competing for this market:

- **Mainframe system management vendors that are moving to client/ server.** This group includes Computer Associates (CA) with *Unicenter*, Legent with *XPE*, Candle with *CT Object Framework*, and IBM with *NetView*. In May 1995, CA acquired Legent for $1.78 billion. In May 1996, it acquired Digital's *PolyCenter*—a move that further consolidates this market. The mainframe vendors have a deep understanding of IS requirements for total systems management, especially at the application level. These systems typically provide accounting, security, storage, and workload management at the application level.

- **Unix network management vendors.** This group includes SunSoft with *Solstice Enterprise Manager* and *SunNet Manager*; HP with *OpenView*; IBM with *SystemView, Tivoli/TME*, and *NetView/6000*; Digital with *PolyCenter NetView*; and Cabletron with *Spectrum*. These are all system vendors with a long history in distributed system management and open frameworks. They all have large portfolios of third-party tools that run on their management platforms. In addition, these vendors are now extending their reach beyond network management; they now provide application and system management suites. However, PCs and LANs are still treated like second class citizens by SNMP managers. The good news is that some vendors are starting to provide bilingual agents that can do both SNMP and DMI.

- **LAN system management vendors.** This group includes Microsoft with *System Management Server (SMS)*, Intel with *LANDesk Management Suite*, Symantec with *Norton Administrator*, Novell with *ManageWise*, Digital with

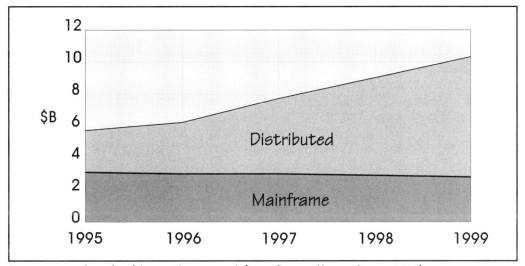

Figure 33-12. Network and System Management Software Revenue (Source: Gartner, 1995).

ManageWORKS, and IBM with *LAN NetView* and *OS/2 SystemView*. These vendors have a long history in managing PCs, NOS servers, and departmental LANs. The information they collect feeds the management food chain. Historically, these systems have not been able to provide enterprise-wide management solutions.

So who will win? It's too early to make this call. Look for acquisitions and mergers everywhere. Client/server management is far too complicated for a monolithic "one size fits all" answer. Prebundled suites of monolithic products are not the answer either—they are too inflexible. The vendors that are best positioned provide open management frameworks built on top of a distributed object bus (such as CORBA).

Open frameworks can be complemented by hundreds of "plug-in" modules from third parties. Frameworks bring best-of-breed point management products together in an integrated customer solution. Together, these plug-ins (and their frameworks) should be able to manage PCs, LANs, WANs, applications, servers, and the Web. Future plug-ins will be built using component technology.

As we go to press, the leaders in object-oriented distributed system management frameworks are Tivoli's *TME*, SunSoft's *Solstice Enterprise Manager*, Cabletron's *Spectrum*, CA/Legent's *Unicenter with CORBA frameworks*, and IBM's *SystemView/Karat*. Symantec and HP may also be offering distributed object frameworks by the time you read this.

CONCLUSION

Intergalactic client/server systems will fail if they cannot be managed. The spread of the Internet and Intranets will further exacerbate the problem. Distributed management systems are still in their infancy. And their agents are from the Stone Age. For example, SNMP agents are totally passive—they speak only when spoken to. We need a new generation of smart agents that can act independently of the management systems. We need component-based management systems that are built on a distributed object foundation. We need better object standards for managing applications. And we need it all now.

Unfortunately, the standards bodies are moving far too slowly. The IETF wasted three precious years on its SNMPv2 wars. The OSF's DME and UI's Atlas were aborted efforts. OSI's CMIP is a market failure. And the OMG is moving far too slowly in the area of system management. The two bright stars in this otherwise dismal picture are the DMTF and Tivoli. The DMTF's DMI is getting wide market acceptance and is now tackling the issues of application management. Tivoli created the *de facto* object standard for system management based on CORBA and DMI MIFs. Tivoli is now tackling the issue of Web system management with help from JavaSoft. So there is some hope.

Part 10

Bringing It All Together

An Introduction to Part 10

*T*he future is bright, fruitful, and positive.

— Bob Marley

Are you Martians still with us? All that talk of problem management and disaster recovery didn't faze you? We're reaching the end of our journey. We realize this tour was really long, but client/server is a broad topic. You probably want us to net it all out for you: Which technology do I pick? How do I get an application out in record time? What help can I expect? It turns out these are the one million dollar questions of client/server.

Which technology do I pick? This is like predicting the future. Anybody can predict it, but the trick is getting it right. We'll give you our two cents worth on where we think this technology is going. You Martians know how to surf now, so we'll throw in a wave theory of client/server. The idea is to look at technology cycles and figure out which wave to ride. If you read this book, you won't be too surprised by the answers.

How do I get an application out in record time? This takes us into the subject of tools. Here on Earth, we've had tools since the dawn of our civilization to help us with our work. The job of toolmakers is to look at all the raw technologies and create the tools that ordinary mortals can use to get a job done. With tools, we can develop client/server applications quickly. The better tools can even help us deploy and manage our client/server applications. Toolmakers are constantly trying to keep up with the types of information presented in this book; they use it to decide the raw technology on which to build their tools. Picking a tool is not easy. It locks you into a client/server paradigm. And we know that there's more than one way to do client/server; in fact, there are hundreds of ways to do it. So we'll answer the question by throwing a model at you on how to pick a tool. Then you'll have to decide which tool is best for your job.

What help can I expect? You'll need a good tool, a working methodology, and lots of good luck. You'll mostly be on your own—but that's when the real fun starts. This book provides a Survival Guide; it's just one more aid that will help you filter the signal from the noise in this overhyped field. Of course, you can always get the advice of consultants and attend seminars. But good advice doesn't come cheap. This final part gives you an overview of tools and methodologies. Are you Martians ready for your return trip home? Time does fly when you're having fun.

Chapter 34

Client/Server Tools and Application Development

Tool evaluation is fun. There are literally hundreds of products. How do you make a decision? One possibility is to stay in tool evaluation mode until you're told that the decision is due tomorrow. Then just pick one!

— **Anonymous MIS Developer**

The million dollar question is: Which magical tool can take the pain out of client/server application development and deployment? And a related question is: Does client/server require a new approach to application development? All these questions are very dear to your authors' hearts. For many years, we were involved in building client/server application development tools. Our elusive goal was to create the perfect tool for developing, deploying, and maintaining client/server applications *quickly*. However, we learned the hard way that you have to make some serious compromises. There is no such thing as a "one size fits all" client/server tool. And there is no magical tool (including ours). So the next best thing we can do is leave you with a model for how to evaluate them. We'll even throw in our two cents on client/server development methodologies.

CLIENT/SERVER APPLICATION DEVELOPMENT TOOLS

Development tools are the linchpin in client/server. Tools encapsulate the client/server technology described in this book and make it easier for users to write applications. The best tools are highly visual. Most of today's client/server tools are used to create departmental decision-support systems. However, Internet tools are just starting to take off. They may set the stage for blasting the tools market out of its departmental bunkers. So how do we classify those client/server tools? Which is the right tool for the right job? Like everything else in client/server, it seems everyone has an opinion on tools. So we present in this section a classification scheme that works for us.

The Latest and Greatest Model of Client/Server Tools

Yes, client/server tool evaluation can be a lot of fun. You're probably being bombarded with tons of glossy advertisements for tools that all promise to deliver instant and hassle free client/server solutions. At trade shows, you've probably watched those slick demonstrations that seem to create entire client/server applications with a few mouse clicks. But with over 300 tools on the market, which do you pick for evaluation? These days, we could probably safely assume that you don't have an infinite budget for tools or the time to evaluate all 300 of them. You could start pruning tools by platform, but most seem to run on all the popular platforms. Or you could prune them by price, but you could end up getting what you paid for. Or you could prune them by brand name and miss out on the most avant-garde tools with the latest and greatest features.

To help you with your evaluation, we propose a simple model that breaks the tool market around four axes (see Figure 34-1):

■ **Roots.** What's the tool's ancestry? At one end of the axis are tools that originated on mainframes; they tend to have a CASE-centric focus. At the other end of the axis are tools that originated on PC LANs; they tend to have a GUI-centric, event-driven focus. Somewhere in between are the supermini 4GL tools. The approach (or paradigm) a tool uses for application development is intimately tied to its roots.

■ **Distributed Technology.** What's the client/server technology? What applications does the tool create? The axis moves from fat clients with thin servers that specialize in decision support to thin clients with fat servers that do OLTP. In the middle are Groupware and Distributed Objects, which split the logic more evenly.

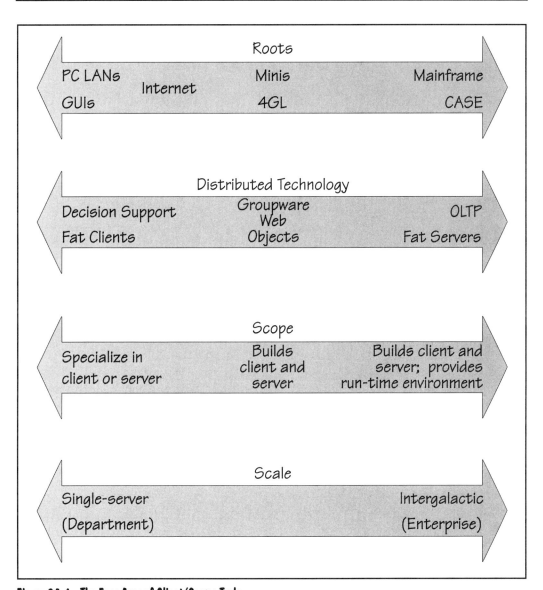

Figure 34-1. The Four Axes of Client/Server Tools.

■ *Scope.* How much of the client/server function does the tool provide? The axis ranges from tools that specialize in the client, the server, or the middleware to tools that provide all three (see Figure 34-2). Some tools may even go as far as bundling a run time that includes system management, resource managers, and single point of installation. This may sound like heresy, but the more bundling the tool provides, the less integration you have to do. Integration is a major headache in client/server systems.

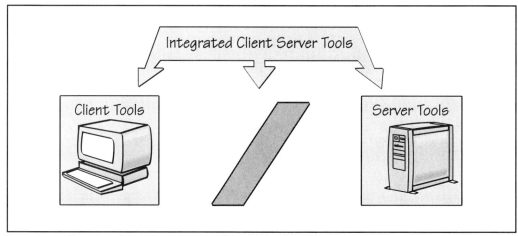

Figure 34-2. How Much Client/Server Coverage Does the Tool Provide?

■ **Scalability.** How well does the tool scale for enterprise solutions? The axis moves from single-server tools to multiserver intergalactic tools. The middleware that the tool targets becomes an important factor in the more intergalactic tools.

You'll need all four axes to understand where a tool fits in the scheme of things and what it can do for you.

Will the Ideal Tool Please Stand Up?

The ideal tool is the one that does the job for you. For us, it's a tool that helps us create 3-tier client/server applications for the Object Web. No one is offering such a tool, but let's put together a set of requirements in the hope that someone builds it. So here's what we would like to see in such a tool:

■ **A visual place-builder for the first tier.** The tool should let you build visual containers that you can then populate with components such as ActiveXs, OpenDoc parts, and Java applets. The container is a compound document. The tool should provide prebuilt containers (or *places*) that we can then extend to meet our needs. Of course, these places must be portable across client platforms. They must also be *shippable*, which means the tool must provide hooks to associate security policies and rules with each place.

■ **A business-object builder for the second tier.** The tool must provide prebuilt frameworks for different object services such as persistence, security, transactions, locking, metering, and versioning (i.e., CORBA services). You should be able to start with a raw business-object template and then extend it with the services you need (via mixins). Ideally, the tool should let us do the mixing via drag-and-drop. We also need a server-side Java environment to write the business logic and associate it with the object.

■ *Frameworks that encapsulate the third tier.* The tool must provide frameworks that encapsulate existing server environments such as DBMSs, groupware, TP Monitors, MOM, e-mail, and workflow. These back-end services are typically invoked by the middle-tier objects.

■ *A visual environment for assembling components.* The tool must provide visual facilities for connecting (or assembling) objects across tiers and within tiers. For example, you should be able to associate a client event in the first tier with a CORBA or OLE method invocation on a business object in the second tier. The CORBA IDL and Interface Repository can play a major role in tying together these components.

■ *A component repository.* The tool must support teams of developers by providing a shared repository of reusable components, places, and server objects. The repository must, of course, provide check-in/check-out facilities and other such features.

We also expect the tool to provide run-time facilities that let you split the business objects at many different points—between the client, the server, and, more importantly, across servers.

We could keep this list going. But what are the odds of getting all these facilities in our current lifetimes? Actually, the odds are quite favorable. Most major tool vendors—including Microsoft, Oracle, Borland, Symantec, Sybase, and IBM—are now adding support for both components and the Internet in their tools. So it's only a matter of time before they add the 3-tier client/server features we've described to support the Object Web.

CLIENT/SERVER APPLICATION DESIGN

Mainframe application designers and programmers have had it easy. In the past, user interfaces were simple constructs driven by simple terminals. The primary focus was on the database and transaction code, leaving the human to simply respond, like an extension of the application. But with client/server applications, the tables have turned. The ultimate goal of client/server solutions is to provide mission-critical applications that have the ease-of-use and responsiveness of stand-alone PCs. In this section, we present a methodology for designing 3-tier client/server applications.

Client/server is primarily a relationship between programs running on separate machines. As such, it requires an infrastructure to do things standalone PCs never had to worry about. For example, robust interprocess communications over LANs or WANs must be included in the design. Graphical interfaces using GUIs and OOUIs must be exploited to make applications look and feel more like real-world objects instead of programming processes. User interfaces are becoming complex, responsive, ad hoc environments that put the emphasis on the human task. OOUI clients bring humans into the distributed loop, which inevitably adds a host of complications. Humans make lots of errors, do unexpected things, and typically require lots of information from diverse sources. The more advanced OOUIs—such as compound documents and shippable places—turn the client workstation into virtual worlds where many parallel dialogs are conducted with a variety of servers.

OOUIs also give the user much more freedom than GUIs or terminal-based systems. Users are free to organize their visual objects (and desktop) in any way they please. They are not tied to the rigid logic of task-oriented applications. OOUIs have no main panels and navigation screens. They make it hard to tell where one application starts and another ends (or what an application object is versus a system object). There are just visual objects everywhere. This begs two important questions: Does client/server require a new approach to system development? Where design used to predominantly start at the database, which comes first now: the client or the server?

What Makes Client/Server Different?

Traditional (terminal-based) system design started with the data. The screens were developed primarily to drive the process of filling in the database, so they were designed after the transactions and tables were defined. Client/server applications, on the other hand, require a far more complex design approach:

■ The interface is more flexible than terminals, and the user is allowed more latitude.

■ The object-based, front-end designs place a lot more intelligence on the client-side of the application.

■ The messages between the client and the server are custom-built and application-specific.

■ The design must be optimized to take advantage of the parallelism inherent in the distributed application.

This leads us to a design approach unique to client/server applications: You must start your design with both the client and the server. So, you have two starting points in a client/server application: the GUI/OUUI and the data (unless the data for a business process is already in place). The GUI/OOUI and data designs come together at the application objects in the middle tier. The application objects map the visual objects to the database, and vice versa. They encapsulate the shared data and the business rules. Does this seem complex? Don't worry: It's not nearly as ominous as it sounds.

Rapid Prototyping Is Essential

One way to avoid a "chicken and egg" situation from developing—like the one in Figure 34-3—is to use a rapid prototyping methodology. Rapid prototyping allows you to develop your system incrementally. You start with the client, and then work your way iteratively towards the server. You always move in small steps, constantly refining the design as you go along. Make sure to involve your end-user during all the stages of the interface design. In this form of delta development, the system is incrementally refined until you develop a working prototype that is mature enough to be placed into production. This approach may place a larger burden on the programmer than the traditional approaches, which rely on up-front analysis and design. And, with rapid prototyping, you also run the risk that a cost-cutting management decision may place a non-optimized "working" prototype prematurely into production. At the other extreme, you may encounter another risk: the perpetual prototyping syndrome.

These risks are easily outweighed by the benefits that rapid prototyping provide in developing an OOUI client/server system. In client/server environments, it is

Figure 34-3. The Client/Server Chicken and Egg.

difficult to determine beforehand how the system is supposed to work (the OOUI design, the network performance, and multiuser loading). It has been our experience that user specifications cannot anticipate all the needs of the users. They cannot adequately account for the potential OOUI technology offers. If you ask the users for guidance, the chances are that they'll give you the wrong answers based on existing solutions (GUI or terminal-based solutions). Instead, you should show them what the technology can do for them and what new visual dimensions OOUIs offer; then work with them on developing the application.

Invariably, OOUIs can capture more of the business process than either GUIs or terminal-based front-ends. A rapid prototype will help in the discovery of the application objects (or business objects). Users will find it easier to discuss visual business objects, and the visual prototype will help develop the design specifications.

So build a prototype and try it out. The trick is to be able to build the application many times. It is easier to talk about something that can be demonstrated live and used. Moreover, it is important that the prototype be developed in an environment where the issues of client/server performance, network overheads, system management, and transaction server design can be tested live. Client/server systems require a lot of monitoring, fine-tuning, and administration. It is better for you to get acquainted with these issues early in the game.

From Prototype To Working System

The OOUI objects permeate the entire application and determine its shape. An application can be seen as a collection of visual business objects. The design of the application starts from the objects (and views) the user sees on the screen, and then works its way towards the server objects and the database structure. Prototypes are used to identify, with your customer's participation, the user model: What business objects are needed, and what do they do? Prototyping is an iterative activity with many false starts. Here is how the typical prototype evolves:

1. ***Understand the business process***. It is a prerequisite that you understand what the application is all about at the business level. So gather the requirements and study the tasks: What does the customer really want?

2. ***Design the visual places.*** Remember, a *place* provides the visual metaphor that ties together the components a user sees. It's the container that creates the virtual world. Or, if you prefer, it's the simulation of the real world. In a world of components, the place becomes your application. We recommend that you hire a visual artist to sketch out each place including its visual components.

3. ***Define the components or business objects***. What the user sees in a place are objects containing views that react to user input and actions. The objects are manipulated according to the requirements of the business process. You should create user objects that correspond to real-life entities; for example, a seat on an airplane. What are the main object types in the application? What other objects do they contain? What are the attributes of the objects? What functions do they have? How do they behave? What are the relationships between objects? What are the "composed of" relationships (is-part-of)? What are the dependency and collaboration relationships (is-analogous-to, is-kind-of, depends-upon)?

4. ***Work on the detailed object views***. What context menu actions apply to each object? What views are required? Are business form views required? Can the views be grouped in Notebook pages? What widgets controls—including input/output fields, list boxes, pushbuttons, menus, sliders, and value-sets—will appear in the views? What level of help is needed? What data validation at the field level is required? What level of triggers are required (on error, on message, and so on)? How are external procedures or methods invoked?

5. ***Develop dry-run scenarios***. You can create your screen objects and animate the application (OOUI tools should provide this capability). Use the scenarios to validate the object model of the user interface. The scenarios should also help you identify the major event-driven interactions.

6. ***Walk through a system scenario***. Such a scenario should follow a transaction from its source through its execution. Identify the protocols that link the visual objects with the middle-tier server objects. Use CORBA IDL to define and document the object interfaces. Blow up this scenario in areas that require more detail. Run an application scenario for each business object. Identify redundant behaviors. Which objects can be reused?

7. ***Identify transaction sources***. A client/server system can be thought of as a client-driven event system. The server is, in a sense, passively waiting on requests from clients. The client, in turn, is driven by the user who is at the "controls" within the confines of the business process. The drag-and-drop of visual objects is typically the source of transactions. Information required upon opening a container or view may also be the source of a transaction. Object/action intersections almost always lead to the generation of a transaction. There is also a high probability that events such as data entry, menu selections, pushing a button, and action dialogs will generate transactions. The visual client interface will eventually be "brought to life" by writing the distributed object invocations that are triggered by the user interaction.

8. ***Define your server objects***. You are now in a position to take a first stab at defining the database objects that correspond to the visual business objects you just created. Iterate on this step until you get it right. Many trade-offs are

involved. The object/action orientation of the client design can help transform the visual objects into an entity-relationship model for database objects. The actions translate into method invocations on middle-tier server objects that encapsulate the persistent data. You can store the data in variety of data-stores—including HTML files, DBMSs, ODBMSs, Lotus Notes, mainframes, and flat files. The middle-tier server object is the integration point for the data. Clients can only manipulate data by invoking these server objects. The server objects can choose to cache the extracted data in an ODBMS or keep it in memory. It's all transparent to the client.

9. ***Publish the IDL for the server objects***. The publication of the IDL advertises to the world what a server object does. It's a binding contract between the server object and its clients. IDL defines the functions exported by the server object. It provides a higher level of abstraction than messages. For example, you could use the DCE RPC IDL or, better yet, CORBA, whose Interface Repository offers a way to discover services dynamically. And, by the time you read this, Network OLE will also be an option.

10. ***Develop your code one business object at a time***. This means developing code on all three tiers for each object. Validate the user interface and the performance of the system with your customer.

11. ***Move from prototype to working system***. A working system is the sum of all the business objects it contains. It's the implementation of a place. You are developing your system incrementally, so you will have a full working system when you've coded your last business object.

We're not done yet. After you develop an acceptable prototype, you can then start experimenting with distribution issues. Where will the places be stored? How are they shipped from the server to the clients? How will you secure these places? These are the issues we covered in Part 8. So are we done? Not yet. You must also use the prototype to understand how to balance loads across servers. The beauty of 3-tier objects is that they scale both downward and upward. At one extreme, you run all your objects on a single machine. At the other extreme, you can give each object its own machine. So use your prototype to play with your loads. It's a dynamic load-balancing act between the clients and the server and between servers.

CONCLUSION

Client/server technology offers developers the potential to create revolutionary new visual applications. Creating these kind of applications requires the seamless integration of OOUI technology, operating systems, ORB technology, and DBMSs. To succeed, we will need new approaches to systems development that emphasize rapid prototyping and the end-user involvement. Doing that will allow us to exploit the synergy between client and server objects. We will also be in a better position to understand, early in a project, the opportunities (for example, parallelism) and pitfalls (for example, performance and error recovery) introduced by splitting an application across a network.

The prototype-based approach to design eliminates the need for lengthy specifications. More importantly, this approach allows the customer to participate in the specification of the product and its stepwise refinement. The approach also lends itself well to the design of distributed applications because you can refine and fine-tune the distribution of function as you learn more about your system's real-life behavior.

So, the successful 3-tier client/server design starts in parallel with both the client and the server. The two starting points are the OOUI objects and the data objects. The "glue" that ties them together are the business objects in the middle. Start with the client and move towards the server, or vice versa. In either case, move in small steps and iterate. The visual prototype brings the design to life early. So, which comes first: the client or the server? They both come first!

Chapter 35

Which Way
Client/Server?

This is the chapter that's going to bring it all together. We'll bring out our infamous
crystal ball and speculate on where client/server technology is heading. We may even
jump on a Soapbox and give you a fearless forecast of which technology wave looks
most promising. Of course, there should be no surprises at this late stage of the
book. You may have even guessed what we're going to see in this famous crystal ball.
So what can we do to build the suspense? We'll tell you the following story.

Two of your authors recently taught a graduate-level course on client/server computing. In the course, we presented all the material that's in this book. Then we
gave our students a choice of client/server projects. We told them they could use
for their projects any of the client/server technologies we covered—including file
servers, DBMSs, TP Monitors, groupware, distributed objects, and the Web. So
which ones did they pick? Over 70% picked the Web for their client/server platform.

In addition, the Web students spent an inordinate amount of time on their projects—they did much more work than we asked for. Some just camped out in our lab.

So what is the moral of this story? It says that client/server programming with the Web is very popular with our graduate students, many of whom are also professional programmers. In addition to being popular, programming for the Web can be addictive and fun. But as you know from this book, we need the Object Web to do real client/server work. Luckily, the Object Web is just as much fun to program, if not more. So the Web is making client/server development fun. It is also bringing it to the masses in a big way.

WHICH WAY CLIENT/SERVER?

In Chapter 2, on page 20, we introduced the idea that client/server is transitioning from the *Ethernet era* to the *Intergalactic era*. We then spent most of this book going over the client/server technologies that can bring about this change. So what is the bottom line?

We offer Figure 35-1 as the answer to the question: Which way client/server? The Ethernet era of client/server saw a file-centric application wave (the NetWare wave) followed by a database-centric wave (the Oracle wave); TP Monitors and Groupware generated minor ripples. The Object Web is the next big wave. We believe that distributed objects combined with the Internet are essential for making the intergalactic client/server vision real.

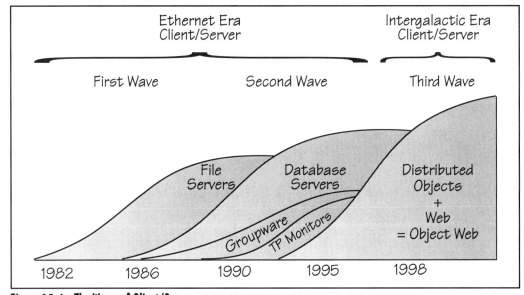

Figure 35-1. The Waves of Client/Server.

Once the Object Web technology takes off, it will subsume all other forms of client/server computing—including TP Monitors, Database, and Groupware. Distributed objects can do it all, and better. Objects will help us break large monolithic applications into more manageable multivendor components that live and coexist on the intergalactic bus. They are also our only hope for managing and distributing the millions of software entities that will live on intergalactic networks. The Web is the killer application that will bring objects to the masses in a big way.

Which Wave Should I Ride?

We shouldn't have to get on a Soapbox to state the obvious: the Object Web is the future of client/server technology. Objects and the Web encompass all aspects of distributed computing—including OOUIs, compound documents, transactions, groupware, database, and system management. So the million dollar question is: Should you invest in interim technologies, or should you just catch the Object Web wave? It's a trade-off between using proven technologies and the ones that are at the "bleeding edge." We're really at a painful technological juncture. Mixing paradigms typically gives you the worst of both worlds. Like our students, we have the urge to immediately ride the Object Web wave and see where it will take us. However, we also hear a voice of caution that tells us the Object Web is still not ready for intergalactic prime time. The Web and objects will eventually morph, but do we want to be first to ride this wave?

The Client/Server Scalability Issue

In addition to technology waves, we must factor the issue of scalability into the choice of a client/server platform. It is much easier to deploy client/server in small enterprises and departments. Over 80% of the existing client/server installations are single server and have less than 50 clients. The small installations are typically easier to deploy and manage. Almost all of the existing client/server tools address that market. These tools can successfully be used to create client/server applications for decision support, e-mail, and groupware. They provide excellent facilities for building GUI front-ends and are adept at working with shrink-wrapped middleware and server packages (mostly SQL DBMSs and Lotus Notes). However, even at the low end, we don't have adequate tools for creating mission critical solutions. By this we mean applications you can depend on to run your everyday business operations. These types of applications, especially at the low end, must support transactions, built-in system management, and high-availability.

Intergalactic client/server is much more complex. It requires the sophisticated middleware described in this book—including MOM, distributed transactions, and ORBs. It requires proven tools that can take advantage of this middleware. Intergalactic client/server is by definition multiserver. So the tools should be able to deploy applications on multiple servers, manage transactions that are distributed across them, perform some form of load-balancing, deploy the software to the clients and servers, and manage the multiserver environment. To be open, these tools are expected to do all this on multivendor operating systems, multivendor resource managers, and multiple GUI front-ends. They must also use standard middleware.

In short, IS people are demanding the level of cohesiveness and scalability they have grown accustomed to on single-vendor mainframe platforms, but now they want it for an open client/server world that runs on Intranets. Of course, we're nowhere close to meeting these expectations. As we explained in this Survival Guide, much of the technology and standards that are needed to make this happen are finally coming together; it will be another year before the tools can catch up. Perhaps the Object Web is a bit premature. Yes, we can create client/server applications for it today using Java and some rudimentary tools that help build the front-end clients, but it won't be a picnic (see the next Soapbox). However, some tool vendors seem to understand the requirements, and perhaps in the near future we'll have the luxury of being able to create intergalactic client/server applications by pointing and clicking (or better yet, dragging and dropping).

The Secret Shame of Client/Server

Soapbox

There's another scam in progress. People are stampeding toward client/server because they're being told it's easy, and that's just not true. No matter what application development tools you choose, it's extremely difficult to design a high-performance client/server application. It's worse than black art.

> — Patricia Seybold, "The Secret Shame of
> Client/Server Development,"
> ComputerWorld (August, 1993)

The real secret is that there are two client/server paradigms: PC LAN client/server and intergalactic client/server. Some call it "Small Client/Server" and "Large Client/Server." Let's face it, client/server started as a PC LAN phenomenon and has done quite well there. It doesn't take a rocket scientist to deploy a NetWare server or write a Lotus Notes application. And how difficult is it to write a client application using PowerBuilder, Delphi, Centura, VisualAge, or Visual Basic? In general, the PC world has been babystepping into client/server from the bottom up, and most of us have been quite happy with the pace of progress. So there is really no "secret shame of client/server" in the PC LAN side of the house—things are on track and moving at a fast pace.

The secret shame may be in the intergalactic side of the house. Perhaps all the relentless client/server hype has led some to believe that they could junk all the mainframes that couldn't fit on a desktop and instantly recreate their 100,000 terminal-based airline reservation systems using Visual Basic. Of course, we can't do this right now.

But you can see from the extensive technology we covered in this book that a solid foundation for intergalactic client/server is coming together. The important standards are behind us. The DCE and MOM infrastructures are almost ready for prime time, SQL servers are in their second generation, open TP Monitors are now a reality, and open platforms for distributed system management are here today. A little bit further out on the horizon are CORBA-based distributed objects and the services that surround them. And, we're finally getting ready for the Object Web that promises to revolutionize the way client/server applications are written and deployed. So there is not much to be ashamed of.

We believe that client/server for PC LANs is ready for business today. You would be at a disadvantage not to make immediate use of the technology PC LANs provide. The tools are not stellar, but they're adequate (we can always do better when it comes to tools). We also believe that you should start laying out some of that intergalactic client/server foundation we've talked about in this Survival Guide. You can do that by introducing some pilot projects that can help you stay on top of the technology as it evolves.

Pssst...Here's the Real Secret to Client/Server Success

But since we're on the topic of "secrets," we'll offer you an opinion that may sound like heresy. (Hopefully, it's too late for a refund now.) With our deep apologies to the open movement, we believe that the *real secret* to client/server success today is to apply the KISS (Keep It Simple Stupid) principle. Pick a client/server platform, limit the number of vendors, limit mix-and-matching, keep the project simple, and get the system up and running fast. Don't think in terms of posterity. Instead, think in terms of *disposable* client/server solutions.

If it takes six weeks to develop and deploy an application that runs on PC LANs or the Internet, then it won't hurt you to dispose of it when something better comes along (the PCs can be salvaged). Of course, you should also stay on top of all that "strategic" intergalactic client/server stuff. However, only deploy it when it's as easy and simple as the "disposable" client/server technology. The rule is: If it's easy, then it's ready for prime time. The corollary is: If it's that easy, then it's disposable. So you're constantly introducing new technology by rapidly creating and deploying "disposable" client/server applications. ❑

IT'S TIME TO SAY GOOD-BYE

The only way to successfully predict the future is to invent it.

— *Alan Kay, PC Guru*

Yes, the journey was a long, tumultuous one. We hope you enjoyed the guided tour as much as we enjoyed playing guides. To our friends from Mars, we hope you have a safe trip home—it was a pleasure having you here. We hope you'll find that client/server gold somewhere. Don't forget to tell your friends on Mars about our guided tour. We also have a companion book for those of you that are thinking about getting into objects. It's called **The Essential Distributed Objects Survival Guide** (Wiley, 1996). This 600-page book gave us the luxury of exploring CORBA, OLE, and OpenDoc in depth.

We're scratching our heads and trying to come up with some words of wisdom to leave you with at the end of this long tour. But we don't have much to add that wasn't already said. We just want to say that this was our attempt to make some sense out of this traumatic shift our industry is going through. It's a very painful shift for

many of us; for others, it's the start of a new dawn in computing with the sky being the limit. OK, enough of that fluffy stuff. We'll say good-bye with a parting Soapbox on where things are going.

Can We Survive the Client/Server Revolution?

Soapbox

Yes, but to do that we need 100,000 new applets. How did we come up with that number? Client/server technology makes it possible to redeploy most of our computer applications on commodity hardware, where the profit margins are razor thin. If we keep recomputerizing the same application base, using PC LANs and Intranets instead of mainframes, most of us will end up without jobs. This is because we're going after a downsized pie, where the profits are dramatically lower. If our profits are lower, we cut down on the research that helps us create these new technologies. And our customers won't get new applications or technology. Everybody ends up losing. It's called the "cannibalizing effect."

Instead, we need to take advantage of client/server technology to extend the boundaries of computerization. In other words, we need to move on to new frontiers like the information highway. But can we create thousands of new client/server applications *quickly* to populate these new frontiers? To do that effectively, we need a technology base, standards, and tools. This Survival Guide makes the case that the technology base, standards, and some solid products are here today. However, still missing are a set of adequate tools that can help us mine the new frontier. It's not enough to create the application; it must also be effectively packaged, deployed, and managed.

So who's going to package, deploy, and manage these applications? We can't expect everyone to read this entire book just to become client/server literate (don't get us wrong—we would love the sales). Instead, we need to simplify the packaging and distribution of our client/server products. Of all the technologies discussed in this book, the Object Web offers the best hope for creating—in record time—new client/server applications that can go where no other applications have gone before. So we're excited about the long-term prospects. However, in the short term, we're in for some rough times. So we'll be in the doldrums until we can figure out how to unleash the true power of this technology. This is sad—but true. The good news is that after we get over that rough hump, those of us who are still around will be headed straight for a new gold rush. As the Chinese proverb puts it, "We're condemned to live in interesting times." ❏

Index

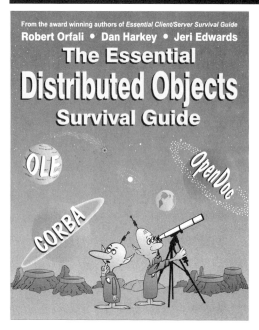